The History of American Education

A Great American Experiment

L. Dean Webb
Arizona State University

PEARSON

Merrill
Prentice Hall

Upper Saddle River, New Jersey
Columbus, Ohio

Library of Congress Cataloging in Publication Data

Webb, L. Dean.
  The history of American education : a great American experiment/L. Dean Webb.
    p. cm.
  Includes bibliographical references and index.
  ISBN 0-13-013649-2
  1. Education—United States—History.   I. Title.

LA205.W43 2006
370′.973—dc22

2004059324

Vice President and Executive Publisher: Jeffery W. Johnston

Executive Editor: Debra A. Stollenwerk

Senior Editorial Assistant: Mary Morrill

Associate Editor: Ben M. Stephen

Production Coordination: Linda Zuk, WordCrafters

Production Editor: Linda Hillis Bayma

Design Coordinator: Diane C. Lorenzo

Photo Coordinators: Monica Merkel and Lori Whitley

Cover Designer: Terry Rohrbach

Cover image: Corbis

Production Manager: Susan Hannahs

Director of Marketing: Ann Castel Davis

Marketing Manager: Darcy Betts Prybella

Marketing Coordinator: Brian Mounts

This book was set in Janson by Pine Tree Composition, Inc. It was printed and bound by Courier Stoughton, Inc. The cover was printed by Courier Stoughton, Inc.

Photo Credits: pp. 2, 375: L. Dean Webb; p. 14: Scott Cunningham/Merrill; p. 30: John Eder/Getty Images Inc.-Stone Allstock; p. 42: © Dorling Kindersley Media Library; p. 50: Getty Images Inc.-Hulton Archive Photos; pp. 53, 71, 136, 152, 187, 230, 269, 280, 307: Corbis/Bettmann; pp. 66, 75, 117, 141, 153: North Wind Picture Archives; pp. 56, 76, 96, 104, 113, 170, 173, 181, 196, 212, 251: Courtesy of the Library of Congress; p. 221: Jacob Riis/Corbis/Bettmann; pp. 242, 336, 342, 358: AP Wide World Photos; p. 260: U.S. Army Photo; p. 294: Mark Richards/PhotoEdit; p. 298: Jim Macmillan/AP Wide World Photos; p. 320: Paul Shambroom/Photo Researchers, Inc.; p. 363: Tony Freeman/PhotoEdit.

Chapter 1 of this book has been adapted for use in this book from materials that originally appeared in *Foundations of American Education*, 1st and 4th editions, by L. Dean Webb, Arlene Metha, and K. Forbis Jordan, copyright © 1992, 2003 by Pearson Education, Inc.

Pearson Education Ltd.
Pearson Education Singapore Pte. Ltd.
Pearson Education Canada, Ltd.
Pearson Education—Japan

Pearson Education Australia Pty. Limited
Pearson Education North Asia Ltd.
Pearson Educación de Mexico, S.A. de C.V.
Pearson Education Malaysia Pte. Ltd.

10 9 8 7 6 5 4 3 2 1
ISBN: 0-13-013649-2

Preface

Nonhistorians often view history as simply a chronicle of past events, serving basically the same function as a newspaper article that chronicles current events. Others think of history as a collection of names, dates, and facts. However, history is much more than this. It is, in short, a recounting of past events and the struggles, successes, and failures of humankind.

History is an interpretive framework through which historians organize and interpret the human experience (Gabella, 1994). This framework is often constructed to answer questions deemed important to the historian. Learning history is not simply a matter of finding facts, "but a process of finding meaning in facts sought and encountered, relating to a web of actors, events, and interpretations" (Gabella, 1994, p. 343).

In addition to being an interpretive framework, history is also a science. Like physical scientists in laboratories, historians are concerned with collecting accurate and complete information and providing accurate interpretation of that information. When history is done well, it is reliable in the sense that the story it tells, the picture it paints, conforms to the historical evidence. However, like all things, history can be abused and misused (Wecter, 1995). A dull narrator can make even the most significant history seem "drab and unimaginative—an act of exhumation, followed by a grim inventory of the bones" (Wecter, 1995, p. 39). History can be abused when the facts are handled carelessly or used to sensationalize. Even worse, "the muse called Clio can be sold down the river to become the handmaid of propaganda, brazenly perverting the truth" (Wecter, 1995, p. 39).

Historians who have sought to interpret the actions, events, and artifacts of the history of education in the United States have offered various interpretations. In the early part of the 20th century, celebrationist or traditionalist historians such as Elwood P. Cubberly and Freeman Butts presented the history of American education as a struggle between positive and negative societal forces in which "the positive forces prevailed because of their inherent 'rightness' and because of the inherent democratic/egalitarian nature of our political, social, and economic system" (Ellis, 1995, p. 4). The traditionalists saw the schools as vehicles for social and economic mobility and celebrated their successes.

Beginning in the 1920s, the traditionalist interpretation was challenged by the liberal or liberal-democratic historians. These historians, although not rejecting the positive forces of American education, acknowledged a history that included conflicts and the competition of ideas.

The late 1960s saw the rise of the revisionist or radical-revisionist perspective, which suggests that the evolution of education in the United States has paralleled the Marxist historical dialectic and developed out of a need to produce an educated workforce for an increasingly capitalist, industrial society dominated by an economic elite (Ellis, 1995). According to revisionists such as Michael Katz and Joel Spring, the schools have served as instruments of social control and have perpetuated the discriminatory treatment of immigrants, racial and ethnic minority groups, and women.

In the 1980s and 1990s the conservatism of the Reagan-Bush era was reflected in the work of conservative historians such as Diane Ravitch. Although not as celebratory as the traditional historians, these historians emphasized consensus and the shared national culture while detailing how the schools had been harmed by efforts to promote social and political reform.

During the same time another group of historians, called postmodern historians by some and new social historians by others (Foner, 2002), looked at history from the perspective of critical theory. They attempted to show that history cannot be told from a single perspective, but that the past is a complex story of interactions that must be examined from the multiple perspectives of race, ethnicity, class, gender, and sexual orientation. These historians sought to give voice to groups neglected or marginalized by many other historians. In so doing, they were criticized for giving too much attention to minor events or historical figures and slighting those events and figures that foster pride in our nation's accomplishments (Foner, 2002).

Given the availability of new historical sources and new interpretive methodologies, it is perhaps understandable that new or different historical interpretations would emerge. Although nonhistorians sometimes view these reinterpretations with suspicion, "historians view the constant search for new perspectives as the lifeblood of historical understanding" (Foner, 2002, p. xvi). Students of educational history should be aware of the varying perspectives, not so they can balance the perspectives, but so they can "think about history as opposed to being a passive recipient of facts" (Spring, 2001, p. 1).

However, thinking about history, according to historian Sam Wineburg (1999), is an "unnatural act" because it requires us to encounter the tension between the familiar and the strange. If we seek familiarity in the past to find relevance to our present, we miss the benefits that can come from encountering the strangeness of that past whose "applicability is not immediately manifest." "The past should not be comfortable. The past should not be a familiar echo of the present, for if it is familiar why revisit it?" (White, cited in Wineburg, 1999, p. 492). Encountering this less familiar past can teach us the limits of our own experience and enhance our ability to perceive the experiences of others in the present as well as the past. "Coming to know others, whether they live on the other side of the tracks or the other side of the millennium" is what history "gives us practice in doing" (Wineburg, 1999, p. 498). The study of history, therefore, can help us in our encounters with the issues of diversity and globalization that dominate present-day discussions of social issues and public policy.

A tale from Wineburg illustrates this point well:

> On his journey from China to India, Marco Polo ventured into Basman, believed to be Sumatra, where he chanced upon a species he had never before seen: the rhinoceros. But he did not see it that way. As his diary records, he saw instead "Unicorns, which are scarcely smaller than elephants. They have the hair of a buffalo . . . (and) a single large, black horn in the middle of the forehead. They do not attack with their horn, but only with their tongue and their knees; for

their tongues are furnished with long, sharp spines. . . . They are very ugly brutes to look at . . . not at all such as we describe them when . . . they let themselves be captured by virgins."

Our own encounters with history present us with a choice: to learn about rhinoceroses or to learn about unicorns. We naturally incline toward unicorns: they're prettier and tamer. But it is the rhinoceros that can teach us far more than we could ever imagine. (p. 498)

Recognizing that the selection of the primary source readings, references, and pictorial evidence for this text can represent a particular historical perspective, every effort has been made to base selection decisions on the historical accuracy of the written material or the historical merit of the illustration, photograph, or other graphic representation, rather than on the extent to which they advance a particular perspective. Accordingly, the title of this text, *The History of American Education: A Great American Experiment*, should not be taken to mean that this history espouses either the celebrationist or postmodern perspective. It does, however, come from the perspective that the educational system that has evolved in this country is, indeed, "great" and has been the result of an "experiment"—a test of various philosophies, ideas, and institutions.

Special Features

Primary Source Readings   It is important not only to be able to evaluate and analyze alternative interpretations of historic information, but also to access primary source documents. For this reason this text presents relevant primary source materials in every chapter. The use of primary source documents not only facilitates a better understanding of the past, but the process of critical evaluation and analysis provides students the opportunity to recognize bias and viewpoint and, in the end, to interpret history through their own eyes and construct their own meaning.

Each Primary Source Reading is accompanied by a set of **Questions for Discussion** designed to encourage the student to reflect on the reading. Although the questions are placed at the end of the reading, if students are directed to them prior to the reading, the questions may be used as advance organizers to focus their reading.

For Your Reflection and Analysis   These boxed questions are woven throughout each chapter and encourage students to apply their understanding of the chapter, to reflect on their personal experiences, or to share their insights or knowledge related to the material presented.

For Discussion and Application   Each chapter ends with questions that provide opportunities for students to synthesize and reflect on the major concepts presented in the chapter. The questions may be used as oral or written assignments or topics for class discussion. At least one question in each set invites students to apply the information presented in the chapter to their own lives and school settings.

Historical Art and Photographs   Historical art and photographs are also important features of the text. Photographs represent a different reality. Photographs "transgress the norms of time, freezing to infinity a moment of the past. . . . They present a reality that once was, but in representation is now something else. The significance of this something else, as with paintings and texts, must be constructed, and this construction is bound up inextricably in the multiple contexts (historical, intellectual, political, social, etc.) of both the photographer and the observer" (Gabella, 1994, p. 352).

References   The text makes extensive reference to the works of historians who have expertise in a particular topic. These references are included not only to support the statements being made, but also to provide the reader with references for further study.

Acknowledgments

The author wishes to recognize the many persons who have contributed to the preparation of this text. First, the experience of researching and writing this history has given me a new and deeper appreciation of the debt we owe to all the educators, from the colonial dames in their kitchens to the nuclear scientists in their university laboratories, who have devoted themselves to expanding and enriching the educational opportunities of the young people and adults of this country. Second, I wish to acknowledge the diverse scholars, past and present, who have provided a record of the development of education in the United States. Third, I want to thank my professional colleagues for their critical comments and suggestions at every stage of the project. A very special thanks goes to Arlene Metha, my friend and co-author on *Foundations of American Education* (Merrill/Prentice Hall), who provided most of the material for the chapter on the philosophy of education.

I extend my special thanks and appreciation to Executive Editor Debbie Stollenwerk, who believed in the project for a number of years; her assistant, Mary Morrill, who is always there and always helpful; and to Associate Editor Ben Stephen, whose advice and assistance saw the project through its development. Sincere thanks are also extended to the reviewers. Their constructive comments made the book far better than it would ever have been without their involvement. For their efforts, I extend appreciation to Judy Arnold, Lincoln Memorial University; Carlton E. Beck, University of Wisconsin–Milwaukee; Richard L. Farber, The College of New Jersey; Dennis Herschbach, University of Maryland; Karen Keifer-Boyd, The Pennsylvania State University; Ann M. Knupfer, Purdue University; Douglas MacIsaac, Stetson University; Janet McNellis, Troy State University; Stephen D. Oates, Northern Michigan University; Susan M. Perlis, Marywood University; Patrick M. Socoski, West Chester University; Carol Winkle, Aquinas College; Karl Wolfe, Pepperdine University; Penelope Wong, California State University, Chico; and Harold S. Wright, Jr., University of Mary Washington.

Educator Learning Center
An Invaluable Online Resource

Merrill Education and the Association for Supervision and Curriculum Development (ASCD) invite you to take advantage of a new online resource, one that provides access to the top research and proven strategies associated with ASCD and Merrill—the Educator Learning Center. At **www .EducatorLearningCenter.com** you will find resources that will enhance your students' understanding of course topics and of current educational issues, in addition to being invaluable for further research.

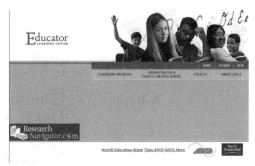

How the Educator Learning Center Will Help Your Students Become Better Teachers

With the combined resources of Merrill Education and ASCD, you and your students will find a wealth of tools and materials to better prepare them for the classroom.

Research

- More than 600 articles from the ASCD journal *Educational Leadership* discuss everyday issues faced by practicing teachers.
- A direct link on the site to Research Navigator gives students access to many of the leading education journals, as well as extensive content detailing the research process.
- Excerpts from Merrill Education texts give your students insights on important topics of instructional methods, diverse populations, assessment, classroom management, technology, and refining classroom practice.

Classroom Practice

- Hundreds of lesson plans and teaching strategies are categorized by content area and age range.
- Case studies and classroom video footage provide virtual field experience for student reflection.
- Computer simulations and other electronic tools keep your students abreast of today's classrooms and current technologies.

Look into the Value of Educator Learning Center Yourself

A four-month subscription to Educator Learning Center is $25 but is **FREE** when packaged with any Merrill Education text. In order for your students to have access to this site, you must use this special value-pack ISBN number **WHEN** placing your textbook order with the bookstore: 0-13-168672-0. Your students will then receive a copy of the text packaged with a free ASCD pincode. To preview the value of this website to you and your students, please go to **www.educatorlearningcenter.com** and click on "Demo."

Brief Contents

Chapter 1   Philosophy and Education   2

Chapter 2   Education in the Old World and the "New"
             Old World Before Jamestown   42

Chapter 3   Education in Colonial America   66

Chapter 4   Education in the Revolutionary and Early
             National Periods   104

Chapter 5   The Common School Movement   136

Chapter 6   Education in the Post–Civil War Era   170

Chapter 7   The Progressive Era in Education   212

Chapter 8   Depression, War, and National Defense   242

Chapter 9   The Struggle for Equal Educational
             Opportunity: 1954–1980   280

Chapter 10   Renewed Conservatism and Reform   320

Chapter 11   Education in a New Century   358

Contents

Chapter 1   Philosophy and Education   2

Branches of Philosophy   4

Metaphysics: What Is the Nature of Reality?   4
Epistemology: What Is the Nature of Knowledge?   4
Axiology: What Is the Nature of Values?   4

Traditional Philosophies and Their Educational Implications   5

Idealism   5   Realism   8
Theistic Realism (Thomism)   10

Contemporary Philosophies and Their Educational Implications   12

Pragmatism   12   Existentialism   14
Analytic Philosophy   17

Philosophies of Education   19

Perennialism   19   Progressivism   23
Essentialism   25   Social Reconstructionism   27
Postmodernism   29

Primary Source Reading: The Allegory of the Cave *by Plato   35*

Primary Source Reading: Preparing for Today and Tomorrow *by Elliot W. Eisner   37*

Chapter 2   Education in the Old World and the "New" Old World Before Jamestown   42

The Renaissance and Education   44

Education During the Reformation   45

Luther   45   Calvin   46   Vernacular Schools   47

Spanish and French Exploration and Education in the New World   47

New Spain   48   Spanish Missions of
La Florida   48   Mission Schools in the
Southwest   49   New France   51

Education of Native Peoples in Precolonial America   53

Basic Courses of Native Education   55   Native Philosophy of Education   56   Core Values of Native Educational Practice   57

Primary Source Reading: The Education of Young Children *by Desiderius Erasmus   60*

Primary Source Reading: The Socialization of Nampeyo *by Barbara Kramer   63*

Chapter 3   Education in Colonial America   66

Education in the New England Colonies   68

Massachusetts Education Laws of 1642 and 1647   69   Elementary Schooling   70
Instruction and Instructional Materials   74
Secondary Education: Latin Grammar Schools   76
Supervision and Support of the Schools   77
Higher Education in Early New England   78

Education in the Mid-Atlantic Colonies   79

Influence of Denominational Variations   79
New York   80   New Jersey   81
Pennsylvania   81   Delaware   83

Education in the Southern Colonies   83

Influence of Social and Economic Systems   83
Elementary and Secondary Education   84
Higher Education: The College of William and Mary   86

Education During the Later Colonial Period   87

Impact of the Enlightenment   87   Impact of Social and Economic Changes on Education   89
Rise of the Academy   90   Expansion of Higher Education   91

The Colonial Schoolmaster   92

Teacher Licensing and Pay   94

Education of Minorities in Colonial America   95

Primary Source Reading: A Dame School in Plymouth, Massachusetts *by Laura Russell*   98

Primary Source Reading: School-Management (Schul-ordnung) *by Christopher Dock*   100

Chapter 4   Education in the Revolutionary and Early National Periods   104

Education Under the Articles of Confederation and the Constitution   106

Northwest Land Ordinances of 1785 and 1787   106

Nationalism and Education   107

Republican Educational Theorists   108

Thomas Jefferson   108   Benjamin Rush   110 Noah Webster   112

New Providers of Elementary Education   114

Monitorial Schools   114   Sunday Schools   115 Infant Schools   116

Town and District Schools: Organization and Instruction   116

Growth of the Academy   118

Academies for Women   119

Emergence of the Public High School   122

Developments in Higher Education in the Early National Period   123

Defense of the Classical Curriculum: The Yale Report of 1828   124   Dartmouth College Case   125

Education of Women in the New Republic: The Cult of Domesticity   125

Primary Source Reading: A New England District School, circa 1801   128

Primary Source Reading: A Plan for Improving Female Education *by Emma Willard*   130

Chapter 5   The Common School Movement   136

Moving Forces   138

Changing Demographics: A Larger, More Diverse, and Urban Population   138   Demands of a Growing Working Class   139   Social Control   139   The Frontier Movement   140

Extended Suffrage   140   Education Journals and Organizations   140   Protestant Religious Accommodation   142

Leading Proponents of the Common School   142

Horace Mann   142   James G. Carter   144 Henry Barnard   145   Catherine Beecher   145

Opposition to the Common School Movement   146

Growth of State and Local Support and Supervision   146

Increased Tax Support   146   Creation of State Boards and State Superintendents of Education   148 Development of Local School Districts and Superintendents   148   Regional Variations   150

Teaching and Textbooks in the Common Schools   151

Pestalozzian Influence   153

The Failure of the Common Schools: The Schooling of Catholics   155

Education of Teachers   156

Establishment of Normal Schools   158   Teacher Institutes   160

Primary Source Reading: Proposal for Tax-Supported Schools *by Thaddeus Stevens   162*

Primary Source Reading: Intolerance in the City of Brotherly Love *by Jim Carnes   166*

Chapter 6   Education in the Post–Civil War Era   170

The Kindergarten Movement   172

The Secondary School Movement   173

The Kalamazoo Case and Increased Tax Support   174   Compulsory Attendance and Increased Literacy   176   NEA Committee of Ten and the Standardization of the Curriculum   177   Seven Cardinal Principles of Secondary Education   177   The Manual Training Movement   179   Vocational Education   180   The Comprehensive High School   181   Emergence of the Junior High School   182

Expansion of Higher Education   183

The Morrill Acts and the Land Grant College Movement   183   Higher Education for Women   184   Emergence of the Modern

University *187*   *Founding of Junior*
Colleges *189*

Improved Teacher Training and
Professionalism 189

Strengthening of the Normal School Curriculum and
Standards 189   *Universities Enter Teacher*
Training 190   *Teacher Certification 191*
Teacher Organizations 192

New Directions in the Education of Native
Americans and African Americans 194

From Mission Schools to Public Schools: 150 Years
of Indian Education 194   *Education of Free*
and Freed Blacks 197   *The Higher Education*
Debate: Booker T. Washington and W. E. B.
Du Bois 198   *Segregation of the Public*
Schools 200

Primary Source Reading: Some Aspects of
Kindergarten *by Susan E. Blow 202*

Primary Source Reading: Summer School Teacher *by*
W.E.B. DuBois 208

Chapter 7   The Progressive Era in
Education   212

Population and National Growth 214

Politics and Economic Growth: The Bright and
Dark Sides 214

Progressive Reformers 218

Changes in Education 218

Progressivism in Education 221

Administrative Progressivism: The Efficiency
Movement 221   Pedagogical
Progressivism 223

Child Study Movement 227

The Measurement Movement 228

Progressive Education After the War 230

Progressive Education Association 231

Influence of the Progressive Education Movement
on Higher Education 231

Primary Source Reading: The Problem of the
Children *by Jacob A. Riis 233*

Primary Source Reading: Court Decisions versus
Social Progress *by Ella Flagg Young 237*

Chapter 8   Depression, War and
National Defense   242

The Depression Begins 244

Impact of the Depression on Education 245

New Deal Education Programs 249

Civilian Conservation Corp 249   National
Youth Administration 249   Public Works
Administration 250   Works Projects
Administration 250   General Federal Aid
Debate 251

The Indian New Deal 252

Efforts to Refocus the Schools
and the Curriculum 254

Social Reconstructionism 254   The Eight-Year
Study 255   William C. Bagley and the
Essentialists 256

Impact of the Second World War
on the Schools 256

Impact of the War on Elementary and Secondary
Schools 258   Impact of the War on Higher
Education 259   Higher Education and the War
Effort 259

Education in the Postwar Era 262

Life Adjustment Education and the Education Critics
of the 1950s 262

Curriculum Reform in the Aftermath
of *Sputnik* 264

New Learning Theories 267

Education and the Red Scare 268

Primary Source Reading: Dare the Schools Build a
New Social Order? *by George S. Counts 271*

Primary Source Reading: A Teacher at Topaz *by*
Eleanor Gerard Sekerak 274

Chapter 9   The Struggle
for Equal Educational Opportunity:
1954-1980   280

The Civil Rights Movement 282

School Desegregation 282

The Carrot and the Stick: The Civil Rights Act
of 1964 and the Elementary and Secondary
Education Act of 1965 284

Education and the War on Poverty 287

Expanding the Rights of Language Minority
Youth   289

Indian Education and the Drive for Self-
Determination   290

Expanding Educational Opportunities for Mexican
Americans   292

The Education of Asian Americans   294

    The First to Come: Chinese Americans   294
    Japanese Americans   295

Gender Equity in Education   297

Expanding Access to Children
with Disabilities   300

School Finance Reform   302

The Students' Rights and Antiwar
Movements   305

Primary Source Reading: U.S. Supreme Court,
Brown v. Board of Education   *310*

Primary Source Reading: Indian Education:
A National Tragedy *by U.S. Senate Special
Subcommittee on Indian Education   313*

Chapter 10   Renewed Conservatism and Reform   320

Conservatism Takes Center Stage   322

The School Reform Movement   323

    *Reform: The First Wave   326   Reform:
The Second Wave   326   Reform: The Third
Wave   329*

Essentialism, Perennialism, and Progressivism
Revisited   331

National Goals, National Standards, and
Accountability   333

School Choice   337

    *Vouchers   338   Charter Schools   338
Private Contractors   339*

Cultural and Gender Wars   340

    *Bilingual Education Debate   340   Multicultural
Education Under Fire   342   Gender Wars   343
Resegregation   344*

The End of a Presidency, a Decade,
a Century   345

Primary Source Reading: The Manufactured Crisis:
Myths, Fraud, and the Attack on America's Public
Schools *by D. C. Berliner and B. J. Biddle   347*

Primary Source Reading: An Educator's Primer on
the Gender War *by David Sadker   351*

Chapter 11   Education in the New Century   358

An Education President, Again   360

No Child Left Behind and the New Federal
Role   360

Expanded State and Local Responsibilities   361

Raising the Stakes on High-Stakes Testing and
Accountability   362

Sanctions   365

Teacher Crisis: Issues of Quantity
and Quality   367

Funding an Adequate Education   370

Brown + 50: What's Changed, What's Not   371

The Achievement Gap   373

Resegregation   374

School Choice   374

Primary Source Reading: Taproots for a New
Century: Tapping the Best of Traditional and
Progressive Education *by David B. Ackerman   377*

References   382

Name Index   393

Subject Index   395

NOTE: Every effort has been made to provide accurate and current Internet information in this book. However, the Internet and information posted on it are constantly changing, and it is inevitable that some of the Internet addresses listed in this textbook will change.

The History
of American Education

A Great American Experiment

CHAPTER 1

Philosophy and Education

The philosophy of the classroom is the philosophy of the government in the next generation.

—*Abraham Lincoln*

"The great force of history comes from the fact that we carry it within us, are unconsciously controlled by it in many ways, and history is literally present in all that we do" (Balwin, cited in Foner, 2002, p. ix). Like history, philosophy is also literally present in all that we do. History and philosophy influence our interpretation of both past events and present actions. Both challenge us to question our beliefs regarding the past. Philosophy raises questions about reality, knowledge, and conduct. History analyzes and raises questions about past events. Philosophy and history are social constructions—that is, our perceptions and views of the past color our perspective of the present. Conversely, the way we experience the present influences the way we interpret the past.

The formal study of philosophy helps us to better understand who we are, why we are here, and where we are going. It empowers us to recognize the meaning of our personal existence. The study of the philosophies of education enables us to recognize educational principles that define our views about the purposes of schooling, curriculum and instruction, teaching, and learning—in effect, our educational philosophy. One cannot be concerned with education without being concerned with philosophy. In fact, John Dewey (1916) went so far as to say that to the extent that "we are willing to conceive education as the process of forming fundamental dispositions; intellectual and emotional, toward nature and fellow men, philosophy may even be defined as the general theory of education" (p. 383).

This chapter begins with an explanation of the three branches of philosophy—metaphysics, epistemology, and axiology—and their interpretation by the major traditional (idealism, realism, theistic realism) and contemporary (pragmatism, existentialism, analytic) philosophies. The position of each philosophy in regard to the purposes of schooling, the most appropriate curriculum and methods of instruction, the nature of the learner, and the role of the teacher is discussed, along with its leading proponents. Attention then turns to the educational philosophies of perennialism, progressivism, essentialism, social reconstructionism, and postmodernism. Each is discussed in terms of its major principles and its beliefs regarding the purposes of schooling, curriculum and instruction, the classroom environment, the role of the teacher, and assessment, as well as its major proponents.

Branches of Philosophy

As a discipline, philosophy is said to have three branches: metaphysics, epistemology, and axiology. These branches are concerned with answering three questions that are important in describing any philosophy:

- What is the nature of reality?
- What is the nature of knowledge?
- What is the nature of values?

Metaphysics: What Is the Nature of Reality?

Metaphysics is the branch of philosophy that is concerned with the nature of reality and existence, as well as with the nature of the person or self. It addresses such questions as whether human nature is basically good, evil, spiritual, mental, or physical.

 For Your Reflection and Analysis

Should schools be involved in discussions of the origins of the universe? Why, or why not?

Metaphysics can be subdivided into ontology and cosmology. *Ontology* raises some fundamental questions about what we mean by the nature of existence and what it means for anything "to be." *Cosmology* raises questions about the origin and organization of the universe or cosmos.

Of the three basic questions, What is the nature of reality? is perhaps the most difficult to answer because its elements are vague, abstract, and not easily identifiable. However, in spite of its abstraction and vagueness, most philosophers would agree that the nature of reality (the meaning of existence) is one of the key concepts in understanding any philosophy.

Epistemology: What Is the Nature of Knowledge?

The branch of philosophy that is concerned with the investigation of the nature of knowledge is known as *epistemology*. To explore the nature of knowledge is to raise questions about the limits of knowledge, the sources of knowledge, the validity of knowledge, the cognitive processes, and how we know. There are many "ways of knowing," including scientific inquiry, intuition, experience, sensing, feeling, trial and error, scientific research, and logic. Logic is primarily concerned with making inferences, reasoning, or arguing in a rational manner, and includes the subdivisions of deduction and induction. *Deductive logic* is reasoning from a general statement or principle to a specific point or example. *Inductive logic* is reasoning from the specific to a more general conclusion.

Axiology: What Is the Nature of Values?

Whereas epistemology explores the nature of knowledge, *axiology* seeks to determine what is of value. To evaluate, to make a judgment, or to value literally means to apply a set of norms or standards to human conduct or beauty. Axiology is divided into two spheres: ethics and aesthetics. *Ethics* is concerned with the study of human conduct

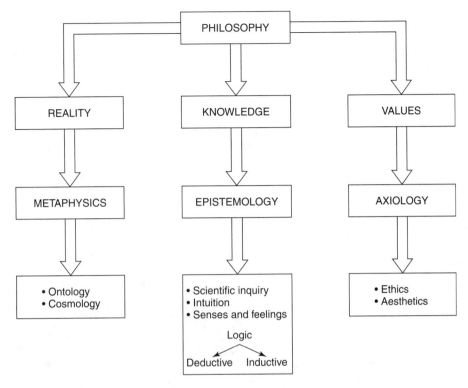

FIGURE 1.1 Summary of the Branches of Philosophy
Source: Webb, L. Dean, Metha, Arlene, & Jordan, K. Forbis (2003). *Foundations of American education,* 4th edition, © 2003. Reprinted by permission of Pearson Education, Inc., Upper Saddle River, NJ.

and examines moral values—right, wrong, good, and bad. *Aesthetics* is concerned with values in beauty, nature, and the "aesthetic experience."

Traditional Philosophies and Their Educational Implications

The so-called traditional philosophies include the oldest Western philosophies of idealism, realism, and theistic realism (neo-Thomism). These philosophies all include the belief in certain preestablished metaphysical truths. The interpretations and applications of these preestablished truths have played a major role in the history of Western civilization.

Idealism

Idealism is considered the oldest philosophy of Western culture, dating back to ancient Greece and Plato. For the idealist, the world of the mind, ideas, and reason is primary.

Metaphysics

Idealism stresses mind over matter. For the idealist, nothing exists or is real except ideas in the minds of people or the mind of God, the Universal Mind. The universe can be explained as a creative and spiritual reality that includes the notions of permanence, order, and certainty.

If the mind is prior, or ultimate, then material things either do not exist (i.e., are not real), or if they do exist, their existence depends in some fashion on the mind. For example, an idealist would contend that there is no such thing as a chair; there is only the idea of a chair. The idealist's concept of reality considers the self as one in mind, soul, and spirit. Such a nature is capable of emulating the Absolute or Supreme Mind.

Epistemology

Because idealism accepts a primarily mental explanation for its metaphysics or reality, it is not surprising that idealists also accept the premise that all knowledge includes a mental grasp of ideas and concepts. And, because the mind is the primary reality, it is important to master the science of logic—in particular, deductive logic. Logic provides the framework for unifying our thoughts. Although traditional idealists consider reason, logic, or revelation to be primary ways of "knowing," modern idealists also accept intuition as a way of knowing.

Some idealists believe that the search for truth, rather than truth itself, is the ultimate challenge. But they also believe that most of us resort to the lowest level (mere opinions about truth) and never reach "Ultimate Truth." Nonetheless, although we may never grasp Ultimate Truth, we do have the potential to aspire to wisdom, improve the quality of our ideas, and move closer to Ultimate Truth.

Axiology

Just as the idealists believe that order is an important element of reality, they also believe that order is basic to understanding the nature of values. Values, they believe, can be classified and ordered into a hierarchy or classification system. To the idealist, values are rooted in existence and are part of reality. "We enjoy values not only because our emotions and sentiments are appropriately aroused but because the things we value are realities that have existence themselves and are rooted in the very structure of the cosmos" (Butler, 1966, p. 74).

Values also are absolute. The good, the true, and the beautiful basically do not change from generation to generation, or from society to society. They are not created by man but are part of the very nature and being of the universe (Kneller, 1971). They are, in fact, reflections of the Absolute Good, the Absolute Truth, and the Absolute Beauty-God.

Leading Proponents

The Greek philosopher Plato (427–347 B.C.) is considered the father of idealism. In his famous "Allegory of the Cave," from *The Republic* (360 B.C./1921), Plato inferred that each of us lives in a cave of shadows, doubts, and distortions about reality (an excerpt of Plato's "Allegory" appears as a Primary Source Reading at the end of this chapter). However, through education and enlightenment, the real world of pure ideas can be substituted for those distorted shadows and doubts.

Judaism and Christianity have both been influenced by Plato's philosophy of idealism. According to Plato, ultimate reality can be found in the "idea" through the mind. Judeo-Christian teaching suggests that ultimate reality can be found in God through the soul. St. Augustine (354–430), a prominent theologian of the fourth and fifth centuries, applied a number of Plato's assumptions to Christian thought, providing the rationale for the religious idealism and theistic realism that influenced Western thought for centuries (Ozmon & Craver, 2003).

Idealist thought influenced the writings of a number of major philosophers, including René Descartes, Immanuel Kant, and Georg Wilhelm Friedrich Hegel. The French philosopher Descartes (1596–1650), in his famous dictum, "*Cogito, ergo sum*— I think, therefore I am," declared that as humans we may doubt everything, but we cannot doubt our own existence. Descartes not only accepted the concepts of the finite mind and ideas as advanced by Plato, but also determined that all ideas, save one, depend on other ideas. The only idea that does not depend on any idea other than itself is the idea of Perfect Being or God. Descartes influenced a number of fields of inquiry, including the sciences (Ozmon & Craver, 2003).

Immanuel Kant (1724–1804) also incorporated the major tenets of idealism by postulating that certain universal moral laws known as *categorical imperatives* guide our actions or behaviors. One of Kant's categorical imperatives was "above all things, obedience is an essential feature in the character of a child." This moral maxim has become a primary basis for moral training or character development in education (Ozmon & Craver, 2003).

The German idealist Georg Wilhelm Hegel (1770–1831) approached reality as a "contest of opposites," such as life and death, love and hate, individual and society. According to Hegel, each idea (thesis) has its own opposite (antithesis). The confrontation between the idea (thesis) and its opposite (antithesis) results in a more comprehensive idea (synthesis).

Educational Implications

Purpose of Schooling.   For the idealist, the purpose of the school is to promote spiritual and intellectual development. Idealists believe that even though students may never fully achieve Ultimate Truth, the school can provide the educational environment that will improve the quality of their ideas and move them closer to Ultimate Truth. The ideal school emulates Plato's model and is designed to produce competent and self-actualized adults who will become useful citizens of the state (Noddings, 1995).

Curriculum and Instruction.   Idealists consider the "ideal" curriculum one that stresses the eternal ideas of the past. As early as middle school and secondary school, students are encouraged to read, study, and reflect on the great works of literature, philosophy, politics, history, and the arts. And, because the enduring truths and values are eternal and unchanging, the curriculum stresses the *Great Books* of the past. Mathematics (algebra, geometry, and calculus) as well as the physical and natural sciences also occupy a prominent place in the idealist's curriculum. For idealists whose

For Your Reflection and Analysis

What, if any, eternal truths or values do you believe should be shared with all students?

religion is an important aspect of their value orientation, the curriculum includes a variety of holy and sacred books (Gutek, 2004).

The preferred methods of instruction for the idealist educator are lecture, discussion, reflection, and the Socratic method. The Socratic method or dialogue is a questioning process used by the teacher that was employed by Socrates, Plato's teacher. The teacher asks questions to lead students to certain conclusions based on their own experiences.

Nature of the Learner. Although the idealist might perceive the student as immature and perhaps misguided, the basic philosophy of idealism is that every student has a mind, soul, and spirit capable of emulating the Absolute Mind. The expectation is that students will broaden their understanding of the world by absorbing ideas from books and teachers.

Role of the Teacher. The idealist teacher serves as the "ideal" role model who has extensive knowledge about the Great Books of the Western World and is able to motivate students to want to become familiar with the universal and timeless lessons from the classics. He or she is familiar with and employs a variety of processes of logical thinking and reasoning. The idealist views the teacher as the source of authority for students.

Realism

Realism, like idealism, is one of the oldest philosophies of Western culture, dating to ancient Greece and Aristotle. Classical, or Aristotelian, realism is the antithesis of idealism. For the realist, the universe exists whether the human mind perceives it or not. Matter is primary and is considered an independent reality. The world of things is superior to the world of ideas.

Metaphysics

Realism stresses the world of nature or physical things and our experiences and perceptions of those things. For the realist, reality is composed of both matter (body) and form (mind). Matter can only be shaped or organized into being by the mind. Moreover, the interaction of matter and form is governed not by God but by scientific, natural laws. Unlike the idealists, who believe reality is in the mind and internal, realists believe reality is external and can be verified.

Epistemology

The major ways of knowing for realists are perception, rational thinking, and sensing. *Sense realism* is a school of realism that asserts that knowledge comes through the senses, which gather data and transmit them to the mind to be sorted, classified, and categorized. From these data we make generalizations. Some realists, such as Aristotle, believed that perception (knowledge acquired through the senses) was not sufficient to understand reality. Aristotle argued that the use of deductive logic is more effective than perception in understanding the physical world. The process of deduction entails the establishment of a first or major premise, followed by a second or minor premise, and the drawing of a conclusion (*syllogism*) from them. For other realists, knowledge is established by the *scientific method*, which includes the systematic reporting and analysis of what is observed and the testing of hypotheses formulated from the observations.

Axiology

Realists believe that values are derived from nature. Natural law and moral law are the major determinants of what is good. Whatever reflects the orderliness and rationality of nature is valued. Goodness depends on leading a virtuous life, one in keeping with natural and moral laws. Although they do not adhere to any hard-and-fast rules regarding ethics, realists do believe that deviating from moral truth will cause injury both to the individual and to society (Power, 1982).

Leading Proponents

Aristotle (384–322 B.C.), a pupil of Plato, is considered the father of realism. Aristotle disagreed with Plato that only ideas are real. For Aristotle, reality, knowledge, and value exist independent of the mind, and their existence is not predicated by our ideas. According to Aristotle, material things have existed since the beginning of time, prior to our knowledge of their existence, and they will continue to exist after we depart (Power, 1982).

Other proponents of realism were Francis Bacon (1561–1626) and John Locke (1632–1704). Bacon, both a philosopher and a politician, advanced a scientific form of realism that depended on the inductive method of inquiry. Locke's advocacy of sense realism stemmed from his study of human knowledge. One of Locke's major concepts was the *tabula rasa* concept. According to this concept there are no such things as innate ideas. We come into the world with a mind like a blank slate (a *tabula rasa*). Knowledge is then acquired through sensory perception.

Other major philosophers who contributed to realism were John Amos Comenius (1592–1670), the Czech educator and theologian, and Jean-Jacques Rousseau (1712–1778), the French philosopher known for his political and educational theories (both discussed in chapter 3). Another realist and a follower of Rousseau was Johann Heinrich Pestalozzi (1746–1827), the Swiss educator known for his child-centered philosophy discussed in chapter 5. Pestalozzi along with Rousseau had a profound influence on progressive education.

Educational Implications

Purpose of Schooling.   Realists argue that the purpose of schooling is to teach moral and intellectual virtue, to help the student to know, and to arrive at the causes of things (Spangler, 1998). Realists believe the school should provide an educational environment designed to develop students' power of reasoning and to help them master the principles of scientific inquiry.

Curriculum and Instruction.   Realists advocate a curriculum that focuses on the natural laws and emphasizes the basics, including mathematics, science, language, literature, and history. Realists give theoretical subjects such as mathematics and the sciences a higher priority than the "practical arts."

Realists prefer a variety of instructional methods, including the use of deductive logic; observation, classification, and categorization; and the scientific method. The content of the curriculum is determined by authority figures or experts.

Nature of the Learner. Realists view the student as an orderly, sensing, and rational being capable of understanding the world of things. Both the teacher and the student are considered learners, and teaching and learning are considered an unending interactive process (Jacobsen, 2003).

Role of the Teacher. The role of the teacher, according to the realist, is to emphasize and model reasoning, observation, and experimentation. Teachers' major function is to teach students how to think clearly and understand the material world.

Theistic Realism (Thomism)

Theistic realism or its antecedent, *Thomism* (sometimes referred to as *neo-Thomism* or religious realism), dates to the time of St. Thomas Aquinas (1225–1274). Theistic realism represents a combination of theism (belief in God) and realism (belief in external and objective reality guided by natural law)(Gutek, 2004). For the theistic realist, God exists and can be known by both faith and reason.

Metaphysics

Theistic realists believe that God gives meaning and purpose to the universe. God is the Pure Being that represents the coming together of essence and existence. Things exist independently of ideas. However, both physical objects and human beings, including minds and ideas, are created by God. Thus, although both physical objects and God are real, God is preeminent. Theistic realists believe that human beings are rational beings with souls, modeled after God, the Perfect Being.

Epistemology

Although some philosophers believe that one can come to know God only through faith or intuition, theistic realists believe that we come to know God through both our faith and our capacity to reason. They also believe in a hierarchy of knowing. At the lowest level is scientific or synthetic knowing. At the second level is analytic or intuitive knowing. And at the highest level is mystical or revelatory knowing (Morris & Pai, 1976). Aquinas clarified that truth or knowledge could not deviate from, or be inconsistent with, revelation (Jacobsen, 2003).

Axiology

For the theistic realist, ethically speaking, goodness follows reason. That is, values are unchanging moral laws established by God that can be discerned by reason. As a corollary, ignorance is the source of evil. If people do not know what is right, they cannot be expected to do what is right. If, on the other hand, people do know what is right, they can be held morally responsible for what they do. In terms of aesthetics, the reason, or intellect, is also the perceiver of beauty. That which is valued as beautiful is also found pleasing to the intellect (Morris & Pai, 1976).

Leading Proponents

Thomas Aquinas, a theologian of the 13th century from whom neo-Thomism or Thomism takes its name, is credited with interfacing the secular ideas of Aristotle and the Christian teachings of St. Augustine. Both Aristotle and Aquinas viewed reality via reason and sensation. Aquinas believed that God created matter out of nothing and gave meaning and purpose to the universe. In his most noted work, *Summa Theologica*, he used the rational approach suggested by Aristotle to answer questions regarding existence and Christianity. As a result, many of the supporting arguments of Christian beliefs rely on Thomas Aquinas. Roman Catholicism considers Thomism its leading philosophy (Ozmon & Craver, 2003).

Educational Implications

 For Your Reflection and Analysis

What, if any, conflicts can you see in developing both the intellect and the spiritual nature of the student?

Purpose of Schooling. For the theistic realist the school has a dual purpose: to cultivate the intellect and to develop the spiritual nature of the individual. Theistic realists also believe that although formal education may end, learning is a lifelong process.

Curriculum and Instruction. For theistic realists, the cultivation of the intellect and the development of the spiritual nature are accomplished by offering a strong liberal arts curriculum while stressing faith and reason through a relationship with God. Subjects such as philosophy (metaphysics and logic), theology, language and literature, mathematics, science, history, geography, political science, sociology, economics, and the arts are central to the curriculum of the theistic realist (Gutek, 2004).

The methods of instruction preferred by the theistic realist are those that discipline the mind. These include drill and practice, demonstration, recitation, the teaching for mastery of factual and basic skills, and training in the rules of conduct.

Nature of the Learner. Theistic realists believe that all students have the potential to learn and are rational beings with souls modeled after God, perfection. The student exemplifies value and worth.

Role of the Teacher. The major role of the teacher in theistic realist philosophy is to be an exemplary intellectual, moral, and spiritual model for students. The teacher is also responsible for providing a program of studies that reinforces mental discipline and exercises students' rational faculties.

Contemporary Philosophies and Their Educational Implications

The modern or contemporary philosophies have their beginnings in the early 20th century and include pragmatism, existentialism, and analytic philosophy. These philosophies share the belief that there are no preestablished truths. At best there is a relative truth.

Pragmatism

Pragmatism, also known as *experimentalism* or *instrumentalism*, focuses on experience.

Metaphysics

Unlike the traditional philosophers, who view reality as a given, pragmatists regard reality as an event, a process, a verb (Morris & Pai, 1976). As such, it is subject to constant change and lacks absolutes. Meaning is derived from experience, which is simply an interaction with one's environment (Garrison, 1994).

Epistemology

According to pragmatism's theory of knowledge, truth is not absolute but is determined by function or consequences. In fact, pragmatists shun the use of the word *truth* and at best speak of a "tentative truth" that will serve the purpose until experience evolves a new truth. Knowledge is arrived at by scientific inquiry, testing, questioning, and retesting—and is never conclusive.

Axiology

Whereas traditional philosophers concentrate on metaphysics and epistemology, pragmatists focus primarily on axiology or values. As with truths, values to the pragmatist are only tentative. They are also constructed from experience and are subject to testing, questioning, and retesting. For the pragmatist, whatever works, or leads to desirable consequences, is ethically or morally good. The focus on consequences is not to imply that the pragmatist is only concerned with what works for the self. In fact, the pragmatist is concerned with social consequences. "What works" is what works for the larger community. For Dewey, democracy was the key component of pragmatism. He was convinced that democracy cannot exist without community. Democracy is more than government; it includes a free community capable of influencing the political, social, and economic institutions that affect its citizenry (Brosio, 2000).

Regarding aesthetic values, for pragmatists what is beautiful is not determined by some objective ideal but by what we experience when we see, feel, and touch. Accordingly, art is a creative expression and shared experience between the artist and the public.

Leading Proponents

Two individuals who had a profound impact on the pragmatist philosophy were Auguste Comte (1798–1857) and Charles Darwin (1809–1882). Comte influenced pragmatism by suggesting that science could solve social problems. For pragmatists, problem solving is a key ingredient in scientific inquiry. Darwin's theory of natural selection implied that reality was open-ended, not fixed, and subject to change. Pragmatists applied Darwin's ideas to education, which they inferred was also open-ended and subject to biological and social development (Ozmon & Craver, 2003).

Pragmatism is primarily associated with the Americans Charles Sanders Peirce (1839–1914), William James (1842–1910), and John Dewey (1859–1952). In fact, Peirce, a mathematician and logician, is credited with developing the theory of pragmatism. He believed that true knowledge depends on verification of ideas through experience. Ideas are merely hypotheses until tested by experience. Peirce regarded learning, believing, and knowing as an intimate part of doing and feeling and lamented that educators often ignored this important relationship (Garrison & Neiman, 2003).

William James, a psychologist and philosopher, incorporated his views of pragmatism in both psychology and philosophy. James emphasized the centrality of experience. According to James, there are no absolutes, no universals, only an ever-changing universe. He suggested that experience should take precedence over abstractions and universals because experience is open-ended, pluralistic, and in process (Ozmon & Craver, 2003).

James's contemporary, John Dewey, had the greatest influence on American pragmatism. As discussed in more detail in chapter 7, for Dewey, experience, thought, and consequence were interrelated:

> [Thought] is the discernment of the relation between what we try to do and what happens in consequence. No experience having a meaning is possible without some element of thought. . . . We simply do something, and when it fails, we do something else, and keep on trying until we hit upon something which works, and then we adopt that method as a rule of thumb measure in subsequent procedures. (Dewey, 1916, pp. 169–170)

Educational Implications

Purpose of Schooling.   Pragmatists consider the purpose of the school to be modeling a progressive democratic society. Dewey envisioned such a democratic community to be pluralistic in nature and include moral, economic, educational, and political goals. The primary purpose of education is to stress function or experience through problem solving and the scientific method.

Curriculum and Instruction.   Unlike the traditional philosophies that stress a prescribed set of subjects, pragmatism favors a curriculum that integrates several subjects such as history, geography, and the sciences. Dewey suggested having students experience "a personally unified curriculum—one that makes sense to them in terms of human experience, in particular, in terms of their own experience. Subjects such as geography and history are particularly relevant as they can be used as examples of explaining human activity or solving social problems" (Noddings, 1995, pp. 37–38).

The preferred instructional methods for pragmatists include learning by doing, problem solving, experimentation, hands-on activities, collaborative learning, and

For Your Reflection and Analysis

Give examples of the use of the scientific method in a music class and a Spanish class.

methods that incorporate deductive thinking. Pragmatists also place a high priority on instructional methods that involve social interaction and group activities.

Nature of the Learner.   Pragmatists consider students to be evolving and active beings capable of interacting with their environment. Students are seen as individuals capable of setting objectives for their own learning. They are also capable of working together to solve common problems, establishing the rules for governing the classrooms, and testing and evaluating ideas for the improvement of learning and classroom life (Noddings, 1995).

Role of the Teacher.   Pragmatists believe that the teacher should model the most authentic type of knowledge, namely, experimental knowledge. The teacher is viewed as the research or project director and is expected to model reflective thinking, which questions all assumptions, claims of knowledge, evidence, and one's own thought processes. The pragmatist teacher also stresses the application of the scientific method, which includes the systematic reporting and analysis of what is observed and the retesting of hypotheses formulated from observation.

Existentialism

Existentialism appeared a century ago as a revolt against the mathematical, scientific, and objective philosophies that preceded it. Existentialism voiced disfavor with any effort directed at social control or subjugation. Existentialism focuses on personal and

Pragmatists encourage instructional methods that stress social activities.

subjective existence. For the existentialist, the world of existence, choice, and responsibility is primary.

Metaphysics

Unlike the realists and theistic realists, who believe that essence precedes existence, the existentialists believe that existence precedes essence. For the existentialist there is neither meaning nor purpose to the physical universe. We are born into the universe by chance, and because there is no world order or natural scheme of things into which we are born, we owe nothing to nature but our existence (Kneller, 1971). Existentialists believe that because we live in a world without purpose, we must create our own meaning (Gutek, 1988).

In addition to existence, the concept of choice is central to the metaphysics of existentialism. To decide who and what we are is to decide what is real. Is it God? Reason? Nature? Science? By our choices we determine reality. According to the existentialist, we cannot escape from the responsibility to choose, including the choice of how we view our past.

Epistemology

Similar to their position concerning reality, existentialists believe that the way we come to know truth is by choice. The individual self must ultimately decide what is true and how we know. Whether we choose logic, intuition, scientific method, or revelation is irrelevant; what matters is that we must eventually choose. The freedom to choose carries with it a tremendous burden of responsibility that we cannot escape. Because no absolutes, no authorities, and no single or correct way to the truth exist, the only authority is the self.

Axiology

For the existentialist, choice is imperative not only for determining reality and knowledge but also for determining value. Every act and every word is a choice and hence an act of value creation. And here is the dilemma, say the existentialists: Because there are no norms, standards, or assurances that we have chosen correctly or rightly, choice is frustrating and exasperating at times. It is often much easier to look to a standard or benchmark to determine what is right, just, or of value than to take responsibility for the choices we make. Yet, the existentialists suggest, this is a very small price to pay for our free will.

Leading Proponents

The leading proponent of existentialism, indeed the father of existentialism, was the Danish philosopher-theologian Søren Kierkegaard (1813–1855), who renounced scientific objectivity for subjectivity and personal choice. He believed in the reality of God and was concerned with individual existence.

Another expositor of existentialism was Martin Buber (1878–1965), a Jewish philosopher-theologian. He incorporated the principle described as an "I-Thou" relationship whereby each individual recognizes the other's personal meaning and reality. Buber suggested that both the divine and the human are related, and that through personal relationships with others one can enhance one's spiritual life and relationship with God (Ozmon & Craver, 2003).

Also contributing to the development of existential thought were Edmund Husserl (1859–1938), who developed a philosophical method called *phenomenology,* or the study of phenomena (referring to objects, events, or things we perceive or experience), and Martin Heidegger (1889–1976), who expanded and revised phenomenology to create another philosophical method known as *hermeneutics,* or the interpretation of lived experience (Ozmon & Craver, 2003). Phenomenology had a major influence on the critical theory and postmodern movements that followed.

Undoubtedly, the most widely known existentialist was Jean-Paul Sartre (1905–1980). Sartre claimed that free choice implies total responsibility for one's own existence. There are no antecedent principles or purposes that shape our destiny. Sartre's major work, *Being and Nothingness* (1956), is considered one of the major philosophic treatises of the 20th century. According to Sartre, because there is no God to give existence meaning, humanity exists without any meaning until we construct our own.

Existentialism had a major impact on educators such as John Holt (1981), Charles Silberman (1970), and Jonathan Kozol (1972, 1991), who were supporters of the open schools, free schools, and alternative schools that flourished during the mid-1960s. One of the most well known educational existentialists was A. S. Neill (1883–1973), who founded Summerhill School outside London shortly after World War I. Summerhill offered an educational experience built on the principle of learning by discovery in an atmosphere of unrestrained freedom (Neill, 1960).

One of the current spokespersons for the existential philosophy of education is Nel Noddings. Noddings (1992) offered an existential educational model that stresses the *challenge to care:*

> As human beings, we care what happens to us. We wonder whether there is a life after death, whether there is a deity who cares about us, whether we are loved by those we love, whether we belong anywhere; we wonder what we will become, who we are, how much control we have over our own fate. For adolescents these are among the most pressing questions: Who am I? Who will love me? How do others see me? Yet schools spend more time on the quadratic formula than on any of these existential questions. (p. 20)

Educational Implications

Purpose of Schooling.   According to the existentialists, the school should prepare students to take responsibility for, and to deal with, the results of their actions. The purpose of education is to foster self-discovery and explain the importance of the freedom of choice and the responsibility for making choices.

Curriculum and Instruction.   Unlike progressivism, which emphasizes group learning, existentialism emphasizes the individual and personal learning. The curriculum is student centered and provides a variety of existential situations that authenticate the student's own personal experience. The favored subject matter is the humanities because it provides evidence of the suffering that accompanies the human condition. Existentialists assert that by concentrating on the unpleasant idea of meaninglessness or nothingness and its accompanying anxiety and absurdity, we ultimately create an affirmation of self and find a purpose in life. Such a curriculum awakens the learner to a subjective awareness called "the existential moment." Unlike the curriculum of the traditional philosophies, which stresses Absolute Truth, the curriculum of the existentialists fosters "personal truth."

The preferred methods of instruction for the existentialist include nondirective humanistic values education, which engages students in cognitive discussions along with affective experiences. These so-called affective approaches are used in conjunction with the Socratic dialogue, a method existentialists believe will lead to self-knowledge and self-discovery.

Nature of the Learner.   Existentialists believe that the student is a free individual capable of authentic and responsible choices. Furthermore, students are capable of self-discipline and self-discovery and can be responsible for their own learning.

Role of the Teacher.   The role of the existentialist teacher is to become an example of authenticity for students. Moreover, the teacher's goal is to help all students achieve their potential while striving for self-actualization (Greene, 1967). The existentialist educator encourages a more personal and interactive teacher–student relationship. He or she is concerned with the cognitive as well as the affective development of the individual. Because the major thrust of existentialism is the search for meaning and purpose, the teacher is viewed as an individual who is comfortable with being introspective and reflective. Imagination and insight are also important qualities of the existentialist teacher.

Analytic Philosophy

Analytic philosophy, also called *philosophical analysis* or *linguistic analysis*, is a philosophy concerned with clarifying language and establishing meaning. Analytic philosophy criticizes the traditional and modern philosophies, as well as the way they are described, for being prescriptive, making normative judgments, and rendering philosophical statements that are jargon ridden and not verifiable.

The analytic philosophy movement came into being during the post–World War I era when a group of European natural scientists and social scientists formed what became known as the Vienna Circle. These scholars focused their attention on analysis and clarification of the language and concepts that philosophers use. The resulting analytic movement was less concerned with the underlying assumptions about reality, truth, and values addressed by the traditional and contemporary philosophies and more concerned with the clarification, definition, and meaning of language.

Metaphysics

Analytic philosophers are not concerned with metaphysics because they regard issues of "truth," or "reality," as theoretical, impractical, and nonempirical. Their main concern is with choosing terms that have clear meaning and are expressed in common or scientific/professional language.

Epistemology

Philosophical analysis assumes that language statements have immediate meaning because of their inner logic, or that they have the possibility of being made meaningful by being stated in empirical terms that can be verified and tested. According to analytic philosophers, if language has no method of verification, it has no meaning. Many of the words or statements we use are emotional or subjective and have meaning specific to the person who used them (Gutek, 2004). For example, the terms *adaptation, inclusion, adjustment, professionalism, reform, growth,* and *tolerance* imply multiple meanings and would be defined in different ways by different disciplines. Similarly, philosophical statements such as "Existence precedes essence" or "Self-actualization is the highest goal for mankind" are not verifiable and hence have limited meaning.

 For Your Reflection and Analysis

Give examples of words or phrases in your discipline that could be considered jargon or have subjective multiple meanings.

Axiology

Analytic philosophers differ with the traditional and contemporary philosophers in their concern with the formation of values and the encouragement of particular behaviors. Analytic philosophers are not interested in which values are true, which behaviors are good, or which art is most beautiful. They are only concerned with questions such as, *Can these values or behaviors be tested empirically, and do they have meaning to the reader?*

Leading Proponents

Two leading and early spokespersons for the analytic philosophy movement were Bertrand Russell (1872–1970) and Israel Scheffler (b. 1923). Russell focused on the connection between language and reality and espoused that reality could be analyzed and reduced to "irreducible elements or relations" (Noddings, 1995). Scheffler, in *The Language of Education* (1960), focused attention on how philosophical analysis can help teachers formulate their beliefs, arguments, and assumptions about topics that are particularly important to the teaching and learning process.

A more contemporary analytic philosopher, Jonas Soltis (1978), also underscored the importance of philosophical analysis for teachers:

> We must be clear about its intent [language of education] and meaning and not be swayed by its imagery and poetry. The analytic temperament and techniques should prove very useful to all practicing educators in getting them to think through with care and precision just what it is they are buying from theorists, and more importantly, just what it is they're after and how best it might be achieved. (p. 88)

Educational Implications

Purpose of Schooling. Analytic philosophers are not concerned with statements relative to the purpose of education. Instead, they are concerned with making certain that the language used by educators in the school is not vague or ambiguous and can be understood by the student and the public.

Curriculum and Instruction.   Analytic philosophers do not prescribe curriculum or instruction. They are concerned that educators who are involved in curriculum development be cognizant of how the language is being used to describe and implement the curriculum. They advocate the use of philosophical analysis as a tool for teachers and curriculum developers because it offers a system of checks and balances to guard against the use of ambiguous and confusing nomenclature. They also believe that all students should be introduced to the importance and value of analyzing the language because it is the cornerstone of communication. They suggest that the tools of analysis should be introduced as early as the elementary grades and should be reinforced though secondary and higher education.

The preferred method of instruction for analytic philosophers is for teachers to model what analytic philosophers profess. That is, teachers should be attentive to how and what they are communicating to their students, their peers, and the public.

Nature of the Learner.   Analytic philosophers believe that students of all ages are capable of understanding and applying the analytic process. However, students need reinforcement for practicing good communication skills.

Role of the Teacher.   The role of the teacher, according to analytic philosophers, is to model the use of language and logic. And, because the field of education encompasses a variety of ideas that have originated in other disciplines (i.e., philosophy, psychology, history, sociology, and religion), the teacher should be well versed in how these disciplines interpret and define their particular language and ideas. Most important, the teacher should always be attentive to choosing terms that are clear and meaningful to the student.

Table 1.1 presents a summary of the educational implications of the traditional and contemporary philosophies.

Philosophies of Education

The major philosophies of education (also referred to as theories of education) are perennialism, progressivism, essentialism, social reconstructionism, and postmodernism (also referred to as postmodern constructivism). Each of these philosophies developed as a protest against the prevailing social and educational climate of the time. For example, perennialism, the first philosophy of education discussed, was a protest against secularization and the excessive focus on science and technology at the expense of reason, which dominated society and its educational institutions at that time.

Perennialism

Eternal or perennial truths, permanence, order, certainty, rationality, and logic constitute the ideal for the perennialist. The philosophies of idealism, realism, and theistic realism (neo-Thomism) are embedded in the perennialist philosophy of education. The educational focus of *perennialism* is on the need to return to the past, namely, to universal truths and such absolutes as reason and faith. The views of Aristotle and Aquinas are represented in this educational philosophy. Although

TABLE 1.1   Educational Implications of Traditional and Contemporary Philosophies

	Purpose of Schooling	Curriculum and Instruction	Nature of the Learner	Role of the Teacher	Leading Proponents
Idealism	• Promote spiritual and intellectual development • Transmit eternal truths and values	• Liberal arts • Great Books • Socratic dialogue • Lecture • Discussion • Reflection	• Mind • Soul • Spirit	• Stress eternal ideas of past	• Plato • Descartes • Kant • Hegel
Realism	• Teach moral and intellectual virtue	• Liberal arts • Deductive logic • Scientific method	• Orderly • Sensing • Rational being	• Stress natural law, scientific inquiry	• Aristotle • Bacon • Locke • Comenius • Rousseau • Pestalozzi
Theistic Realism (Neo-Thomism)	• Cultivate the intellect • Develop spirituality	• Liberal arts • Basic skills • Drill and practice • Demonstration • Recitation • Rules of conduct	• Rational being with soul, modeled after God	• Stress faith and reason	• Augustine • Aquinas
Pragmatism	• Stress function and experience • Model democracy	• Integrated • Problem solving • Deductive logic, scientific method • Group projects, experimentation	• Evolving, active being	• Research and project director • Model reflective thinking	• Comte • Darwin • Peirce • James • Dewey
Existentialism	• Stress self-discovery, choice, and responsibility	• Humanities • Student centered • Self-discovery • Personal truth • Socratic method • Values education	• Free, capable, authentic, responsible chooser	• Stress authenticity, responsibility, self-discovery, and choice	• Kierkegaard • Buber • Husserl • Heidegger • Sartre
Analytic Philosophy	• Stress clarification, definition, and meaning of language	• Analysis of language, communication skills	• Capable of understanding and applying linguistic analysis	• Stress clear and meaningful language • Model and use appropriate language and logic	• Russell • Scheffler • Soltis

perennialism has been associated with neo-Thomism and the teachings of the Roman Catholic Church, it has also received widespread support from lay educators.

Purpose of Schooling

Whether one is an ecclesiastical (Thomist) or lay perennialist, one would contend that the purpose of schooling is to cultivate the rational intellect and to provide knowledge of the eternal truths. For the ecclesiastical perennialists the highest goal of education is union with God.

Curriculum and Instruction

For the ecclesiastical perennialist, Christian doctrine is an important aspect of the curriculum. The holy scriptures, the catechism, theology, and the teaching of Christian dogma play a significant role. Wherever possible, theistic works take precedence over purely secular works (Morris & Pai, 1976).

Both the ecclesiastical and lay perennialists emphasize a concern for subject matter because through the mastery of subject matter intellect is trained and eternal truths are revealed. The cognitive subjects of philosophy, mathematics (especially algebra and geometry), history, languages, the fine arts, literature (in particular, the Great Books), and science occupy a central position in the perennialist curriculum. In addition, perennialists contend that character training and moral development have an appropriate place in the design of the curriculum.

 For Your Reflection and Analysis

If you were a perennialist teacher, what 10 books would you choose as the Great Books? At what age or grade level should they be introduced to students?

Perennialists such as Mortimer Adler viewed the curriculum as the context for developing intellectual skills through reading, writing, speaking, listening, observing, computing, measuring, and estimating. Adler maintained that education involves confronting the problems and questions that have challenged people over the centuries. Adler (1984) suggested three specific methods of instruction: "(1) didactic teaching by lectures or through textbook assignments; (2) coaching that forms the habits through which all skills are possessed; and (3) Socratic teaching by questioning and by conducting discussions of the answers elicited" (pp. 8–9).

Prior to studying the great works of literature, philosophy, history, and science, students are taught methods of critical thinking and questioning strategies to prepare them to engage in "dialogue" with the classical writers. Ecclesiastical perennialists encourage any type of teaching method that brings the learner into direct contact with the Supreme Being.

Classroom Environment

Perennialists are concerned with training not only the intellect, but also the will. They believe that the teacher has the obligation to discipline the student in order to train the will. They consider the most appropriate classroom environment for training the will to be one that reinforces time on task, precision, and order. The ecclesiastical perennialists add to this a learning environment that also reflects an appreciation for prayer and contemplation.

Role of the Teacher

Perennialists view the teacher who is well educated in the liberal arts to be the authority figure and instrument that provides for the dissemination of truth. If the teacher is the disseminator, then the student is the receptacle for learning. The metaphor "director of mental calisthenics" has been used to describe the perennialist teacher (Morris & Pai, 1976).

Another metaphor that describes the perennialist teacher is an "intellectual coach" who can engage students in Socratic dialogue. The perennialist teacher must be a model of intellectual and rational powers. He or she must be capable of logical analysis, be comfortable with the scientific method, be well versed in the classics, have a good memory, and be capable of the highest forms of mental reasoning.

Assessment

The standardized, objective examination is the favored evaluation tool of the perennialist. Because the study of the classical tradition of the Great Books promotes an exchange of ideas and insights, the essay examination is also used.

Leading Proponents

Jacques Maritain (1882–1973), a French Catholic philosopher who served as ambassador to the Holy See, was perhaps the best spokesperson for the ecclesiastical perennialist position. According to Maritain (1941), intelligence alone is not sufficient to comprehend the universe fully. One's relationship to a Spiritual Being is also necessary. Robert M. Hutchins (1899–1977), the former chancellor of the University of Chicago discussed in chapter 8, was a noted spokesperson for the lay perennialist perspective. Both Maritain (1943) and Hutchins (1936) argued that the ideal education is one designed to develop the mind, and that can best be done by a curriculum that concentrates on the Great Books of Western civilization.

As discussed in chapter 10, the 1980s witnessed a resurgence of perennialism. In *The Paideia Proposal: An Educational Manifesto* (1982), Mortimer Adler, like Hutchins, opposed the differentiated curricula (i.e., vocational, technical, academic) and contended that all students in a democratic society should have access to the same high-quality education. Also, like Hutchins, Adler favored the Great Books tradition and maintained that by studying the great works of the past, one can learn enduring, relevant lessons about life.

Allan Bloom, another prominent perennialist figure of the 1980s, was concerned with what he perceived as the crisis of liberal education, particularly in the university. In his book *The Closing of the American Mind* (1987), Bloom contended that "cultural illiteracy" is the crisis of our civilization. Like Hutchins and Adler, Bloom advocated teaching and learning about the Great Books.

Perennialist curricula can be found in elementary and secondary schools ranging from low-income multicultural public schools to elite academies (Ruenzel, 1997). The curriculum of St. John's College at Annapolis, Maryland, and Santa Fe, New Mexico, which emphasizes the importance of studying the Great Books tradition, is an excellent example of the perennialist curriculum in higher education.

Progressivism

Progressivism is an educational philosophy that embraces the notion that the child is an experiencing organism who is capable of "learning by doing." The philosophy of pragmatism is embedded in the progressivist philosophy of education and is grounded in the scientific method of inductive reasoning. It encourages the learner to seek out processes that work, and to do things that best achieve desirable ends.

Purpose of Schooling

Progressivists believe that the school should model life, particularly a democratic society. To prepare students to best operate in this democracy and in the larger democratic society, the school should encourage cooperation and develop problem-solving and decision-making skills.

Curriculum and Instruction

The progressivist curriculum can best be described as experience centered, relevant, and reflective. Such a curriculum integrates several subjects but does not reflect universal truths, a particular body of knowledge, or a set of prescribed core courses. Instead it provides a series of experiences to be gained. The curriculum is responsive to the needs and interests of the individual, which vary from situation to situation. Lerner (1962) described such a curriculum as child centered, peer centered, growth centered, action centered, process and change centered, and equality centered. The progressivist is not interested in studying the past, but is governed by the present. Unlike the perennialists and essentialists, who advocate the cultural and historic roots of the past, progressivists advocate that which is meaningful and relevant to the student today.

    For the progressivist, because there is no rigid subject matter content and no absolute standard for what constitutes knowledge, the most appropriate teaching methods include group work and the project method. Katz and Chard (2000) contended that project work can be used as early as first grade (age 6) to complement systematic instruction. The instructional strategy used along with the project method is the scientific method. However, unlike the perennialists and essentialists, who view the scientific method as a means of verifying truth, progressivists view scientific investigation as a means of verifying experience.

 For Your Reflection and Analysis

Describe a project that could be used in the first grade to teach Science.

    Classroom activities in critical thinking, problem solving, decision making, and cooperative learning are examples of some of the methods that are incorporated in the progressivist curriculum. The curriculum is also community centered. For example, students experience the arts by frequenting museums and theaters, experience social studies by interacting with individuals from diverse social groups and social conditions, and experience science by exploring their immediate physical world (Westheimer & Kahne, 1993).

Classroom Environment

The progressivist teacher fosters a democratic classroom environment that emphasizes citizenship. Teachers advocate parent involvement and democratic decision making with regard to the administration of the school. Students and parents are encouraged to form their own councils and organizations to address educational issues and advance social change.

Role of the Teacher

The metaphor of the teacher as facilitator or director of learning might best describe the progressivist teacher. Such a teacher is not considered to be the authority or disseminator of knowledge or truth, as is the perennialist or essentialist teacher. Rather, he or she is viewed as a guide who facilitates learning by helping the student sample direct experience. Progressivism by its very nature is socially oriented; thus the teacher is a collaborative partner in making group decisions, keeping in mind the ultimate consequences for the students.

Assessment

Because progressivism supports the group process, cooperative learning, and democratic participation, its approach to assessment differs from that of the more traditional approaches. For example, the progressivist engages in *formative evaluation*, which is process oriented and concerned with ongoing feedback about the activity underway rather than with the measurement of outcomes. Monitoring what students are doing, appraising the skills they still need to develop, and resolving unexpected problems as they occur are typical examples of the type of evaluation progressivists use.

Leading Proponents

As discussed in chapter 7, progressivism had its impetus in the first decades of the 20th century at a time when many liberal thinkers alleged that American schools were out of touch with the advances that were being made in the physical and social sciences and technology. As discussed in that chapter, Francis W. Parker (1837–1902), superintendent of schools in Quincy, Massachusetts, and later head of the Cook County Normal School in Chicago, is considered the father of progressive education. However, as also discussed, John Dewey (1859–1952) and his work at the laboratory school at the University of Chicago provided the clinical testing ground for progressivism. From his position at the University of Chicago and Teachers College, Columbia University, Dewey served as one of the chief spokespersons for the progressive education movement.

Ella Flagg Young (1845–1917), a colleague of Dewey's at the University of Chicago and former superintendent of the Chicago Public Schools, also served as an important spokesperson for progressivism by emphasizing the central role of experimentation and democracy in the classroom and the school. William H. Kilpatrick (1871–1965) further advanced progressive education by introducing the experience-centered curriculum, including the use of the project method.

Progressivism fell into disfavor in the years following World War II, but as Ravitch (2000) noted, it never really disappeared. As discussed in chapter 10, in the late

20th century progressivism experienced somewhat of a revival and can be seen in the work of individuals such as Theodore Sizer. It has also been associated with the pedagogical theory of social reconstructionism discussed later in this chapter.

Essentialism

If one were to choose an adjective that best describes *essentialism*, it would probably be *eclectic*. The philosophies of idealism and realism are embedded in the essentialist philosophy of education. As described in chapter 8, essentialism began as a protest against the perceived decline of intellectual rigor and moral standards in the schools. Essentialists charged that the curriculum was watered down and full of frills, and that in an attempt to provide equality, educational standards had been lowered and the more able students were badly served. Moreover, they contended that the school lost sight of its major purpose, to train the intellect and prepare students for life by teaching them the culture and traditions of the past.

 For Your Reflection and Analysis

What subjects in the curriculum today would an essentialist probably consider frivolous?

Purpose of Schooling

For the essentialist the primary purposes of schooling are to train the intellect and teach students the culture and traditions of the past. It should also provide the student with the skills and knowledge necessary to successfully participate in a democratic society.

Curriculum and Instruction

The curriculum of the essentialist school provides a basic education that includes instruction in the "essentials," including reading, writing, and mathematics in the primary grades, and history, geography, natural science, and foreign languages in the upper elementary grades. At the secondary level, the curriculum places a major emphasis on a common core that includes 4 years of English, 3 years of mathematics, 3 years of science, 3 years of social studies, a half year of computer science, and for the college-bound, foreign languages.

The methods of instruction to support such a curriculum include the more traditional instructional strategies, including lecture, recitation, discussion, and Socratic dialogue. Written and oral communication also occupy a prominent place in the instructional milieu of the essentialist school. Like perennialists, essentialists view books as an appropriate medium for instruction. Essentialists have also found various educational technologies supportive of their educational theory.

In general, essentialists prefer instructional materials that are paced and sequenced in such a way that students know what they are expected to master. Detailed syllabi and lesson plans, learning by objectives, competency-based instruction, computer-assisted instruction, and audio-tutorial laboratory methods are other examples of teaching strategies that are acceptable to the essentialist.

Classroom Environment

Esssentialists not only advocate intellectual discipline, but they also maintain that moral discipline and character training deserve an important place in the curriculum. Accordingly, the essentialist classroom is defined by clear expectations for behavior and respect for others.

Role of the Teacher

The essentialist educator is viewed as either a link to the so-called "literary intellectual inheritance" (idealism) or a demonstrator of the world model (realism). To be an essentialist teacher is to be well versed in the liberal arts, humanities, and sciences; to be a respected member of the intellectual community; to be technically skilled in all forms of communication; and to be equipped with superior pedagogical skills to ensure competent instruction. One of the most important roles of the teacher is to set the character of the environment in which learning takes place (Butler, 1966).

Assessment

Of all the philosophies of education, essentialism is perhaps most comfortable with testing. In fact, the entire essentialist curriculum reflects the influence of the testing movement. IQ tests, standardized achievement tests, diagnostic tests, and performance-based competency tests, as well as the current "high-stakes testing" mandated by the No Child Left Behind Act (2001) discussed in chapter 11 are examples of the widespread application of measurement techniques. Competency, accountability, mastery learning, and performance-based instruction have gained increasing popularity as a result of the essentialists' influence on educational practice.

Leading Proponents

Although essentialism can be traced to Plato and Aristotle, its greatest popularity has come in the 20th and 21st centuries. As discussed in chapter 8, the major proponents of essentialism in the middle decades of the 20th century were William C. Bagley (1874–1946), Arthur E. Bestor (1908–1994), and Admiral Hyman G. Rickover (1900–1986).

A major revival of essentialism occurred in the 1970s with the *back-to-basics movement* and was echoed in the recommendations of the education reform reports of the 1980s discussed in chapter 10. For example, *A Nation at Risk* (National Commission on Excellence in Education, 1983), the premier of these reports, recommended a core of *new basics:* English, mathematics, science, social studies, and computer sciences, and for the college-bound, a foreign language. Many of the other reports not only proposed similar cores, but also called for improvement in their content and increased rigor in their standards. The success of the essentialist position is evidenced by the steps taken in a number of states to strengthen graduation requirements and enforce high-stakes testing to meet the federal mandates of the No Child Left Behind Act (2001). Essentialism is the dominant educational philosophy in our schools today.

Social Reconstructionism

Throughout history individuals have aspired to improve, change, or reform society, including its educational institutions. These social reconstructionists or change agents differ from revolutionaries in that they believe not only that society is in need of change or reconstruction, but also that education must take the lead in this reconstruction. John Dewey suggested the term *reconstructionism* in the title of his book, *Reconstruction in Philosophy* (1920).

Modern *social reconstructionism* had its beginnings in Marxist philosophy. According to Karl Marx (1818–1883), capitalism and its emphasis on competition and the control of property in the hands of a few led to an alienated workforce who found little meaning or purpose in their work. Marx's later writings recommended a total social revolution against the ruling class by the working class.

Purpose of Schooling

For social reconstructionists, the purpose of schooling is to critically examine all cultural and educational institutions and recommend change and reform as needed. In addition, the school's purpose is to teach students and the public not to settle for "what is," but rather to dream about "what might be." Most important, the purpose of schooling is to prepare students to become change agents.

Curriculum and Instruction

Because the majority of social reconstructionists believe in the importance of democracy and the proposition that the school is the fundamental institution in modern society, the curriculum of the social reconstructionist school reflects democratic ideals and emphasizes *critical literacy* and the development of critical thinking skills. Such a curriculum denounces any form of the politics of exclusion. Rather, it challenges all unequal power relationships and focuses on power as applied to class, gender, sexuality, race, and nationalism (Blake & Masschalein, 2003). Rather than concentrate on separate subjects, students consider societal problems such as the place of biomedical ethics in improving the quality of life, the need to conserve our natural resources, and the issues of foreign policy and nationalism. In addition to the formal or official curriculum, attention is given to the "hidden curriculum" which "represents the knowledge claims and values of the dominant group or class that controls the schools" (Gutek, 2004, p. 319).

> *For your Reflection and Analysis*
>
> *How would a social reconstructionist respond to proposals to include values education in the curriculum?*

Teaching strategies include problem solving and focus on activities outside the school, such as teaching younger students who need help, public clean-up projects, writing an editorial, or promoting consumer legislation. Activities such as these contextualize skills learned at school in a way that helps students appreciate their usefulness (Kincheloe, Slattery, & Steinberg, 2000). Instead of merely reading and studying about the problems of society, students spend time in the community becoming acquainted with and immersed in the problems and their possible solutions. They analyze, research, and link the underlying issues to institutions and structures in the community and larger society. Finally, they take some action or responsibility in planning for change.

Classroom Environment

The classroom environment of the social reconstructionist is a climate of inquiry in which teachers and students question the assumptions of the status quo and examine societal issues and future trends. In such a classroom there is less emphasis on management and control, and more focus on community building (Kincheloe et al., 2000). An atmosphere that promotes analysis, criticism, and action research best describes this type of classroom environment. Conflict resolution and differences in worldviews are encouraged and reinforced.

Role of the Teacher

The metaphors "shaper of a new society," "transformational leader," and "change agent" aptly describe the social reconstructionist teacher. Social reconstructionist teachers must also be willing to engage in ongoing renewal of their personal and professional lives. They must be willing to critique and evaluate the conditions under which they work and extend their educative role outside the domains of the classroom and school. They must have a high tolerance for ambiguity, be comfortable with constant change, and be willing to think about their own thinking and the cultural and psychosocial forces that have shaped it. As an educational reformer, such a teacher detests the status quo and views the school as a particular culture in evolution. Moreover, he or she views the larger society as an experiment that will always be unfinished and in flux. The social reconstructionist teacher must be willing to engage in and form alliances with community groups, neighborhood organizations, social movements, and parents to critique and question the practice of school democracy and school policy.

 For Your Reflection and Analysis

How comfortable are you with ambiguity? Constant change?

Assessment

The type of evaluation that is appropriate for both students and teachers in a social reconstructionist school is *authentic assessment*. This includes formative evaluation, which entails a cooperative effort between student and teacher, student and student, teacher and administrator or supervisor, and community and teacher. Information is shared regularly during periodic formal and informal conferences, and the student or teacher being evaluated is an active participant in the process. Such an evaluation requires participants to have the ability and willingness to think in critical terms and to expose underlying assumptions and practices. Standardized testing, including teacher competency testing, is only used if mandated by state or federal law.

Leading Proponents

As discussed in chapter 8, George S. Counts (1889–1974), Theodore Brameld (1904–1987), and Harold Rugg (1886–1960) were perhaps the best known of the American social reconstructionists who, in the early part of the 20th century, attempted to bring about major educational reform. Each of these individuals advocated the transformation of society and envisioned an ideal and more equitable world.

Two more contemporary social reconstructionists are Ivan Illich (1926–2002) and Paulo Freire (1921–1997). In his *Deschooling Society*, Illich (1974) maintained that because schools have corrupted society, one can create a better society only by abolishing schools altogether and finding new approaches to education. Illich called for a total political and educational revolution. Freire, who was born, was educated, and taught in Latin America, proposed that education be drawn from the everyday life experiences of the learners. In his *Pedagogy of the Oppressed* (1973), Freire maintained that students should not be manipulated or controlled but should be involved in their own learning. According to Freire, by exchanging and examining their experiences with peers and mentors, students who are socially, economically, and politically disadvantaged can plan, initiate, and take action for their own lives.

Although few modern educators consider themselves to be social reconstructionists, many are currently practicing and implementing the beliefs and values aligned with social reconstructionism. In addition, many principles of social reconstructionism are reflected in the critical theory and postmodern movements discussed next.

Postmodernism

Postmodernism, also called *postmodern constructivism*, has been defined as a contemporary philosophy, ideology, movement, and process. It represents a combination of the philosophies of pragmatism, existentialism, and social reconstructionism and uses the technique of *critical theory*. Critical theory is a process of analyzing and critiquing political, economic, social, and educational institutions. Critical theorists make assumptions and generalizations about the political nature of those institutions. They raise such questions as, *Who controls the school? Who chooses the curriculum? Who hires the teachers? Who chooses the textbooks?* and *Who writes the textbooks?* In short, *Who has the power?* From their analysis, they uncover examples of disequity between the dominant culture (male, White, middle-class) and disenfranchised or marginal groups (the poor, African Americans, Hispanics, women, gays, lesbians, the transgendered, and the aged) (Gutek, 2004).

Postmodernists believe that there are no eternal universal truths and values. They suggest that reality is subjective; it is not found in our ancient past, but in the eye of the beholder. Postmodernists believe that individuals construct their own meaning from personal experience and that history is itself a construction (Newman, 1998). This theme is prevalent throughout the writing of postmodernists such as Jacques Derrida (1976), Jean-Francois Lyotard (1985), and Richard Rorty (1998).

Postmodernists also question "scientific realism" by refuting epistemological claims that science (in particular the scientific method) is objective and unbiased.

Critical theorists raise questions about the unequal distribution of power in society.

They claim that objective observation is not possible because the observer affects what is observed. Postmodernists suggest that the way we arrive at knowledge is not by science alone but by examining "the human past and present to see how claims of truth have originated, been constructed and expressed, and have had social, political, and educational consequences" (Gutek, 2004, p. 130). They question the dominance of objectivity, universal explanations, truth, and rationality (Kincheloe et al., 2000). In their place they substitute critical inquiry and political awareness (Henderson, 2001); diversity, inclusion, and multiplicity (McLaren & Torres, 1998); and the limitations of language or the meaning of words (Biesta, 2001).

 For Your Reflection and Analysis

Give examples of other "myths" that are perpetuated by the schools and by other institutions.

Purpose of Schooling

Postmodernists believe the purpose of schooling is to prepare students to become vigilant and aware of the variety of myths that are presented as "truths." Examples of such myths include "equal educational opportunity," "apolitical curriculum," "fair housing," "level playing field," and "open enrollment."

Curriculum and Instruction

Postmodernists encourage reading a wide variety of materials. For example, postmodernists might suggest the reading of the Great Books. However, they would not use the Great Books as a model for truth as do the perennialists, but as a model for questioning, critiquing, and analyzing what constitutes truth.

In the postmodernist classroom students are taught the concepts of *constructivism* and *deconstruction*. Constructivism is a learning theory that originated from the cognitive development research of both Jean Piaget (1948) and Jerome Bruner (1960). The major theme of constructivist theory is that learning is an active process in which learners construct new ideas or concepts based on current or past knowledge. The learner selects and transforms information, constructs hypotheses, and makes meaningful decisions. By reflecting on their own experiences, learners construct their own understanding of the world.

Students are also involved in *deconstructing* or *decoding*, a method of "getting inside the text" to identify how the knowledge presented, the meanings, and the interpretations in the text affect our ideas and beliefs. Examples of questions that would be asked when deconstructing or decoding a text include: "What texts represent official knowledge in the curriculum? How are these texts interpreted in order to establish and maintain power relationships between different groups? Which texts (experiences) are excluded? What did the text mean at the time it was written? And, what does the text mean for different groups today?" (Gutek, 2004, p. 131).

At the end of this chapter, Elliott W. Eisner's article, "Preparing for Today and Tomorrow," exemplifies the concepts of constructivism and deconstruction.

Classroom Environment

The postmodern classroom environment is nonthreatening, supportive, and open to discussions of many controversial subjects and topics. Students are encouraged to reflect on their experiences and share their personal stories and narratives. Questioning and critiquing are not interpreted as negative actions or behaviors. Rather, they are perceived as positive actions toward bringing about change. A constructivist learning environment stimulates group problem solving and collaborative, experiential group activities.

Role of the Teacher

The postmodernist teacher's role is to practice and model the "doing of critical theory." These teachers practice and model questioning, critiquing, and analyzing. At the same time, they recognize the power and influence they have over their students, their peers, parents, and the larger community. As professionals, they constantly check how they are communicating to determine whether they are alienating or offending others, while always respecting the rights of all individuals to take issue and disagree.

Assessment

A variety of assessment techniques are used by the postmodernist teacher, including student and teacher self-assessments. Students are encouraged to keep journals and write personal narratives to chronicle their progress. Teachers solicit ongoing

TABLE 1.2 Educational Implications of Philosophies of Education

	Purpose of Schooling	Curriculum and Instruction	Classroom Environment	Role of the Teacher	Assessment	Leading Proponents
Perennialism	• Cultivate intellect • Promote moral development • Transmit eternal truths and values	• Liberal arts • Christian doctrine • Great Books • Character training • Enduring truths • Problem solving • Discussion • Socratic dialogue • Lecture • Critical thinking	• Train will • Time on task • Orderliness • Highly structured	• Disseminator of truth • Director of mental calisthenics • Mental disciplinarian • Model intellectual and rational powers • Intellectual coach • Authoritarian	• Objective exam • Essay exam	• Aristotle • Aquinas • Maritain • Hutchins • Adler • Bloom
Progressivism	• Promote democratic society	• Experience centered • Relevant • Reflective • Integrative • Student centered • Cooperative learning • Project method • Scientific method • Problem solving • Critical thinking	• Emphasize citizenship • Collaborative • Democratic • Community centered	• Facilitator • Director of learning • Collaborative partner • Research director	• Formative evaluation • Ongoing monitoring of student progress	• Parker • Dewey • Young • Kilpatrick • Rugg • Sizer

Essentialism	• Train intellect • Develop cultural literacy	• Back to basics • Uniform • Common core • Lecture • Recitation • Discussion • Socratic dialogue • Mastery of facts • Computer assisted • Learning by objectives • Competency based	• Moral discipline • Behavioral expectations • Respect • Character training	• Teacher as demonstrator • Teacher as intellectual • Authoritarian	• Standardized tests • Mastery learning • Performance based	• Bagley • Bestor • Rickover • Bennett • Ravitch • Hirsch
Social Reconstructionism	• Critique cultural and social institutions • Prepare change agents	• Critical literacy • Politics of change • Human relations • Community involvement • Expose "hidden curriculum" • Problem solving	• Climate of inquiry • Community building • Conflict resolution	• Transformational leader • Change agent • Shaper of new society • Educational reformer	• Cooperative effort • Formative evaluation • Authentic assessment	• Counts • Brameld • Rugg • Illich • Freire
Post-modernism	• Critically examine all institutions • Examine myths	• Analysis of language • Critical literacy • Constructivism • Deconstruction • Discussion • Self-reflection • Problem solving	• Nonthreatening • Supportive • Collaborative	• Facilitator • Model critical theory	• Ongoing feedback • Student self-assessment • Teacher self-assessment • Journaling	• Derrida • Lyotard • Rorty • Apple • Giroux • Bowles • Gintis • McLaren • Cherry-holmes

feedback from students. They invite students to evaluate their teaching effectiveness and interactions with others.

Leading Proponents

Some of the major proponents of postmodern constructivism are Michael W. Apple (2004), Stanley Aronowitz (2003), Henry A. Giroux (2003), Joe L. Kincheloe (2004), Colin Lankshear (2003), and M. Knobel and Peter L. McLaren (2003). Their major contribution has been to demonstrate how history's claim to universal truth has legitimized and empowered elites at the expense of marginal groups in our society.

Table 1.2 presents a summary of the educational implications of the philosophies of education discussed in this chapter.

Conclusion

A review of the major philosophical approaches as well as the contexts within which each emerged suggests an interdependent relationship between the two. Each philosophical orientation was influenced by the changes, challenges, and concerns confronting society at that particular time in history. The contribution of each philosophical orientation, therefore, cannot be fully appreciated without careful consideration of the social, political, and economic forces that may have necessitated the need to examine critical assumptions such as who should be educated and by whom, what they should learn, and the purpose of education. As the philosophies introduced in this chapter are revisited in the chapters that follow, their relationship to these forces will become more evident. In a similar vein, as we look toward the future, we can assume that the rapid demographic and social changes in American society, coupled with political and historical events in the United States and abroad, will result in another paradigm shift in the philosophy of education.

For Discussion and Application

1. Prepare a reflection paper entitled "My Philosophy of Life." In your paper respond to the following questions: (a) Are human beings basically good or evil? (b) How is knowledge determined? (c) Are there certain moral or ethical values that are universal?
2. What critical thinking skills are most important in your discipline or subject area? Which teaching methods would you use to help your students develop those critical thinking skills?
3. As a social reconstructionist, list five major changes that you would propose for education and schooling in the 21st century.
4. Philosophical analysis is a technique used to eliminate ambiguities and clarify language. Select five terms relevant in your subject area and discuss some of the beliefs, arguments, and assumptions underlying those terms.
5. Prepare a reflection paper entitled, "My Philosophy of Education." In your paper answer the following questions: (a) Are there certain universal truths that should

be taught? If yes, identify those truths. (b) What is the ideal curriculum? (c) If you were to choose one method or instructional strategy, what would it be? (d) What type of learning environment is most conducive to learning? (e) How will you know that your students have learned?

6. Construct a personal time line that illustrates how your philosophy of life has changed. Include critical experiences and events that influenced the change(s).

Primary Source Reading

Plato, a disciple of Socrates, operated a school in Athens in which he often taught using the Socratic method, metaphors, and allegories. Of these, The Allegory of the Cave *is probably the most famous. The allegory contains the essence of Plato's philosophical assumptions regarding what is real, how we know, and the nature of knowledge. As you read the excerpt of the story, try to make a mental picture of the cave as Socrates in the story asked Glaucon to do.*

The Allegory of the Cave

Plato

[Socrates] And now, I said, let me show in a figure how far our nature is enlightened or unenlightened:—Behold! human beings living in an underground cave, which has a mouth open towards the light and reaching all along the cave; here they have been from their childhood, and have their legs and necks chained so that they cannot move, and can only see before them, being prevented by the chains from turning round their heads. Above and behind them a fire is blazing at a distance, and between the fire and the prisoners there is a raised way; and you will see, if you look, a low

Source: Plato (360 B.C./1921). *The Republic of Plato*, Book VII, (B. Jowett, trans.). London: Oxford University Press.

wall built along the way, like the screen which marionette players have in front of them, over which they show the puppets.

[Glaucon] I see.

[Socrates] And do you see, I said, men passing along the wall carrying all sorts of vessels, and statues and figures of animals made of wood and stone and various materials, which appear over the wall? Some of them are talking, others silent.

[Glaucon] You have shown me a strange image, and they are strange prisoners.

[Socrates] Like ourselves, I replied; and they see only their own shadows, or the shadows of one another, which the fire throws on the opposite wall of the cave?

[Glaucon] True, he said; how could they see anything but the shadows if they were never allowed to move their heads?

[Socrates] And of the objects which are being carried in like manner they would only see the shadows?

[Glaucon] Yes, he said.

[Socrates] And if they were able to converse with one another, would they not suppose that they were naming what was actually before them?

[Glaucon] Very true.

[Socrates] And suppose further that the prison had an echo which came from the other side, would they not be sure to fancy when one of the passers-by spoke that the voice which they heard came from the passing shadow?

[Glaucon] No question, he replied.

[Socrates] To them, I said, the truth would be literally nothing but the shadows of the images.

[Glaucon] That is certain.

[Socrates] And now look again, and see what will naturally follow if the prisoners are released and disabused of their error. At first, when any of them is liberated and compelled suddenly to stand up and turn his neck round and walk and look towards the light, he will suffer sharp pains; the glare will distress him, and he will be unable to see the realities of which in his former state he had seen the shadows; and then conceive someone saying to him, that what he saw before was an illusion, but that now, when he is approaching nearer to being and his eye is turned towards more real existence, he has a clearer vision, what will be his reply? And you may further imagine that his instructor is pointing to the objects as they pass and requiring him to name them, will he not be perplexed? Will he not fancy that the shadows which he formerly saw are truer than the objects which are now shown to him?

[Glaucon] Far truer.

[Socrates] And if he is compelled to look straight at the light, will he not have a pain in his eyes which will make him turn away to take and take in the objects of vision which he can see, and which he will conceive to be in reality clearer than the things which are now being shown to him?

[Glaucon] True.

[Socrates] And suppose once more, that he is reluctantly dragged up a steep and rugged ascent, and held fast until he's forced into the presence of the sun himself, is he not likely to be pained and irritated? When he approaches the light his eyes will be dazzled, and he will not be able to see anything at all of what are now called realities.

[Glaucon] Not all in a moment, he said.

[Socrates] He will require to grow accustomed to the sight of the upper world. And first he will see the shadows best, next the reflections of men and other objects in the water, and then the objects themselves; then he will gaze upon the light of the moon and the stars and the spangled heaven; and he will see the sky and the stars by night better than the sun or the light of the sun by day?

[Glaucon] Certainly.

[Socrates] Lastly he will be able to see the sun, and not mere reflections of him in the water, but he will see him in his own proper place, and not in another; and he will contemplate him as he is.

[Glaucon] Certainly.

[Socrates] He will then proceed to argue that this is he who gives the season and the years, and is the guardian of all that is in the visible world, and in a certain way the cause of all things which he and his fellows have been accustomed to behold?

[Glaucon] Clearly, he said, he would first see the sun and then reason about him.

[Socrates] And when he remembered his old habitation, and the wisdom of the cave and his fellow-prisoners, do you not suppose that he would felicitate himself on the change, and pity them?

[Glaucon] Certainly, he would.

[Socrates] And if they were in the habit of conferring honors among themselves on those who were quickest to observe the passing shadows and to remark which of them went before, and which followed after, and which were together; and who were therefore best able to draw conclusions as to the future, do you think that he would care for such honors and glories, or envy the possessors of them? Would he not say with Homer,

Better to be the poor servant of a poor master, and to endure anything, rather than think as they do and live after their manner?

[Glaucon] Yes, he said, I think that he would rather suffer anything than entertain these false notions and live in this miserable manner.

[Socrates] Imagine once more, I said, such as one coming suddenly out of the sun to be replaced in his old situation; would he not be certain to have his eyes full of darkness?

[Glaucon] To be sure, he said.

[Socrates] And if there were a contest, and he had to compete in measuring the shadows with the prisoners who had never moved out of the cave, while his sight was still weak, and before his eyes had become steady (and the time which would be needed to acquire this new habit of sight might be very considerable) would he not be ridiculous? Men would say of him that up he went and down he came without his eyes; and that it was better not even to think of ascending; and if any one tried to loose another and lead him up to the light, let them only catch the offender, and they would put him to death.

[Glaucon] No question, he said.

[Socrates] This entire allegory, I said, you may now append, dear Glaucon, to the previous argument; the prison-house is the world of sight, the light of the fire is the sun, and you will not misapprehend me if you interpret the journey upwards to be the ascent of the soul into the intellectual world according to my poor belief, which, at your desire, I have expressed whether rightly or wrongly God knows. But, whether true or false, my opinion is that in the world of knowledge the idea of good appears last of all, and is seen only with an effort; and, when seen, is also inferred to be the universal author of all things beautiful and right, parent of light and of the lord of light in this visible world, and the immediate source of reason and truth in the intellectual; and that this is the power upon which he who would act rationally, either in public or private life must have his eye fixed.

Questions for Discussion

1. What does the light from the fire in the cave represent in the allegory? What does the sun outside the cave represent in the allegory?

2. Plato chose the metaphor of the 'cave' and the prisoner to convey his message. What other metaphors might he have chosen to convey the same message?

3. Based on the lesson in the allegory, describe the limits of sense realism as a way of knowing. According to Plato, how can we come to know the real world?

4. If you have seen the movie *The Matrix*, would you agree or disagree that *The Matrix* can be viewed as a modern version of *The Allegory of the Cave?* Explain why or why not.

Primary Source Reading

Elliot Eisner, professor of education and professor of art at Stanford University and former president of the John Dewey Society, is concerned with the development of aesthetic intelligence and the way the arts affect and transform consciousness. He proposed the use of critical methods from the social sciences in studying and improving education.

In this selection Eisner asserts that the primary goal of education should be to enable students to learn how to invent themselves—to learn how to create their own minds. According to Eisner, the schools must refine the students' capacities for judgment, critical thinking, literacy, collaboration, and service so that they are adequately prepared for the future.

Preparing for Today and Tomorrow

Elliot W. Eisner

At first glance, the idea of designing a curriculum that prepares students for the future seems unassailable. After all, education is not only for the present. Students will be living in a world different from the one they now occupy, and schools should enable them to deal with that world.

Source: Eisner, E. W. (2003/2004). Preparing for today and tomorrow. *Educational Leadership, 61* (4), 6–10.

As unassailable as such an idea appears, who among us can tell what the future will look like? Projections about lifestyles, social arrangements, and problems that will be encountered are notoriously difficult. Who could have predicted 20 years ago the challenges that adults address today? Indeed, some of the most significant weaknesses of education policy stem from the belief that the aims and content of education can be justified on the basis of preparation. "Some day you will need this" is a familiar refrain heard both in schools and around the kitchen table. Alas, such an exhortation does little to stimulate or motivate students.

If an unknowable future is not a sound basis on which to plan curriculum and instruction, then what is? From my perspective, we can best prepare students for the future by enabling them to deal effectively with the present. School curriculums based on the preparatory conception of education are often intellectually irrelevant or become little more than hoops through which students learn to jump in order to move ahead. Too much of what we do now in schools is of the hoop-jumping variety.

What I desire is an education process that is genuinely meaningful to students, challenging them with problems and ideas that they find both interesting and intellectually demanding. I want to assess that process by the depth of its engagement in students' lives.

Of course, regardless of their view of the future, people have different beliefs about what is important for students to learn in the here and now. For example, many educators value the development of critical mindedness, but some parents may reject this goal because critical mindedness can challenge values promulgated at home. The point is that even if we agree that education should address the present, what constitutes appropriate preparation for the present is itself a contested issue. That, in a democracy, is as it should be. The last thing we need is a one-size-fits-all curriculum with one single set of goals for everyone. Diversity yields richness, and diversity in schooling is a source of richness for our culture. Having said that, let me comment on a number of aims that I embrace as being appropriate for our schools.

What Should Schools Teach

Judgment

The best way to prepare students for the future is to focus on the present in a way that enables students to deal with problems that have more than one correct answer. The problems that matter most cannot be resolved by formula, algorithm, or rule. They require the exercise of that most exquisite human capacity that we call judgment. Judgment is not mere preference, but rather the ability to give reasons for the choices that we make. Good judgment requires good reasons. The dispositions and critical acumen that make good judgment possible are among the most important abilities that schools can cultivate in students.

To cultivate this quality, the curriculum needs to consist of problems that permit judgment. Such problems require deliberation and yield multiple possible resolutions. Note that I say *resolutions* rather than solutions. Problems of a substantial magnitude usually need to be considered from various angles and can only be temporarily resolved. The majority opinions of the U.S. Supreme Court justify the Court's findings, but an acceptable finding in one period in the nation's history may no longer be appropriate at another time. We should teach students that the practices of deliberation and judgment go hand in hand.

Critical Thinking

A second ability that schools need to develop in students is the ability to critique ideas and to enjoy exploring what one can do with them. To develop this ability, students must be presented with ideas that are worth exploring. Several decades ago, Jerome Bruner identified three questions to guide the development of his curriculum *Man—A Course of Study:* What is human about man? How did he get that way? What can make him more so? Each of these three ideas can be explored and discussed in class at a level appropriate to the student's age.

Powerful ideas are those that have legs that take students someplace. The idea of random mutation and natural selection, the relationship between culture and personality, and the protection of minority rights in a government in which the majority rules are examples of the ideas that students might critically examine, explore, and explicate. Each of these ideas is inexhaustible. The problem for students is to tease out their implications and to apply those implications not to tomorrow, but to today.

Meaningful Literacy

A third aim for schools is to cultivate multiple forms of literacy. Literacy is normally conceived of as the ability to read and write. Sometimes computational skill, or numeracy, is added to the concept. I mean something considerably broader, however. Literacy involves the ability to encode or decode meaning in any of the symbolic forms used in the culture. For example, one can be literate in one's ability to experience and derive meaning from music, from the visual arts, or from dance.

Our lives are enriched by the ability to secure wide varieties of meaning. Schools that neglect some cultural forms, such as the arts, guarantee that they will graduate semiliterate students—students for whom the arts will be other people's pleasures. Of course, these students may well respond to the popular arts. But we cannot anticipate that they will be responsive to the more classical and complex forms that represent extraordinarily high levels of artistic accomplishment. The ability to experience such forms meaningfully requires instruction.

But I don't want to lose the larger point. By defining literacy broadly, we can identify areas in which some school programs are lacking. Programs that focus essentially on the conventional use of language or the formal use of numbers can limit students' ability to secure meaningful experience from other forms of representation.

Different forms of representation evoke, develop, and refine the modes of thinking that contribute to the cultivation of what is broadly called *mind*. The school curriculum that excludes such resources neglects the development of mind to its fullest capacities. Although brains are primarily biological, mind is mainly a form of cultural achievement. The provision of opportunities in the school curriculum for students to encounter a variety of forms of representation not only engenders meaning that is specific to each form, but also promotes the growth of mind.

To push this idea even further, we might say that the primary aim of education is to enable youngsters to invent themselves—to learn how to create their own minds. Cultural literacy provides not only *recreation* but also *re*-creation. What we recreate throughout life is the self.

Collaboration

A fourth aim for schools that can make a difference in the lives of students here and now is the provision of opportunities to learn to work with others collectively, cooperatively, and in harmony. We tend to think about schools as producing solo performances. We also need to think about schools as helping students learn to work collaboratively with others, particularly with students who are culturally different from themselves. What we ought to seek through education is both individuation and integration.

By individuation, I mean that schools ought to cultivate what is personally and productively idiosyncratic about each student. Schools ought to promote the realization of each student's distinctive talents, aptitudes, and proclivities. And at least to some degree, schools ought to help students identify their individual strengths and make it possible for them to follow their bliss.

But schools should also help students learn how to work with others on meaningful projects. The process of collaboration gives birth to new ideas and develops social skills that matter in a democracy. Schools should provide ample opportunity for such activities to take place and for the forms of learning that those activities promote to be realized. Education, after all, is more than an individual affair. At a time when a sense of community seems to be dissipating in our neighborhoods, the opportunity to form community through collaborative work in schools is especially important.

Service

Related to collaborative work is a fifth aspiration for schools today: the creation of conditions through which students can make a contribution to the larger community. Schooling should be about more than individual achievement intended to serve one's own personal ambitions. Providing payback to the community makes sense, not only as a form of appropriate socialization, but also as a moral virtue.

Service learning moves in this direction. In addition to formal service learning programs, schools should plan opportunities for all students to have some connection with cultural centers, social agencies, medical institutions, and other community resources to which they might make some contribution. We are so wrapped up in test scores that we often marginalize the importance of developing socially responsible citizens who are willing to contribute to the larger social welfare and who know how to do so. This aim, too, is appropriate for schools today.

What Schools Must Become

To achieve the aims I have described, we need a radically different conception of what matters in education. Test scores need to take a back seat to more educationally significant outcomes. As long as schools treat test scores as the major proxies for student achievement and educational quality, we will have a hard time refocusing our attention on what really matters in education.

The issue is not one of having accountability or not having accountability. We are all accountable: The question is how. We need an approach to accountability that is wider than measurement and more sensitive to nuances that

count. Such an approach will require a radically different view of where we look to find out how well students are learning. After all, the major lessons of schooling manifest themselves outside the context of schools. The primary aim of education is not to enable students to do well in school, but to help them do well in the lives they lead outside of school. We ought to focus on what students do when they can choose their own activities.

We also need to revise our school programs so that they address the important issues outlined here. So much of what we do in our schools is simply a reflection of traditional categories that basically serve as selection mechanisms. We need to question these traditions. How do we justify what we require students to pay attention to? Do most students need a course in calculus? How about one in chemistry? Do we believe that the subjects we teach develop the students' minds? Do we think that these subjects are relevant to tasks beyond schooling? Do we teach these courses because they are sources of satisfaction to students? We need to raise such questions and develop thoughtful responses. When our answers to these questions are found wanting, revision is in order.

Finally, we need to embrace a broader view of mind, by which I mean a broader view of the ways in which thinking occurs. By no means is thinking limited to what words alone can carry. The limits of our cognition are not defined by the limits of our language. As Michael Polanyi commented, "We know more than we can tell." The acknowledgement that thinking occurs in any of the sensory modalities that humans possess—sight, sound, touch, taste, smell—opens up the door for the development of programs that can do justice to the ways in which humans do think and have thought throughout their history on this planet. We may not want to address every aspect of mind that can possibly be cultivated, but we should pay attention to our options and make selections on the basis of grounds that we can justify.

Preparation for tomorrow is best served by meaningful education today. The development of mind is a form of cultural achievement in which schools have an important role to play. If we endorse these propositions, we will realize that genuine reform of our schools requires a shift in paradigms from those with which we have become comfortable to others that more adequately address the potential that humans possess for shaping not only the world, but themselves.

Questions for Discussion

1. Explain what Eisner meant when he said, "We can best prepare students for the future by enabling them to deal effectively with the present."

2. Give examples of curriculum in your content area that would incorporate the teaching of judgment, critical thinking, and meaningful literacy.

3. Which educational philosophy would most likely agree with the statement that "the primary aim of education is to enable youngsters to invent themselves—to learn how to create their own minds"? Which is least likely to agree? Support your choices.

Education in the Old World and the "New" Old World Before Jamestown

The grandfathers and the grandmothers are in the children; teach them well.

—Ojibwa proverb

The system of education that operates in the United States is unique. It has been shaped and framed by what has been referred to as the American Experience; hewn out of the rocky New England countryside and the tidewaters of the East Coast, refined by the needs of a people that built an unparalleled industrialized state, and spread by the prairie schooners that plowed the western frontiers. Although the American educational system is unique, it is not without its European heritage. The colonists who came first by the dozens and then by the thousands to settle along the Atlantic coast brought with them educational ideas and experiences that provided the seeds for the American educational system that evolved.

These settlers called the land they settled the "New World." To them it was new. But to the native peoples who lived there it was not a new world; "it was their old world; it was their home" (Hakim, 1999a, p. 60). Although the Europeans considered the native peoples uncivilized and uneducated, they were neither. They were only lacking the type of civilization and knowledge possessed by the Europeans.

To better understand the American educational system that developed in the "New" Old World, in this chapter we first look briefly at its European precolonial heritage and how it was influenced by two dominant forces: the humanist philosophy of the Renaissance and the religious philosophy of the Protestant Reformation, which reinforced the importance of education, in particular, the classical humanist education. We then turn to a brief review of the initial exploration and colonization of the Spanish in Florida and the Southwest, in particular their vast system of missions, and those of the French in Canada and the Ohio and Mississippi valleys.

The chapter ends with a discussion of the formal and informal Native American educational systems in place at the time of the European exploration and colonization. These systems emphasized the development of survival skills, the transmission of cultural heritage, and spiritual awareness, and were grounded in the belief that the human being is comprised of a spirit, a mind, and a physical body.

The Renaissance and Education

The Renaissance, which began in the 14th century and reached its high point in the 16th century, was so called because it represented a *renaissance*, or rebirth, of interest in the cultures of ancient Greece and Rome. It was a period of great change: the decline of the feudal system; the rise of nation-states and nationalism; the growth of cities; a revival of commerce; the introduction of gunpowder; new forms of art, literature, and architecture; and the exploration of new worlds. The dominant philosophy of the Renaissance was humanism, which viewed human nature as its subject. It stressed the dignity of the individual, free will, and the value of the human spirit and all of nature. Rejecting scholasticism and the model of the scholar-cleric as the educated man, the humanists considered the educated man to be the secular man of learning described in the classics. They also looked to the classics, primarily the works of the Roman educator Quintilian, for commentary on education. Quintilian's *Institutio Oratoria* (Institutes of Oratory) had been found and brought to Italy by Byzantine scholars when Constantinople (Istanbul) fell to the Muslims in 1453.

The foremost humanist of the Renaissance and the one with the greatest impact on educational thought was Desiderius Erasmus (1466–1536) of the Netherlands. Erasmus studied at the University of Paris and Oxford University and was a professor at Cambridge in England. Like other humanists, Erasmus believed in the importance of teaching Latin and Greek. His *Colloquies* used dialogues not only to teach Latin style but also to instruct students in religion and morals; they were among the most important textbooks of his time. The use of text to teach both language and Christian doctrine and morals provided a model for the *New England Primer*, which was to become the most important textbook in colonial America.

In the *Education of Young Children*, a portion of which is included as a Primary Source Reading at the end of this chapter, Erasmus argued for early childhood education. In *Upon the Method of Right Instruction*, he proposed the systematic training of teachers who he believed should be both broadly educated and experts in their subjects, be of gentle disposition, and have unimpeachable morals. His views on pedagogy are found in his treatise *Of the First Liberal Education of Children*, in which he asserted that the needs and interests of the student take precedence in the selection of materials and methods, not those of the church or the medieval guilds. In this treaty he, as had Quintilian 15 centuries earlier, deplored the use of corporal punishment. Quintilian claimed that "study depends on the good will of the student, a quality that cannot be secured by compulsion."

Erasmus believed in the potential of the individual to improve himself (he did not address the education of females) as well as in the importance of education to the development of the intellect and morality. In his emphasis on individuality and inherent human rights Erasmus was ahead of his time and pointed the way to the Enlightenment that was to follow (see the discussion in chapter 3).

 For Your Reflection and Analysis

Can corporal punishment serve a legitimate purpose in the school besides coercing students to study?

The first educational products of the Renaissance can be seen in the famous Italian court schools connected to the courts of reigning families. Perhaps the best known were those operated by Vittorino da Feltre at Mantua from 1423 to 1446 and by Guarino da Verona at Ferrara from 1429 to 1459. Like many modern preparatory boarding schools, they housed boys from ages 8 or 10 to age 20. They emphasized what Woodward (1906) called the "doctrine of courtesy"—the manners, grace, and dignity of the antique culture. At the court schools a humanist curriculum was taught that included the so-called seven liberal arts (grammar, logic, rhetoric, arithmetic, geometry, astronomy, and music), as well as reading, writing, and speaking in Latin; study of the Greek classics; and, for the first time, the study of history. Following the teachings of Quintilian, the court schools emphasized games and play, recognized individual differences, and discouraged punishment. The goal was to produce well-rounded, liberally educated courtiers—the ideal personality of the Renaissance—to fill positions as statesmen, diplomats, or scholars.

For Your Reflection and Analysis

Which, if any, of the seven liberal arts should be required subjects today? Why?

The classical humanist curriculum, if not the humanist student-centeredness, is reflected in the Latin grammar school, the dominant form of secondary education in colonial New England discussed in chapter 3. Moreover, the humanist belief that the human condition could be improved by education is reflected in the educational writings of many of the Founding Fathers. And, although the Protestant reformers discussed next are generally not considered humanists, they also shared the humanist belief in the importance of education, the responsibility of the individual in determining his destiny, and the role of the school in teaching moral principles.

Education During the Reformation

The period of history known as the Reformation formally began in 1517 when an Augustinian monk and professor of religion named Martin Luther (1483–1546) nailed his Ninety-five Theses questioning the authority (and abuses) of the Roman Catholic Church to the door of the court church in Wittenburg, Germany. In the years that followed, a religious revolution swept the European continent, resulting in a century of war and the reformation of the Roman Catholic Church. Those who protested the authority of the church came to be known as Protestants. The invention of the printing press enabled their doctrine and the Bible translated in the vernacular to spread rapidly. Whereas the Renaissance produced educational thought and practice that prestaged secondary education in America, the Reformation did the same for elementary education.

Luther

One of the major practices rejected by Martin Luther and other leaders of the Reformation was that priests read and interpreted the scriptures for the people because most of the people were illiterate. Luther not only objected to the power and authority this provided the church, but he also believed that every individual was responsible for his or her salvation, a salvation that came through faith, not works, and that could best be obtained by prayer and reading and studying the scriptures. To do this, however, it was necessary that every child be provided a free and compulsory elementary education. Luther believed that education should be supported by the state, and that the state should have the authority and responsibility to control the curriculum, the textbooks, and the instruction. In his 1524 *Letters to the Mayors and Aldermen of All Cities of Germany in Behalf of Christian Schools,* Luther stressed the spiritual, economic, and political benefits of education. The curriculum he recommended included classical languages, grammar, mathematics, science, history, physical education, music, and didactics (moral instruction). Theology was also taught and the study of Protestant doctrines accomplished through the catechism (a question-and-answer drill).

Although formal schooling was important to the establishment of a "priesthood of believers," Luther thought it should occupy only part of the day. At least 1 or 2 hours a day should be spent at home in vocational training, preparing for an occupation through an apprenticeship. Secondary schools, designed primarily as preparatory schools for the clergy, taught Hebrew as well as the classical languages, rhetoric, dialectic, history, mathematics, science, music, and gymnastics. A university education, whose purpose was seen as providing training for higher service in the government or the church, was available only to young men who demonstrated exceptional intellectual abilities.

Calvin

One of the major theologians of the Protestant Reformation, and perhaps the one most important to American history, was John Calvin (1509–1564). Raised as a French Catholic, Calvin, like Luther, came to reject the authority of the Catholic Church and accepted the doctrine of salvation by faith through prayer and the study of the scriptures. Calvin's views on education were very similar to those of Luther. He too stressed the necessity of a universal, compulsory, state-supported education that would not only enable all individuals to read the Bible themselves and thereby attain salvation, but also profit the state through the contributions of an orderly and productive citizenry. The school was also seen as a place for religious indoctrination through catechistic instruction. Calvin also supported a two-track educational system consisting of common schools for the masses and secondary schools teaching the classical, humanist curriculum for the preparation of the leaders of church and state.

Calvin's influence was widespread, both in the Europe of his day and later in the colonies of the New World. His advocacy of a universal primary education provided by the vernacular schools (described next) was adopted by Protestant theologians and educators throughout Europe. It was brought to the New World by the Puritans (English Calvinists who sought to purify or reform the Church of England) who settled in New England, as well as members of the Dutch Reformed Church who settled in New York, and Presbyterian Scotch Calvinists who settled in the middle and southern colonies. The efforts of each of these groups reflect the Calvinist emphasis on the importance of education to the religious, social, and economic welfare of the individual and the state. The legal mandates adopted by Calvinist communities in

Europe (e.g., holding parents responsible for the education of their children) became the models for similar laws in the New England colonies. The Calvinist proposal for state-supported education also had great appeal to the growing middle classes in Europe and the American colonies.

Vernacular Schools

The initial product of the belief that each person should be able to read the scriptures was the establishment of vernacular schools—primary or elementary schools that offered instruction in the mother tongue or "vernacular." Instruction in the native tongue also reflected and served to reinforce the spirit of nationalism that had begun to emerge during the Renaissance. The vernacular schools provided a basic curriculum of reading, writing, mathematics, and religion.

Vernacular schools were established throughout Germany by Philip Melanchthon and Johann Bugenhagen following Luther's teachings. Elementary schools also began to appear in other Protestant strongholds, especially those in the Netherlands, Scotland, and Switzerland, that followed the teachings of Calvin. The vernacular school also served as the model for the elementary schools that were established in colonial America.

For Your Reflection and Analysis

What are the disadvantages of teaching in the vernacular?

The Reformation took place against the backdrop of many other sweeping changes that marked the Renaissance in Europe. The rise of nation-states and a growing and more prosperous middle class combined with a revival of commerce and a quest for new markets to encourage willing explorers to find new routes to reach the treasures of the Orient or to capitalize on the riches of the newly discovered Americas.

Spanish and French Exploration and Education in the New World

Despite the notoriety given to Columbus' "Voyage of Discovery," the Spanish were by no means the first foreigners to reach the North American continent. Neither were the 10 Native Americans Columbus carried back with him to Europe in 1493, the first Native Americans to come to Europe. Buddhist texts tell of five beggar monks sailing from China to the Western Hemisphere as early as 458, and Cherokee oral tradition tells of Black men coming by sea before Columbus but being driven away. It has also been well documented that the Vikings landed and traded with the natives of Greenland and Canada 500 years before Columbus. And, as early as 1009, Native American captives were taken to Norway, and in 1420 captured Inuits were displayed there (*American Journey*, 1998).

Although many European explorers came before the Spanish, these early explorers came and went without making any imprint. It was the Spanish first, then the French, English, Dutch, and other Europeans, who would transform the land and the peoples with whom they came in contact.

New Spain

Beginning with the voyage of Columbus in 1492, the Spanish undertook a series of voyages to explore the Western Hemisphere. The primary purpose of the initial voyages was not to colonize the lands but to secure whatever wealth could be gleaned from the land and its inhabitants and return it to Spain. In the course of these voyages Spain established an empire in the New World that included, at various times, parts of South America, all of Central America, the entire southwestern United States, Florida, and southern California.

The tale of the Spanish conquest and the process by which the Spanish deliberately and ruthlessly stamped out the cultures, and sometimes the people, they defeated has been told many times; nothing can be gained by its repetition here. Rather, our primary interest is in their educational ventures, which were extensive. The Spanish operated an extensive system of mission and other church-sponsored schools throughout their vast empire. Their printing presses produced scores of books and, 85 years before the founding of Harvard, the first of the English colonial colleges, they had founded universities at Mexico City and Lima, Peru.

Spanish Missions of La Florida

In August of 1565 the Spanish established the first permanent European settlement in what was to become the United States. Unlike their previous excursions into Mexico, this expedition, commanded by Don Pedro Menendez de Aviles, newly appointed governor of La Florida, included not only 500 soldiers and settlers but farmers, craftsmen, and 26 families. Ten Jesuit missionaries were also among the 600 individuals who landed near present-day St. Augustine, Florida. The Jesuit missionaries soon began their work of attempting to convert the natives to Christianity and to instruct them in the Spanish culture and language. However, they met with little success; indeed, several Jesuits were killed. In 1572 the Jesuits abandoned their conversion efforts in Florida and moved to Mexico.

The Franciscans who came the next year initially concentrated their efforts in and around St. Augustine, and in 1606 the first school in what was to become the United States was established to teach the children of the Spanish settlers. Not dissuaded by the experiences of the Jesuits, the Franciscans also moved out into the surrounding wilderness. From their base in St. Augustine they moved along the coast north into what was to become Georgia and into the interior of Florida, establishing missions from which to undertake their conversion and educational work. Usually a mission was established in a village where the chief lived and where the chiefdom's council house was located. The mission itself was really only a small compound within a much larger Indian community and typically included the church and a friary where the priest lived ("Georgia's Spanish Missions," 2003).

By 1650 there were 50 missions with approximately 25,000 Indian converts in what was called La Florida (White, cited in Vega, 1984).

 For Your Reflection and Analysis

What was the strategy behind locating the missions in the chief's village?

However, 50 years later the dramatic decline in the native population had reduced the number of missions to two. Many Native Americans had died from common European diseases for which they had no natural immunities. Others died in wars with the Europeans, and others were subjected to forced resettlement. By 1710 the only remaining mission was the one at St. Augustine.

Mission Schools in the Southwest

A quarter century after the settlement at St. Augustine and 2,000 miles to the west, the Spanish settled the village of San Gabriel in northern New Mexico. The 1598 settlement at San Gabriel was the first permanent Spanish settlement in what is now the western United States. The Franciscan priests who accompanied Don Juan de Onate's expedition from Mexico to the pueblo where San Gabriel was founded had a clear mission: to spread the holy Catholic faith and convert the natives. The Spanish expedition into New Mexico was one of a series of expeditions into the Southwest that followed Cortez' conquest of Mexico in 1519. The mission established at San Gabriel was part of a vast network of missions established by Spanish priests and friars throughout Central America, as well as a territory that covered most of what are now the states of New Mexico, Arizona, Texas, and California.

The operation of the mission system in New Spain was based on the Spanish concept of the appropriate division of duties and responsibilities between the cross and the crown. According to this theory,

> The duty and privilege of the church was to teach, the obligation of the state was to provide the material means for the church to accomplish its spiritual task. This task was primarily to mold the minds of the people according to a set pattern of instruction in the Christian doctrine, and secondly, to enhance the knowledge of this religious faith by the teaching of academic subjects.
>
> This approach to education was not unique. It was rather commonplace in both Europe and (later) in the thirteen American colonies. In the sixteenth and seventeenth centuries education was the patrimony of the clergymen and those who, one way or another, could assist the church in its task of salvation of human souls. (Vega, 1984, p. 551)

The proposed relationship between church and state was made clear as early as 1503 by King Ferdinand of Spain in an order to the governor of New Spain that "in each town already built or to be built in the future, a house should be erected for the Indian children to come twice a day to be instructed in the arts of writing and reading, as well as other things pertaining to the Christian Faith" (Konetzke, cited in Vega, 1984, pp. 81–82).

In keeping with the Spanish concept of the role of the mission school, the friars taught both Christian doctrine and reading and writing. Catechisms, prepared by Franciscan friars in Mexico as early as 1540, used easily understood pictographs to do both. The friars also set up workshops in the schools where the Indians were taught trades and industrial arts, as well as the fine arts. And, unlike the English settlers who

Pictograph on wall of Canyon de Muerto (Arizona) depicts Spanish soldiers and priest exploring the Southwest.

 For Your Reflection and Analysis

Why would the English have wanted the Native Americans to abandon their former industries?

tried to get the Native Americans to abandon their former industries, the Spanish tried to use the industry or mechanical progress the Indians already possessed as the basis for improvement (Shea, 1978).

By 1628 the friars had established 50 missions throughout the Rio Grande and Pecos valleys: A year later new missions were added in the Acoma, Zuni, and Hopi pueblos (Taylor, 2001). A 1630 report by the supervisor of the Franciscan missions in New Mexico included the following references to the educational work of the missions:

> The Tompiras Nation . . . extends in that direction more than fifteen leagues, and has fourteen or fifteen pueblos, with more than ten thousand inhabitants. It has six very good friaries and churches. All of the inhabitants have been converted. . . . In their schools all the trades are taught as elsewhere. . . .
>
> The Pecos Nation. Continuing to the north four more leagues one reaches the pueblo of the Pecos. . . . These Indians are well trained . . . and, like the others, have their schools where reading, writing, singing, and instrumental music are taught. . . .
>
> The Town of Sante Fe. Seven leagues west of the aforesaid pueblo is the town of Sante Fe, capital of the kingdom. . . . There the friars are already teaching the Spaniards and the Indians to read, write, play musical instruments, sing, and to practice all the arts of civilized society. (Lynch, cited in Vega, 1984, p. 121)

The missions educated not only the Native Americans, but as the previous reference to the mission in Sante Fe indicates, in some cases the children of the Spaniards. By the time of the Revolutionary War, 20,000 Spanish-speaking settlers had migrated north from Mexico into New Mexico, Texas, and Arizona. Although some of the children of the Spanish settlers attended the mission schools, children of the more affluent settlers were schooled at home by tutors or were sent to schools in Mexico or Spain.

For 200 years the missions played a central role in the conversion and education of Native Americans. By the 18th century, however, their influence began to decline. The missions became secularized: They changed from being churches under the control and support of the central church or a particular religious order, notably the Franciscans, to parish churches supported by members of the parish and served by Dominicans, nonorder priests. In the process of secularization the lands of the mission were divided, efforts to convert and civilize the Native Americans were abandoned, and most of the mission schools fell by the wayside (Berger, 1947; Vega, 1984).

New France

By the late 16th century the French had also completed a number of voyages of exploration to the New World. Initial colonization attempts by the French in the Carolinas and Florida were failures. In 1605 the first permanent French settlement in North America was founded at Port Royal, Nova Scotia, but it was destroyed by the English in 1614. In 1608 Samuel de Champlain, the governor of French Canada and the explorer who had conducted much of the exploration, founded the first enduring French colony in North America at what is now Quebec. Eventually, the French empire spread from Canada down the Ohio and Mississippi valleys to the Gulf of Mexico (see Figure 2.1).

Unlike the Spanish, and later the English, French ventures in the New World were not directed at establishing permanent settlements but commercial outposts for the vast fur-trading empire that developed. The fur-trading Company of New France undertook most of the exploration and actually owned Canada until 1663; it "saw little purpose and no profit in the costly business of transporting people to a colony dedicated to the fur trade" (Taylor, 2001, p. 365). The colonization of New France also did not benefit from the immigration of religious dissidents as did the colonization of New England. Although there were many religious dissidents in 17th century Catholic France who might have been anxious to immigrate to New France to escape persecution, French policy after 1632 forbade their immigration. This policy deprived Canada of an especially promising set of colonists, the Protestant Huguenots, who were similar to the English Puritans in terms of their Calvinist faith and middle-class status as artisans, shopkeepers, and merchants (Taylor, 2001).

 For Your Reflection and Analysis

Why would the French government want to forbid the immigration of dissidents rather than let them leave as most other nations did?

Because there were few settlers in New France, there were no schools except in the largest towns. These schools were operated for the children of the settlers, not the Native Americans. However, in a pattern that was similar to that of the Spanish, French priests, particularly the Franciscans and the Jesuits, followed the explorers and fur traders into the wilderness to convert and educate the

FIGURE 2.1   European Powers in North America, 1770

Native Americans. The Jesuits, a teaching order that had been influential in establishing a number of secondary schools and universities in Europe, established the first elementary and secondary school in New France in Quebec in 1616. The Ursulines, an order of teaching sisters, opened a girls' school in the same city in 1642, long before such schools were even being considered in the New England colonies. The Jesuits were also successful in establishing a number of missions. However, the Black Robes, as they were called by the Indians, had limited success in converting the Indians. But as explorers, educators, and cartographers, the Jesuits accomplished a great deal. Catholic influence on education in the United States can be traced to the Jesuits as well as to orders of teaching nuns.

 For Your Reflection and Analysis

Which of the major colleges and universities in the United States were founded by Jesuits?

Of all the European settlers, the French were probably the most congenial to the Indians. Whereas the Spanish did not consider the Indians human beings until a papal decree in 1527 declared them to be humans and capable of embracing the Catholic faith, the French "often became absorbed in Indian life, adopting Indian

French missionaries followed the explorers into the wilderness.

customs and dress, learning native languages and intermarrying" (Nabokov & Vine, 2000, p. 19).

By 1660 New France had fewer than 3,000 colonists compared to 58,000 colonists in New England. Concern that they were losing in the race to colonize North America led the French crown to attempt to stimulate immigration by paying the passage of immigrants to New France. However, most of the male immigrants were soldiers or indentured servants, over two thirds of whom returned to France after their terms of service were over. When the government stopped subsidizing the migration in 1673, it ground to a halt (Taylor, 2001). In the absence of a population to demand or support them, schools in New France were scarce. In contrast, as described in chapter 3, in the English colonies schools had sprung up in towns and villages all along the eastern seaboard.

The native peoples that these early Spanish and French missionaries and English colonists sought to "educate" were not uneducated. Although they did not share the dominant European educational philosophies or their formal educational practices, they did have well-developed systems of educating the young that are described in the following section.

Education of Native Peoples in Precolonial America

The pre-Columbian population of what is now the United States has been estimated to have been as many as 11 million native people, if not twice that many (Adovasio & Page, 2002). (By 1900, only 250,000 remained.) These several million people represented 300 different cultures and spoke over 200 different languages (Nabokov & Vine, 2000; Reagan, 2000) (see Figure 2.2). The first Europeans that came to the New England and Mid-Atlantic colonies would have encountered one of the many Algonquian-speaking tribes. As they traveled inland, they would have met the members of another language family, the Iroquoian, including the five tribes who made up the Iroquois League (Mohawk, Oneida, Onondaga, Cayuga, and Seneca). In the southeast they would have encountered the Muskogean-speaking Indians who came to make up the loosely knit Creek Confederacy. And in Virginia they would have found the Powhatan Confederacy, which linked 200 villages and 30 different tribes. These groups were as culturally different from one another as were the nations of Europe (Nabokov & Vine, 2000).

The education of these millions of native people did not originate with the mission schools. In fact, prior to the arrival of Europeans in the New World, each native

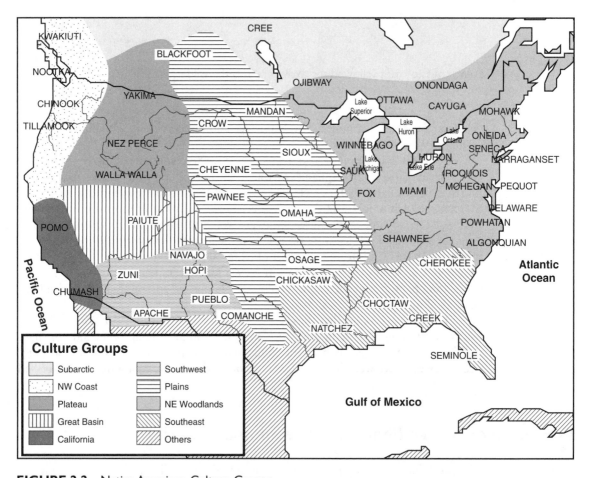

FIGURE 2.2 Native American Culture Groups

Source: Stefoff, R. (2001). *The colonies.* Tarrytown, NY: Benchmark Press, p. 21. Copyright © Marshall Cavendish Corporation.

group had a comprehensive formal and informal system for educating and training their children and youth. However, the free and spontaneous nature of Native American education, which relied on oral tradition, not the written word, was very different from the more formalized approach of the Europeans. As a result, the European colonists perceived it as unreliable and as a lesser form of education than the traditional school model they employed (Hale, 2002).

Basic Courses of Native Education

Prior to being accepted as a mature member of a native society, a child was expected to master certain skills. These skills, described by Tuscarura as the "three basic courses" of native education, fall into three areas: (1) economic or survival skills; (2) knowledge of cultural heritage; and (3) spiritual awareness (Szasz, 1988).

Economic or Survival Skills

Training for survival was dependent on a knowledge of the physical sciences, including geography, temperature, access to water, and so on. For example, those tribes that lived in the southwestern deserts needed a different type of survival training than those who lived in the subarctic. Regardless of the geographic differences, all native children were taught at an early age that survival was dependent on a harmonious relationship with nature. To achieve that harmony, a proper attitude toward the earth and all animate and inanimate life living on it was necessary (Szasz, 1988). Last, training for survival included the development of physical skills.

 For Your Reflection and Analysis

Many courses today carry the title "survival skills." How do they compare with the survival skills taught to Native American youth?

Knowledge of Cultural Heritage

Throughout history all peoples have sought to pass on the history and heritage of their culture. The heritage of the indigenous people of North America represented a wide range of cultural patterns, norms, social structures, and behaviors (Reagan, 2000). Song, dance, drama, simple or complex symbols, and the written word were used. Among the native peoples of North America the art of storytelling was seen as the most effective strategy for imparting the culture to children. "Storytelling was taught on many levels, with the tales reinforcing cultural ideals learned in more daily and mundane lessons, and moral instruction punctuating the lives of native youth" (Szasz, 1988, p. 13). Medicine men, ritual leaders, and members of the oldest living generation often bore the responsibility for transmitting the knowledge and culture to the next generation (Szasz, 1988).

Spiritual Awareness

The need for spiritual awareness was not limited to the medicine man, shaman, or priest. Spiritual awareness was required of all youth. Some native groups worshipped a creator or Great Spirit. Others perceived a single and all-powerful supernatural power. Most acknowledged a creative force in all things on Earth, suggesting that one could not separate the spiritual and the material, the natural and the supernatural, or the human and the animal (Szasz, 1988).

The search for spiritual awareness began early in development. Spiritual attitudes were shared by family and older members of the tribe, as well as through ritual and ceremony. Spiritual training intensified dramatically as the youth neared puberty. In some tribes a specific ceremony might last several days, whereas in others, such as at the Taos pueblo, boys left their homes and lived in a kiva for a year and a half where they were trained by a spiritual leader. Among some tribes in the Northwest both boys and girls went on "spiritual quests" (solitary days of fasting and physical hardships) to obtain a guardian spirit in the form of an animal or any living creature who would guide them for the rest of their lives (Szasz, 1988).

 For Your Reflection and Analysis

Give examples of various "coming of age" ceremonies or practices in non-Native American cultures.

Native Philosophy of Education

The native philosophies of child-rearing, education, and youth development that were practiced at the time of the European colonization had been refined over 15,000 years of civilization and preserved via oral tradition. Many continue to be practiced

Young Native American completes his physical quest.

by native families and tribes today. At the center of Native American educational thought and practice is the belief that the human being is comprised of a spirit, a mind, and a physical body. Of these three elements, the spirit is the most important: "the first step that parents take towards the education of their children is to prepare them for future happiness, by impressing in their tender minds, that they are indebted for their existence on a great and benevolent Spirit" (Heckewelder, cited in DeJong, 1993, p. 12). Another core educational belief relates to health, which is not only a physical condition but also a spiritual condition. Through the combined spirit, mind, and body the individual achieves the ultimate goal of harmony. Although harmony is the ultimate goal of education, the prevention of disharmony is also an important educational goal.

> One cannot be in a state of disharmony caused by suppressed anger, frustration, heartache, or fear without sooner or later developing unwellness in the physical body from that disharmony. Disharmony may be a vague feeling of things "not being right" in one's life, and a time of meditation may be needed in which to discover what is not right. (Locust, cited in Reagan, 2000, p. 87)

Self-worth or self-esteem is also a central concept in the native philosophy of education. Self-esteem is considered to have four basic elements: significance, competence, power, and virtue. Each of these components collectively and individually contributes to a child's view of self-worth. Significance is found through the acceptance, attention, and affection of others. Those who are rejected and ignored and do not feel that they belong lack significance.

Competence evolves as one masters one's environment. Competence leads to success, satisfaction, and self-efficacy. In contrast, chronic failure extinguishes motivation. Power suggests that the individual has control over his or her own behavior. It also assumes that he or she has gained the respect of others. Powerlessness leads to helplessness. Virtue includes worthiness and is demonstrated by the cultural values and the values of significant others. The lack of virtue leads to a life without spiritual fulfillment (Coppersmith, cited in Brendtro, Brokenleg, & Van Bockern, 1991).

Core Values of Native Educational Practice

Each of the four elements of self-esteem are embedded in the traditional core values of native educational practices. These core values are (1) the spirit of belonging, (2) the spirit of mastery, (3) the spirit of independence, and (4) the spirit of generosity (Brendtro et al., 1991).

Spirit of Belonging

Like Nampeyo, whose education is described in the Primary Source Reading for this chapter, Native American children are nurtured and reared by a large circle of significant and caring others not limited to biological relations. All adults had the duty to serve as the teachers and caregivers of the young. Although all adults contributed to the education of the young, their roles varied: The role of the father or mother was different from that of the grandfather or grandmother, whose role was different from that of an aunt or uncle, and so forth. The spirit of belonging transcended human relationships and extended to nature as well. Animals, plants, people, and streams were all considered interdependent (Brendtro et al., 1991).

Spirit of Mastery

Children and adults strive for competence or mastery of their environment. An important goal of native education was to develop cognitive, physical, social, and spiritual competence. Numerous techniques were used to teach mastery. For example, children were taught wisdom through ceremonies and oral history. Competence was also taught through games and creative play. As recalled by one Cheyenne woman:

> In my girlhood days we played what we girls called "tiny play." This play imitated the customs and ways of grownup people. . . . After a time as I became a little older we played what we called "large play." The boys would go out hunting. . . . We girls would pitch our tipis and make ready everything as if it were a real camp life. . . . Some of the boys would go on the warpath, and always came home victorious. (cited in Szasz, 1988, p. 23)

Perhaps the most important lesson that was taught in teaching mastery was that success was to be shared by all:

> The simple wisdom of Native culture was that since all need to feel competent, all must be encouraged in their competency. Striving was for attainment of personal goals, not being superior to one's opponent. Just as one felt ownership in the success of others, one also learned to share personal achievements with others. Success became a possession of the many, not the privileged few. (Brendtro et al., p. 8)

Spirit of Independence

Individual freedom was highly valued in the native culture. However, the native spirit of independence differed in several ways from the White culture's emphasis on independence, assertiveness, and competition. For example, native people believed that the young must first experience dependency and then learn to respect and value elders. Equally important was to be taught through explanation and the modeling of appropriate behavior. By approaching children with maturity and dignity, native people believed they would teach them responsibility. Children were never rewarded for their achievement. Rather, the achievement itself was viewed as the reward. Modeling, group influence, discussion, and positive expectations were used in lieu of rewards and punishment. Sanctions served a corrective role in the educational process (DeJong, 1993).

Spirit of Generosity

The highest virtue in the Native American culture was to be generous and unselfish. Training in altruism began in early childhood and continued throughout life. The values of simplicity, generosity, and nonmaterialism were important in the native culture. The capacity to care, to share, and to accept some responsibility for the welfare of all in the community were central to the spirit of generosity (Brendtro et al., 1991).

The system of education among native peoples, one that had served them so well in teaching their children to become mature and responsible members of their tribes, was challenged by the arrival of the Europeans. The Europeans believed the Native American children should have a different education and acquire a different view of spiritual awareness (Szasz, 1988). European educational principles and practices, particularly those of the English, as well as their efforts to compel the Native Americans to adopt European culture and religion, are described in the chapters that follow.

 For Your Reflection and Analysis

To what extent are the core values of Native American educational practice found in non-Native American education today?

Conclusion

Despite the controversy often surrounding it, religion has been one of the most powerful forces in shaping the history of the United States. Even before their first expedition the Spanish explorers had been charged by the Catholic king of Spain with converting and educating the natives. The desire to bring Christianity to the natives led Spanish priests into the wilderness to establish a vast system of missions throughout the southwestern United States and Central America. Beginning with these Spanish missions and continuing through the mission schools on Indian reservations in the 20th century, religious groups have played a major role in bringing literacy to Native Americans.

The meeting of the European and Native American cultures was marked by an imbalance of power and the conflict that often accompanies the first meeting of people from very different cultures. Those from both cultures undoubtedly had their disappointments and misperceptions: The Europeans were not gods as the Native Americans originally thought, and not all Native Americans were "noble savages, as some Europeans characterized them." The experiences of the Spanish and French with the Native Americans were different, primarily because of the nature of their relationships. The interactions of the Spanish were more negative, primarily because their interactions were marked by exploitation and forced assimilation. The interactions of the French were generally more positive because they, for the most part, did neither of these things. They were trappers and did not go in search of Native American gold and silver. Also the French did not build missions and force assimilation.

Many of the perceptions and practices that would characterize race relations in America for more than three centuries had their origins in precolonial America. The perception that the native population was uncivilized and uneducated led to a devaluing and rejection of their cultural traditions and served to justify, in the minds of many colonists, their forced assimilation. These attitudes and behaviors, first manifest with the Native Americans, have been evidenced in all subsequent interactions between minorities and the dominant Anglo culture. American history has been characterized by efforts to force the assimilation of various ethnic and racial minorities. The school's role in these efforts is described throughout the remainder of this text.

For Discussion and Application

1. In what ways is the humanist philosophy reflected in contemporary educational practice?
2. How would those on both sides of the bilingual education debate respond to the concept of vernacular schools?
3. How did the exploration of the New World by the Spanish and French compare in terms of intent and outcomes?
4. Compare the formal and informal education of Native Americans youth in pre-colonial America with that of children in Calvinist communities in Europe.
5. Compare the Native American philosophy of education with that of a contemporary educational philosophy practiced in a school with which you are familiar.

Primary Source Reading

The following excerpts were written by Desiderius Erasmus in 1529 to William, Duke of Cleves, following the birth of the duke's son. Erasmus took advantage of this opportunity to instruct the Duke of Cleves about the importance of education for his newborn son. In doing so, he also outlined some of the major educational principles that embody educational psychology, educational theory, and parenting. These principles have stood the test of time and continue to have relevance for parents and educators today. As you read the following passages, consider how these basic principles have relevance for your life personally and professionally.

The Education of Young Children

Desiderius Erasmus

The Argument at Large

I desire to urge upon you, Illustrious Duke, to take into your early and serious consideration the future nurture and training of the son lately born

Source: De Pueris Instituendis as quoted in Desiderius Erasmus concerning the aim and method of education (W. H. Woodward, Ed. and Trans.). (Cambridge, MA: 1529/1904), pp. 180–186.

to you. For, with Chrysippus, I contend that the young child must be led to sound learning whilst his wit is yet unwarped, his age tender, his mind flexible and tenacious. In manhood, we remember nothing so well as the truths which we imbibed in our youth. Wherefore I beg you to put aside all idle chatter which would persuade you that this early childhood is unmeet for the discipline and the effort of studies.

The arguments which I shall enlarge upon are the following. First, the beginnings of learning are the work of memory, which in young children is most tenacious. Next, as nature has implanted in us the instinct to seek for knowledge, can we be too early in obeying her behest? Thirdly, there are not a few things which it imports greatly that we should know well, and which we can learn far more readily in our tender years. I speak of the elements of Letters, Grammar, and the fables and stories found in the ancient Poets. Fourthly, since children, as all agree, are fit to acquire manners, why may they not acquire the rudiments of learning? And seeing that they must needs be busy about something, what else can be better approved? For how much wiser to amuse their hours with Letters, than to see them frittered away in aimless trifling!

It is, however, objected, first, that such knowledge as can be thus early got is of slight value. But even so, why despise it, if so be it serve as the foundation for much greater things? For, if in early childhood a boy acquire such useful elements he will be free to apply his youth to higher knowledge, to the saving of his time. Moreover, whilst he is thus occupied in sound learning he will perforce be kept from some of the temptations which befall youth, seeing that nothing engages the whole mind more than studies. And this I count a high gain in such times as ours.

Next, it is urged that by such application health may be somewhat endangered. Supposing this to be true, still the compensation is great, for by discipline the mind gains far more in alertness and in vigour than the body is ever likely to lose. Watchfulness, however, will prevent any such risk as is imagined. Also, for this tender age you will employ a teacher who will win and not drive, just as you will choose such subjects as are pleasant and attractive in which the young mind will find recreation rather than toil.

Furthermore, I bide you remember that a man ignorant of Letters is no man at all, that human life is a fleeting thing, that youth is easily enticed to sin, that early manhood is absorbed by clashing interests, that old age is unproductive, and that few reach it. How then can you allow your child, in whom you yourself live again to lose even one of those precious years in which he may begin to acquire those means whereby he may elevate his whole life and keep at arm's length temptation and evil?

The First Law: Education Must Begin From the Very Earliest Years

I rejoice at your determination that your son shall be early initiated into the arts of true learning and the wisdom of sound philosophy. Herein consists the full duty of fatherhood, the care and guidance of the spirit of him for whose creation you are responsible. And now for my first precept. Do not follow the fashion, which is too common amongst us, of allowing the early years of childhood to pass without fruit of instruction, and of deferring its first steps until the allurements of indulgence have made application more difficult.

The Supreme Importance of Education to Human Well-Being

To dumb creatures Mother Nature has given an innate power or instinct, whereby they may in great part attain to their right capacities. But Providence in granting to man alone the privilege of reason has thrown the burden of development of the human being upon training. Well, therefore, has it been said that the first means, the second, and the third means to happiness is right training or education. Sound education is the condition of real wisdom. And if an education which is soundly planned and carefully carried out is the very fount of all human excellence, so, on the other hand, careless and unworthy training is the true source of folly and vice. This *capacity for training* is, indeed, the chief aptitude which has been bestowed upon humanity. Unto the animals nature has given swiftness of foot or of wing, keenness of sight, strength or size of frame, and various weapons of defence. To Man, instead of physical powers, is given a mind apt for training; in this single gift all others are comprised, for him, at least, who turns it to due profit. We see that where native instinct is strong—as in squirrels or bees—capacity for being taught is wanting. Man, lacking instinct, can do little or nothing of innate power; scarce can he eat, or walk, or speak, unless he be guided thereto. How then can we expect that he should become competent to the duties of life unless straightway and with much diligence he be brought under the discipline of a worthy education? Let me enforce this by the well-known story of Lycurgus, who, to convince the Spartans, brought out two hounds, one of good mettle, but untrained and therefore useless in the field, and the other poorly bred and well-drilled at his work; "Nature," he said, "may be strong, yet Education is more powerful still."

Other Parents Neglect the Duty of Education Until Too Late

Further, there are those—sometimes men of repute for practical wisdom—who err in deferring education till a stage when the boy finds the rudiments of learning irksome to acquire. Yet these same fathers will be over-anxious for their children's future fortune even before they be born. We hear of astrologers called in: "the child," it is affirmed, "will be a born soldier." "Then let us plan to enter him into the king's service." "He will be the very type of a churchman." "Then let us work for a bishopric or an abbey for him." And this is not thought to be taking care prematurely for a career yet far-distant. Why then refuse to provide not less early that the boy may be worthily prepared to fill it: so that he grow up not only to be a captain of a troop, but a fit and reputable officer of the commonwealth; not merely to be called a bishop, but to be worthy of his charge? Men seem to me to have regard to nothing less than to that end to which all these other ends are subordinate. Lands, castles, furnishings, dress, servants, all are well cared for, and are of the best: the son of the house alone is left untrained, untaught, ignorant, boorish. A man buys a slave; he may be useless at first, as knowing nothing. Straightway he is tried, and it is quickly found what he can best do, and to that craft he is diligently trained. But the same man will wholly neglect his son's upbringing. "He will have enough to live upon," he will say. "But *not* enough to live a worthy life," I rejoin. "What need of learning? He will have wealth." "Then the more need of all the guidance that Letters and Philosophy can bestow." How active, for instance, do princes show themselves to get for their sons as large a dominion as they can, whilst no men seem to care less that their heirs should be duly educated to fulfill the responsibility that must fall to them. The saying of Alexander is often quoted: "Were I not Alexander I would be Diogenes." But Plutarch is right in his reflection, that the very fact that he was lord of so great an empire was, had he known it, reason enough for him to desire to be a philosopher as well. How much more does that father give his son who gives him that by which he may *live worthily* than he who merely gives that whereby he may live!

The Error of Those Who Think That Experience Gives All the Education That Men Need

They err, therefore, who affirm that wisdom is won by handling affairs and by contact with life, without aid from the teaching of philosophy. Tell me, can a man run his best in the dark? Or, can a gladiator conquer if he be blindfold? The precepts of philosophy—which is knowledge applied to life—are, as it were, the eyes of the mind, and lighten us to the consciousness of what we may do and may not do. A long and manifold experience is, beyond doubt, of great profit, but only to such as by the wisdom of learning have acquired an intelligent and informed judgment. Besides, philosophy teaches us more in one year than our own individual experience can teach us in thirty, and its teaching carries none of the risks which the method of learning by experience of necessity brings with it. For example, you educate your son to the mystery of medicine. Do you allow him to rely on the method of "experience" in order that he may learn to distinguish between poisons and healing drugs? Or, do you send him to the treatises? It is an unhappy education which teaches the master mariner the rudiments of navigation by shipwrecks: or the Prince the true way of kingship by revolutions, invasions or slaughter. Is it not the wise part to learn beforehand how to avoid mischiefs rather than with the pains of experience to remedy them? Thus Philip of Macedon put his son Alexander to school with Aristotle that he might learn philosophy of him, to the end that when a king he should be saved from doing things which must be repented of. Thus education shews us in brief what we should follow, what avoid: she does not wait till we have suffered the evil results of our mistakes, but warns us in advance against courses which will lead to failure and misery. Let us, therefore, firmly knit up this threefold cord: let Nature . . . by Training, thus united, be made perfect by right Practice.

When we observe animal life, we notice that each creature learns, first of all, to perform those things which preserve life and to avoid those things which make for pain and destruction. This is true not less of plants, as we can see when we contrast the close-knit tree of the exposed seacoast and its fellow spreading luxuriantly in warmth and shelter. All living things strive to develop according to their proper nature. What is the proper nature of Man? Surely it is to live the life of Reason, for reason is the peculiar prerogative of man. And what is it that in man makes for pain and destruction? Surely it is Folly, which is life without reason. It is, then, certain that desire for excellence and aversion to folly come readily to man if only his nature, as yet empty of content, be from the outset of life filled with right-activities. Yet we hear extravagant complaints "how prone is child-nature to wrong, how hard to win to excellence." But herein men accuse nature unjustly. Parents themselves are to blame in taking little heed for that which the child imbibes in his early years.

Questions for Discussion

1. Discuss how you might apply the following principle to early childhood education today: "The young child must be led to sound learning whilst his wit is yet unwarped, his age tender, his mind flexible and tenacious."

2. Prepare an argument that either agrees or disagrees with the following principle and explain its relevance for your professional life: "Nature . . . may be strong, yet Education is more powerful still."

3. Give examples of how the following principle applies to your personal life: "Philosophy teaches us more in one year than our own individual experience can teach us in thirty, and its teaching carries none of the risks which the method of learning by experience of necessity brings with it."

Primary Source Reading

Every culture has its own unique way of socializing its young. This socialization process enables each member of the group or clan to learn the values and norms of his or her particular society. Regardless of the culture, one of the most important ways that children learn is by observation, imitation, and practice. The following is an account of the socialization of a young Hopi-Tewa female named Nampeyo. As you read the story of Nampeyo, note the variety of individuals who were responsible for her early socialization and training.

The Socialization of Nampeyo

Barbara Kramer

The Tewas call it Tewa Village, but it is commonly known as Hano. On the narrow top near the gap in the mesa, each Tewa clan built stone dwellings similar to those of the Hopis, and, in the traditional matriarchal society, the house belonged to the woman. When a daughter married, the husband moved to her home. As a clan increased in numbers, second- and sometimes third-story rooms would be added atop the rooms below. Dwellings that expanded outward and upward eventually enclosed a dirt plaza where ceremonial activities and social dances took place, where members of a clan seated on sheep skins and rabbitskin blankets celebrated a marriage or the harvesting of crops with a feast. Young men courted maidens through open windows while, inside, near the grinding stones, the girls kneeled at their task of preparing cornmeal. In the northeast corner of the plaza, the Monete Kiva provided an underground chamber for the ceremonies, dances, clan functions, and social gatherings of men. Activity was so confined around the

Source: From *Nampeyo and her pottery*, by Barbara Kramer. © 1996 Barbara Kramer. Reprinted by permission of the University of Arizona Press.

plaza that everyone knew everyone else's life almost as intimately as his own.

The Corn clan rooms, however, did not face inward toward the plaza but stood behind the Tobacco clan dwelling, facing east where they caught the first rays of the morning sun. The main room of entry contained "curious belongings hung on the wall or thrust above the great ceiling beams—strings of dried [herbs], . . . gaily painted dolls, blankets, arrows, feathers, and other objects enough to stock a museum."

Nampeyo was born in one of those Corn clan rooms. . . . The precise date is unknown, because time was not marked off in numbered segments by a people whose lives were governed by the position of the sun and the rhythm of nature. Whatever the year, it was what elders call "the old time," when families woke to the voice of a village crier calling announcements from a rooftop at dawn and went about their tasks barefoot until dark, setting aside their chores only to prepare for or to celebrate a ceremony. . . .

Nampeyo's father, Quootsva of the Hopi Snake clan, lived with his family in Walpi until he married her mother, White Corn, and moved to her home in Hano. Among both Hopis and Hopi-Tewas, a child was born into the clan of its mother; thus the children of Quootsva and White Corn were all of the Tewa Corn clan. . . .

According to custom, one of the whitewashed rooms in the stone house was darkened by hanging rabbitskin quilts at the window openings and the doorway. During her labor, White Corn was comforted and assisted by her mother and her mother's sisters. After the birth, Quootsva's mother was called to cut the umbilical cord, and the paternal grandmother remained with mother and child for twenty days, caring for them in the darkened room. For the mesa people, the transition from womb to world was an unhurried one.

As was customary during confinement, White Corn ate only cornmeal gruel and water boiled with juniper, and every fifth day Quootsva's mother administered a sweatbath by pouring water over a heated stone. The infant was washed frequently, rubbed with fine ash, and given the maternal love innate to Hopi and Tewa women.

To supplement this human nurturing, an ear of white corn was placed next to the child to guard it from evil spirits.

Following tradition, all the women of Quootsva's Snake clan gathered in Walpi early on the twentieth day after Nampeyo's birth. With only the stars and moon lighting their way, a quiet procession passed through the middle village to the whitewashed room where White Corn and her baby waited. While a clansman sang, gifts were presented, and each woman in turn dipped an ear of corn into yucca-root suds, then touched it to the infant's head with a prayer and the whisper of a name related to the father's clan. The child was then placed into a new cradleboard together with four ears of corn, wrapped around and around with a sash into secure immobility, and carried from the house by the paternal grandmother as the yellow line of dawn gradually illumined the sky. When the first rays of sun touched the stone house and the gathered clan members, the grandmother said a blessing. Then, speaking to the child, she said, in effect, "You have come out to see the sun," and she gave her a childhood name. Later, when Nampeyo reached puberty, she was given the name "Nung-beh-yong," Tewa for Sand Snake. . . .

Nampeyo passed her infancy secured within a cradleboard lined with cedar shavings to provide padding and absorption. Oftentimes the board hung from a viga, from which it was swung by grandparents or little brothers passing by. Sometimes White Corn strapped the board to her back, rocking the infant while she worked and sang lullabies. The infant was never left alone, lest, they believed, a spirit of the dead hold the child and the child too would die.

During Nampeyo's lifetime, observers commented that the instinctive affection given to children by the mesa people instilled a security of being and belonging. They rarely heard a child cry or saw one scolded by an adult. Every member of the family in the course of his daily tasks enfolded a newborn, so that it assimilated the activities that would constitute its later life. A mother making pottery would give her child a piece of clay to mold, letting it learn with its own hands what she too had learned in the same way. A father would pick up an infant to his chest while he chanted a song and danced a few steps. Chores, song, and ceremonial dance thus became part of the rhythm of life.

The child Nampeyo followed her mother about and learned where to dig clay, how to wash impurities from it, how to shape little pots and to fire them. She and White Corn collected beeweed, which they boiled into paint, and they chewed the tough leaves of yucca to make brushes. Making utilitarian pottery was a continuing, time-consuming task, and skill was required to shape the various vessels: cooking pots and large storage jars, stew bowls and water jars, large bowls for mixing batter for piki (tissue-thin blue cornbread that is rolled or folded), seed jars for storing crop seeds for the next year's planting, and cups and ladles.

Small water canteens were fashioned for the men to carry into the fields, but for themselves, women made the cumbersome flat-sided three- to six-gallon canteens that they used to collect water from the spring at the base of the mesa. Tying the pottery jug on her back with a shawl that was then secured around her forehead, the woman made her way down the trail to the spring to wait her turn among her neighbors. Greetings would be exchanged—"*lo-la-mi! lo-la-mi!*"—and gossip shared. Shifting the filled jug to her back and bending to support the increased weight, she would trudge slowly, barefoot, back up the narrow trail, stopping occasionally to rest and to let others pass. This daily ritual, passed on from White Corn's mother to White Corn and then to Nampeyo, gradually produced a strange gait, a sort of waddle in which their stocky bodies leaned forward as if into the wind.

Most chores, prayers, and celebrations related to corn, the staple of life. . . . White Corn's mother, then White Corn, and eventually Nampeyo herself kneeled before the three flat grinding stones every day. Each of the stones produced a successively finer meal under the mano (handheld stone) that was pushed back and forth to prepare it for gruels, puddings, or batter for piki.

White Corn's house had a separate cooking room, where the child watched and learned how to make the tissue-thin blue piki. Rolled or folded and stacked in layers on a flat basket, piki was a staple with meals, presented as gifts, and given to men preparing for and participating in ceremonies in the kivas. . . .

As was the practice of all mesa women, White Corn periodically plastered and whitewashed the rooms of her house and kept it in repair. Because hers was the oldest Corn clan dwelling in Hano, it housed clan fetishes and ceremonial objects in a separate chamber safeguarded by the women. In this house of "our oldest mother" of the clan, clan meetings were held to discuss land problems and rituals. Prior to a ceremony, a smoke meeting was held in the clan house to determine the auspicious time for it to begin, which was then announced from a rooftop the following dawn. . . .

All this the daughter learned so that she could carry on tradition in the Corn clan dwellings at the top of the trail.

Lengthy, repetitive dances performed in costume and associated with religious and social ceremonies were held in the kiva during winter and on the dirt plaza the remainder of the year. Before, during, and after the dances, homes were opened to members of the extended families, some of whom traveled from distant pueblos. Uninvited guests also were welcomed, including Navajos, who "sprawl into and over the houses and fairly crowd the Hopi women out of their own houses." Folded quilts of rabbit fur or sheepskins served as cushions for the guests, who were served bowls of stew and piki by their hostess.

So days were filled in the old way. Where adults went children always followed, absorbing, listening, and watching in preparation for their future responsibilities.

Questions for Discussion

1. How do your experiences of early socialization and training compare with those of Nampeyo?
2. How would you describe how children were educated in the Tewa village?
3. Describe the most important values and norms reflected in Nampeyo's culture. How do these compare with those reflected in your culture?

CHAPTER 3

Education in Colonial America

All other nations have come into being among peoples whose families had lived for time out of mind on the same land where they were born. Englishmen are English, Frenchmen are French, Chinese are Chinese. While their governments come and go; their national states can be torn apart and remade without losing their nationhood. But Americans are a nation born out of an idea; not the place, but the idea, created the United States Government.

—Theodore H. White
American Pulitzer Prize–Winning
political writer

Between 1607, when the first permanent English colony was founded in Jamestown, and 1733, when Georgia was founded by former inmates from English debtors' prisons, the British managed to establish a dozen colonies along the Atlantic seaboard. These colonies varied widely in their economies, their political traditions, and their religions. Their provisions for education reflected these differences. In the New England colonies, a tradition of government and religious involvement and support of education developed. The ethnic, language, and religious differences in the Mid-Atlantic colonies were reflected in a pattern of pluralistic, parochial schools, with no government support. Educational opportunity in the southern colonies, where the established church did not involve itself in the provision of education, was determined almost exclusively by social class. In all areas the two-track system of petty schools and Latin grammar schools dominated, and instruction was primarily religious and authoritarian. And in all areas religion played a major role in determining the selection of schoolmasters, the majority of whom received no formal training for their role.

In the later colonial period the ideology of the Enlightenment, which emphasized rationality and scientific inquiry, combined with an increasing commercialized economy to demand a more practical education than that offered by the Latin grammar school. The result was the rise of the academy, which offered an education to the sons (and later daughters) of the mercantile gentry that was, in Benjamin Franklin's terms, both "ornamental" and "useful." Similar disillusionment with the curriculum of the university also brought changes that reflected the growing secularization of society.

The education system or systems that evolved in colonial America, although grounded in the European heritage of the colonists, was no less a product of their colonial experience and developing culture. Some practices were transplanted and took root, whereas other practices (e.g., reliance on private support for the schools) failed or were discarded. In this chapter we look at the first steps in this evolving process.

Education in the New England Colonies

The English exploration of North America began with the voyages of John Cabot along the coast between Chesapeake Bay (Virginia) and Newfoundland in 1497 and 1498. However, it was not until almost a century later that the English attempted to colonize any of this territory. In 1583 Sir Humphrey Gilbert unsuccessfully attempted to establish a colony in Newfoundland. The next year his half-brother, Sir Walter Raleigh, established what became known as the Lost Colony of Roanoke (North Carolina), which was equally unsuccessful. However, in the first decade of the 17th century economic prosperity in England, the Protestant Reformation, English naval supremacy following the defeat of the Spanish Armada, and the newly achieved peace with Spain combined with a desire for the riches of the New World to create a renewed English interest in establishing a presence in North America.

In 1606 King James of England granted a charter for a settlement in the New World to a joint stock company known as the Virginia Company. The next year, 104 settlers recruited by the Virginia Company established the first permanent English settlement in the New World on the tidewater plains of Chesapeake Bay at Jamestown, Virginia. The first year saw 66 of the colonists die from disease, hunger, and Indian attack. More settlers arrived only to see a fire destroy most of the buildings in 1608, and the "starvation winter" of 1609–10 reduce their numbers from 500 to 60.

But the colony did survive, and land grants attracted more settlers. Tobacco from the West Indies was introduced in 1612. The cultivation of tobacco was responsible for not only the growth and economic prosperity of the colony, but also a demand for cheap labor. By 1619, when a Dutch ship captain sold the first Blacks as indentured servants, the colony was already experiencing a shortage of laborers for the tobacco fields. Attempts to enslave the native population proved unsuccessful and led to what seemed to be an inevitable demand for slave labor.

James I disliked what he called that "stinking smoke" and also distrusted the Virginia House of Burgesses that had been authorized by the Virginia Company. In 1624 he revoked the charter of the Virginia Company, making Virginia a royal colony under the direct control of a governor appointed by the crown. That same year, farther to the north, the Dutch established a colony, New Netherlands, at the lower end of Manhattan Island.

In 1620 another group of religious dissidents, the Pilgrims, separatist Puritans who wanted to purify and separate from the Church of England, set sail for northern Virginia but landed their ship, the Mayflower, 225 miles to the northeast at Plymouth (Massachusetts). Within 10 years the population of the Plymouth Bay Colony was estimated to be 5,700.

That same year a group of nonseparatist Puritans led by John Winthrop founded the Massachusetts Bay Colony at Boston. This colony became a focal point of migration and the base from which the other New England colonies (Rhode Island, New Haven [Connecticut], New Hampshire) developed (Cohen, 1974b). Over 20,000 settlers (mostly farmers, merchants, and artisans) came during the Great Migration from 1630 to 1642 (Milner, O'Conner, & Sandweiss, 1996). Although immigration decreased significantly after 1642, high birthrates and low infant mortality rates contributed to a rapid growth of the colony. By 1700 the descendents of these settlers constituted 40% of the colonial population of North America (Milner et al., 1996). According to Cubberley (1934), the Puritans "contributed most that was of value for our future educational development" (p. 14). Although some later historians (e.g., Cremin, 1970) would deny that Puritan education represented the foundation of our public school system, there is no denying that the New England colonists sustained a vigorous emphasis on education even within a hostile new environment.

The Puritan interest in education stemmed from both the fact that they were generally well educated themselves and therefore valued education, and the importance of education to the Puritan way of life. The Puritans shared many of the educational views of the Reformation, namely, that education was necessary for religious instruction and salvation, economic self-reliance, and the exercise of citizenship by a literate laity.

Initially the Puritans attempted to follow English practice regarding the establishment and support of schools by relying on private donations from wealthy benefactors and limiting the role of the state. However, the lack of a pool of wealthy benefactors, as well as the fears that parents were neglecting the education of their children, soon led them to consider a more direct role for the state.

Massachusetts Education Laws of 1642 and 1647

The first major indication of the role that the state would come to play in American education, indeed the first education law in the colonies, was the Massachusetts Education Law of 1642. This law was aimed at not only promoting literacy but also strengthening the social order. The law ordered the selectmen of each town to ascertain whether parents and masters of apprentices were providing for the education of their wards. The selectmen were to determine the ability of the child to "read and understand the principles of religion and the capitall lawes of this county." The parent or master of any child failing to meet this obligation could be fined and the child could be apprenticed to a new master who would be required to fulfill the law. Although the law required neither the establishment of schools nor compulsory attendance, it is significant that only 22 years after stepping ashore in the New World, the colonists were enacting legislation that did, in fact, require compulsory education.

Five years later, the colony enacted the Education Law of 1647, also called the Old Deluder Satan Law because of its first line: "It being one chief project of that old deluder, Satan, to keep men from knowledge of the Scriptures." This law actually required the establishment of schools: It ordered every township of 50 households to "appoint one within their town to teach all such children as shall resort to him to write and reade" and all town-

 For Your Reflection and Analysis

Give examples of existing education laws or policies that are directed at maintaining or strengthening the social order. How effective are they?

ships of 100 or more households to "set up a grammaer schoole, the master thereof being able to instruct youth so farr as they may be fited for the university, provided that if any towne neglect the performance hereof above one year, that every such towne shall pay £five to the next school till they shall perform this order."

In Your Reflection and Analysis

What are the pros and cons of having education be a local responsibility?

It is important to note that neither the Education Law of 1642 nor the Education Law of 1647 made any mention of the church or a minister. Rather, education was made a direct responsibility of the people and their elected officials. This initial action laid the foundation for what was to become the cornerstone of the American educational system—local responsibility. The laws also served as models for other colonies: Three years after the Massachusetts Old Deluder Satan Law, the colonists in Connecticut enacted similar legislation with a similar caution against Satan.

Elementary Schooling

The New England colonists not only shared Calvin's view of the aim of education, but they also adopted the two-track system advocated by Calvin and the other scholars of the Reformation. Town schools were established by an official act of the town, acting as a corporate body, to provide an elementary education. The town schools are often referred to as common schools because they were open to children of all social classes. Rarely, however, were they tuition-free. Parents usually paid a head tax for each child in attendance, although the township often supplemented the fees.

In some towns girls were allowed to attend the town school. However, they were generally allowed to attend only when the boys were not in attendance (before or after the regular school day) or during the summer when the older boys would be working on the farm. It was also during the summer session when women teachers were most likely to be employed to teach younger children of both sexes, as well as the older girls.

The most common provider of elementary education, especially in the early colonial days and for the youngest children, was the *dame school*. The dame school was an old English institution operated for children under 7 or 8 years of age; it was essentially a household school held in the kitchen or living room of a neighborhood woman (often a widow) with minimal education, like the "Marm" described in the Primary Source Reading for this chapter, who received a modest fee for her efforts.

Dame schools were established to educate the children of the common folk in the basics of spelling and reading. Occasionally, if the dame knew any herself, she might teach basic writing and arithmetic. Girls were often taught cooking and needlework along with their letters. In Puritan New England the view was that a little reading, spelling, and needlework was all the education that was needed or appropriate for females. Girls needed to be able to read so that they could study the Bible, but writing, arithmetic, grammar, and geography were considered unnecessary. There was no need for girls to learn to write because they had few if any acquaintances outside their own town to communicate with, and there was no need for them to learn anything but enough arithmetic to count their eggs or stitches because men conducted all business affairs (Littlefield, 1965).

Some towns designated the dame school mistress as the town teacher and thereby claimed to be in compliance with the Law of 1647. In the later colonial years

The dame school provided the only education that many colonial children received.

some towns also began paying the dame school teachers directly rather than relying on parental payments. Thus, what was a private institution came to be viewed as a public enterprise. One reason for public support of the dame school was to subsidize education for the children of the poor (as in Marblehead in 1700, Charleston in 1712, and Salem in 1729) (Perlman, Siddali, & Whitescarver, 1997). Another reason was to provide inexpensive educational services to hamlets surrounding a town as towns grew and populations dispersed. Thus,

> Farmington voted in 1713 "to settle school dames in each quarter of the town." Plymouth in 1725 supported a grammar school in the center of town and permitted the hamlets at "each end of town, which for some years past had a woman's school among them" to deduct the costs of the woman's schools from their contribution to the grammar school. Brookline in 1727 arranged to have two schoolhouses, each with a woman's school operating at the time the master was at the other's schoolhouse. Dudley in 1743 supported a school dame for three months at each end of the town and a schoolmaster for three months at the center of town. And, Westminister in 1766 allowed that "a woman's school be kept seven months in the outskirts of town." (Perlman et al., 1997, p. 127)

Also operating at the elementary level were the so-called "reading schools" and "writing schools," which were concerned with the teaching of these disciplines. These schools operated on a fee basis, although in the later colonial period some of these also received some public support. In colonial schools, reading was taught independent of, and prior to, writing. The reading school was the more elementary of the two types of schools, concentrating on the learning of the ABCs with perhaps some religious instruction (Butts & Cremin, 1953). The writing school focused on the skills that were needed in commerce—writing, arithmetic, double-entry bookkeeping—but not uncommonly gave some attention to reading. These schools were almost always taught by men because they were the ones who possessed these skills. Writing schools typically did admit girls. However, few parents were both willing and able to pay the fees for their daughters, and for most girls their education ended with the dame school.

Yet another provider of elementary education was the *charity* or *pauper school.* These schools were primarily operated by the various denominations, but sometimes by wealthy benefactors, for the children of the poor who could not afford to attend other schools. They operated mainly in the South and in the larger towns and cities. Even in the communities where they did operate, they did not serve all the needy children. The child might be needed to work, or the parents might be unwilling to go through the humiliating process of declaring themselves paupers. The pauper schools offered only a basic curriculum, "strongly laced with religious exercises and the memorization of scripture. The goal was to produce adults who would be minimally literate, who would have a chance at religious salvation, and who would act according to the morality the schools taught" (Kaestle, 1983, pp. 31–32).

An apprenticeship system whereby a child was apprenticed to a master to learn a trade was also the means by which some children were educated. The apprenticeship system stemmed from the guild system of the Middle Ages. The child could be entered into an apprenticeship voluntarily by the parent or involuntarily under certain circumstances. The laws of some colonies mandated that all children whose parents were unable to provide for them were to be placed in apprenticeships. The apprenticeship was also used as a way to provide for the very poor or orphans. Both boys and girls served as apprentices, as did some free Blacks. Female apprentices usually were given fewer educational opportunities than male apprentices and were most often apprenticed as cooks and bakers or domestic servants, or in weaving, spinning, or needlecraft. The need for skilled workers in the colonies served to strengthen the apprenticeship system and the attention given to the relationship between the master and the apprentice. For example, Benjamin Franklin's brother, to whom he had been apprenticed, beat him and as a result was jailed for a month.

The master was typically required by the terms of the indenture to ensure that the apprentice could at least minimally read and write (See the 1772 schoolmaster apprentice contract in Figure 3.1). Sometimes the master provided the instruction, but often, especially in the New England and Mid-Atlantic colonies where schools were more readily available, he paid for others to provide the instruction. The Education Laws of 1642 and 1647 strengthened the educational component of the apprenticeship system.

 For Your Reflection and Analysis

Compare the apprenticeship described in Figure 3.1 with the student teaching experience.

Registered for Mr. George Brownell Schoolmaster
ye 18th day of July 1722.

   This Indenture Wittnesseth that John Campbel Son of Robert Campbell of the City of New York with the Consent of his father and mother hath put himself and by these presents doth Voluntarily put and bind himself Apprentice to George Brownell of the Same City Schoolmaster to learn the Art Trade or Mystery and with the Said George Brownell to Serve from the twenty ninth day of May one thousand seven hundred and twenty one for and during the Term of ten years and three Months to be Compleat and Ended During all which term the said Apprentice his said Master and Mistress faithfully Shall Serve their Secrets keep and Lawfull Commands gladly everywhere obey he Shall do no damage to his said Master or Mistress nor suffer it to be done by others without Letting or Giving Notice thereof to his said Master or Mistress he shall not Waste his said Master or Mistress Goods or Lend them Unlawfully to any he shall not Committ fornication nor Contract Matrimony within the Said Term at Cards Dice or any other unlawfull Game he shall not Play: he Shall not absent himself by Day or by Night from his Said Master or Mistress Service without their Leave; nor haunt Alehouses Taverns or Playhouses but in all things behave himself as a faithfull Apprentice ought to Do towards his said Master or Mistress during the Said Term. And the said George Brownell Doth hereby Covenant and Promise to teach and Instruct or Cause the said Apprentice to be taught and Instructed in the Art Trade or Calling of a Schoolmaster by the best way or means he or his wife may or can if the Said Apprentice be Capable to Learn and to find and Provide unto the Said Apprentice sufficient meat Drink Apparel Lodging and washing fitting for an Apprentice during the Said Term: and at the Expiration thereof to give unto the Said Apprentice one Suit of Cloth new Consisting of a coatvest coat and Breeches also one New hatt Six New Shirts Three pair of Stockings one pair of New Shoes Suitable for his said Apprentice. In Testimony Whereof the Parties to these Presents have hereunto Interchangeably Sett their hands and Seals the third day of August in the Eighth year of the Reign of our Sovereign Lord George King of Great Brittain &c. Anno Domini One thousand seven hundred and Twenty-One. John Campbel. Signed Sealed and Delivered in the presence of Mary Smith Cornelius Kiersted Memorandum Appeared before me John Cruger Esq. Alderman and One of his Majesties Justices of the Peace for this City and County. John Campbell and Acknowledged the within Indenture to be his Voluntary Act and Deed New York the 9th Aprill 1722.

John Cruger.

FIGURE 3.1 Apprentice Contract for a Schoolmaster, 1722

Source: Citty of N. Yorke indenture, 1694-1727, translated by Saybolt, cited by Cubberley, E. P. (1934).
Readings in public education in the United States. New York: Houghton Mifflin, pp. 71–72.

Instruction and Instructional Materials

Instruction in colonial schools was primarily religious and authoritarian. Its goal was preparation for eternity. The curriculum stressed the four *R*s: readin', 'ritin', 'rithmetic, and religion. Memorization and recitation were the dominant instructional processes. The schoolmaster relied on fear to motivate children and to keep them in order. It was not uncommon for a gag to be put in the mouth of a child who talked too much or for a child who did not perform well to be made to stand in the corner, sometimes on a stool, wearing a dunce cap.

Classes often lasted from about 7 a.m. to 5 p.m., with a 2-hour break for lunch, for 8 months (March to October) and 8 a.m. to 4 p.m. for 4 months (November to February). In the early colonial period classes were held in the house of the schoolmaster or the town meeting house. Later, when schoolhouses were built, they were scarcely more than a narrow log box with a master's desk and crude wooden student benches. "Many schoolhouses did not have glass set in the small windows but newspaper or white paper greased with lard were fastened in the rude sashes, or in holes cut in the wall, and let in a little light" (Glubok, 1969, p. 120).

Paper was expensive and was rarely used for practice in the schools. Rather, the white bark from birch trees was often used instead of paper, and narrow pieces of actual lead (not lead pencils) or quill pens made from goose feathers were used for writing. Books were rare and expensive. Most primary students learned their basic lessons from the *hornbook*, so called because the material was written on a sheet of parchment, placed on a wooden board shaped like a paddle, and covered with a thin sheath of cow's horn for protection (see Figure 3.2). The board had a handle with a hole in it so it could be strung around the child's neck. The typical lessons on the hornbook were the ABCs, the Lord's Prayer, verses with either a scriptural or moral theme, and some stanzas of poetry for memorizing. At the top on the side of some hornbooks was the biblical emblem of the cross, which was soon referred to as Crisscross—Christ's Cross. Others had little pictures around the four edges to aid in memorization (e.g., B-Bear; H-Horse; O-Owl; etc.). A further aid to memory was a row of nonsense jingles such as the following:

> Art we add
> Ben is bad
> Cat she can
> Dad or dan
> Ear and eye
> . . .
> (Meriwether, 1978, pp. 29–30)

The *New England Primer* was used with slightly older children. It was basically an enlargement of the hornbook, constructed along the same religious lines, and has been referred to as "the little Bible of New England" (Meriwether, 1978, p. 19). Although different editions of the primer varied somewhat in the 200 years of its publication (1690–1886), it usually began with an alphabet and spelling guide, followed by

FIGURE 3.2   A hornbook

one of the things that made the primer famous—24 little pictures, mostly biblical incidents, with alphabetical rhymes as illustrated in Figure 3.3.

After the alphabetic rhymes came "The Dutiful Child's Promise," which required the child to promise as follows:

> I will fear GOD, and honor the KING.
> I will honor my Father and Mother.
> I will Obey my Superiors.
> I will Submit to my Elders.

The primer also included the Lord's Prayer, the Apostle's Creed, the Ten Commandments, a listing of the books of the Bible, and a list of numbers from 1 to 100, using both Arabic and Roman numerals. Another prominent feature of the primer was a poem, the exhortation of John Rogers to his children, from John Foxe's *Book of Martyrs*, with a picture of the martyr burning at the stake as his wife and children look on. The primer ended with a shortened version of the Puritan catechism (Ford, 1962).

After the primer the child was ready for the study of grammar—not English grammar, but Latin grammar. This instruction was provided by private tutors, or most often, at the Latin grammar school.

FIGURE 3.3   *A New England Primer*

Secondary Education: Latin Grammar Schools

The Latin grammar school was the primary secondary school during the early colonial period. Public and private Latin grammar schools existed for the further education of the male children of the well-to-do. Latin grammar schools were intended to serve as preparatory schools for the university, where proficiency in Latin was required for admission. The school day was typically 8 hours long and was held 6 days a week.

 For Your Reflection and Analysis

Why was proficiency in Latin so central to secondary and higher education in colonial America? How valid are these reasons today?

Education at the grammar school was quite different from that of the dame or town school. The emphasis was on Latin, with some Greek and occasionally Hebrew. Other disciplines included those necessary for the classical education of the Renaissance concept of the educated man. The course of study in the grammar school lasted fairly intensively for 6 to 7 years. Students tended to withdraw and return depending on family circumstances, but because school was conducted on a year-round basis and instruction was organized around particular texts, it was not difficult for a student to resume study after an absence (Cremin, 1970).

The first Latin grammar school was established in Boston in 1635. The Boston Latin Grammar School became the model for similar schools throughout New England. Within a decade of the founding of the Boston Latin Grammar School, and before the Law of 1647 required them to do so, 7 of the 22 towns in the Bay Colony had voluntarily established grammar schools (Kraushaar, 1976). However, the public Latin grammar schools did not necessarily restrict themselves to the classical curriculum. In towns with only one or two Latin pupils, the schoolmaster spent most of his time teaching reading, writing, and spelling to both older and younger students (Herbst, 1996). Only in larger cities, with several Latin schools, could the master devote himself to teaching the classical languages and leave the task of teaching in the lower grades to his assistant, the usher (Herbst, 1996).

For Your Reflection and Analysis

Speculate on the reasons the private girls schools did not seriously consider the academic training of females until the second half of the 18th century.

Girls did not attend Latin grammar schools. The only girls who received a secondary education were those from the more affluent families that could afford to hire a private tutor or to send them to one of the private schools or female seminaries that began to emerge in the second half of the 18th century. Most of these were boarding schools of the finishing school type. Initially these institutions were concerned with preparing girls for marriage and motherhood. Their training focused on the development of social and domestic skills. It was not until the second half of the 18th century that they began to seriously concern themselves with academic training.

Supervision and Support of the Schools

Schools in colonial America were supported by various means, including tuition, selected taxes and fees (e.g., marriage and liquor licenses), and endowments. Dorchester (Massachusetts) is credited with having made the first public provision for a school by direct taxation of its inhabitants. The Dorchester Town Records of May 20, 1639 read as follows:

> there shall be a rent of £20 a year forever imposed upon Thompson's Island to be paid by every person that hath propriety in the said Island according to the proportion that any such person shall from time to time enjoy and possess there and this towards the maintenance of a school in Dorchester. This rent of £20 yearly to be paid to such a schoolmaster as shall undertake to teach English, Latin, and other tongues, and also writing. The said schoolmaster to be chosen from time to time by the freemen, and it is left to the discretion whether maids shall be taught with the boys or not. (Littlefield, 1965, p. 70)

As the town of Dorchester did in regard to Thompson's Island, it was common practice for a town to set aside a parcel of land—often referred to as "school fields" or "school meadows"—and use the rental income from the land for the support of the town school. However, this money was generally not enough and was supplemented by taxation or tuition.

Public funding led to public administration. Dorchester is also said to have been the first town to appoint a special school committee to oversee the school (Littlefield, 1965). Initially the schools in each town were managed directly by the general public at the town meeting. As the towns grew in size, they began to authorize the selectmen, or councilmen, to manage the schools. In time the selectmen formed special school committees to help with the management of the schools, or, as in Dorchester beginning in 1645, they were elected by the town as a whole. According to the Dorchester Town Records, three "able and efficient" men were to be chosen wardens or overseers of the grammar school and were given the following responsibilities: (1) to ensure that the school is "supplied with an able and sufficient schoolmaster," (2) to ensure that the school is kept in good repair (the selectmen were given the power to "tax the town with such sums as shall be requested for the repairing of the school-house"), (3) to ensure that before the end of September "there be brought to the school-house twelve sufficient cart loads of wood for fuel" (the wardens were given the authority to tax the students for the cost of the wood), and (4) to ensure that the schoolmaster faithfully performs his duties (Littlefield, 1965).

Higher Education in Early New England

The major function of the Latin grammar school was to prepare young men for college. As previously noted, despite their location and circumstances, the colonists had a great interest in higher education. This might be because, by some accounts, one out of every 30 of the first settlers of Massachusetts was a graduate of Cambridge University in England (Meriwether, 1978). Still others had graduated from Oxford or other English universities.

The first college in the American colonies, Harvard College, was established in 1636 when the General Court of Massachusetts supplemented the bequest of the Reverend John Harvard of his library and half his estate with an appropriation of £ 400 for a "schoale or college." Harvard also received twelve pence a year and a peck of corn from every family in the colony, as well as the revenue from the ferry between Newtown (Charlestown) and Boston (Tunis, 1957).

 For Your Reflection and Analysis

What might account for the fact that the average English colonist had far more education than Englishmen of the day?

The primary motivation for the founding of Harvard College was religious—to ensure that there would be an educated ministry for the colony. Fearful that there would be no replacements for the ministers who first came with them, the colonists dreaded "to leave an illiterate Ministry to the churches, when our present Ministers should lie in the Dust." However, despite their concern for the training of ministers, neither Harvard nor the other colonial colleges were intended to be seminaries. According to its charter of 1650, Harvard was established for "The advancement and education of youth in all manner of good literature, Artes and Sciences." The 1701 charter of Yale College (originally the Collegiate School) stated its purpose to be to prepare youth to be "fitted for Publick employment both in Church and Civil State."

Attendance at Harvard and the other colonial colleges was limited almost exclusively to the children of the well-to-do. Even within this group a well-defined class system operated. As late as 1769 the roster of students at Harvard was not listed alphabetically, but according to social status (Hakim, 1999b). Because of the size of the eligible population, as well as their tuition and exclusivity, the enrollment at the colonial colleges was small. Beginning with its first graduating class of 9 in 1642, for the next 50 years Harvard graduated fewer than 10 students per year.

Until near the end of the 18th century the faculty of the typical colonial college consisted of a president (usually a minister) and a few tutors (seldom more than three) who were themselves often young men studying for the ministry. Few instructors could be considered "professors"—mature men with command of their subject matter (Boorstin, 1958).

Under these circumstances it is not surprising that the curriculum of the university in the early colonial period was based on the classically oriented pattern of the

English university from which the ministers and tutors, as well as the Puritan leaders, had matriculated. As Cohen (1974b) described it:

> The undergraduate courses revolved around the traditional Trivium and Quadrivium but without musical studies, the Three Philosophies (Metaphysics, Ethics, Natural Science), and Greek, Hebrew, and a chronological study of ancient history. As in English universities logic and rhetoric were the basic subjects in the curriculum. . . . Compositions, orations, and disputations were given the same careful scrutiny as at English universities. (p. 66)

Latin dominated the curriculum. Most of the textbooks were in Latin, and the president gave his lectures in Latin. Logic and rhetoric required that the student use the Latin language correctly and effectively (Herbst, 1996). The epitome of efforts to apply the language were the recitations, declamations, and deputations (debates):

> Students recited and declaimed to break the monotony of listening to lectures and of outlining systems. These oral exercises also served as examinations and as demonstrations of the students' acquired verbal skills . . . [this training] increased the students' nimbleness of mind and taught them to think quickly on their feet, to express themselves accurately and with precision, and to speak effectively, compellingly, and elegantly—all skills of inestimable value to a future lawyer, minister, physician, statesman, or politician." (Herbst, 1996, p. 16)

Although their curriculum resembled that of the English universities, colonial colleges differed in one very important respect from their English ancestors. English universities operated under a form of academic self-government that reflected their origins as medieval guilds of learned men. Because no such guilds existed in the colonies, for the simple reason that there was no sizable body of learned men, control of the colonial colleges fell to representatives of the community (Boorstin, 1958). Another important way colonial colleges differed from English colleges was that, unlike Oxford and Cambridge, which were removed from major commercial and political centers, the early colonial colleges tended to be located at the center of each colony's affairs, thereby symbolically connecting learning and public life (Boorstin, 1958).

 For Your Reflection and Analysis

What effect might the location of the colonial colleges have had on their role and function in colonial social and public life?

Education in the Mid-Atlantic Colonies

Influence of Denominational Variations

Whereas the New England colonies had been settled primarily by English colonists who shared the same language, traditions, and religion, the settlers of the Mid-Atlantic colonies (New York, New Jersey, Pennsylvania, and Delaware) came from a variety of national and religious backgrounds. Many had fled Europe because of religious persecution and were generally more distrusting of secular authority than were the New England colonists. Thus, although the schools in the Mid-Atlantic colonies were as religious in character as those in New England, because of the diverse religious backgrounds of the settlers, it was not possible for the government in any colony to agree on the establishment of any one system of state-supported schools. It fell to each denomination to establish its own schools. The consequence of this pattern of pluralistic, parochial schooling was the absence of any basis for the establishment of a system of public schools or for state support or regulation of the schools. As a result, many young people, especially those in rural areas, had no access to education beyond what might be provided in the home.

New York

The colony of New Netherlands was established in 1621 by the Dutch. Earlier exploration of the region had been undertaken by Henry Hudson, an Englishman in the employ of the Dutch East India Company. Although the early immigrants to New Netherlands were motivated more by the prospect of profits from the fur trade than a quest for religious freedom, the relationship between church and state that characterized the New England colonies was also found in New Netherlands. That is, the close ties between learning and the established faith that existed in Holland were recreated in New Netherlands, and the state was expected to promote the official church (Cohen, 1974b). Company records indicate that the schools in 11 communities were established by the Dutch West India Company, some at the insistence of the Dutch settlers who, like those in New England, were concerned lest their children grow up without the education necessary for the practice of their religion. And, those who were organizing new settlements were instructed to include both a minister and a schoolmaster in their plans (Kraushaar, 1976). Although the Dutch West India Company paid the schoolmasters, the schools were operated by the Dutch Calvinist Church, which also saw to the licensing and supervision of the masters. Two years before the Boston Latin School was founded, Master Adam Roelansten was employed by the Dutch West India Company to direct a school at New Amsterdam (Kraushaar, 1976).

After New Netherlands was seized by the British and became the royal colony of New York in 1674, state responsibility and support of schooling was withdrawn. Except for a few town schools and a limited number of charity schools, formal schooling became a private concern. Education at the elementary level was provided by private tutors for the upper class, private venture schools for the middle class, and denominational schools such as those operated by the Anglican Missionary Society for the Propagation of the Gospel in Foreign Parts (SPG) for the lower class. Dame schools were rarely in operation in New York, but the apprenticeship system was very strong and provided the means by which some children gained a basic education. Overall, however, because only a few towns established schools, and because the provision of education was principally left to the will or ability of parents to send their children to private or denominational schools, the illiteracy rate in New York was high (Cohen, 1974b).

Education at the secondary level was even more exclusively private or parochial. Most schools had a religious or ethnic affiliation. By 1762 New Amsterdam (New York City) could boast that it had 10 English, 2 Dutch, 1 French, and 1 Hebrew tuition schools (Kraushaar, 1976).

Higher education was unavailable for any but the few who could afford to leave the colony. Not until 1754 did the first institution of higher education, Kings College, now Columbia University, open in the colony. In its initial advertisements Kings College said that it would offer a practical curriculum, but once it began operation, its curriculum differed little from the classical curriculum of the other colonial colleges (Butts & Cremin, 1953). Kings College was the first of the colonial American universities to open a law school, in 1755.

New Jersey

New Jersey was originally part of New Netherlands. Once taken over by the English, it became first a proprietorship and then a royal colony. As in New York, education in New Jersey was primarily private and denominational. Religious diversification was extensive, and each of the sects—Dutch Reformed, Puritan, Quaker, German Lutheran, Baptist, and Scotch-Irish Presbyterian—established its own schools. The SPG also operated schools for the poor. A few towns, mainly those in the eastern region settled by the Puritans, established town schools. Secondary education was limited. Because of the primarily rural, agrarian economy, the private venture secondary schools found in other Mid-Atlantic colonies were absent. However, proximity to New York and Philadelphia did provide access to their secondary institutions for those who could afford them (Cohen, 1974b).

The colony of New Jersey most distinguished itself in the realm of higher education. Prior to the Revolutionary War it had founded more colleges than any other colony: the College of New Jersey, now Princeton University, in 1746, and Queens College, now Rutgers University, in 1766.

Pennsylvania

The Pennsylvania colony was founded in 1681 by a Quaker, William Penn, as an asylum for his fellow believers. The Quakers, or Society of Friends, were very tolerant of other religions; consequently, a number of different religious groups or sects, including the Dunkards, Lutherans, Moravians, Mennonites, and Scotch-Irish Presbyterians, settled in Pennsylvania. Each of these groups tended to segregate itself and operate its own schools. Although William Penn advocated free public education "so that youth may be trained up in virtue and useful knowledge and arts," and despite the fact that the Pennsylvania Assembly enacted a law in 1683 providing that all children be instructed in reading and writing and be taught "some useful trade or skill," largely as a result of the great diversity among the settlers, Pennsylvania did not develop a system of free public education. The apprenticeship system did operate in Pennsylvania, and the Pennsylvania apprenticeship law, like the Massachusetts law, placed obligations on the master to ensure that the apprentice could read and write. A few community-supported schools were established, but as in the other Mid-Atlantic colonies, formal education was primarily a private or denominational affair.

The major difference between Pennsylvania and the other Mid-Atlantic colonies was that the various denominations did, in fact, establish a fairly widespread system of schools in Pennsylvania. Of the various denominational groups active in Pennsylvania, the Quakers were the most significant in terms of educational endeavors. More than any other, the Quakers were responsible for the spread of a liberal philosophy of schooling that envisioned schools that were both public and private, had English and classical curricula, were cultural and practical in orientation, and were open to girls as well as boys (Kraushaar, 1976). The Quaker belief that all were created equal under God led not only to the education of both sexes and to the free admission of the poor, but also to the education of Blacks and Native Americans. A school for Black children was established in Philadelphia by the Quaker schoolmaster, Anthony Benezet, as early as 1770. Benezet, who had earlier (1754) opened a school for girls, operated the school until his death in 1784 and then endowed it with all his possessions.

Because Quakers do not have ministers, they were not as interested in the establishment of secondary schools leading to that vocation. In their secondary schools they emphasized practical knowledge rather than the classical curriculum studied at most secondary schools at that time.

 For Your Reflection and Analysis

With what social movements in U.S. history have the Quakers been prominently associated?

Other denominations were also working in Pennsylvania to both provide education and advance their religious doctrines. The SPG founded a number of charity schools, including a school for Black children in Philadelphia in 1758. The Moravians also established a number of elementary schools, including the first nursery school in the colonies. They were also active in efforts to Christianize and educate the Native Americans. They devised a written script for several Native American languages and translated the Bible and other religious materials into these languages. In 1746 the Moravians established a boarding school for girls at Bethlehem, one of the first in the colonies. In their pedagogical practices they were influenced by the educational philosophy of the Moravian bishop Jan Amos Comenius, which stressed sensory experiences as the basis for learning, respect for the individual, freedom, creative activity, instruction in the vernacular, and universal education.

The various denominations also operated schools at the secondary level. In addition, a number of private secondary schools were opened in Pennsylvania during the later colonial period, many offering such practical subjects as navigation, gauging, accounting, geometry, trigonometry, surveying, French, and Spanish. *Practical* did not mean that the arts were neglected. Notwithstanding the rumblings of the more stern Quakers, private schools offering drawing, painting, music, and dance for both sexes prospered (Kraushaar, 1976). Among the private secondary schools operating in Philadelphia was Benjamin Franklin's Philadelphia Academy, opened in 1751.

Franklin was also instrumental in the founding of the College of Philadelphia, now the University of Pennsylvania, in 1753. Unlike its sister institutions, the College of Philadelphia was nonsectarian in origin (although it later came under

Anglican control). The curriculum of the college was perhaps more progressive than that of other institutions. Students were allowed a voice in the election of courses, and the curriculum emphasized not only the classics but also mathematics, philosophy, and the natural and social sciences. A medical school was established in connection with the college, the first such college in the colonies.

Delaware

Delaware, founded in 1638 as a Swedish colony, New Sweden, fell under Dutch control in 1655, then under the rule of the English with their conquest of New Netherlands in 1664. It was later incorporated into the province of Pennsylvania, but in 1703 organized its own separate government. Education in Delaware was greatly influenced by Pennsylvania, and Pennsylvania's general abandonment of the responsibility for the provision of education to private or denominational groups after 1683 was followed in Delaware. Although a number of elementary schools were established in the colony, the level of literacy remained low. During the colonial period formal secondary education was available on a very limited basis, and no institution of higher education was established in the colony (Cohen, 1974b).

Education in the Southern Colonies

Influence of Social and Economic Systems

The Southern colonies (Maryland, Virginia, the Carolinas, and Georgia) differed in significant ways from the New England and mid-Atlantic colonies. The southern colonies were royal colonies administered by governors responsible directly to the king. Unlike the New England Puritans, who sought to reform the Church of England, the colonist in the southern colonies accepted the Church of England as the established state church. (The exception was Maryland, which was founded by Lord Baltimore as a refuge for English Catholics.) And, the Church of England asserted that parents were responsible for educating their children, not the government or the church. In fact, Sir William Berkeley, governor of Virginia in the 17th century and a Royalist (a supporter of the English king), thanked God that there were no free schools or printing presses in Virginia: "for learning has brought disobedience and heresy and sects into the world; and printing has divulged them and libels against the government." As a result of such sentiments, no legislation was enacted requiring local governments to support schools.

Another factor influencing the educational development of the southern colonies was the economic system operating there. Compared to the New England economy, which was based on small farms and commerce, the economy of the southern colonies was based on large plantations where tobacco, rice, indigo, and later cotton were cultivated by slaves. Many of the original

 For Your Reflection and Analysis

Why was the Church of England less interested in ensuring the education of the young than the Puritans were?

settlers in the southern colonies had been granted large tracts of land known as "hundreds." As tobacco and cotton became profitable crops, they expanded their holdings into even larger tracts, which became plantations. As a result of the plantation system, the relatively small population of the southern colonies was widely dispersed. This factor mitigated against the development of towns or the concentration of populations necessary to support public schools.

Elementary and Secondary Education

As a result of the social and economic structure of the southern colonies, educational opportunities were determined largely by social class. Although class distinctions existed in all the colonies (see Figure 3.4), they were most pronounced in the South. The South had an aristocratic upper class made up of the plantation owners, a small middle class, and a large lower class of slaves.

The children of the plantation owners and the wealthy commercial classes in the Tidewater cities received their education from private tutors or at private Latin grammar schools before being sent to universities. Sometimes one wealthy plantation owner would hire a tutor who would teach not only his children but those of relatives or neighbors at what was, in effect, a plantation boarding school. The tutors typically taught both the sons and the daughters of the planters. However, these females were the exception. In fact, the majority of females in the southern colonies were totally uneducated and illiterate (Spruell, cited in Szasz, 1988).

In the early colonial period the plantation aristocracy often sent their male children to New England or, more commonly, to Britain to receive their secondary or, more often, their university education; to the Scottish universities for medicine; to the Inns of Court in London for law; or to Oxford or Cambridge for mathematics, rhetoric, or philosophy (Bobrick, 1997). In fact, schoolmasters in England looked for clients in the colonies, and some kept advertisements in newspapers in the colonies (Meriwether, 1978). One such advertisement, which appeared in 1769 in the *Virginia* (Williamsburg) *Gazette*, reads as follows:

> At the Academy in Leeds, which is pleasantly situated in the county of York in England, Young Gentlemen are genteely boarded, and diligently instructed in English, the Classicks, Modern Languages, Penmanship, Arithmetick, Merchants Accounts, Mathematicks, Modern Geography, Experimental Philosophy, and Astronomy, for twenty guineas per annum, if under twelve years of age, by Mr. Aaron Grimshaw, and able masters. Drawing, Musick, and Dancing, are extra charges. Due regard is paid to the young Gentlemens health, morals and behavior. (Cohen, 1974a, p. 473)

By the later colonial period, as the number of colonial colleges grew in number and stature, the practice of going abroad to receive a university education was on the decline.

With the exception of the children of the plantation aristocracy or the wealthy Tidewater merchants, most other free children in the southern colonies received at best only an elementary education. This education was provided informally through

Upper Classes of Free Men

In Towns	*In Rural Regions*
Merchants	
Magistrates and officials	Landed gentry
	Magistrates
Established clergy	Established clergy

In Rural Regions — Landed gentry:
planters
country gentlemen
patroons

Middle Classes of Free Men

In Towns	*In Rural Regions*
Substantial shopkeepers	Substantial farmers
Master craftsmen	Dissenting clergy
Lawyers and college teachers	

Lower Classes of Free Men

In Towns	*In Rural Regions*
Mechanics, artisans	Small freehold farmers
Clerks in business	Renters and tenants
Fishermen and sailors	
Teachers	

Servile Classes of Unfree Men

In Towns	*In Rural Regions*
Indentured white servants	Indentured white servants and workers
Negro servants	Negro slaves

FIGURE 3.4 Class System in Colonial America

Source: From *A history of education in American culture (p. 32).* by Butts. © 1953. Reprinted with permission of Wadsworth, a division of Thomson Learning: www.thomsonrights.com. Fax 800-730-2215.

the apprenticeship system or formally at endowed free schools, denominational schools, "old field schools," or private venture schools. Virginia was the most active of the southern colonies in attempting to ensure the education of apprenticed children, especially orphaned children.

The endowed free schools were few in number and never educated more than a small number of poor children. The charity schools were operated by the various denominations: The Catholics operated schools in Maryland; the Presbyterians and Moravians opened schools for their followers in Virginia, the Carolinas, and Georgia; and the Anglican SPG was active in all the colonies. The SPG helped supply teachers, books, and financial support to operate schools for the most disadvantaged and provided the closest thing to a public school system found in the South before the Revolutionary War (Cohen, 1974b). The SPG was also almost the only group attempting to provide education to the slaves.

In some rural areas where other schooling was not available, several small planters or farmers used old tobacco sheds or built rough schoolhouses on abandoned tobacco fields. These "old field schools" generally charged a fee and offered only the most basic education. Often the teacher was a local clergyman supplementing his salary. According to one historian, the majority of children who received an education in 17th-century Virginia received their schooling at old field schools (Bracey, cited in Szasz, 1988). In fact, George Washington received a significant portion of his education at an old field school.

Private venture elementary schools were found in many of the larger cities of the South. Private venture schools also operated at the secondary level, as did public grammar schools, in the larger towns or cities. However, because there were so few towns of any size, the private venture schools were the primary providers of education at the secondary level in the southern colonies. Even these were few. As a result of the public neglect of education, overall the educational level of the southern colonies was below that of most of the other colonies, especially those in New England.

Higher Education: The College of William and Mary

The only institution of higher education established in the South prior to the Revolutionary War was the College of William and Mary, established in Virginia in 1693 under a charter from King William III and Queen Mary II of England. An earlier attempt by the Church of England to establish a college for Native Americans at Henrico, Virginia, had been unsuccessful. The charter of William and Mary charged it with training ministers and bringing Christianity to the Indians.

Like Harvard, its sister institution in New England and the only older institution of higher education in the colonies, William and Mary also originally offered the traditional curriculum. However, by the second quarter of the 18th century, it began to broaden its curriculum. It was the first college to offer an elective system in which students chose their own course of study. And, perhaps foreshadowing Virginian supremacy in the public affairs of the country, William and Mary emphasized law and politics earlier than any other college in the country, and encouraged the study of history, mathematics, and modern languages (Meriwether, 1978). In fact, one educational historian stated that by 1779 its curriculum was probably the most advanced in the United States (Cohen, 1974b).

Figure 3.5 presents on overview of education in Colonial America.

 For Your Reflection and Analysis

In what way might the history, geographic, or cultural location of William and Mary have contributed to its broader and less rigid curriculum?

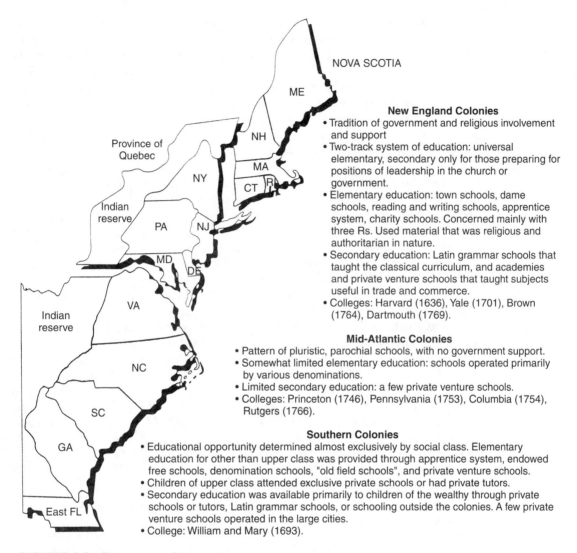

New England Colonies
- Tradition of government and religious involvement and support
- Two-track system of education: universal elementary, secondary only for those preparing for positions of leadership in the church or government.
- Elementary education: town schools, dame schools, reading and writing schools, apprentice system, charity schools. Concerned mainly with three Rs. Used material that was religious and authoritarian in nature.
- Secondary education: Latin grammar schools that taught the classical curriculum, and academies and private venture schools that taught subjects useful in trade and commerce.
- Colleges: Harvard (1636), Yale (1701), Brown (1764), Dartmouth (1769).

Mid-Atlantic Colonies
- Pattern of pluristic, parochial schools, with no government support.
- Somewhat limited elementary education: schools operated primarily by various denominations.
- Limited secondary education: a few private venture schools.
- Colleges: Princeton (1746), Pennsylvania (1753), Columbia (1754), Rutgers (1766).

Southern Colonies
- Educational opportunity determined almost exclusively by social class. Elementary education for other than upper class was provided through apprentice system, endowed free schools, denomination schools, "old field schools", and private venture schools.
- Children of upper class attended exclusive private schools or had private tutors.
- Secondary education was available primarily to children of the wealthy through private schools or tutors, Latin grammar schools, or schooling outside the colonies. A few private venture schools operated in the large cities.
- College: William and Mary (1693).

FIGURE 3.5   Education in Colonial America.
Source: Webb, L. D., Metha, A., & Jordan, K. F. (2003). *Foundations of American Education,* (4th ed., p. 99). Upper Saddle River, NJ: Merrill/Prentice Hall.

Education During the Later Colonial Period

Impact of the Enlightenment

The Age of the Enlightenment, or the Age of Reason, that swept the Western world in the 17th century had found its way to the shores of the American colonies by the 18th century. As in Europe, it brought greater concern for independent rationality, an examination of all beliefs, repudiation of supernatural explanations of phenomena, and a greater questioning of traditional religious dogma. Philosophers, scientists, and scholars of the period believed that observation and scientific inquiry were the avenues to the discovery of the "natural laws" that dictated the orderly operation of the universe. The Enlightenment was a period of rapid expansion of the knowledge base in the natural and physical sciences, mathematics, and engineering: Newton proposed his theory of gravity, Leeuwenhoek identified bacteria, the first inoculation against smallpox was given, and the first suspension and iron bridges were built. It also spawned the invention of the first steam engine, water turbine, power loom, cotton gin, and many other machines and processes that made the Industrial Revolution possible.

Enlightenment philosophers argued that the natural laws that governed nature also imbued man with certain rights that existed in nature before men entered civil society. Their rational examination of all beliefs led them to reject the authority of the church and the absolute rights of monarch. They believed not only in the right of the people to govern themselves but also in their ability to do so. They considered education an instrument of social reform and improvement—a belief shared by not only the Founding Fathers, but all generations of Americans since.

One of the important philosophers of the Enlightenment was the English philosopher John Locke. Locke is best known for his political theories, which served as the basis for the American and French constitutions. However, he also had a profound influence on education. As discussed in chapter 1, Locke is associated with the school of thought called sense realism and favored the inductive and scientific method, which proposes that man learns best through sensory experiences. In *Some Thoughts Concerning Education*, Locke recommended a curriculum that included, beyond the three *R*s, history, geography, ethics, philosophy, science, and conversational foreign languages, especially French. Mathematics was also emphasized, not to make the scholar a mathematician, but to make him a reasonable man. The curriculum Locke recommended anticipated that of the academy described in the next section. As evidenced in the writings of the Founding Fathers on which he had such an influence, Locke believed the goal of education was to create the moral, practical individual who could participate effectively in the governing process.

Locke's political philosophy, in keeping with his respect for the lessons of science, proposed that there were inherent laws of nature and that associated with these natural laws man had certain natural rights. These natural rights came from God or nature, not from rulers or governments. Among these rights, according to Locke, were those espoused in the Declaration of Independence—life, liberty, and the pursuit of happiness.

A century later, another philosopher who is best remembered for his political theories, but who also had a profound effect on educational theory, Jean-Jacques Rousseau, continued to advance the natural law argument. Rousseau is associated with an educational movement called naturalism. Its emphasis on freedom and the individual has had a significant influence on educational theory and practice. His book *Social Contract* had a major influence on the thinking of those involved in both the French and American revolutions.

Impact of Social and Economic Changes on Education

At the same time that the philosophy of the Enlightenment was sweeping the colonies, the population of the colonies was increasing rapidly and its economy outgrowing its localized base of farming and fishing. Transportation and communication improved, trade and commerce increased, and cities and towns flourished. The application of the concept of natural laws to economics and capitalism (e.g., the ownership of property and the profit motive) was associated with the emergence of a new mercantile gentry and a growing middle class.

The growth in trade and commerce placed new demands on education. For example, the ship owners of New England needed navigators to chart courses for their ships, surveyors were needed to lay out the lands of the expanding frontier, and bookkeepers and scribes were needed to keep the accounts and records of ever larger businesses and agricultural enterprises. At the same time, the budding city life supported by increased affluence and leisure time created demands for the "arts of polite society" (Cohen, 1974a, p. xvii).

The classical curriculum of the Latin grammar school was not prepared to meet these needs. As a result, during the first half of the 18th century numerous private venture schools, the so-called "English schools," sprang up in the larger towns, teaching subjects useful in trade and commerce (as well as the classical languages for those who wanted them). The newspapers of the time were filled with advertisements for these schools. One such advertisement, appearing in 1723, read as follows:

> There is a school in New York, in the Broad Street, near the Exchange, where Mr. John Walton, late of Yale College, Teacheth Reading, Writing, Arethmatick, whole Numbers and Fractions, Vulgar and Decimal, The Mariners Art, Plain and Mercators Way; Also Geometry, Surveying, the Latin Tongue, the Greek and Hebrew Grammers, Ethicks, Rhetorick, Logick, Natural Philosophy and Metaphysicks, all or any of them for a Reasonable Price. The School from the first of October till the first of March will be tended in the Evening. If any Gentlemen in the Country are disposed to send their Sons to the said School, if they apply themselves to the Master he will immediately procure suitable Entertainment for them, very Cheap. Also if any Young Gentlemen of the City will please to come in the Evening and make some Tryal of the Liberal Arts, they may have the opportunity of Learning the same things which are commonly Taught in Colledges. (*American Weekly Mercury*, cited in Cubberly, 1934, p. 83)

The private venture schools were operated by ministers, teachers, enterprising tradesmen or craftsmen, or dames who set up their own shops and charged what the traffic would bear to whomever could afford to pay for it (Kraushaar, 1976). Day schools, evening schools, early morning schools, even correspondence schools offered group or tutorial instruction (Cohen, 1974a). Girls were allowed to attend the English schools but often had to attend in separate classes. The private venture or English schools served an important role in the transfer of vocational education from the family and apprenticeships to the school (Cohen, 1974a).

Rise of the Academy

Although the private venture or English schools played an important role as providers of education in colonial America, their role was not permanent. Rather, they served as a transition between the grammar school and the academy. Academies as educational institutions in the colonies began to emerge in the mid-18th century. One of the earliest and strongest supporters of the academy was Benjamin Franklin. Franklin believed that "the rigid classical curriculum had degenerated into a shibboleth of the learned class and that the grammar school, whose chief beneficiaries were the ministry, the scholar, and the gentleman, was an anachronism" (Kraushaar, 1976, p. 19).

Franklin was strongly influenced by the philosophy of the Enlightenment, particularly that of John Locke, and was a proponent of a practical education to prepare the skilled craftsmen, businessmen, and farmers needed in the colonies. In his 1747 *Proposals Relating to the Education of Youth in Pennsylvania*, Franklin laid out the plan for an academy in which English rather than Latin was to be the medium of instruction. This break with tradition was important because it proposed, in effect, that vernacular English could be the language of the educated person. Also breaking with tradition, Franklin made no provision for religious instruction other than for a course in the history of religion. He proposed that students be taught "those Things that are likely to be most useful and most ornamental. Regard being had to the several Professions which they are intended."

From this statement of principle Franklin went on to detail what should be the specific subject matter of the academy:

> All should be taught "to write a fair hand" and "something of drawing"; arithmetic, accounts, geometry, and astronomy; English grammar out of Tillotson, Addison, Pope, Sidney, Trenchard, and Gordon; the writing of essays and letters; rhetoric, history, geography, and ethics; natural history and gardening; and the history of commerce and principles of mechanics. Instruction should include visits to neighboring farms, opportunities for natural observations, experiments with scientific apparatus, and physical exercise. And the whole should be suffused with a quest for benignity of mind, which Franklin saw as the foundation of good breeding and a spirit of service, which he regarded as "the great aim and end of all learning." (Cremin, 1970, p. 7)

 For Your Reflection and Analysis

Would Franklin consider today's service learning requirements to fulfill this "great aim"?

In 1751, with the support of several wealthy Philadelphians, Franklin's academy opened. Very soon it became clear that Franklin's vision for the school was not to be realized. Although he had believed that Latin and Greek were useless for all but a very limited number of pursuits, he had included them in the curriculum for those who might want them. However, the person hired to head the academy, the Anglican minister, Reverend William Smith, was an avowed classist who favored the classical masters over the English masters. For example, the Latin master was paid £200 per year to teach 20 students, whereas the English master was paid £100 to teach 40 students. And, while the Latin master was given £100 to spend on books and maps, the English master was given nothing (Blinderman, 1976). As time passed, Franklin's academy gave less emphasis to the practical studies and came to more closely resemble the Latin grammar school. In 1753 it was rechartered as the College, Academy, and Charitable School of Philadelphia.

Although Franklin's academy did not survive as he intended, others, such as Phillips Andover Academy founded in 1778, did. As will be discussed in chapter 4, from its beginnings in New England, the academy movement spread west and south and became the primary provider of secondary education prior to the Civil War.

Expansion of Higher Education

Until 1747 there were only three colleges in the colonies—Harvard, Yale, and William and Mary. Then, the Great Awakening of religious fervor that swept the colonies in the mid-18th century brought with it an increased sectarianism that resulted in every religious sect wanting to establish its own college. By the beginning of the Revolutionary War nearly every major Christian sect had established its own institution of higher education: the New-Side Presbyterians founded Princeton; Dutch Reformed revivalists founded Rutgers; Baptist revivalists founded Brown; and the Anglicans and Presbyterians cooperated in the founding of Kings College (Columbia) and the College of Pennsylvania (Boorstin, 1958). In 1769 Dartmouth College was established by a Congregational minister, Eleazer Wheelock, as a college for Native Americans. According to its charter, Dartmouth was to educate the "youth of the Indian tribes in this land in reading, writing, and all parts of learning which shall appear necessary and expedient for civilizing and Christianizing the Children of gajens, as well as in all liberal arts and sciences." On a per capita basis the nine colonial colleges represented a much greater dispersion of higher education than was to be found in England, where higher education was reserved for the privileged few (Cohen, 1974a).

In the period from 1717 to 1747 about 1,400 people graduated from the colonial colleges; in the next 30 years more than twice that number graduated. About half of these had matriculated from the newly founded colleges. However, even though each new college had been founded by a particular denomination, and the president was a member of that denomination, few places had enough college-bound youth of a particular denomination to compose an entire student body. The student bodies of these colleges, therefore, were interdenominational (Boorstin, 1958).

The curriculum of many of the colleges of this era began to reflect the growing secularism of the society. In 1722 Harvard established its first professorship in the secular subjects of mathematics and natural philosophy. By 1760 the scientific subjects accounted for 20% of the curriculum. Another sign of the growing secularism was the change in graduates' careers. Although theology remained the most popular career, an increasing number of graduates were turning to law, medicine, trade, and commerce as the New England colleges became centers of independence, stimulation, and social usefulness (Cohen, 1974b).

The Colonial Schoolmaster

In colonial America teachers ranged from the widows or housewives in dame schools to college-educated masters in the grammar schools. Most teachers were men who were not intending to make teaching a career. Often they were young men who taught for only a short time before studying for the ministry or were established clergymen needing to supplement their income. Unfortunately, then as now, some individuals taught because they either were not admitted to or had failed at their chosen professions. Given the strong relationship between church and education, more often than not teachers were chosen more for their religious orthodoxy than their educational qualifications. The criteria for the licensing of teachers outlined in the Massachusetts Act of 1654 clearly demonstrate that religious, not professional, qualification was the primary consideration in the hiring of a teacher.

> Forasmuch as it greatly concernes the welfare of this countrje that the youth thereof be educated, not only in good literature, but sound doctrjne, this Court doth therefore commend it to the serious consideratjon and special care of the Overseers of the colledge and the selectmen in the severall tounes, not to admit or suffer any such to be contjnewed in the office or place of teaching, educating, or instructing of youth or child in the colledge or schooles that have manifested themselves vnsound in the faith or scandalous in theire lives, and not giving due satisfaction according to the rules of Christ.

For Your Reflection and Analysis

Should teachers today be held to a higher standard of moral conduct than other members of the community?

Colonial teachers at the secondary level were often viewed as assistant pastors and in addition to their teaching duties were expected to perform various duties related to the functioning of the church, including such things as ringing the bell for worship, leading the choir, leading prayers, or filling in for the pastor in his absence. Typical of the teaching duties expected of the grammar school master were those detailed by the town of Dorchester in 1645 and presented in Figure 3.6.

It was not uncommon in colonial America to find teachers who were indentured servants—persons who had sold their services for a period of years in exchange for passage to the New World. Many of these indentured servant teachers, especially during the 18th century, were Irish schoolmasters. Indeed, a large number of nonindentured Irish schoolmasters came to the colonies after the passage in Ireland of the Laws for the Suppression of Popery, commonly known as the Penal Laws. The Penal Laws of 1695 forbade any Catholic from teaching school upon penalty of fine or imprisonment. Many of the Irish teachers were graduates of prestigious Trinity College in Dublin. They were generally the younger sons of well-to-do families who, unable to obtain suitable employment at home, "sought the congenial employment of teaching for which there was a demand in the various American communities" (Houston, cited in O'Brien, 1917, p. 54). In some colonies, especially Pennsylvania and New York, the provision of education was almost totally dependent on the immigrant Irish schoolmasters (O'Brien, 1917).

"First. That the schoolmaster shall diligently attend his school and do his utmost endeavor for benefiting his scholars according to his best discretion.

"Second. That from the beginning of the first month until the end of the seventh, he shall every day begin to teach at seven of the clock in the morning and dismiss his school at five in the afternoon. And for the other five months, that is, from the beginning of the eighth to the end of the twelfth month he shall every day begin at eight of the clock in the morning and end at four in the afternoon.

"Thirdly. Every day in the year the usual time of dismissing at noon shall be at eleven and to begin again at one, except that

"Fourthly. Every second day in the week he shall call his scholars together between twelve and one of the clock to examine them what they have learned on the sabbath day preceding, at which time he shall take notice of any misdemeanor or outrage that any of his scholars shall have committed on the sabbath to the end that at some convenient time due admonition and correction may be administered.

"Fifthly. He shall equally and impartially receive and instruct such as shall be sent and committed to him for that end whether their parents be poor or rich, not refusing any who have right and interest in the school.

"Sixthly. Such as shall be committed to him he shall diligently instruct, as they shall be able to learn, both in humane learning and good literature, and likewise in point of good manners and dutiful behaviour towards all, especially their superiors as they shall have occasion to be in their presence whether by meeting them in the street or otherwise.

"Seventhly. Every sixth day in the week at two of the clock in the afternoon he shall catechise his scholars in the principles of Christian religion, either in some Catechism which the wardens shall provide and present, or in defect thereof in some other.

"Eighthly. And because all man's endeavors without the blessing of God needs be fruitless and unsuccessful, therefore it is a chief part of the schoolmaster's religious care to commend his scholars and his labors amongst them unto God by prayer morning and evening, taking care that his scholars do reverently attend during the same.

"Ninthly. And because the rod of correction is an ordinance of God necessary sometimes to be dispensed unto children, but such as may easily be abused by overmuch severity and rigor on one hand, or by overmuch indulgence and lenity on the other, it is therefore ordered and agreed that the schoolmaster for the time being shall have full power to administer correction to all or any of his scholars without respect of persons, according as the nature and quality of the offence shall require." The rule further requires that the parents "shall not hinder the master therein" but if aggrieved they can complain to the wardens "who shall hear and impartially decide between them."

FIGURE 3.6   Duties of a Schoolmaster, 1645

For Your Reflection and Analysis

The shortage of teachers in some districts today has resulted in the recruiting of teachers in a number of countries, including Ireland. Compare the personal and professional immigration experiences of Irish teachers of the 17th century with those of today.

Colonial teachers received no formal training. Perhaps the closest to any teacher preparation was that received by those individuals who entered teaching after serving as apprentices to schoolmasters. The first book on pedagogy printed in America was written by Christopher Dock, an 18th-century German schoolmaster in Pennsylvania. In *School-Management/Schulordnung*, a selection from which serves as a Primary Source Reading for this chapter, Dock admonished schoolmasters to use corporal punishment only as a last resort and asserted that it was better to bring a child to do something out of love than the fear of punishment. He advised the use of group praise or rebuke to motivate or punish. He also advised that teachers recognize pupils' individual differences, including religious differences.

Teacher Licensing and Pay

The hiring and licensing of teachers in New England was deemed to be the responsibility of the selectmen of a town, often with the assistance of the minister. The role of the minister was made clearer and stronger in 1701 by an act of the Massachusetts General Court (the colonial legislature), which required that every grammar school master "be approved by the ministers of the town, and the ministers of the two next adjacent towns, or any two of them, by certificate under their hand" (*Acts and Resolution*, 1701, p. 470). The law sought not only to ensure that those most able to judge the qualifications of the grammar school master to teach Latin and Greek were involved in the selection of the master, but also to prevent favoritism by requiring the signature of at least one out-of-town minister (Cole, 1956).

The act of 1701 applied only to the licensing of grammar school masters. Less than a dozen years later, in 1712, the Massachusetts General Court gave the selectmen of each town the authority to license elementary teachers: "no person or persons shall or may presume to set up or keep a school for the teaching or instructing of children or youth in reading, writing, or any other science, but such as are of sober and good conversation, and have the allowance and approbation of the selectmen of the town in which any school is to be kept" (*Acts and Resolutions*, 1712, p. 681–682). Typically, the selectmen would involve the minister in the selection of the schoolmaster. Thus, by 1712 the system of licensing schoolmasters had been established: The legislature established general qualifications that were applied at the local level. This was in keeping with the general philosophy of local control that characterized the educational systems of the New England colonies (Cole, 1956) and that came to characterize education in all 50 states.

In the Mid-Atlantic colonies teachers were certified by the royal proprietor, the royal governor, or the religious group who employed them (e.g., the SPG). In New Netherlands the governor, acting under the authority of the Dutch West India Company, certified teachers. In the South, where the Church of England was the established church, as in England, teachers were certified by the Bishop of London.

The pay given the colonial schoolmaster was often not in hard currency, but in room and board. Schoolmasters often moved from the home of the parents of one student to that of another, a practice referred to as "boarding 'round." Teachers were also paid in whatever kind of product or produce might be available to parents. According to some accounts, in one school in Salem, "one scholar was always seated at the windows to study and also to hail passers-by and endeavor to sell to them the accumulations of corn, vegetables, etc., which had been given in payment to the teacher" (Glubok, 1969, p. 18).

Education of Minorities in Colonial America

As previously noted, the first Blacks came to the American colonies in 1619, not as slaves, but as indentured servants. However, the demand for cheap labor for the southern plantations soon brought an extension of the African slave trade to the colonies. For the same price that an English or Irish servant could be bought for 7 years, an African slave could be bought for life (Bennett, 1976). Acting in a way that would change American history, in the 1660s Virginia and Maryland enacted legislation that made all bonded slaves, as well as the children of all female slaves, slaves for life. By the beginning of the Revolutionary War half a million Blacks lived in the colonies, most as southern slaves.

What education was provided to most Blacks, free or slave, was provided by missionary or charitable organizations, although a limited number of slave owners did provide minimal literacy training to their slaves so they could read the Bible or better attend to their owners' affairs. The missionary group that showed the greatest interest in the education of both Blacks and Native Americans was the SPG. The SPG was active in establishing schools for Black children in larger towns such as New York and Philadelphia, where concentrations of slaves could be found. They also ventured into Puritan New England and were, in fact, encouraged by such prominent Puritans as Cotton Mather, who for a short period himself operated a charity school for Blacks and Native Americans.

The SPG was also very active in the southern colonies. The SPG sought to assure the slave owners that they could allow slaves to become Christians and literate without letting them be free. In one unique endeavor the SPG purchased two slaves and trained them to serve as teachers in a school in Charleston, South Carolina. The school was apparently well attended, although probably more by free Blacks than slaves as had been originally intended. In 1740, following a slave rebellion, South Carolina made teaching a slave to write a crime. Georgia followed suit in 1770. In 1800 South Carolina expanded the prohibition against educating slaves to slave meetings "for purposes of mental instruction." The fear that education contributed to slave unrest led slave owners in other states to curtail any educational activities for or by slaves. Nevertheless, some religious groups, slave owners, and slaves continued in their efforts. And, although there is no real way to determine how many slaves were literate, it has been estimated that despite the obstacles 5% of the slave population was literate in 1860 on the eve of the Civil War (King, 1995).

Many of the denominational and philanthropic groups that were involved in the education of Blacks were also involved in efforts to bring education to the Native

For Your Reflection and Analysis

Why did White Americans try to force assimilation on Native Americans but block the assimilation of Black Americans?

Americans. As noted previously, a few schools were established in the larger towns by the SPG, Quakers, Moravians, and other denominations. Yet their activities were undertaken in near total ignorance and disregard for tribal methods of education. The schools engaged in both "deculturation and enculturation of an absolute kind. They generally accepted Indian potential for 'uplift,' but sought the utter extirpation of the tribal culture and the inculcation of English ideas of religion and 'civility,' down to the smallest details of appearance and behavior" (Coleman, 1993, p. 37).

Another approach, one that continued into the 20th century, was to separate the "civilized" or would-be civilized Indians from the tribe. In 1651 John Eliot, the "Apostle to the Indians," established the first of the so-called "praying towns" where converted Native Americans lived like the English, were subject to English laws, attended church and school, and were discouraged from the practice of traditional Native American customs and habits. Eliot learned the Algonquian language from an Indian servant and translated the New Testament into Algonquian. In 1664 Eliot published the complete Bible in Algonquian—the first Bible printed in the American colonies.

Although some Native Americans did settle in the praying towns, attend denominational schools, and even attend such colleges as Harvard and Dartmouth, many did so because they saw it as a way of survival. Most Native Americans were not

John Eliot, "Apostle to the Indians."

convinced of the superiority or even equality of the education offered by the colonial schools and were unwilling to pay the price to receive it, that is, to convert to Christianity and to give up their Native American customs and traditions. Nonetheless, and despite its limited success, the colonial approach to Native American education continued in modified form into the 20th century. Missionaries, subsidized by private and public funds, continued to carry both Christianity and "civilization" to the Indians. Reading, writing, arithmetic, and religious catechism remained at the heart of their efforts, and parents continued to be asked to give their children over to boarding schools to be educated and civilized. To the English colonists, and later to the Anglo Americans, the school became the tool for assimilation of the Native American.

Conclusion

Much has changed in the almost 400 years since the first settlers arrived at what became the American colonies. But in many very important ways the beliefs, ideas, and practices of colonial America are reflected in 21st-century American life. The beliefs and values of Protestant New England—that perseverance and hard work are virtues and will lead to success (and conversely that poverty is the result of laziness) that self-improvement and education are the vehicles for upward mobility, and that every person must be literate and that education contributes to the general welfare of society—as well as the whole set of virtues associated with what has become known as the Protestant work ethic—are touted as core values and beliefs of American culture.

In the colonial period some of the basic foundations of the present educational system were established. Perhaps the most fundamental and treasured of these is local control. Almost 400 years after the first selectmen met to make decisions about the local school, boards of local citizens still meet to hire teachers, select textbooks and teaching materials, and decide on the support to be given the local schools. An important corollary foundation laid during the colonial period was public support for the schools. Although the schools were not yet free, and the early education laws were not enforced, the precedent for public support was established.

Unfortunately, the seeds were also planted in colonial New England for some of the least positive aspects of American life, particularly those related to issues of social justice. The institution of slavery was established during this period, and the marked class differences that had been so much a part of the colonists' European heritage continued to dominate almost all aspects of colonial life. Then, as is unfortunately still true, the wealth of the parent was a major determinant of the quality and quantity of education the child received. Also still remaining, many education critics would argue (see, for example, Spring, 2001; Orfield, 2001), are the racism and sexism that characterized colonial education. In addition, the colonial belief that the best way to "civilize" the Native Americans was to separate them from the tribe continued into the 20th century.

The colonial legacy is also evident in many other aspects of American education. For example, some of the regional educational differences among the colonies exist today: In many parts of the South, for example, schools still struggle to overcome the neglect that had its origins in colonial governments. In many ways the status of the teacher has not changed significantly since the days of Christopher Dock and Master Adam Roelasten. That is to say, although teaching has come to be considered a profession with established requirements for entry and licensure, it remains a relatively low-status, low-paying occupation.

For Discussion and Application

1. What, if any, reminders of Puritan education were evident in the schools you attended?
2. In the interest of the "general welfare," should the federal government attempt to eliminate regional educational differences?
3. Franklin proposed that students be taught those things that are "most useful" and "ornamental." On what basis should these be determined by a school or community?
4. Explain the influence of the philosophy of the Enlightenment on education in the later colonial period.
5. Interview a practicing teacher (or draw from your own experience as a teacher) and compare the personal and professional roles and expectations of colonial teachers, with those of contemporary teachers.

Primary Source Reading

Dame schools run by widows or housewives in their homes provided the most basic education to young children of both sexes. The one described in this selection from the memoir of Laura Russell was located in Plymouth, Massachusetts. Laura began attending the school at about age 2 and for the sum of 8¢ a week received instruction in reading, spelling, and sewing from "Marm."

A Dame School in Plymouth, Massachusetts

Laura Russell

Our education began at a very early age, from twenty months to two years being considered a proper time for us to enter the infant school. As

Source: Reprinted from *Witnessing America* © by Noel Rae and The Stonesong Press, LLC, and used with permission of The Stonesong Press.

one child after another was added to the family and our mother's cares increased, this school served as a sort of day-nursery. It was but a short distance from our house and was taught by an old dame whom we always addressed as "Marm." She was an excellent woman and filled the duties of nurse as faithfully as those of teacher. She usually wore an Indigo blue calico gown with small white spots, a mob cap with a broad band of black ribbon tied into a large bow in front and round-eyed spectacles, with heavy iron frames. The house was old and small and there seemed to be a perpetual colony of skunks under it which occasionally caused great excitement among us and was a source of much annoyance to the old lady who tried in vain to hire some one to rout them. She used to say that if needle, thimble and scissors would do it she need not call upon anybody for help. . . .

The schoolroom was small and of irregular shape with an open fireplace in one corner. . . . Next to the fireplace was a closet where among the dishes always stood a little black teapot whose supply of the drink which cheers seemed to be as unfailing as that of the widow's cruse, for though "Marm" made frequent demands upon it, the contents were never exhausted. Her method of drinking was somewhat primitive and would hardly meet with favor at a fashionable afternoon tea. She considered a cup quite unnecessary preferring the simpler way of taking the spout into her mouth.

The old lady began each morning's session by reading a chapter from the Bible, rapping on its cover with her steel tailor's thimble as a signal for us to range ourselves in a semicircle about her chair and listen to the Holy Word. It is doubtful if these lessons had the intended effect for the only recollection of them which I retain is the frequent repetition of the word "Selah" from which it may be inferred that the Psalms were her favorite selection. In after years when asked the meaning of the word, she frankly replied that she did not know, and being further questioned as to why she read it, she answered, "Because it's in the Bible, dear." The great Bible lay upon a table under the looking-glass between the windows and, with the Old Farmer's Almanac, constituted the old lady's entire library. On the sacred volume and the almanac was a small wooden box into which at the close of each day we dropped our little brass thimbles and our bit of patchwork with its irregular, blackened stitches piled one upon another after having been many times picked out and re-sewed with squeaking, crooked needle and tear-dimmed eyes.

The white unpainted floor of the schoolroom was bare with the exception of a braided mat in front of "Marm's" chair, but in place of a carpet there was a liberal sprinkling of beach sand which was renewed every week, and ornamented by being herring-boned with a broom. The only school furniture was a number of low wooden crickets which were placed in a row through the middle of the room, and which were sometimes supplemented with a block or two under the windows, when the school was crowded. The crickets were worn smooth and shiny from long wriggling of the little unsupported forms daily seated upon them, the knots being conspicuous for their high polish. Each child carried its cricket at night into the adjoining room, and returned it to its place the next morning, the school room serving also for parlor and bedroom.

Occasionally we got a slight rap on the head from the tailor's thimble, but the only other punishment that I remember was when an aggravated offence brought from "Marm" the command, "Take your cricket and go down to Bantam," Bantam being the farther corner of the room occupied by an old roundabout chair. I have never been able to trace the origin of this word nor do I know whether it referred to the corner or the chair, but the punishment was resorted to as an extreme measure and to us meant not only deep disgrace but almost Siberian exile.

Into this seminary we were initiated at the tender age before-mentioned and sent with undeviating regularity twice a day with the exception of Saturday when we were allowed a half-holiday. No storm was so fierce, no snow so deep, no cold so intense as to interfere with the inflexible rule of daily attendance at school. . . . When the weather was unfavorable, it was our custom as well as that of other children to take a little basket of luncheon and remain through the noon recess. As "Marm" depended upon her after dinner nap, our amusements were necessarily much restricted. When we grew too noisy, we were checked with the admonition, "Let your victuals stop your mouth." The old dame must have looked forward to Saturday with delightful anticipation. At the close of the morning session she was not only relieved of all care of the children till the following Monday, but was at liberty to pass the rest of the day with her son and his family. In winter she donned her scarlet cloth cloak with its numerous little capes, being kept from these weekly visits only by sickness or very severe weather.

In the room adjoining the schoolroom a bucket of water always stood on a table and near it a large pewter vessel in size and shape somewhat resembling a beer-mug. When we were very good, we were allowed to hand water around to the children, passing the pewter mug from one to another without refilling till the supply was exhausted. This was a much coveted office, but like other positions of honor and trust, it had its drawbacks. When my turn came, I remember that the weight of the mug frequently caused cramps in my small hands. Then the kind old dame would call me to her side and carefully wrap them in the red flannel nightgown which she thought had a peculiar virtue from its color. She also laid me on the bed in her little spare dark bedroom for the daily nap, an indulgence which did not seriously interfere with my education since only reading, spelling and sewing over and over were taught.

Our tuition cost the moderate sum of eight cents a week. . . . This modest charge did not include the fuel, for the following item was added to an autumn bill still in my possession: "If she comes this winter, one dollar for fire-money."

Questions for Discussion

1. What educational experience impressed you the most about the dame school described in Laura Russell's memoir? Explain why it impressed you.
2. Prepare an announcement of vacancy for the position of dame school teacher. Describe the desired qualifications and benefits.
3. Describe the physical environment of the dame school. What artifacts made the most impression on you? Give reasons why.

Primary Source Reading

One of the most famous teachers in colonial America was Christopher Dock, a Mennonite, who taught in various German communities in Pennsylvania for over 50 years. Dock's book, Schul-ordnung, *published in 1770, was the first book on pedagogy published in America. In the selection included here Dock discusses "how he receives children at school." As you read the material, consider the period in history and the informal preparation of teachers.*

School-Management (Schul-ordnung)

Christopher Dock

Concerning Friend Saur's first question, how I receive the children at school, I proceed as follows: the child is first given a welcome by the other children, who extend their hands to him. Then I ask him if he will be diligent and obedient. If he promises this, he is told how to behave; and when he can say his A B C 's and point out each letter with his index finger, he is put into the Ab. When he reaches this class his father owes him a penny, and his mother must fry him two eggs for his diligence, and the same reward is due him with each advance; for instance, when he enters the word class. But when he enters the reading class, I owe him a present, if he reaches the class in the required time and has been diligent, and the first day this child comes to school he receives a note stating: "Diligent. One pence." This means he has been admitted to the school; but it is also explained to him that if he is lazy or disobedient his note is taken from him. Continued disinclination to learn and stubbornness causes the pupil to be proclaimed lazy and inefficient before the whole class, and he is told that he belongs in a school for incorrigibles. Then I ask the child again if he will be obedient and diligent. Answering yes, he is shown his place. If it is a boy, I ask the other boys, if a girl, I ask the girls, who among them will take care of this new child and teach it. According to the extent to which the child is known, or its pleasant or unpleasant appearance, more or less children express their willingness. If none apply, I ask who will teach this child for a certain time for a bird or a writing-copy. Then it is seldom difficult to get a response. This is a description of my way of receiving the child into school. . . .

Source: Brumbaugh, M. G. (1908). *Life and works of Christopher Dock, America's pioneer writer on education.* Philadelphia: J. B. Lippincott, pp. 104–111.

The children arrive as they do because some have a great distance to school, others a short distance, so that the children cannot assemble as punctually as they can in a city. Therefore, when a few children are present, those who can read their Testament sit together on one bench; but the boys and girls occupy separate benches. They are given a chapter which they read at sight consecutively. Meanwhile I write copies for them. Those who have read their passage of Scripture without error take their places at the table and write. Those who fail have to sit at the end of the bench, and each new arrival the same; as each one is thus released in order he takes up his slate. This process continues until they have all assembled. The last one left on the bench is a "lazy pupil."

When all are together, and examined, whether they are washed and combed, they sing a psalm or a morning hymn, and I sing and pray with them. As much as they can understand of the Lord's Prayer and the ten commandments (according to the gift God has given them), I exhort and admonish them accordingly. This much concerning the assembling of pupils. But regarding prayer I will add this additional explanation. Children say the prayers taught them at home half articulately, and too fast, especially the "Our Father" which the Lord Himself taught His disciples and which contains all that we need. I therefore make a practice of saying it for them kneeling, and they kneeling repeat it after me. After these devotional exercises those who can write resume their work. Those who cannot read the Testament have had time during the assemblage to study their lesson. These are heard recite immediately after prayer. Those who know their lesson receive an O on the hand, traced with crayon. This is a mark of excellence. Those who fail more than three times are sent back to study their lesson again. When all the little ones have recited, these are asked again, and any one having failed in more than three trials a second time is called "Lazy" by the entire class and his name is written down. Whether such a child fear the rod or not, I know from experience that this denunci-

ation of the children hurts more than if I were constantly to wield and flourish the rod. If then such a child has friends in school who are able to instruct him and desire to do so, he will visit more frequently than before. For this reason: if the pupil's name has not been erased before dismissal the pupils are at liberty to write down the names of those who have been lazy, and take them along home. But if the child learns his lesson well in the future, his name is again presented to the other pupils, and they are told that he knew his lesson well and failed in no respect. Then all the pupils call "Diligent" to him. When this has taken place his name is erased from the slate of lazy pupils, and the former transgression is forgiven.

The children who are in the spelling class are daily examined in pronunciation. In spelling, when a word has more than one syllable, they must repeat the whole word, but some, while they can say the letters, cannot pronounce the word, and so cannot be put to reading. For improvement a child must repeat the lesson, and in this way: The child gives me the book, I spell the word and he pronounces it. If he is slow, another pupil pronounces it for him, and in this way he hears how it should be done, and knows that he must follow the letters and not his own fancy.

Concerning ABC pupils, it would be best, having but one child, to let it learn one row of letters at a time, to say forward and backward. But with many, I let them learn the alphabet first, and then ask a child to point out a letter that I name. If a child is backward or ignorant, I ask another, or the whole class, and the first one that points to the right letter, I grasp his finger and hold it until I have put a mark opposite his name. I then ask for another letter, etc. Whichever child has during the day received the greatest number of marks, has pointed out the greatest number of letters. To him I owe something—a flower drawn on paper or a bird. But if several have the same number, we draw lots; this causes less annoyance. In this way not only are the very timid cured of their shyness (which is a great hindrance in learning), but a fondness for school is increased. Thus much in answer to his question, how I take the children into school, how school proceeds before and after prayers, and how the inattentive and careless are made attentive and careful, and how the timid are assisted.

Further I will state that when the little ones have recited for the first time, I give the Testament pupils a verse to learn. Those reading newspapers and letters sit separately, and those doing sums sit separately. But when I find that the little ones are good enough at their reading to be fit to read the Testament, I offer them to good Testament readers for instruction. The willing teacher takes the pupil by the hand and leads him to his seat. I give them two verses to try upon. But if I find that another exercise is necessary after this (such as finding a passage in Scripture, or learning a passage, in which case each reads a verse), I give only one verse, which is not too hard for those trying to read in the Testament. If pupils are diligent and able, they are given a week's trial, in which time they must learn their lesson in the speller with the small pupils and also their lesson with the Testament pupil. If they stand the test they are advanced the next week from the spelling to the Testament class, and they are also allowed to write. But those who fail in the Testament remain a stated time in the ABC class before they are tested again. After the Testament pupils have recited, the little ones are taken again. This done they are reminded of the chapter read them, and asked to consider the teaching therein. As it is the case that this thought is also expressed in other passages of Holy Writ, these are found and read, and then a hymn is given containing the same teaching. If time remains, all are given a short passage of Scripture to learn. This done, they must show their writing exercises. These are examined and numbered, and then the first in turn is given a hard word to spell. If he fails the next must spell it and so on. The one to spell correctly receives his exercise. Then the first is given another hard word, and so each receives his exercise by spelling a word correctly.

As the children carry their dinner, an hour's liberty is given them after dinner. But as they are usually inclined to misapply their time if one is not constantly with them, one or two of them must read a story of the Old Testament (either from Moses and the Prophets, or from Solomon's or Sirach's Proverbs), while I write copies for them. This exercise continues during the noon hour.

It is also to be noted that children find it necessary to ask to leave the room, and one must permit them to do this, not wishing the uncleanness and odor in the school. But the clamor to go out would continue all day, and sometimes without need, so that occasionally two or three are out at the same time, playing. To prevent this I have driven a nail in the door-post, on which hangs a wooden tag. Any one needing to leave the room looks for the tag. If it is on the nail, this is his permit to go out without asking. He takes the tag out with him. If another wishes to leave, he does not ask either, but stands by the door until the first returns, from whom he takes the tag and goes. If the tag is out too long, the one wishing to go inquires who was out last, and from it can be ascertained to whom he gave the tag, so that none can remain out too long.

To teach the uninitiated numbers and figures, I write on the blackboard (which hangs where all can see) these figures

1   2   3   4   5   6   7   8   9   0

far apart, that other figures can be put before and behind them. Then I put an 0 before the 1 and explain that this does not increase the number. Then I erase the 0 and put it after the 1, so that it makes 10. If two ciphers follow it makes 100, if three follow, 1000, etc. This I show them through all the digits. This done I affix to the 1 another 1, making 11. But if an 0 is put between it makes 101, but if it be placed after, it makes 110. In a similar manner I go through all the digits. When this is done I give them something to find in the Testament or hymnal. Those who are quickest have something to claim for their diligence, from me or at home.

As it is desirable for intelligent reading to take note of commas, but as the inexperienced find this difficult, I have this rule: If one of the Testament pupils does not read on, but stops before he reaches a comma or period, this counts one-fourth failure. Similarly if one reads over a comma, it is one-fourth failure. Repeating a word counts one-half. Then all failures are noted, and especially where each one has failed. When all have read, all those who have failed must step forward and according to the number of errors stand in a row. Those who have not failed move up, and the others take the lowest positions.

Regarding the correspondence, I may say that for twelve years I kept two schools, as already said, and for four summers (during the three months that I had free owing to the harvest) I taught school at Germantown. Then the pupils in Skippack, when I went to Sollford, gave me letters, and when I returned, the Sollford pupils did likewise. It was so arranged that pupils of equal ability corresponded. When one became his correspondent's superior, he wrote to another whose equal he tried to be.

The superscription was only this: My friendly greeting to N. N. The contents of the letter consisted of a short rhyme, or a passage from Scripture, and they told something of their school exercises (their motto for the week and where it is described, and &c.). Sometimes one would give the other a question to be answered by a passage of Scripture. I doubt not, if two schoolmasters (dwelling in one place or not) loving one another and desiring their pupils to love one another, were to do this in the love of God, it would bear fruit.

This is a piecemeal description of how children are taught letters, and how their steps are led from one degree to the next, before they can be brought to the aim that we have in view to the glory of God and for their own salvation, and which will be last discussed.

Questions for Discussion

1. Of the teaching methods used by the Schoolmaster Christopher Dock, which appear to have been most effective? Least effective? Give reasons why.
2. Consider the variety of classroom management techniques used by Schoolmaster Dock. To what extent are some of those classroom management techniques being used today?
3. A variety of "ways of knowing" (e.g., scientific inquiry, intuition, insight, experience, logic, the senses, etc.) are embedded in any philosophy of education. Which ways of knowing would you attribute to Schoolmaster Dock's philosophy of education?

Education in the Revolutionary and Early National Periods

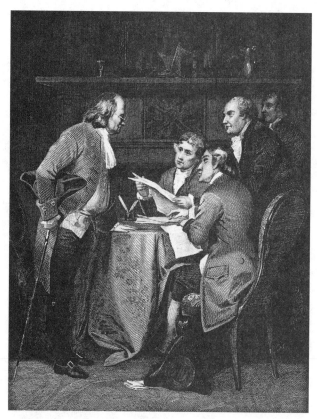

There is but one method of preventing crimes and of rendering a republican form of government durable, and this, by disseminating the seeds of virtue and knowledge through every part of the state by means of proper places and modes of education, and this can done effectively only by the interference of the Legislature.

—*Benjamin Rush, 1788*

On July 4, 1776, the 13 colonies declared their independence from England. Education was one of the casualties of the war that followed. Many schools closed or cut back their operations as funds and teachers became scarce. Loyalist teachers and professors were either forced out of their positions, or like the head of the Boston Latin Grammar School, chose to leave on their own. Other teachers left to join the fighting on the side of the colonies, as did many college students. A number of schools and college buildings were used to house troops; others were destroyed or cannibalized for the war effort (e.g., a half ton of lead was removed from the roof of Harvard Hall to make bullets).

Being independent and no longer part of a large empire brought not only the freedom to act, but also the challenges that accompanied the actions. Independence did not mean that the colonies immediately discarded all vestiges of the institutions that had developed under European governance. What independence did bring was the freedom to develop a native American culture and institutions.

The Founding Fathers were aware that changing their form of government was only the beginning of the revolution. As Benjamin Rush remarked, "We have only finished the first act of the great drama. We have changed our form of government, but it remains yet to effect a revolution in our principles, opinions, and manners so as to accommodate them to the forms of government we have adopted."

In the next act in the drama, the leaders of the new nation set about the business of devising a government and institutions that would encompass the ideas for which they had fought. One of the most important institutions to the survival of the new nation, they believed, was the school. The school would promote nationalism and produce the educated and orderly citizenry required for the functioning of a democratic republic. Consistent with this belief, various proposals were made for systems of education. Among these were those made by Thomas Jefferson and Benjamin Rush for statewide, publicly supported education systems. Although these were not to be fully realized for over a century, educational opportunities were expanded during the early national period, primarily to children of the poor through the monitorial schools, Sunday schools, and infant schools. At the same time, the growth of the academy expanded opportunities at the secondary level for a broader range of students, especially those from the growing middle class and females. The academy also paved the way for the American high school.

Perhaps more important, the early republic also witnessed the growth of what was to be the bedrock of the American education system, the common school. The growth of an increasingly urban population not only provided the enrollment, but also increased the demand for a common system of education that would provide individuals from all classes the opportunity to succeed. The common school movement is explored in detail in chapter 5, but not before its antecedents and the forces supporting the movement are examined in the present chapter.

Education Under the Articles of Confederation and the Constitution

The first attempt at self-governance, the Articles of Confederation and Perpetual Union, was adopted by the Continental Congress and went into effect after ratification in 1781. The government established under the Articles of Confederation was an attempt to organize the 13 separate colonies under a national government that was given little authority and included no executive or judicial branches. It also proved unable to tax, regulate commerce, or enforce civil law. Perhaps more important to the citizens of the new United States of America, it did not provide the framework for the establishment of a strong national government that would be able to bring 13 disparate governments into a unified whole. Fearing that the confederation would collapse and that anarchy would prevail, delegates from each state met in the summer of 1787 and drafted the Constitution, which after ratification in 1789 launched the new republic.

Perhaps because of the former colonists' suspicion of a strong central government, or perhaps because of the association of education with theology, neither the Articles of Confederation nor the Constitution mentioned education. Education was considered to be one of the powers reserved to the states by the Tenth Amendment, which states: "The powers not delegated to the United States by the Constitution, nor prohibited by it to the States, are reserved to the States respectively, or to the people."

Northwest Land Ordinances of 1785 and 1787

Despite the fact that neither the Articles of Confederation nor the Constitution mentioned education, there can be no doubt that the nation's founders recognized the importance of education to a form of government in which the quality of representation depended on citizens' ability to make informed choices at the ballot box. To ensure that the settlers in the Northwest Territory did not neglect education, Congress passed perhaps the most important piece of legislation under the Articles of Confederation, the Land Ordinance of 1785. This ordinance prescribed the terms for admitting new states into the union from the Northwest Territory, and required that the 16th section of land in each township in the Territory be set aside for the support of education. The land could be sold or leased, but the proceeds were to go to fund education. The 16th section, which was the section closest to the geographical center of the township (see Figure 4.1), was a strategic choice for the possible location of a school.

Although it would be three-quarters of a century and the passage of the Morrill Land Grant Act before federal government again participated in any meaningful way in the support of public education, the Northwest Ordinance not only provided the precedent for that act, but also established the principle for federal support of education. The precedent of setting aside land for the support of education was followed in all subsequent government grants to states and territories and provided the basis for the permanent school fund that still exists in most of these states. Ultimately, 80 million acres of land were distributed for the support of public education under the terms of the Northwest Ordinance. Two years after the first ordinance, in Article

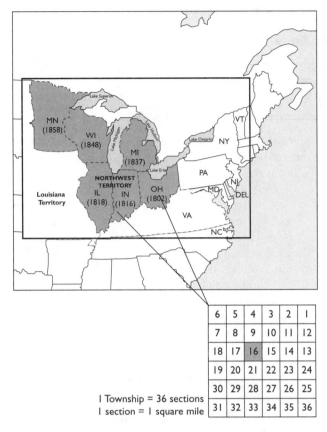

FIGURE 4.1   Northwest Territory and Township. The 16th section of each township in the Northwest Territory was set aside for the support of education.

Three of the Northwest Ordinance of 1787, which incorporated the Northwest Territory, Congress reiterated the importance of education: "Religion, morality, and knowledge being necessary to good government and the happiness of mankind, schools and the means of education shall be forever encouraged."

Nationalism and Education

The spirit of nationalism that dominated the new republic shaped the view of the Founding Fathers regarding what type of education was needed for the new nation. Whereas the primary purpose of colonial education had been sectarian, emphasis was now placed on citizenship and the nation-state. Education was seen as the best way to both prepare citizens to participate in a republican form of government and maintain order. The Founding Fathers were well aware (and were reminded by the Whiskey Rebellion in Pennsylvania in 1794 and Shays' Rebellion in Massachusetts in 1787) of the uncertain existence of the national government. Although influenced by the

For Your Reflection and Analysis

What paradox might you see today in our nation's attempt to model democracy and maintain security?

philosophy of the Enlightenment, they also knew the lessons of history, which suggested that republics had a tenuous existence. Education, they believed, especially one based on Protestant principles and morals, was essential to preparing virtuous and orderly citizens. At the same time they wanted to preserve the principles of liberty and equality for which they had fought. In their search for ordered liberty they accepted a paradox: "the free America was to be, in political convictions, the uniform America," and in the end "saw conformity as the price of liberty" (Tyack, 1967, pp. 84–85).

Although they differed on many details, the republican leaders held at least four beliefs regarding education in common: (1) That education must be relative to the form of government; hence, a republic needs an educational system that prepares citizens to function effectively in a republican form of government; (2) that what was needed was a truly American education purged of all vestiges of older, monarchical forms and dedicated to the creation of a cohesive and patriotic citizenry; (3) that education should be genuinely practical, aimed at the improvement of the human condition, with the new sciences at its heart; and (4) that American education should be exemplary and a means through which America could teach the world the glories of liberty and learning (Cremin, 1982).

Republican Educational Theorists

It was generally acknowledged that the condition of education at the end of the revolutionary period was deplorable. This conviction led a number of the Founding Fathers to draft legislation or make other formal proposals designed to improve and extend schooling and to make it increasingly state supported. This is not to say that their idea of a publicly supported education system was adopted in the new republic, but as the historian David Tyack (1967) reminded us, "The concept of uniform, systematic education serving republican purposes did not disappear. Later, when challenges confronted society during the period of the common school crusade, the ideas would emerge again, fortified by added sanctions and new anxieties" (p. 92). Although many of the Founding Fathers expressed their views on the importance of education, the three who stand out as having the greatest influence on the education that developed in the new republic are Thomas Jefferson, Benjamin Rush, and Noah Webster.

Thomas Jefferson

Of the Founding Fathers, perhaps none is so well known for his views on education as Thomas Jefferson (1743–1826). Jefferson was strongly influenced by the philosophy of Locke and believed that government must be by the consent of the governed and that men were entitled to certain rights that could not be abridged by the government. Jefferson was one of the chief proponents of the addition of a Bill of Rights to the Constitution. According to one educational historian, "Few statesmen in

American history have so vigorously strived for an ideal [liberty]; perhaps none has so consistently viewed education as the indispensable cornerstone of freedom" (Rippa, 1984, p. 68).

Plan for a State Education System

Jefferson's *Bill for the More General Diffusion of Knowledge*, introduced in the Virginia legislature in 1779, provided for the establishment of a system of public schools for Virginia. In the preamble Jefferson gave what was the prototypic republican, nationalistic argument for the importance of state-supported education for republican citizenship:

> When it becomes expedient for promoting the publick happiness that those persons, whom nature hath endowed with genius and virtue, should be rendered by liberal education worthy to receive, and able to guard the sacred deposit of the rights and liberties of their fellow citizens, and that they should be called to that charge without regard to wealth, birth or other accidental condition or circumstance; but the indigence of the greater number disabling them from so educating, at their own expense, those of their children who nature hath fitly formed and disposed to become useful instruments for the public, it is better that such should be sought for and educated at the common expense of all than that the happiness of all should be confined to the weak or wicked.

The bill called for each county to be subdivided into parts called *hundreds;* each hundred was to provide an elementary school, supported by taxes. Attendance would be free for all White children, male and female, for 3 years. The curriculum would be reading, writing, arithmetic, and history. Jefferson believed that through the study of history students would learn to recognize tyranny and support democracy. The bill went on to propose that the state be divided into 20 districts and that a boarding grammar school be built at public expense in each district. Those attending would be not only those boys whose families could afford the tuition, but also the brightest of the poorer students from the elementary schools whose tuition would be paid by the state. The curriculum of the grammar school was to include Latin, Greek, geography, English, grammar, and higher mathematics. Finally, upon completion of grammar school, 10 of the scholarship students would receive 3 years' study at the College of William and Mary at state expense. The remaining scholarship students, according to Jefferson, would most likely become masters in the grammar schools.

Although this plan, viewed in today's light, appears strikingly elitist, in Jefferson's day it was considered excessively liberal and philanthropic. In fact, it was defeated by the Virginia legislature in 1789, in 1797, and again in 1817. Its defeat can be attributed in large part to the unwillingness of the wealthy to pay property taxes for the education of the poor.

Nonetheless, the plan is considered important because it reflects Jefferson's commitment to the concept of a system of universal, free public education, if only for 3 years, and his

 For Your Reflection and Analysis

How different are the wealthy of today from the wealthy of Jefferson's time in terms of their willingness to pay additional taxes to support the public schools?

belief in its necessity for a democracy. As he expressed in one of his most well-known quotes: "If a nation expects to be ignorant and free it expects what never was and never will be."

Founding the University of Virginia

Jefferson's interest in education also extended to establishing the University of Virginia. After leaving the presidency of the United States in 1809, he devoted much of his energies to that effort. He created the project (sometimes called "Mr. Jefferson's University") in every detail: He designed the buildings and landscape (he even bought the bricks and picked out the trees to be used as lumber), chose the library books, designed the curriculum, and selected the students and faculty. In the selection of the faculty and textbooks what has been described as Jefferson's "rigid liberalism" (Tyack, 1967) was much in evidence. Apparently, Jefferson's tolerance did not extend to what he considered political "heresy": Jefferson insisted that students be protected from exposure to Federalist faculty and texts.

 For Your Reflection and Analysis

What explanation would there be for Jefferson not considering serving as president one of his greatest accomplishments?

The University of Virginia opened in 1825, a year before Jefferson's death on July 4, 1826. So important was the University of Virginia to Jefferson that he requested that its founding be included on his tombstone among what he considered his other greatest accomplishments: writing the Statute of Virginia for Religious Freedom and authoring the Declaration of Independence. Serving as president of the United States was not included.

Benjamin Rush

Benjamin Rush (1746–1813), a medical doctor and professor, was a graduate of both the University of Edinburgh (Scotland) and Princeton. At the outbreak of the Revolutionary War he was a professor at the College of Philadelphia. Rush was deeply interested in education as well as a broad range of social issues: He was strongly opposed to the death sentence and encouraged penal reform and the establishment of institutions for the mentally ill. Together with Benjamin Franklin he organized the first abolition society in Philadelphia, the Society for the Relief of Free Negroes Unlawfully Held in Bondage.

Rush wanted to establish a system in Pennsylvania and eventually the entire nation that would provide for public support for free schools. According to the plan he laid out in *A Plan for the Establishment of Public Schools and the Diffusion of Knowledge in Pennsylvania*, a plan similar to Jefferson's plan for Virginia, Rush proposed that in every town of 100 or more families a free school be established where children would be taught to read and write English and German as well as arithmetic. An academy was to be established in each county "for the purpose of instructing youth in the learned languages (Latin and Greek), and thereby preparing them to enter college." The higher education provisions of the plan included four colleges where males would be instructed in mathematics and the "higher branches of science" as well as one university located in the state capital where "law, physic, divinity, the law of nature and nations economy, etc. be taught . . . by public lectures in the winter season, after the manner of the European universities." Rush's education plan was intended to tie together the whole education system: The university would supply the masters for the academies and free schools, and the free schools, in turn, would supply the students for the academies. More than perhaps the other leading republican theorists, Rush was concerned about the quality and character of the teachers and the financial support they might receive:

> It will be no purpose to adopt this or any other mode of education unless we make choice of suitable masters to carry our plans into execution. Let our teachers be distinguished for their abilities and knowledge. Let them be grave in their manners, gentle in their tempers, exemplary in their morals, and of sound principles in religion and government. Let us not leave their support to the precarious resources to be derived from their pupils, but let such funds be provided for our schools and colleges as will enable us to allow them liberal salaries. (Rush, cited in Rudolph, 1965, p. 21)

 For Your Reflection and Analysis

What aspects of Rush's proposal do you think are necessary ingredients of teacher quality? Not necessary?

Rush was an advocate of the education of women and founded one of the first female academies in the United States, the Young Ladies Academy of Philadelphia. However, he was not an egalitarian. In fact, in Rush's opinion, education would serve to make women more subservient to men and to recognize and accept their natural inferiority and that men were by intent and design the natural leaders of the world (Campbell, 2000). To a large extent Rush's support of women's education was based on his view of their particular duties in a republic. In his *Thoughts Upon Female Education* (1787), Rush espoused the idea of "republican motherhood," the idea that women's primary duty was to bring up their sons to be virtuous citizens. To best prepare them to do so, Rush proposed that women be instructed in not only the three *R*s, but also "some knowledge of figures and bookkeeping . . . [and, since] there are certain occupations in which she may assist her husband with this knowledge, and should she survive him and agreeably to the custom of our country be the executrix of his will, she cannot fail of deriving immense advantage of it"; geography; "the first principles of astronomy and natural philosophy, particularly with such parts of them as are calculated to prevent superstition"; history; vocal music and dance; English literature; moral philosophy; and the Christian religion.

Rush was also an advocate for the education of Blacks. Rush saw the education of Blacks to be a moral and economic imperative: "Let the young negroes be educated in the principles of virtues and religion . . . let them be taught to read and write—and afterward instructed in some business whereby they may be able to maintain themselves" (Blinderman, 1976, p. 21).

Rush was perhaps the harshest of the republican theorists in terms of achieving discipline and political conformity—indeed, indoctrination—through education. The following quotes from Rush provide what Kaestle (1983) called a "chilling reminder of the harsh side of revolutionary educational thought":

In the education of youth, let the authority of our masters be as absolute as possible. The government of schools like the government of private families should be arbitrary, that it may not be severe. By this mode of education we prepare our youth for the subordination of laws and thereby qualify them for becoming good citizens of the republic. I am satisfied that the most useful citizens have been formed from those youth who have never known or felt their own wills till they were one and twenty years of age. . . .

From the observations that have been made it is plain that I consider it is possible to convert men into republican machines. (pp. 16–17)

A major goal of Rush, one he shared with George Washington and all the presidents up to Andrew Jackson, was to establish a national university. For Rush and many others a national university would not only serve the purpose of educational equality, but also would be an avenue for promoting nationalism. Rush went so far as to propose that Congress pass a law to prevent any person 30 years after the founding of the university from holding office who had not graduated from the federal university (Tyack, 1967). An equally strong proposal by Jefferson included bringing the entire faculty of the College of Geneva, Switzerland, to become the core for a national university (Butts & Cremin, 1953).

 For Your Reflection and Analysis

Is there a place in today's education system for a system of federally operated national universities?

Many of the other leaders of the new nation supported the creation of a national university. In fact, the proposal was considered by the drafters of the Constitution but rejected because it would require the inclusion of too much detail. Nevertheless, each of the first six presidents of the United States voiced his support for what historian David Madsen (1966) called an "Enduring Dream of the U.S.A."—a national university. Although not to be realized in the form envisioned by its early proponents, the national military academies realized at least part of the dream, to train leaders for the "militia" and the navy.

Noah Webster

Jefferson and Rush proposed legislation and established colleges, but it was a teacher, Noah Webster (1758–1843), who had the most influence on education in the new republic. Although Webster could probably be considered more a Federalist than a Jeffersonian Republican, he did share the view of his contemporaries that education was central to ensuring stability and liberty in the nascent republic. Webster believed that the primary purpose of education should be the inculcation of patriotism, and that what was needed was a truly American education rid of its European influence (Madsen, 1974). These goals could best be accomplished, he believed, by creating a distinctive national (American) language and curriculum. To this end Webster prepared a three-part *Grammatical Institute of the English Language* containing spelling, grammar, and reading books to replace the English texts then in use. He also produced an American version of the Bible and what became the world-famous *American Dictionary of the English Language* as a vehicle for promoting an American language.

Of his textbooks the most popular was the *Elementary Spelling Book*, published in 1783, often referred to as the "blue-back speller" because of the color of the binding. By 1875, 75 million copies of the speller had been sold (Spring, 2001), many of which were used again and again. The book included both a federal catechism with political and patriotic content and a moral catechism, whose content was related to respect for honest work and property rights, the value of money, the virtues of industry and thrift, and the dangers of liquor. Instruction was also given on how to behave in school (e.g., "He that speaks loud in school will not learn his lesson well, nor let the rest learn theirs"). According to the noted historian Henry Steele Commager (1977), "No other secular book had ever spread so wide, penetrated so deep, lasted so long" (p. 74).

Webster supported the concept of free schools in which all children would receive at least 4 months of schooling annually and in which they would be taught the necessary patriotic and moral precepts. As a member of the Massachusetts legislature during the early 1800s, he worked for the establishment of a state system of education and is credited by some as initiating the common school movement that culminated in Horace Mann's work in the 1830s (Spring, 2001). He also supported the education of women because they would be the mothers of future citizens and the teachers of youth. However, he was firmly opposed to parents sending their daughters to "demoralizing" boarding schools. A staunch patriot whose proposals sometimes bordered on the fanatic (e.g., the proposal that the first word a child learned should be *Washington*), Webster has been called the Schoolmaster of the Republic.

Through his dictionary and textbooks, Webster sought to create a distinctive American language.

New Providers of Elementary Education

Although the education proposals of Jefferson, Rush, and others were not adopted, other proposals for expanding educational opportunities were implemented in the early republic. And, despite the fact that Webster and others promoted the establishment of a uniquely American education, some of the major innovations in American education in this period were of European origin. Among these were the monitorial school, the Sunday school, and the infant school. None of these survived in its initial form, but they promoted the common school movement discussed in chapter 5 by both illuminating the need for education and giving the common people a taste for learning.

Monitorial Schools

Monitorial schools originated in England and were brought to America by a Quaker, Joseph Lancaster. In the Lancasterian monitorial system, one paid teacher instructed hundreds of pupils through the use of monitors or student teachers who were chosen for their academic abilities. Monitorial education was concerned with teaching only the basics of reading, writing, and arithmetic. The first monitorial school in the United States was opened in New York City in 1806, and the system spread rapidly. One such school in Pennsylvania designed to accommodate 450 students was described as follows:

> The teacher sits at the head of the room on a raised platform. Beneath and in front of the teacher are three rows of monitors' desks placed directly in front of the pupils' desks. The pupils' desks are divided into three sections . . . and each section is in line with one of the rows of monitors' desks . . . . A group of pupils would march to the front of the room and stand around the monitors' desks, where they would receive instruction from the monitors. When they finished, they would march to the rear part of their particular section and recite or receive further instruction from another monitor. While this group was marching to the rear, another group would be marching up to the front to take their places around the monitors. When finished, the pupils would march to the rear, and the group in the rear would move forward to the second part of their section to receive instruction from yet another monitor. Because each of the three sections had a group in front, one in the rear, and one in the middle working on different things, a total of nine different recitations could be carried on at one time. (Spring, 2001, pp. 71–72)

The monitorial system was attractive not only because it provided an inexpensive system for educating the poor, but also because submission to the system was supposed to instill the virtues of orderliness, obedience, and industriousness. The system gained wide appeal. In fact, Kaestle (1983) asserted that it was "the most wide-spread and successful educational reform in the Western world during the first 30 years of the nineteenth century" (pp. 41–42).

 For Your Reflection and Analysis

What virtues do the schools attempt to instill today?

The Lancasterian system was considered ideal for the charity schools operated by the free school societies for the children of the poor in urban areas not being served by the denominational charity schools. Overall, the free schools were not a major factor in the history of education; nonetheless, for a period they did provide the only education some children received. For example, by 1820 the Free School Society of New York City (renamed the Public School Society in 1826 and placed under the city department of education in 1853) was teaching more than 2,000 children (Cremin, 1982). They were also important in providing the basis for the public school systems that developed in many American cities in the mid-19th century (Kaestle, 1983).

In time the monitorial system declined. It appeared to be suited more to large cities with large numbers of students than to small towns and rural areas. Even in the large cities it was not always considered successful. Among the many criticisms of the system was that often the peer monitors were not able to command respect and maintain discipline and that the schools afforded only the most basic education. Yet, instead of being an educational dead end, as depicted by many educational historians, Lancasterian monitorialism may have been the model for the factorylike urban schools that emerged in the United States in the late 19th century (Gutek, 1986).

 For Your Reflection and Analysis

To what extent would Jefferson or Rush have supported the monitorial system?

Sunday Schools

The *Sunday school*, a form of charity school, was begun in 1780 in England by Robert Raikes. The first Sunday school in America opened in 1786 in Virginia. Its purpose was to offer moral instruction and the rudiments of reading and writing to children who worked during the week, primarily in the factories of the larger cities. Historians have estimated that as much as 40% of the laborers in the factories at the time were children. The Sunday school was seen as serving a secular purpose by providing these working children with an alternative to roaming the streets on Sunday.

By 1800 more than 2,000 students were in Sunday schools in Philadelphia. Sunday schools were also in operation in New York, Richmond, and other eastern cities. In some locations Sunday schools were able to obtain some public support for their operations. The Sunday and Adult School Union, a national organization established in 1817 that was reorganized as the American Sunday School Union in 1824, promoted the spread of the movement across the country. The Union published and distributed reading and spelling books, religious books, and books for moral guidance and instruction. The Union also distributed sets of "Sunday School Libraries" which served, *de facto*, as the only public libraries in many rural communities (Boylan, 1988).

It has been estimated that, by 1827, 200,000 children attended Sunday schools (Kaestle, 1983). In a number of communities, and even on plantations, Black adults and children were among those who took advantage of the opportunity to learn to read and write on Sunday, albeit in separate classes.

The typical Sunday school operated from 6 to 10 in the morning and from 2 to 6 in the afternoon. The remainder of the day was spent at morning and evening worship. Classes were small and typically were taught by young female volunteers. Like the other forms of charity education, the curriculum of the Sunday school emphasized basic literacy with a heavy emphasis on reading and memorizing the scriptures.

The original Sunday schools were not adjuncts of the church, but were established by laypeople and rarely met in churches. However, by 1830 the initial secular purpose of the Sunday school had been superseded by religious interests and, although they continued to teach reading, they came to be religious institutions operated by Sunday school societies with primarily evangelical missions. They grew in number, reaching out to the frontier and becoming available to children from homes of all sorts. Like the monitorial schools, the free schools, and the infant schools discussed next, although the Sunday schools had a limited existence, they were important to the evolution of the American educational system in that they expanded educational opportunity to many children and focused attention on education. In many communities Sunday schools not only served as the precursor of the common school but also, according to historian Ann Boylan (1988), rivaled the common school in importance.

Infant Schools

The last of the major educational innovations introduced in the early republic was the *infant school*. The infant school was established in England in 1816 by Robert Owen to provide for the children of mothers working in his factory. Within a decade the concept had crossed the Atlantic. In 1827 infant schools were opened in New York and Philadelphia and later in other eastern cities. The infant schools were taught by women and were designed for poor children ages 2 to 7. They were intended to provide basic literacy and moral training to those who, because they would go to work in a factory at a very early age, probably would not receive any other schooling. Like the Sunday school, the infant school was a product of the charity school movement and reflected the sentiment that education, especially moral education, was necessary to mitigate against the potentially antisocial effects of poverty.

Primary schools designed along this model did not survive. In fact, by 1840 infant schools had basically vanished from the American educational scene. However, they were important in serving as another vehicle for drawing public attention to early childhood education, and more generally, to the need to support education. In the few cities where infant schools had been designed by those who advocated early childhood education for all children, poor or not, as preparatory to the elementary school, the infant schools survived and became part of the town school system. And, as discussed in chapter 6, in the 1850s the infant school was revived in the form of the kindergarten by the followers of Friedrich Froebel.

Town and District Schools: Organization and Instruction

The monitorial school, the Sunday school, and the infant school all played a role in bringing an elementary education to the young people of the new nation, but it was the town and district schools, the so-called common schools, that continued to grow in number and enrollment throughout the early national period. This growth was in large part a result of the rapid growth in the population, especially the population of urban centers. Between 1790 and 1830 the population more than tripled, from 3.9 million to 12.9 million (see Table 5.1). In 1790 no city in the United States had a population of 50,000, but by 1830 seven cities had populations of more than 50,000. The growth of the common schools also reflected the demands of the ever larger immigrant population that saw education as the vehicle for upward social and economic mobility as well as the demand for skilled workers to serve the growing industrial sector.

Also contributing to the increased enrollment of the common schools was the increased admission of females, especially in the rural areas and small towns. Enrollments were also encouraged by the decentralized district system of control whereby each community took responsibility for the provision of education. The district system received legal status in several of the former colonies in the late 18th century (e.g., Connecticut in 1760, Vermont in 1782, Massachusetts in 1789, and Rhode Island in 1799) and moved west with the passage of the Northwest Ordinance. The district system meant that schools were located closer to pupils' homes, and therefore were more convenient to attend. Also, because they were "local schools," people were more willing to pay taxes for their support.

The enrollment and curriculum of the district schools varied greatly. Although the urban schools of the period are thought of as having large classes and being overcrowded, it was also not unusual in the winter months for 60 or 70 students to be shut up in a one-room rural school barely large enough for 30. Because there was no

"HER EYES ARE LIKE AN AMETHYST,
HER FINGERS DOVE-TAILED, LIPS APART."

District schools enrolled male and female children of all ages.

For Your Reflection and Analysis

Had you been a teacher in a rural school during this time which pedagogical challenge would you have found most difficult? Why?

standard age for beginning school, it was also not unusual in rural areas, more so than in urban areas, for children to begin attending school as early as 3 years old. The range in age of the students added to the challenges facing the rural school teacher.

Another pedagogical challenge to district school teachers was that children often studied from the texts their families supplied them. According to one historian, in some Wisconsin schools there were sometimes as many different textbooks in use as there were children (Kaestle, 1983).

The pedagogical challenges combined with the low pay did not attract or keep the most qualified persons in the ranks of the rural teacher or keep them in the job for very long. The New England district school described in the Primary Source Reading for this chapter had at least 37 different teachers in 30 years. Rural schoolmasters of the period are most often discussed using terms such as *ignorant* or *transient*. Typically, because of the low wages, teachers worked at another job to make ends meet. In rural areas little more than reading, spelling, writing, and basic arithmetic might be taught. And, given the tie between the school and the community in rural areas, the teacher often taught in a foreign language if it was the dominant language in the community (e.g., German in parts of Pennsylvania) or emphasized the religious principles or practices dominant in the community.

In some cases the public Latin grammar schools often functioned as *de facto*, common schools. As previously noted, a smaller town might insist that the schoolmaster teach English as well as Latin and offer Latin only to boys whose parents specifically requested it (Herbst, 1996). As a result, in towns with only a few Latin pupils, the schoolmaster would spend most of his time teaching reading and writing to children of all ages, and often to both sexes.

Growth of the Academy

By the outbreak of the Revolutionary War, the Latin grammar school tradition had virtually collapsed. Towns refused to support the Latin grammar schools, and the courts, in turn, refused to enforce the law requiring this support. At the same time, the academy movement continued to grow.

Although today the term *academy* brings to mind an exclusive private institution with a college preparatory curriculum, or perhaps providing military training, in the late 18th and early 19th centuries the term was more broadly applied. Some academies were indeed prestigious and exclusive. Others were nothing more than log cabins. Stimulated by the founding of the United States Military Academy at West Point in 1802 and the Naval Academy at Annapolis in 1848, many were indeed established as military schools. Admission to some academies was open to all comers; others catered to special clients. Some were boarding schools; some were day schools. Some were teacher owned, others were organized by groups of parents or individuals, and yet others were organized by denominations or philanthropic individuals or groups.

The establishment of academies was encouraged in many states by the public support given them, sometimes by grants of land and sometimes by grants of state funds. For example, Georgia and Tennessee developed an academy plan for counties that involved grants of land and public funds. In part because of this support, by 1831 over 100 academies had been established in Georgia (Kraushaar, 1976).

The curriculum of the academy usually depended, at least in part, on the students enrolled: Some students' preparation was seriously lacking and therefore needed remediation, and adjustments had to be made for other students whose attendance alternated seasonally between the farm and the academy. The better academies were on par with the colleges, whereas the poorer ones offered little more than the common schools (Kraushaar, 1976). In the larger academies, a classical department offered a curriculum of Latin and Greek and an English department offered English grammar, geography, arithmetic, and other studies deemed "practical" or in demand. (See, for example, the 1818 curriculum for the Phillips Exeter Academy in Figure 4.2.)

The academy also played an important role in the introduction of pedagogy and other courses in teacher education. In fact, what is credited with being the first normal school in the United States was incorporated as the Concord Academy in 1822. Later, when the public high school replaced the academy as the primary provider of secondary education, many academies experienced a rebirth as normal schools and for several decades were the main providers of teachers for the common schools (Kraushaar, 1976).

By the mid-19th century more than 6,000 academies were operating in every state and territory in the United States, enrolling 263,000 students. The academy is considered by most education historians as the forerunner of the American high school. Its broad range of curricular offerings responded to the demands of the growing middle class and demonstrated that there was an important place in the educational system for a secondary educational institution for non-college-bound as well as college-bound youth. The broadened curriculum of the academy, combined with its more liberal entrance requirements, allowed the entrance of people of various religious and social backgrounds and was a major step in the democratization of American secondary education (Rippa, 1984).

Academies for Women

Girls first began attending academies by attending the traditionally all-male academies. A number of the male academies admitted girls as a way to fill up the school. However, girls typically were taught in a separate room or even a separate building, during different hours, or during the summer. Soon, however, a number of female-only academies were established. Unlike the private venture schools, which tended to be located only in larger towns, many of the female academies were located in small towns and took boarders from all over the country. Also, unlike the private venture schools, many of which tended to have somewhat of a tenuous existence, many of the academies "were able to develop an established base, acquiring permanent buildings, hiring more staff relative to the number of students, and relying on financial support from their communities. With their more permanent standing, the academies were able to develop their curricula more fully and offer more to students" (Campbell, 2000, p. 16).

CLASSICAL DEPARTMENT

First Year: Adam's Latin Grammar; Liber Primus, or a similar work; Viri Romani, or Caesar's Commentaries; Latin Prosody; Exercises in reading and making Latin; Ancient and Modern Geography; Virgil; Arithmetic.

Second Year: Virgil; Arithmetic; Exercises in reading and making Latin, continued; Valpey's Greek Grammar; Roman History; Cicero's Select Orations; Delectus; Dalzel's Collectanea Graeca Minora; Greek Testament; English Grammar and Declamation.

Third Year: The same Latin and Greek authors, in revision; English Grammar and Declamation, continued; Sallust; Algebra; Exercises in Latin and English translations, and Composition.

Fourth Year: Collectanea Graeca Majora; Q. Horatius Flaccus; Titus Livius; Parts of Terence's Comedies; Excerpta Latina, or such Latin and Greek authors as may best comport with the student's future destination; Algebra; Geometry; Elements of Ancient History; Adam's Roman Antiquities.

ENGLISH DEPARTMENT

[For admission into this Department the candidate must be at least 12 years of age, and must have been well instructed in Reading and Spelling; familiarly acquainted with Arithmetic, through simple Proportion with the exception of Fractions, know Murray's English Grammar through Syntax, and must be able to parse simple English sentences.]

First Year: English Grammar, including exercises in Reading, Parsing, and Analyzing, in the correction of bad English; Punctuation and Prosody; Arithmetic; Geography; and Algebra, through Simple Equations.

Second Year: English Grammar, continued; Geometry; Plane Trigonometry, and its application to heights and distances; Mensuration of Sup. and Sol.; Elements of Ancient History; Logic; Rhetoric; English Composition; Declamation, and exercises of the Forensic kind.

Third Year: Surveying; Navigation; Elements of Chemistry and Natural Philosophy, with experiments; Elements of Modern History, particularly of the United States; Moral and Political Philosophy; English Composition, Forensics, and Declamation.

FIGURE 4.2   Phillips Exeter Academy Curriculum, 1818
Source: Bell, cited in Cubberley, E. P. (1934). *Readings in public education in the United States* (pp 223–224). New York: Houghton Miffflin.

Some female academies were called seminaries and were important in the training of female teachers, teaching being about the only profession open to women at the time. In 1821 the Troy Female Seminary in New York was opened by Emma Willard, a lifelong activist for women's rights. Opposed to the ornamental curriculum common to the female academies of the period, Willard proposed a curriculum that

For Your Reflection and Analysis

How did Willard's proposal for an academy compare with Franklin's?

was "solid and useful." The proposed curriculum is included in a Primary Source Reading for this chapter.

Mount Holyoke Female Seminary, founded in 1837 by Mary Lyon, also provided a demanding curriculum, one that included courses in philosophy, mathematics, and science comparable to those offered at Amherst, and used the same texts. To be admitted to Mount Holyoke, as at many of the leading seminaries, students had to demonstrate mastery of not only the basics, but also Latin. Mount Holyoke, like Troy, was oriented to the training of teachers. Its success is indicated by the fact that more than 70% of the alumnae from the first 40 years taught at one time.

Catherine Beecher, the sister of Harriet Beecher Stowe, the noted abolitionist and author of *Uncle Tom's Cabin*, founded the Hartford (Connecticut) Female Seminary in 1828. The institution was immediately successful and outgrew its quarters twice within the first 3 years (Marr, 1959). Beecher designed and offered the first system of calisthenics for women. Moving west, in 1832 she founded the Western Institute for Women in Cincinnati and was instrumental in the founding of female seminaries in Iowa, Illinois, and Wisconsin. While championing the intellectual abilities of women, Beecher did not totally reject the doctrine of the cult of domesticity (discussed later) and believed that homemaking was the true profession of women. The role of education was to prepare women for their roles and responsibilities in the family as homemaker and in the public as teacher. Beecher also advanced a plan for a nationwide system of teacher training schools and worked vigorously to extend education to the West.

Following the path forged by the female seminaries in New England, seminaries sprang up in other regions of the country, especially in the South. In the West, Catholic female schools, the convent academies, began appearing in relatively larger numbers. In fact, the swift response of the sisterhoods to the demand for girls' schools made them pioneers in female education in many western states (Oates, 1994). In 1829 Nazareth Academy, near Bardstown, Kentucky, and neighboring Loretto Academy became the first female academies to receive charters in that state. Similarly, the Sinsinawa Female Academy in Wisconsin, opened in 1847 by Dominican Sisters, was the first private girls' school in the former Northwest Territory to receive a state charter. St. Joseph's Academy, opened in St. Paul, Minnesota Territory, in 1851 by the Sisters of St. Joseph, became the first girls' school in the state of Minnesota (Oates, 1994).

Initially these schools were much like many of the female academies of the era and offered curricula designed to prepare females for their domestic roles as wives and mothers. However, the criticisms of convent schools by education reformers such as Catherine Beecher, Emma Willard, and Mary Lyon encouraged the sisterhoods to strengthen the curricula and make sure their teachers were well educated (Oates, 1994). As a result of their reputation for having a well-prepared and dedicated staff and providing a safe and happy environment for young females, the Catholic female academies were popular with middle- and upper-class parents of all denominations. In fact, Protestant girls made up the majority of the academies' enrollments (Oates, 1994).

Although the female academies did expand the educational opportunities afforded females in the early republic, they also presented at least three fundamental

For Your Reflection and Analysis

Catholic high schools continue to be popular with non-Catholic students. To what do you attribute their success?

problems with respect to female education. First, because most of the academies were private, attendance was limited to those who could afford the tuition, namely middle- and upper-class families. Second, the academies perpetuated the bias against educating girls and boys together. And, third, with notable exceptions, the curriculum offered females, both in the female and coeducational academies, was typically more limited than that offered males (Tozer, Violas, & Senese, 2002).

After the Civil War, female academies and seminaries began to lose ground to the growing number of women's colleges. Competition also came from traditionally all-male colleges and universities as they began to admit women. Some, such as Mount Holyoke, were able to become respected colleges. Others were incorporated into other institutions of higher education, whereas still others became high schools. Most simply closed, but not before collectively playing a major role in expanding educational opportunity beyond elementary school for females.

Emergence of the Public High School

Public *secondary schools* offering education beyond the elementary school did not become a firmly established part of the American educational scene until the last quarter of the 19th century. However, the beginnings of the movement occurred well before the Civil War. Boston inaugurated the high school movement in 1821 with the opening of the English Classical School for Boys, renamed the Boston English High School in 1824. In calling for community support, the Boston school committee made it clear that they wished to provide an alternative to the Latin grammar school and to provide locally "an education that shall fit him [the child] for active life, and shall serve as a foundation for eminence in his profession, whether Mercantile or Mechanical" (Binder, 1974, p. 107). Such an education could otherwise be obtained only by sending the child to a private academy.

The English High School became an instant success. As will be discussed in chapter 5, other towns soon followed this example. The success of the high school for boys encouraged school reformers to attempt to convince taxpayers and city officials that a high school for girls would be equally beneficial. They made the case that the city would benefit if girls received further education for their roles as wives and mothers. In addition, they argued, "before marriage and motherhood or as widows and spinsters, women, young and old, could aid the city as teachers in the common schools" (Herbst, 1996, p. 44). Their arguments were persuasive, and in 1826 the city opened a high school for girls.

Like the boys' school, the girls' school was an immediate success. In fact, too successful, according to Mayor Quincy:

"From the known circumstances of females, between the age of eleven and sixteen," complained Mayor Quincy, "there is no reason for believing that any one, once admitted to the school, would voluntarily quit it for the whole three years; unless, indeed, in the case of marriage." As Quincy saw it, sending girls to high school was not cost-efficient. Girls were neither trade- nor profession-minded and, unlike boys, rarely obtained employment or other opportunities before they graduated from school. Thus their stay in school, argued the mayor, was but a waste of the taxpayers' money. (Herbst, 1996, p. 44)

Despite the success of the girls' high school, city officials apparently agreed with the mayor, and the school was closed after only 3 years of operation. It would be a quarter of a century before a public secondary education was made available to the girls of Boston. However, other public high schools for girls opened in towns such as Worester (1824); New York City (1826); East Hartford, Connecticut (1828); and Buffalo, New York (1828) and did remain open.

 For Your Reflection and Analysis

What, if any, are the advantages of single-sex secondary schools?

In 1827, largely through the efforts of James G. Carter, Massachusetts passed the first law in the United States to require the establishment of public high schools. The law read, in part:

> Be it enacted, That each town or district within this Commonwealth, containing fifty families, or householders, shall be provided with a teacher or teachers, of good morals, to instruct children in orthography, reading, writing, English grammar, geography, arithmetic, and good behavior, for such terms of time as shall be equivalent to six months for one school in each year . . . one hundred families, or householders . . . equivalent to eighteen months . . . five hundred families, or householders . . . twenty-four months . . . shall also be provided with a master of good morals, competent to instruct, in addition to the branches of learning aforesaid, in the history of the United States, bookkeeping by single entry, geometry, surveying, algebra; and shall employ such a master . . . at least ten months in each year . . . and in every city, or town, and district containing four thousand inhabitants, such master shall be competent in addition to all foregoing branches, to instruct the Latin and Greek languages, history, rhetoric, and logic.

Like the earlier Massachusetts Law of 1647, initially this law was not rigidly enforced, and the number of high schools in the state grew slowly. In fact, 10 years after its passage fewer than 20 high schools had been established in Massachusetts. In one sense the law was ahead of its time. In a period when the majority of the population had not completed an elementary education there was limited popular demand for the high school. As will be discussed in chapter 6, it was not until after the Civil War that various political, social, and economic factors converged to create this demand.

Developments in Higher Education in the Early National Period

In the period following the Revolutionary War, the same nationalistic, democratic spirit that gave rise to the common school also produced an increase in public institutions of higher education. The first state institutions of higher education were established in the South: the University of Georgia in 1785, the University of North

Carolina in 1789, the University of Tennessee in 1794, and the University of South Carolina in 1801. In the second quarter of the 19th century the movement spread to the Midwest: Indiana University in 1820, the University of Michigan in 1837, and the University of Wisconsin in 1848.

The increase in the number of public institutions was a result of not only the fact that in most states the policies governing the granting of college charters were very liberal, but also of the fact that as people moved westward they wanted colleges close at hand. Another factor contributing to their growth, as mentioned in chapter 3, was the fact that many denominations chose to establish their own colleges rather than have their members educated at colleges operated by other denominations. The result, according to some historians, was that the progress of colleges in moving away from serving narrow sectarian interests that had been achieved in the last decades of the 18th century was reversed (Hofstadter, 1955).

A large number of the private institutions did not survive, primarily because of insufficient funding. By and large those that did survive, indeed even the established private and public colleges, were very small. For example, Harvard did not have a graduating class of 100 until after the Civil War. In both public and private institutions lecture and recitation remained the most common modes of instruction, and discipline remained strict. And, although the curriculum of public institutions gave more emphasis to the sciences and modern languages than the curriculum of the denominational institutions, over growing objection, the classical curriculum remained dominant in both public and private institutions of higher education in the early national period.

Defense of the Classical Curriculum: The Yale Report of 1828

As had already happened at the secondary level, the 19th century brought increasing pressures on colleges to make the curriculum more relevant to commerce, industry, and agriculture. The classical curriculum, its critics charged, was useless to a generation that was to subdue mountains, dig canals, construct turnpikes and railroads, throw bridges across rivers, and turn woods and plains into granaries and pastures. Moreover, the critics complained, the colleges were unwilling to admit the sons and daughters of farmers and workingmen; rather, all they did was to promote the snobbishness of the upper class (Herbst, 1996).

In response to such charges, and in response to a request of Judge Noyes Darling, one of Yale's own alumni and a member of the college corporation, the faculty of Yale prepared what came to be called the Yale Report of 1828. In the report the Yale scholars defended the study of the classics on the basis that they provided the foundation of the literatures of every Western nation, their study helped develop mental discipline and proper character, their study provided the best preparation for professional study, and to abandon their study would devalue a college degree. They also, in effect, rejected specialization in the curriculum and advocated a broad, general education.

The Yale Report was a major contributor to the debate that waged about the appropriate

 For Your Reflection and Analysis

What required subjects in the curriculum of colleges and universities of today, if removed, would devalue the degree?

curriculum for the colleges and universities of the new nation. It also provided the rationale for the continuation and inclusion of the liberal arts or "college prep" curriculum in the secondary schools of the growing industrialized nation.

Dartmouth College Case

In 1816 the New Hampshire legislature, dominated by the more liberal Jeffersonian Republicans, and concerned by what appeared to be the antiliberal sentiments of the board of trustees of Dartmouth College, enacted legislation to convert Dartmouth College from a private to a state institution. The college had been established in 1769 under the authority of a royal charter from King George of England. The legislature based its legal claim for doing so on the fact that the majority of the funds for the operation of the college were public funds.

In the Dartmouth College case (*Trustees of Dartmouth College v. Woodward*, 1819), the U.S. Supreme Court upheld the original contract from the king of England that had given private status to the college. The case was important not only in affirming the constitutional principle that the state could not impair contracts, but in providing a foundation for the system of private colleges secure from government control that we have today.

Education of Women in the New Republic: The Cult of Domesticity

As discussed, the early national period was one of uncertainty and concern about what was necessary to maintain the stability of the republican form of government that had been established. The lessons from classical history suggested that the health and welfare of republics depended on their ability to maintain virtue and discipline. Because the new republic had no standing army and had rejected the establishment of religion, the family assumed a significant political role because it was the only social unit that could provide both moral training and discipline for the young (Conway, 1978). At the same time that the family unit was seen as having this critical role, the growing and changing market economy led many men to work outside of the home. As a result, a new division of labor between the sexes developed: Men were to have economic (and political) responsibility, and women were to have the primary responsibility for managing the home and educating the young. With this responsibility came the responsibility to serve as moral guardians for the young (Conway, 1978).

The role of guardian of society's moral standards was critically important to the new republic, but it clearly placed women in a position of servitude, which apparently did not trouble the republican males who had espoused that all men were created equal. It also apparently did not cause any consternation among the first generation of women educators born in the new republic: Both Emma Willard and Catherine Beecher celebrated the new calling that republican culture had created for the patriotic woman teacher (Conway, 1978). Similarly, numerous articles appearing in such education reform journals as the *Common School Journal* and the *American Journal of Education* supported the model of the educated woman based on the importance of her role as wife and mother (Woody, 1929).

The "cult of domesticity," as this understanding of the female role has been come to be known, became a way of pacifying women with a doctrine of "separate but equal": Women were said to be equally as important as men, but separate and different (Zinn, 1980). The ideology of the cult of domesticity was reinforced by 19th-century "scientific" observations of male and female differences, which led to the conclusion that females were both physically and mentally inferior to men. Included among these observations were that women were generally physically smaller than men, women menstruated and therefore were believed physically incapacitated every month, and women had smaller brains than men (scientists measured cranial capacity and brain weight and correlated these with intelligence) ("The Cult of Domesticity and True Womanhood," n.d.).

For Your Reflection and Analysis

What scientific evidence regarding gender differences exists today?

The more positive side of the cult of domesticity was that it created a need for women, who were to be the early childhood educators and guardians of society's morals, to become more educated. As a result, most schools, especially those in New England, began admitting girls, if only before or after the regular program. As a consequence, from 1780 to 1840 women's literacy doubled. As elementary education became more universal, advocates of women's education directed their efforts to securing equality of educational opportunity for women at the secondary level.

Another positive result of delegating to women the responsibility for educating the young was that it opened wide the door for women to become teachers of the young of both sexes. Now it was argued that women were naturally suited to be teachers and that because the law, medicine, religion, and politics were exclusively (and rightfully) men's professions, teaching was a women's profession.

Conclusion

Despite the fact that neither the Articles of Confederation nor the U.S. Constitution mentioned education, the Founding Fathers recognized that education was central to the prosperity of the new nation. This Enlightenment view of the role of education in securing the national welfare has been the driving force behind many of the efforts to reform education that have had major impacts on its direction. In the last century this has been visible in the curriculum reforms that followed the launching of Sputnik in 1957 (see chapter 8), the reform movement that followed the release of *A Nation at Risk* in 1983 (see chapter 10), and the passage of the No Child Left Behind Act in 2001 (see chapter 11).

At times the republican founders' goals of promoting freedom, maintaining order, and promoting nationalism seemed in conflict, as they often have in American history. So too, Rush's desire to convert men into "republican machines" stands in stark contrast to notions of individual freedom. Similarly in contrast is the fact that Jefferson argued for human equality while owning slaves and accepting women's inferior social, political, and educational status. However, when placed against the backdrop of the early 19th century and in the context of the uncertain process of nation building, the ideology of the republican theorists seems perhaps more liberal.

Although the leaders of the new republic never doubted that an expanded education system would benefit the nation and its people, most were not so egalitarian as to propose that this meant *all* the people. The monitorial schools, Sunday schools, and infant schools did extend education to the children of the poor (and also served what was perceived as another important goal of providing the moral training that would deter the student from a life of crime and immorality), but their impact was marginal in terms of the number of students served. A large portion of the children from the lower classes received little, if any, education. Native Americans and African Americans were for all intents and purposes excluded from the schools. And, despite increased access, girls had limited opportunities for anything beyond an elementary education. Even the education made available in the new female academies reflected what was later made even more patently clear with regard to the education of minorities—that separate was rarely equal.

However, although the American education system in the early national period was far from meeting any of the descriptors with which it is currently referenced— "free," "public," or "universal"—it did support the growth of what was to be the core of the system, the common school. Already the new nation was feeling the effects of a growing population, urbanization, and industrial development. In a pattern that was to be repeated for more than a century, immigration and industrialization brought a demand for education for citizenship and for work. As the nation prospered, it developed the need and capacity to support an expanded education system. The push to achieve this system, the common school movement, is the topic of the next chapter.

For Discussion and Application

1. In what ways were Thomas Jefferson's plans for an educational system elitist? Egalitarian?
2. What might Benjamin Rush have considered the ideal "republican machine"?
3. What are the dangers of thinking that education can play a major role in promoting and maintaining discipline in society?
4. Consider the monitorial schools, Sunday schools, and infant schools. What contributed to their ultimate success or failure in becoming a part of the American education system?
5. Do you believe the schools should teach moral values? If so, who should determine what values to teach?
6. The ideology of the cult of domesticity was reinforced by so-called "scientific" observations of sex differences. Choose one of the observations regarding sex differences and refute the observation with current scientific evidence.

Primary Source Reading

Writing in 1831, an anonymous New England teacher described the schoolhouse he attended as a boy, his instructors, and the instruction. He also described some of the changes he observed that had taken place over the last 30 years. Girls were apparently allowed to attend the school, and he did not distinguish how their instruction differed from that of the boys. He did, however, note the extreme difference in pay between male and female teachers.

A New England District School, circa 1801

School House and General Arrangements

The school house stood near the centre of the district, at the junction of four roads, so near the usual track of carriages, that a large stone was set up at the end of the building to defend it from injury. Except in the dry season the ground is wet, permitting small collections of water on the surface, and the soil by no means firm. The spot is peculiarly exposed to the bleak winds of winter; nor are there at present any shade trees near, to shelter the children from the scorching rays of the summer's sun during their recreations. There were a few formerly; but they were cut down many years ago. Neither, is there any such thing as an outhouse of *any kind*, not even a wood shed.

The size of the building was twenty two feet long, by twenty broad. From the floor to the ceiling, it was seven feet. The chimney and entry took up about four feet at one end, leaving the school room itself, twenty feet by eighteen.

Source: History of a common school, from 1801 to 1831. (October 1831). *American Annals of Education*, pp. 468–472.

Around three sides of the room, were connected desks, arranged so that when the pupils were sitting at them, their faces were towards the instructor and their backs towards the wall. Attached to the sides of the desks nearest to the instructor, were benches for small pupils. The instructor's desk and chair occupied the centre. On this desk were stationed a rod or ferule; sometimes both. These, with books, writings, inkstands, rules, and plummets, with a fire shovel, and a pair of tongs (often broken), were the principal furniture.

The windows were five in number, of twelve panes each. They were situated so low in the walls, as to give full opportunity to the pupils, to see every traveller as he passed, and to be easily broken. The places of the broken panes, were usually supplied with hats, during the school hours. The entry was four feet square. A depression in the chimney on one side of the entry, furnished a place of deposit for about half of the hats, and spare clothes of the boys; and the rest were left on the floor, often to be trampled upon. The girls generally carried their bonnets, etc. into the school room. The floor and ceiling were level, and the walls were plastered.

The room was warmed by a large and deep fire place. So large was it, and so little efficacious in warming the room otherwise, that I have seen about *one eighth of a cord of good wood*, burning in it at a time. In severe weather, it was estimated that the amount usually consumed, was not far from a cord, or one hundred and twenty eight feet, a week.

The new building erected about five years since, has many improvements upon the former. It is of brick; the room is larger and higher; it is better lighted, and has an improved fire place. The writing desks for the pupils are attached to the walls, and the seats for the smaller pupils have backs. Besides, the local situation of the house is changed. It stands two or three rods from the road side, on a firm soil; but there are no shade trees near, nor any out houses. Like the former house, it has a cold bleak situation in winter. With regard to an entry, however, there now is none. The whole building forms but one room.

The school was not unfrequently broken up for a day or two for want of wood in former years; but since they have used a smaller fire place, this occurrence has been more rare. The instructor or pupils were, however, sometimes compelled to cut or saw it, to prevent the closing of the school. The wood was left in the road near the house, so that it was often buried in the snow or wet with the rain. At the best, it was usually burnt green. The fires were to be kindled, about half an hour before the time of beginning the school. Often, the scholar, whose lot it was, neglected to built it. In consequence of this, the house was frequently cold and uncomfortable about half the forenoon, when the fire being very large, the excess of heat became equally distressing. Frequently too, we were annoyed by smoke. The greatest amount of suffering, however, arose from excessive heat, particularly at the close of the day. The pupils being in a free perspiration when they retired, were very liable to take cold.

The ventilation of the school room, was as much neglected as its temperature; and its cleanliness, more perhaps than either. Situated as the house was, the latter might seem to be in a measure unavoidable. There were, however, no arrangements made for cleaning feet at the door, or for washing floors, windows, etc. In the summer the floor was washed, perhaps once in two or three weeks.

The winter school has usually been opened about the first of December, and continued from twelve to sixteen weeks. The summer school is commenced about the first of May. Formerly this was also continued about three or four months; but within ten years the term has been lengthened usually to twenty weeks. Males have been uniformly employed in winter, and females in summer.

The instructors have usually been changed every season, but sometimes they have been continued two successive summers or winters. A strong prejudice has always existed against em-ploying the same instructor more than once or twice in the same district. This prejudice has yielded in one instance, so far that an instructor who had taught two successive winters, twenty five years before, was employed another season. I have not been able to ascertain the exact number of different instructors who have been engaged in the school during the last thirty years; but I can distinctly recollect *thirtyseven*. Many of them, both males and females, were from sixteen to eighteen years of age, and a few, over twentyone.

Good moral character, and a thorough knowledge of the common branches, were formerly considered as indispensable qualifications in an instructor. The instructors were chiefly selected from the most respectable families in town. But for fifteen or twenty years, these things have not been so much regarded. They have indeed been deemed desirable; but the most common method now seems to be, to ascertain as near as possible the dividend for that season from the public treasury, and then, fix upon a teacher who will take charge of the school three to four months, for this money. He must indeed be able to obtain a license from the Board of Visitors; but this has become nearly a matter of course, provided he can spell, read, and write. In general, the candidate is some favorite or relative of the District Committee. It gives me great pleasure, however, to say that the *moral* character of almost every instructor, so far as I know, has been unexceptionable.

Instructors have usually boarded in the families of the pupils. Their compensation has varied from seven to eleven dollars a month for males; and from sixtytwo and a half cents to one dollar a week for females. Within the last ten years, however, the price of instruction has rarely been less than nine dollars in the former case, and seventy five cents in the latter. In the few instances in which the instructors have furnished their own board, the compensation has been about the same; it being supposed that they could work at some employment of their own, enough to pay their board, especially females. The only exceptions which I can recollect are two; both within five years. In one of these instances the instructor received twelve dollars, and in the other, eleven dollars and fifty cents a month.

It often happens that no family of the district is prepared to receive the instructor. In such cases it is expected he will repair to the house of the District Committee. Some, however, from delicacy, or other causes, choose to go to their own homes, when near, until a place is provided.

Two of the Board of Visitors usually visit the winter schools twice during the term. In the summer, their visits are often omitted. These visits usually occupy from one hour to an hour and a half. They are spent in merely hearing a few hurried lessons, and in making some remarks, general in their character. Formerly, it was customary to examine the pupils in some approved catechism; but this practice has been omitted for twenty years.

The parents seldom visit the school, except by special invitation. The greater number pay very little attention to it at all. There are, however, a few who are gradually awaking to the importance of good instruction; but there are also a few, who oppose every thing which is suggested, as at the least, useless; and are scarcely willing their children should be governed in the school.

The school books have been about the same for thirty years. Webster's Spelling Book, the American Preceptor, and the New Testament, have been the principal books used. Before the appearance of the American Preceptor, Dwight's Geography was used as a reading book. A few of the Introduction to the American Orator were introduced about twelve years since, and more recently, Jack Halyard.

Until within a few years, no studies have been permitted in the day school, but spelling, reading and writing. Arithmetic was taught by a few instructors, one or two evenings in a week. But in spite of a most determined opposition, arithmetic is now permitted in the day school, and a few pupils study geography.

Questions for Discussion

1. What were some of the changes that had taken place at the school in the 30 years since the writer left?
2. Describe the typical teacher, how teachers were selected, and their compensation.
3. Speculate on the reason for the "strong prejudice [that] has always existed against employing the same instructor more than once or twice in the same district."

Primary Source Reading

Emma Willard, the founder of the Troy Female Academy, delivered an address to the New York Legislature in 1819 proposing a plan for a state-supported seminary for females. In her address she outlined the problems with the present mode of female education, one that relied heavily on "private adventurers," detailed the principles that should guide the education of females, provided a plan for a female seminary with a detailed discussion of the proposed curriculum, and argued the benefits society would receive from such a seminary. The principles and benefits sections are excerpted here.

A Plan for Improving Female Education

Emma Willard

The object of this Address, is to convince the public, that a reform, with respect to female education, is necessary; that it cannot be effected by

Source: Willard, Emma. (1819). *An address to the public, particularly to the members of the legislature of New York, proposing a plan for improving female education,* 2nd Ed. Middlebury, VT: J. W. Copeland.

individual exertion, but that it requires the aid of the legislature: and further, by shewing the justice, the policy, and the magnanimity of such an undertaking, to persuade that body, to endow a seminary for females, as the commencement of such reformation. . . .

Of the Principles by Which Education Should be Regulated

To contemplate the principles which should regulate systems of instruction, and consider how little those principles have been regarded in educating our sex, will show the defects of female education in a still stronger point of light, and will also afford a standard, by which any plan for its improvement may be measured.

Education should seek to bring its subjects to the perfection of their moral, intellectual and physical nature: in order, that they may be of the greatest possible use to themselves and others: or, to use a different expression, that they may be the means of the greatest possible happiness of which they are capable, both as to what they enjoy, and what they communicate.

Those youth have the surest chance of enjoying and communicating happiness, who are best qualified, both by internal dispositions, and external habits, to perform with readiness, those duties, which their future life will most probably give them occasion to practice.

Studies and employments should, therefore, be selected, from one or both of the following considerations; either, because they are peculiarly fitted to improve the faculties; or, because they are such, as the pupil will most probably have occasion to practice in future life.

These are the principles, on which systems of male education are founded; but female education has not yet been systematized. Chance and confusion reign here. Not even is youth considered in our sex, as in the other, a season, which should be wholly devoted to improvement. Among families, so rich as to be entirely above

labour, the daughters are hurried through the routine of boarding school instruction, and at an early period introduced into the gay world; and, thenceforth, their only object is amusement. Mark the different treatment, which the sons of these families receive. While their sisters are gliding through the mazes of the midnight dance, they employ the lamp, to treasure up for future use the riches of ancient wisdom; or to gather strength and expansion of mind, in exploring the wonderful paths of philosophy. When the youth of the two sexes has been spent so differently, is it strange, or is nature in fault, if more mature age has brought such a difference of character, that our sex have been considered by the other, as the pampered, wayward babies of society, who must have some rattle put into our hands, to keep us from doing mischief to ourselves or others?

Another difference in the treatment of the sexes is made in our country, which, though not equally pernicious to society, is more pathetically unjust to our sex. How often have we seen a student, who, returning from his literary pursuits, finds a sister, who was his equal in acquirements, while their advantages were equal, of whom he is now ashamed. While his youth was devoted to study, and he was furnished with the means, she, without any object of improvement, drudged at home, to assist in the support of the father's family, and perhaps to contribute to her brother's subsistence abroad; and now, a being of a lower order, the rustic innocent wonders and weeps at his neglect. . . .

One of these is, that, without a regard to the different periods of life, proportionate to their importance, the education of females has been too exclusively directed, to fit them for displaying to advantage the charms of youth and beauty. Though it may be proper to adorn this period of life, yet, it is incomparably more important, to prepare for the serious duties of maturer years. Though well to decorate the blossom, it is far better to prepare for the harvest. . . .

Another error is that it has been made the first object in educating our sex, to prepare them to please the other. But reason and religion teach, that we too are primary existences; that it is for us to move, in the orbit of our duty, around the Holy Centre of perfection, the companions, not the satellites of men; else, instead of shedding around us an influence, that may help to keep them in their proper course, we must accompany them in their wildest deviations.

I would not be understood to insinuate, that we are not, in particular situations, to yield obedience to the other sex. Submission and obedience belong to every being in the universe, except the great Master of the whole. Nor is it a degrading peculiarity to our sex, to be under human authority. Whenever one class of human beings, derive from another the benefits of support and protection, they must pay its equivalent, obedience. Thus, while we receive these benefits from our parents, we are all, without distinction of sex, under their authority: when we receive them from the government of our country, we must obey our rulers; and when our sex take the obligations of marriage, and receive protection and support from the other, it is reasonable, that we too should yield obedience. Yet is neither the child, nor the subject, nor the wife, under human authority, but in subservience to the divine. Our highest responsibility is to God, and our highest interest is to please him; therefore, to secure this interest, should our education be directed.

Neither would I be understood to mean, that our sex should not seek to make themselves agreeable to the other. The errour complained of, is that the taste of men, whatever it might happen to be, has been made a standard for the formation of the female character. In whatever we do, it is of the utmost importance, that the rule, by which we work, be perfect. For if otherwise, what is it, but to err upon principle? A system of education, which leads one class of human beings to consider the approbation of another, as their highest object, teaches, that the rule of their conduct should be the will of beings, imperfect and erring like themselves, rather than the will of God, which is the only standard of perfection.

Having now considered female education, both in theory and practice, and seen, that in its present state, it is in fact a thing "without form and void," the mind is naturally led to inquire after a remedy for the evils it has been contemplating. Can individuals furnish this remedy? It has heretofore been left to them, and we have seen the consequence. If education is a business, which might naturally prosper, if left to individual exertion, why have legislatures intermeddled with it at all? If it is not, why do they make their daughters illegitimates, and bestow all their cares upon their sons?

It is the duty of a government, to do all in its power to promote the present and future prosperity of the nation, over which it is placed. This prosperity will depend on the character of its citizens. The characters of these will be formed by their mothers; and it is through the mothers, that the government can control the characters of its future citizens, to form them such as will ensure their country's prosperity. If this is the case, then it is the duty of our present legislators to begin now, to form the characters of the next generation, by controling that of the females, who are to be their mothers, while it is yet with them a season of improvement.

But should the conclusion be almost admitted, that our sex too are the legitimate children of the legislature; and, that it is their duty to afford us a share of their paternal bounty; the phantom of a college-learned lady, would be ready to rise up, and destroy every good resolution, which the admission of this truth would naturally produce in our favour.

To shew that it is not a masculine education which is here recommended, and to afford a definite view of the manner in which a female institution might possess the respectability, permanency, and uniformity of operation of those appropriated to males; and yet differ from them, so as to be adapted to that difference of character and duties, to which the softer sex should be formed, is the object of the following imperfect . . . .

Benefits of Female Seminaries

Let us now proceed to inquire, what benefits would result from the establishment of female seminaries.

They would constitute a grade of public education, superior to any yet known in the history of our sex; and through them, the lower grades of female instruction might be controlled. The influence of public seminaries, over these, would operate in two ways; first, by requiring certain qualifications for entrance; and secondly, by furnishing instructresses, initiated in their modes of teaching, and imbued with their maxims.

Female seminaries might be expected to have important and happy effects, on common schools in general; and in the manner of operating on these, would probably place the business of teaching children, in hands now nearly useless to society; and take it from those, whose services the state wants in many other ways. . . . If then women were properly fitted by instruction, they would be likely to teach children better than the other sex; they could afford to do it cheaper; and those men who would otherwise be engaged in this employment, might be at liberty to add to the wealth of the nation, by any of those thousand occupations, from which women are necessarily debarred.

But the females, who taught children, would have been themselves instructed either immediately or indirectly by the seminaries. Hence through these, the government might exercise an intimate, and most beneficial control over common schools. Any one, who has turned his attention to this subject, must be aware, that there is great room for improvement in these, both as to the modes of teaching, and the things taught; and what method could be devised so likely to effect this improvement, as to prepare by instruction, a class of individuals, whose interest, leisure, and natural talents, would combine to make them pursue it with ardour. Such a class of individuals would be raised up, by female seminaries. And therefore they would be likely to

have highly important and happy effects on common schools . . . .

What is offered by the plan of female education, here proposed, which may teach, or preserve, among females of wealthy families, that purity of manners, which is allowed, to be so essential to national prosperity, and so necessary, to the existence of a republican government.

1. Females, by having their understandings cultivated, their reasoning powers developed and strengthened, may be expected to act more from the dictates of reason, and less from those of fashion and caprice.

2. With minds thus strengthened they would be taught systems of morality, enforced by the sanctions of religion; and they might be expected to acquire juster and more enlarged views of their duty, and stronger and higher motives to its performance.

3. This plan of education, offers all that can be done to preserve female youth from a contempt of useful labour. The pupils would become accustomed to it, in conjunction with the high objects of literature, and the elegant pursuits of the fine arts; and it is to be hoped, that both from habit and association, they might in future life, regard it as respectable.

To this it may be added, that if housewifery could be raised to a regular art, and taught upon philosophical principles, it would become a higher and more interesting occupation; and ladies of fortune, like wealthy agriculturalists, might find, that to regulate their business, was an agreeable employment.

4. The pupils might be expected to acquire a taste for moral and intellectual pleasures, which would buoy them above a passion for show and parade, and which would make them seek to gratify the natural love of superiority, by endeavouring to excel others in intrinsic merit, rather than in the ex-

trinsic frivolities of dress, furniture, and equipage.

5. By being enlightened in moral philosophy, and in that, which teaches the operations of the mind, females would be enabled to perceive the nature and extent, of that influence, which they possess over their children, and the obligation, which this lays them under, to watch the formation of their characters with unceasing vigilance, to become their instructors, to devise plans for their improvement, to weed out the vices from their minds and to implant and foster the virtues . . . .

Thus, laudable objects and employments, would be furnished for the great body of females, who are not kept by poverty from excesses. But among these, as among the other sex, will be found master spirits, who must have preeminence, at whatever price they acquire it. Domestic life cannot hold these, because they prefer to be infamous, rather than obscure. To leave such, without any virtuous road to eminence, is unsafe to community; for not unfrequently, are the secret springs of revolution, set in motion by their intrigues. Such aspiring minds, we will regulate, by education, we will remove obstructions to the course of literature, which has heretofore been their only honorable way to distinction; and we offer them a new object, worthy of their ambition; to govern, and improve the seminaries for their sex.

In calling on my patriotic countrymen, to effect so noble an object, the consideration of national glory, should not be overlooked. Ages have rolled away;—barbarians have trodden the weaker sex beneath their feet;—tyrants have robbed us of the present light of heaven, and fain would take its future. Nations, calling themselves polite, have made us the fancied idols of a ridiculous worship, and we have repaid them with ruin for their folly. But where is that wise and heroic country, which has considered, that our rights are sacred, though we cannot defend them? that tho' a weaker, we are an essential part of the body politic, whose corruption or improvement must affect the whole? and which, having thus considered, has sought to give us by education, that rank in the scale of being, to which our importance entitles us? History shows not that country. It shows many, whose legislatures have sought to improve their various vegetable productions, and their breeds of useful brutes; but none, whose public councils have made it an object of their deliberations, to improve the character of their women. Yet though history lifts not her finger to such a one, anticipation does. She points to a nation, which, having thrown off the shackles of authority and precedent, shrinks not from schemes of improvement, because other nations have never attempted them; but which, in its pride of independence, would rather lead than follow, in the march of human improvement: a nation, wise and magnanimous to plan, enterprising to undertake, and rich in resources to execute. Does not every American exult that this country is his own? And who knows how great and good a race of men, may yet arise from the forming hand of mothers, enlightened by the bounty of that beloved country,—to defend her liberties,—to plan her future improvement,— and to raise her to unparalleled glory?

Questions for Discussion

1. What does Willard give as the most compelling reasons for educating women?
2. Give examples of mistaken principles that hindered the education of women during Willard's time. To what extent are these mistaken principles in effect today?
3. Explain what Willard meant by the metaphor, "Though well to decorate the blossom, it is far better to prepare for the harvest." What

implications can be derived from this metaphor relative to the education of women?

4. Which of the following descriptors would best describe Emma Willard: (a) politically moderate activist committed to women's equity, (b) apolitical educator attempting to reform female education, (c) feminist committed to women's rights, or (d) seasoned and savvy educator who happens to be a female? Support your choice.

The Common School Movement

Be ashamed to die until you have won some victory for humanity.

—*Horace Mann, 1859*
Final address to the graduating
class of Antioch College

The period from 1830 to 1860 has been called the age of the common school movement in American education history. The movement was built on the vision of statewide school systems and the role of education espoused by the republican educational theorists discussed in chapter 4. Horace Mann, James G. Carter, Henry Barnard, Catherine Beecher, and other common school reformers shared the republican vision of a publicly supported and publicly controlled educational system that would promote nationalism, ensure social order, and prepare the educated citizens and skilled workforce needed for the increasing industrialized society. They disseminated their ideology via educational periodicals and educational organizations such as the American Lyceum.

The common school movement was made possible by a number of political, social, and economic factors that transformed not only education but also other institutions in the 19th century. Among the most important were the demands of a larger and more urban population, the extension of suffrage to the common man, the demands for skilled workers to serve the increasingly industrialized economy, and an increase in immigration, with larger numbers coming from countries whose languages and religions were neither English nor Protestant. Whereas many immigrants saw the schools as the vehicle for upward mobility, many other Americans saw the schools as instruments of assimilation.

One of the major goals of the common school movement was to increase state support for education. The movement had some success when the rate bill was abolished and state support from the revenue of public lands and taxation increased. Control followed with the creation of state boards and state superintendents of education and the evolution of local school boards and local superintendents vested with increased administrative responsibilities.

Another major goal of the common school movement was to bring some degree of standardization to textbooks and instruction and to improve teacher qualifications and training. The formal preparation of teachers began in the private seminaries and academies. The growth of the common schools and the push by common school reformers for better trained teachers led to the establishment of state-supported normal schools. Nonetheless, even into the 20th century the majority of teachers did not receive training at normal schools but at teacher institutes, which offered short courses in the theory and practice of teaching.

The common school movement was not without its opposition, primarily from defenders of local control, those opposed to or suspicious of increased governmental involvement in the schools, those opposed to increased taxation to support the schools, and sectarian interests. Although not rejecting the concept of or need for public schools, Catholics saw the Protestant-dominated public schools as a threat to their religious values. Following conflict and rejection of their requests for reform or exclusion from participation in Protestant religious practices, Catholics in many parishes chose to establish their own schools.

In this chapter the major forces and figures behind the common school movement are discussed. A brief summary is also given to the opposition to the common schools and the conflict between Catholics and Protestants over the Protestant sectarian nature of the common schools. Also examined are the evolution of state and local governmental structures that supported the common schools and the institutions that were established to train the teachers for the common schools.

Moving Forces

Changing Demographics: A Larger, More Diverse, and Urban Population

Between 1830 and 1860, 1,220,178 square miles of territory were added to the United States. During the same period the population exploded from 13 million to 31.5 million (see Table 5.1). Of these, 4 million were immigrants. Whereas before this time the majority of immigrants had come from Northern Europe and shared much the same language and cultural and religious backgrounds of the Americans, these new immigrants did not. Beginning in the 1830s and 1840s larger numbers came from Ireland, Germany, and Southern Europe; they were often Roman Catholic and often spoke a language other than English. Most settled in the larger cities of the Northeast and Midwest, providing the much needed labor for the growing industrial complex, but at the same time contributing to the problems facing growing urban areas.

As the United States was growing rapidly in size, it was also becoming increasingly urban. The new immigrants tended to settle in the cities, and more people moved from the farm to the city. Improved methods of agriculture made farming less labor intensive at the same time that employment opportunities were created by the growing number of factories. In 1820 only 12 cities in the then 23 states had populations of over 10,000; by 1860 the number of cities had increased to 101, and eight had populations of over 100,000 (Binder, 1974).

The growth in the cities was a result of the growth in industrialization. For example, in 1807 only 15 cotton mills were in operation in the United States; by 1831 there were 801 mills employing 70,000 workers (Rippa, 1984). Industrial growth was promoted by inventions such as the steam engine, which powered not only industrial equipment but also the boats and railroads that traversed the country moving people and materials in ever shorter times.

TABLE 5.1   Area and Population of the United States, 1790–1890

Year	Land Area (square miles)	Population
1790	864,746	3,929,214
1800	864,746	5,308,483
1810	1,681,824	7,239,881
1820	1,749,462	9,638,453
1830	1,749,462	12,865,020
1840	1,749,462	17,069,453
1850	2,940,042	23,191,876
1860	2,969,640	31,443,321
1870	2,969,640	39,818,449
1880	2,969,640	50,155,783
1890	2,969,640	62,947,714

Source: U.S. Bureau of the Census. (1975). *Historical statistics of the United States, colonial times to 1970* (p. 8). Washington, DC: U.S. Government Printing Office.

Demands of a Growing Working Class

The increasing urbanization of America resulted in concentrations of children who needed schooling and a more industrialized economy required a more literate and skilled workforce. The working class, who could not afford to educate their children at private expense, saw the common schools as avenues for upward social and economic mobility without the taint of pauperism associated with the charity schools.

The newly emerging workingmen's organizations were open in their support of tax-supported common schools. While rejoicing in their new political equality, they were concerned that the growing industrialization and concentration of wealth would restrict their economic opportunity and social mobility (Tyack, 1967). The common schools were seen as providing the education necessary for protection against abuses of the factory system and the tyranny of the upper class. Echoing the traditional republican position, the workingmen's organizations also argued that common schools were necessary to attain "those cardinal principles of republican liberty which were declared in '76 and which can only be sustained by the adoption of an ample system of public instruction, calculated to impart equality as well as mental culture." According to the workingmen of Pennsylvania's *Call for an Equal and Republican System of Mental Instruction*, their object was "to secure the benefits of education for those who would otherwise be destitute, and to place them mentally on a level with the most favored in the world's gifts. As poverty is not a crime, neither is wealth a virtue" (Tyack, 1967, p. 145). The demand for increased educational opportunity was a major call of the workingmen's political parties throughout the 1830s.

> *For Your Reflection and Analysis*
>
> *How do you interpret what was meant by the quote: "As poverty is not a crime, neither is wealth a virtue?"*

Social Control

Some of the strongest support for the common schools came from the dominant English-speaking, middle- and upper-class Protestants. They viewed the common schools as agencies of social control over the lower socioeconomic classes and as the best hope of "Americanizing" the children of the immigrants and socializing the multitudes to conform to the values and beliefs necessary to maintain the existing social order. According to Gutek (1986), social control in this context meant

> imposing by institutionalized education the language, beliefs, and values of the dominant group on outsiders, especially on the non-English speaking immigrants. Common schools were expected to create such conformity in American life by imposing the language and ideological outlook of the dominant group. For example, by using English as the medium of instruction, the common schools were expected to create an English-speaking citizenry; by cultivating a general value orientation based on Protestant Christianity, the schools were expected to create a general American ethic. (pp. 87–88)

Most social groups also saw the common schools as a means of controlling crime and social unrest. Knowledge was seen as the solution to intemperance: "In proportion as we elevate men in the scale of existence . . . so do we reclaim them from all temptation of degrading vice and ruinous crimes" (Binder, 1974, p. 32).

The Frontier Movement

Interest in education and the establishment of common schools was not limited to the industrialized regions of the East. As the frontier moved steadily westward, the one-room schoolhouse, often the only public building in a community, became the symbol of civilization and the center of efforts to keep literacy, citizenship, and civilization alive in the wilderness (Gutek, 1986). Contrary to what is often depicted, the frontier did not attract only the misfits and the uneducated. Many Harvard and Yale graduates, as well as common school graduates, followed the National Road, Cumberland Trail, Erie Canal, or other paths and waterways to the frontier and brought with them the desire to maintain education. One of the most visible examples was the so-called "coonskin library" founded by settlers of Athens County, Ohio, who trapped raccoons and sold the pelts to Boston merchants to buy books ("Ohio Mileposts—Feb. 2, 1804," 2003).

The spirit of the frontier movement itself also contributed to the common school movement. The frontier movement was fueled by people who valued the individual more than social class. Moreover, the frontier was a place where a practical education was more important than the ability to read or write Latin. In effect, the philosophy of the common school was consistent with, and supportive of, the values of the frontier.

Extended Suffrage

On the political front, the age of the common school coincided with the age of the common man. In the early years of the republic the right to vote in many states was limited to those who owned property. Gradually this began to change, and many states, especially those on the frontier, extended suffrage to all White males. In 1828, after the abolishment of the property requirement, Andrew Jackson became the first "common man" to be elected president. The result of the extension of suffrage was not only increased office-holding by the common man, but also his desire for the education necessary to exercise his political powers wisely. One way the common man exercised his political power was to pressure for direct taxation to support the common schools, which he saw as the vehicle for the upward mobility of his children.

Education Journals and Organizations

Two of the most important mechanisms for spreading the ideology of the common school were education periodicals and education organizations. Between 1825 and 1850 more than 60 education journals came into existence (Spring, 2001). Among the most important were the Massachusetts *Common School Journal* and the prestigious *American Journal of Education*. Although many of these journals did not survive, collectively they served both to popularize education and to keep teachers informed of educational innovations and ideas from both home and abroad.

Of the education organizations, the most noteworthy was the American Lyceum. The lyceum was a local association for "mutual instruction and information in the arts and sciences." The first lyceum in the United States was established in 1826 in Mill-bury, Massachusetts, by Josiah Holbrook, a Yale-educated Connecticut farmer and traveling lecturer on science and technology. Holbrook borrowed the concept from the mechanics institutes, a form of adult education used first in England to provide training to "mechanics," a term used at the time to include various artisans, trades-men, and industrial workers. Holbrook promoted his vision of a national system of lyceums through newspaper advertisements and articles, articles in education journals, and numerous public lectures. From its beginning in Massachusetts the concept spread throughout the East and Midwest (the then-frontier). The lyceum never really caught on in the South, however, because "southern aristocrats feared that education of poor whites and slaves would damage the economy . . . (and) the South lacked a large middle class, the main patronage of lyceums" (Fithian, 2000, p. 2).

In 1831 the hundreds of local lyceums united in a national organization, the American Lyceum. By 1839 there were 4,000 to 5,000 local lyceums in the United States providing adult education through concerts, demonstrations, vocational train-ing, debates, performances, and lectures on topics of current interest delivered by local as well as national speakers, including such persons as Ralph Waldo Emerson, Henry David Thoreau, Oliver Wendell Holmes, Dewitt Clinton, and Horace Greeley.

A Meeting at Cooper Union.

The lyceum provided adult education through lectures, demonstrations, con-certs, and performances.

Many of these speakers, Horace Mann among them, were in favor of school reform and in support of the common school.

The lyceum movement was a reflection of the Enlightenment principles of education for self-improvement and education for utility and played an important role in communicating new discoveries and inventions. It also reflected the republican belief in the role and potential of education to preserve democracy and right social ills.

The lyceum was an important provider of education at a time when many communities did not have a public school. Many lyceums created libraries. A few actually established schools, and most contributed directly to the public schools or indirectly by creating both a desire for knowledge and an acceptance of the need for public schools. The lyceum movement reached its peak in about 1840 and then slowly faded as the functions of lyceums was taken over by public libraries and public schools.

Protestant Religious Accommodation

Religious intolerance had been part of American life since the earliest colonial days. Roger Williams and Anne Hutchinson, the founders of Rhode Island, were banished from the Massachusetts Bay Colony because of their disagreement with Puritan practices. Historically, public support for the schools was rejected if the result would be support being given to another's religion. Common school reformers addressed the problem by proposing that the schools practice nondenominational Protestantism. Thus, as will be discussed later in this chapter, although Catholicism would be excluded, the schools would not be Protestant nonsectarian. They would promote republican virtues and Christian morality, but free of the doctrine and without the interpretation of any particular Protestant denomination (Kaestle, 1983). This accommodation was criticized in those parts of the country where sectarian bias was strong, but support for the common schools could not have been obtained without it.

Leading Proponents of the Common School

Horace Mann

If any one person were to be given the title father of American education, that person would be Horace Mann (1796–1859). Elected to the Massachusetts legislature in 1827, Mann soon became the spokesperson for the common school movement. He led a campaign to organize the schools in Massachusetts into a state system and to establish a state board of education.

Upon the creation of the Massachusetts state board of education in 1837, the first in the nation, Mann gave up his political career and a chance at the governorship to become the board's first secretary and the chief state school officer. He served in this position for 12 years and used it as a platform for proclaiming the ideology of the common school movement, as well as other social causes. In addition to his numerous lectures, writings, and editorship of the Massachusetts *Common School Journal*, each year Mann wrote a report to the legislature reciting current educational practices and conditions and making recommendations for improvement. These reports were distributed in other states and abroad, and were significant in influencing education legislation and practice throughout the country. In his final report Mann (1848) spelled out his vision of the common school:

> It knows no distinction of rich and poor, of bond and free, or between those who, in the imperfect light of this world are seeking through different avenues, to reach the gate of heaven. Without money and without price, it throws open its doors, and spreads the table of its bounty, for all the children of the state. Like the sun, it shines, not only upon the good, but upon the evil, that they may become good, and like the rain, its blessings descend, not only upon the just, but upon the unjust, that the unjust may depart from them and be known no more.

In his own state, Mann campaigned vigorously to increase public support for education and public awareness of the problems facing education in the form of dilapidated, unsanitary facilities and substandard materials, as well as the shortcomings of the local school committees. Mann was also critical of the status of the teaching profession. As a result of his efforts, state appropriations to education were doubled, 50 new secondary schools were built, textbooks and equipment were improved, teachers' salaries in Massachusetts were raised more than 50%, and the minimum length of the school year was extended to 6 months.

 For Your Reflection and Analysis

Who in contemporary America could be considered a champion of education? Name some of that person's activities.

Mann also fought to improve the professional training of teachers and established three normal schools (teacher training institutions), the first such state-supported schools in America. The first of these normal schools (taken from the French *école normale*) was established in 1839 at Lexington, Massachusetts. At its dedication, Mann (1839) proclaimed that without normal schools "Free Schools themselves would be shorn of their strength and their healing power and would at length become mere charity schools and thus die out in fact and in form."

Mann was also one of the first to recognize in a concrete fashion the contribution education makes to the economic growth of a nation as well as to the social and economic advancement of the individual. Although he did not advance his argument as far as the human capital theorists of the next century did, he did argue, in his Fifth Annual Report (1841) in particular, that an educated public would increase economic wealth and that it was therefore in the self-interest of business and industry to support education through taxation. Further arguments in favor of tax support of education because of its benefits to society are presented in the Twelfth Annual Report (1848).

In his Tenth Annual Report (1846) Mann asserted that education was the right of every child and that it was the state's responsibility to ensure that every child was provided an education. Although Mann himself did not promote compulsory attendance but regular attendance, this report was instrumental in the adoption by the Massachusetts legislature of the nation's first compulsory attendance law in 1852.

Like several other prominent educators of his time, Mann had visited the Prussian schools and observed the Pestalozzian methods. His Seventh Report (1843) gave a positive report of his observations. A humanitarian in all things (treatment of the mentally ill, abolition of slavery, etc.), he was particularly impressed with the love and rapport shared by the teachers and students involved in these schools. He also shared Pestalozzi's and Catherine Beecher's belief that women were the better teachers for the common schools.

Mann's belief that the common school would promote social harmony and ensure that the republic would be guided by an intelligent, moral citizenry was not original or unique; it was an echo of the arguments of Rush and the other republican thinkers. But at a time when the common school movement was spreading across the nation, when it came to defining its basic principles and articles of faith, he was unquestionably the chief spokesperson (Binder, 1974).

James G. Carter

James G. Carter (1795–1845) began his pioneering work in school reform in Massachusetts after his graduation from Harvard in 1820. Carter experienced life in a district school firsthand as a teacher while working his way through Groton Academy and Harvard College. In a series of newspaper articles beginning in 1821, two of which also appeared as pamphlets in 1824 and 1826, Carter attacked the deplorable conditions of the underfunded schools in the commonwealth. Carter warned:

> If the states continue to relieve themselves of the trouble of providing for the instruction of the whole people, and to shift the responsibility upon the towns, and the towns upon the districts, and the districts upon individuals, each will take care of himself and his own family as he is able, and as he appreciates the blessing of a good education . . . [with the result that] the institution which has been the glory of New England will, in twenty years more, be extinct.

Through Carter's efforts the Massachusetts Law of 1827, which required the establishment of tax-supported secondary schools, was passed. He was also instrumental in the 1834 passage of an act that increased public support by establishing a permanent school fund, the interest of which was to go to the maintenance of the common schools. In addition, as a member of the Massachusetts House of Representatives and chairman of its Committee on Education, Carter drafted the legislation that in 1837 created the Massachusetts state board of education. The board, on which Carter served, was given the authority to appoint a secretary who would serve as the chief state school officer. The board immediately chose Horace Mann.

Carter was dedicated to the improvement of teacher training and is often credited as being the father of the normal school. When the Massachusetts legislature rejected his plan to establish a state teacher training institution, he invested his own funds to establish one in Lancaster. Financial problems and the resistance of local residents contributed to its short life. Not

 For Your Reflection and Analysis

What recommendations would you propose to improve the training of today's teachers?

deterred, Carter was instrumental in founding the American Institute of Instruction, which played a major role in advancing the normal school movement.

Henry Barnard

Another major leader of the common school movement was Henry Barnard (1811–1900). Like Mann, he served in the state (Connecticut) legislature, worked to establish a state board of education, and then became the board's first secretary (1838–1842). He then served in a similar capacity in Rhode Island, as chancellor of the University of Wisconsin, and as president of St. John's College. In 1871 Barnard became the first U.S. Commissioner of Education.

Like Mann, Barnard saw education as the best means of promoting economic and social progress and good citizenship. Although his successes in Connecticut were more limited than those of Mann in Massachusetts, as secretary of the state board of education in Rhode Island he was instrumental in establishing a state system of free common schools and in significantly increasing public financial support for the schools in that state. He also urged better teacher preparation, the establishment of normal schools, and higher salaries for teachers.

Much of Barnard's influence on educational theory and practice came through his numerous lectures and writings, and more important, through his editorship (1855–1870) of the *American Journal of Education*, the only educational journal of national significance at the time. Barnard is also credited with initiating the teachers institute movement: He held the first institute in Connecticut in 1839. As discussed later in the chapter, the teachers institute was a meeting lasting from a few days to several weeks, at which teachers met to be instructed in new techniques and informed of the most modern material.

Barnard's greatest success lay in his democratic philosophy, "schools good enough for the best and cheap enough for the poorest," and his role as a disseminator of information about better schools. He is sometimes called the father of American school administration.

Catherine Beecher

Catherine Beecher (1800–1878), the previously mentioned founder of the Hartford Female Seminary and the Western Institute for Women, was a strong supporter of the common school and saw her task as focusing the attention of the nation on the need for a corps of female teachers to staff the common schools. She was especially active in campaigning for more schools and teachers for the frontier and in 1852 founded the American Women's Education Association to recruit and train teachers for the frontier schools. Beecher published numerous pamphlets and lectured nationwide promoting not only the common school but also a plan for a nationwide system of teacher training seminaries. Although the plan was not adopted, her efforts on behalf of the common school were a force in its acceptance, and her work on behalf of women pointed to a new American consensus concerning female roles (Cremin, 1982).

Opposition to the Common School Movement

Despite the well-reasoned arguments given in support of the common school movement (see, for example Thaddeus Stevens' speech before the Pennsylvania House of Representatives that serves as a Primary Source Reading for this chapter), the common school movement did not proceed without opposition. Like today, many people were opposed to increased taxation, for whatever purpose. Others, especially those with a sectarian or ethnic bias, opposed the idea of paying taxes to educate other people's children. Catholics, in particular, objected to paying taxes to support schools that were openly teaching Protestantism. Opposition also came from schools that served each of these groups, as well as owners of private schools.

Another faction of opposition came from those who were concerned about the loss of local control or those who were suspicious of state control. They argued, as do many today, that decisions about education should remain in the hands of those who are closest to the child and who are paying the most for the support of the schools.

The common school debate lasted for a number of years and was waged in state after state. Indeed, the full ideal of the common school reformers was not realized until the 20th century.

For Your Reflection and Analysis

Has the ideal of the common school reformers been realized? If not, in what ways has it fallen short?

Growth of State and Local Support and Supervision

Increased Tax Support

The idea of having universal common schools was one thing, but paying for them through direct taxation of the general public was another. With perhaps the exception of Connecticut, which had sold all of its land in the Western Reserve territory and set up a permanent school fund, the interest from which was distributed to localities (Kaestle, 1983), there was little ongoing state aid to education. Local or county property taxes, taxes levied on specific activities (e.g., liquor licenses or marriage fees), even lotteries provided partial support for the schools, but the remainder of the expenses was charged to the parents in the form of a *rate bill*. The rate bill was, in effect, a tuition fee based on the number of children attending school or the number of days the child attended. (See the copy of an 1825 rate bill in Figure 5.1.) Even though the fee might be small, poor parents often could not afford it, so their children either did not attend school or took turns attending. In some states, school districts were allowed to levy a school tax if the majority of the voters agreed. However, if the tax proceeds were insufficient to support the schools, the rate bill was used.

One of the major goals of the common school movement was to secure increased state support for the common schools. Beginning in the first quarter of the 19th century several states began to follow the example of Connecticut and provide aid to the schools from funds derived from the interest on a permanent school fund

County of Livingston, ss:

To the collector of school district No. 15 in the towns of York and Leicester in the County aforesaid greeting

In the name of the people of the state of New York you are hereby commanded and required to collect from each of the inhabitants of said district in the anexed tax list named the sum of money set opposite to his name in said list and within thirty days after receiving this warrant to pay the amount thereof collected by you (retaining your fees for collection) into the hands of the trustees of said district or some or one of them and take his or their receipt thereof and if any of the said inhabitants shall refuse or neglect to pay said sum after lawful demand thereof you are hereby further commanded to levy the same by distress and the sale of the goods and chattels of such delinquents together with the costs and charges of such distress and sale according to law

Given under our hands and seals this 21st day of september in the Year of our Lord one thousand eight hundred and twenty five

Job Holbrook }
Noah Cooley   } Trustees

List of taxes payable by the following persons freeholders and inhabitants of school district No. 15 in the towns of York and Leicester made by the trustees of said district on the 21st day of September in the year 1825 in conformity with the act for the support of common schools.

NAMES OF PERSONS	NUMBER OF DAYS	AMOUNT OF TAX
Amos Avery	15	$0.10 cts
Job Holbrook	83	0.56
Alanson Holbrook	138	0.93
Noah Richardson	164	1.11
Urias Story	172	1.16
Harry Wheelock	88	0.60
Noah Cooley	85½	0.58
Allen Hubbard	80	0.54
John Eastwood	108½	0.73
Sterling Case	257	1.74
Otis Hinkley	60½	0.41
Benjamin Clark	191	1.29
Banim Case	63	0.42
George Denmark	242½	1.64
whole number of days	1748	

11.81 the amount of tax
.56 collectors fee
11.25
4.75 public money
16.00 teachers wages

FIGURE 5.1 New York Rate Bill of 1825

Source: Cubberely, E P. (1934). *Readings in public education in the United States* (p. 185). New York: Houghton Mifflin.

For Your Reflection and Analysis

State support for education varies among the states, with states paying from 35 to 95% of total operating expenditures. What is the state's share in your state?

established with the proceeds of the sale of public lands. Other states imposed direct taxation for the support of education; in 1825 Illinois became the first state to enact a public school tax. Still other states made appropriations from the general fund to support education. Conditions were usually placed on their receipt, for example, that local support must equal or exceed state support or that the schools must be kept open a minimum number of days per year and provide free heat, books, and supplies.

By 1865 systems of common schools had been established throughout the northern, midwestern, and western states, and more than 50% of the nation's children were enrolled in public schools. As enrollment in the common school grew, the pressure to make them completely tax supported increased. As previously noted, labor groups in particular pressed hard for the schools to be free. In 1827 Massachusetts was the first state to eliminate the rate bill. In 1834 Pennsylvania's Free School Act became a model for eliminating the pauper school concept. Although other states soon followed these examples, and by constitutional or legislative enactment adopted the concept of public support for public schools open to all children, it was not until 1871 that the last state (New Jersey) abolished the rate bill, making the schools truly free.

Creation of State Boards and State Superintendents of Education

As is usually the case, increased support was accompanied by increased efforts to control. The effort to establish some control or supervision of the common schools was marked by the creation of an office of state superintendent or commissioner of education and a state board of education. In 1812 New York became the first state to appoint a state superintendent, Gideon Hawley. His tenure in office was filled with such controversy that in 1821 he was removed from office and the position was abolished and not recreated until 1854. Nonetheless, by the outbreak of the Civil War, 28 of the 34 states had established state boards of education and chief state school officers. By and large these officers and boards were vested with more supervisory power than real control. Initially their major responsibilities were involved with the distribution of the permanent school funds and the organization of a state system of common schools.

Development of Local School Districts and Superintendents

The creation of a state system of common schools paralleled the development of local school districts and the establishment of local and county superintendents. As noted in chapter 4, the New England states instituted the district system in the late 18th century and it spread westward during the first quarter of the next century. Initially the districts were administered by a school committee that was responsible for the selection and certification of teachers, the selection of textbooks, the maintenance and repair of school buildings, and school visitations.

School visitations, conducted primarily for the purpose of examining students, were an important supervisory task in the colonies and early republic. Initially the visits were conducted by ministers or interested selectmen. Once the school committee was established and assumed this duty, it was natural that one member of the committee might have more interest or ability in visiting the schools than others. If no member had the ability or interest, the committee would appoint a minister or some other layman to perform this duty (National Education Association, 1933a). From this practice emerged the position of the "school visitor" or "school inspector."

In states in which the county was the unit for operation of schools, primarily the southeastern states, a person already holding public office, such as the county clerk, the county judge, a justice of the peace, or a land commissioner, was often given the task. In 1829 Delaware became the first state to appoint a county official whose only responsibilities were to supervise the schools and conduct school visitations. This was the beginning of the office of the county superintendent (National Education Association, 1933a).

The evolution of the office of city school superintendent was somewhat different. As cities grew in size and school enrollments increased, the number of schools to be visited and the complexity of the operation of the schools grew accordingly. To handle their increased responsibilities, the school committees, or what now may be referred to as school boards, increased their size and divided themselves into subcommittees that were responsible for particular aspects of the operation of the schools.

This system worked well in the towns and smaller cities in which the board and number of subcommittees were small. In the larger cities, however, the large number of subcommittees (at one time Chicago reportedly had 79 and Cincinnati had 74) often thwarted the completion of even the most basic tasks (Gilland, 1935). Moreover, the magnitude of the tasks made it difficult to find competent people willing to devote the time necessary to accomplish them. For example, in 1847 the Boston school committee reported that there was no one:

- Whose duty it is to find the best and most economical plans for schoolhouses, their ventilation and warming, and their apparatus, seats, desks, and other furniture.
- To look out for the best teachers, when a vacancy occurs, or in preparation for a vacancy.
- To find out what is the most successful teaching in all the schools, and to point it out for the benefit of all. . . .
- Whose special duty it is to see whether the best course of studies is pursued, or to suggest improvement from the experience of the best schools elsewhere.
- To see whether the schools are adopted to the population, and all classes of children brought into them. . . .
- To supervise the transfer of children from school to school, and from one set of schools to another.
- To oversee the organization of new schools.
- To say what libraries should be in the schools, for teachers or pupils. (*Annual Reports, School Committee, 1847*, cited in Rheller, 1935)

Situations such as this led school committees to recognize the need for an executive office to perform or oversee the performance of the functions it could not. This executive officer in time became recognized as the superintendent of schools.

Buffalo, New York, is credited with having appointed the first superintendent of schools in 1837. In fact, this was a layperson who served for no salary and functioned primarily as the school inspector. He resigned after only a few months and was replaced by a man who received a salary of $75 per year. The next year Louisville and several other Kentucky cities appointed "agents of public schools" who were paid only a modest salary. In 1840 St. Louis named a school superintendent with no salary. However, that same year Providence, Rhode Island, named Nathan Bishop as superintendent with an annual salary of $1,250, a sizable salary at the time (National Education Association, 1933a).

Following these initial appointments, the number of superintendents grew slowly. Thirty years after the appointment of the first superintendent, only 30 cities had appointed superintendents. There were a number of obstacles to the appointment of superintendents. A major obstacle was the dependence of the school board on the city council: The city council often refused the school board's request to appoint a superintendent or simply failed to act on the request (American Association of School Administrators [AASA], 1952). Also working against the appointment of superintendents was (a) fear by the school board, principals, and teachers that they would lose control; (b) the public's fear of "one man control"; (c) a lack of qualified men for the position; (d) a concern over the legality of establishing such a position; (e) concern about the cost of the position; (f) satisfaction with current conditions; and (g) a general resistance to change (Young, 1976).

The early superintendents functioned mostly as assistants or representatives of the school board. Most boards continued to operate as both executive and legislative bodies and were reluctant to delegate any of their executive functions to the superintendent. The subcommittee arrangement continued, and the superintendent was expected to supplement not replace them. Gilland's (1935) analysis of the duties and responsibilities of the first superintendents found that most of the responsibilities were related to instruction, particularly the supervision and visitation of the schools, and few were related to finance. Because many school board members were businessmen, they considered themselves more competent to conduct the financial affairs of the district than the superintendent (AASA, 1952). It was not until the second half of the 19th century that superintendent and school board relationships began to change and the superintendent began to assume the powers and duties associated with a chief executive officer.

 For Your Reflection and Analysis

How has the relationship between the superintendent and the school board changed over time?

Regional Variations

The growth of the common school was not uniform across the country. Enrollment and attendance rates were lowest in rural areas and among minorities. In the predominantly rural South, with the highest concentration of minorities, the common school movement advanced slowly and enrollments were lowest. In the one-room rural schools, controlled by farmer-parents (Angus & Mirel, 2000), progress was not marked by movement from one grade to another, but by completing one text and beginning another. "Rural schools operated on a calendar that reflected the rhythms and labor needs of farm life and consequently enrolled higher percentages of children than the city schools, although for much shorter school terms" (Angus & Mirel, 2000, p. 6).

A different pattern emerged in urban areas, where instruction was offered in large schools organized by grades and controlled by elected or appointed boards of education (Angus & Mirel, 2000). Regional differences also were evident in how teachers were trained (rural teachers largely at teacher institutes) and how much teachers were paid (rural teachers received lower salaries).

Teaching and Textbooks in the Common Schools

Rote memorization and recitation was the most common form of "teaching" in the common schools. The textbook dictated the curriculum: Students studied books, not subjects (Tyack, 1967). Consistent with the prevailing republican philosophy, textbooks were intended to teach morality and religious principles and to celebrate the American culture and democratic form of government. Their goal was to promote patriotism and to shape a uniform national character. The virtues of obedience, honesty, industriousness, courage, sobriety, and charity were taught by positive and negative example. Disobedient or sinful children were often depicted as ending up in pitiful situations or, worse, dead. Of greater concern about the content was that

> *For Your Reflection and Analysis*
>
> *To what extent does the textbook dictate the curriculum in the schools today?*

the textbooks so selected their themes as to disguise the real world, not to reveal it; to repress anxieties, not to confront them; to foster complacency among established groups rather than to include the disposed. In an urban and industrial society, whose agriculture was fast becoming mechanized and aimed at a world market, the schoolbooks painted a sentimental picture of rural bliss. In a period of great stress on the family, they drew a cloying picture of home sweet home. In times of industrial violence they ignored the condition of labor and described unions as the evil plan of foreigners, anarchists, and Communists. In the midst of unparalleled political corruption they portrayed statesmen of stainless steel. The Negro appeared infrequently in the texts, and then usually in the guise of Sambo. People of other nations often appeared as foils to illustrate the superior virtue of Americans. A pervasive Protestantism colored the readers and downgraded other religions either openly or by implication. A pluralistic, expansive society undergoing great intellectual, social, economic, and political change was reduced in the textbooks, as Ruth Elson has observed, to a "fantasy made up by adults as a guide for their children, but inhabited by no one outside the pages of schoolbooks." (Tyack, 1967, p. 184)

The most widely used textbooks in the common schools were the *Eclectic* series of readers prepared by the Reverend William Holmes McGuffey (see Figure 5.2). Six

FIGURE 5.2   Page from a McGuffey Reader
Source: McGuffey, W. H. (1879, 1920). *McGuffey's third eclectic reader* (pp. 52–54). New York: John Wiley & Sons.

readers in all, the first appeared in 1836. Although they did have a very moralizing tone, it was not as harsh as that of the *New England Primer*. They did, however, project a social doctrine that reinforced the existing social and economic order, including slavery and the role of women. Although they contained excellent literature, they were often criticized for being overly literary and formal: For example, the fifth reader contained poetry and prose "designed for elocutionary exercises to increase articulation, inflection, pitch, accent, rate, emphasis and gesture" (Payne, 2003). Over 100 million copies of the readers were sold. McGuffey's original agreement with the publisher was that he was to receive 10% of the royalties until this reached $1,000. Then the books became the property of the publisher. In later years the publisher voluntarily paid McGuffey an annuity to use his name (Cubberley, 1934). Some believe that the readers have had a greater influence on literary tastes in the United States than any other book except the Bible (Payne, 2003).

 For Your Reflection and Analysis

In what ways do textbooks today reinforce the existing social order?

By the second quarter of the 19th century a greater variety of textbooks were being published for use in the common schools. Moreover, their authors began to promote the more modern educational teachings. For example, whereas the *McGuffey Readers* continued to teach morality and patriotism, the stern preachments of earlier schoolbooks were replaced or complemented with selections designed to appeal to youthful interest (Cremin, 1982).

Instructional methods were also changing. Although rote learning and drill and practice did not disappear from the classroom, a more progressive approach that reflected the teachings of Pestalozzi was making some inroads. As noted, the Pestalozzian methods were admired and reported on in the leading education journals by such eminent common school reformers as Horace Mann and Henry Barnard.

Pestalozzian Influence

Johann Heinrich Pestalozzi (1746–1827) was a Swiss educator whose philosophy of education incorporated the child-centered, sensory experience principles of Rousseau. Like Rousseau, he believed in the natural goodness of human nature and individual differences in "readiness" to learn. Perhaps more than Rousseau, Pestalozzi recognized the importance of human emotions in the learning process. He believed in the importance of giving the child feelings of self-respect and emotional security and in treating the child with love. In fact, it can be said that the ideal of love governs Pestalozzi's philosophy of education.

Pestalozzi believed that instruction must begin with the concrete and proceed to the abstract. Materials should be presented slowly, in developmental order, from simple to complex. Pestalozzi advanced the concept of the *object lesson*, which involved tailoring the lesson to the stages of child development and centered on handling, counting, and naming concrete materials (i.e., objects) within the child's natural environment. For example, "in an arithmetic lesson dealing with the number 'three,' the child should handle three objects, then progress from sight and touch to abstract

Pestalozzi's child-centered philosophy of education emphasized treating children with love.

For Your Reflection and Analysis

What instructional practice today can best be compared to the object lesson?

concepts of number and the idea contained in the word 'three'" (Gillett, 1966, p. 218). Using the object lesson, discussion and oral presentation replace rote learning.

Pestalozzi established a school in Verdun, Switzerland, to put his ideas into practice. A num-

---

LESSON ON PLANTS

Flowers

1. Require the children to look at some flowers and say in what they are alike. (They all have *leaves;* they all have *stems;* nearly all have the outer leaves (calix) of a *green color.*) Let the children smell the flowers—they all have some kind of *smell.* Ask how they are produced (from *slips* or *seeds*). If a slip or seed be put into the ground and gets proper nourishment, what takes place? (They grow.) All flowers are grown. What happens to flowers when taken out of the ground and left without water, etc? (They decay.) Who made the flowers? Children repeat in what flowers are alike.

2. Having found out in what flowers are alike, lead the children to discover in what they differ. By the sense of smell they will discover that some have a sweet scent, others a strong scent, and others a faint, soft scent. By the sense of sight they will discover that flowers differ in size. Let them name the large flowers, the small ones, and find examples of each from memory. Also that flowers differ in shape. Some have leaves that spread out as the Iris, others with leaves closely packed together as the Rose, some with broad flat leaves, others with curled leaves. Also flowers differ in color. Let the children name the different colors of different flowers. Next, let them compare the color of the stamens and leaves. Some are dark green, and others a light green. Then, by reference to flowers gathered and placed in water; some of which have to be thrown away on the morrow, while others may be kept. Draw from that that some decay directly, while others last a longer time.

3. Let the children say of whom we should think when we look at flowers. Would they rather have them or not? Why would they have them? Why flowers are made of different colors? Why not all green, all blue, all of the same shade? (They are prettier as they are.) What their beauty shows about God? That He not only gives us what we need, but gives us things to please us and make us happy. Whom they should thank when they gather flowers.

"Such instruction," says Dearborn, "was intended to lay the foundations for the formal acquisition of knowledge in the later grades by providing the children with proper habits of study, and by providing them with the primary elements of knowledge considered basic to their later elementary school work."

FIGURE 5.3   An Object Lesson on Plants, Prepared by E. A. Sheldon at Oswego
Source: Cubberley, E. P. (1934). *Readings in public education in the United States* (pp. 347–348). New York: Houghton Mifflin.

ber of branch schools were opened, including one for girls. Pestalozzi had a profound impact on education throughout much of the Western world. Educators came from all over the world, including the United States, to observe and study his methods. Horace Mann and Henry Barnard came under his influence. Edward A. Sheldon, superintendent of schools in Oswego, New York, established a normal school at Oswego in 1861 that followed Pestalozzi's methods. The almost 1,400 graduates of the Oswego Normal School carried the object teaching methodology to classrooms and normal schools all over the country. The result was classrooms that placed a greater emphasis on developmental learning and the individuality of the child. Figure 5.3 shows an example of a typical object lesson on plants prepared by Sheldon.

The Failure of the Common Schools: The Schooling of Catholics

Beginning in the 1830s the first substantial influx of Roman Catholic immigrants came to the United States. Most of these were Irish. In cities such as New York, Boston, and Philadelphia the Irish formed a visible community with their own taverns, clubs, and newspapers (Binder, 1974). As their numbers grew, so did the prejudice against them. They were described in the newspapers as "Irish niggers" and "a mongrel mass of ignorance" (Carnes, 1995). The Irish were regularly discriminated against in housing and employment and given the most menial and demeaning jobs. Because of their willingness to work for lower wages, they sometimes displaced native workers and were seen as an economic threat to them.

Others saw a far greater danger. Although two centuries had passed since the religious persecutions of the Reformation, many Protestants still distrusted all things and people "Popish." Matters were not helped when, in 1829, Bishop John England of Baltimore assembled the first Provincial Council of Catholicity, which encouraged Catholics to build schools for their own children and to resist the singing of sectarian hymns and the reading of the Protestant Bible in the schools. From the Catholic perspective, the common schools posed a threat to their religious values. Dominated by Protestants, the schools included Protestant hymns and prayers and the reading of the Protestant Bible (the King James Version), as well as texts and other materials with an openly anti-Catholic bias, as a regular part of instruction.

 For Your Reflection and Analysis

How does the prejudice against the Irish compare with the prejudice against immigrants today? Which groups experience the most prejudice and distrust? Why?

The animosity between Catholics and Protestants in New York City came to a head in 1840 when Governor William H. Steward, concerned that the vast majority of New York City's Catholic children were not attending the city's schools because of the anti-Catholic atmosphere, proposed to the legislature that Catholic schools be included as part of state school system and be provided state support. The proposal was welcomed by the Catholic community but was opposed by the Protestants, particularly the Public School Society, a Protestant philanthropic society chartered to provide elementary education for poor children. The Society received the majority of the state school funds allocated to New York City and protested the use of public funds to support Catholic schools.

The Catholic community, encouraged by Steward's proposal, petitioned the New York City Common Council for a share of the common school fund. In their petition they cited the anti-Catholic sentiments expressed in the schools that had forced them to establish their own schools, despite the fact that they were paying taxes to support the common schools. Recognizing the potential legal issues involved in using public funds to support the exercise of religion, the petitioners said they were willing to postpone religious instruction until after the school day. The Protestants responded that if the Catholics were willing to postpone religious instruction until after the school day, they should be willing to do the same after spending the day in the common school (Spring, 2001). Under pressure from the Protestant churches and the Public School Society, the Council rejected the petition.

The Catholics then carried their petition to the state legislature. Bombarded from both sides, the response of the legislature was to pass a law that forbade the use of public funds in schools that taught any religious doctrine, including those of the Public School Society. The result was that although the Catholics did not receive access to state support, by law, if not by practice, sectarian influences were excluded from the school. However, feelings continued to run high. In 1842 a riot between Catholics and Protestants broke out in New York City that involved an attack on the bishop's home.

The next year the Philadelphia school board granted Bishop Francis Patrick Kenrick's request that Catholic children be permitted to read the Douay (Catholic) Bible instead of the King James Version. Protestants were outraged, and Protestant newspapers and "nativist" groups were vocal in their objections. Anti-Catholic feelings escalated, culminating in the 1844 riot described in a Primary Source Reading for this chapter. Churches and many other buildings were burned, and several people were killed.

Protestant and Catholic conflict occurred in several other locations as Catholics continued to protest the heavily sectarian practices in the common schools and school boards continued to reject their requests for reform or excusal from participation in Protestant religious practices. In fact, in *Donahoe v. Richards* (1854) the Supreme Court of Maine said that a school board could expel from school students who refused to read the Protestant Bible being used in the school. In the end, many Catholics felt they had no choice but to establish their own schools.

Education of Teachers

Most histories of education identify the Colombian School at Concord, Vermont, established by the Reverend Samuel Hall in 1823, as the first formal teacher training institution. Hall had gone to Concord as a supply (temporary) pastor in 1822 and in the first year observed the poor condition of the schools. He came to believe that better trained teachers were central to school improvement. When he accepted the permanent pastorate in 1823, he did so with the provision that he be allowed to open a school to train teachers. Beginning in an unused part of a store, but soon moving to a new brick building constructed by the town, the school was incorporated as the Concord Academy and received a share of the county school fund (Marr, 1959).

At the Concord school, Hall offered a review of the subjects taught in the common school, plus advanced mathematics, chemistry, natural and moral philosophy, logic, astronomy, and "the art of teaching." Students also had the opportunity to observe and practice teaching during the winter term in the surrounding schools (Lemlech & Marks, 1976). In 1829 Hall published the first professional textbook on teacher education in the English language, *Lectures on Schoolteaching*. (A chapter outline of the work is presented in Figure 5.4.) The next year he left Concord to head the teacher training seminary that was to open at Phillips Academy at Andover, Massachusetts. After his departure the Concord Academy ceased to operate as a teacher training institution.

Although most historians consider the Concord Academy to be the first normal school, others argue that the first such institution was actually the previously mentioned

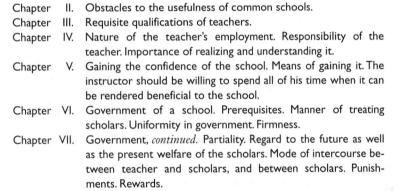

Chapter	I.	Indifference to the importance, character, and usefulness of common schools; its origin and influence.
Chapter	II.	Obstacles to the usefulness of common schools.
Chapter	III.	Requisite qualifications of teachers.
Chapter	IV.	Nature of the teacher's employment. Responsibility of the teacher. Importance of realizing and understanding it.
Chapter	V.	Gaining the confidence of the school. Means of gaining it. The instructor should be willing to spend all of his time when it can be rendered beneficial to the school.
Chapter	VI.	Government of a school. Prerequisites. Manner of treating scholars. Uniformity in government. Firmness.
Chapter	VII.	Government, *continued*. Partiality. Regard to the future as well as the present welfare of the scholars. Mode of intercourse between teacher and scholars, and between scholars. Punishments. Rewards.
Chapter	VIII.	General management of a school. Direction of studies.
Chapter	IX.	Mode of teaching. Manner of illustrating subjects. Spelling. Reading.
Chapter	X.	Arithmetic. Geography. English Grammar. Writing. History.
Chapter	XI.	Composition. General subjects, not particularly studied. Importance of improving opportunities when deep impressions are made on the minds of the school.
Chapter	XII.	Means of exciting the attention of scholars. Such as are to be avoided. Such as are safely used.
Chapter	XIII.	To female instructors.

FIGURE 5.4 Chapter Outline from *Lectures on Schoolkeeping* by Samuel R. Hall
Source: Cubberley, E. P. (1934). Readings in public education in the United States (pp 324–325). New York: Houghton Mifflin.

Troy Female Seminary opened by Emma Willard in 1821. The primary (but not the only) purpose of the seminary was to train female teachers in both the subject areas and pedagogy. Willard bestowed on each graduate a signed certificate confirming her qualifications to teach. In fact, long before the first state-supported normal schools were opened, the Troy Seminary as well as a number of other academies were preparing males and females for the teaching profession. In fact, recognizing the need for trained teachers, and being unable to gain legislative support for state-sponsored normal schools, many of the common school advocates encouraged the academies to undertake the training of teachers. In New York, the legislature, unwilling to create normal schools, in 1823 authorized the distribution of state aid to private academies to encourage a supply of qualified teachers for the common schools. Similar action was taken in Wisconsin.

In some academies teacher training was the primary course of study. Others offered teacher education, as Barnard had encouraged them to do, by offering classes in the winter and spring for females, who taught summer terms in the schools, and again in the summer for males, who taught in the winter when the older boys were in attendance (Marr, 1959).

The total number of teachers trained in the academies is not known, but an examination of the records of individual schools suggests that the numbers were significant and that the academies were especially important in preparing teachers for the newly opened west. The catalog of one school, the Ipswich Female Seminary, provides the following list of students and their occupations:

Whole number of students	1458
Missionaries	21
Teachers in New England and Middle States	400
Teachers in West	57
Teachers in South	31
Total	509

(Marr, 1959, p. 244)

If these figures are typical, we can assume that at least one third of the graduates of the female academies entered the ranks of teaching.

Despite the important role played by the academies, the common schools needed more teachers than those who could afford to finance their own education at the mostly private academies. In addition, the teachers needed more advanced training in teaching than was offered at most academies. These needs gave rise to the publicly supported normal school.

 For Your Reflection and Analysis

Approximately what percentage of graduates of colleges of education actually become classroom teachers?

Establishment of Normal Schools

The normal school was the single greatest force in increasing the professional training of teachers. As we have seen, Horace Mann, James Carter, Henry Barnard, Catherine Beecher, and others who had worked for the establishment of common schools also recognized that their success depended on the preparation of a sufficient quantity of adequately trained teachers. This could best be accomplished, they believed, by the establishment of institutions for the specific training of teachers, that is, normal schools.

As noted previously, the first state-supported normal schools were in Massachusetts. The growing enrollments in the common schools led other states to follow suit. In 1844 the New York State Normal School at Albany was opened under the direction of David P. Page. His book, *Theory and Practice of Teaching or the Motives and Methods of Good School Keeping*, published in 1847, became the standard text in teacher education. The normal schools were generally coeducational, although the majority of students were women. Mann, Beecher, and other common school reformers believed that women made better teachers than men at the elementary level, but they were also practical and recognized that women were less expensive to hire. This is borne out by the data on teacher salaries presented in Table 5.2.

Admission to the normal school typically required only an elementary education. Admission was free to residents of the state, but often a tuition equal to that of an academy was charged to out-of-state residents. The course of study lasted 1 or 2 years and included a review of material to be taught in the common school, instruction in methods of teaching, "mental philosophy" (i.e., educational psychology), and classroom management. Overriding the curriculum was a concern for the development of moral character. A prominent feature of these normal schools was the model school, the forerunner of the laboratory school, where students could practice teaching. If a model school was not present, students were often provided the opportunity to practice teach in a neighboring school.

To meet the ever-increasing demand for teachers in urban areas, a number of larger cities operated normal schools while also including a "normal department" in some high schools that trained teachers for the common schools. These normal schools typically had higher entrance requirements than did the state or private schools (generally the completion of 2 or 3 years of high school) and also provided the opportunity for much more observation and practice experience. In most instances they were authorized to issue teaching certificates (Angus & Mirel, 2000).

TABLE 5.2 Average Weekly Salary of Teachers, 1841–1864

	Rural		City	
Year	Men	Women	Men	Women
1841	$4.15	$2.51	$11.93	$4.44
1845	3.87	2.48	12.21	4.09
1850	4.25	2.89	13.37	4.71
1855	5.77	3.65	16.80	5.79
1860	6.28	4.12	18.56	6.99
1864	7.86	4.92	20.78	7.67

Source: Spring, J. (1986). *The American School: 1642–1985. Varieties of historical interpretation of the foundations and development of American education.* Copyright © the McGraw-Hill Companies, Inc.

By 1865 over 50 normal schools were in operation, and by 1900 almost 350 normal schools were operating in all 45 states. Most, but not all, normal school students intended to be teachers, but others took advantage of the low cost and convenience afforded by the normal school to obtain a higher education. As discussed in chapter 6, in the beginning of the 20th century normal schools expanded and strengthened their curricula and transitioned into state teachers colleges.

Teacher Institutes

Despite the spread of normal schools, as late as 1900 the majority of teachers had not attended normal schools. Before this, and even into the 20th century, the most important institution in the training of teachers, especially rural teachers, was the *teacher institute*. A common practice of school districts was to hire individuals with no formal training with the condition that they attend a teacher institute. The typical institute met once or twice a year for a period of several days to 4 weeks, usually in the summer months. They were most often organized and conducted by the county superintendent of schools. Some were offered in connection with normal schools or other institutions of higher education. Others appear to have been initiated by a lyceum. The American Sunday School Union also held teacher institutes for its teachers.

The curriculum of the teacher institutes "consisted of reviews of the basic subjects offered in the country schools, a few opportunities to be tutored in more advanced subjects, a few lectures on principles and methods of good teaching given by successful teachers chosen by the county superintendent, and the opportunity to prepare for the county teachers examination that was often given as the concluding event of the institute" (Angus & Mirel, 2000, p. 9). The institute also gave great emphasis to elevating the moral character of the teacher (Spring, 2001). In rural areas young people who did not intend to be teachers attended the institutes because they were their only opportunity for an education beyond the county school; the institutes were, in effect, "the rural young people's colleges" (Fuller, cited in Angus & Mirel, 2000, p. 9).

Conclusion

The common school movement was essentially a movement directed at transforming the collection of unequal and underfunded public and semipublic schools attended on an uneven basis by students who were kept, not taught, by inexperienced and untrained teachers into a system of universal, free, tax-supported schools. The success of the movement can be measured in higher rates of school attendance; longer school terms; improved facilities; increased state support; and improved teacher quality, training, and pay. State departments of education were created, state supervision increased, school administration was professionalized, and some degree of standardization in textbooks and school practices occurred.

The success of the school reform movement can be attributed to the fact that it was able to gain the support of what might otherwise be seen as opposing groups.

One the one hand the common school reformers were able to convince the leaders of business and industry that the common schools were a good economic investment and would produce the kind of workforce they needed. On the other hand they were able to convince workers and those at the other end of the socioeconomic spectrum that the schools were the vehicles for their upward mobility. Also important was the fact that the religious nondenominational compromise satisfied Protestant religious interests.

Despite the success of the movement, it is not without its critics. Some critics saw the rhetoric of the common school reformers as undemocratic, racist, and anti-immigrant. In their goal to promote state supervision and control and improve education for the many, common school reformers dismissed the interests of others. One of the most consistent criticisms of the movement was its sectarianism bias. Consistent with republican ideology, the common schools were considered an important vehicle for teaching Christian morality and values. The schools did not just promote Christian doctrine, however; they promoted exclusively Protestant doctrine. While perhaps providing a common value system to replace the "outworn Calvinist doctrine," this practice carried with it the loss of a multicultural society in which all individuals are free to choose values that are compatible with their own religion and culture (Tozer, Violas, & Senese, 2002).

Another major criticism of the common school movement has been what some see as its attempt at social control. Supporters of the common schools thought they should teach the children of immigrants and the poor the morals and customs of the dominant culture and the skills and habits that would best serve business and industry. Others have seen this as not only an attempt at forced assimilation and social control, but also paternalistic and undemocratic.

Despite opposition, the common school reformers were successful in firmly establishing the cornerstone of the American public educational system and gaining wide acceptance of public support for its operation. The advancement of these concepts at the secondary level in the years following the Civil War is a major topic of chapter 6.

For Discussion and Application

1. How do the political, economic, and social factors shaping education today compare with those that shaped the schools in the first decade of the 19th century?
2. Consider the immigration of the Irish in the 1800s and the immigration of Hispanics today. Describe some of the common problems and challenges of both groups as they attempt(ed) to benefit from the concept of public education for all.
3. How does the conflict over religious practices in the common schools compare with that over the separation of church and state today?
4. In what ways do the concerns regarding teacher education expressed in the 19th century compare with the concerns expressed today?
5. Give examples in your own subject field of Pestalozzi's application of the following developmental principle: "Instruction must begin with the concrete and proceed to the abstract."

Primary Source Reading

Thaddeus Stevens is perhaps best known as an aboli-
tionist. However, he was also an avid supporter of the
common school movement. His April 11, 1835, speech
against the repeal of the Pennsylvania Free School Act
of 1834 before the Pennsylvania House of Representa-
tives, part of which is reprinted in this reading, was
not only key to saving the bill, but also a good example
of the ideology of the common school reformers. In par-
ticular he pointed to the importance of providing
equality of opportunity and the stigmatizing affects of
the charity/pauper schools. He also spelled out the cost
savings of the common schools over the present system
and decried in the strongest terms those who would
deprive the children of the state this educational op-
portunity.

Proposal for Tax-Supported Schools

Thaddeus Stevens

Mr. Speaker,—I will briefly give you the reasons
why I shall oppose the repeal of the school law. . . .
will attempt to show that the law is salutary, useful and important; and that consequently, the last
legislature acted wisely in passing, and the present would act unwisely in repealing it. That instead of being oppressive to the people, it will
lighten their burdens, while it elevates them in
the scale of human intellect. . . .

If an elective republic is to endure for any
great length of time, *every* elector must have sufficient information, not only to accumulate wealth,
and take care of his pecuniary concerns, but to direct wisely the legislatures, the ambassadors, and
the executive of the nation—for *some* part of all
these things, *some* agency in approving or disap-
proving of them, falls to every freeman. If then,

Source: Stevens, T. (May 2, 1835). General education—
Remarks of Mr. Stevens in the Pennsylvania House of
Representatives. *Hazard's Register of Pennsylvania*, 15
(18), 283–287.

the permanency of our government depends upon
such knowledge, it is the duty of government to
see that the means of information be diffused to
every citizen. This is a sufficient answer to those
who deem education a private and not a public
duty—who argue that they are willing to educate
their *own* children, but not their *neighbor's* children.

But while but few are found ignorant and
shameless enough to deny the advantages of general education, many are alarmed at its supposed
burthensome operation. A little judicious reflection, or a single year's experience, would show that
education, under the free school system will cost
more than one one-half less, and afford better and
more permanent instruction than the present disgraceful plan pursued by Pennsylvania.—Take a
township of six miles square and make the estimate—such townships, on an average, will contain
about 200 children to be schooled. The present
rate of tuition generally (in the country) is two dollars per quarter. If the children attend school two
quarters each year, such township would pay $800
per annum. Take the free school system—lay the
township off into districts three miles square; the
farthest scholars would then have one mile and a
half to go, which would not be too far. It would require four schools. These will be taught I presume,
as in other states, three months in the winter by
male, and three months in the summer by female
teachers; good male teachers can be had at from
sixteen to eighteen dollars per month and board
themselves; females at nine dollars per month—

Take the highest price, eighteen dollars for three months, would be	$54.00
And then for females at $9 for three months,	27 00
Each school would cost	81 00
Four to a township	4
	324 00
The price now paid for the same is	800 00

Saving for each township of six miles square,
$476.00 per annum.

If the instruction of 200 scholars will save
by the free school law $476, the 500,000 children

in Pennsylvania will save [$]1,190,000! Very few men are aware of the immense amount of money which the present expensive and partial mode of education costs the people. Pennsylvania has half a million of children, who either do, or ought to go to school six months in the year. If they *do* go, at two dollars per quarter, their schooling costs two millions of dollars per annum! If they do *not* go when they are able, their parents deserve to be held in disgrace. Where they are unable, if the state does not furnish the means, she is criminally negligent. But by the free school law, that same amount of education, which would now cost two millions of dollars, could be supplied at less than one-third of this amount. The amendment which is now proposed as a substitute for the school law of last session, is, in my opinion, of a most hateful and degrading character. It is a re-enactment of the pauper law of 1809. It proposes that the assessors shall take a census, and make a record of the *poor;* This shall be revised, and a new record made by the county commissioners, so that the names of those who have the misfortune to be poor men's children shall be forever preserved, as a distinct class, in the archives of the county! The teacher, too, is to keep in his school a *pauper* book, and register the names and attendance of poor scholars. Thus pointing out and recording their poverty in the midst of their companions. Sir, hereditary distinctions of rank are sufficiently odious; but that which is founded on poverty is infinitely more so. Such a law should be entitled "an act for branding and marking the poor, so that they may be known from the rich and proud."—Many complain of this tax, not so much on account of its amount, as because it is for the benefit of others and not themselves. This is a mistake. It is for *their own* benefit, inasmuch as it perpetuates the government, and ensures the due administration of the laws under which they live, and by which their lives and property are protected. Why do they not urge the same objection against all other taxes? The industrious, thrifty, rich farmer pays a heavy county tax to support criminal courts, build jails, and pay sheriffs and jail keepers, and yet probably he never has and

never will have any direct personal use of either. He never gets the worth of his money by being tried for a crime before the court, allowed the privilege of the jail on conviction; or receiving an equivalent from the sheriff or his hangman officers! He cheerfully pays the tax which is necessary to support and punish convicts; but loudly complains of that which goes to prevent his fellow being from becoming criminal, and to obviate the necessity of those humiliating institutions.

This law is often objected to, because its benefits are shared by the children of the profligate spendthrift equally with those of the most industrious and economical habits. It ought to be remembered, that the benefit is bestowed, not upon the erring parents, but the innocent children. Carry out this objection and you punish children for the crimes or misfortunes of their parents. You virtually establish castes and grades founded on no merit of the particular generation, but on the demerits of their ancestors; An aristocracy of the most odious and insolent kind—the aristocracy of wealth and pride.

It is said that its advantages will be unjustly and unequally enjoyed, because the industrious, money-making man keeps his whole family *constantly* employed, and has but little time for them to spend at school; while the idle man has but little employment for his family and they will constantly attend school. I know sir, that there are some men, whose whole souls are so completely absorbed in the accumulation of wealth; and whose avarice so increases with success that they look upon their very children in no other light than as instruments of gain—that they, as well as the ox and the ass within their gates, are valuable only in proportion to their annual earnings. And according to the present system, the children of such men are reduced almost to an intellectual level with their co-laborers of the brute creation. This law will be of vast advantage to the offspring of such misers. If they are compelled to pay their taxes to support schools, their very meanness will induce them to send their children to them to get the worth of their money. Thus it will extract good out of the very penuriousness of the miser. Surely a system, which will work such wonders, ought to be as greedily sought for, and more highly prized than that coveted alchymy, which was to produce gold and silver out of the blood and entrails of vipers, lizards and other filthy vermin!

Why, sir, are the colleges and literary institutions of Pennsylvania now, and ever have been, in a languishing, sickly condition? Why, with a fertile soil and genial climate, has she, in proportion to her population, scarcely one-third as many collegiate students, as cold, barren, New England? The answer is obvious—She has no free schools. Until she shall have, you may in vain endow college after college, they will never be filled; or filled only by students from other states. In New England free schools plant the seeds and the desire of knowledge in *every* mind, without regard to the wealth of the parent or the texture of the pupil's garments. When the seed thus universally sown, happens to fall on fertile soil, it springs up and is fostered by a generous public, until it produces its glorious fruit.—Those who have but scanty means and are pursuing a collegiate education, find it necessary to spend a portion of the year in teaching common schools; thus imparting the knowledge which they acquire, they raise the dignity of the employment to a rank which it should always hold, honorable in proportion to the high qualifications necessary for its discharge. Thus devoting a portion of their time to acquiring the means of subsistence, industrious habits are forced upon them, and their minds and bodies become disciplined to a regularity and energy which is seldom the lot of the rich. . . .

But we are told that this law is unpopular; that the people desire its repeal. Has it not always been so with every new reform in the condition of man? Old habits, and old prejudices are hard to be removed from the mind. Every new improvement, which has been gradually leading man from the savage through the civilized up to a highly cultivated state, has required the most strenuous, and often perilous exertions of the wise and the good. But, sir, much of its unpopularity is chargeable upon the vile arts of unprinci-pled demagogues. Instead of attempting to remove the honest misapprehensions of the people, they cater to their prejudices, and take advantage of them, to gain low, dirty, temporary, local triumphs. . . .

It is the duty of faithful legislators to create and sustain such laws and institutions, as shall teach us our wants—foster our cravings after knowledge, and urge us forward in the march of intellect.—The barbarous and disgraceful cry, which we hear abroad in some parts of our land, "that learning makes us worse—that education makes men rogues," should find no echo within these walls. Those who hold such doctrines any where, would be the objects of bitter detestation, if they were not rather the pitiable subjects of commiseration. For even voluntary fools require our compassion as well as natural idiots! . . .

In giving this law to posterity, you act the part of the philanthropist, by bestowing upon the poor as well as the rich the greatest earthly boon, which they are capable of receiving: you act the part of the philosopher by pointing, if you do not lead them up the hill of science: you act the part of the hero, if it be true as you say, that popular vengeance follows close upon your footsteps. Here then, if you wish true popularity, is a theatre on which you may acquire it. What renders the name of Socrates immortal, but his love of the human family, exhibited under all circumstances and in contempt of every danger? But courage, even with but little benevolence, may confer lasting renown. It is this which makes us bow with involuntary respect, at the names of Napoleon, of Caesar and of Richard of the Lion heart. But what earthly glory is there equal in lustre and duration to that conferred by education?—What else could have bestowed such renown upon the Philosophers, the Poets, the Statesmen, and Orators of antiquity? What else could have conferred such undisputed applause upon Aristotle, Demosthenes, and Homer; on Virgil, Horace, and Cicero? And is learning less interesting and important now than it was in centuries past, when those statesmen and orators charmed and ruled empires with their eloquence?

Sir, let it not be thought that those great men acquired a higher fame than is within the reach of the present age. Pennsylvania's sons possess as high native talents as any other nation of ancient or modern time! Many of the poorest of her children possess as bright intellectual gems, if they were as highly polished, as did the proudest scholars of Greece or Rome.—But too long—too disgracefully long, has coward, trembling, procrastinating legislation permitted them to lie buried in "dark unfathomed caves."

If you wish to acquire popularity, how often have you been admonished to build not your monuments of brass or marble, but make them of ever-living mind!—Although the period of yours, or your children's renown, cannot be as long as that of the ancients, because you start from a later period, yet it may be no less brilliant. Equal attention to the same learning; equal ardor in pursuing the same arts and liberal studies, which has rescued their names from the rust of corroding time, and handed them down to us untarnished from remote antiquity, would transmit the names of your children, and your children's children in the green undying fame down through the long vista of succeeding ages, until time shall mingle with eternity.

Let all, therefore, who would sustain the character of the philosopher or philanthropist. sustain this law.—Those who would add thereto the glory of the hero, can acquire it here; for in the present state of feeling in Pennsylvania, I am willing to admit, that but little less dangerous to the public man is the war-club and battle-axe of savage ignorance, than to the Lion Hearted Richard was the keen scimitar of the Saracen. He, who would oppose it, either through inability to comprehend the advantages of general education; or from unwillingness to bestow them on all his fellow citizens, even to the lowest and the poorest; or from dread of popular vengeance, seems to me to want either the head of the philosopher, the heart of the philanthropist or the nerve of the hero.

All these things would be easily admitted by almost every man were it not for the supposed cost. I have endeavored to show that it is not expensive; but admit that it were somewhat so, why do you cling so closely to your gold? The trophies which it can purchase; the idols which it sets up, will scarcely survive their purchaser. No name, no honor can long be perpetuated by mere matter. Of this, Egypt furnishes melancholy proof. Look at her stupendous pyramids, which were raised at such immense expenses of toil and treasure.—As mere masses of matter they seem as durable as the everlasting hills, yet the deeds, and the names which they were intended to perpetuate, are no longer known on earth. That ingenious people attempted to give immortality to matter, by embalming their great men and monarchs. Instead of doing deeds worthy to be recorded in history, their very names are unknown, and nothing is left to posterity but their disgusting mortal frames for idle curiosity to stare at. What rational being can view such soulless, material perpetuation with pleasure? If you can enjoy it, go, sir, to the foot of Vesuvius; to Herculaneum, and Pompeii, those eternal monuments of human weakness. There, if you set such value on material monuments of riches, may you see all the glory of art, the magnificence of wealth, the gold of Ophir, and the rubies of the East preserved in indestructible lava along with their haughty wearers, the cold, smooth, petrified, lifeless, beauties of the "Cities of the Dead."

Who would not shudder at the idea of such prolonged material identity? Who would not rather do one living deed, than to have his ashes forever enshrined in ever-burnished gold. Sir, I trust, that when we come to act on this question we shall all take lofty ground—look beyond the narrow space which now circumscribes our vision—beyond the passing, fleeting point of time on which we stand: and so cast our votes that the blessing of education shall be conferred on every son of Pennsylvania—shall be carried home to the poorest child of the poorest inhabitant of the meanest hut of your mountains, so that even he may be prepared to act well his part in this land of freemen, and lay on earth, a broad and a solid foundation for that enduring knowledge, which goes on increasing through increasing eternity.

Questions for Discussion

1. Which 20th-century political leader(s) would be most likely to deliver a speech similar to Thaddeus Stevens' defense of equal educational opportunity?
2. How does the stigma associated with the pauper schools compare with basing eligibility for certain educational programs today on socioeconomic status?
3. Thaddeus Stevens was an abolitionist as well as a champion for educating the underclass. He also had great faith in a liberal arts education. Which philosophy best describes Stevens? Explain your choice.

Primary Source Reading

The anti-Catholic and anti-Irish intolerance that existed in the United States in the 19th century reflected a lengthy history of hatred and violence between the English and Irish that predated the colonization of America. As you read the essay "In the City of Brotherly Love," consider the underlying economic and social factors that contributed to this conflict.

Intolerance in the City of Brotherly Love

Jim Carnes

In Pennsylvania Public Schools in the 1840s, daily lessons from the King James Bible were required by law. In the opinion of Philadelphia's Protestant majority, this practice provided the moral underpinning of education.

To the city's growing minority of Irish Catholics, however, the "Bible law" represented

Source: Carnes, J. (1995). In the city of brotherly love. *Us and them: A history of intolerance in America* (pp. 41–47). New York: Oxford University Press.

forced indoctrination into the Protestant faith. The Catholic Church recognized a different version of the Christian scriptures, known as the Douai-Reims Bible, but Philadelphia authorities prohibited its use in the schools.

The mostly poor, working-class Irish immigrants of suburbs like Kensington and Southwark didn't yet have much of a voice in Philadelphia politics. But the resolution of a similar controversy in New York City inspired Philadelphia's Catholic bishop to petition the school board. Daily Bible reading was fine, Bishop Francis Kenrick wrote in November 1842, so long as Catholic students were allowed to use their own Bibles and were excused from Protestant devotional lessons. In January 1843, school officials granted the request.

The board's action didn't attract much notice at first. Eventually, however, a teacher lodged a complaint that the divided devotional was disrupting her classroom. When a Catholic board member and city alderman from Kensington named Hugh Clark advised the teacher to suspend all religious instruction until a better compromise could be reached, the issue threw Philadelphians into a face-off.

There was more at stake on both sides of this conflict than a simple choice of Bibles. For the city's largely native-born Protestants, control of school curriculum was just one of the many privileges enjoyed by the majority. All descendants of early settlers in this cradle of the republic, they believed that the rising tide of immigrants threatened the long-standing political, economic, social and religious institutions of "native Americans."

The Irish Catholics, on the other hand, felt that they were entitled to a voice in their children's education and other areas of public life. Most of them had fled to the United States after Ireland's potato crops began to fail in the early 1800s. The emerging factory system in the Northeast allowed them to begin new lives, if only on the lowest rung of the economic ladder.

This same system was taking jobs away from the skilled artisan class, to which most native Anglo-Saxon Protestants belonged. As a result, the ancient hatred between the English and the Irish quickly took root in American soil. Religious differences provoked open confrontation. In Philadelphia, as in Boston, New York and most other large cities, anti-Catholic and "nativist" organizations opposed the integration of new immigrants into U.S. society.

One such organization was the American Republicans, a Protestant political party in Philadelphia that became heavily involved in the school Bible controversy. The party held a rally to demand the resignation of alderman Hugh Clark from the school board. Nativist leaders sponsored a referendum in the 1844 spring election asking the public whether Catholic students should be permitted to read from the Catholic Bible.

Various groups used the campaign as an opportunity to denounce Catholicism as an evil foreign influence. Newspapers alleged that the Pope in Rome was pursuing a secret plan to seize control of American schools. Political candidates joined the local press in opposing the naturalization of foreigners as U.S. citizens. Protestant voters soundly rejected the two-Bible policy.

Alderman Hugh Clark introduced before the city legislature a resolution to ban Bible reading in the public schools. Again, the nativists united to defend the old state law. Their victory so-angered Clark that he walked into Kensington School one morning during devotional, grabbed the Protestant Bible from the teacher's hands and proceeded to tear it page from page.

Events began to spiral out of control. As soon as word of Clark's defiance reached nativist leaders, they scheduled a protest meeting in the heart of Kensington. Residents of the district warned that such a gathering would bring trouble. As the outdoor rally assembled on Friday evening, May 3,1844, Irish Catholics darted in and destroyed the speakers' platform. Onlookers began throwing bricks and rocks to disperse the crowd.

Philadelphia during this era lacked a police force capable of handling a large public disturbance. Only the sheriff of Philadelphia County had jurisdiction over the entire city, and his force was too small to concentrate in one troubled district. In the absence of effective law enforcement

agencies, the nativists announced their plan to return to Kensington the following Monday.

Several thousand people heeded the call. In the middle of one of the opening speeches, an unexpected downpour swept over the area, scattering the multitude through the streets to find shelter. Most found their way to Nanny Goat Market, a pavilion large enough to accommodate the meeting.

Just as the speaker resumed addressing his rainsoaked and restless audience, someone fired a gun. A number of witnesses blamed a sniper from the nearby station house of the Hibernia Hose Company, an Irish fire brigade; others claimed that an argument within the crowd had sparked the shooting. Either way, one of the nativist protesters, an 18-year-old named George Schiffler, lay gravely wounded.

The assembly erupted in pandemonium. Nativists by the hundreds stormed through the neighborhood, dislodging cobblestones to hurl through the windows of Irish stores and homes. Four men carried George Schiffler to an apothecary shop, where he died within an hour. Back at Nanny Goat Market, a band of Kensington residents attacked the remaining protesters with brickbats and pistols. One old Irishman in a sealskin cap took potshots with a musket.

The Irish and nativist factions regrouped on opposite sides of the market, skirmishing periodically throughout the evening. Philadelphia County Sheriff Morton McMichael arrived with several of his marshals during a lull around 7 p.m. and saw no need to exercise his authority.

By 10 o'clock, however, the nativists had swelled their ranks and were surging down Second Street toward the Female Roman Catholic Seminary. Faced with a rampage, Sheriff McMichael ordered his men to fire their rifles over the heads of the crowd. An assault on the seminary was averted, but angry nativists roamed the streets past midnight.

The next morning—Tuesday, May 7— Philadelphians awoke to an uneasy calm. The *Native American* newspaper appeared with its front page banded in black for mourning. The guns were quiet, but on streetcorners around the city the usual commerce was punctuated by spontaneous anti-Catholic harangues. Bishop Kenrick issued a formal statement condemning Catholic participation in the turmoil and had copies posted in all districts. Within hours the nativists had removed these notices and folded them into paper hats.

Nativist leader Thomas Newbold announced a meeting to be held downtown that afternoon at 3 o'clock in Independence Square, a location that still symbolizes Philadelphia's role in the American Revolution. There the protesters passed voice-vote resolutions asserting their right to gather peaceably and charging the Catholics with attempting to drive the Bible out of the schools. Despite the pleadings of several leaders, the group elected to march once again into Kensington.

The Irish neighborhood was located about a mile and a half north of Independence Square. Along the way, the marchers shouted nativist slogans and waved a tattered American flag that they said had been trampled by Irishmen. With minimal warning, Kensington residents prepared to defend their homes and themselves. A distant roar and the shattering of windows announced the approaching mob.

No sooner had the market area begun to fill with nativists than a shot rang out from a house across the street, instantly killing one marcher. The crowd's attempt to charge the house was halted by a volley of gunfire from rooftops and windows. In sporadic confrontations over the next hour, three more marchers died. Still refusing to disband and flee, the nativists sent a small party to torch a building in which several snipers were hiding. The fire quickly consumed that structure and spread along the block. Within minutes, nearly 30 buildings were in flames, including Nanny Goat Market. As soon as the Hibernia and Carroll fire brigades arrived on the scene, the rioters attacked them. Two engines and four carriages were destroyed.

Brig. Gen. Thomas Cadwalader, commander of the Pennsylvania militia, had had his men on alert since the day before. At 9 p.m. on Tuesday, at the height of the market fire, Sheriff McMichael called for Cadwalader to station his troops on the outskirts of Kensington. Around midnight, the order came to occupy the ravaged district. The soldiers succeeded in intimidating the mob without further violence by setting up loaded cannons in the streets. Under military escort, the fire companies hosed down the smoldering ruins.

By Wednesday morning, only three men—all Irish—had been arrested for their role in the disturbance. Following his arraignment for murder, John Taggert was escorted by several deputies to Northern Liberties Jail, thought to be a safe distance from Kensington. Along the way, a band of nativists seized Taggert, brutally beat him and got his neck in a noose before the deputies returned with enough help to save him.

Early in the afternoon, nativists began making their way back toward Kensington. The smell of smoke still hung in the air. Here and there, speakers railed against the Pope and demanded vengeance for the deaths of their comrades. Anticipating a replay of the night before, Irish Protestant and nativist residents of the district hung American flags and signs reading "Native American" in their windows. Some simply tacked up copies of the newspaper by that name. Each display drew a cheer from the passing throng.

Militia units patroling the area were unable to quell the unrest. As momentum gathered, marchers forcibly entered Irish homes to search for weapons. New fires, deliberately set, destroyed or damaged several more blocks by late afternoon. Emboldened by these exploits, the nativists broadened their aim and struck out toward downtown Philadelphia.

Mayor John Morin Scott, summoned from his daughter's birthday party, met the mob as it reached St. Augustine's Roman Catholic Church, at the corner of Fourth and Vine. The mayor spoke from the church steps, calling for reason and calm and denying a rumor that the building contained stored weapons. With this he explained that he himself was carrying the key.

Suddenly, a hurled stone hit the mayor in the chest, knocking the breath out of him. Police guards hurriedly bundled him away. The rioters, now confident that the church was undefended, lifted two boys over the fence to begin the destruction. The youngsters broke in through a window and set fire to curtains and furnishings. According to plan, someone ruptured the building's gas line, and the leak ignited just as the intruders escaped. Again, the crowd blocked firefighters' access to the blaze.

Similar assaults that afternoon destroyed St. Michael's Roman Catholic Church, from which the priest barely escaped, and the Female Seminary that had been spared two days earlier. The mob roared as the burning steeples toppled. The fires produced columns of smoke that were visible for miles. As the flames diminished, the fury of the nativists also seemed to subside. In a final flare-up, a remnant of the mob ransacked the home of Alderman Hugh Clark. The streets were empty before sundown.

In crowded and barricaded rooms in Kensington, many Irish Catholic families made plans to leave Philadelphia. Others argued that only by standing their ground could they ever make a home in America.

On Thursday morning, May 9, Mayor Scott convened a meeting in Independence Square to begin the process of restoring the public peace. In the three days of upheaval, 20 people had been killed, scores more injured and two Catholic churches and more than 50 Irish homes destroyed.

By acclamation, those present—many of whom had participated in the rioting—agreed to the appointment of special police units to patrol each neighborhood. Even the editors of the *Native American* voiced shock and regret: "No terms that we can use are able to express the deep reprobation that we feel for this iniquitous proceeding; this wanton and uncalled-for desecration of the Christian altar."

Despite the general contrition and heightened security, isolated groups and individuals continued the campaign of anti-Catholic vandalism. Bishop Kenrick cancelled Sunday Mass throughout Philadelphia to avoid further confrontation. When posters boldly printed with the words "Fortunio and his Seven Gifted Servants" began appearing around the city, a rumor circulated that the strange slogan was a secret message from the Pope ordering Catholics to take up arms. The rumor died when a businessman revealed that the signs advertised a play coming soon to a local theatre.

The nativist/Irish conflict erupted again in Philadelphia later that summer. Organizers of the city's annual Independence Day celebration staged a procession honoring the widows and orphans of nativists who had died in the riots. The display rekindled bitter memories, and soon new suspicions arose that the Catholics were planning an uprising in the suburb of Southwark. Again the militia was called in, and the fighting that broke out was as fierce as that in Kensington. This time, the death toll reached 13.

Several months after these episodes, Philadelphia County complied with state law by repaying Catholics for damages incurred to their property in the mob violence. The riots of 1844 damaged the public image of the nativist movement, which would later seek new legitimacy in the political system. The establishment of a separate Catholic school system in Philadelphia solved the Bible problem but did little to heal the rift between the two communities. That process would take place some years later as nativists and Irish immigrants and soldiers of all stripes joined forces to preserve the federal union.

Questions for Discussion

1. What important economic and social differences existed between the Irish Catholics who had recently migrated to the United States in the 1840s and the native-born Protestants who lived in Philadelphia at that time?

2. Discuss how the conflict between the Philadelphia Protestants and Irish Catholics might have been addressed and resolved peacefully.

3. What are some of the current examples of religious intolerance that has emerged in America since the War on Terrorism and 9/11? What are some nonviolent methods of resolving these religious disputes?

CHAPTER 6

Education in the Post–Civil War Era

Education and work are levers to uplift a people. Work alone will not do it unless inspired by the right ideals and guided by intelligence. Education must not simply teach work—it must teach life.

—*W. E. B. DuBois*
The Negro Problem, 1903

The later decades of the 19th century saw a continuation of the trend toward urbanization as the rural migration and influx of immigrants continued. Beginning in 1885 a large migration from eastern and southern Europe, known as the New Migration, brought millions of new immigrants to America (see Table 7.1). As in earlier decades, the schools were seen as both the path to upward mobility and a weapon in the war on urban poverty, juvenile delinquency, and the perceived moral derogation of society.

In the period after the Civil War the common school spread beyond its New England beginnings to the remainder of the nation. Increased enrollment in the common schools translated into a growing demand for education beyond the common school. In response, the late 19th and early 20th centuries witnessed the rapid and national expansion of another educational institution, the comprehensive high school, as well as the introduction of a new secondary institution, the junior high school. In higher education this was also a time of institution building—the junior college—as well as a period of expansion and redefinition of existing institutions. Normal schools expanded their curricula and became teachers colleges involved in the training of both elementary and secondary teachers. And, what were essentially small liberal arts colleges transformed into large universities involved in graduate education and research. At the other end of the spectrum, the kindergarten was introduced.

A number of forces worked to bring about these changes. The demands of workingmen, farmers, and a growing middle class; the ongoing demand for skilled workers; concern over U.S. competition in the world market; and major national reform reports on the curriculum were key factors in the transformation of the high school as well as the movement to introduce vocational education into the curriculum. Additional impetus for growth and change in higher education came from the Morrill Acts and the increased number of women entering higher education. At the end of the period the framework of the American educational system we know today, from the kindergarten through the comprehensive high school and the multipurpose research university, was in place.

During this period in American education history major changes were taking place not only in public elementary, secondary, and postsecondary education, but also in the education of two groups that had traditionally been excluded from these schools—Native Americans and African Americans. After the Civil War the federal government became involved in the education of the former slaves while also assuming greater responsibility for the education of Native Americans. However, as the century progressed, the government withdrew its support for the education of Blacks, which fell into neglect in the hands of the states. At the same time, federal programs for Native Americans expanded and became institutionalized under the Bureau of Indian Affairs. The condition of the education of Blacks and Native Americans did not significantly improve until the middle of the next century.

The Kindergarten Movement

The first kindergarten was established in 1837 in Germany by Fredrich Froebel (1782–1852), who gave it the name that is now used in almost every language—*kindergarten* (in German, "children's garden"). Froebel studied at Pestalozzi's institute in Switzerland and accepted many of his ideas associated with sense realism, child-centeredness, and the object lesson, but he was more concerned with activity than was Pestalozzi. According to Froebel, the primary aim of the school should be the development of the native endowments of the individual child through self-expression. Self-expression was encouraged by an active curriculum that included games, singing, or any number of creative and spontaneous activities. Froebel believed that the education process should begin with the child as early as 3 or 4 years of age.

Froebel developed highly stylized materials that were mass produced, boxed with instructions for their use, and distributed throughout the Western world. *Mother and Nursery Songs* was a collection of songs, poems, pictures, instructions, games, and suggested activities designed for instruction of the young at home (Gillett, 1966). As described in the Primary Source Reading for this chapter, the so-called *gifts* and *occupations* were to be used. The gifts were play objects that did not change their form (e.g., wooden spheres or cubes). They were symbols of the fundamentals of nature and were designed to assist the child in understanding the concept each represented. The occupations were materials used in creative construction or design activities whose shape changed in use (e.g., clay, sand, or paper). Used together, they were said to ensure the progressive self-development of the child.

Froebel's system of education emphasized play as an environment for instruction because it was the traditional avenue of growth and learning for children. It also included projects in gardening and construction that were organized in great detail. In fact, every aspect of group and individual activity and interaction was minutely prescribed to promote the development of social relationships.

One of Froebel's pupils, Margaretha Schurz, opened the first kindergarten in the United States in Watertown, Wisconsin, in 1856. Other German-speaking communities soon followed. Four years later the first English-speaking kindergarten was established in Boston by Elizabeth Peabody, a sister-in-law of Horace Mann. This school served as an educational stepping-stone to the elementary school for students from well-to-do families. However, the first large-scale adoption of the kindergarten in St. Louis in the 1870s was not targeted to the well-to-do, but to the children of the urban poor. Begun as charity kindergartens by a young socialite, Susan Blow, who had observed the kindergarten firsthand in Germany, their success led to their adoption by the school board. With the encouragement of Superintendent William T. Harris, the kindergarten was expanded, and Miss Blow opened a school to train fellow teachers in Froebel's methods. Other, mostly urban, districts followed the lead of St. Louis. The kindergarten movement also expanded in the private arena with assistance from philanthropic individuals and societies who saw the kindergarten as a way to combat the ills of urban poverty. The success of the "charity kindergartens" and the support given the kindergarten movement by the National Education Association, which in 1884 established a department of kindergarten instruction, contributed

Kindergarten at the North-End Industrial Home in Boston, Massachusetts, in 1881.

to the adoption of the kindergarten by public school systems. By 1918, although not universally established (only 10.5% of the 4.5 million children between 4 and 6 years of age were enrolled in a kindergarten [Butts & Cremin, 1953]), the kindergarten had undoubtedly been accepted as the first rung of the American education ladder.

The Secondary School Movement

While the kindergarten movement was preparing children for entry into school, the secondary school movement was providing opportunities for young people to stay in school longer. Although the high school had been introduced onto the American education scene as early as 1821, in the years before the Civil War the high school movement had grown slowly. Ten years after its introduction, in 1831, the first American *comprehensive* (and coeducational) *high school*, offering both English and classical courses of study, was opened in Lowell, Massachusetts. High schools were also soon opened in several other larger cities. However, the movement was slow in developing. By 1860 there were only 300 high schools in the nation compared to more than 6,000 academies. Of the 300, more than 100 were located in Massachusetts, the only state that had enacted legislation requiring communities to provide secondary level education.

The slow growth of the high school movement can be partially explained by the fact that, unlike the common school, the high school had not yet been overwhelmingly demanded by the masses. Rather, it appeared to be more a reformer's response to urbanization and industrialization. Middle- or upper-class reformers, adopting the philosophy and rhetoric of the common school advocates, viewed their efforts as democratizing secondary education and providing a means of maintaining social values, addressing the social problems centered in urban centers, and promoting economic progress. As a result, prior to the Civil War, most high schools were located in urban areas, where a sufficient number of students and sufficient tax support were most often found.

In the years after the Civil War, however, a number of factors came together to create a greater demand for secondary education. These factors were similar to those that fueled the common school movement: population growth caused in large part by increased immigration, and a rapid growth in industry and technological change that intensified the demand for skilled workers. At the same time, a high school education was increasingly seen as necessary to the full realization of one's social and economic goals. This was as true for artisans and small entrepreneurs in the cities as it was for businessmen and professionals in rural communities (Herbst, 1996). Lastly, economic growth created a larger tax base that could be used to support an expanded education system.

The convergence of these factors created a demand for secondary education that brought a dramatic increase in the number of public high schools—from about 500 in 1870 to 6,000 in 1900. During the 1880s the number of high schools increased tenfold and surpassed the number of academies. By the end of the century free public high schools had pushed out the majority of fee-paying academies. Although still only a small percentage of the eligible population attended high school, in 1900 over half a million students were enrolled and 62,000 graduated (see Table 6.1).

The Kalamazoo Case and Increased Tax Support

The public secondary school movement was given impetus by the decision of the Michigan Supreme Court in the famous *Kalamazoo* case (1874). The case originated when the school board of Kalamazoo, Michigan, moved to establish a publicly supported high school and hire a nonteaching superintendent. Three taxpayers brought suit to prevent the board from levying a tax to support the high school. They charged that because the instruction in the schools was not practical and therefore not necessary or beneficial to the majority of people, but instead benefited only a few, these few should be the ones to pay for it (*Stuart et al. v. School District No. 1 of the Village of Kalamazoo*, 1874). The taxpayers based their suit on the fact that the Michigan constitution authorized the establishment of common schools and a university but did not mention secondary or high schools, as well as the fact that the constitution specified that English was to be the language of instruction in the schools, not Latin (the curriculum of the high school was primarily college prep and did emphasize Latin). The Michigan Supreme Court ruled in favor of the school board. According to the rationale of the court, it would be inconsistent with the intent of the framers of the Michigan constitution to have set up elementary schools and a state university and then

TABLE 6.1 Summary of Public Elementary and Secondary School Statistics: 1869–70 to 1929–30

Item	1869–70	1879–80	1889–90	1899–1900	1909–10	1919–20	1929–30
1	2	3	4	5	6	7	8
Population, pupils, and instructional staff							
Total population, in thousands	38,558	50,156	62,622	75,995	90,490	104,514	121,878
Population aged 5–17 years, in thousands	11,683	15,066	18,473	21,573	24,011	27,571	31,414
Percent of total population 5–17	30.3	30.0	29.5	28.4	26.5	26.4	25.8
Total enrollment in elementary and secondary schools, in thousands	7,562	9,867	12,723	15,503	17,814	21,578	25,678
Kindergarten and grades 1–8, in thousands	7,481	9,757	12,520	14,984	16,899	19,378	21,279
Grades 9–12, in thousands	80	110	203	519	915	2,200	4,399
Enrollment as a percent of 5-to 17-year-olds	64.7	65.5	68.9	71.9	74.2	78.3	81.7
High school graduates, in thousands	—	—	22	62	111	231	592
Average daily attendance, in thousands	4,077	6,144	8,154	10,633	12,827	16,150	21,265
Average length of school term, in days	132.2	130.3	134.7	144.3	157.5	161.9	172.7
Total instructional staff, in thousands	—	—	—	—	—	678	880
Supervisors, in thousands	—	—	—	—	—	7	7
Principals, in thousands	—	—	—	—	—	14	31
Teachers, librarians, and other nonsupervisory instructional staff, in thousands	201	287	364	423	523	657	843
Men, in thousands	78	123	126	127	110	93	140
Women, in thousands	123	164	238	296	413	585	703

Source: National Center for Education Statistics, U.S. Department of Education. (2002). *Digest of education statistics, 2002.* Washington, DC: U.S. Government Printing Office.

expect citizens to obtain a private secondary education. The court also held that it was within the power of the school board to have a superintendent and that when the voters of the district had voted to support a high school it was within the authority of the school board to decide the curriculum.

By ruling that the legislature could tax for the support of secondary schools, the Michigan Supreme Court provided the precedent for public support of secondary education. As a result of the growth in secondary education, in the decade between school years 1879–80 and 1889–90, total expenditures for the public schools increased 81%, from $78 million to $141 million (National Center for Education Statistics [NCES], 2003).

Compulsory Attendance and Increased Literacy

The *Kalamazoo* decision having quashed the argument that public funds could not be used for secondary education, compulsory attendance laws soon followed. Although Massachusetts had passed the first compulsory attendance law in 1852 (requiring all children between ages 8 and 14 to attend school 12 weeks a year, 6 of them consecutively), the push for compulsory attendance laws did not take place until after the Civil War. Compulsory attendance laws were a complement to child labor laws. Although not directed at school attendance, child labor laws had the effect of regulating school attendance. For example, child labor laws enacted in Massachusetts in 1836 and Connecticut in 1842 said that no child under 15 could be employed in any business or industry without proof of having attended school 3 out of the past 12 months. The passage of similar child labor laws in other states was instrumental in driving the adoption of compulsory attendance laws. Concomitant with the adoption of child labor laws were the technological advances in industry that decreased the need for child labor.

By 1918 all states had enacted laws requiring full-time attendance until the child reached a certain age or completed a certain grade. The passage of such laws was not accompanied by full and immediate compliance, but the laws did combine with other factors to raise the attendance rate from 50% in 1865 to 72% in 1900. Also by 1900 children attended school an average of 99 days per year, twice as many as they had a century earlier (NCES, 2003).

One result of the increase in school attendance was a declining illiteracy rate: from 20% of all persons over 10 years of age in 1870, to 7.7% in 1910 (Graham, 1974). However, illiteracy rates varied by segment of the population and region. As a result of the pre–Civil War prohibitions on teaching Blacks and the provision of an inadequate education after the war, Blacks had the highest illiteracy rate, 30.4% in 1910. The illiteracy rate was also high among the older population, which had not been the beneficiary of universal, compulsory education. Whites who were the children of a foreign-born parent had the lowest illiteracy rate, 1.1%. And, the South, which not only had the most Blacks but also had been the slowest in developing systems of common schools, had the highest illiteracy rate (Graham, 1974).

NEA Committee of Ten and the Standardization of the Curriculum

In its origins the high school had been viewed as a provider of a more practical education than that of the academy. However, although its curriculum may have been more practical than that of the academy, at the end of the 19th century it was still oriented toward preparing students for college, despite the fact that the majority of students did not go to college. As high school enrollment increased, there was growing concern that the needs of the terminal student were not being met and that, as a consequence, many dropped out. Many questions arose regarding the proper relationship between the elementary school and the high school, and the high school and higher education, as well as what should be taught at each level. Then, as now, institutions of higher education complained about the preparation provided by the high schools, and the high schools complained about the varied and conflicting entrance requirements of colleges and universities.

In an attempt to address some of these issues, and in an effort to standardize the high school curriculum and college entrance requirements, in 1892 the National Education Association (NEA) established the Committee of Ten. The committee was chaired by Charles Eliot, the much-respected president of Harvard University, and was largely composed of representatives of higher education. The *Report of the Committee on Secondary School Studies* was issued in late 1893. Four different curricula were recommended by the committee: classical, Latin-scientific, modern language, and English. However, while maintaining that the purpose of secondary schools was not to prepare students for college and acknowledging that few secondary students went on to college, the committee used the same mental discipline rationale as had the framers of the Yale Report to suggest that the subjects that prepared a student for college would be useful to all students because they trained the powers of reasoning, observation, memory, and expression. Vocational training, they believed, should come after high school.

Although the recommendations of the Committee of Ten came under immediate attack from many educators, they did serve to determine the standardized curricular patterns for several decades. They also laid the groundwork for recurring proposals for a core curriculum that were made throughout the 20th century. The report of the Committee of Ten also had a major influence on the work of the Carnegie Foundation for the Advancement of Teaching, which resulted in the establishment of the Carnegie Unit as the standard unit of credit for a yearlong high school course.

 For Your Reflection and Analysis

If the Committee of Ten were charged today with selecting the subject matter of the high school, what changes might it propose?

Seven Cardinal Principles of Secondary Education

The opposition to the recommendations of the Committee of Ten that greeted their announcement did not diminish with time, and within 25 years little support could be found. Concerns remained that high schools were not able to attract and retain students, who were then left to roam the streets. In 1913 the National Education

Association responded by appointing another committee, the Commission on the Reorganization of Secondary Education (CRSE), to review the curriculum and organization of secondary education in light of the many changes that had taken place in society and the workplace, as well as in the secondary school population and educational learning theories.

Unlike the Committee of Ten, which was made up almost exclusively of university representatives, the CRSE included high school teachers and principals, school district administrators, normal school teachers and administrators, representatives of state departments of education, the U.S. commissioner of education, and other representatives of the U.S. Bureau of Education. After 5 years of work the CRSE issued its report, the *Cardinal Principles of Secondary Education* (U.S. Bureau of Education, 1918).

The underlying philosophy of the CRSE was that schools in a democracy should be organized such that "the individual and society may find fulfillment each in the other" (U.S. Bureau of Education, 1918, p. 9). A second major theme of the *Principles* was the concept of social efficiency. The "cult of efficiency" that had gained favor in the business community found life in the schools in the curriculum theory of social efficiency discussed in more detail in chapter 7. Social efficiency argued that in order for society to function efficiently, students to use their time more efficiently, and schools to operate more efficiently, education should help students understand their function in society and should offer them only those subjects that would prepare them most directly for what their lives had in store (Kliebard, 1995).

The report identified seven objectives that should guide the curriculum: (1) health; (2) command of fundamental processes (reading, writing, and oral expression); (3) worthy home membership; (4) vocation; (5) citizenship; (6) worthy use of leisure; and (7) ethical character. As compared to the recommendations of the Committee of Ten, only one of the objectives, command of fundamental processes, was concerned with college preparation. And, unlike the Committee of Ten report, which focused on the four curricula, the *Principles* focused on goals or objectives outside the curriculum; the curriculum was the instrument through which students would achieve the goals.

 For Your Reflection and Analysis

Of the seven cardinal principals, which ones have the most relevance today?

The *Cardinal Principles* were widely accepted and represented two significant reforms: "First, they directly facilitated the assimilation of all students into a common culture, and second, this was the first time that the school curriculum became the means through which nonacademic goals were to be attained" (Horn, 2002, p. 35). After a decade of debate over whether secondary education in the United States should follow the European model of dual systems (academic and vocational/industrial) or a unitary, "democratic" system, the *Principles* provided the blueprint for the American comprehensive high school and its distinguishing feature—academic and vocational studies under the same roof (Wraga, 2000). The comprehensive high school would serve two complementary functions: a specialized function that would address the variegated needs of a heterogeneous student body and a unifying function that would promote the social interaction of students from different backgrounds (Wraga, 2000). Social interaction was facilitated by extracurricular activities and the intermingling of students in those parts of the curriculum that would be common to all students (e.g., health, citizenship, and ethics). The report revised the curricular philosophy of the high school while also preparing the foundation for the comprehensive high school as the institutional expansion of that philosophy (Kliebard, 1995).

The Manual Training Movement

Concurrent with the high school movement, and anticipating the more functional emphasis of the *Cardinal Principles*, was the manual training movement. Manual training prepared the way for vocational education. Manual training began in the 1870s with the training of engineers, but soon spread to public education and was promoted by President John Runkle of the Massachusetts Institute of Technology. Manual training, as opposed to vocational training or the mechanical arts, was intended to develop perception, dexterity, hand–eye coordination, and visual accuracy and was not specific to any trade or vocation or the manufacture of any product (Herbst, 1996).

Manual training was welcomed at the secondary level by many who did not welcome the involvement of business and industry in the curriculum of the school. Separating instruction from production provided manual and mental training for future draftsmen, engineers, and craftsmen, while also providing all students the opportunity to discover and pursue their mechanical interests and talents and encouraging them to remain in school. These arguments, most persuasively and forcefully made by Calvin Woodward, dean of the O'Fallon Polytechnic Institute of Washington University, a manual training high school, appealed to educators, parents, and others who were critical of the narrow academic focus of the traditional high school (Herbst, 1996).

The movement to integrate manual training into the public schools did not go unchallenged. Some educators agreed with the Committee of Ten's contention that the public schools were not in the business of preparing workers for business or the crafts. Criticism from the opposite direction came from those who saw little relationship between the skills gained in manual training and those needed by industry. Others objected to manual training because of its association with reform schools, where it was considered the appropriate program for students who were unprepared or unable to benefit from academic instruction. Manual training had also traditionally been associated with the schooling of Native Americans and Blacks, and a number of the critics of these programs, most notably W. E. B. DuBois, questioned the limits manual training placed on the occupational and economic advancement of these minorities.

Despite these and other objections, manual training was introduced in numerous schools, typically in the form of drafting, art education, or mechanics. However, manual training never really gained a lasting place in the curriculum. It was never able to gain the support of a critical mass of educators. In part this may have been due to the low esteem in which it was held by many educators (manual training was conspicuous by its absence from the report of the Committee of Ten). However, manual training did play a major role in setting the stage for another movement—the vocational education movement.

Vocational Education

By the turn of the 20th century, business leaders had become increasingly concerned that the United States was losing ground in competition in world markets, particularly to Germany. The success of the German technical schools in preparing highly skilled workers was seen as a major factor in Germany's economic success. Industry's interest in vocational education coincided with progressive education's criticism of the public schools. By 1910 business leaders, public officials, unions, and progressive educators had come together to create the vocational education movement (Cuban, 2001). They pressured the schools to do more than simply link theory and practice but to offer a separate vocational curriculum.

The initial response of school districts, especially those in the larger cities, was to open trade, technical, and industrial high schools. The next major step came with the introduction of day and evening continuation schools for youth already at work, and cooperative education programs jointly sponsored by the schools and industry. The later arrangements freed the public schools from investing in shops, kitchens, and other specialized work spaces. Equally important, artisans, master craftsmen, and other experienced tradespersons served as instructors, leaving the high school teachers to concentrate on academic and citizenship education (Herbst, 1996).

 For Your Reflection and Analysis

Should requirements be placed on noneducators before they can teach in the public schools?

Vocational education programs tended to be concentrated in the cities, and those to whom the programs were initially directed, the children of immigrants, responded enthusiastically to them. In the South vocational education was initially geared to Blacks. According to one historian's interpretation, both immigrants and Blacks occupied a somewhat analogous position—numerically large and politically weak. Both groups were also accustomed to the dominant group, native-born Whites, making educational policy decisions for them. In this instance the dominant group had decided that vocational training would be good for "others" (Graham, 1974).

Labor leaders were originally opposed to the concept of a differentiated vocational curriculum; they saw it as exacerbating class differences. However, they came to accept the argument that the benefits vocational education offered in keeping students in school and providing them the skills necessary for higher paying jobs outweighed this negative. They also believed, or at least hoped, that as long as vocational education was part of the comprehensive high school, students from different social classes would have the opportunity to interact.

Vocational education was already established in the high school curriculum when a business-led coalition succeeded in securing federal support for vocational education through the Smith-Hughes Act of 1917. The Smith-Hughes Act provided federal funds to help pay for the preparation and salaries of teachers in the agriculture, trade and industrial, and home economics fields.

Vocational education was one of the most successful reform initiatives of the 20th century (Horn, 2002) and key to attracting larger numbers and a wider range of students to the high school. Not only was a new curricular option created, but also

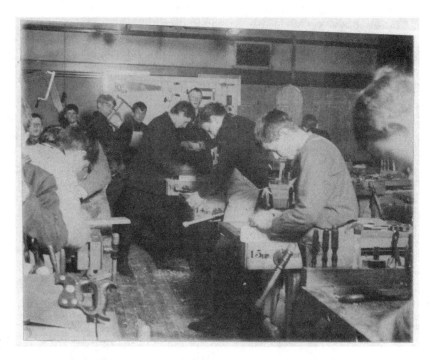

Vocational education was one of the most successful educational reforms of the 20th century.

many existing subjects were infused with criteria taken from vocational education; for example, courses such as business mathematics and business English were accepted as legitimate substitutes for the traditional forms of these subjects (Kliebard, 1995). By the late 1920s separate vocational tracks and vocational guidance counselors were in place in most urban comprehensive high schools; vocational education had become a fundamental part of the public school system.

The Comprehensive High School

By the mid-1920s the work of the CRSE and the introduction of vocational education had given shape to the American comprehensive high school. It was an institution based on the concept of democracy that offered a range of curricula to students of differing abilities and interests. Four basic curricula were offered: (1) the college preparatory program, which included courses in English language and literature, foreign languages, mathematics, the natural and physical sciences, and history and social sciences; (2) the commercial or business program, which offered courses in bookkeeping, shorthand, and typing; (3) the industrial, vocational, home economics, and agricultural programs; and (4) a modified academic program for students who planned to terminate their formal education upon high school completion. Students self-selected different educational tracks based on their abilities, goals, interests, or prospects for further education. As guidance counselors became more common, standardized tests were used to sort students into the different curricular tracks.

For a variety of reasons, despite the opportunity for alternative curricula, the college prep curriculum remained the dominant curriculum track in most comprehensive high schools. In his study of the high school curriculum during the 1920s Counts (1926) attributed this to the social prestige associated with the traditional curriculum. In other schools, especially in small high schools, enrollments and resources typically could not support all four curricula, and despite efforts to break the stranglehold of the college preparatory curriculum and the inroads made by vocational education, often the only program offered was the academic program.

The domination of the traditional academic curriculum, as well as a structure that anticipated students moving through graded classrooms, studying the same subjects in the same ways, and taking exams for promotion resulted in many students being left behind. Retarded students aged 10 to 15, many from poor and immigrant families, crowded the upper elementary grades "shamed and bored as individuals and collectively producing what educators called 'waste'—a social sin in an age that glorified the concept of social efficiency" (Tyack & Cuban, 1995, p. 186).

Emergence of the Junior High School

The *junior high school*, which appeared in the first decade of the 20th century, offering Grades 6 and 7, or 6, 7, and 8, was designed, in part, to address the problems of the high school. It was also a response to the Committee of Ten's recommendation that academic work begin earlier and that elementary schooling be reduced from 8 to 6 years and secondary education be extended down 2 years. The concept appealed to several groups of reformers. One group was concerned about attrition and preparing students for the world of work. They felt the junior high school would prevent dropping out and would provide students the opportunity to explore their vocational interests or even receive vocational training before high school. Another group was encouraged by the work of developmental psychologists such as G. Stanley Hall that emphasized the developmental differences between childhood and preadolescence, and between preadolescence and postadolescence, and suggested that for educational purposes children at these stages were better kept separate. According to Hall and his contemporaries, the junior high school period was one in which "differences of abilities or extra-school conditions and of prospects will acutely manifest themselves, forcing us to differentiate curricula" (Snedden, cited in Kliebard, 1995, p. 96).

 For Your Reflection and Analysis

What are some of the ways "extra-school conditions" differ during the junior high school period?

A third group of reformers was concerned with transforming the curriculum of the entire school system. These reformers wanted to break the rigidity of the traditional classroom and introduce new subjects and new ways of teaching. They believed that reorganizing the intermediate grades would provide the impetus for reorganizing the entire public school system (Tyack & Cuban, 1995).

Although the concept of the junior high school did receive widespread support, its adoption and incorporation into school systems was slow. The first junior high school was established in Columbus, Ohio, in 1909 and was followed by a second the next year in Berkeley, California. Ten years later 94% of the secondary schools in the country were still following the traditional pattern of 8 years of elementary school and 4 years of high school. Two decades later this pattern still characterized about two thirds of the secondary schools (Tyack & Cuban, 1995). It was not until after World War II and a rapid growth in enrollments and new school construction that school reorganization driven by overcrowding and space availability brought an end to the dominance of the 8–4 pattern and cemented this rung of the U.S. education system ladder.

Expansion of Higher Education

The Morrill Acts and the Land Grant College Movement

Throughout the first half of the 19th century, as the population grew and expanded westward, the number of colleges grew rapidly. By the outbreak of the Civil War 20 states had established colleges supported largely from public lands. In 1862 additional incentive was provided by the Land Grant College Act, also known as the Morrill Act after its sponsor, Representative Justin Morrill of Vermont. A growing recognition among farmers and laborers that education would contribute to an improved economic condition, and that the curriculum of the majority of the existing colleges was irrelevant to their needs, led them to urge the establishment of institutions that would provide a more practical education related to their needs. In response, with the backing of industrial interests, but over the objections of many private colleges, the first Morrill Act was passed by Congress and signed by President Lincoln in 1862. The act granted 30,000 acres of public land to each state for each senator and representative it had in Congress based on the 1860 census. The income from the land was to be used to support at least one college that would teach subjects related to "agriculture and mechanical arts." The money could be used to establish agricultural and mechanical schools at existing colleges, to add support to existing programs, or to open new colleges. Within a decade 24 land grant colleges were enrolling 2,600 students, 13% of the total U.S. collegiate population (Williams, 2003). Among the first of the new institutions were the universities of Maine (1865), West Virginia and Illinois (1867), California (1868), Nebraska and Purdue (1869), Ohio State (1870), and Arkansas and Texas A & M (1871).

Despite these numbers, the quarter century after the Civil War was not positive for land grant colleges. Their faculties were inadequate, and they attracted far more engineering students than agricultural students (Williams, 2003). However, the passage of the Hatch Act in 1887, which established and funded agricultural experimental stations at land grant colleges, and the Morrill Act of 1890, which provided for direct annual grants to each state to support educational programs at land grant colleges, gave strength to the movement. The second Morrill Act also mandated that no grant

For Your Reflection and Analysis

What is the land grant college in your state? Was it established as a land grant college, or did it become one with the Morrill Act?

be given to any state that denied admission to its land grant colleges because of race without providing "separate but equal" institutions. Soon after, 17 states, mostly in the South, also established separate land grant colleges for Blacks.

The two Morrill Acts provided the incentive for a shift from the classical to a more applied curriculum and for greatly expanded state systems of higher education. The acts provided the financial stability land grant colleges needed and at the same time promoted state support (Williams, 2003). They also marked a major shift in the federal government's involvement in the provision of education. For the first time the federal government sought to influence the direction of education and for the first time made a significant and direct financial contribution to education. The 106 land grant colleges and universities are listed in Table 6.2

Higher Education for Women

Another group for whom opportunities for higher education expanded in the period after the Civil War was women. As previously noted, a number of women's seminaries and a few women's colleges had been opened prior to the Civil War. Although most were not equal to the best men's colleges in terms of admission standards or degree requirements, they probably compared favorably with the majority of male institutions of the period that claimed collegiate status (Newcomer, 1959). Some, such as Mary Sharp College, which was founded in 1850 and required both Latin and Greek for graduation, were comparable to the finest men's colleges (Woody, 1929). Prior to the Civil War, Georgia Female College (1836), Oxford Female College (1852), Illinois Conference Female College (1854), Ingram University (1857), and Vassar College (1861) were among the women's colleges offering a four-year course leading to an A.B. degree (Newcomer, 1959). In addition to the women's colleges, several formerly all-male institutions (e.g., Oberlin in 1833; Antioch in 1853; and the State University of Iowa in 1858) began admitting women prior to the Civil War.

Although the door to higher education for women was opening, it was not yet opened very wide. Prior to the Civil War only 3,000 women in the entire nation were attending colleges or universities that offered A.B. degrees (Newcomer, 1959). Women's higher education only really began to flourish after the Civil War. Several private women's colleges (e.g., Wellesley, 1875; Smith, 1875; Radcliff, 1879; and Bryn Mawr, 1880) were established that offered programs comparable to those found in the men's colleges. In 1884 Mississippi chartered the first public-supported state women's college, Mississippi State College for Women. In addition, an increasing number of state universities began admitting women, albeit selectively.

Women had an increased presence in higher education for a number of reasons. The growth of public secondary education was no doubt a major factor. The Civil War itself was another contributing factor in that it brought a decline in male college enrollments that women were eager to fill. The opening of several professions to women also increased their interest in higher education: Although overall the numbers were small, more and more women were becoming physicians and ministers, and

TABLE 6.2 Land Grant Colleges and Universities

Alabama
  Alabama A&M University
  Auburn University
  Tuskegee University
Alaska
  University of Alaska System
American Samoa
  American Samoa Community College
Arizona
  University of Arizona
  Dine College
Arkansas
  University of Arkansas, Fayetteville
  University of Arkansas at Pine Bluff
California
  University of California
  D-Q University
Colorado
  Colorado State University
Connecticut
  University of Connecticut
Delaware
  Delaware State University
  University of Delaware
District of Columbia
  University of the District of Columbia
Federated States of Micronesia
  College of Micronesia
Florida
  Florida A&M University
  University of Florida
Georgia
  Fort Valley State University
  University of Georgia
Guam
  University of Guam
Hawaii
  University of Hawaii
Idaho
  University of Idaho

Illinois
  University of Illinois
  Fort Peck Community College
  Little Big Horn College
  Salish Kootenai College
  Stone Child College
Nebraska
  University of Nebraska
  Nebraska Indian Community College
  Little Priest Tribal College
Nevada
  University of Nevada, Reno
New Hampshire
  University of New Hampshire
New Jersey
  Rutgers, The State University of New Jersey
New Mexico
  Crown Point Institute of Technology
  New Mexico State University
  Southwestern Indian Polytechnic Institute
  Institute of American Indian Arts
New York
  Cornell University
North Carolina
  North Carolina A&T State University
  North Carolina State University
North Dakota
  North Dakota State University
  Cankdeska Cikana Community College
  Fort Berthold Community College
  Sitting Bull College
  Turtle Mountain Community College
  United Tribes Technical College
Northern Marianas
  Northern Marianas Colleges
Ohio
  The Ohio State University
Oklahoma
  Langston University
  Oklahoma State University

(continued)

TABLE 6.2   Land Grant Colleges and Universities (continued)

Oregon	Montana
Oregon State University	Montana State University
Pennsylvania	Blackfeet Community College
The Pennsylvania State University	Dull Knife Memorial College
Puerto Rico	Fort Belknap Community College
University of Puerto Rico	Rhode Island
Indiana	University of Rhode Island
Purdue University	South Carolina
Iowa	Clemson University
Iowa State University	South Carolina State University
Kansas	South Dakota
Kansas State University	South Dakota State University
Haskell Indian Nations University	Oglala Lakota College
Kentucky	Sinte Gleska University
Kentucky State University	Sisseton Wahepton Community Colleges
University of Kentucky	Si Tanka College
Louisiana	Tennessee
Louisiana State University System	Tennessee State University
Southern University and A&M College	University of Tennessee
Maine	Texas
University of Maine	Prairie View A&M University
Maryland	Texas A&M University
University of Maryland Eastern Shore	Utah
University of Maryland, College Park	Utah State University
Massachusetts	Vermont
University of Massachusetts, Amherst	University of Vermont
Michigan	Virgin Islands
Michigan State University	University of the Virgin Islands
Bay Mill Community College	Virginia
Minnesota	Virginia Polytechnic Institute & State University
University of Minnesota	Virginia State University
Fond Du Lac Tribal and Community College	Washington
Leech Lake Tribal College	Washington State University
White Earth Tribal and Community College	West Virginia
Mississippi	West Virginia University
Alcom State University	West Virginia State University
Mississippi State University	Wisconsin
Missouri	University of Wisconsin-Madison
Lincoln University	Wyoming
University of Missouri System	University of Wyoming

Source: U.S. Department of Agriculture, Natural Resources Conservation Service (2003). Land Grant Colleges and Universities. Retrieved November 8, 2004, from NRCS website: www.nrcs.usda.gov/technical/land/lgif/m27831.g.f.

After the Civil War, women increasingly sought higher education.

 For Your Reflection and Analysis

What social issues are the focus of the women's rights movement today?

to a lesser extent, lawyers. Another major factor contributing to the push for higher education for women was the women's rights movement. Many women turned the energies that had been given to emancipation to securing equal political and economic rights for women.

Whatever the combination of factors, and despite the prejudices against higher education for women, the number of women attending colleges and universities increased markedly after the Civil War. As depicted in Table 6.3, only 5 years after the war ended, one in every five college students was female, and in 10 years this had increased to one in three. However, a majority of these were attending normal schools, teaching remaining the most accessible and socially acceptable profession for women.

Emergence of the Modern University

Some historians have called the period between the end of the Civil War and the beginning of the 20th century the Age of the University. During this period over 200 new colleges were established in the United States. Feeding the growth in higher education was the rapid growth in technology, industry, and commerce.

As the number of institutions of higher education grew, so did their role. Many of the new institutions, as well as many of the older institutions, bore the name *university*. However, it was difficult to tell an American college from a

TABLE 6.3 Number of Institutions of Higher Education, Staff, Enrollments, and Degrees Granted, 1869–70 to 1919–20

Item	1869–70	1879–80	1889–90	1899–1900	1909–10	1919–20
1	2	3	4	5	6	7
Total Institutions	563	811	998	977	951	1,041
Professional staff	5,553	11,522	15,809	23,868	36,480	48,615
Male	4,887	7,328	12,704	19,151	29,132	35,807
Female	666	4,194	3,105	4,717	7,348	12,808
Instructional staff	—	—	—	—	—	—
Total fall enrollment	62,839	115,850	156,756	237,592	355,430	597,880
Male	49,467	77,994	100,453	152,254	214,779	314,938
Female	13,372	37,856	56,303	85,338	140,651	282,942
Bachelor's, total	9,371	12,896	15,539	27,410	37,199	48,622
Male	7,993	10,411	12,857	22,173	28,762	31,980
Female	1,378	2,485	2,682	5,237	8,437	16,642
Master's, total	—	879	1,015	1,583	2,113	4,279
Male	—	868	821	1,280	1,555	2,985
Female	—	11	194	303	558	1,294
Doctor's, total	1	54	149	382	443	615
Male	1	51	147	359	399	522
Female	0	3	2	23	44	93

Source: National Center for Education Statistics, U.S. Department of Education. (2003). *Digest of education statistics, 2002.* Washington, DC: U.S. Government Printing Office.

university, at least by its name. The first major step in creating institutional differences in patterns as well as practice was made by Johns Hopkins University. From its inception in 1876 Johns Hopkins had patterned itself after the German universities, placing heavy emphasis on graduate studies and research. In 1885 the University of Pennsylvania and Bryn Mawr followed Johns Hopkins' lead and began admitting students to newly created graduate departments. Bryn Mawr admitted students with a diploma from a college of acknowledged standing into a degree program leading to a master's and doctorate.

Following the lead of these innovators, other colleges and universities began to examine their programs. A number of more established private institutions (e.g., Harvard, Columbia, and Yale) and the larger state institutions (e.g., Michigan, Minnesota, Pennsylvania, and Wisconsin) began moving in the direction of establishing graduate programs and emphasizing research. In most of these institutions graduate study was open to women, and a number of women took advantage of the opportunity to study what had previously been possible only by "special arrangements" (Woody, 1929).

Another major curricular innovation in higher education was the introduction of the elective principle, championed by Harvard's President Eliot. Although the concept met stiff resistance on many campuses, many leading colleges and universities adopted it. By the end of the 19th century the American university had come to look much as we know it today, with an undergraduate college of liberal arts and sciences, a graduate college, and various professional colleges.

Founding of Junior Colleges

While some university presidents were moving to add a graduate level, others were attempting to become less involved in undergraduate education by introducing what eventually became the free-standing junior college. Some university presidents and deans viewed the first 2 years of higher education as more appropriate to secondary education and wanted to free their faculties from what they considered secondary education responsibilities so that they could devote themselves more to research and graduate education. Others, such as President William Rainey Harper who had put a 2–2 plan in place at the University of Chicago, felt the arrangement would meet the needs of those who could not afford to attend 4 years, as well as those who were not interested in research or were not academically qualified for it. In 1892, under President Harper's leadership, the University of Chicago initiated a reorganization whereby the freshman and sophomore years were designated the "academic college" and the junior and senior years the "university college." Four years later they were renamed the junior and senior colleges, and students were awarded an associate in arts degree upon completion of the junior college (Butts & Cremin, 1953).

In 1901 the first free-standing junior college was established, the Joliet (Illinois) Junior College. President Harper was also instrumental in its development. Although initially established to offer courses that would transfer to 4-year institutions, it soon began to also offer terminal and vocational programs as well (Gutek, 1986). Other junior colleges, some former academies or small liberal arts colleges, were established in several other parts of the country. The junior college was a popular choice for women, who were still denied admission at many 4-year institutions.

A major impetus for the junior college movement came in California. In 1907 California passed a law permitting school boards to "prescribe a post graduate course of study for the graduates of such high school or other schools, which courses of study shall approximate the studies prescribed in the first two years of university courses." By the early 1920s the concept of the junior college was well established. During the late 1920s, encouraged by the Smith-Hughes Act, which provided federal aid to vocational education, junior colleges developed more extensive vocational and technical education programs. By the end of the decade over 400 junior colleges were in operation, enrolling more than 50,000 students.

Improved Teacher Training and Professionalism

Strengthening of the Normal School Curriculum and Standards

Between the end of the Civil War and 1900 the number of normal schools exploded: from 50 to nearly 350. As their numbers increased, improvements in the quality of facilities, faculties, and students were matched by an expansion of the curriculum. A burgeoning population had created an increased demand for elementary or common school teachers, while the secondary school movement created a concomitant demand for secondary teachers. To meet this demand, normal schools began to broaden their curricula to include the training of secondary school teachers. At the same time, they began to require high school completion for admission.

A major change in the operation of normal schools occurred during the second and third decades of the 20th century as they expanded their programs from 2 to 3 years and eventually to 4 years. The passage of teacher certification statutes that specified the amount and type of training required of teachers contributed to this move as did the requirement by accrediting agencies that secondary school teachers have bachelor's degrees. By this time many normal schools were beginning to call themselves state teachers colleges and offering B.A. degrees. Between 1911 and 1930 there were 88 such conversions (Tyack, 1967). In time, with the broadening of the curriculum to embrace many of the liberal arts, the "teacher" designation was dropped and most became simply "state colleges." Some of these former normal schools have become among the largest and most respected universities in the United States.

Universities Enter Teacher Training

The development and growth of teachers colleges was paralleled by the establishment of departments or chairs of pedagogy in colleges and universities. Teacher training at the college or university level, typically consisting of one or two courses in the "science and art" of teaching, had been offered at a limited number of institutions as early as the 1830s. However, universities did not become involved in teacher preparation to any significant extent until after the Civil War. Their involvement stemmed in part from the increased demand for secondary school teachers. The universities had always been institutions for the education of those who taught in the Latin grammar schools, academies, and high schools. However, they did not prepare these students as teachers per se, but as individuals who had advanced knowledge of certain subject matter. The increased demand for secondary school teachers, the entrance of the normal schools into the training of secondary school teachers (to which the universities objected), and the growing recognition that the professionalization of teaching demanded study of its theory and practice led to the increased involvement of universities in teacher education.

The University of Iowa established the first permanent chair of pedagogy (education) in 1873. Other midwestern universities followed, and in 1892 the New York College for the Training of Teachers became a part of Columbia University. By the turn of the century teacher training departments had become commonplace in the major colleges and universities.

An important outgrowth of the involvement of universities in teacher education was the movement to develop a science of education and the scientific investigation of educational problems. One of the earliest contributors to this movement was the German philosopher and educator, Johann Friedrich Herbart (1776–1841).

 For Your Reflection and Analysis

In what ways can education be considered a science?

Herbartianism

Herbart believed that the development of character was the primary goal of education and could best be achieved by a scientific approach to the learning process that placed greater emphasis on the development of ideas and less on emotion and feeling. Herbart proposed, much along the lines of current thinking in brain research, that learning takes place through the process of apperception by which the child interprets new information in light of past experiences. By this process two or more ideas become related and will continue to be related and will relate to future ideas or experiences. Thus, teaching must ensure the association of ideas by making sure the student understands how new material is related to previous material. Because instruction is most successful if it stimulates interest, the curriculum should be directed at arousing student interest. Such a curriculum, with its emphasis on the relationship of concepts and information, was designed to break down the isolation of disciplines found in the traditional curriculum.

Herbart maintained that any suitable material could be learned if presented systematically and in successive steps. The five steps in the Herbartian methodology are as follows:

1. *Preparation*—preparing the student to receive the new material by arousing interest or recalling relevant past material or experiences.
2. *Presentation*—presenting the new material.
3. *Association*—relating or combining old and new ideas.
4. *Generalization*—formulating general ideas or principles based on both old and new material and experiences.
5. *Application*—applying the ideas or principles to new situations.

Herbart's ideas had a significant influence on American education. Before the end of the 19th century teachers across the country were organizing lessons around the five steps in the Herbartian methodology. Although many of them may have done so rather mechanically, the process did force attention to methodology. The National Herbartian Society was founded in 1892 and 8 years later became the National Society of the Scientific Study of Education. Although the Herbartian movement was short-lived, the Herbartian ideas and pedagogy had a profound influence on teaching methods and the curriculum, particularly at the elementary level, long after the movement itself faded (Kliebard, 1995). Most books on teaching methods published between 1895 and World War I were pervaded by Herbartian ideas, and as late as the 1950s the Herbartian steps could be found in teacher education tests (Connell, 1980). The Herbartians provided a well-articulated and methodical approach to education at a time when teachers and teacher education were seeking just such a systematic and comprehensive view (Connell, 1980). Herbart demonstrated not only the significance of methodology in instruction, but equally important, that education could become a science.

Teacher Certification

The growing public school system demanded not just more teachers but *qualified* teachers trained in the most recent educational pedagogy and psychology. The traditional method of assessing teacher quality had been certification following a written

For Your Reflection and Analysis

What regional or district bias can arise in teacher hiring today?

examination and often an oral examination by a lay committee. However, the ability and objectivity of these panels was always suspect. In a Baptist area Congregationalist teachers might not be hired, or vice versa. In the South, prospective teachers might be hired only if they said that states' rights had caused the Civil War, and in the North only if they blamed slavery (Tyack, 1967). The written exams in most states, although free of bias, tested only what might be expected of a common school graduate and contained no questions on pedagogy.

By the mid-19th century, state departments of education had become involved in teacher certification. In 1843 New York authorized the state superintendent to set examinations and issue certificates that would be valid statewide. Indiana followed in 1852, Pennsylvania in 1854, and by the end of the century the superintendents of most other states were given the same authority (Angus & Mirel, 2000). By 1921, 26 states issued all certificates, 7 states developed the regulations and examinations but the county issued the certificate, and 12 states developed regulations and questions but the county administered the examination and issued the certificate (Butts & Cremin, 1953).

At the same time that certification was being centralized at the state level, certification requirements were being upgraded. In 1900 no state required high school graduation for certification. In the first decade of the 20th century this changed as a few states began to require high school graduation for an elementary school teaching certificate and in others the number of years of secondary school completion required for certification was increased to 2, 3, or 4. By 1921, 4 states required high school graduation plus some professional training of their teachers, and 14 states required high school graduation but no professional training. Thirty states did not yet specify any academic requirement for certification (Butts & Cremin, 1953). Nonetheless, the trend toward increasing certification requirements had clearly begun. In the years to come certification requirements would increasingly define who was qualified to teach and what knowledge teachers should possess.

Teacher Organizations

In the 19th century, as now, the ability and willingness of policy makers to provide teachers a salary commensurate with their training and responsibilities was a major issue. The salary issue and concerns over working conditions were major factors leading to the establishment of teacher organizations. Teachers had begun organizing in state associations in the 1840s. In 1857 the president of the New York Association, with the support of the presidents of nine other state associations, issued a call to teachers to meet in Philadelphia on August 26, 1857, for the purpose of organizing a National Teachers Association (NTA). A copy of the call is presented in Figure 6.1.

In 1870 the NTA merged with the American Normal School Association and the National Association of School Superintendents to become known as the National Education Association (NEA). Although the NEA concerned itself with broad educational issues, it was originally dominated by college presidents and school superintendents and did not concern itself with teacher welfare. In fact, originally it did not even have a teachers' division.

The eminent success which has attended the establishment and operations of the several teachers' associations in the states of this country is the source of mutual congratulations among all friends of popular education. To the direct agency and the diffused influence of these associations, more, perhaps, than to any other cause, are due the manifest improvement of schools in all their relations, the rapid intellectual and social elevation of teachers as a class, and the vast development of public interest in all that concerns the education of the young.

That the state associations have already accomplished great good, and that they are destined to exert a still broader and more beneficial influence, no wise observer will deny.

Believing that what has been accomplished for the states by the state associations may be done for the whole country by a National Association, we, the undersigned, invite our fellow teachers throughout the United States to assemble in Philadelphia on the 26th day of August next, for the purpose of organizing a National Teachers' Association.

We cordially extend this invitation to all practical teachers of the North, the South, the East, and the West, who are willing to unite in a general effort to promote the general welfare of our country by concentrating the wisdom and power of numerous minds, and by distributing among all the accumulated experiences of all; who are ready to devote their energies and their means to advancing the dignity, respectability, and usefulness of their calling; and who, in fine, believe that the time has come when the teachers of the nation should gather into one great educational brotherhood.

As the permanent success of any association depends very much upon the auspices attending its establishment, and the character of the organic laws it adopts, it is hoped that all parts of the Union may be largely represented at the inauguration of the proposed enterprise. Signed by:

> T. W. Valentine, President of the New York Teachers' Association.
> D. B. Hagar, President of the Massachusetts Teachers' Association.
> W. T. Luckey, President of the Missouri Teachers' Association.
> J. Tenny, President of the New Hampshire Teachers' Association.
> J. G. May, President of the Indiana Teachers' Association.
> W. Roberts, President of the Pennsylvania Teachers' Association.
> C. Pease, President of the Vermont Teachers' Association.
> D. Franklin Wells, President of the Iowa Teachers' Association.
> A. C. Spicer, President of the Wisconsin Teachers' Association.
> S. Wright, President of the Illinois Teachers' Association.

FIGURE 6.1   Call for a Convention to Organize a National Teachers' Association, 1857
Source: Cubberley, E. P. (1934). *Readings in public education in the United States* (pp. 506–507). New York: Houghton Mifflin.

Rather than organizing as a professional association, especially one that was controlled by administrators, many teachers felt that the best prospect for improving their status was to form labor unions and ally themselves with the growing labor organizations. The first such teachers' labor union was the Chicago Teachers Federation (CTF), formed in 1897. In 1902 the CTF affiliated with the Chicago Federation of Labor (CFL), an action that was condemned by the Chicago school board. The

CTF severed the tie with the CFL when it lost a battle with the school board over the school board's arbitrary decision prohibiting union membership. Even with this setback the CTF continued to grow.

Following the lead of the Chicago teachers, teachers in several other cities formed local unions. In 1916 several local unions merged into one organization, the American Federation of Teachers (AFT). Immediately thereafter the AFT affiliated with the American Federation of Labor. Although its membership was only 2,800 in 1918, the membership of both the AFT and the NEA continued to grow as teachers sought to follow the lead of the growing labor movement and improve working conditions through organizational representation and membership.

 For Your Reflection and Analysis

Are you currently a member of, or do you plan to join, a teacher organization? What do you perceive as a benefit of membership?

New Directions in the Education of Native Americans and African Americans

While educational opportunities at all levels were expanding for White Americans in the post–Civil War era, two minority racial groups, Native Americans and Blacks, were finally gaining access. The education of Native Americans had historically been provided, with government support, by various religious groups. After the Civil War the federal government came to play a more direct role. The government operated the controversial boarding schools as well as a growing number of on-reservation day schools through the Bureau of Indian Affairs (BIA). However, as documented in the 1928 Meriam Report, the quality of these schools and the education they offered was inferior. Significant reform would not come for several decades.

The emancipation of the slaves brought not only freedom from bonds but also the freedom to be educated. During the period of Reconstruction great strides were made in establishing schools for Blacks. However, the gains of Reconstruction were short-lived, and the end of Reconstruction brought not only an end to these efforts, but also a reversal of many of the gains. By the end of the century debate within the Black community centered on what kind of education Blacks should have and the best way to achieve social and civil rights. The separate but unequal education system was in place that would characterize American education for more than half a century.

From Mission Schools to Public Schools: 150 Years of Indian Education

In the period between the Revolution and the Civil War the policy of the federal government was one of pushing the Indians ever farther westward. The federal government negotiated treaties in which the Indian tribes ceded tribal land in exchange for money payments, promises of land ownership, and the provision of various protections and services, including education. The primary way the federal government met its treaty obligations to provide education was through financial support of mission schools operated on the reservations by various religious groups. The objective of the education was to assimilate the Indian into American society. Most of the schools followed a program of studies known as the 50/50 curriculum: half of the time was spent in the traditional common school academic subjects, as well as the religion of the sponsoring denomination, and the other half of the time in vocational and agricultural training for boys and domestic arts for girls. Native language and culture were excluded from the curriculum (Hale, 2002).

While the European Americans were attempting forced assimilation of Native Americans and the eradication of Native American language and culture, most Native Americans continued to resist the assimilation efforts and sought to preserve their language and culture. For example, in 1821 a Cherokee named Sequoyah (1770–1843) developed an 86-character phonetic Cherokee alphabet. Because each character represented a sound in the Cherokee language, it was easy for the Cherokee to master and to learn to read and write using it. By 1828 a printing press using the characters was turning out pamphlets, hymns, the Bible, and a newspaper.

For Your Reflection and Analysis

Give examples of current efforts of Native Americans to pursue their language and culture. How successful have they been?

The Indian Removal Act of 1830 resulted in the forced removal of the so-called Five Civilized Tribes (Cherokee, Chickasaw, Choctaw, Creek, and Seminole) from the Southeast to the Indian Territory of Oklahoma and temporarily interrupted missionary efforts. However, the missionaries soon resumed their work, with increased federal aid, and remained the primary providers of education to Native Americans into the 20th century (Coleman, 1993). In fact, it was not until 1917 that this arrangement, which in effect constituted government support of sectarian education, ended and educational programs became institutionalized in the Bureau of Indian Affairs.

The mission school experience was not a positive one for most Indians or for the missionaries. The missionaries failed to recognize that Indians were intensely religious and were invested in preserving their religion and culture at all cost (DeJong, 1993). The federal government provided a little money but no standards. The net result of 100 years of effort and hundreds of thousands of dollars was "a small number of poorly attended mission schools, a suspicious and disillusioned Indian population, and a few hundred alumni who for the most part were considered outcasts by whites and Indians alike" (DeJong, 1993, p. 59).

Boarding Schools

After the Civil War the assimilation approach to Indian education became popular. This approach advocated the incorporation of Native Americans into the predominant White culture and, like the praying towns of colonial times, was established on the belief that the most lasting and efficient way this assimilation could take place was to remove children from their tribal setting and subject them, in a strict disciplinary setting, to an infusion of American language and customs.

The first major boarding school was established in 1879 at Carlisle, Pennsylvania, by General Richard Henry Pratt. At the boarding school students were given new names and forbidden to speak in their native tongue. They were required to wear uniforms and boys to keep their hair short and follow a strict regimen. The boarding schools provided only the rudiments of a common school education along with a basic vocational and industrial education. Manual labor was required to keep the schools self-supporting. Discipline was strict and harsh. Disease and death were common, especially in the early years (Adams, 1995). By the turn of the century, 25 off-reservation boarding schools had been established enrolling 6,000 students annually along with 81 on-reservation boarding schools with over 8,000 students in attendance (Coleman, 1993).

Despite their numbers, the boarding schools were subject to much criticism. The physical and living conditions were often unhealthy and substandard. Dropout rates were high. Students often returned to the reservation rather than enter White society and upon their return often found reentering life on the reservation difficult. They also found either that they were unable to apply the training they had received, or that it was irrelevant. In the end the boarding schools failed to produce the assimilated and educated Indian that had been envisioned at their inception. As former commissioner of Indian affairs Francis Leupp wrote in 1910, "the Indians did not fail in their quest for an education, but the educational system failed the Indians" (Dejong, 1993, p. 129).

Reservation Day Schools and Public Schools

In the last quarter of the 19th century, in part as a response to the criticisms of the boarding schools, and in part as a result of President Grant's efforts to institutionalize education programs under the BIA, government schooling expanded rapidly in the form of BIA-operated day schools on the reservations. The on-reservation day

Boarding schools sought to force assimilation of Native American Youth.

schools offered some advantages over the off-reservation boarding schools: They were less expensive to operate, and they were more acceptable to parents. As a consequence, the number of day schools increased from 150 in 1877 to 301 in 1900 (Coleman, 1993).

Also increasing in numbers were public schools located on the reservations. Native Americans in the eastern United States who were not under the jurisdiction of the federal government had attended off-reservation public schools for years. A newer phenomenon was the public school located on the reservation. These schools were initially built to accommodate the White people who rented land on some reservations. But early in the 20th century Native American children began to attend public schools both on and off the reservations in ever-increasing numbers: In 1900 only 246 Native American students attended public schools, but by 1930 over half of the 72,000 Native American children in school attended public schools (Coleman, 1993).

Despite the progress made in providing access and the attempts by Congress to compel and coerce attendance, as late as the 1920s large numbers of Indian children did not attend school. And, the goal of Indian education providers remained what it had from colonial times: assimilation of the Indian into the White man's culture and society. The education was typically low on academics and high on practical, vocational education. It was not until after the very critical 1928 Meriam Report discussed in chapter 9 that any significant changes were initiated in Native American education.

Education of Free and Freed Blacks

As discussed earlier, during the colonial period and the early republic various missionary and denominational groups provided limited and sporadic schooling to Blacks, both free and slave. However, by the third decade of the 19th century the rise of militant abolitionism and the fear of slave revolts had led several southern states to enact the so-called "Black Codes," which, among other things, prohibited the education of slaves. In the North, although most states had abolished slavery, little public support was given to educating free Blacks, and most grew up without any formal education. Those who did attend school more often than not found themselves in segregated schools. An important legal support for this segregation (and also for segregation for the remainder of the century) was provided by the Massachusetts Supreme Court decision in *Roberts v. City of Boston* (1850), which said that separate but equal schools did not violate the rights of the Black child.

Despite these obstacles, some free Blacks did obtain an education. The outbreak of the Civil War in 1861 found about 4,000 Blacks in schools in the slave states and 23,000 in the free states (West, 1972). A few blacks even obtained a higher education. A small number went abroad to England or Scotland; a few attended the limited number of American colleges that admitted Blacks, notably Oberlin in Ohio and Berea in Kentucky; and others attended the three Black colleges established before 1860: Cheyney State College (1839) and Lincoln University (1854) in Pennsylvania and Wilberforce University (1856) in Ohio.

Many of the free Blacks who gained a higher education prior to 1860 did so under the auspices of the American Colonization Society, which was established in 1817 to send free Blacks to the colony of Liberia in Africa, founded by the society in

1822. The education of the free Blacks was undertaken to provide the doctors, lawyers, teachers, clergy, and civil servants needed by the new colony. Although not all those educated by the society went to the colony, and some who went did not remain, enough did to provide the colony and the Republic of Liberia, which it became in 1847, with its leadership elite (Pifer, 1973).

Reconstruction

During the post–Civil War period known as the Reconstruction (1865–1877), hundreds of teachers supported by various northern churches, missionary societies, and educational foundations moved to the South to educate the newly liberated Blacks. The first of the educational foundations, established in 1867, was the Peabody Fund for the Advancement of Negro Education in the South. It later merged with the Slater Fund to support industrial education and teacher preparation. Among the other groups involved in the education of southern Blacks, the largest was the General Education Board set up by John D. Rockefeller in 1902 (Pifer, 1973; West, 1972).

Another major force in Black education in the South during Reconstruction was the Freedmen's Bureau. The bureau was responsible for the establishment of some 3,000 schools, and by 1869 some 114,000 students were in attendance in bureau schools. These schools followed the New England common school model in terms of their curriculum (reading, writing, grammar, geography, arithmetic, and music) and moral outlook (the importance of certain values and the responsibility of citizenship), but added a new dimension—industrial training. Consistent with the rationale for the education of immigrants and Native Americans, vocational and industrial training was considered the best education to prepare Blacks for the occupations they were most suited to perform (Gutek, 1986).

 For your Reflection and Analysis

Why was assimilation a goal of Native American education but not of African American education?

The Higher Education Debate: Booker T. Washington and W. E. B. DuBois

One of the first and most important institutions of higher education for Blacks in the immediate post–Civil War period was the Hampton Normal and Agricultural Institute, founded in 1868 by General Samuel Chapman Armstrong, a representative of the Freedmen's Bureau. The Hampton Institute was founded for the education of Blacks, but beginning in 1878 also admitted Native Americans. Industrial education was the basic mission of the Hampton Institute. Booker T. Washington (1856–1915) was one of the hundreds of young Blacks who flocked to the few normal schools or colleges that admitted Blacks. At Hampton, Washington developed the education ideas that led to his establishment of the Tuskegee Institute in 1881. Washington emphasized the dignity of labor and, rather than an academic education, advocated a practical education that would provide Blacks the marketable skills that would allow them to be self-sufficient.

Washington and the "Tuskegee Doctrine" were much favored by the philanthropic foundations and politicians. In what was to be known as the very controversial

"Atlanta Compromise," at an address at the Cotton States Exposition in 1895 Washington assured his audience that Blacks were not seeking social and political equality, but to earn economic independence and the respect of Whites by taking their places as industrious laborers and skilled tradesmen. Washington (1895) declared:

> Our greatest danger is that in the great leap from slavery to freedom we may overlook the fact that the masses of us are to live by the productions of our hands, and fail to keep in mind that we shall prosper in proportion as we learn to dignify and glorify common labour and put brains and skill into the common occupations of life. . . . No race can prosper till it learns that there is as much dignity in tilling a field as in writing a poem. (p. 343)

Washington believed that when Blacks had shown their loyalty, established themselves as valued workers, been successful in their trades or businesses, and owned property, they would deserve and be given their civil and political rights. Man may discriminate, he said, but the laws of commerce and trade do not.

Others, such as W. E. B. DuBois (1868–1963), the first Black to earn a Ph.D. from Harvard, disagreed with Washington and what they considered a position of accommodation or compromise. They argued that such a position was wrong and that giving Blacks only one educational direction (industrial) and Whites several undermined the achievement of civil and political equality. DuBois criticized what he called Washington's "gospel of work and money" as depriving the "Talented Tenth" of the Black population of the education they needed to become the leaders of their race. This group, he believed, should receive the classical education provided prospective leaders of White society (DuBois, 1903).

DuBois encouraged political activism and in 1909 joined a multiracial group of social activists in founding the National Association for the Advancement of Colored People. Whereas Washington was criticized for being too politically accommodating, DuBois was criticized for being the opposite. Whereas Washington avoided the issue of racism and even forbade his faculty and students from talking about it, DuBois in his many publications chronicled the racist practices and abuses in the United States. Whether Washington's accommodation approach to civil rights or DuBois' militant approach hindered the movement, or whether any other approach would have made any difference is open to conjecture. What is known is that by the time Washington began his work at Tuskegee, not only had Reconstruction begun to decline, but a backlash against Blacks had begun. The education he advanced was perhaps the only one that would have been permitted and supported in the openly racist political and social climate that pervaded the South at the end of the 19th and the beginning of the 20th century (Tozer, Violas & Senese, 2002).

Whatever the debate, Washington's efforts were successful: Tuskegee was transformed from a couple of dilapidated buildings to a thriving institution. Ten years after its founding, Tuskegee had a faculty of 88 and a student body of 1,200, making it one of the largest institutions of higher education in the South. It is also significant to note that Tuskegee and especially the Hampton Institute were important as centers for the training of Black teachers. The traditional attention given to Tuskegee and Hampton as agricultural and industrial schools has obscured the fact that they were founded and maintained primarily to train Black teachers for the South. Indeed, between 1872 and 1890, 604 of Hampton's 723 graduates became teachers (Anderson, 1978). Many of these teachers, along with Tuskegee's alumni, were instrumental not only in establishing and teaching in the public schools, but also in establishing normal schools in rural areas throughout the South.

In addition to Hampton and Tuskegee, several other distinguished Black colleges and universities were established in the immediate post–Civil War years. These include Atlanta University, founded in 1865 by the American Baptist Mission Society; Howard University, chartered in 1868 by the Congregationalists; Fisk University, established in 1866 by the American Missionary Association; and Mehary Medical College, originally Walton College, founded in 1865 by the Methodist Episcopal Church. Somewhat later, as a result of the Second Morrill Act of 1890, Black land grant colleges were established in each of the southern and border states—17 in all (Pifer, 1973).

Segregation of the Public Schools

Another factor changing the face of education in the South during the Reconstruction period was legislation leading to the establishment of tax-supported public school systems. Many freedmen recently elected to state legislatures were a force in this movement. Many of these Black legislators, as well as some White legislators, advocated integration in the newly established schools. In fact, many of the state statutes or constitutional provisions established the schools without making reference to either integration or segregation. However, none of the southern states actually instituted an integrated system, and what began as custom became law in all the southern states. Yet the efforts of the various groups and agencies did result in a dramatic reversal of the educational status of Black Americans: from a literacy rate estimated at 5% or 10% at the outbreak of the Civil War to one of 70% by 1910.

As impressive as these figures are, they hide the condition of the education of Blacks in the South, which deteriorated after the end of Reconstruction. Following Reconstruction the pay of Black teachers fell to less than half that of White teachers, as did expenditures for Black schools. These differences translated into shorter school terms, inadequate textbooks and materials, and dilapidated facilities (Anderson, 1988). The Primary Source Reading at the end of this chapter describes one such school in rural Tennessee taught by W. E. B. DuBois. Perhaps not surprisingly, in 1900 the enrollment rate for Black school-age children was 31% compared to 54% for Whites (Snyder, 1993).

After the 1870s the federal government effectively withdrew from the promotion of the civil and educational rights of Blacks. As a result, the system of racial segregation that was established in the South remained in effect until the desegregation movement of the 1950s and 1960s. The practice of segregation was sanctioned by the 1896 U.S. Supreme Court decision in *Plessy v. Ferguson*, in which the Court said that separate railroad cars did not violate the Constitution.

During this same period, ever-increasing numbers of White children from immigrant and lower socioeconomic families were entering the enlarged public school system; between 1880 and 1895 White enrollment in the public schools increased 106% compared to 59% for Black enrollment (Frazier, cited in Hare, & Swift, 1976). The "rise of the poor Whites" placed increased financial demands on public revenues and often resulted in funds being diverted from Black schools to improve other schools (Gutek, 1986). To this was added the disenfranchisement of Blacks by many southern states and the delegation of authority to local school boards to divide state education funds as they saw fit. From the Court approval of segregation, the Blacks' loss of political power, and the decreased financial support for Black education emerged the "separate but inferior" system that marked so much of the South until the Supreme Court reversal of *Plessy v. Ferguson* in 1954 and the subsequent civil rights movement discussed in chapter 9.

Conclusion

The dramatic expansion of education in the period between the Civil War and World War I occurred in an environment of rapid change in all aspects of society and in a climate of debate concerning the nature and purpose of education. It also coincided with an incredible growth in the knowledge base and in what was seen as necessary to know in order to operate successfully in society (Graham, 1974). At the same time, education took on a progressively more important role in preparing the trained workforce needed to maintain America's place in world markets. In an increasingly technical society corporate leaders began to look to the schools to provide the vocational preparation previously provided by the family or through the apprenticeship. For the first time the federal government joined in supporting educational programs in both the public schools and the colleges and universities.

As the education system expanded, so too did what the attainment of a particular level of education came to signify. As Graham (1974) explained, if one were to ask an American at the end of the Civil War to define an "educated man," the response would probably have been a man with a knowledge of the classics. By World War I the definition would likely be a man who had been to college. At the same time, compulsory attendance laws

> *For your Reflection and Analysis*
> *How would you define an educated person?*

shifted emphasis from remaining in school until the mastery of certain knowledge to remaining in school until a certain age.

Underlying all the changes in this period was a debate, one visible between Washington and DuBois about the type of education that was best for minorities, the poor, and the children of immigrants. The debate centered around questions such as, Whose interests are being served if students are educated for employment rather than for development of the intellect? and What is the role of the school in promoting social stability and social reform? These fundamental questions were debated even more loudly in the progressive era discussed in chapter 7 and to a large extent remain unanswered today.

For Discussion and Application

1. Given that the women's colleges (i.e., Vassar, Wellesley, Smith, etc.) offered academic programs comparable to those in the colleges for men, what were the advantages and/or disadvantages of enrolling in a single-sex institution?
2. Compare Herbart's learning theories with constructivist learning theory.
3. What might be the advantage to a teacher organization to affiliate with a labor union?
4. Was Booker T. Washington a realist or an accommodationist? Support your answer.
5. Examine copies of two education journals from the period 1870–1900. List the major topics/issues discussed. Compare and contrast those topics with the major issues being discussed by educators today.

Primary Source Reading

In 1873, with the support of Superintendent William T. Harris, Susan Blow opened the first public kindergarten in America at the Des Peres School in St Louis. The next year she opened a school to train teachers in the philosophy of Fröebel and the principles of the kindergarten, which she also described, in part, in this article. St. Louis soon became the focal point of the kindergarten and Blow its intellectual leader. She was a prolific writer and between 1905 and 1909 was a lecturer at Teachers College, Columbia University.

Some Aspects of the Kindergarten

Susan E. Blow

The Kindergarten is many-sided. Herein lies its greatest merit and its greatest danger. To every different point of view it presents a different face. To some it is a play-school, to others a workshop, to others an improved system of object lessons. Its sole aim is declared successively to be physical development, technical training, the formation of habits of cleanliness, order and courtesy, the strengthening of observation and the pleasant

Source: Blow, S. E. (1881). Some aspects of the kindergarten. *American Journal of Education, 31,* 595–616.

teaching of useful facts. All are right and all are wrong. The Kindergarten is all of these things, and yet no one of them, nor even a combination of them. Every part is necessary to the whole, and yet the whole is something more than the sum of its parts. . . .

The Kindergarten is organic, therefore a variety in unity. It recognizes that life is essentially activity, therefore aims mainly to develop power; it knows that objective truth is the mind's air and food, therefore values knowledge; it sees that the prizes of life fall to the capable and industrious, therefore trains the child to work; it takes note of the increasing complexity of social relationships, therefore strives to initiate him into all the amenities of life; it conceives the child in his threefold nature—as a physical, intellectual and moral being,— therefore emphasizes equally the training of the body, of the mind, and of the affections and will. Finally it grasps all these different phases of education in the unity of a single thought, and in the nature and laws of self-consciousness finds its method and its aim. It beholds the child through expression struggling towards self-knowledge, and it comes to his aid with material which appealing to his total nature calls forth his total activity. It helps him to complete expression that it may lead him to clear insight, and holds up before him all his relationships, that he may realize all his possibilities. Such at least was the Kindergarten in the idea of its founder. . . .

The program of the theoretical Kindergarten includes garden work, songs, games, stories, talks, lunch and exercises, in the Fröbel gifts and occupations. . . .

The life of man began in a garden; his first occupations were to "dress it and keep it" and to name the beasts of the field and the fowls of the air. So the little child should dig and plant his own garden, and feed and care for his dog, his cat, or his bird. Practical doing awakens love and thought. Sympathy with nature is intensified by digging in the ground. Dependence is realized through waiting for the results of work. Curiosity is excited by the miracle of growth. The beauty of law is seen in the life of trees and flowers, and the unconscious lawfulness of nature inclines the heart to free obedience. . . .

The Kindergarten songs are either taken from the "Mother Play and Nursery Songs," or inspired by its spirit. The one essential requirement is that they shall present the same idea to thought, feeling and will. The music must correspond to the words, and both must be illustrated by gestures. . . .

He was a wise man who said, "Let me make the songs of a nation and I care not who may make its laws." He is a wiser man who aims not only to write a nation's songs but to influence its games. . . .

If we watch the games of children we shall notice that they fall, broadly speaking, into three classes. In the first class are included games of running, wrestling, throwing, and all other plays whose charm lies mainly in the exertion of physical strength and skill; the second class of which the "King William" we all so well remember, is a type, reproduces the child's observations and experiences,—and the third which may be illustrated by "hide the handkerchief" and "turn the platter" is characterized by its appeal to the activities of the mind. In the Kindergarten these different types reappear transfigured. Fröbel has studied instinctive play—grasped its underlying idea, and perfected its form. He has arranged a variety of pure movement games, each one of which calls into play important muscles,—he has reproduced life in a series of dramatic games representing the flowing of streams, the sailing of boats, the flying of birds, the swimming of fishes, the activities of the farmer, the miller, the baker, the carpenter, the cobbler,—in short, all the activities of nature and of man; he disciplines the senses through games appealing to sight, touch, hearing, smell and taste, and rouses pure mental activity through games which stimulate curiosity by suggesting puzzles.

A comparison of Fröbel's plays with the traditional games of different nations would do much to show the purifying and elevating tendency of the Kindergarten. The limits I have set myself permit, however, only one or two suggestive illustrations.

The Kindergarten games, like the songs, express the same thought in melody, in movement and in words. They differ from the songs in that their representations require the combined action of many different children. In the play of the birds' nest, for instance, a given number of children represent trees, imitating, with arms and fingers, the branches and leaves, while others, like birds, fly in and out, build nests, and finally drop their little heads in sleep. So in the ship game, the children standing around the circle, by a rhythmical undulating movement, represent waves, while a half-dozen little children, with intertwined arms, form the ship, and with a movement corresponding to that of the waves, imitate its sailing. Each child has something to do, and if a single child fails to perform his art, the harmony of the representation is destroyed. The games, therefore, tend strongly to develop in the children mutual dependence and sympathy, as in all life nothing draws us nearer to each other than united action for a common end. . . .

The daily talk with the children is one of the most important and yet one of the most neglected features of the Kindergarten. It is neglected because it cannot be done by rule, it is important because through it the varied activity of the Kindergarten is concentrated in the unity of its idea. What should be talked about depends on what the children have been doing, and the whole idea of the conversation is lost when it is perverted into an object lesson. What the children have expressed in play, in their block-building, in their stick-laying, in their weaving and cutting and modeling, that also should they learn to express in words. What they see around them in the room, what they have noticed on their way to the Kindergarten, the pebbles they have picked up, the insects they have caught, the flowers they have brought with loving, smiling eyes to their motherly friend—in one word, in all the thronging impressions which besiege the mind from without, and in all the crude activity which shows the tumultuous forces within, the true Kindergartner finds suggestions for her talks with the little ones. . . .

The stories have one distinct object, which they realize in a twofold way. They aim to show the child himself, and to attain this end offer him both contrasts and reflections. The wise Kindergartner alternates the fairy tales which startle the child out of his own life and enable him to look on it from an alien standpoint, with symbolic stories of birds and flowers and insects, and with histories of little boys and girls in whose experiences she simply mirrors his own. Using the "Mother Play and Nursery Songs," she leads the children toward the past, and, as they grow older, reproduces, in the legends of heroes and demi-gods, and in the touching narratives of the Bible, the infancy and childhood of the human race. Moving thus from the known to the unknown, and from the near to the remote, she holds himself up to him first in the glass of nature, then in the glass of childhood, and at last in the glass of history. . . .

In what I have to say of Fröbel's gifts and occupations I wish to be distinctly understood as stating only their theoretic possibilities. Their adaptations to children of different ages and characters can only be learned by experience. . . .

With this general understanding pass we now to a detailed consideration of the gifts and

occupations, and of their relationship to each other and to the child.

The First Gift consists of six soft worsted balls of the colors of the rainbow.

The Second Gift consists of a wooden sphere, cube and cylinder.

The Third Gift is a two-inch cube divided equally once in each dimension, producing eight small cubes.

The Fourth Gift is a two-inch cube divided by one vertical and two horizontal cuts into eight rectangular parallelopipeds. Each of these parallelopipeds is two inches long, one inch broad and half an inch thick.

The Fifth Gift is a three-inch cube divided equally twice in each dimension into twenty-seven small cubes.

The Sixth Gift is a cube of three inches divided into twenty-seven parallelopipeds of the same dimensions as those of the Fourth Gift.

The Seventh Gift consists of square and triangular tablets. Of the latter there are four kinds, viz: Equilateral, right and obtuse isosceles and right scalene triangles.

The Eighth Gift is a connected slat,—the Ninth consists of disconnected slats.

The Tenth Gift consists of wooden sticks of various lengths, and the Eleventh Gift of whole and half wire rings of various diameter.

Looking at the gifts as a whole we see at once that their basis is mathematical, and we notice that they illustrate successively the solid, the plane and the line. We perceive, too, that they progress from undivided to divided wholes, and from these to separate and independent elements. Finally, we observe that there is a suggestiveness in the earlier gifts which later ones lack, while on the other hand the range of the latter far exceeds that of the former. . . .

The great problem of education is to effect the necessary mediation without destroying originality, and this can only be done by organizing experiences which shall conduct to a preconceived end. This truth is now widely realized, and everywhere we find increasing demand for experiments in natural science and illustrations in all branches of study. But only Fröbel has seen that this same method should be applied to the youngest children and to the most familiar facts, and by a series of objects in which essential qualities are strongly contrasted, aims to excite the mind to conscious antithesis. . . .

The contrasts of nature are so blended into harmony that their opposition is lost, yet this very opposition must be felt before their harmony can be realized. Fröbel simply accelerates the natural tendency of thought by carefully abstracting from material things their essential qualities, and then so arranging his gifts that each one shall throw some distinctive attribute into relief. Thus in the first gift he presents contrasts of color; in the second, contrasts of form; in the third, contrasts of size; in the fourth, contrasts of dimension; in the fifth he offers both contrasts of angles and contrasts of number; while in the sixth he repeats, emphasizes and mediates the contrasts of the preceding gifts. Passing to the plane in the seventh gift he offers subtler contrasts of form, while the connected and disconnected slats render these still more striking by showing how they are produced. The sticks and rings which, properly speaking, are one gift, contrast the straight and curved line, and offer striking perceptions of position and direction. And finally the solids, planes and lines are mutually illustrative, and the child learns both clearly to distinguish the different parts of his solids and to connect his planes and lines with them, identifying at last his stick, the embodiment of the straight line, with the axis of the sphere, the edge of the cube and the side of the square, and the ring which embodies the curve with the circumference of the sphere and the edge of the cylinder.

These contrasts of color, size, form, number, dimension, relation, direction and position illustrated in the gifts are applied in the occupations, and supplemented in the games and songs by contrasts of smell, taste, movement and sound. There is no salient attribute of material things which is not thus thrown into light, and as a consequence sharply defined and firmly grasped by the mind.

We realize the significance of this result more fully when we reflect that by the perception of analogies between the material and spiritual world, the words designating the acts, objects, qualities and relations of the one have been adapted to express the acts, powers, states and relations of the other. There is no single word of our intellectual or moral vocabulary which was not originally applied to something apprehensible by the senses, and many of the most important of them refer to physical facts and qualities with which the child gets acquainted in his earliest years. When, for instance, we speak of great men, great actions, greatness, the analogy is obviously to size; when we call a man *straightforward*, allude to *crooked* dealings or describe a character as *angular*; we borrow from the language of lines and their relations; when we talk of lives *rounded* into completeness and actions that are fair and *square*, we are debtors to analogies with form; when we speak of *high* station, *deep* truths, *broad* views, we refer, however, unconsciously to the "threefold measure which dwells in space;" and when we mourn of *dark* sorrows and *black* crimes, we steal our words from the vocabulary of color. It was part of Fröbel's ideal to make the child sensible of these relationships by connecting his first perception of the moral force of words directly with the physical fact to which they stand in analogy. To give only a single illustration, in the game of the joiner the child alternates long and short movements while imitating the act of planning. The long and short of movement is then connected with the long and short of sound, the long and short of form, and the long and short of time; and finally, through the story of Goliath and David, in telling which the contrast between the tall giant and the stripling who defied and conquered him is emphasized, the distinction between physical and moral greatness is foreshadowed to the mind. The mark of the true Kindergarten is the all-pervading connection between the things of sense and the things of thought. . . .

There is a growing belief among educators that the mind should be kept in constant relation with all the essential branches of knowledge, but that the method of study should vary with the progressive stages of mental development. Thus they would present the sensible facts of any given science to the perceptions of the child, the relations of these facts to the understanding of the youth, and the synthesis of these relations to the reason of the mature student. By this method there is secured continuity of thought and the ultimate inclusive principle is made to register the results of a vivid personal experience. . . .

The Kindergarten deals with the first stage of this double development and offers to the mind perceptions, and to the heart presentiments. Moreover it deals not with special branches of study, but with primal facts, not with special moral obligations, but with fundamental moral relationships. And finally it appeals not separately to the mind and heart, but through the same objects and exercises touches both at once. In all this the Kindergarten is in accord with the nature of the child. . . .

It seems to me, therefore, quite reasonable when Fröbel claims that the deepest and most universal truths should determine what we do for children and how we do it, and *that precisely these deepest truths are the ones that the child will most readily recognize, though of course only tinder limited forms and applications.* The deepest of all truths to Fröbel is that self-recognition is effected through self-activity. . . .

All the features of the Kindergarten thus far alluded to are simply results of a single ruling thought,—flowers and fruit of one hidden root. When we comprehend this prolific thought we comprehend Fröbel. Until then we can only see in the Kindergarten a system of more or less valuable detail. Briefly stated this root thought is that as God knows himself through creation so must man, or in other words that to truly live we must constantly create, and that the condition of

a complete self-consciousness is a complete reflection. The life of the soul is a struggle towards self-knowledge, and self-knowledge comes only through self-externalization. As Fröbel puts it, "The inward as in-ward can never be known, it is only revealed by being made outward. The mind like the eye sees not itself but by reflection." . . .

Fröbel's merit lies not in the recognition of this truth, but in its application. Many thinkers have stated it more clearly than he, and other educators have traced it in the ceaseless bubbling over of the child's speech and in the ardor of his play. But Fröbel alone, with in-sight into the end the child blindly seeks, has aimed to aid the instinctive struggle towards self-consciousness, and by wisely organized material to stimulate and direct creative activity. . . .

However we may criticize the basis of Fröbel's thought, no fair observer will question the results of his method. Let a child try to fashion his lump of clay into a bird's nest, and though his effort yield no other result it will certainly lead him to examine carefully the next bird's nest he sees. Let him make an apple and a pear and he must feel their difference in form as he would never have done had he simply looked at the two fruits. Let him attempt to lay with his sticks the outline of a house and his attention cannot fail to be caught by facts of direction and proportion. Let him apply numbers in weaving and their relations grow interesting to him. Lead him to construct symmetrical figures and he must feel the laws of symmetry. Teach him rhythmic movements and he must recognize rhythm. All *things* are revealed in the doing, and productive activity both enlightens and develops the mind. . . .

The order of the Kindergarten gifts follows the order of mental evolution, and at each stage of the child's growth Fröbel presents him with his "objective counterpart." "The child," he says, "develops like all things, according to laws as simple as they are imperative. Of these the simplest and most imperative is that force existing must exert itself,—exerting itself it grows strong—strengthening it unfolds—unfolding it represents and creates—representing and creating it lifts itself to consciousness and culminates in insight." This perception of the course of development determines his idea of the stages of early education. It should aim, first, to strengthen the senses and muscles conceived as the tools of the spirit,—second, to prepare for work by technical training, and to aid self-expression by supplying objects which through their indefiniteness may be made widely representative,—third, to provide material adapted to the conscious production of definite things and diminish the suggestiveness of this material in direct ratio to the increase of creative power, and fourth, by analysis of the objects produced, and the method of their production lift the child to conscious communion with his own thought. The first stage of this educational process is realized through the "Songs for Mother and Child,"—the second through the Kindergarten games, the simpler occupations and the first two Gifts,—the third through the exercises with blocks, tablets, slats, sticks and rings, and the work in drawing, folding, cutting, peas work and modeling, and the fourth through the wise appeal of the Kindergartner to the thought of the child as she leads him slowly from the what to the how, and from the how to the why and wherefore of his own action. . . .

From this imperfect survey of the Gifts let us turn now to the Occupations. These are Perforating, Sewing, Drawing, Intertwining, Weaving, Folding, Cutting, Peas work, Card-board and Clay Modeling. . . .

Taken as a whole the occupations apply the principles suggested by the gifts and give permanence to their vanishing transformations. It will be observed that particular occupations connect with particular gifts. Thus pricking, sewing and drawing, which are essentially one, connect with the sticks and rings, intertwining and mat plaiting connect with the slats, folding and cutting with the tablets and peas work, card-board and clay modeling with the undivided and divided solids of

the first six gifts. It is also noticeable that while the gifts move from the solid to the surface, the line and the point, the occupations, reversing this movement, develop from point to line, surface and solid, and that while the determined material of the gifts limits to the combination and arrangement of unchangeable elements, the plastic material of the occupations is increasingly subservient to the modifying thought and touch of the embryo artist.

As has been repeatedly said the aim of the Kindergarten is to strengthen and develop productive activity. But we must be conscious of ideas before we can express them, and we must gain the mastery of material before we can use it as a means of expression. Hence the first use of the gifts is to waken by their suggestiveness the mind's sleeping thoughts, and the first use of the occupations to train the eye and the mind to be the ready servants of the will. While the child is still imitative in the occupations he becomes inventive in the gifts, but as he grows to be more and more a law unto himself he turns from the coercion of his blocks, tablets and sticks to obedient paper and clay, and ultimately outgrowing the simpler occupations, concentrates his interest in the exercises of drawing, coloring and modeling. These artistic processes, with a technical training according to the very successful Russian plan, might it seems to me be profitably introduced into our regular school course. . . .

Describing the influences which had most strongly affected the evolution of his own thought, Fröbel said that the field had been his schoolroom and the tree his tutor; the nursery his university, and little children his professors. From the tree he learned the continuity of life and traced the successive differentiations which mark the process of organic growth; studying children he beheld the continuity of life melt into the varied unity of creative thought, and learned to see in the course of development through progressive differentiations the embodiment of thought's external distinction of the self from the self. Hence his final word is that there is nothing true but thought, and his fundamental educational maximum to teach children to think by training them to do. In development through an activity which is both receptive and productive lies the secret of his method and the explanation of the child's otherwise inexplicable growth in "self-reverence, self-knowledge, self-control;" the three, that "alone lead life to sovereign power."

Questions for Discussion

1. Give examples of the connections between "the things of sense and the things of thoughts" found in the contemporary kindergarten curriculum.
2. According to Susan Blow, we can comprehend Fröebel when we comprehend the following: "To truly live we must constantly create, and that the condition of a complete self-consciousness is a complete reflection."
3. Compare Fröebel's belief that "all things are revealed in the doing and productive activity" with the philosophy of John Dewey.
4. Rewrite Fröebel's metaphor that "the field had been his schoolroom and the tree his tutor, the nursery his university, and the little children his professors" in contemporary language and application.

Primary Source Reading

W. E. B. DuBois was a student at Fisk University in Nashville, Tennessee. During the summer he worked as a teacher in rural Tennessee. What follows is what he describes as the "enthralling experience" of teaching 30 young scholars in a log hut that used to be a storage shed for corn. The description he provides is both vivid and compelling.

Summer School Teacher

W. E. B. DuBois

There was a Teachers' Institute at the county seat; and there distinguished guests of the superintendent taught the teachers fractions and spelling and other mysteries—white teachers in the morning, Negroes at night. This was to supplement the wretched elementary training of the prospective teachers. . . .

There came a fine day when all the teachers left the Institute and began the hunt for schools. I learned from hearsay (for my mother was mortally afraid of fire-arms) that the hunting of ducks and bears and men is wonderfully interesting, but I am sure that the man who has never hunted a country school in the South has something to learn of the pleasures of the chase. I see now the white, hot roads lazily rise and wind and fall before me under the burning July sun; I feel the deep weariness of heart and limb as ten, eight, six miles stretch relentlessly ahead; I feel my heart sink heavily as I hear again and again "Got a teacher? Yes." So I walked on and on—horses were too expensive—until I had wandered beyond railways, beyond stage lines, to a land of "varmints" and rattlesnakes, where the coming of a stranger was an event, and men lived and died in the shadow of one blue hill.

Sprinkled over hill and dale lay cabins and farmhouses, shut out from the world by the forests and the rolling hills toward the east. There I found at last a little school. Josie told me of it; she was a thin, homely girl of 20, with a dark brown face and thick, hard hair. I had

Source: DuBois, W. E. B. (1996). Summer school teacher. In N. Rae (Ed.), *Witnessing America, the Library of Congress book of firsthand accounts of life in America 1600–1900* (pp. 71–75). Reprinted from *Witnessing America* © by Noel Rae and The Stonesong Press, LLC, and used with permission of The Stonesong Press.

crossed the stream at Watertown, and rested under the great willows; then I had gone to the little cabin in the lot, where Josie was resting on her way to town. The gaunt black farmer made me welcome and Josie, hearing my errand, told me anxiously that they wanted a school over the hill; that but once since the Civil War had a teacher been there; that she herself longed to learn—and thus she ran on, talking fast and loud, with much earnestness and energy.

Next morning I crossed the tall round hill, lingered to look at the blue and yellow mountains stretching toward the Carolinas, then plunged into the wood, and came out at Josie's home. It was a dull frame cottage with four rooms, perched just below the brow of the hill, amid peach trees. The father was a quiet, simple soul, calmly ignorant, with no touch of vulgarity. The mother was different—strong, bustling, and energetic, with a quick, restless tongue, and an ambition to live "like folks." There was a crowd of children. Two boys had gone away. There remained two growing girls; a shy midget of eight; John, tall, awkward and 18; Jim, younger, quicker and better looking; and two babies of indefinite age.

Then there was Josie herself. She seemed to be the center of the family; always busy at service, or at home, or berry-picking; a little nervous and inclined to scold, like her mother, yet faithful, too, like her father. She had about her a certain fineness, the shadow of an unconscious moral heroism that would willingly give all of life to make life broader, deeper and fuller for her and hers. I saw much of this family afterwards, and grew to love them for their honest efforts to be decent and comfortable, and for their knowledge of their own ignorance. There was with them no affectation. The mother would scold the father for being so "easy"; Josie would roundly berate the boys for carelessness; and all knew that it was a hard thing to dig a living out of rocky side-hill. I found a place where there had been a Negro public school only once since the Civil War; and there for two successive terms

during the summer I taught at 28 and 30 dollars a month.

It was an enthralling experience. I remember the day I rode horseback out to the commissioner's house with a pleasant young white fellow who wanted the white school. The road ran down the bed of a stream; the sun laughed and the water jingled, and we rode on. "Come in," said the commissioner, "come in. Have a seat. Yes, that certificate will do." I was pleasantly surprised when the superintendent invited me to stay for dinner; and he would have been astonished if he had dreamed that I expected to eat at the table with him and not after he was through.

The schoolhouse was a log hut, where Colonel Wheeler used to store his corn. It sat in a lot behind a rail fence and thorn bushes, near the sweetest of springs. There was an entrance where a door once was, and within, a massive rickety fireplace; great chinks between the logs served as windows. Furniture was scarce. My desk was made of three boards reinforced at critical points, and my chair, borrowed from my landlady, had to be returned every night. Seats for the children—these puzzled me much. I was haunted by a New England vision of neat little desks and chairs, but, alas the reality was rough plank benches without backs, and at times without legs. They had the one virtue of making naps dangerous, possibly fatal, for the floor was not to be trusted. All the appointments of my school were primitive: a window-less log cabin; hastily manufactured benches; no blackboards; almost no books; long, long distances to walk. On the other hand, I heard the sorrow songs sung with primitive beauty and grandeur. I saw the hard, ugly drudgery of country life and the writhing of landless, ignorant peasants. I saw the race problem at nearly its lowest terms.

It was a hot morning late in July when the school opened. I trembled when I heard the patter of little feet down the dusty road, and saw the growing row of dark solemn faces and bright eager eyes facing me. First came Josie and her brothers and sisters. The longing to know, to be a student in the great school at Nashville, hovered like a star above this child-woman amid her work and worry, and she studied doggedly. There were the Dowells from their farm toward Alexandria—Fanny, with her smooth black face and wondering eyes; Martha, brown and dull; the pretty girl-wife of a brother, and the younger brood.

There were the Burkes—two brown and yellow lads, and a tiny haughty-eyed girl. Fat Reuben's little chubby girl came, with golden face and old-gold hair, faithful and solemn. Thonie was on hand early—a jolly, ugly, good-hearted girl, who slyly dipped snuff looked after her little bow-legged brother. When her mother could spare her, Tildy came—a midnight beauty, with starry eyes and tapering limbs; and her brother, correspondingly homely. And the big boys—the hulking Lawrences; the lazy Neills, unfathered sons of mother and daughter; Hickman, with a stoop in his shoulders, and the rest.

There they sat, nearly 30 of them, on the rough benches, their faces shading from a pale cream to a deep brown, the little feet bare and swinging, the eyes full of expectation, with here and there a twinkle of mischief, and the hands grasping Webster's blue-back spelling book. I loved my school, and the fine faith the children had in the wisdom of their teacher was truly marvellous. We read and spelled together, wrote a little, picked flowers, sang, and listened to stories of the world beyond the hill.

At times the school would dwindle away, and I would start out. I would visit Mun Eddings, who lived in two very dirty rooms, and ask why little Lugene, whose flaming face seemed ever ablaze with the dark red hair uncombed, was absent all last week, or why I missed so often the inimitable rags of Mack and Ed. Then the father, who worked Colonel Wheeler's farm on shares, would tell me how the crops needed the boys; and the thin slovenly mother, whose face was pretty when washed, assured me that Lugene must mind the baby. "But we'll start them again next week." ...

On Friday nights I often went home with some of the children—sometimes to Doc Burke's farm. He was a great, loud, thin black, ever working, and trying to buy the 75 acres of hill and dale where he lived; but people said that he would surely fail, and the "white folks would get it all." His wife was a magnificent Amazon, with saffron face and shining hair, uncorseted and barefooted, and the children were strong and beautiful. They lived in a one-and-a-half-room cabin in the hollow of the farm, near the spring. The front room was full of great fat white beds, scrupulously neat; and there were bad chromos on the walls, and a tired center table. In the tiny back kitchen I was often invited to "take out and help" myself to fried chicken and wheat biscuits, "meat" and corn pone, string beans and berries.

On this visit, at first I was a little alarmed at the approach of bedtime in the one lone bedroom, but embarrassment was very deftly avoided. First, all the children nodded and slept, and were stowed away in one great pile of goose feathers; next, the mother and the father discreetly slipped away to the kitchen while I went to bed; then, blowing out the dim light, they retired in the dark. In the morning all were up and away before I thought of waking. Across the road, where fat Reuben lived, they all went outdoors while the teacher retired, because they did not boast the luxury of a kitchen.

I liked to stay with the Dowells, for they had four rooms and plenty of good country fare. Uncle Bird had a small, rough farm, all woods and hills, miles from the big road; but he was full of tales—he preached now and then—and with his children, berries, horses, and wheat he was happy and prosperous. . . . Best of all I loved to go to Josie's, and sit on the porch, eating peaches, while the mother bustled and talked; how Josie had bought the sewing machine; how Josie worked at house service in winter, but that four dollars a month was "mighty little" wages; how Josie longed to go away to school, but that it "looked like" they never could get far enough ahead to let her.

Questions for Discussion

1. Give examples from the reading that explain what DuBois meant in the opening quote of the chapter that "Education must not simply teach work—it must teach life."

2. What lessons did DuBois learn from his students, their families, and the community?

3. Had you been the summer school teacher instead of DuBois, which experiences would have presented the greatest challenges to you? Explain.

CHAPTER 7

The Progressive Era in Education

The educational process has no end beyond itself; it is its own end.

—*John Dewey*
Democracy and Education, *1916*

The progressive reform movement describes a range of efforts at the turn of the 20th century that were designed to promote social and education reform in the context of and in response to staggering demographic and industrial changes in the United States. Efforts were directed at regulating the labor of women and children, improving working conditions, combating unfair business practices, overturning corruption in politics at all levels, making government more democratic and responsible to the people, and improving conditions in urban slums.

The progressive reform movement in education in its initial phase, before World War I, was directed at providing a new type of education to a diverse student population, especially the growing population of urban poor. It was concerned with making the educational enterprise more efficient and making the child the center of the educational process. The efficiency movement addressed not only the efficiency of operations but also the efficient delivery of a differentiated curriculum to students based on their vocational or educational goals.

The efficiency movement was supported by the child study and mental measurement movements and the development of new learning theories. The child study movement recognized that emotional growth and personality development were of equal importance to cognitive development in understanding the child. The measurement movement stressed that if education was to be studied using the principles of scientific inquiry, and if education is concerned with change, then those changes must be measurable.

The child-centeredness philosophies of Rousseau, Froebel, and Pestalozzi influenced pedagogical progressives such as Francis W. Parker, John Dewey, Ella Flagg Young, and William H. Kilpartick, who emphasized "learning by doing." These reformers sought to replace the teacher-dominated, subject-centered curriculum with an activity and discovery curriculum focused on the needs and interests of the child and on preparation for participation in a changing democratic society.

After World War I educational progressivism, while retaining its child-centered focus, changed its curriculum as well as its focus from schools serving the urban poor to suburban and private "progressive" schools. As discussed in chapter 8, by the beginning of the Depression, progressive education had already begun to decline.

Population and National Growth

The 20th century brought marked changes in American social, economic, political, and educational life. Population growth continued at a staggering rate: from 76 million in 1900 to 106 million in 1920 and 123 million in 1930. And, although birthrates declined, improvements in medicine and sanitation led to lower infant mortality, a lower overall death rate, and a longer life expectancy for all segments of the population. By World War I most infectious diseases had been brought under control, and medical education was greatly improved (Bonner, 1963).

As in the last decades of the 19th century, a significant portion of the population growth was the result of immigration. In the first 2 decades of the 20th century the average number of immigrants arriving in this country doubled from the previous 2 decades, from an average of 450,000 immigrants per year to an average of almost 900,000 per year (see Table 7.1). Also, continuing the trend that had begun in the last century, the majority of these immigrants, the "new" immigrants, were from southern and eastern Europe—Italy, Poland, Russia, Austria-Hungary—and were primarily Catholic or Jewish. Many were peasants or refugees from the ghettos of Poland or Russia. Concerns that the new immigrants were of an undesirable "racial stock" and tended to be illiterate, criminal, and "ill-fitted to the demands of a Teutonic civilization" led to demands in the popular media that immigration be restricted (Ravitch, 2001, p. 65).

 For Your Reflection and Analysis

What are some of the most pressing problems facing "new immigrants" to the United States today?

At the same time that the population was experiencing rapid growth it was becoming increasingly urban. The urban population rose 39% between 1900 and 1910 and, in 1920, for the first time in our nation's history the number of those living in towns of 2,500 (54.3 million) exceeded the number of those living in rural areas (51.8 million) (see Table 7.2). As a result, towns and cities grew. Much of the growth of the cities came from the new immigrants. The immigrants tended to congregate in crowded segregated neighborhoods in tenement houses. Living conditions in the slums and tenements in many of the major American cities equaled or exceeded the squalor, poverty, and unsanitary conditions of the European slums the immigrants had left behind.

America experienced growth not only at home, but also on the international scene. In the last years of the 19th century and the beginning of the 20th century the United States acquired Guam, the Philippines, Puerto Rico, the Hawaiian Islands, the Virgin Islands, and the Panama Canal Zone. The nation also engaged in a war with Spain; landed troops in Mexico, Nicaragua, and Haiti; helped put down a revolt in China; and in 1917 entered World War I and the fight to make the world safe for democracy.

Politics and Economic Growth: The Bright and Dark Sides

The economic growth of the United States during this period was even more profound than the population growth. Whereas the population increased less than four-fold in the post–Civil War to pre–World War I period, production increased tenfold

TABLE 7.1 Immigration by Country, 1871 to 1950

Region and country of last residence	1871–80	1881–90	1891–1900	1901–10	1911–20	1921–30	1931–40	1941–50
All countries	2,812,191	5,246,613	3,687,564	8,795,386	5,735,811	4,107,209	528,431	1,035,039
Austria-Hungary	72,969	353,719	592,707	2,145,266	896,342	63,548	11,424	28,329
Belgium	7,221	20,177	18,167	41,635	33,746	15,846	4,817	12,189
Czechoslovakia					3,426	102,194	14,393	8,347
Denmark	31,771	88,132	50,231	65,285	41,983	32,430	2,559	5,393
France	72,206	50,464	30,770	73,379	61,897	49,610	12,623	38,809
Germany	718,182	1,452,970	505,152	341,498	146,945	412,202	114,058	226,578
Greece	210	2,308	15,979	167,519	184,201	51,084	9,119	8,973
Ireland	436,871	655,482	388,416	339,065	146,181	211,234	10,973	19,789
Italy	55,759	307,309	651,893	2,045,877	1,109,524	455,315	68,028	57,661
Netherlands	16,541	53,701	26,758	48,262	43,718	26,948	7,150	14,860
Norway	95,323	176,586	95,015	190,505	66,395	68,531	4,740	10,100
Sweden	115,922	391,776	226,266	249,534	95,074	97,249	3,960	10,665
Poland	12,970	51,806	96,720	—	4,813	227,734	17,026	7,571
Portugal	14,082	16,978	27,508	69,149	89,732	29,994	3,329	7,423
Romania	11	6,348	12,750	53,008	13,311	67,646	3,871	1,076
Soviet Union	39,284	213,282	505,290	1,597,306	921,201	61,742	1,370	571
Spain	5,266	4,419	8,731	27,935	68,611	28,958	3,258	2,898
Switzerland	28,293	81,988	31,179	34,922	23,091	29,676	5,512	10,547
United Kingdom	548,043	807,357	271,538	525,950	341,408	339,570	31,572	139,306
Yugoslavia					1,888	49,064	5,835	1,576

Source: U.S. Bureau of Citizenship and Immigration Services. (2004). Retrieved July 30, 2004 from USCIS website: uscis.gov/graphics/shared/aboutus/statistics/imm/98excel/Table2_2xls.

TABLE 7.2 U.S. Urban and Rural Population, 1790–1990

Total population	Number of places of 2,500 or more	Urban Population	Rural Population	Percentage of total population	
				Urban	Rural
248 709 873	8 510	187 053 487	61 656 386	75.2	24.8
226 542 199	7 749	167 050 992	59 494 813	73.7	26.3
203 302 031	6 433	149 646 617	53 565 309	73.6	26.3
179 323 175	5 445	125 268 750	54 045 425	69.9	30.1
151 325 798	4 307	96 846 817	54 478 961	64.0	36.0
179 323 175	5 023	113 063 593	66 259 582	63.1	36.9
151 325 798	4 077	90 128 194	61 197 604	59.6	40.4
132 164 569	3 485	74 705 338	57 459 231	56.5	43.5
123 202 624	3 183	69 160 599	54 042 025	56.1	43.9
106 021 537	2 728	54 253 282	51 768 255	51.2	48.8
92 228 496	2 269	42 064 001	50 164 495	45.6	54.4
76 212 168	1 743	30 214 832	45 997 336	39.6	60.4
62 979 766	1 351	22 106 265	40 873 501	35.1	64.9
50 189 209	940	14 129 735	36 059 474	28.2	71.8
38 558 371	663	9 902 361	28 656 010	25.7	74.3
31 443 321	392	6 216 518	25 226 803	19.8	80.2
23 191 876	237	3 574 496	19 617 380	15.4	84.6
17 063 353	131	1 845 055	15 218 298	10.8	89.2
12 860 702	90	1 127 247	11 733 455	8.8	91.2
9 638 453	61	693 255	8 945 198	7.2	92.8
7 239 881	46	525 459	6 714 422	7.3	92.7
5 308 483	33	322 371	4 986 112	6.1	93.9
3 929 214	24	201 655	3 727 559	5.1	94.9

Source: U.S. Bureau of the Census. Retrieved September 10, 2003, from Website: www.census.gov/population/censusdata /table-4.pdf.

(Gray & Peterson, 1974). This was also a period of rapid growth for the railroads and other transportation and communication industries. The expansion of the railroads brought an end to the frontier, which by 1890 was considered officially closed by the Bureau of Census (i.e., they could not draw a line of demarcation beyond which the population was less than two persons per square mile). Railroads now linked all parts of the nation, as did an ever-expanding network of telephone lines. At the same time, the transatlantic cable and transworld shipping linked this nation with others. The expansion in the transportation industry opened up new markets for the growing agricultural and manufacturing industries. By 1920 the United States had become the largest manufacturing nation in the world.

Paradoxically, this period of stellar economic growth is also regarded as a dark chapter in American history because of the abuses in industry and politics. The business leaders who helped bring about the growth also contributed to the abuses and have been referred to as "robber barons" who placed both their personal and business fortunes ahead of the welfare of their workers and those who consumed their products. Muckraking journalists filled the tabloids with descriptions of the plight of workers (including children) in factories, the unsafe and unsanitary working conditions, the horrors of industrial accidents, the filth and disease of the meat packing industry, and descriptions of life in the poverty-ridden slums. (See the treatise on children in the slums by Jacob Riis in the Primary Source Reading for this chapter.)

 For Your Reflection and Analysis

What commonalities exist between the "robber barons" during the turn of the century and the executives involved in the Enron scandal of 2002?

The excesses in industry were facilitated by the corruption in politics. Disregard for the welfare of workers and consumers was matched by disregard for the welfare of taxpayers. Corruption was evident at all levels of government, including the local school district. School boards and school systems were exposed as cesspools of patronage and corruption: Politically appointed school board members put unqualified friends and relatives into teaching and administrative positions and took bribes to award construction contracts or to purchase textbooks and supplies. Politicians not only stole from the public trust, but they also sold the public trust.

The most visible symbol of corruption in government was Tammany Hall, the name given to the corrupt political machine that dominated New York City politics from before the Civil War to the early 1930s. For over 70 years the Tammany machine directed the flow of money, patronage, and votes in New York City politics. Doing any business with the city required not only the payment of a bribe, but also the padding of subsequent bills to keep the payments going to the machine. In the end taxpayers might pay 10 times the actual cost to build a city building or operate a streetcar. Millions and millions of dollars every year were swindled from the city. Bribery, graft, and other forms of corruption brought in millions more.

Progressive Reformers

The response to the negative business and political practices was a reform movement that came to be known as the progressive movement. Decrying the excesses of big business, the progressives challenged the cherished ideal of limited government and urged the government to protect consumers against unfair monopolistic practices, workers (particularly women and children) against exploitation, and the less fortunate against any form of social injustice. Labor legislation sought to regulate the labor of women, limit child labor, bar children from hazardous occupations, regulate wages and hours, and improve health and safety conditions in factories. On the local, state, and national levels progressives sought to wrest control of government from the business community and use it to bring about social change. They were successful advocates of the passage of antitrust legislation, which sought to control monopolies and their unfair business practices.

Workers in settlement houses such as Jane Adams' Hull House in Chicago joined other social reformers in crusades to improve the conditions in urban slums. The majority of those affected by the deleterious conditions in the unsanitary, filthy, and overcrowded tenements were immigrants and their children. In addition to attempting to improve their living conditions, social reformers sought to provide them with language training, vocational skills, and citizenship training. Many of the educational progressives, including John Dewey, aligned themselves with and contributed to the work of the social reformers.

Laborers also sought to improve their plight through labor unions and strikes. Increased union activity met with harsh resistance and persecution; violence and loss of life were not uncommon. Yet by 1920 one fifth of all nonagricultural workers in the nation were organized; in view of employer hostility, this was a considerable achievement (Kirkland, 1969).

The progressive movement also gained momentum in the political arena after 1900. Progressives maintained a firm belief in representative democracy and individual freedom and were instrumental in extending democracy through the direct election of judges, local school board members, and U.S. senators; the initiation of the referendum, the recall, the initiative, and the secret ballot; and the extension of women's suffrage. Progressive reformers also fought corruption in government and sought to expand civil service and promote efficiency in government operations.

Changes in Education

Significant changes in the educational arena accompanied those in the social, economic, and political arenas. The urbanization of the population and the popularity of the automobile made possible the building of larger schools and contributed to the consolidation of many rural school districts. The number of school districts in the United States continued to decrease gradually from over 130,000 at the turn of the century to approximately 119,000 in 1937 and 40,000 by 1960 (National Center for

Education Statistics [NCES], 1993). Although the number of districts declined, the differences between urban and rural districts remained. Students in rural schools (67% of all students in 1910) attended school for fewer weeks than urban students did and received only 57% of the per pupil expenditure of urban students ($26.13 vs. $45.74) (Cuban, 1984).

Instruction at the turn of the 20th century was still very teacher centered and the curriculum very subject centered and, consistent with the recommendations of the Committee of Ten, geared toward the college preparation curriculum. Cuban (1984) described it as follows:

> Generally, classes were taught as a group. Teacher talk dominated verbal expression during class time. Student movement during instruction occurred only with the teacher's permission. Classroom activities clustered around teacher questions and explanations, student recitation, and the class working on textbook assignments. Except for laboratory work done in science classrooms, uniformity in behavior was sought and reflected in classroom after classroom with rows of bolted-down desks facing the blackboard and the teacher's desk. (p. 30)

As the nation entered the new century, the school population was increasing more rapidly than the overall population. School enrollment more than doubled between 1890 and 1930. Moreover, students stayed in school longer, and high school enrollment rose dramatically, from 519,000 in 1900 to 4.4 million in 1930. To accommodate this growth, new schools were being opened at the rate of one per day (Cuban, 1984). The growth in the student population and school facilities was accompanied by an almost doubling in the number of teachers and other nonsupervisory personnel between 1900 and 1930 (see Table 6.1, p. 175). During the same period the average length of the school term increased by 27 days. More teachers and longer terms translated into a tenfold increase in expenditures between 1900 and 1930 (see Table 7.3).

A significant portion of the increase in school enrollment, especially in the larger cities, came from the new immigrants or the children of new immigrants. As had been

TABLE 7.3 Revenues and Expenditures, 1889–90 to 1929–30 (in unadjusted dollars)

School year ending	1890	1900	1910	1920	1930
Total revenues, in millions	143	220	433	970	2,089
Federal government	—	—	—	2	7
State government	26	38	65	160	354
Local sources	97	149	312	808	1,728
Total expenditures, in millions	141	215	426	1,036	2,317
Expenditures per pupil in average daily attendance	17	20	33	64	108

Source: U. S. Department of Education, National Center for Education Statistics. (1993). *120 Years of American education: A statistical portrait.* Washington, DC: U.S. Government Printing Office.

For Your Reflection and Analysis

*Which of the most recent "new immigrants"
to the United States had an easier time
assimilating? A more difficult time? Why?*

true for generations of earlier immigrants, these immigrants saw education as the best route to improve their life in their new homeland. "So powerful was the lure of education that on the day after a steamship arrived, as many as 125 children would apply to one New York school" (Bernard & Mondale, 2001c, p. 73). Urban schools, already overcrowded and often in disrepair, faced the task of teaching these children, many of whom spoke no English and were living in conditions of abject poverty. Overcrowding meant that many children were only able to attend school part time.

As discussed in the previous chapter, the response of some education reformers to the burgeoning immigrant enrollment was a push to expand the industrial and vocational offerings of the public schools. Many school districts introduced multiple vocational tracks to prepare "hand-minded" immigrant children to become industrial and commercial workers, domestic workers, or housewives (Ravitch, 2001). Many others saw the school as the means to Americanize the immigrant. In their desire to do so, schools added classes in civics and American history, and, as the nation moved toward war, many schools adopted an English-only curriculum. After the Allied victory in 1918 the movement accelerated and soon 35 states mandated that instruction be in English only. American heroes and anthems were emphasized, the Bible was read, the Lord's Prayer was recited, and Christian holidays were celebrated, even in cities such as New York where a large part of the student population was Jewish (Bernard & Mondale, 2001c).

Jacob Riis photo of children in a New York tenement.

Progressivism in Education

The progressive reform movement, which had such a widespread impact on political, social, and economic life, also found expression in education. The use of the word *expression* here has been carefully chosen because defining exactly what should be considered part of the progressive education movement has been the subject of some debate. Some historians have viewed the progressive education movement as the educational phase of the larger progressive movement that swept American political and social life (Cremin, 1959). Others have challenged this analysis as failing to include those social and political reformers who had a vision of a corporate society that depended on the replacement of rugged and independent individualism with a socialized and cooperative man with an occupational specialization—a vision that led them to advocate training for both social cooperation and a special slot in society (Spring, 1970). Still others have taken the position of this text, namely that in its first stage, before World War I, progressive education was an expression of the same middle-class drive that gave form and energy to the progressive movement, but that in the years following the war progressive education reflected a very different set of social values and took a very different direction.

In the prewar period, paralleling the call of the social and political reformers, in addition to curricular and administrative reforms, education reformers, particularly those in the cities, called for making the schools more sanitary, more open to air and sunlight, and more conducive to creative activity; lowering pupil–teacher ratios; and adding the provision of basic health care and food services to the responsibilities of the school. In some areas schools were kept open in the evening to provide classes for adults, primarily immigrants, or evening study hours for children living in crowded tenement houses. In other areas attempts were made to have the schools serve as community centers.

The impact of progressivism in education was most evident in the areas of administration and pedagogy. Progressivism in administration was manifest in the efficiency movement, or what Callahan (1962) dubbed the "cult of efficiency." In pedagogy, progressivism was evidenced in a variety of efforts to make the child the center of the educational process.

Administrative Progressivism: The Efficiency Movement

The efficiency movement was an attempt to apply the principles of scientific management to the operation of the schools. Scientific management, which grew out of the work of Frederick W. Taylor, an engineer at Bethlehem Steel, was aimed at increasing production at lower cost while at the same time instilling order, standardization, and discipline into the process. Scientific management as a technique involved a careful analysis of the task to be performed, a detailing of the timing of the actions and materials used in performing the task, and a determination of the order of the quickest and best steps and the elimination of any unnecessary steps.

Many of the leaders of the progressive movement, as well as many members of boards of education, were members of the business community. At a time when the schools were being criticized for their ineffectiveness and inefficiency, these individuals increasingly urged that the principles and practices of business be applied to the operation of the schools. Beginning in the second decade of the century, school boards and superintendents themselves stepped up their efforts to apply the "science" of management to the educational enterprise and adopted the language and ideology of corporate America.

The influence of the efficiency movement was evidenced by the attention given to job analysis and specialization, supervision, standardization of tasks, teacher evaluation, accountability, cost accounting, and the introduction of incentive pay plans. Another very visible manifestation was the reduction in the size of school boards. School boards in the larger cities were often very large: At one time the Philadelphia School Board had 42 members and New York City had 46. In some cases the size of the board reflected the political division of the city into wards and the fact that each ward demanded a representative on the board. In many cases board members were politically appointed, not elected. Administrative progressives, as these reformers have been called, believed that reducing the size of the board would increase its efficiency, and that moving to nonpartisan elections would reduce the influence of patronage and bribery. At the same time that school boards were becoming smaller, their membership moved from being dominated by upper-class and professional men to increased representation from the middle and upper middle classes.

Reformers were also convinced that schools would be more efficient if decisions were made or informed by experts. This belief led to the vesting of greater decision making in the most acknowledged expert, the superintendent, and the centralization of power and authority around the office of the superintendent, as well as the introduction of a more hierarchical and bureaucratic educational structure. It also led to the establishment of efficiency departments patterned after Taylor's "planning departments" and the hiring of so-called educational "efficiency experts." These departments and experts were actively involved in conducting surveys appraising every aspect of the school operation and making recommendations for improvement.

For Your Reflection and Analysis

What are some of the current proposals being suggested to make the schools more efficient?

The administrative progressives in education were the first generation of professional educators trained in graduate schools of education (Tyack & Cuban, 1995). They were made up primarily of urban superintendents, professors of education, state and federal officials, and leaders of the professional education organizations. By 1930, through the efforts of administrative progressives within and outside of education, most school boards had been transformed into smaller, more businesslike operations divorced from partisan politics (Cuban, 2001). The administrative progressives were also instrumental in increasing state funding and certification requirements for teachers and in bringing greater standardization to textbooks and the curriculum.

Social Efficiency

The desire to maximize the efficient operation of the schools also contributed to the social efficiency movement mentioned in chapter 6. According to the educators involved in this movement, schools would be more efficient if they did not "waste" specific instruction on students who would never need or use it. Accordingly, they believed that the "efficient" curriculum should be differentiated in an array of academic and vocational tracks and students would be tracked into the curricula that would contribute most directly to their vocational or educational goals. The social efficiency movement, in its belief that assessment could provide a scientific basis for the placement of students, was clearly influenced by the mental measurement movement and Thorndike's work in human intelligence, both discussed later in this chapter. Both of these supported efforts to vocationalize the curriculum.

According to Kliebard (1995), no one epitomized the efficiency-minded curriculum planners more than John Franklin Bobbitt (1876–1956). Bobbitt developed an approach to curriculum development that was adapted from Taylor's concepts of job and task analysis and was based on the belief that the curriculum should be developed on the basis of an analysis of adult vocational, occupational, social, and political roles. In his 1912 article, "The Elimination of Waste in Education," Bobbitt used the factory metaphor to articulate how such a curriculum could be adapted to the production of "the finished product for which it is best adapted" (p. 269), that is, the provision of an education based on the predicted social and vocational role of the child.

Bobbitt was very impressed with the school system that had been established by Superintendent William Wirt in Gary, Indiana, a city that had basically been founded by the U.S. Steel Corporation in 1906. Wirt studied with Dewey at the University of Chicago, and the system he established in Gary reflected Dewey's concern for the interdependence between the school and the community. The Gary plan, known as the platoon or work-study-play plan, involved organizing the student body into two platoons. While one platoon was involved in academic subjects in the morning, the second platoon was involved in physical activities, manual or vocational training, or cultural pursuits. In the afternoon the pattern was reversed. Such a program was intended to maximize the intellectual, social, cultural, and physical abilities of the child. It also aimed at making the most efficient use of school facilities. His concern for efficiency and maximization also led Wirt to open the schools at night, on weekends, and during the summers.

By 1929 the platoon system had been adopted by over 200 school districts. However, it had also been the subject of considerable controversy. Although those social efficiency reformers who saw the platoon system and similar efforts to differentiate the curriculum as enabling the schools to operate more efficiently, many of their contemporaries, as well as many parents, objected to the presumption of predicting the future roles of children. Others saw them as nothing more than attempts at social control and as a way to ensure industry a supply of trained workers. In New York City the plan was abandoned after protest from immigrant and working-class parents concerned that their children were being overwhelmingly tracked into the vocational curricula.

Pedagogical Progressivism

Pedagogical progressivism traces its intellectual roots to Froebel and Pestalozzi. The emphasis Froebel and Pestalozzi placed on educating the whole child and on the importance of the needs and interests of the child are clearly reflected in progressivism, as is their advocacy for an activity curriculum. The beginning of pedagogical progressivism in this country can be traced to Francis W. Parker, superintendent of schools in Quincy, Massachusetts.

Francis W. Parker

Francis W. Parker (1837–1902) studied in Europe and became familiar with the work of Pestalozzi and Froebel. He shared their belief that learning should emanate from the interests and needs of the child and that the most appropriate curriculum was an activity-based one that encouraged children to express themselves freely and creatively. He also shared their belief in the importance of loving and respecting the child. In all things, Parker's aim was to make the child the center of the educational process.

Parker left the superintendency in Quincy to become principal of the Cook County Normal School in Chicago. There Parker was able not only to influence the training of teachers but also to put his ideas into practice at the practice (lab) school associated with the school. The practice school of Cook County Normal School was organized as a model democratic community. Art was an integral part of the curriculum, as were nature studies, field trips, and social activities. Rather than deal with multiple, discrete subject matter, the curriculum attempted to integrate subjects in a way that made it more meaningful to the learner. For example, reading was taught in conjunction with history and literature and mathematics was taught in relationship with other activities. The concept of integration became one of the tenets of progressivism.

Parker's educational ideas were spread through his many publications and speeches. Numerous educators and other interested persons came to observe his theories in practice at the lab school. Later, when he joined the faculty at the University of Chicago, his influence extended to his colleagues John Dewey and Ella Flagg Young.

John Dewey

John Dewey, professor of philosophy and pedagogy at the University of Chicago and professor of philosophy at Columbia University, first came into contact with Parker as a parent of children at Parker's practice school. Dewey was impressed with the philosophy and methods of the school and in 1896 established his own laboratory school at the University of Chicago. Unlike other similar schools associated with colleges or universities, Dewey did not intend that his school be a practice school for training teachers, but a laboratory where ideas could be tested. Implicit in this was the belief that education was a legitimate area for scientific investigation and that a science of education did indeed exist.

Dewey's progressive educational theories reflected his philosophy of pragmatism. As described in chapter 1, pragmatism holds that there are no absolutes: Truth results from the application of scientific thinking to experience. Dewey rejected the old, rigid, subject-centered curriculum in favor of the child-centered curriculum in which learning came through experience, not rote memorization of facts and figures. "Learning by doing" was the motto of his lab school. At the lab school the classroom was a miniature of society, and learning was integrated into real-life experiences. The problem-solving method was the preferred method at the lab school, and motivation

For Your Reflection and Analysis

To what extent did your elementary school experience reflect the progressive child-centered philosophy?

was at the center of the learning process. Motivation was stimulated by focusing on the needs and interests of the children and their natural inquisitiveness. However, although Dewey proposed that children be given the opportunity for creative self-expression, and that their interests be considered in the learning process, he did not believe that this should be unfettered. Dewey believed that order was important and in later life became critical of some of the more extreme versions of child-centeredness, which he considered anti-intellectual. For Dewey the child's experience with the environment "must be mediated by reflective thinking and problem solving" and the learning experience must maintain a "pragmatic balance between the consequences of education for the student and for society" (Horn, 2002, p. 38).

The goal of education for Dewey was to promote individual growth and to prepare the child for full participation in a democratic society. The relationship between education and democracy and school and society was central to Dewey's vision of the school. However, Dewey was not in favor of using the school to prepare children for a predetermined vocation or place in life. Dewey believed the school as a miniature democratic institution should be the place where the child develops a "spirit of social cooperation and community life." Only by enabling the child to develop to his or her maximum potential would the community realize its own. In one of his most widely read books, *The School and Society* (1899), Dewey argued that what the best and wisest parents want for their children, the community should want for all children.

For Your Reflection and Analysis

How do you reconcile the views of Dewey and Bobbitt, both of whom are considered progressive educators?

Dewey maintained that the child should be viewed as a total organism and that education is most effective when it considers not only the intellectual but also the social, emotional, and physical needs of the child. He thought that education was a lifelong process and that the school should be an integral part of community life, a concept that supported the development of the community school.

Dewey wrote some 500 articles and 40 books. His classic *Democracy and Education* (1916) provided perhaps the strongest statement of his educational theories and provided the rationale for a generation of progressive educators. Dewey's influence was felt not only in philosophy and education, but also in law, political theory, and social reform. Dewey provided the intellectual foundation for progressive education, and is also said to be "the real spokesman for intellectual America in the Progressive Era" (Bonner, 1963, p. 44).

Ella Flagg Young

Ella Flagg Young (1845–1917), the first woman superintendent of a large city school system (Chicago, 1907–1915) and the first woman president of the National Education Association (1910), was an important figure in the progressive education movement, both in her own right and through her influence on and collaboration with her colleague at the University of Chicago, John Dewey. Dewey acknowledged that he was constantly getting ideas from her: "More times than I could say I didn't see the meaning or force of some favorite conception of my own until Mrs. Young had given it back to me . . . it was from her that I learned that freedom and respect for freedom meant regard for the inquiring and reflective processes of individuals" (McManis, 1916, p. 121).

Young served as supervisor of instruction at Dewey's lab school. Like Dewey, Young proposed that teaching methods should give fullest expression to the individual interests of the child, that education should recognize the total experiences the child brings to the school, and that the curriculum should provide the child with experiences that build on his or her natural interests and dispositions (Webb & McCarthy, 1998).

Young shared Dewey's belief that the school should mirror the democratic society it served. She espoused democratic administration and organized teachers' councils to provide teachers with a greater voice in decision making. In her public voice as well as in her administrative practices she encouraged the extension of the principles of democracy throughout the educational system, the individual school, and into the classroom. She decentralized many administrative responsibilities and encouraged the development of principals as instructional leaders.

Although she was one of the most respected and well known superintendents of her day, Ella Flagg Young was one of a handful of superintendents who did not join the cult of efficiency. She rejected attempts to mechanize the work of the teacher. In fact, her approach was just the opposite. She gave teachers a voice in decision making, sought to raise their salaries and increase the professionalism of teaching, and, as evidenced in the Primary Source Reading for this chapter, supported their right to unionize. As a principal she started teacher clubs in which teachers could meet to discuss various issues facing the schools and the profession. In a short time Ella Flagg Young Clubs could be found in elementary schools throughout Chicago.

From her professional positions as principal of the Chicago Normal School, superintendent of Chicago schools, and president of the National Education Association, as well as through her numerous presentations and publications, Young was able to play a visible and important role in promoting progressive education in the years leading up to World War I.

William H. Kilpatrick

William H. Kilpatrick was the most prominent advocate of progressive education in the period between World War I and World War II (Graham, 1967). Kilpatrick, a professor at Teachers College, translated Dewey's philosophy into a practical educational methodology, the *project method*. The project method was an attempt to make education as child centered and "practical" as possible by engaging the child in projects consistent with the child's own goals and interests. For Kilpatrick "wholehearted purposeful activity" should be at the heart of the educative process. Conduct of projects should proceed through four steps: purposing, planning, executing, and judging. Kilpatrick rejected the scientific, efficiency curriculum planning of Bobbitt. Rather, he believed that the curriculum should be built around the "purposeful act." Kilpatrick and his followers were not proposing:

that one kind of content was somehow better than another. They were, in effect, arguing that selection of content was a matter of secondary importance at best ... [rather] the child's own purposes should provide the basis for the development of the curriculum with subject matter employed instrumentally as it bore on the accomplishment of those purposes. .... Kilpatrick proposed a curriculum that deemphasized the acquisition of knowledge in favor of a curriculum that was synonymous with purposeful activity. .... Kilpatrick was, in effect, reconstructing what we mean by a curriculum, and an interesting side effect of that redefinition was that the *project method* had become a curriculum. (Kliebard, 1995, pp. 143–44)

The project method gained widespread favor as an alternative to social efficiency as a curriculum development methodology. Despite concerns that the project method failed to ensure the acquisition of the knowledge needed by future citizens, and that standardization of the process came to overshadow the child-centered goal, the movement continued to grow. By the 1930s the movement outgrew its identification with the project per se and was reinvented as the activity or experience curriculum (Kliebard, 1995).

 For Your Reflection and Analysis

Describe a project that you completed as part of your elementary or secondary schooling. To what extent was it a "purposeful learning activity"?

Kilpatrick played a major role in advancing the progressive education movement through not only his many presentations and publications (perhaps the most widely distributed being his 1918 article, "The Project Method"), but through the over 35,000 students he taught in his quarter century at Teachers College.

Child Study Movement

During the first 2 decades of the 20th century, as the progressive movement was gaining momentum, two related movements were also taking place that would have far-reaching consequences—the child study movement and the measurement movement. Child study, through the observation of children at school or at play, was considered a scientific approach to determining individual differences among children upon which curricular decisions could be made. The child study movement began with the pioneering work of G. Stanley Hall (1849–1924). Hall received a doctorate in psychology from Harvard, the first in the United States. His 1883 paper on what preschoolers know and do not know is said to mark the beginning of the child study movement.

Hall established a center for applied psychology at Johns Hopkins University in 1884, the year Dewey graduated from the same institution. Five years later he was named president of Clark University in Worcester, Massachusetts. Hall is credited with the founding of the American Psychological Association (APA) in 1892 and served as its first president.

Under Hall's leadership at Clark University considerable research was conducted on educational issues and child development. Hall and his colleagues recognized that emotional growth and personality development were just as important as cognitive development and physical development in understanding the child. Hall was influenced by Charles Darwin's theory of evolution and advanced the recapitulation theory of child development, which saw the child as an evolving organism who developed through a series of recognizable and successively related stages that paralleled the development or evolution of civilization. Hall believed that once educators understood how the child developed, they would be better able to foster that development by tailoring developmentally appropriate learning activities. In effect, Hall was advocating individualized instruction. These early efforts at child study were important in laying the foundations for educational psychology and developmental psychology and reinforced the progressives' promotion of child-centered reform.

The Measurement Movement

One expression of the progressive influence on education was a growing interest in the science of education. If education were to be studied using the principles of scientific inquiry, and greater efficiency were to be obtained, things must be measured. As Edward L. Thorndike (1918), one of the leaders in the development of the science of education, explained:

> Whatever exists at all exists in some amount. To know it thoroughly involves knowing its quantity as well as its quality. Education is concerned with changes in human beings; a change is a difference between two conditions; each of these conditions is known to us only by the products produced by it—things made, words spoken, acts performed and the like. To measure any of these products means to define its amount in some way so that competent persons will know how large it is, better than they would without measurement. (p. 7)

Although intelligence and aptitude measures had been in use for some time, the real breakthrough came when French psychologists Alfred Binet and Theodore Simon developed an instrument based on an intelligence scale that allowed comparison of individual intelligence to a norm. The goal of the test was to enable French schools to identify mentally challenged students for appropriate placement. Of the many adaptations of the Binet-Simon scale, the most important for education was the so-called Stanford revision by Lewis Terman, one of Cubberly's colleagues at Stanford University. The Stanford-Binet Intelligence Test extended the Binet test to the average and gifted student and is still today the most widely used individually administered intelligence test in America. Terman also included the *intelligence quotient* (IQ), a number indicating the ratio between mental age and chronological age.

One of the major American figures in the measurement movement was the educational psychologist Edward L. Thorndike (1874–1949). He taught the first university course in educational measurement and wrote the first textbook on the use of social measurements, *An Introduction to the Theory of Mental and Social Measurements* (1904). Thorndike was also a major contributor to efforts to develop standardized intelligence and achievement tests. He wrote and taught about test construction, and he and his students at Columbia developed achievement tests in several areas. As a member of the U.S. Army's Committee on Classification of Personnel, Thorndike supervised the development of the Beta form of the Stanford-Binet test used with illiterate World War I recruits.

In fact, the massive mobilization of manpower needed during World War I was a major factor in the growth of the measurement movement. The military needed a way to determine which men were suited for service and for what type of service. Out of this need a number of group intelligence tests were developed and ultimately were administered to 1.75 million recruits during World War I.

One unexpected result of this massive testing was the discovery of a large number of young men with educational (as well as physical) deficiencies: Approximately one quarter of all recruits were judged illiterate. Deficiencies were particularly high among rural youth, which confirmed the inadequacies of many rural school systems.

The success of the wartime use of the tests led to what seemed their next logical use—to identify and sort students for alternative educational placements. According to Heffernan (1968), the "apparent objectivity of the test results had a fascination for school administrators and teachers. Certainty seemed somehow to attach to these mathematically expressed comparisons of pupil achievement" (p. 229). Throughout the country students were classified, assigned, and compared on the basis of tests. However, the tests were not without their critics.

Criticism came from a number of fronts. Progressives such as John Dewey voiced their concerns that the tests were used to indiscriminately label students and to make subjective judgments about their potential, thereby undermining the democratic purpose of schooling. Essentialists such as William C. Bagley, also of Teachers College, also criticized the use of tests when they were used under the umbrella of

The testing of World War I recruits was a major step in the development of intelligence tests.

For Your Reflection and Analysis

How has the use or misuse of testing reinforced upward mobility or social control?

social efficiency to unnecessarily limit the educational opportunities afforded children. And, because the children whose opportunities were most likely to be limited were minorities and immigrants, members of the lower class also challenged the use of the tests. Yet, despite these objections the measurement movement moved forward; by the end of the 1920s several million schoolchildren had taken intelligence tests, and measurement had become a permanent part of American education.

Progressive Education After the War

The 1920s brought a rise in the stock market, telephone poles, and women's skirts. The car replaced the horse and buggy as the primary means of transportation, and sound came to the big screen. With a rising economy and the country riding a wave of patriotism after having "made the world safe for democracy," social and political progressivism declined. Educational progressivism, while not necessarily declining, took a different turn. In fact, the progressive reform movement after the war bore little similarity to the reform movement before the war (Graham, 1967).

Before the war reform in education had been directed toward the public schools serving the urban poor. The goal of the reforms was not to alter the school's primary role as a place of instruction, but to expand public school facilities and curricular offerings. Progressive reformers sought to add to the school's primary role various measures designed to improve the lot of the children of the working poor and to equip them to more easily and fully participate in American life; "hence the vocational schools, the health and nutrition programs, the hot meal schedules, and the rest" (Graham, 1967, p. 8).

After the war progressive education was primarily an affair of so-called "progressive" private schools or the public schools in suburbs serving middle- or upper-class families. These parents were not interested in the social services provided by the school or the vocational training it offered; they were impressed by the "new psychology" and the references to child-centeredness and creativity and wanted to see these ideas expanded to their schools (Graham, 1967).

Location was not the only difference between the prewar and postwar "progressive schools." They differed in their curricula and the very source of the initiation of the reforms.

> While Gary had gone in for efficiency of school operation, individualized instruction stamped the Winnetka (a Chicago suburb) plan. Gary achieved an *expanded* curriculum including vocational courses; Winnetka featured a *revised* curriculum stressing social studies and a newly integrated subject matter. Impetus for reform at Gary had come from old-line civic progressives and local community planners. . . . Initiative for school revision in Winnetka, on the other hand, had come from the residents and parents of the modish suburb who wanted to improve local educational opportunities for their children. (Graham, 1967, p. 10)

Progressive Education Association

The founding of the Progressive Education Association (PEA) in 1919 gave progressives a formal organizational voice. The association adopted seven guiding principles: (1) the child's freedom to develop naturally; (2) interest as the motivation for all work; (3) the teacher as guide in the learning process; (4) the scientific study of pupil development; (5) greater attention to everything that affects the child's physical development; (6) cooperation between the school and home in meeting the natural interests and activities of the child; and (7) the Progressive School should be a leader in educational movements (*Progressive Education*, 1924).

In the years after its founding the PEA was considered the official expression of the progressive education movement and at its height had over 10,000 members. The PEA published a journal, *Progressive Education*, from 1924 to 1955, as well as a large number of books and reports, perhaps the best known being the report of the Eight Year Study discussed in chapter 8.

In its early years the PEA was dominated by headmasters from "progressive" private schools. Later, leadership shifted to public school administrators and professors of education, many of whom were affiliated with Teachers College, Columbia University. Although many of its leaders considered themselves disciples of Parker and Dewey, Dewey was often critical of the activities of the PEA, which he did not believe were based on a fully developed and articulated philosophy. However, he did share with the members of the PEA a concern that in a somewhat desperate attempt to be "scientific" education had overlooked the fact that the child should be the most important consideration (Hissong & Hissong, 1930).

> *For Your Reflection and Analysis*
>
> *Is Dewey's concern about attempts to bring science to education valid today? Explain.*

Despite their common grounds, as Graham (1967) detailed in her history of the Progressive Education Association, the PEA did not reflect the concerns of the majority of the pre–World War I leaders of the progressive movement. And yet in the end the innovations of the prewar progressives were taken up into the mainstream of American education, whereas many of those urged by the PEA's leaders and contemporaries, although popular for a decade or two, soon passed from vogue (Graham, 1967). The decline of the progressive movement and some of the reasons for it are discussed in chapter 8.

Influence of the Progressive Education Movement on Higher Education

The influence of the progressive education movement was also felt in higher education. The great model of progressive higher education was the University of Wisconsin. The Wisconsin model was based on the idea that "the obligation of the university was to undertake leadership in the application of science to the improvement of the life of the citizenry in every domain" (Cremin, 1988, p. 246). This was to be accomplished through research and service, the training of experts, and extended education.

The movement to establish a science of education also affected colleges and universities. Departments of pedagogy and education were established offering graduate degrees in educational administration, elementary and secondary teaching, and educational psychology. Faculty in these departments conducted research and published their findings in scholarly journals.

 For Your Reflection and Analysis

How has the progressive movement influenced curricular reform in higher education?

The teachers colleges and normal schools, like the universities, adopted the progressive service orientation: "They presumed to prepare scientifically trained experts; they extended their learning to all comers; and they prided themselves on their sensitivity to popular need" (Cremin, 1988, p. 248). By 1940 there were over 200 teachers colleges and normal schools located in 42 of the 48 states. As previously noted, many had become state colleges. Almost all granted the bachelor's degree, many the master's degree, and a few the doctoral degree (President's Commission on Higher Education, 1948).

College and university enrollment rose steadily during the pre–World War I years and then surged after the war, partly as a result of those who had come to higher education as part of the Student's Army Training Corps and then stayed after the war ended. Higher education enrollment rose from almost 600,000 in 1919–20 to 1.1 million in 1929–30.

Most of these students were seeking a professional or technical education, primarily in education, business, and engineering, and were enrolled not in the universities but in the growing number of junior colleges and the teacher education institutions. The number of junior colleges increased from 52 in 1920 to 277 in 1930 and 456 in 1940 (U.S. Bureau of the Census, 1975).

Conclusion

More than any education reform movement in U.S. history, the progressive education movement was part of a larger reform movement directed at reforming almost every aspect of American life. Fundamental changes in American life at the turn of the 20th century forced the school not only to assume many new responsibilities but also to formulate new responses to the basic question of what type of education would best prepare youth for participation in society.

Progressive education's response was a rejection of the traditional teacher-centered, subject-centered curriculum in favor of a child-centered curriculum. In so doing it was criticized for being anti-intellectual. The progressive education movement was also criticized, as had been the common school movement, of being an attempt by White, Protestant, middle- and upper-class reformers to impose their values on the lower classes. Some historians (e.g., Hofstadter, 1955) have gone so far as to suggest that the motives of the reformers were less to improve the plight of others than to gain power for themselves; that is, that their crusade against corruption in local governments was less about removing corrupt politicians than it was about removing lower-class politicians and restoring political power to themselves.

In the end, despite conservative accusations or liberal accolades to the contrary, progressive education never took over American education in the 1920s and 1930s. Despite the visibility of figures such as Dewey and Kilpatrick, it was not the progressive changes in the classroom that had the most lasting impact, but those outside the classroom. The social efficiency and organizational and operational reforms advocated by the administrative progressives became part of the policy and practice of American education. Nevertheless, progressive education has had a profound impact far beyond its place in time and has never disappeared as a way of looking at the curriculum and the learning process. Progressive educational ideas were behind the establishment of alternative and free schools in the 1960s and 1970s and the constructivist educational theory that came to favor in the 1990s. Progressive educational ideas continue to be a lightning rod for conservative criticisms of the schools, perhaps because many of the conditions that gave rise to them still exist.

For Discussion and Application

1. Give examples of how the search for efficiency has affected the operation of today's schools.
2. Various historians have defined progressive education differently. Present your definition of progressive education.
3. G. Stanley Hall was influenced by Charles Darwin's theory of evolution. Explain Hall's application of evolution to the study of the young child.
4. Explain the various ways that the measurement movement has become a permanent part of American education today.
5. According to Thorndike's concept of "psychological connectionism," learning depends on a reward being given when an appropriate connection is made between a stimulus and a reward. Ask students at the elementary, secondary, and postsecondary levels what would be the most effective reward for them.

Primary Source Reading

Jacob A. Riis arrived in New York City in 1870 at the age of 21. Like millions of other eager young immigrants, he envisioned America as the "Promised Land." His early struggle and experience of being homeless, penniless, and suicidal culminated in his moving account, How the Other Half Lives: Studies Among the Tenements of New York. *As you read this selection from* How the Other Half Lives, *imagine yourself tagging along with Riis as he explores tenement living through the eyes of a newcomer to America and through the eyes of an innocent child, whose major goal in life is survival.*

The Problem of the Children

Jacob A. Riis

The problem of the children becomes, in these swarms, to the last degree perplexing. Their very number makes one stand aghast. I have already given instances of the packing of the child population in East Side tenements. They might be continued indefinitely until the array would be

Source: Riis, J. A. (1890). The problem of the children. In J. A. Riis, *How the other half lives: Studies among the tenements of New York* (pp. 177–185). New York: Charles Scribner's Sons.

enough to startle any community. For, be it remembered, these children with the training they
receive—or do not receive—with the instincts
they inherit and absorb in their growing up, are
to be our future rulers, if our theory of government is worth anything. More than a working
majority of our voters now register from the tenements. I counted the other day the little ones, up
to ten years or so, in a Bayard Street tenement
that for a yard has a triangular space in the centre
with sides fourteen or fifteen feet long, just room
enough for a row of ill-smelling closets at the
base of the triangle and a hydrant at the apex.
There was about as much light in this "yard" as in
the average cellar. I gave up my self-imposed task
in despair when I had counted one hundred and
twenty-eight in forty families. Thirteen I had
missed, or not found in. Applying the average for
the forty to the whole fifty-three, the house contained one hundred and seventy children. It is not
the only time I have had to give up such census
work. I have in mind an alley—an inlet rather to a
row of rear tenements—that is either two or four
feet wide according as the wall of the crazy old
building that gives on it bulges out or in. I tried
to count the children that swarmed there, but
could not. Sometimes I have doubted that anybody knows just how many there are about. Bodies of drowned children turn up in the rivers right
along in summer whom no one seems to know
anything about. When last spring some work-
men, while moving a pile of lumber on a North
River pier, found under the last plank the body of
a little lad crushed to death, no one had missed a
boy, though his parents afterward turned up. The
truant officer assuredly does not know, though he
spends his life trying to find out, somewhat illogi-
cally, perhaps, since the department that employs
him admits that thousands of poor children are
crowded out of the schools year by year for want
of room. There was a big tenement in the Sixth
Ward, now happily appropriated by the beneficent spirit of business that blots out so many foul
spots in New York—it figured not long ago in the

official reports as "an out-and-out hog-pen"—
that had a record of one hundred and two arrests
in four years among its four hundred and seventy-
eight tenants, fifty-seven of them for drunken and
disorderly conduct. I do not know how many
children there were in it, but the inspector reported that he found only seven in the whole
house who owned that they went to school. The
rest gathered all the instruction they received
running for beer for their elders. Some of them
claimed the "flat" as their home as a mere matter
of form. They slept in the streets at night. The
official came upon a little party of four drinking
beer out of the cover of a milk-can in the
hallway. They were of the seven good boys and
proved their claim to the title by offering him
some.

The old question, what to do with the boy,
assumes a new and serious phase in the tenements. Under the best conditions found there, it
is not easily answered. In nine cases out of ten he
would make an excellent mechanic, if trained
early to work at a trade, for he is neither dull nor
slow, but the short-sighted despotism of the
trades unions has practically closed that avenue to
him. Trade-schools, however excellent, cannot
supply the opportunity thus denied him, and at
the outset the boy stands condemned by his own
to low and ill-paid drudgery, held down by the
hand that of all should labor to raise him. Home,
the greatest factor of all in the training of the
young, means nothing to him but a pigeon-hole
in a coop along with so many other human animals. Its influence is scarcely of the elevating
kind, if it have any. The very games at which he
takes a hand in the street become polluting in its
atmosphere. With no steady hand to guide him,
the boy takes naturally to idle ways. Caught in the
street by the truant officer, or by the agents of the
Children's Societies, peddling, perhaps, or beg-
ging, to help out the family resources, he runs the
risk of being sent to a reformatory, where contact
with vicious boys older than himself soon develops the latent possibilities for evil that lie hidden

in him. The city has no Truant Home in which to keep him, and all efforts of the children's friends to enforce school attendance are paralyzed by this want. The risk of the reformatory is too great. What is done in the end is to let him take chances—with the chances all against him. The result is the rough young savage, familiar from the street. Rough as he is, if any one doubt that this child of common clay have in him the instinct of beauty, of love for the ideal of which his life has no embodiment, let him put the matter to the test. Let him take into a tenement block a handful of flowers from the fields and watch the brightened faces, the sudden abandonment of play and fight that go ever hand in hand where there is no elbowroom, the wild entreaty for "posies," the eager love with which the little messengers of peace are shielded, once possessed; then let him change his mind. I have seen an armful of daisies keep the peace of a block better than a policeman and his club, seen instincts awaken under their gentle appeal, whose very existence the soil in which they grew made seem a mockery. I have not forgotten the deputation of ragamuffins from a Mulberry Street alley that knocked at my office door one morning on a mysterious expedition for flowers, not for themselves, but for "a lady," and having obtained what they wanted, trooped off to bestow them, a ragged and dirty little band, with a solemnity that was quite unusual. It was not until an old man called the next day to thank me for the flowers that I found out they had decked the bier of a pauper, in the dark rear room where she lay waiting in her pine-board coffin for the city's hearse. Yet, as I knew, that dismal alley with its bare brick walls, between which no sun ever rose or set, was the world of those children. It filled their young lives. Probably not one of them had ever been out of the sight of it. They were too dirty, too ragged, and too generally disreputable, too well hidden in their slum besides, to come into line with the Fresh Air summer boarders.

With such human instincts and cravings, forever unsatisfied, turned into a haunting curse; with appetite ground to keenest edge by a hunger that is never fed, the children of the poor grow up in joyless homes to lives of wearisome toil that claims them at an age when the play of their happier fellows has but just begun. Has a yard of turf been laid and a vine been coaxed to grow within their reach, they are banished and barred out from it as from a heaven that is not for such as they. I came upon a couple of youngsters in a Mulberry Street yard a while ago that were chalking on the fence their first lesson in "writin'." And this is what they wrote: "Keeb of te Grass." They had it by heart, for there was not, I verily believe, a green sod within a quarter of a mile. Home to them is an empty name. Pleasure? A gentleman once catechized a ragged class in a down-town public school on this point, and recorded the result: Out of forty-eight boys twenty had never seen the Brooklyn Bridge that was scarcely five minutes' walk away, three only had been in Central Park, fifteen had known the joy of a ride in a horse-car. The street, with its ash-barrels and its dirt, the river that runs foul with mud, are their domain. What training they receive is picked up there. And they are apt pupils. If the mud and the dirt are easily reflected in their lives, what wonder? Scarce half-grown, such lads as these confront the world with the challenge to give them their due, too long withheld, or ——. Our jails supply the answer to the alternative.

A little fellow who seemed clad in but a single rag was among the flotsam and jetsam stranded at Police Headquarters one day last summer. No one knew where he came from or where he belonged. The boy himself knew as little about it as anybody, and was the least anxious to have light shed on the subject after he had spent a night in the matron's nursery. The discovery that beds were provided for boys to sleep in there, and that he could have "a whole egg" and three slices of bread for breakfast put him on the best of terms with the world in general, and he decided that Headquarters was "a bully place." He sang "McGinty" all through, with Tenth Avenue variations, for the police, and then settled down to the serious business of giving an account of himself. The examination went on after this fashion:

"Where do you go to church, my boy?"

"We don't have no clothes to go to church." And indeed his appearance, as he was, in the door of any New York church would have caused a sensation.

"Well, where do you go to school, then?"

"I don't go to school," with a snort of contempt.

"Where do you buy your bread?"

"We don't buy no bread; we buy beer," said the boy, and it was eventually the saloon that led the police as a landmark to his "home." It was worthy of the boy. As he had said, his only bed was a heap of dirty straw on the floor, his daily diet a crust in the morning, nothing else.

Into the rooms of the Children's Aid Society were led two little girls whose father had "busted up the house" and put them on the street after their mother died. Another, who was turned out by her step-mother "because she had five of her own and could not afford to keep her," could not remember ever having been in church or Sunday school, and only knew the name of Jesus through hearing people swear by it. She had no idea what they meant. These were specimens of the overflow from the tenements of our home— heathen that are growing up in New York's streets to-day, while tender-hearted men and women are busying themselves with the socks and the hereafter of well-fed little Hottentots thousands of miles away. According to Canon Taylor, of York, one hundred and nine missionaries in the four fields of Persia, Palestine, Arabia, and Egypt spent one year and sixty thousand dollars in converting one little heathen girl. If there is nothing the matter with those missionaries, they might come to New York with a good deal better prospect of success.

By those who lay flattering unction to their souls in the knowledge that today New York has, at all events, no brood of the gutters of tender years that can be homeless long unheeded, let it be remembered well through what effort this judgment has been averted. In thirty-seven years the Children's Aid Society, that came into existence as an emphatic protest against the tenement corruption of the young, has sheltered quite three hundred thousand outcast, homeless, and orphaned children in its lodging-houses, and has found homes in the West for seventy thousand that had none. Doubtless, as a mere stroke of finance, the five millions and a half thus spent were a wiser investment than to have let them grow up thieves and thugs. In the last fifteen years of this tireless battle for the safety of the State the intervention of the Society for the Prevention of Cruelty to Children has been invoked for 138,891 little ones; it has thrown its protection around more than twenty-five thousand helpless children, and has convicted nearly sixteen thousand wretches of child-beating and abuse. Add to this the standing army of fifteen thousand dependent children in New York's asylums and institutions, and some idea is gained of the crop that is garnered day by day in the tenements, of the enormous force employed to check their inroads on our social life, and of the cause for apprehension that would exist did their efforts flag for ever so brief a time.

Nothing is now better understood than that the rescue of the children is the key to the problem of city poverty, as presented for our solution to-day; that character may be formed where to reform it would be a hopeless task.

The concurrent testimony of all who have to undertake it at a later stage: that the young are naturally neither vicious nor hardened, simply weak and undeveloped, except by the bad influences of the street, makes this duty all the more urgent as well as hopeful. Helping hands are held out on every side. To private charity the municipality leaves the entire care of its proletariat of tender years, lulling its conscience to sleep with liberal appropriations of money to foot the bills. Indeed, it is held by those whose opinions are entitled to weight that it is far too liberal a paymaster for its own best interests and those of its wards. It deals with the evil in the seed to a limited extent in gathering in the outcast babies from the streets. To the ripe fruit the gates of its prisons, its reformatories, and its workhouses are opened wide the year round. What the showing would be at this end of the line were it not for the barriers wise charity has thrown across the broad highway to ruin—is building day by day—may be measured by such results as those quoted above in the span of a single life.

1. What were the major factors contributing to the conditions described by Riis in "The Problem of the Children"?
2. How does Riis' description of the lives of the urban poor compare with the condition of the urban poor in many large U.S. cities today?
3. How have our attitudes toward immigration and immigrants changed since Riis' time?
4. Although not specifically states by Riis, it is possible that the 70,000 children for whom the Children's Aid Society "found homes in the West" were taken there on the so-called "orphan trains." It is estimated that, between 1854 and 1930, as many as 150,000 to 200,000 abandoned, orphaned, and neglected children were relocated to the West and Midwest via the orphan trains operated primarily by the Children's Aid Society. The trains went from town to town, where the children were cleaned up, off-loaded, and paraded before prospective parents. Unfortunately many of these parents were seeking cheap labor. Imagine you were one of the relocated children. What might be your response to the challenges and opportunities presented by the experience?

Primary Source Reading

In this 1917 article, Ella Flagg Young, the first female superintendent of a large city school system (Chicago) and the first woman president of the National Education Association, compares the U.S. Supreme Court decision in the Dred Scott case that said Blacks did not have the same rights as Whites, with the decision of the supreme court of Illinois in a case that involved teachers' rights versus the school board's right to deny employment to teachers who had joined a union.

Court Decisions versus Social Progress

Ella Flagg Young

In 1857 people living north of the "Mason and Dixon Line" were startled upon reading the opinion rendered by the Supreme Court of the United States in what is known as the "Dred Scott case." The opinion, concurred in by six associate justices, was rendered by the Chief Justice. The two remaining associate justices presented dissenting opinions. Discussions ran high on the streets, in the homes, in the daily papers, and in assemblies. In the discussions it seemed as if only two persons were involved in the case: the negro, Dred Scott, and the Chief Justice, Roger B. Taney. A most interesting phase of the Chief Justice's opinion was his review of public opinion in 1775 and 1788. It seemed a strong argument with the Chief Justice that it would be difficult in 1857 to realize the attitude of the public mind toward the negro when the Declaration of Independence and the Constitution were adopted. The attitude of the public toward slavery when the decision in the Dred Scott case was rendered had no weight apparently with

Source: Young, E. F. (1917). Court decisions versus social progress. *Proceedings of the National Education Association* (pp. 350–354). Washington, DC: NEA.

the Chief Justice. The leading line of his argument was that the civil rights of negroes were not mentioned in the Constitution. William H. Seward, the Secretary of State at the time when President Lincoln was assassinated, met that argument with his famous saying "There is a higher law of right and morality than that of the Constitution."

The decision of the Supreme Court settled, however, for the time being the question of the social welfare of a race; but it burned into the memories of thousands the quoted expression which was accepted as Chief Justice Taney's own attitude of mind: "They [the negroes] had no rights which the white man was bound to respect." You are all familiar with events which, beginning three years later, followed the decision: the Civil War, the Emancipation Proclamation, the Thirteenth Amendment abolishing slavery, the Fourteenth Amendment guaranteeing civil and political rights to all citizens, native-born and naturalized.

It was the irony of fate that Chief Justice Taney lived as chief justice to witness the promulgation of the Emancipation Proclamation, and also action by Congress, preliminary to the adoption of the Thirteenth Amendment. Here was a man with an intellectual grasp that enabled him to hold the highest judicial position under the Constitution until his death at the advanst age of eighty-seven years; and yet with his intellectuality, his training in the law, and his experience, he was unable to break away from the bondage of race antipathy and race superiority. No vision of the rights of another race beside the one to which he belonged had influenst his conception of the meaning of *humanity*.

Sixty years after the opinion in the Dred Scott case was rendered there was delivered an opinion on the rights of public-school teachers in the state of Illinois, by Chief Justice Cooke, of the Supreme Court of Illinois. Tho the language in the decision presented by Chief Justice Cooke is not identical with that in the Dred Scott case, yet there are resemblances that suggest the subject of this paper in relation to an important question in school administration—the reemployment of teachers.

Chief Justice Taney said, "The right of property in a slave is distinctly and expressly affirmed in the Constitution." Chief Justice Cooke says, "The Board has the absolute right to decline to reemploy any applicant *for any reason or for no reason at all*." If to dispense, *for no reason at all*, with the services of a teacher, thus casting that teacher, discredited and dishonored professionally, into the open market is not an exercise of property rights, then, I ask, what are property rights? Both chief justices saw organizations superior to the supreme courts; Chief Justice Taney held that "this Court has no jurisdiction to revise the judgment of a state court upon its own laws"; Chief Justice Cooke held that "questions of policy are solely for the determination of the Board, and when they have once been determined by it, the Courts will not enquire into their propriety." As Chief Justice Taney failed to recognize the force of the strong undercurrent of public opinion that was to change the legal status of a race, so Chief Justice Cooke failed, even by reference, to recognize the current that had caused the Board itself, in Chicago, in the latter part of the nineteenth century, to adopt a rule guaranteeing a statement of cause, thirty days' notice, and a trial, before a refusal to reelect was enforst, thus transferring teachers from the property class to that of human beings with legal rights.

In the Dred Scott decision, Chief Justice Taney wandered from the point at issue and took occasion to express personal opinions on other points. In the decision in Illinois, Chief Justice Cooke said, "This leaves, then, *as the sole question* to be determined, whether the Board of Education has the right, in the selection of teachers, to discriminate between those who are members of a federation or union and those who are not members of any such federation or union, and whether its action in *this regard* violates any constitutional or statutory provision." Here is stated definitely the question before the court. Chief Justice Cooke wandered from the point at issue, to present *obiter dicta* on other issues. I am not asking you to consider the question of membership of teachers in a federation or union; I am presenting for your consideration the remarkable personal opinions of Chief Justice Cooke and their out-of-date attitude toward teachers as an efficient force in human welfare and therefore in the social progress of this nation. If all boards of education should have, as he says the board in Illinois has, the absolute right to decline to reemploy any teacher for *any reason whatever* or *for no reason at all*, the question arises, In this land of increasing opportunities what kind of men and women will eventually be found choosing teaching as a life-work? The Chief Justice borders on the garrulous as he adds, "It is immaterial whether the reason for the refusal to employ him is because the applicant is married or unmarried, is of fair complexion or dark." The Chief Justice does not state which he, if a member of a board of education, would refuse to reemploy, the blonde benedicts or the brunette bachelors.

In recognizing the power placed in the hands of the board as discretionary, common sense should be used by the court in its interpretation of the term discretionary. The restriction to the exercise of discretion and judgment, as set by the plain citizen and the great American and English dictionaries, should be recognized.

A lawyer and statesman, John C. Calhoun, said, "There is no power of government without restrictions; not even the so-called discretionary power of Congress." Another lawyer and statesman, Alexander Hamilton, in writing on taxation said, "The genius of liberty re-reprobates everything arbitrary or discretionary in taxation." What would he have said about discretion in reemploying teachers?

Two associate justices dissented from Chief Justice Taney's opinion, and two in the Illinois court from Chief Justice Cooke's opinion; they "did not concur in all the *reasoning* of the opinion, but they concurred in the *conclusion!*" They dissented from the *obiter dicta*. Here is their language:

> The board of education is charged with the maintenance of the public schools and the employment of teachers therein. It may enact all reasonable rules for the promotion of the effi-

ciency of the schools under its control. This power does not, however, include the power to adopt any kind of an arbitrary rule for the employment of teachers it may choose to adopt, for a rule can easily be imagined the adoption of which would be unreasonable, contrary to public policy, and on the face of it not calculated to promote the best interests and welfare of the schools. In our opinion courts would have the power, in the interests of the public good, to prohibit the enforcement of such an arbitrary rule.

The decision of the Supreme Court of the United States affected a race many of whose people nurst and cared for the children of the dominant race. The decision of the Supreme Court of Illinois affected the men and women who are charged with the education of those future citizens who are receiving their training in the public schools, elementary and high. If the law as interpreted by the Illinois court were to apply to all public schools in the United States, there would have been at the close of this school year as many men and women teachers liable to ejection from their positions in the public schools, *for no reason at all*, as there were soldiers who died in the Union and Confederate forces in the Civil War—about 600,000.

As in the days of slavery a negro might be separated from family and home for no reason due him or her, so under the decision rendered by Chief Justice Cooke, men and women public-school teachers might be dropt from their positions all unexpectedly, and for no reason due to them or for no reason at all. The records show that it has been done in cities in Illinois having 100,000 or more inhabitants.

Turning to social progress in this country let me ask, What has been the tendency, the direction of legislation on questions involving human welfare? It has been to give a sense of freedom from the terrors that accompany the fear of unseen malignity. England is a more conservative country than the United States. I will quote from the official report of a debate lasting three days in the House of Lords in July, 1916.

Lord Sheffield: In local activity another element to which I look for securing the real growth of our public education is a great respect for the freedom and the individuality of the teachers. If you are to get the best out of your teachers, you must encourage them to think for themselves, and to have freedom in their methods, and *for that* you must secure that those who have the appointment and promotion of teachers shall be so constituted that they have regard only to the character and efficiency of teachers *as* teachers in appointing and promoting them. I wish for no subsidiary aims of another character.

The Marquis of Crewe: If the training of the nation is to be advanst, there must be greater *honor* for the teaching profession in the different grades. . . . Nor do I forget the necessity of maintaining and safeguarding the independence of the teacher in leading the life and expressing the opinions which he or she is entitled to hold.

Compare these opinions with that exprest by the Chief Justice of the Supreme Court of Illinois.

I infer that Chief Justice Cooke and the associate justices do not indorse this statement in the Ritchie case, Supreme Court of Illinois, 1909: "What we know as men we cannot profess to be ignorant of as judges." I infer this because of two events that occurred on two consecutive days in Springfield, Ill.: On April 19, 1917, Chief Justice Cooke presented the decision containing his *obiter dictum* that the board has the absolute right to decline to reemploy an applicant, *for no reason at all;* on April 20, 1917, Governor Lowden of Illinois signed a bill that had been adopted on the third reading in the legislature of Illinois and contained this amendment:

No teacher or principal who has been or shall be appointed by said Board of Education shall (after serving a probationary period of three years) be removed except for cause, and then, only by a majority of all members of the Board, upon written charges presented by the superintendent of schools, to be heard by the Board or a duly authorized committee of the same, after 30 days' notice, with copy of the charges, is served upon

the person against whom they are preferred, who shall have the privilege of being present with counsel, offering evidence and making defense thereto.

It may be objected that the Court does not, as did the Board, possess discretionary power; that it must interpret the law as it is written, not in combination with present-day understanding of human welfare. Justice Brewer, of the Supreme Court of the United States, stated in the *Muller v. Oregon* case, 1907, that "the Court took judicial cognizance of all matters of general knowledge"; he admitted the empirical evidence presented by Mr. Louis D. Brandeis, then attorney, now associate justice of the Supreme Court of the United States, whose argument bound together the welfare of the workers and the welfare of the nation. The Illinois chief justice would have done well to recognize conditions that make for the welfare and efficiency of teachers and consequently of the state, instead of injecting into his decision his *obiter dicta* that would terrify and unnerve teachers.

Speaking about the decision in the Dred Scott case, Abraham Lincoln made many telling points, a few of which I quote:

Judicial decisions are of greater or less authority as precedents according to circumstances. . . . If this important decision had been made by the unanimous consent of the judges [you may recall that in Illinois two did not concur in all the reasoning] and *without any apparent partisan bias* . . . it might be factious not to acquiesce in it as a precedent. But when, as is true, we find it wanting in these claims to public confidence, it is not factious, it is not even disrespectful, to treat it as not having yet quite establisht a settled doctrine for the country, or if, wanting in some of these, it had been before the Court more than once, and had there been affirmed and reaffirmed thru a course of years, it then might be, perhaps would be, factious, nay even revolutionary, not to acquiesce in it as a precedent.

Following Abraham Lincoln's line of reasoning, I conclude that it is not factious, it is not even disrespectful to treat the decision and the *obiter dicta* of Chief Justice Cooke of Illinois as not having quite yet established a settled doctrine of school administration in democratic America.

Questions for Discussion

1. Explain what Dr. Young meant by the title, "Court Decisions Versus Social Progress."
2. Give examples of other court decisions that presented arguments similar to the Dred Scott case in denying individual rights.
3. How does the attitude of boards of education toward union membership by teachers in 1917 compare to current feelings of boards, politicians, and the general public toward the NEA or NFT?
4. The day of the decision by the Illinois Supreme Court which Dr. Young is criticizing in this article, a bill adopted by the Illinois legislature was signed by the governor that, in effect, nullified the court decision. Give other examples in which the U.S. Congress or a state legislature has taken similar action.

CHAPTER 8

Depression, War, and National Defense

The gains of education are never really lost. Books may be burned and cities sacked, but truth, like the yearning for freedom, lives in the hearts of humble men.

—*Franklin D. Roosevelt*
Speech to the Democratic National
Convention, June 27, 1936

Following a sharp economic slump at the end of World War I, overall, the decade after the war was one of prosperity. Mass production of new products such as the washing machine, refrigerator, and vacuum cleaner not only made them more affordable, but contributed to corporate profits and business expansion. Despite falling prices in the agriculture sector and economic warnings that stock values were grossly inflated and that factories were overproducing, consumer optimism led more and more people to invest their life savings or borrowed money in the stock market. Then, in mid-October of 1929 stock prices began to decline and some investors began to sell their stocks. The few became the many, and the many led to panic. In less than 2 weeks more than 28 million shares had been sold. The massive selling led the market to crash on Tuesday, October 29.

The Depression that followed in the wake of the stock market crash had a serious impact on schools. Many schools were closed, programs eliminated, teacher salaries cut, and positions eliminated. Beginning in 1933, the federal government became actively involved in education through New Deal programs that fundamentally changed the relationship between the federal government and the schools, one that would become more involved and complex after the Depression was over.

The experience of the Depression elicited a new interest in social change and social reform. One group of social reformers, the so-called Frontier Thinkers, advocated that the schools become more involved in the social issues of the time. At the other end of the spectrum were essentialists who argued that progressivism had gone too far by attending to the interests of the young child and ignoring basic skills.

As America sought to reverse the economic crisis that gripped the nation in the 1930s, Europe faced not only its own depression but also the rise of dictatorships in Italy, Spain, and Germany. America's attempt to stay neutral ended with the Japanese attack on Pearl Harbor in December of 1941. World War II had a heavy impact on education. Higher education in particular played an important role in preparing personnel for military service as well as for the war industries and essential civilian activities.

After the war, public attention that had been focused on the Depression and World War II was refocused on the schools. Schools became the targets of conservative anticommunist witch hunts while also being criticized for their lack of rigor and inattention to academics. The response to this criticism, as well as to the technological competition that followed the Russian launching of the spaceship Sputnik in 1957, was a wave of reform supported in part by the National Defense Education Act (NDEA). The NDEA marked not only a significant increase in federal funds to education but also a new purpose for education. During the Cold War, for perhaps the first time in American history, the role of the schools was seen as not merely to support the war effort, but to be an important weapon in it.

The quarter century between the crash of the stock market in 1929 and the *Brown* decision ending legal segregation in the schools saw a major shift in the role of the federal government in education and the role of the schools in securing and maintaining the nation's economic and military preeminence. This chapter provides an overview of the events contributing to the transformations of these roles.

The Depression Begins

When the stock market crashed in October of 1929 investors lost not only their own life savings, but also the money they had borrowed from the banks. When they could not repay the banks, the banks could not return money to the depositors who rushed to the banks to withdraw "hard cash." Similar to the rush to sell off stocks, the rush to the banks caused many banks to crash or close, over 9,000 by 1933, causing millions of people to lose their life savings.

With the crash of the market and the banks came a crash in consumer confidence. Those with money were reluctant to spend it. Production slowed and, in some areas, ground to a halt. The gross national product dropped by almost half between 1929 and 1933. Reduced production led to more layoffs and more unemployment, leading to more bankruptcies and more people being unable to pay their bills. Before it was over, more than 55,000 businesses had failed and 13 million people, 25% of the civilian labor force, were unemployed. Many others were working at much lower wages or reduced hours. Many of the unemployed or underemployed became homeless. Unemployment was particularly high among minorities and young people. As many as 6 million young people were out of school and unemployed between 1933 and 1935. Many had no occupational training or experience. In a labor market overrun with experienced workers, they had few opportunities for employment (National Policies Commission, 1941).

The initial response of the federal government to the worsening economic condition and the massive unemployment, homelessness, and literal hunger was to do nothing to provide aid to individuals:

> People were going hungry, even starving, while farmers were driving sheep off cliffs because they could not afford to ship them to market; leather factories were boarded up while Baltimore teachers collected used shoes so that children could come to school; people languished in hovels and tin shacks while construction workers stood in soup lines. In the midst of all this, governmental leaders before the New Deal seemed incapable of acting to relieve the most elemental needs of the people. The governor of West Virginia told hungry miners that the Constitution forbade him to give them food. (Tyack, Lowe, & Hansot, 1984, p. 14)

At the beginning of the Depression, the Republican president, Herbert Hoover, who believed in minimal government, did not believe the federal government should be involved in providing direct aid to individuals. Hoover looked to private charities and state and local agencies to address the needs of the homeless and unemployed. Hoover directed the resources of the federal government toward underwriting banks and loans to businesses and industries, believing that if they became healthy, they would rehire employees and restart the economy. However, when this did not work and economic conditions worsened, the voters replaced him with a Democrat, Franklin Delano Roosevelt. Roosevelt promised a New Deal for the American people. Over the remainder of the decade Roosevelt initiated a series of work relief and public works programs that fundamentally changed the relationship between the federal government and the American people.

Impact of the Depression on Education

For the first 2 years the schools escaped the brunt of the Depression. In fact, from 1929 until 1931 enrollments and staff grew and salaries and total expenditures remained somewhat stable. Most superintendents viewed the current economic condition as a temporary storm they could weather by "creative retrenchment" and greater "compactness and efficiency" (Tyack et al., 1984). They still had faith in scientific management and the cult of efficiency. However, as school districts began to feel the impact of the Depression and educators daily saw its impact in the lives of their children, their faith failed and they, like most other Americans, began to blame greedy business leaders for the plight of the nation.

By 1932 schools were in serious financial trouble. The schools competed with other public institutions for limited tax revenues. And, the unemployed millions paid no taxes. Businesses and homeowners were often seriously in arrears in paying the property taxes on which the schools depended. By the end of the school year 1933–34, although total enrollments had increased by 750,000 since 1930, total revenues were down by almost $278 million (National Center for Education Statistics [NCES], 1993). The decline in revenues led many states, especially those in the hard-pressed South and Southwest, to close schools or shorten the school year. For example, in Alabama in 1933, 85% of the public schools were closed and 7,000 teachers were out of work (Moreo, 1996). By the first quarter of 1934 an estimated 20,000 schools nationwide had closed, affecting over 1 million pupils. Ten states were estimated to have schools with school terms of less than 3 months and 22 with terms of less than 6 months (National Education Association [NEA], 1933b).

One of the initial retrenchment strategies of the schools was to increase class size, especially at the secondary level. In many districts adult education, summer schools, kindergarten, and everything but the most basic subjects were eliminated. Similarly, many but the most necessary positions were eliminated. School nurses, supervisory specialists, and elementary principals were among the first to go. Schools for the handicapped were also eliminated or radically curtailed (Carlson, 1933). The schools that did stay open were usually short on equipment and supplies. Old and damaged textbooks were the norm. As the Depression deepened, students were increasingly asked to bring their own supplies, or in extreme cases, to pay tuition. In one such community the NEA (1933b) reported that 200 parents were unable to pay the $3 per month tuition for grade school students or $5.50 for high school students. Some students had to stop attending school because they could not afford the materials. Many others were not able to attend because they did not have the clothes or shoes in which to attend. Testimony before the U.S. Senate estimated that 3.5 million young people were unable to attend high school because of poverty (Moreo, 1996).

The Depression also had a serious impact on teachers. They were public employees, mostly unorganized, and worse, in terms of being able to exercise any political pressure, 80% were female. Female teachers were particularly vulnerable to arbitrary dismissal on the basis of age, health, marriage, weight, or some minor infraction of a bureaucratic rule (Moreo, 1996). Being married put females at particular risk. Removing more senior married teachers for new, unmarried teachers was an

For Your Reflection and Analysis

To what extent are female teachers today more vulnerable to layoffs in times of financial cutbacks?

economic measure as well as an attempt to limit the incomes of families in which both the husband and wife were public employees, as was often the case. Eighteen states considered bills to bar married women from teaching, many districts adopted policies of not hiring married women, and "Married Teachers Not Wanted" signs were common (Moreo, 1996).

Throughout the country, most teachers who retained their positions saw their salaries cut. Between 1930 and June 1933 the average salary reduction in the cities was 13.7%. Half the rural teachers were being paid less than $750 per year, and one in five was receiving less than $450 per year (NEA, 1933b). In many districts teachers received no salary for months or were paid in script (certificates of indebtedness or tax anticipation warrants) with the school board promising to pay them when revenues were collected. These warrants sometimes were accepted by merchants, but often were not. Banks might cash the warrants but often charged a fee or discounted the warrant. In other areas teachers worked for room and board, reverting back to the colonial practice of "boarding 'round." In some rural areas teachers were reported to live in the schoolhouse and cook gift vegetables on the wood-burning stove (Graves, 2002; Moreo, 1996).

The response of teachers and other educators to their declining economic conditions and the encroachment on their professionalism was mixed. Some, like the social reconstructionists discussed later in this chapter, called for social engineering through education. Others called for school personnel to become more politically active and to organize to fight tax cuts and tax policies that unduly favored the business community. Membership in the NEA, AFT, and state and local associations grew. Educators entered the once distained arena of politics as candidates and lobbyists. Most of their efforts were directed at the state level. By and large their campaigns for greater state aid were successful: The state share of school budgets almost doubled during the 1930s, from 16.9% in 1929–30 to 30.3% in 1939–40. Teachers also sought greater state regulation of certification and curriculum oversight, and greater protection through teacher tenure (Tyack et al., 1984).

 For Your Reflection and Analysis

What were the greatest challenges that teachers faced during the Great Depression?

Table 8.1 shows the changes in school terms, staff, and expenditures for rural and city schools, and the percentage of change in expenditures by state universities between 1930 and 1934, the time when a number of the New Deal programs described in the following pages began to reach education. Overall, as the data indicate, rural schools in the South, Appalachia, and the Dust Bowl were particularly hard hit. Higher education expenditures were also heavily affected by the Depression. Nationwide, universities decreased their spending by almost 18%; in nine states the decrease was 30% or more, and one, Mississippi, had a staggering 81% decrease.

The financial plight of the schools was beyond the ability of most states to solve. In time some relief did come from the federal government—not as direct federal aid, but through the series of New Deal programs described in the next section.

TABLE 8.1 Changes in School Conditions by State, 1930–1934

States	Rural schools: Percentage of change, 1930–1934			City schools: Percentage of change, 1931–1934			Higher education: Percentage of change, 1930–1934 in expenditures by state universities
	Term	Staff	Total expenditures	Staff	Current expenditures	Capital outlay	
1	2	3	4	5	6	7	8
Continental United States	−4	−3	−23	−4.6	−19.5	−80.1	−17.7
Alabama	−36.0	+6	−47	−6.5	−32.4	−93.9	−27
Arizona	0.0	−15	−31	−16.3	−42.8	−62.6	—
Arkansas	−2.7	−14	−39	−15.6	−41.8	−20.5	—
California	−0.6	−1	−21	−4.6	−15.1	−80.6	−28
Colorado	−4.0	−4	−27	−11.6	−38.2	−97.8	−36
Connecticut	+0.5	−2	+3	−3.5	−19.5	—	−6
Delaware	0.0	+6	+15	—	—	—	—
Florida	−18.0	+3	−27	−1.3	−35.9	−84.3	−1
Georgia	−20.0	0	−23	−0.7	−18.4	...	+23
Idaho	−1.0	−10	−30	−6.5	−33.7	−66.1	−7
Illinois	−6.0	−2	−28	−7.9	−32.2	−68.0	−21
Indiana	−1.0	+1	−26	−8.7	−31.1	−79.8	−2
Iowa	+0.5	−4	−17	−7.4	−29.0	−54.1	—
Kansas	−0.6	−4	−29	−5.6	−28.8	−84.0	−39
Kentucky	−5.0	+6	−30	−3.6	−16.0	−50.2	−26
Louisiana	−24.0	+3	−18	+0.6	—	—	+59
Maine	−2.0	−2	−19	−1.8	−15.2	—	−7
Maryland	0.0	−1	−19	—	—	—	−8
Massachusetts	−0.6	−2	−11	−2.7	−4.9	−98.8	—
Michigan	−19.0	−6	−37	−13.0	−37.9	−91.1	+1
Minnesota	0.0	−1	−23	−3.1	−18.1	−94.3	−9
Mississippi	−4.0	−4	−42	−5.7	−23.5	—	−81
Missouri	−4.0	−1	−39	+0.9	−25.6	−93.2	−22

(continued)

TABLE 8.1 Changes in School Conditions by State, 1930–1934 (Continued)

States	Rural schools: Percentage of change, 1930–1934			City schools: Percentage of change, 1931–1934			Higher education: Percentage of change, 1930–1934 in expenditures by state universities
	Term	Staff	Total expenditures	Staff	Current expenditures	Capital outlay	
1	*2*	*3*	*4*	*5*	*6*	*7*	*8*
Montana	−2.0	−7	−35	−7.8	−9.7	−85.6	−23
Nebraska	0.0	−2	−35	−6.5	−14.0	−97.2	−31
Nevada	−5.0	+6	−3	—	—	—	−18
New Hampshire	0.0	−3	−22	−3.2	−11.9	+9.7	−11
New Jersey	−0.5	+2	−18	−0.8	−24.4	−54.7	—
New Mexico	−5.0	−3	−17	−6.3	−35.4	—	−18
New York	0.0	+2	−18	−2.3	−13.1	−97.0	—
North Carolina	+5.0	−3	−47	−2.2	−31.4	—	−1
North Dakota	−5.0	−7	−39	−7.7	−24.4	−86.3	—
Ohio	−9.0	−5	−31	−11.9	−20.1	−45.4	−11
Oklahoma	−10.0	−5	−26	−8.5	−24.9	−76.6	−21
Oregon	−4.0	−1	−14	−14.7	−36.1	−51.6	−56
Pennsylvania	0.0	0	−13	−2.0	−14.8	−71.2	−30
Rhode Island	0.0	+2	+3	+1.3	−12.7	−88.9	−12
South Carolina	−4.0	−9	−32	−5.2	−39.4	—	−43
South Dakota	−2.0	−21	−20	−10.1	−25.2	−89.1	−24
Tennessee	−2.0	+1	−23	−3.4	−17.0	+1.9	−40
Texas	+2.0	0	−15	−10.5	−28.4	−88.4	—
Utah	0.0	−6	−38	−2.4	−23.5	−99.6	−23
Vermont	+0.6	−5	−18	−7.1	−18.8	—	—
Virginia	−5.0	−3	−22	+2.2	−21.9	−90.6	+21
Washington	+3.0	−6	−29	−5.8	−29.5	+47.6	−42
West Virginia	−26.0	−3	−44	−13.3	—	—	—
Wisconsin	−0.6	−1	−27	−1.3	−15.6	−74.5	—
Wyoming	−4.0	−8	−25	−13.2	−22.2	−98.2	−17

Source: National Education Association. (1933). *Current conditions in our nation's schools.* Washington, DC: Author.

New Deal Education Programs

Until the Great Depression the relationship of the federal government to education was clear: The provision of education was viewed as the responsibility of the states and local school districts. However, beginning with the creation of the Civilian Conservation Corps (CCC), the Public Works Administration (PWA), and later the National Youth Administration (NYA) of the Works Progress Administration (WPA) in 1933, this established relationship changed. The New Deal reformers were concerned that the schools did not serve the poor well. So, although the New Deal was not directed at education, each of these New Deal programs either had an educational component or worked with the schools to accomplish its goals. Like other New Deal programs, they were not directed at the general school population but were designed for the poor and staffed mainly by people on relief. Not designed by education experts, but based on the belief that all kinds of people can teach and that learning can take place in all kinds of locations, these New Deal ventures constituted a new vision of public education (Tyack et al., 1984).

Civilian Conservation Corp

The CCC was one of the federal emergency agencies created under President Roosevelt's New Deal to provide "work relief" for the unemployed. The CCC provided temporary work for over 2 million people 18 to 25 years of age on various conservation projects, including reforestation, wildlife preservation, flood control, and forest fire prevention. Most of these young people were from rural backgrounds and had not finished high school.

Not long after it began, the CCC introduced an educational component. The army, which administered the CCC camps, also administered the education program. Instruction was provided by Forest Service and army officers, local public school teachers, WPA and NYA employees, or other qualified persons, many of whom were volunteers. Attendance in the classes was voluntary. About one third of the courses were vocational, one third were academic, one fifth were remedial, and the remainder were avocational. Many of the courses were offered in conjunction with the work of the camps and, being administered by the army, stressed discipline along with content (Tyack et al., 1984).

National Youth Administration

The NYA administered two programs: (1) a work relief and employment program for needy out-of-school youth aged 16 to 25 and (2) a program that provided part-time employment to needy high school and college students to help them continue their education. Money was allocated to high schools based on the number of children from poor families in attendance. Between 6 and 10% of secondary students were in the NYA during its 9 years of operation. They worked in school offices, cafeterias, shops, laboratories, and as groundskeepers.

Under the terms of the NYA college student employment program, the college selected the students to participate and supervised the work to be done. Approximately

98% of the eligible institutions, including junior colleges and normal schools, participated in the program, as did 12% of all college students. Students worked on research projects, in libraries, in clerical positions, and in community service projects. Sixty percent of the participating students were male, and 6% were Black or from other minority groups (Lindley & Lindley, 1938). A special affirmative action fund for promising Black graduate students enabled about 200 Blacks to receive their Ph.D.s during the 1930s compared to 41 in the period from 1900 to 1930 (Tyack et al., 1984).

College enrollment, which had dropped in the first years of the Depression, would have dropped further without the NYA support of undergraduate and graduate students. At its peak in 1939–40, approximately 750,000 students in 1,750 colleges and 28,000 secondary schools participated in NYA programs.

The second major NYA work relief program, one for out-of-school youth, pioneered a new concept in education—education through work. That is, 2.7 million youth working in various community projects and for various state and local agencies and institutions, as well as in its cooperative residential centers, were involved in learning by doing. A boy on a construction project might have a related training class in blueprint reading, and a youth on an agricultural project might have a class on the chemistry of soils (Tyack et al., 1984).

Public Works Administration

The Public Works Administration was critically important to schools, colleges, and universities faced with not only growing enrollments but also unsafe and dilapidated buildings. Between 1934 and 1939, $1.7 billion in federal funds (with $300 million state and local matching funds) provided for the building of 102 public libraries and 59,614 classrooms (Moreo, 1996), including almost 13,000 schools.

Works Projects Administration

Whereas the PWA was a lifesaver to schools in providing facilities, the Works Projects Administration, the largest of the New Deal programs directed specifically at putting men and women back to work, employed 100,000 teachers to teach adult education and in the 1,500 WPA-operated preschools across the country. The preschools taught some 150,000 children. The WPA also operated summer schools for students who had failed subjects during the regular school year, as well as programs that provided special enrichment activities, including field trips.

The WPA adult education program served as many as 4 million adults primarily in their own communities, in classes taught by unemployed people with similar backgrounds. Perhaps its most important program was the adult literacy program. Between 1933 and 1938, 1.5 million adults were taught to read, about one third of them Black. Other adult education programs ran the gamut from

> cooking and nutrition to family budgeting, personal hygiene, care of the sick, and other family welfare concerns. . . . All the more remarkable was the fact that despite reductions in the number of classes and teachers, enrollments continued to climb. In

An 82-year-old former slave reading to her class in a WPA education program in Alabama.

addition, as waves of immigrants fleeing Nazi Germany arrived, they immediately sought out classes in English and citizenship training. (Moreo, 1996, p. 126)

The WPA also employed relief workers to perform a variety of noninstructional work in the schools. WPA workers repaired and painted schools; constructed or repaired school furniture, fixtures, and equipment; worked in the cafeteria; and performed a variety of other tasks.

Another important noninstructional program of the WPA was the WPA nutrition project, which used surplus food to provide free hot lunches to needy children, primarily in the cities. For example, in New York City almost 120,000 lunches were served per day (Moreo, 1996).

 For Your Reflection and Analysis

How appropriate was it for the federal government to bypass state and local school systems in delivering the educational components of the New Deal programs?

General Federal Aid Debate

The general plight of the schools, as well as the major inequalities that existed among the states, led the NEA and other educational groups to conclude that federal aid was necessary. The education establishment also resented the fact that educators were not trusted to operate the educational component of the various New Deal programs and that educational funds were given to the CCC, NYA, and the WPA and bypassed established school systems. What educators wanted was general federal aid with no strings attached. However, even though they were successful in getting sponsors for several general federal aid bills, they were never able to secure passage, largely because of the opposition of President Roosevelt. Roosevelt's lack of support stemmed less from concern about the potential impact of general federal aid on the federal budget, and more from a genuine belief that, compared to other sectors, the schools were in pretty good shape. Roosevelt preferred to target funds to the unemployed and to those who would benefit the most from the new educational services (Tyack et al., 1984).

Roosevelt was not alone in his rejection of general federal aid. Many educators were opposed to federal aid, primarily because of fear of federal control. The fear of federal control was so great that some districts rejected all federal aid. Many feared that federal aid would lead to a national system of education and would undermine local control. Others were concerned that aid would (or would not) go to private, parochial schools. Perhaps the strongest opposition to general federal aid to education came from the southern governors, who feared that with federal aid would come a demand for uniformity that would threaten racial segregation. Yet, southern schools, and particularly the rural schools attended by Black children already disadvantaged in terms of educational expenditures, were hit particularly hard by the Depression-driven cuts in education expenditures. A study during the middle of the Depression found that in the southern states Blacks constituted 25% of the student population but received only 12% of total revenues. Yet, despite these inequities, the number of Blacks attending high school doubled during the 1930s, and the number of graduates tripled (Tyack et al., 1984).

For Your Reflection and Analysis

To what extent are the Depression-era arguments for or against federal aid to education relevant today?

The plight of southern Blacks was exceeded only by that of Native Americans. Even before the Depression the 1929 Meriam Report documented the intolerable conditions on the reservations. Conditions were made only worse by the failing economic conditions associated with the Depression. The response of the Roosevelt administration became known as the Indian New Deal.

The Indian New Deal

As described in previous chapters, historically the education of Native Americans had been viewed as a means of assimilation. By the end of World War I this policy had brought Native Americans to the edge of disaster: "They were suffering from short life expectancy, disease, malnutrition, a diminishing land base, and a stagnant, unrealistic school system" (American Indian Education Foundation [AIEF], 2003, p. 2). The granting of citizenship in 1924 did not bring any improvements. In response to a number of public reports by reformers determined to improve the plight of the Native Americans, the Bureau of Indian Affairs (BIA) commissioned the Brookings Institute for an independent study of the condition of Native Americans. The resultant study, the Meriam Report, noted that much of the poverty of Native Americans was a result of the loss of their land. It also criticized the BIA educational program, exposing the inadequate industrial training, overcrowded dormitories, inadequate diet, and physical punishment in the boarding schools. The report discouraged the use of boarding schools and recommended that they be used only for older children and that younger children be educated in community day schools (Kidwell & Swift, 1976).

Soon after Roosevelt took office, he appointed John Collier, a progressive activist, as Commissioner of Indian Affairs. Several New Deal measures were subsequently enacted and became known as the Indian New Deal. The Indian New Deal was an attempt to remedy the conditions described by the Meriam Report. More important, it signaled a reversal of the policy of assimilation. Collier was convinced that Indian policy should focus on the renewal of Indian sovereignty, establish economic independence, and recognize and value Indian culture and language. Consistent with these beliefs Collier felt the curriculum in the schools should include Indian culture and heritage. And, in an effort to stem the deterioration of tribal languages, as well as to facilitate English language acquisition, Collier supported bilingual education.

Some of Collier's earliest efforts were directed at stopping the sale of tribal Indian land and provided for the organization of tribal councils as legal bodies. Collier believed self-governance was central to both the economic and political recovery of Indian peoples and building a trusting relationship. Many of Collier's ideas were included in the Indian Reorganization Act of 1934. That same year the Johnson-O'Malley (JOM) Act was passed. The JOM provided supplemental funds to public schools to provide for the special needs of Native American students, including transportation, school lunches, or expenses such as those associated with graduation (Kidwell & Swift, 1976).

Overall, however, Indian education policy was not determined by legislation but by the Bureau of Indian Affairs (BIA) and its director. Collier's director of the Education Division of the BIA was a former president of the Progressive Education Association, Willard Beatty. Consistent with progressivist principles, Beatty promoted a child-centered curriculum that was more relevant to the culture and needs of the Indian student and stressed the importance of the relationship between the school and the community it served. Both Collier and Beatty sought to phase out the boarding schools and to replace them with public and day schools. During the 1930s the number of day schools almost doubled and enrollment tripled.

Native American education was also the beneficiary of many of the New Deal work relief programs. Significant funds were allocated through the PWA for the building of hospitals, water and sewer treatment plants, irrigation and drainage projects, and much-needed schools. A separate Indian CCC known as the Indian Emergency Conservation Work (IECW) program was geared to the unique needs of Indians and provided a tremendous opportunity for vocational training. During the 9-year life of the program (April 1933 to July 1942) some 85,000 Indians served in the IECW (Szasz, 1999).

Many of the gains made during the New Deal were lost during World War II and after. During the war funds to the reservations were decreased and renewed emphasis was given to assimilation, including the continued operation of the off-reservation boarding schools.

Efforts to Refocus the Schools and the Curriculum

Although the Depression clearly had a major impact on the schools, the governance of the schools remained the same; what went on behind the schoolhouse door changed little during the Depression. In spite of all the talk about, and attempts to introduce, progressive educational practices, teacher-center instruction continued to dominate in schools in the 1930s (Cuban, 1984).

Moreover, the Depression and the New Deal responses also did little to change the inequalities of educational opportunity that had characterized the educational experience of the poor and minorities throughout American history. For example, in 1930 the national average expenditure per child was $87, per southern White child $44, and per southern Black child $12 (Moreo, 1996). Although the states assumed a larger share of public school expenditures, and although state-supported programs sought to bring greater equalization, the property wealth of the local school district remained the major determinant of per pupil expenditures. The low-property-wealth rural and inner-city schools contained the majority of the poor and minorities. In fact, the number of urban poor grew as Dust Bowl migrants and rural Mexican Americans and Blacks, displaced from the farms, moved to the cities.

Disgust and disagreement with the status quo led some educators to attempt to change the direction of the educational enterprise. One such group, the social reconstructionists, wanted to see the schools move in a completely new direction and take the lead in creating a new social order. Another, the essentialists, wanted the schools to return to the traditional, basic education model.

Social Reconstructionism

The experience of the Depression had a significant impact on many progressive educators, who came to believe that the schools had a responsibility to redress social injustices and bring about social change. At the 1932 convention of the Progressive Education Association, in an address that serves as a Primary Source Reading for this chapter, "Dare the Schools Build a New Social Order?" George C. Counts, a professor at Columbia University, challenged the child-centered doctrine and called on educators to focus less on the child and more on the social issues of the time, to "face squarely and courageously every social issue, come to grips with life in all its stark reality . . . develop a realistic and comprehensive theory of welfare, fashion a compelling and challenging vision of human destiny" (p. 7). In effect, Counts asked the schools to take the lead in planning for the reconstruction of society and the building of a new social order. The social reconstructionists, as these like-minded educators were called, were convinced that much of the economic ills of the country were a result of an outmoded economic model that stressed unbridled competition and individualism. What modern technological society called for, according to Counts, was a planned society and an economic model built not on individualism, but on collectivism.

Counts was joined in his deep concern about socioeconomic conditions in America, his attack on the class bias that permeated the schools, and his belief that educators should do something to address them by liberal progressive educators such as William

For Your Reflection and Analysis

How do the Native American core values of belonging, mastery, independence, and generosity mentioned in chapter 2 reinforce Counts' economic model built on cooperation?

H. Kilpatrick and Harold Rugg. In 1935 these individuals joined with other social reformers to form the John Dewey Society for the Study of Education and Culture and began publishing a journal, *The Social Frontier,* which became the focus of educational extremism during the 1930s. The position of the group of the most radical reconstructionists, the so-called Frontier Thinkers, was sharply criticized by many conservative progressives and was responsible for a deepening schism within the Progressive Education Association and even among the social reconstruction membership itself. In 1937 Counts left the editorship of *The Social Frontier* and began to speak out openly against communism.

Although the social reconstructionism movement never gained much of a foothold among the rank and file of American educators, and *The Social Frontier* never had a circulation above 6,000 (Ravitch, 1983), it served to associate progressive education with "an economic radicalism that smacked of socialism and communism" and ultimately contributed to progressivism's growing unpopularity in the postwar years (Spring, 1989). However, as discussed in chapter 1, its concern with social change presaged the postmodern and critical theory movements that focused on transformative change in society and education.

The Eight-Year Study

While progressive education was under attack by the social reconstructionists, it was simultaneously being vindicated by a long-term study conducted by the PEA under the leadership of Ralph Tyler. The Eight-Year Study (1932–1940) involved 30 high schools willing to experiment with their curricula in order to discover the effectiveness of progressive educational approaches in preparing students for college. Over 250 colleges agreed to waive their admission requirements in regard to completion of a traditional curriculum for the graduates of these schools. The revised curriculum delivered the content from the disciplines in an integrated approach organized around themes rather than as discrete subjects. The study followed 1,475 students in matched pairs from high school to college. The results, published in 1942, showed that students from experimental high schools not only achieved as well as students from traditional high schools, but also were more involved and successful in artistic and cultural activities.

Although the Eight-Year Study and its findings did not have an immediate impact, its results served as the basis for Ralph Tyler, the project director, to develop a theory of curriculum development, the Tyler Rationale, which did influence curriculum development for decades. Tyler saw curriculum development as a rational process that involved the development of objectives and learning activities that facilitated the attainment of the objectives, all integrated from grade to grade and activity to activity (Horn, 2002). The results of the study also provided support for the integrated curriculum, a concept that found renewed favor half a century later.

William C. Bagley and the Essentialists

The Eight-Year Study and the larger cause of progressive education did not go unchallenged. Some of its harshest criticisms came from a group headed by William Bagley, a colleague of Counts' at Teachers College. Taking their name from Bagley's 1938 publication "An Essentialist Platform for Advancement of American Education," the essentialists were critical of progressive education's lack of emphasis on fundamentals. They believed that progressivism had gone too far in attending to the interests of children and ignoring the basic skills. Bagley compared American education with the education systems of other countries such as Germany and judged it to be weak, lacking in rigor, full of "frills," and inadequate in preparing youth for productive participation in society. Bagley advocated an organized, sequential curriculum and an instructional process that, although not ignoring the interest of the child, was teacher initiated and emphasized the transmission of those enduring skills, arts, and sciences that are necessary for the continuation of civilization.

 For Your Reflection and Analysis

Would Bagley be supportive of the seven cardinal principles of secondary education described in chapter 6? Why or why not?

The essentialists also criticized progressive education for ignoring discipline and argued that greater discipline was required in the classroom to prepare students for their participation in the workforce as well as their orderly participation in a democratic society. Bagley proposed in *Classroom Management*, his widely used book on teacher training, a very rigid and structured classroom environment in which students walked in lockstep to class, placed their desks in a prescribed order, and gave immediate response to comments.

The essentialists were also critical of the social reconstructionists. Bagley argued that instead of attempting to reconstruct society and use the schools as agents of social engineering, educators would serve society better by preparing "literate citizens knowledgeable in fundamental skills and knowledge that was of unquestioned value and permanence and that provides the basis for intelligent understanding and for the collective thought and judgment that are the essence of our democratic institutions" (Bagley, 1938, p. 251).

Many of the essentialists' criticisms of progressive education, namely that it was weak, full of frills, and a major negative factor in the nation's position in global economics and military competition, have been echoed by critics of the educational establishment ever since. Although their criticisms lessened during the war that was soon to come, they were revived stronger than ever in the 1950s. Also, the reform reports of the 1980s and 1990s used much of the essentialists' language.

Impact of the Second World War on the Schools

Germany's invasion of Poland in September of 1939 marked the beginning of World War II. Although it would be more than 2 years before America was formally involved in the war, America's Lend-Lease agreement with the Allies meant that American factories increasingly were called on to supply the Allied war effort. This helped the American economy recover from the Depression. The threat of impending war also led educational institutions at all levels to address the task of promoting education for national defense. Before the United States became involved in the war this meant education to strengthen the foundations of democracy. After the Japanese attack on Pearl Harbor and America's entry into the war, this meant using education resources to promote the war effort (Kandel, 1948).

The joint Education Policy Commission (1942) of the NEA and the American Association of School Administrators suggested that the federal government establish an agency to facilitate and coordinate the interaction of government agencies and the schools and colleges. The federal government responded with the establishment of the U.S. Office of Education (USOE) Wartime Commission. The Wartime Commission did not mandate that specific courses be taught in the schools as part of the war effort. However, in its report, *The Best Kind of High School Training for Military Service*, it did outline the type of educational program that would provide the most valuable preinduction training for future members of the armed services. Basically the commission recommended that the schools emphasize health and physical fitness, education for citizenship, the academic subjects, and specialized training in vocational skills.

Six months into the war the war activities of high school youth were brought into focus by the establishment of the High School Victory Corps. The government had forecast that 80% of the 1.3 million high school males between 16 and 18 years of age would enter the armed forces soon after graduation (Ugland, 1979). The Victory Corps was a federal program organized by the USOE to encourage instruction and training in pursuits and services needed in wartime. In addition to their curricular pursuits Victory Corps members were required to participate in at least one wartime activity or service (e.g., air warden, fire watcher, civil defense volunteer, USO volunteer, or home-school-community services such as salvage campaigns). The USOE hoped that the Victory Corps would give substance to the idea of the student reservist and preinduction training and saw this as a way to have a prominent spot in the war effort (Ugland, 1979). However, most schools were realistic about what they could provide in terms of preinduction training. Although they did follow the advice of the USOE and give more attention to applied mathematics and science, manual and industrial arts, and vocational education, they also continued to offer a strong academic curriculum. This was due in part to the fact that most of the students who left school to take jobs in the war industries were not headed for college, and those that remained in school were reluctant to depart dramatically from an academic curriculum (Ugland, 1979).

For what were undoubtedly a variety of reasons the Victory Corps was less successful than its creators had envisioned. One year after its inception less than 25% of eligible students had joined the Victory Corps. Enrollment declined, and the next year the program was discontinued. Nonetheless, the Victory Corps program did have an effect on the curriculum. In combination with the emphasis on preinduction training and the support given vocational training, it served to shape the wartime curriculum toward "education for victory."

Impact of the War on Elementary and Secondary Schools

The war had a heavy impact on the schools, teachers, and students. (The impact on one special group of students, Japanese American students in relocation camps, is the subject of one of the Primary Source Readings for this chapter.) High school enrollments declined from 6.7 million in 1940–41 to 5.5 million in 1943–44. Despite "Go-to-School" drives, it was difficult for the 80% of students who did not plan to go to college to resist either the call to arms or the high wages to be found in the wartime industries. And, even though enrollment had declined, the teacher shortage that had begun before the war now worsened. Not only did large numbers of teachers leave the classroom for the battlefield, but many more left to take higher paying positions in industry. The shortage of teachers, which some historians consider to be the most serious consequence of the war, was felt during the war years and the postwar years as well (Kandel, 1948). By the end of the war more than one third (350,000) of the teachers employed in 1940–41 had left teaching (Kandel, 1948). Teacher shortages occurred both in the subject matter fields that might be expected and in rural and other areas where salaries were far below those paid in the wartime industries. The results of the teacher shortages were similar to those experienced during the Depression: school closures, reduced terms, and fewer course offerings. By the middle of 1943 the teacher shortage was seen as a threat to the students still in the schools. Moreover, it was projected that it would take a decade to make up the deficit created by the teachers leaving the profession and the decline in enrollment in teacher education programs (Kandel, 1948).

Another major impact of the war on the schools was financial. Financial support, already low because of the Depression, was further reduced as funds were diverted from education to other purposes. Once again these financial difficulties highlighted the inequalities of educational opportunity that existed among regions and districts. Reports from the Selective Service on the young men rejected for mental and physical deficiencies showed higher percentages coming from the predominantly rural and southern states, the same areas that had the lowest educational expenditures. The inequalities and their consequences intensified the argument for federal support for education as a national concern. Some financial assistance was provided to those school districts overburdened by an influx of children from families employed in defense industries or on military bases by the Lanham Act of 1941. This so-called "impact aid" was continued under the provisions of Public Laws 815 and 874.

A major war-related initiative sponsored by the federal government was the Vocational-Defense Training Program, later known as the Vocational Training for War Production Workers. Through this program over 5 million people received training in war occupations at public vocational schools. Training was provided to people already employed in war occupations who needed additional skills or knowledge to equip them for more advanced positions, as well as pre-employment training to unemployed persons or persons employed in non-war occupations. One part of the program was designed to provide training to youth, especially rural youth, to assist in the production of food for the war effort. Later called the Food Production War Training Program and extended to include adults, the program enrolled 2.8 million people in courses such as Farm Machinery and Equipment Repair and Construction, Food Conservationism and Preservation, and a variety of courses designed to help reach the wartime food production goals (Henry, 1945b).

Impact of the War on Higher Education

Colleges and universities were also seriously affected by the war. Enrollment declined sharply: Almost 75% of male students went into military service. The instructional staff was also severely reduced as instructors left for military service or to perform research related to the war effort, enter the diplomatic service, or provide expertise and service in the monumental task of conversion of industries from peacetime to wartime.

Institutional finances were also affected by the war. Income in 1943–44 was only 67% of what it had been in 1939–40 (Knight, 1952). Larger institutions involved in the specialized training described later or in government-sponsored research were not as heavily affected as smaller institutions, but basically all institutions were affected by an increase in cost for current operations (Kandel, 1948). The impact of the reductions in enrollments, staff, and finances on the nation's colleges and universities was so serious that toward the end of the war Congress authorized a study of the effects of these reductions as well as the projected impact of the phasing out of the specialized training programs being conducted on college campuses. The results of the study led the committee to recommend emergency federal aid to assist higher education. A bill introduced in May 1945 to provide this aid did not pass, but the next year President Harry Truman appointed the President's Commission on Higher Education in a Democracy to consider the future of higher education in America. Among the recommendations made by the committee in 1947 was that the federal government continue to provide funding for research. Not only was this done, but the magnitude of these vast research enterprises served to transform many universities into what Clark Kerr (1963) termed "federal grant universities."

Higher Education and the War Effort

Individually, and through the American Council on Education, colleges and universities sought to play an active role in the war effort. They were intent on ensuring that the mistakes of World War I not be repeated. At the outbreak of that war the War Department had no plan for involving colleges and universities in the war effort, and when they finally did, they effectively took over college campuses. They also had no plan for training scientific and technical personnel and indiscriminately drafted faculty into the armed services to serve in roles that made no use of their academic training and talents (Cardozier, 1993).

As World War II loomed and then overtook the United States, colleges, college students, and the war department were faced with a dilemma: They recognized that the future need for professionally trained individuals demanded that college students remain in school and that college professors remain in their positions, but at the same time these were the very individuals who were required for positions of leadership in military and government service. One way colleges and universities attempted to meet the manpower demand was by acceleration: moving to four quarters or three semesters and to a 6-day instructional week. This made graduation possible in 2⅔ or 3 years. Even medical schools adopted accelerated programs that reduced the length of medical preparation to 3 years.

One of the most important roles played by colleges and universities during the war was preparing men for military service, for war industries, and for essential civilian activities. By the end of 1943, 380,000 men were involved in specialized training at 489 colleges and universities, many as part of the Army Specialized Training Program, the Army Air Force College Training Program, and the Naval College Training Programs (Knight, 1952). In each case the particular branch of service contracted with the college or university to use its facilities and faculties to provide specialized training that its own training facilities were not prepared to deliver.

In addition to on-campus training of military personnel, over 100,000 service men and women were enrolled in correspondence courses for high school or college credit that were supplied by the United States Armed Forces Institute in cooperation with more than 800 colleges and universities (Henry, 1945a). The experience and interest of military personnel in higher education continued in the postwar period and was a major factor in the postwar boom in higher education enrollment.

Training civilian personnel in areas deemed important to the war effort was provided through the Engineering, Science, and Management Defense (later War) Training Program operated cooperatively by the United States Office of Education and participating colleges and universities. The program supported 12- to 16-week courses designed to address the shortage of engineers, chemists, physicists, and production supervisors in the specialties important to the war effort. The program also provided war courses for high school physics and math teachers as part of the government's efforts to promote preinduction courses in the high schools. Between the end of 1943 and

Colleges and universities played a major role in training military and civilian personnel for the war effort.

For Your Reflection and Analysis

Which of the educational institutions (elementary, secondary, or postsecondary) felt the greatest negative impact of World War II? Give reasons why.

October 1945 more than 1.3 million men and women were enrolled in 12,500 short courses offered by over 200 colleges in 1,000 towns and cities across the country (Kandel, 1948).

Although it is not possible to cite all the contributions the schools, colleges, and teachers made to the war effort, the statement of "Education's Part in the War Effort" issued by the

---

The schools and colleges of the United States made indispensable contributions to the nation's war effort. Among other things they

(1) Laid the foundations upon which a citizens' army was quickly built. In World War I only 20% of the members of the armed forces had more than an eighth-grade education; in World War II, almost 70% had more than an eighth-grade education. . . .

(4) Carried through a training program designed to increase industrial production and the supply of food. Pre-employment courses were given to 2,667,000, supplementary vocational courses to 4,800,000, and agricultural training to 4,188,000 students.

(5) Registered millions of men for the Selective Service. In most communities school buildings were used and thousands of teachers voluntarily gave time as registration clerks.

(6) Registered citizens and distributed 415,000,000 ration books. Many teachers served on the rationing boards—in August 1945, of the 126,000 board members nearly 7,600 were educators.

(7) Participated in the drives to collect waste paper and metal. Out of 25,000,000 tons of paper collected, it is estimated by authorities that the schools collected at least 2,500,000 tons.

(8) Sold two billion dollars worth of war bonds and stamps. In 1945 more than 25,000,000 pupils were participating in school savings plans as compared to 2,500,000 in 1941.

(9) Provided headquarters for civilian defense activities. Partial reports from city school systems indicate that one in ten teachers participated in such activities.

(10) Assisted the Junior Red Cross produce over 35,000,000 comfort and recreational articles for the armed forces. In addition, medical chests, dried milk, and educational gift boxes were sent to children in the war zones.

(11) Gave thousands of hours to war-supporting agencies. Among these were the United Service Organizations, American Red Cross, war relief drives for our Allies, book drives of the American Library Association, and nursery schools and child-care programs.

FIGURE 8.1 Education's Part in the War Effort

Source: National Education Association. (1946). Education's part in the war effort. *Journal of the National Education Association*, May, p.250.

National Education Association in 1946 and presented in Figure 8.1 enumerates some that have not been mentioned in this discussion.

Education in the Postwar Era

Enrollment in both higher education and the public schools surged in the postwar years. Toward the end of the war, in an effort to assist veterans whose schooling had been interrupted by military service, the Servicemen's Readjustment Act of 1944 was passed. The G.I. Bill, as it became known, provided benefits to 7.8 million veterans of World War II to help them further their education. The benefits subsequently were extended to veterans of the Korean, "Cold," and Vietnam wars; eventually almost 15 million veterans were involved. The G.I. Bill also initiated a great postwar popularization of higher education. More men and women representing a greater age range and from various social, economic, cultural, and racial groups attended colleges and universities than ever before (Cremin, 1988) (see Table 8.2).

In addition, while returning servicemen filled college and university classrooms after the war, within a decade the postwar "baby boom" hit the public schools. Between 1946 and 1956 kindergarten and elementary school enrollments increased 37%, from 17.7 million to 24.3 million.

Life Adjustment Education and the Education Critics of the 1950s

The years after World War II constituted a period of not only burgeoning enrollments, but also adjustment—the adjustment of returning servicemen and servicewomen; the adjustment of the economy from wartime to peacetime; the adjustment to life in a new residential configuration, the suburb; and the adjustment to a society that was more transient, more mobile, and more prosperous than ever before (Gutek, 1981). In the midst of postwar changes and uncertainties an education

TABLE 8.2   Degree-Granting Institutions of Higher Education, Faculty, and Enrollments, 1919–20 to 1999–2000

Year	Total institutions	Total faculty	Total enrollment
1919–20	1,041	48,615	597,880
1929–30	1,409	82,386	1,110,737
1939–40	1,708	146,929	1,494,203
1949–50	1,851	245,722	2,659,021
1959–60	2,008	380,554	3,639,847
1969–70	2,525	450,000	8,004,660
1979–80	3,152	675,000	11,569,899
1989–90	3,535	824,220	13,538,560
1999–2000	4,084	1,027,830	14,791,224

Source: U.S. Department of Education, National Center for Education Statistics. (2003). *Digest of education statistics 2002* (Table 171). Washington, DC: U.S. Government Printing Office.

For Your Reflection and Analysis

Give arguments for and against life adjustment education as a tool for making education more relevant for all students.

movement called *life adjustment education* came into prominence. Life adjustment education became associated with progressive education and became the target of a group of critics who held progressive education responsible for a perceived decline in educational standards.

Life adjustment education was formally introduced in 1945 at a vocational education conference sponsored by the U.S. Office of Education. Spurred on by a series of conferences, state and national commissions, and numerous publications, it was seen by many as a natural outgrowth of progressive education's goal of making the schools more relevant to the broad spectrum of students. Focusing on the majority of youth in the middle, those not in the college prep or vocational track, life adjustment education stressed functional objectives such as vocation, family life, and personal hygiene and health, and rejected traditional academic studies. Although other approaches to creating a more functional curriculum had been advanced during the 1930s and 1940s, none gained the favor that life adjustment education did. In less than a decade after its formal introduction, half the states had undertaken some variation of the life adjustment curriculum.

Critics of progressive education found in life adjustment education a perfect target: "It continued an abundance of slogans, jargon, and various anti-intellectualisms; it carried the utilitarianism and group conformism of latter-day progressivism to its ultimate trivialization" (Ravitch, 1983, p. 70). One of the foremost critics of life adjustment education and progressive education in the postwar period was Arthur Bestor. In his most famous critical study, *Educational Wastelands* (1953), Bestor deplored the anti-intellectual quality of American schools, which he claimed had been caused

 For Your Reflection and Analysis

In what ways does Bestor's traditional liberal arts curriculum reflect the educational philosophy of Plato and Aristotle?

by progressive educators who "set forth purposes of education so trivial as to forfeit the respect of thoughtful men, and by deliberately divorcing the schools from the disciplines of science and scholarship" (p. 10). Bestor advocated a return to basics—traditional liberal arts curriculum of well-defined intellectual disciplines and the development of the intellect as the primary goal of education. Like earlier essentialists, Bestor (1956) argued that such a curriculum should be systematic and sequential because "clear thinking is systematic thinking, [and] liberal education involves the logical organization of knowledge" (p. 36). Bestor's criticisms were well received by conservatives and other opponents of progressive education, and he was widely publicized in the popular press. Bestor later became one of the founders of the Council on Basic Education.

Two other leading critics of the contemporary education scene were Robert Hutchins and Admiral Hyman G. Rickover, father of the atomic submarine. Similar to Bestor, Hutchins advocated a return to a more traditional curriculum. But for him the preferred curriculum was the classical liberal arts curriculum. Consistent with the perennialist educational philosophy discussed in chapter 1, Hutchins argued that the ideal education is one that is designed to cultivate the intellect and that this could best be done by a curriculum that concentrates on the Great Books of Western civilization.

Perhaps even more critical of progressivism was Admiral Rickover (1959), who judged it to be "as hopelessly outdated today as the horse and buggy" and declared that "nothing short of a complete reorganization of American education, preceded by a revolutionary reversal of educational aims, can equip us for winning the educational race with the Russians" (p. 188). Rickover's criticism of America's schools was based largely on comparisons to their European counterparts. Based on this comparison Rickover concluded, as had Bestor, that a liberal arts education provided the intellectual discipline needed for critical thinking and problem solving as well as advanced specialized training. He also favored the multitrack, ability grouping of most European educational systems to the American comprehensive high school and focused his attention on the academically talented, who he believed were central to maintaining America's competitive edge with the Soviets.

At the same time that progressivism was coming under attack for its association with life adjustment education, the deepening Cold War brought growing intolerance for progressive ideals. Progressivism was associated with liberal politics, and progressive textbooks that promoted international understanding and discussed socialism and communism were attacked by right-wing groups as being unAmerican (Bernard & Mondale, 2001a).

In the end it was not its critics that killed progressive education. Rather it was a victim of both its successes and its failures. On the one hand, much of what the progressives had initially advocated had been incorporated into the schools: Projects, activities, and pupil experiences had been intelligently integrated into subject-matter teaching, concern for health and vocation had gained a permanent place in the school program, and concern for the individual differences among children had replaced the lockstep institution and rote memorization (Ravitch, 1983). On the other hand, progressive education failed to recognize the extremism of its unrelenting rejection of the traditional curriculum and to give adequate attention to the critical issues facing education in the 1930s and 1940s (Graham, 1967). Basically, progressive education did not seem to be relevant to the time: When the Soviet Union launched Sputnik, the first space satellite, in 1957, to a nation suddenly concerned with intelligence and the need for increased science and mathematics skills, progressive education seemed out of step.

Curriculum Reform in the Aftermath of Sputnik

Few times in history has a single event had such an impact on education as the launching of Sputnik in October 1957. The event seemed to confirm the fear that the United States was losing in the Cold War technological and military races with the Soviet Union. The fear of hydrogen bombs being dropped from a similar craft onto American cities was matched by the humiliation and loss of prestige from being forced into second place in a critically important area of science and technology (McGrath, 1958). The launching of Sputnik seemed to confirm criticisms that the school curriculum lacked rigor and that insufficient attention was being paid to math and science. It also highlighted the consequences of the decades-long underfunding and neglect of education: At the time of the launching of Sputnik there was a reported shortage of 135,000 teachers and 159,000 classrooms. Many more thousands of teachers were operating on temporary or emergency certificates. Some classes in the larger cities held 40 or more children, and 800,000 children nationwide attended school only half day (McGrath, 1958).

The response of the federal government to Sputnik was significant in both its magnitude and its direction. In effect the federal government initiated a national curriculum in the areas of mathematics, science, and modern foreign languages. This was accomplished not by mandate but by support for the development of new curricular materials, the distribution of money to school districts to purchase the new materials, and the training of teachers in the use of the new material and methods. Federal support for the development of math and sciences curricula came through funding provided through the National Science Foundation (NSF). Support for the development of a language curriculum came through the National Defense Education Act of 1958 (NDEA). The NDEA also provided support for students preparing for careers in science, mathematics, foreign languages and engineering; the hiring of science teachers and the purchase of scientific equipment and supplies; the improvement of guidance, counseling, and testing programs, especially those directed at the identification and encouragement of the more capable students; foreign language institutes and laboratories; and increased funding to the NSF.

The fivefold increase in funding to the NSF allowed it to expand its curriculum development and education programs. In 1956 it established the Physical Science Study Committee (PSSC) composed of a number of very prestigious scientists. Federal support for the work of the PSSC allowed it to spend over $1 million per year for several years, beginning in 1958, on the development of curriculum materials for high school physics. Classroom teachers were introduced to the PSSC materials through summer institutes conducted at institutions of higher education under contract with the NSF, as well as through in-service institutes. The institutes were free to teachers. In fact, teachers were given a stipend and sometimes academic credit to attend the institutes. After the passage of the NDEA, school districts could use grant funds to purchase PSSC materials. Within a couple of years the manufacture and distribution of PSSC materials had been turned over to private companies.

Another NSF group, the School Mathematics Study Group (SMSG), was organized in 1958 and developed the "new math," which was based on set theory. A set was

> any collection of things which could be points, lines, vectors, or any philosophical notion, such as brotherhood. By thinking in terms of sets, children were to learn to understand relationships and discover hidden patterns. Supposedly, after developing this habit of thinking, the student would retain a mental discipline that would be useful in advanced mathematical techniques. (Spring, 1989, p. 82)

The SMSG developed a series of widely used mathematics textbooks. The stated purpose of the SMSG was not to compete with commercial publishers but to ensure that its curriculum was being used in the schools. Accordingly, the SMSG established a committee to review commercial math texts each year to determine whether they incorporated SMSG curriculum and, if so, to remove any competing SMSG text. Although the SMSG always denied that its intention was to establish a national curriculum, the pressures it brought on the textbook industry had the effect of forcing the adoption of the SMSG curriculum.

The curriculum development work of the PSSC and the SMSG became models for other areas of the curriculum. In 1965, under a grant from the NSF, the American Institute of Biological Sciences Curriculum Study Group began work on a biological sciences curriculum, and between 1960 and 1963 the Chemical Education Material Study Group developed a range of curriculum materials for that discipline. The cooperative development of these curricula by university scholars and education experts, curricula that stressed structure, abstraction, discovery, and curiosity, tended to counter the complaints of anti-intellectualism that had dogged the schools for a number of years (Spring, 1989). The only drawback for the schools was that the development activities were basically limited to the sciences, mathematics, and foreign languages.

The curriculum reforms initiated by the NDEA were further stimulated by former Harvard University president James Conant's (1893–1978) widely publicized study of secondary education, *The American High School Today* (1959), also known as the Conant Report. Conant's experiences both as an educator and in national defense had convinced him of the critical relationship between education and the welfare of the nation. According to Conant (1953), "If the field of Waterloo was won on the playing fields of Eton, it may well be that the ideological struggles with communism in the next fifty years will be won on the playing fields of the public schools of the United States" (p. 62). The primary conclusion Conant reached from his study of American high schools was that the number of small high schools should be drastically reduced by district reorganization because small high schools typically were not financially able to offer quality academic and vocational programs. Conant recommended that in the larger, reconstituted high schools all students be required to take 4 years of English, 3 or 4 years of social studies, and 1 year each in mathematics and sciences. The more able students would take additional math, sciences, and foreign languages.

Like Rickover, Conant was concerned that the schools were not challenging the academically talented. However, although he did not support separate schools for the academically talented as did Rickover, arguing that the comprehensive high school was more democratic and contributed to social cohesion, Conant did propose that students be grouped by ability within the academic subjects. He also stressed the importance of identifying the academically gifted and channeling them into the university science and technology programs most needed to serve the national interests.

Conant played a major role in the establishment of the Educational Testing Service and advanced placement and was an advocate for the use of standardized tests for college admissions and for increasing the number of guidance counselors in the high schools.

Unlike Bestor and some of the other school critics of the 1950s, Conant did not attack

 For Your Reflection and Analysis

Conant has been criticized for being an educational elitist. Do you agree or disagree? Why?

educators and did not condemn the comprehensive high school or suggest any radical alteration of it. As a result, his recommendations were seen by most educators and school boards as recommendations for improvement, not as attempts to transform the schools. Conant's recommendations had considerable influence on educational planners and policy makers. Over the next decade the number of school districts decreased from 40,520 to fewer than 18,000 (NCES, 1993), when many of the small high schools were consolidated.

New Learning Theories

The importance of psychology to the science of education and to understanding how learning takes place had been advanced in the first quarter of the 20th century by Thorndike and integrated with his work on intelligence testing. Thorndike developed a theory of learning that he labeled *psychological connectionism*. He compared the mind to a switchboard where connections are made between a stimulus and a response. The connection is made as a result of the law of effect: A reward is given when the appropriate connection is made between the stimulus and the response. According to Thorndike's stimulus–response theory, learning depends on this connection being made between the stimulus and the response. Thorndike's suggestion that individuals differ in not only their intelligence but also their innate ability to form connections (i.e., to learn) played a major role in the recognition of individual differences and their importance in learning.

The foundation laid by Thorndike was advanced in the postwar period by Jean Piaget and Jerome Bruner and provided support to the efforts to reform the curriculum. Piaget and Bruner advanced the stage concept of child development. According to Bruner's theory of cognition, learning is a process by which children construct new ideas and concepts based on their previous learning. Moreover, according to this theory, learning occurs in three stages of complexity (enactive, iconic, and symbolic); progress from one stage to another is influenced less by the developmental level of the child (as Piaget believed), and more by the environment. Like the progressives, Bruner also believed that children learn best when they are interested in the material and are engaged in active problem solving. And, learning is easier when teaching is concerned with providing an understanding of structure, the relationship between things, rather than simply the mastery of facts. According to Bruner (1960), "any subject can be taught effectively in some intellectually honest form to any child at any stage of development" (p.33).

Bruner's theories of cognition had a major impact on teachers, curriculum development, and policy making in the 1950s and 1960s. He participated in the work of the NSF and was instrumental in the design and implementation of a number of education programs, including the landmark social studies curriculum development project, "Man: A Course of Study." His stage theory of learning provided the rationale for the *spiral curriculum* sequencing pattern whereby subject matter is presented over a number of grades with increasing complexity and abstraction. His theories of the way children construct knowledge provided the theoretical framework for the constructivist theory discussed in chapter 1.

Education and the Red Scare

The period from 1947 to 1954, the McCarthy era, so named because of the highly publicized congressional search for communists and subversives led by Senator Joseph McCarthy of Wisconsin, was one of zealous anticommunism that touched all aspects of American life. Right-wing extremists used the threat of communist infiltration to discredit individuals or ideas that they considered liberal or progressive. Public schools and universities, because of their role in shaping the minds and values of the young, became leading targets, if not the number one target, of those who were concerned about disloyalty and subversion at the state and local levels (Ravitch, 1983). To a large extent education became the battleground for some of the ideological battles being waged in the larger society as well. Before it was over, the Red Scare had left a significant and enduring mark on American education. More than 600 teachers lost their jobs after having been accused of "un-American" activities. Hundreds more were brought before hearing bodies but allowed to keep their jobs. Tenured university faculty were fired for their left-wing political activities, for refusing to answer questions about their relationship with the communist party, or in the case of 31 California professors, for refusing to pledge "I am not a member of the Communist party, or under any oath, or a party to any agreement, or under any commitment that is in conflict with my obligation under this oath" (Ravitch, 1983, p. 98). Across the country Red Scare tactics were used in an attempt to remove liberal educators, and virtually all teachers were intimidated and lived in fear and anxiety of being called before a state or federal investigative committee, of being arbitrarily labeled a communist in the press, or of becoming the target of some reactionary group (Foster, 2000).

 For Your Reflection and Analysis

Give other examples throughout history of individuals or ideas that have been discredited or dismissed because of their liberal or progressive nature.

The Red Scare also had a profound effect on what teachers taught and the materials they used. While experiencing academic repression from the outside, teachers also self-censored out of fear of being dismissed or being reported for being subversive. In towns and cities across the land textbooks and curriculum materials were vigorously scrutinized lest any subject be included that might induce criticism. Books were withdrawn from use and even burned. In Texas the legislature ordered all school (and university) libraries to remove any and all literature published by the Soviet Union. In Indiana a member of the state textbook commission pressed to have *Robin Hood* banned from the schools because the story was part of "a communist directive in education" which celebrated "robbing the rich to give to the poor" (Foster, 2000, p. 1).

 For Your Reflection and Analysis

What forces in today's political or social climate might lead teachers to self-censor?

The Red Scare also dealt what might be considered the death blow to progressive education and was instrumental in moving the curriculum further to the political

The McCarthy hearings in the U.S. Senate symbolized the Red Scare tactics that resulted in the dismissal of hundreds of teachers.

right (Foster, 2000). The critics of progressive education were effective in linking it to collectivism, and by implication, to communism. To deflect or avoid criticism, educators "frequently played down features of progressive education lest they be construed subversive, and vigorously emphasized the '3 R's,' the 'fundamentals,' and loyalty to American traditions" (Foster, 2000, p. 184).

The height of the Red Scare in education came in 1952 and 1953 with the widely publicized congressional investigations of alleged subversion. Soon after this the tide began to turn. The election of the moderate Republican, Dwight Eisenhower, undermined McCarthy's claims that the government was "soft on communism" (Ravitch, 1983). McCarthy's ever more outlandish and unsubstantiated accusations led to his censure by the Senate in late 1954. The courts were also taking a stand, overturning dismissals and declaring unconstitutional some of the more far-reaching state and local actions. By the mid-1950s the worst of the scare was over. However, the personal and professional damage done to the nation's educators and to the schools where they practiced their chosen profession remained.

Conclusion

Education was not immune to the effects of the Depression, and in some respects the response of many educators was similar to that of the larger population: They looked to the federal government for relief. Many educational leaders called on the federal government to provide general aid to the schools. Their major argument, the same one that has been used ever since, is that federal aid is necessary to overcome the educational inequalities that exist among the states resulting from the inequalities of resources and the ability to support education. The argument continues that only the federal government can address these inequalities, and that it is in the interest of the general welfare for it to do so. Whatever the merits of the arguments, the federal government has continued to refuse to distribute general federal aid to education. In addition to any ideological reasons related to perceptions of the role of the federal government and states' rights, a major reason has undoubtedly been the same one used during the Depression—the cost to the federal government would be too high.

The federal government did involve itself in education during the Depression, however, and in a way and to a degree previously not envisioned. However, much to the chagrin of educators, and over their protests, New Deal education funds and programs were not given to the education community. This distrust of the education community continues to characterize the view of many politicians.

During and after World War II the federal government continued its involvement, not only in providing financial support to education, but also in promoting a curriculum designed to serve national security. The progressive notion of the interest of the child guiding the curriculum gave way to the interest of the state. The postwar years also brought the federal government into the schools in a far less positive way. The U.S. Committee on Un-American Activities, as well as state investigatory committees, engaged in what is generally conceded to be a "witch hunt" to discredit educators who had even the slightest real or imagined connection to communism. In most cases the investigations were used to discredit liberal-leaning educators or simply those who were not liked. Similarly, the heightened nationalism following the terrorist attacks of September 11, 2001, led educators, as well as politicians, the media, and members of the general public to be censored or to self-censor for fear of being labeled "unpatriotic." The brunt of the Red Scare was felt by the more liberal educators, both in the public schools and in colleges and universities. They remain the targets of right-wing conservative ideologues today.

For Discussion and Application

1. Compare the high school curriculum of 1930 with the high school curriculum of 1960.
2. How can the school most effectively serve as an initiator of social change?
3. Trace the changing involvement of the federal government in education in the 20th century.
4. Compare the major criticisms of progressive education during the 1950s with those made by education critics of today.
5. Interview a Depression-era student regarding the impact of the Depression on the students and the school he or she attended. How might you have responded to these circumstances?

Primary Source Reading

In this speech before the Progressive Education Society in 1932, Counts expressed both optimism and pessimism regarding the future and education. He underscored the great faith of the American people in progress and in education. He also pointed to the progressive education movement as a possible remedy or model for hope and change. However, Counts was a realist and suggested that for progressive education to be genuinely progressive, it must have direction. It must free itself from the influence of its liberal-minded upper-middle-class supporters, face each social issue courageously, establish strong community ties, and develop a realistic theory of welfare.

As you read the following excerpts of Counts' speech, ask yourself how you would answer the question posed by his title. Why did the delegates greet his message with silence?

Dare the Schools Build a New Social Order?

George S. Counts

Like all simple and unsophisticated peoples we Americans have a sublime faith in education. Faced with any difficult problem of life we set our minds at rest sooner or later by the appeal to the school. We are convinced that education is the one unfailing remedy for every ill to which man is subject, whether it be vice, crime, war, poverty, riches, injustice, racketeering, political corruption, race hatred, class conflict, or just plain original sin. We even speak glibly and often about the general reconstruction of society through the school. We cling to this faith in spite of the fact that the very period in which our troubles have multiplied so rapidly has witnessed an unprece-

Source: Counts, G. S. (1932). *Dare the schools build a new social order?* (pp. 3–12). Copyright © 1932 by George S. Counts. Reprinted by permission of HarperCollins Publishers Inc.

dented expansion of organized education. This would seem to suggest that our schools, instead of directing the course of change, are themselves driven by the very forces that are transforming the rest of the social order.

The bare fact, however, that simple and unsophisticated peoples have unbounded faith in education does not mean that the faith is untenable. History shows that the intuitions of such folk may be nearer the truth than the weighty and carefully reasoned judgments of the learned and the wise. Under certain conditions education may be as beneficent and as powerful as we are wont to think. But if it is to be so, teachers must abandon much of their easy optimism, subject the concept of education to the most rigorous scrutiny, and be prepared to deal much more fundamentally, realistically, and positively with the American social situation than has been their habit in the past. Any individual or group that would aspire to lead society must be ready to pay the costs of leadership: to accept responsibility, to suffer calumny, to surrender security, to risk both reputation and fortune. If this price or some important part of it is not being paid, then the chances are that the claim to leadership is fraudulent. Society is never redeemed without effort, struggle, and sacrifice. Authentic leaders are never found breathing that rarefied atmosphere lying above the dust and smoke of battle. With regard to the past we always recognize the truth of this principle, but when we think of our own times we profess the belief that the ancient roles have been reversed and that now prophets of a new age receive their rewards among the living.

That the existing school is leading the way to a better social order is a thesis which few informed persons would care to defend. Except as it is forced to fight for its own life during times of depression, its course is too serene and untroubled. Only in the rarest of instances does it wage war on behalf of principle or ideal. Almost everywhere it is in the grip of conservative forces and is serving the cause of perpetuating ideas and institutions suited to an age that is gone. But there is one movement above the educational horizon which would seem to show promise of genuine and creative leadership. I refer to the Progressive Education movement. Surely in this union of two of the great faiths of the American people, the faith in progress and the faith in education, we have reason to hope for light and guidance. Here is a movement which would seem to be completely devoted to the promotion of social welfare through education.

Even a casual examination of the program and philosophy of the Progressive schools, however, raises many doubts in the mind. To be sure, these schools have a number of large achievements to their credit. They have focused attention squarely upon the child; they have recognized the fundamental importance of the interest of the learner; they have defended the thesis that activity lies at the root of all true education: they have conceived learning in terms of life situations and growth of character; they have championed the rights of the child as a free personality. Most of this is excellent, but in my judgment it is not enough. It constitutes too narrow a conception of the meaning of education; it brings into the picture but one-half of the landscape.

If an educational movement, or any other movement, calls itself progressive, it must have orientation: it must possess direction. The word itself implies moving forward, and moving forward can have little meaning in the absence of clearly defined purposes. We cannot, like Stephen Leacock's horseman, dash off in all directions at once. Nor should we, like our presidential candidates, evade every disturbing issue and be all things to all men. Also we must beware lest we become so devoted to motion that we neglect the question of direction and be entirely satisfied with movement in circles. Here, I think, we find the fundamental weakness, not only of Progressive Education, but also of American education generally. Like a baby shaking a rattle, we seem to be utterly content with action provided it is sufficiently vigorous and noisy. In the last analysis a very large part of American educational thought, inquiry, and experimentation is much ado about nothing. And, if we are permitted to push the analogy of the rattle a bit further, our consecration to motion is encouraged and supported in order to keep out of mischief. At least we know that so long as we thus busy ourselves we shall not incur the serious displeasure of our social elders.

The weakness of Progressive Education thus lies in the fact that it has elaborated no theory of social welfare, unless it be that of anarchy or extreme individualism. In this, of course, it is but reflecting the viewpoint of the members of the liberal-minded upper middle class who send their children to the Progressive schools—persons who are fairly well-off, who have abandoned the faiths of their fathers, who assume an agnostic attitude towards all important questions, who pride themselves on their open-mindedness and tolerance, who favor in a mild sort of way fairly liberal programs of social reconstruction, who are full of good will and humane sentiment, who have vague aspirations for world peace and human brotherhood, who can be counted upon to respond moderately to any appeal made in the name of charity, who are genuinely distressed at the sight of *unwonted* forms of cruelty, misery, and suffering, and who perhaps serve to soften somewhat the bitter clashes of those real forces that govern the world; but who, in spite of all their good qualities, have no deep and abiding loyalties, possess no convictions for which they would sacrifice over-much, would find it hard to live without their customary material comforts, are rather insensitive to the accepted forms of social injustice, are content to play the role of interested spectator in the drama of human history, refuse to see reality in its harsher and more disagreeable forms, rarely move outside the pleasant circles of the class to which they belong, and in the day of severe trial will follow the lead of the most powerful and respectable forces in society and at the same time find good reasons for so doing. These people have shown themselves entirely incapable of dealing with any of the great crises of our time—war, prosperity, or depression. At bottom they are romantic sentimentalists, but with a sharp eye on the main chance. That they can be trusted to write our educational theories and shape our educational programs is highly improbable.

Among the members of this class the number of children is small, the income relatively high, and the economic functions of the home greatly reduced. For these reasons an inordinate emphasis on the child and child interests is entirely welcome to them. They wish to guard their offspring from too strenuous endeavor and from coming into too intimate contact with the grimmer aspects of industrial society. They wish their sons and daughters to succeed according to the standards of their class and to be a credit to their parents. At heart feeling themselves members of a superior human strain, they do not want their children to mix too freely with the children of the poor or of the less fortunate races. Nor do they want them to accept radical social doctrines, espouse unpopular causes, or lose themselves in quest of any Holy Grail. According to their views education should deal with life, but with life distance or in a highly diluted form. They would generally maintain that life should be kept at arm's length, if it should not be handled with a poker.

If Progressive Education is to be genuinely progressive, it must emancipate itself from the influence of this class, face squarely and courageously every social issue, come to grips with life in all of its stark reality, establish an organic relation with the community, develop a realistic and comprehensive theory of welfare, fashion a compelling and challenging vision of human destiny, and become less frightened than it is today at the bogies of *imposition* and *indoctrination*. In a word Progressive Education cannot place its trust in a child-centered school.

This brings us to the most crucial issue in education—the question of the nature and extent of the influence which the school should exercise over the development of the child. The advocates of extreme freedom have been so successful in championing what they call the rights of the child that even the most skillful practitioners of the art of converting others to their opinions disclaim all intention of molding the learner. And when the word indoctrination is coupled with education

there is scarcely one among us possessing the hardihood to refuse to be horrified. This feeling is so widespread that even Mr. Lunacharsky, Commissar of Education in the Russian Republic until 1929, assured me on one occasion that the Soviet educational leaders do not believe in the indoctrination of children in the ideas and principles of communism. When I asked him whether their children become good communists while attending the schools, he replied that the great majority do. On seeking from him an explanation of this remarkable phenomenon he said that Soviet teachers merely tell their children the truth about human history. As a consequence, so he asserted, practically all of the more intelligent boys and girls adopt the philosophy of communism. I recall also that the Methodist sect in which I was reared always confined its teachings to the truth!

The issue is no doubt badly confused by historical causes. The champions of freedom are obviously the product of an age that has broken very fundamentally with the past and is equally uncertain about the future. In many cases they feel themselves victims of narrow orthodoxies which were imposed upon them during childhood and which have severely cramped their lives. At any suggestion that the child should be influenced by his elders they therefore envisage the establishment of a state church, the formulation of a body of sacred doctrine, and the teaching of this doctrine as fixed and final. If we are forced to choose between such an unenlightened form of pedagogical influence and a condition of complete freedom for the child, most of us would in all probability choose the latter as the lesser of two evils. But this is to create a wholly artificial situation: the choice should not be limited to these two extremes. Indeed today neither extreme is possible.

I believe firmly that a critical factor must play an important role in any adequate educational program, at least in any such program fashioned for the modern world. An education that does not strive to promote the fullest and most thorough understanding of the world is not worthy of the name. Also there must be no deliberate distortion or suppression of facts to support any theory or point of view. On the other hand, I am prepared to defend the thesis that all education contains a large element of imposition, that in the very nature of the case this is inevitable, that the existence and evolution of society depend upon it, that it is consequently eminently desirable, and that the frank acceptance of this fact by the educator is a major professional obligation. I even contend that failure to do this involves the clothing of one's own deepest prejudices in the garb of universal truth and the introduction into the theory and practice of education of an element of obscurantism.

Questions for Discussion

1. If George Counts were alive today, what specific changes might he propose to his address, "Dare the Schools Build a New Social Order?" Give reasons why.

2. Counts believed that "an education that does not strive to promote the fullest and most thorough understanding of the world is not worthy of the name." What do you believe Counts meant by this statement? Do you agree with his premise? Why or why not?

3. Counts suggested that the weakness of progressive education lies in the fact that it has elaborated limited theories of social welfare (i.e., anarchy or extreme individualism), which reflect the point of view of the liberal-minded upper class who are most apt to send their children to progressive schools. Discuss other forms of social welfare that might be more acceptable to members of all social classes regardless of income or social status.

Primary Source Reading

Eleanor Gerard Sekerak, a teacher at Topaz High School, a War Relocation Authority Camp (WRA) at Topaz, Utah, presents a moving account of her 3-year experience teaching Japanese American students at the internment camp. *Upon her arrival, the school buildings had not been completed, there was a desperate lack of school supplies and textbooks, practically no library existed, and transportation was nonexistent. In spite of these challenges a successful community high school emerged with all the extracurricular offerings of the traditional high school. As you read "Teacher at Topaz," ask yourself how you would have fared as a student or teacher at Topaz High School.*

A Teacher at Topaz

Eleanor Gerard Sekerak

A number of Nisei students attended Technical High School in Oakland, the location of my second supervised teaching assignment. Faculty members worried aloud about their Nisei students. What would happen, especially to the seniors removed from classes before the end of the semester? What about their plans for college? I had no Nisei in my class, but during hall duty I had occasion to admonish, almost daily, a youngster who always dashed by as though on roller skates. Once while reminding him not to run in the halls, I asked his name. "Bill Oshima," he told me.

The halls seemed very quiet after evacuation. From neither the teachers nor the students did I hear any anti-Nisei sentiment; no one identified the "enemy" with our students.

At last, the semester ended and evaluation and interviews occupied my days. One of California's most prestigious districts accepted my application for a teaching position and told me that a contract would be mailed later in the summer. That settled, I happily departed for the summer as a counselor at Camp Sunset in Bartlett, Illinois, near Chicago.

Source: Sekerak, E. G. (1986). A teacher at Topaz. In R. Daniels, S. C. Taylor, & H. H. Kitano (Eds.), *Japanese Americans: From relocation to redress.* Seattle, WA: University of Washington Press (pp. 38–43).

However, the teaching contract did not arrive and, finally, I wrote my dean asking him to inquire. Back came his regrets, informing me that the district had decided to hire a man. This was long before the days when one could rush into court claiming discrimination!

As I wondered what to do next, a telegram arrived from Lome Bell, formerly a YMCA executive in the Los Angeles area and then a regional supervisor for the National Youth Administration. During the early summer of 1942, he had left the NYA to work for the War Relocation Authority. His wire read, "If you have not yet signed a contract, will you consider a position at Topaz, Utah. We are in desperate need of teachers." . . .

I had no illusions about what I would find at Topaz; Lome Bell had warned, "This is an internment camp with barbed wire and military police." The advice at the San Francisco office of the WRA had been, "Take warm clothes; Utah winters are cold at 4,700 feet." And further, "Don't expect gourmet meals—you'll eat mass cooking in a staff dining hall." The preceding three months as a camp counselor proved good preparation for dorm life. . . .

Despite our location in the middle of an alkali desert, we did enjoy one great advantage—we didn't displace any local residents. We were made to feel as welcome as was possible under the distressing conditions. We experienced none of the really nasty episodes that plagued some of the other centers, and I personally credit the basic goodness of our neighboring Mormon residents.

Within hours of arriving at the staff women's dorm, my trunk was delivered by a crew of young men, one of whom shrieked upon seeing me and dropped the trunk on his toes. It was my hall-runner from Technical High. He dashed away shouting, "Guess who's here? That strict teacher from Tech!" By noon, the whole of Topaz knew that a California teacher had arrived.

Charles Ernst, an experienced settlement-house director from Boston, dignified and imposing but warm and considerate, was our first project director. He was an excellent administrator, undaunted by the bureaucratic paperwork

from Washington. With a deep concern for human values, Mr. Ernst kept representatives of the community in touch with developments.

Evening meetings to introduce new staff were one procedure. Never was an ordinary teacher made to feel more welcome. People crowded around to ask questions, shake hands, bow, and thank me for being there. When questioners learned that I was from Oakland and from UC, out of the crowd emerged classmates from University High and a smiling Hiro Katayama who had told us "good-bye" only six months before. Thus on my first day there were three meshings with past experiences.

The next day those teachers who had already arrived met with the administrators and other faculty. For some months I was the only California-credentialed teacher, giving me enormous prestige with the resident families. This standing also gave me an "instant" tool for discipline: I had only to remark to a reluctant student, "Homework not done? I think I'll stop to talk with your folks on the way home," to see an immediate transformation to eager scholar.

Most of our first-year teachers were trained in Utah; at that time a fifth year of college for secondary credentials was not required in Utah. For this reason, the Topaz residents felt shortchanged and worried about their children's academic preparation. However, our superintendent, a Utah native, had a Ph.D. from the University of California, Berkeley, and this mollified the parents. "Appointed," i.e., U.S. Civil Service, faculty were augmented by the resident staff, many of whom had excellent backgrounds but were without formal teacher-training credits. Hiro Katayama joined us in this capacity, having been recruited by Henry Tani. Henry, himself a graduate of Stanford University in business administration, became our administrative assistant. He had organized the high school at the Tanforan Assembly Center and would later become a national staff member with the United Church of Christ. . . .

The school buildings were far from complete when I arrived. A half-block of barracks at each end of the project was to house the two elementary schools, called "Mountain View" and "Desert View." Block 32, midway in the camp, constituted the six-year high school with a total anticipated enrollment of 1,720. Residents were arriving from Tanforan as fast as barracks could be built. Priority for the available carpenter time was to go to the elementary schools; volunteer labor sped up high school construction—the students and teachers all fell to. Alumni still laugh at the memory of Miss Gerard, teetering precariously on a wobbly table, holding a sheetrock slab with both arms while hammer-wielding students banged nails on each edge—and presto, a ceiling!

As soon as the barracks were winterized, huge "pot belly" stoves were moved into the middle of a room, tables and benches brought in to accommodate thirty-six students, and we were in business—it was October 26, 1942. The lack of supplies was desperate, so a phone call to my mother (and we waited hours to place a wartime call) resulted in her calling my former teachers at University High. Thanks to their efforts, outdated "surplus" texts began to arrive. "History is history, government is government," I sternly told my juniors and seniors, "you don't need a brand-new book!" Thus were we launched on an idealistic curriculum designed for us by a summer-session graduate class in curriculum development at Stanford University.

The curriculum began with the concept of the "community school," that is, the school is looked upon as an extended home, the community furnishing observations and opinion. This approach proved most valuable for students in the vocational area, and some of our students (those over sixteen years) were soon spending half their time in apprentice training or work experience. The schools in all relocation centers were to be affiliated with, and to meet the standards of, the states in which they were located. Utah had long been active in the vocational education field, so advisory committees were organized and planning help generously given. Consultants from the state board of education and even the board itself visited us.

The curriculum designed for us was based on a "core" of general education in agriculture, commercial, or college preparatory, and, in addition, a guidance program in which every teacher was expected to have a role. Our sequential theme for the entire school system was to be "Adaptation of Our Socioeconomic Arrangements to the Control and Direction of Technological Development." We were provided with illustrations of how to adapt this theme to the various grades, e.g., in grade one, "How can the yard at school be made more useful and beautiful?" In reality, the yard was dust (or mud) with huge piles of coal, and not a leaf could be coaxed from that alkali soil. In grade eleven, it was suggested, "How may the community take advantage of improved transportation and communication to make better living conditions for its people?" Our transportation consisted of walking the gravel roads of a one-mile square; no one went to Delta unless by special pass and by riding in an army truck.

In the beginning, faculty meetings were an exercise in how to tolerate frustration, as we wrestled with the "how to" of a core curriculum in a community school with few supplies and practically no library. Then we ran into opposition from the community itself—the parents did not want an experimental curriculum. They wanted their children to be prepared for college and to lose no academic ground because of the evacuation. So, with apologies to Stanford's Professor Paul Hanna, we modified the curriculum procedures by combining social studies and English as the "core" for the 1942–43 school year.

The first semester we covered federal, state, county, and city government, and administration. An update on the creation and administration of wartime agencies was included. Then an intensive study of the WRA calling our project a "federally created municipality" followed. Staff members came to class to discuss the various phases of the administration of Topaz, and students took field trips and participated in an actual week of work experience in one phase of the community.

In May 1942 our community participation took a very active form when all seniors and their teachers went into the fields to plant onions and celery in areas of tillable ground scattered beyond the alkali deposits. Thereafter, whenever crooked celery stalks appeared on mess hall tables, much merriment ensued concerning whose responsibility it was to have produced such a deformity.

The second semester each student decided on the town in which he wished to resettle, and we set up a community survey of this locality and state. Using a Russell Sage publication, *Your Community* by Joanna Colcord, they sent for materials (writing model letters), did primary and secondary research, and wrote a term paper in college manuscript form summing up their results. At a recent reunion, there was amusement as alumni recounted that they had arrived at their chosen resettlement destinations knowing more than the natives.

Underlying all this was my personal determination that standards of behavior and of learning and performance were in no way to be lessened. As I faced my first day I wondered how I could teach American government and democratic principles while we sat in classrooms behind barbed wire! I never ceased to have a lump in my throat when classes recited the Pledge of Allegiance, especially the phrase, "liberty and justice for all."

In our opening discussion, the students and I agreed that the whole evacuation process had been traumatic but could not last forever—and we could not permit academic achievement to be interrupted. So they arrived at class on time, with homework completed, worked diligently, took their exams, and otherwise observed normal classroom standards. (We had one exception: the day the first snow fell, the California Bay Area students and their teacher rushed to the window to watch.) All the normal life of a typical high school was set up: school chorus, student newspaper, yearbook, student government, drama, athletics, dances, and the usual senior week activities. Borrowing caps and gowns graciously loaned by the University of Utah, 218 seniors marched across the dusty windswept plaza to outdoor graduation exercises on June 25, services complete with an invocation and a begowned faculty. . . .

On one occasion, I chaperoned the first experimental group of senior girls and young women to work for the summer in a tomato cannery near Ogden. We started with light-hearted attitudes, anticipating hard work but making money. The grim realities of migratory agricultural life met us when we found utterly unacceptable, unsanitary, and crowded housing conditions plus an employer who couldn't or wouldn't consider any improvements. I had to appeal to nearby military to place me in phone contact with our project director. Upon hearing of the conditions, he ordered us back to Topaz, explaining to grateful parents that their daughters were not to be exploited.

To thank me for heading off a potentially embarrassing incident for the WRA administration, the director assigned my roommate and me an apartment in the new staff housing. Until that time we had lived in barracks rooms just as the evacuees did. Unlike some centers, at no time were there barriers between staff and evacuee housing. From then on, our apartment became a center for visitor and student meetings and parties.

My first roommate, Emily Minton, community activities director, was married at Topaz in December 1942. Her husband, Norman Center, arrived from San Francisco carrying Reverend Tsukamoto's altar candlesticks, and Goro Suzuki sang "I'm Dreaming of a White Christmas" at the reception. Mary MacMillan, my second roommate, taught at the high school until she left for graduate work in Nashville, Tennessee. "Mary Mack," much beloved by the students, would later go to postwar Hiroshima to teach. Third to move in was Muriel Matzkin, a biology teacher from New York. Muriel and I later went to Washington, D.C., to help close out the WRA. Later Muriel married Milton Shapp and became "first lady" of Pennsylvania.

Good-byes to those actually relocating to jobs out of the evacuation zone were far happier than parting with those destined for Tule Lake. When the first large group of families left for re-settlement in the East, and not just on seasonal leave, staff and friends crowded around the gate to say their farewells. Voices raised in song— "God be with you till we meet again"—as tears ran unashamedly down dusty cheeks.

Happiest of all leave-takings were those when students left for college. Many educators, such as my faculty colleagues at Technical High, had worried about the evacuee students who were then in college or planning to enter in the spring of 1942, and about those who would be graduating during the war years. During the early summer of 1942, some thirty deans and registrars met to consider the problem. With the eventual cooperation of over 300 colleges and universities, they established five requirements: (1) The student had to be accepted academically by the college while still in camp; (2) students could attend any school approved or "cleared" by the War and Navy departments; (3) students had to be able to provide for themselves financially for one year; (4) they had to be assured of a welcome in the college community; and (5) all students had to provide an autobiography.

The fourth stipulation created problems, as many of the large universities had war-related projects on their campuses; as a consequence, the need for an agency to handle a multitude of details became obvious. John J. McCloy, assistant secretary of war, and Milton Eisenhower, the first director of the WRA, requested that the American Friends Service Committee coordinate the activities of all interested groups, such as the churches, the YMCA, the YWCA, and the Fair Play Committee. The result was the National Japanese American Student Relocation Council funded by church boards and two philanthropic foundations. Thomas R. Bodine was appointed to the position of field director, and thereby hangs a tale of true dedication and commitment. Tom Bodine was a member of the Society of Friends and brought to the position the personal resources of extraordinary patience, understanding, and tremendous good cheer. He had charm,

compassion, integrity, and aplomb with which to cajole, console, and counsel evacuee students and their parents, relocation center high school faculty, foundation boards of directors, and college presidents.

When we finally built a school auditorium at Topaz, had an adequate library, fielded uniformed athletic teams, and had "settled in," Tom made us realize the stagnation of the human spirit that was occurring behind barbed wire. Spurred by him, we set up a student relocation office; our first was run very efficiently by the gracious Louise Watson. It later became a part of the high school, and I was called the "student relocation advisor" so as not to offend the high school "guidance counselor." We organized our own scholarship fund to which both residents and outsiders contributed. (Once, when a dental problem forced me to make a quick train trip home, my only other engagement during that one-day visit was to talk with a group of teachers. Asking me to please wait, they withdrew and returned with a check for a thousand dollars. "If Hayward students are awarded scholarships, tell them Hayward High teachers gave the money, otherwise we are to be anonymous," they said.)

The scholarships awarded, plus a $25 leave grant made when an evacuee departed camp, helped establish the student's financial ability. However, jobs, housing, and community acceptance were the concern and responsibility of the National Japanese American Student Relocation Council. By summer 1945, at least 3,000 students had been placed in various kinds of post-secondary education, having been relocated from all ten centers.

Topaz's closure was official on October 31, 1945, and I left immediately for Washington, D.C. My responsibility there was to handle correspondence concerning student records, especially transcripts, as the relocated students had entered schools all over the nation. Several months later, when all seemed quiet on the school front, Dr. John Provinse and I went to lunch with an official from the National Archives. We turned over the educational records from all the centers, everything in good order and all students accounted for.

Questions for Discussion

1. What similarities and differences existed between the experiences of the Japanese American students who were incarcerated in the War Relocation Authority camps and the American Indian students who were educated under the supervision of the Bureau of Indian Affairs?

2. What were some of the contradictions that the Japanese American students experienced while being educated in a segregated environment?

3. Why did the U.S. government treat Japanese Americans differently from German Americans or Italian Americans, whose countries of origin were also at war with the United States during the same time?

The Struggle for Equal Educational Opportunity: 1954–1980

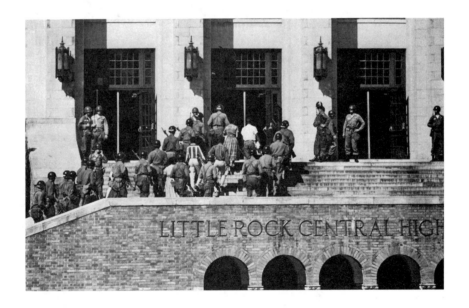

At the desk where I sit, I have learned one great truth. The answer for all our national problems—the answer for all the problems of the world—comes down to a single word. That word is "education."

—Lyndon B. Johnson
Brown University, September 28, 1964

In the mid-20th century the unequal educational opportunities afforded minorities, the poor, immigrants, females, and those with disabilities were part and parcel of an education system that "placed most power in the hands of prosperous, white, male leaders born in the United States who tended to assume the correctness of their own culture and policies" (Tyack & Cuban, 1995, p. 22). In the 1950s, however, the segregated, ill-served, underserved, and nonserved began to challenge the status quo. They pressured state and federal governments and turned increasingly to the courts in pursuit of equity. Their victories were seen not only in increased educational access for Blacks, Hispanics, Asian Americans, those with disabilities, and females, but also in state school finance reforms designed to reduce the inequities between rich and poor districts. The combination of legislation and litigation in the 1970s also brought a much more diversified and culturally responsible curriculum to the schools, colleges, and universities. Special education, immigrant education, bilingual education, and compensatory education programs were expanded, and new programs in ethnic and gender studies begun. At the same time, Native Americans were able to improve their educational experience and achieve a greater say in the governance and education of their people.

These gains did not come easy or without serious costs. The struggle to desegregate the public schools, colleges, and universities met with stiff resistance, even violence. Violence, demonstrations, and other forms of protest were also common on college campuses in the 1960s and 1970s in protest of the Vietnam War and issues of social injustice.

While the schools were serving as the backdrop for much of the civil rights movement, the federal government looked to the schools to assume a key role in another major move to transform American society—the War on Poverty. The War on Poverty was one of the largest domestic programs in our nation's history and was aimed at the 35 million Americans living in poverty and plagued by under- and unemployment. A number of education initiatives were enacted to expand vocational and technical training, preschool readiness for disadvantaged children, and compensatory education. Also adopted was legislation providing direct federal aid to institutions of higher education, as well as scholarships and loans to college students.

In the 1970s frustration with what some considered the extremes in the schools and the largess of the government helped bring in Republican administrations that had a different view of the role of government. Many of the War on Poverty initiatives begun during the Kennedy and Johnson administrations were reduced or eliminated, and administrative and judicial support for enforcement of civil rights waned. As the 1970s ended, education critics were blaming the excesses of the 1960s for the perceived failure of the schools and calling for a return to basics.

The Civil Rights Movement

Throughout their history, Americans had considered a good education to be the vehicle for upward mobility and a hallmark of the American democratic tradition. In reality, however, many young people in America received little or no education or an education that was dramatically unequal and inferior to that received by the majority population. For example, in 1950, 72% of children with disabilities were not enrolled in school (Anderson, 2001).

As the parents of minority children, children with disabilities, and female children became more and more aware of the unequal educational opportunities their children experienced, campaigns to obtain better opportunities became the centerpiece of the larger crusade for civil and political equality. Lacking, for the most part, political or economic influence, "getting the best education possible for their children motivated ordinary citizens to show extraordinary grit, courage, and endurance, challenging Jim Crow and other legal and customary forms of racial, ethnic, gender, and disability subordination" (Anderson, 2001, p. 127). Although the discussion of the civil rights movement begins with Blacks, perhaps because the basic vision of what was wrong was most visible in the history of Blacks in America, the general principles of the movement were later applied to advancing the rights of other racial and ethnic groups, women, and those with disabilities.

School Desegregation

The schools became a stage for much of the drama of the civil rights movement. The 1954 landmark school desegregation decision in *Brown v. Board of Education of Topeka* served as a "major catalyst" in efforts to address the inequities in public education (Tyack & Cuban, 1995). The *Brown* decision, presented as a Primary Source Reading for this chapter, was a reversal of the 1898 Supreme Court decision in *Plessey v. Ferguson*, which had said that separate facilities for Blacks and Whites were not unconstitutional as long as they were equal. Since the 1930s the NAACP had traveled throughout the South gathering evidence that Black schools, always separate, were never equal. In 1954, the year when the *Brown* decision was rendered, per pupil expenditures for Black students in the South were only 60% of those for White students (Patterson, 2001). By the early 1950s the NAACP was ready to take its challenge of separate but equal to the United States Supreme Court (Anderson, 2001). The case, filed as *Brown v. Board of Education of Topeka, Kansas*, a consolidation of four other cases, was argued by Thurgood Marshall of the NAACP Legal Defense Fund. The decision, delivered by Chief Justice Earl Warren on May 17, 1954, said that

> To separate [Black children] from others of similar age and qualifications because of their race generates a feeling of inferiority as to their status in the community that may affect their hearts and minds in a way never to be undone. . . . We conclude that in the field of public education the doctrine of "separate but equal" has no place. Separate educational facilities are inherently unequal. (p. 468)

Recognizing the importance of any order they might make, as well as the uniqueness of each community, and that states would require time to come into compliance with its ruling, the Court set no rigid schedule for compliance but said the states should proceed "with all deliberate speed." School districts were charged with the responsibility of creating desegregation plans under the supervision of the closest federal district court.

At the time of the *Brown* decision, 17 states and the District of Columbia required segregation in the public schools by law (*de jure*); in four others (Arizona, Kansas, New Mexico, and Wyoming) it was permitted. The educational response to the *Brown* decision varied. In the so-called border states the response was mostly calm, and over the next several months a number of districts in Oklahoma, Texas, Kentucky, West Virginia, Missouri, Tennessee, and Arkansas began to integrate (Manchester, 1975). But in the Deep South the decision was met with open hostility, massive resistance, and vows of defiance. Georgia governor Tallmadge vowed that "the people of Georgia . . . will fight for the right . . . to manage their own affairs . . . [and will] map a program to insure continued and permanent segregation of the races" (Manchester, 1975, p. 736). Georgia then passed a bill making it a felony to spend public funds to support an integrated school. That same year the Mississippi legislature passed a state constitutional amendment allowing the legislature to abolish public schools and provide tuition grants for attendance at private schools. The next year the Mississippi legislature made it against the law for a White person to attend a racially integrated school (Watras, 1997).

Southern resistance was not limited to legislative action. Throughout the South, White citizens' councils were formed to resist school integration. Harsh words turned rapidly to violent racial incidents. Black children attempting to attend White schools were subjected to verbal and physical harassment. Politicians and political candidates seemed determined to outdo each other in demonstrating opposition to school integration.

Perhaps the most dramatic physical confrontation in the struggle to integrate the public schools, and certainly the one that got the most media attention, took place in Little Rock, Arkansas. In September of 1957, fighting an uphill battle for reelection, Governor Orval Faubus sought to strengthen his position among his right-wing constituents by using the Arkansas National Guard to block the enrollment of nine Black students in Central High School on the pretext that violence had been threatened. Later, violence did erupt, and evidence suggests that to vindicate himself Faubus was a behind-the-scene instigator (Manchester, 1975). To enforce a court order that the children be allowed to register, President Eisenhower federalized the Arkansas National Guard and sent in the regular army to ensure that the students were safely enrolled.

 For Your Reflection and Analysis

Over 50 years have passed since Brown v. Board of Education of Topeka. *How much longer will it take to achieve full equity and the end of segregation in the United States? Explain.*

The physical violence associated with attempts to desegregate education was not limited to the public schools but accompanied attempts to integrate institutions of higher education in the South. As in Little Rock, on at least two occasions—in 1962 at the University of Mississippi and in 1963 at the University of Alabama—

federal troops had to be used to enforce integration. Also in both cases the governor of the state was attempting to block the integration. The incident at the University of Mississippi involved the death of two people and the injury of numerous others and was one of the most violent episodes in the history of the integration of education.

The saga began when James Meredith, a nine-year veteran of the air force applied for admission to the University of Mississippi. A protracted legal battle following his rejection ended with the Supreme Court ordering the university to admit Meredith. Once again a governor, this time Mississippi Governor Ross Barnett, tried to stand in the way. After four failed attempts by federal marshals to register Meredith and avoid violence, early one Sunday evening in June 1962 federal marshals again escorted Meredith to the Oxford campus to register. That same evening President Kennedy went on national television to explain the situation and to appeal to the students to remain calm and obey the law. But it was not to be. In the violent confrontation that followed, a French correspondent and an Oxford spectator were killed and 166 marshals and 16 national guardsmen were injured. The regular army arrived 5 hours later and, in the process of fighting their way to the campus, 40 of them were also hit by missiles or shotgun blasts. Then, shortly before 8 o'clock the next morning, three marshals accompanied Meredith to the "battered Lyceum. There, at last, he was admitted by a Robert Byron Ellis, the stony-faced registrar." (Manchester, 1975, p. 951)

The Carrot and the Stick: The Civil Rights Act of 1964 and the Elementary and Secondary Education Act of 1965

A decade after *Brown*, school desegregation had made limited progress. Initially, districts attempted to accomplish desegregation by adopting freedom of choice plans. In most instances these plans had little impact on the level of desegregation, and 98% of Black children still attended all-Black schools. However, the civil rights movement that *Brown* had triggered was gaining momentum on other fronts. Freedom rides, sit-ins, boycotts, and other forms of nonviolent protest both appealed to the national conscience and focused national attention on a movement that would not be denied. President John F. Kennedy pressed for the passage of a federal civil rights statute that would end segregation in public facilities, attack discrimination in employment, and require nondiscriminatory practices in programs and institutions receiving federal funds. Five days after his assassination, his successor, Lyndon B. Johnson, appeared before Congress and sought its passage, declaring it the most fitting honor of his memory. Seven months later Congress passed, and on July 2 President Johnson signed, the Civil Rights Act of 1964. The act became one of the most significant pieces of social legislation in U.S. history.

The Civil Rights Act served to further involve the federal government in the activities of the schools. Title VI of the act prohibits discrimination against students on the basis of race, color, or national origin in all institutions receiving federal funds. Title VII forbids discrimination in employment based on race, color, religion, national origin, and as of 1972, sex. Title IV of the act authorized the withholding of federal funds from any institution or agency violating the law. It also authorized the U.S. attorney general to take legal action to achieve school desegregation and provided federal grants for in-service training and technical assistance to school districts to encourage voluntary desegregation or to help districts undergoing court-ordered desegregation.

Title IV of the Civil Rights Act authorized a survey to determine the availability of equal educational opportunities for all peoples in public institutions in the United States. The survey was directed by James Coleman of Johns Hopkins University, and the report was made to Congress in less than 2 years. The now famous Coleman Report, as it became known, seemed to undermine compensatory education by its finding that for most student populations there seemed to be little relationship between school inputs (e.g., expenditures per pupil, class size, number of library books, and facilities) and student achievement. Rather, the single most important variable was the educational and social class background of the family, and the second most important variable was the educational and social class background of the other children in the school.

Although lending little support to compensatory education, as a result of its finding that poor Black students achieved higher in integrated schools, the report provided support for integration, including the controversial practice of busing to achieve racial balance. Subsequent analysis has suggested that the determining factor is really students' socioeconomic status, not their racial or ethnic identity. Nevertheless, the Coleman Report generated considerable discussion over the next 2 or 3 decades concerning the extent to which schools make a difference in student achievement or whether it is too late by the time the child gets to school.

The passage of the Civil Rights Act of 1964 was followed the next year by passage of the Elementary and Secondary Education Act of 1965 (ESEA). As described by President Johnson, the ESEA represented "a major new commitment of the federal government to quality and equality in the schooling that we afford our young people." The passage of the Civil Rights Act and the ESEA, in combination with the growing intolerance of the Supreme Court to the resistance to the *Brown* decision, created a "carrot-and-stick" mechanism that dramatically increased the pace of school desegregation. The carrot was the increased federal support provided by the ESEA, while the stick was the Civil Rights Act. Federal revenues to education increased from $2.0 billion in 1965–66 to $3.2 billion in 1970 and to $4.9 billion in 1974.

The courts also became more proactive in moving the pace of integration. In 1964 the Supreme Court ruled that the time for "all deliberate speed" had run out (*Griffin v. County School Board*). In 1968 the Court said that if freedom of choice plans were not working, other strategies must be used (*Green v. County School Board of New Kent County*). These strategies could include forced busing, pairing of schools, consolidating schools, altering attendance zones, reassigning teachers, and using racial quotas (*Swann v. Charlotte-Mecklenburg Board of Education*, 1971).

At the same time the courts were dealing with *de jure* segregation in the South, they were increasing being asked to address the *de facto* segregation that existed in many communities outside the South. In these communities, state law did not mandate segregation, but local zoning ordinances, housing restrictions, attendance zones, gerrymandering, or other deliberate official actions were designed to segregate minorities. In fact, by the early 1970s Black students in the South were more integrated than those in the North or West.

 For Your Reflection and Analysis

Give examples of de facto *segregation of Blacks and other minorities in education and the larger society.*

An early attempt by the Office of Civil Rights to pressure school districts into desegregating by withholding federal funds as authorized under Title IV had ended in failure. At the time, 1965, Black students in Chicago were attending segregated and seriously overcrowded schools. Many were on shortened double shifts and as a result received less instructional time. Following an investigation, the U. S. Office of Education announced that it was withholding $32 million in funds to the city's schools. However, pressure from Chicago's powerful Mayor Richard J. Daley led President Johnson to urge the Office of Education to settle the dispute. In the end, even though the school board basically did nothing, the federal funds were released.

The entry of the courts into districts with *de facto* segregation was more aggressive. In a case involving Denver, Colorado, *Keyes v. School District No. 1* (1973), the Supreme Court held that when official actions had a segregative intent, they were just as illegal as *de jure* segregation. Moreover, the Court required the school district to desegregate Mexican American as well as Black students. The Court also held that proof of intent to segregate in one part of a district is sufficient to find the district to be segregated and to warrant a districtwide remedy. However, the next year, when a federal judge ordered across-district busing (busing Detroit students to the suburbs and busing suburban students into the city), the Supreme Court ruled that the scope of the remedy could not exceed the scope of the violation and that the suburban school districts were not responsible for the segregated condition of the Detroit schools (*Milliken v. Bradley*, 1974) Continuing with the same rationale, in a subsequent *de facto* case the Court held that the scope of the desegregation remedy cannot exceed the impact of the segregatory practice (*Dayton Board of Education v. Brinkman*, 1977). See Table 9.1 for a summary of Supreme Court desegregation cases.

The actions of the courts and the carrot-and-stick strategy seemed to work, especially in the southern states: By 1972, 91% of southern Black children attended integrated schools. The magnitude of this accomplishment cannot be overstated. As Harvard desegregation researcher Gary Orfield (in Bernard & Mondale, 2001b) noted, during a period of less than 10 years "we took a society that was like South Africa, an apartheid society where everything was defined by race . . . and we made it the most integrated part of the United States . . . an accomplishment very few democracies have ever done in peacetime" (p. 149).

However, despite the apparent movement forward in desegregation, in 1969 the Justice Department of newly elected President Richard Nixon announced that it would no longer withhold federal funds for failure to desegregate but instead would pressure compliance with litigation. That same year the Office of Civil Rights cut back dramatically on the number of compliance reviews, and within 5 years was conducting no reviews (Watras, 1997). Throughout the 1970s the courts had continued to exercise broad powers in ordering desegregation remedies, and significant desegregation was achieved in southern school districts and a number of large, metropolitan school districts outside the South. However, by and large the Nixon administration did not support the court actions. Four retirements on the Supreme Court gave Nixon the opportunity to appoint more conservative justices. By the end of the 1970s attempts to integrate began to slow in some areas, and in many areas there was a drift toward the resegregation discussed in chapter 10. This resegregation involved not only Blacks but other minorities, primarily non-English-speaking Hispanics.

TABLE 9.1 Selected U.S. Supreme Court Cases Related to Desegregation in the Public Schools

Case	Decision
Brown v. Board of Education of Topeka (1954)	The doctrine of separate but equal in educ... of the Fourteenth Amendment.
Green v. County School Board of New Kent County (1968)	Local school boards should immediately take whatever steps are necessary to achieve a unitary system.
Swann v. Charlotte-Mecklenburg Board of Education (1971)	Transportation of students to opposite-race schools is permissible to achieve desegregation.
Keyes v. School District No. 1 (Denver) (1973)	Proof of intent to segregate in one part of a district is sufficient to find the district to be segregated and to warrant a district-wide remedy. For purposes of defining a segregated school, Blacks and Hispanics may be considered together.
Milliken v. Bradley (1974)	In devising judicial remedies for desegregation, the scope of the desegregation remedy (in this case, a cross-district remedy) cannot exceed the scope of the violation.
Dayton Board of Education v. Brinkman (1977)	Judicially mandated desegregation plans cannot exceed the impact of the segregatory practices.
Board of Education of Oklahoma City Public Schools v. Dowell (1991)	Desegregation decrees are not intended to operate in perpetuity, and can be dissolved when a district has made a good faith effort to comply and to the extent practical has eliminated the vestiges of past discrimination.
Freeman v. Pitts (1992)	Lower courts can relinquish supervision of a school district under desegregation decree in incremental stages before full compliance has been achieved in every area of school operations.
Missouri v. Jenkins (1995)	Once the effects of legally imposed segregation have been eliminated, the goal of desegregation plans need not be to maintain racial balance or to attain academic goals unrelated to the effects of *de jure* segregation, but to return control to state and local authorities. Any resegregation of neighborhood schools that may result is not unconstitutional.

Source: Webb, L. Dean, Metha, Arlene, & Jordan, K. Forbis. (2003). *Foundations of American education* (4th ed.) © 2003. Reprinted by permission of Pearson Education, Inc., Upper Saddle River, NJ.

Education and the War on Poverty

In the early 1960s large numbers of Americans became aware that at least one quarter of the population had been bypassed by the postwar prosperity and lived in dire poverty. Books, reports, and high-impact media coverage such as Edward R. Murrow's documentary on migrant farm workers, "Harvest of Shame," brought a flood of interest in the elimination of poverty. As a result, beginning in a modest way by President John F. Kennedy and elevated to "war" status by President Lyndon Johnson, the federal government set out to wage a War on Poverty. In an effort to win the war, legislation was passed to expand welfare services, subsidize low-income housing, improve health care, and improve inner-city schools.

Education was viewed as key to the elimination of poverty. Poor children as well as those of certain minority groups, it was noted, often failed to achieve. In the optimistic view of many politicians, educators, and social scientists, the "cultural deprivation" (i.e., lack of middle-class attitudes and incomes) of the poor was attributable to a lack of education; if the poor were provided the skills and education for employment, they could achieve middle-class economic and social status and break the "cycle of poverty" (Zigler & Valentine, 1979).

The War on Poverty on the education front was waged by a number of initiatives. The Vocational Education Act of 1963 more than quadrupled federal funds for vocational education. The purpose of the act was to enhance occupational training opportunities for persons of all ages through the provision of financial assistance to vocational and technical programs in high schools and nonbaccalaureate postsecondary institutions. The Manpower Development and Training Act, enacted the same year, was directed at providing retraining for unemployed adults.

The Economic Opportunity Act (EOA) of 1964 established the Job Corps to train youth between 16 and 21 in basic literacy skills and for employment. It also established a type of domestic Peace Corps, Volunteers in Service to America (VISTA). Perhaps the most popular and controversial component of the EOA was Project Head Start, a program aimed at disadvantaged children 3 to 5 years old who would not normally attend preschool or kindergarten. President Johnson called Head Start a "landmark," not only in education but in "the maturity of our democracy." Head Start, he foretold, would "strike at the basic cause of poverty" by addressing it at its beginnings—the disadvantaged preschool child. As the name suggests, the intent of the program was to give disadvantaged children a head start in the educational race so that once in school they might be on equal terms with children from nondisadvantaged homes

> *For Your Reflection and Analysis*
>
> *What evidence suggests that compensatory programs such as Head Start have been successful?*

The centerpiece of the education legislation enacted as part of the War on Poverty was the Elementary and Secondary Education Act of 1965. The most far-reaching piece of federal education legislation to date, the ESEA allocated over $1 billion in federal funds annually to education, with no matching requirements. The ESEA included five major sections or titles. The largest, receiving about 80% of the funds, was Title I, which provided assistance to local school districts for the education of children from low-income families. The compensatory education programs funded through Title I were intended to maintain the educational progress begun in Head Start. Title I was to become the major education component of the War on Poverty. Other sections of the ESEA provided funds for library resources, textbooks, and instructional materials; education research and development centers; and strengthening state departments of education. The act was expanded in 1966 and 1967 to include programs for Native American children, children of migrant workers, the handicapped (Title VI), and children with limited English-speaking ability (Title VII).

Another significant act passed during that same session of Congress was the Higher Education Act of 1965, which provided direct assistance to institutions of higher education for facilities construction and library and instructional improvement. The act also provided for the first time in American history federal scholarships to students, termed "Equal Opportunity Grants." It also authorized low-interest, federally insured loans to qualified students and established a National Teacher Corps to recruit young people into teaching. The year 1965 also saw the establishment of the National Foundation of the Arts and the Humanities to promote and encourage production, dissemination, and scholarship in the arts and humanities.

Congress continued to pass legislation affecting education during the remainder of the Johnson presidency, including the Educational Professions Development Act in 1967. In 1968, the last year of Johnson's Great Society, the Vocational Education Act was expanded and its funding authorization doubled. That same year the Higher Education Act was amended to consolidate previous legislation and added a number of new program initiatives.

Between the years 1963 and 1969 Congress passed more than two dozen major pieces of legislation affecting education. These laws dramatically increased federal involvement in education and provided vast sums of money for elementary and secondary schools, vocational schools, and colleges and universities. In 1963–64 federal funds for elementary and secondary schools totaled almost $900 million. By 1968–69 this had skyrocketed to $3 billion, and the federal government's share of the financing of education had risen from 4.4% to 8.8%. Perhaps equally as important as the increased funding was the shift in federal emphasis from identifying the gifted, which had marked the 1950s, to a concern for the disadvantaged. Concern had shifted from the Cold War to the War on Poverty.

While the War on Poverty was being waged, if not war, conflict was also taking place on other fronts as schools became a battleground in the struggle to attain equal rights for minorities, females, and the disabled.

Expanding the Rights of Language Minority Youth

Despite the fact that in many communities in the United States a significant portion of the student population had limited English-speaking ability (LESA), instruction in many of the schools in these communities was given in English only. In the 1960s the growing Hispanic population in the Southwest turned its attention to this problem. Increasing pressure from educators, parents, and special interest groups led Congress in 1968 to amend the ESEA to add the Title VII Bilingual Education Program, also called the Bilingual Education Act (BEA). The BEA was the first federal recognition that LESA students have special needs that must be addressed if they are to have equal educational opportunities. The BEA provided federal funds in the form of competitive grants to school districts to design and implement bilingual education programs for LESA students. However, despite the prospect of federal funds, many school districts did little or nothing to serve their non-English- or limited-English-speaking students.

The major impetus for expanding the educational opportunities of language minority students was provided by the 1974 U.S. Supreme Court decision in *Lau v.*

Nichols. Lau was filed on behalf of the 1,800 limited-English-speaking Chinese students in San Francisco who attended schools that provided instruction only in English. The plaintiffs alleged a violation of both the due process clause of the Fourteenth Amendment of the U.S. Constitution and Title VI of the Civil Rights Act of 1964. Although not ruling on the Fourteenth Amendment claim, the Court did find that the district was in violation of Title VI. According to the Court, "there is no equality of treatment merely by providing students with the same facilities, textbooks, teachers, and curriculum; for students who do not understand English are effectively foreclosed from any meaningful education" (p. 566). The Court ruled that schools must provide assistance to LESA students, but it did not specify whether Title VI requires bilingual education, remedial English instruction, or any other specific instructional model.

The *Lau* decision was effectively extended to all students and all school districts, not just those receiving federal funds, by Title II of the Education Amendments of 1974, which said that language barriers were to be overcome with instructional programs. Many districts were not prepared, financially or technically, to comply with the *Lau* decision or Title II. To assist the many districts affected by *Lau*, in 1974 the Bilingual Education Act was amended to define a bilingual education program and identify its goals; establish regional centers to provide technical support and training; and fund capacity-building efforts of school districts to expand their curricula, staff, and research for bilingual programs. Bilingual education was defined as a program that provides instruction in English and in the native language of the students to allow the student to progress effectively through the education system. The goal of the program is to prepare LESA students to participate in the regular classroom as rapidly as possible.

For Your Reflection and Analysis

What key issues continue to be argued concerning bilingual education for limited-English-speaking students?

Support for bilingual education grew throughout the 1970s. Within a year of the *Lau* decision the number of states providing funding for bilingual education increased from 2 to 11. In 1978 the BEA was amended again to broaden the definition of eligible students from LESA to limited-English-proficiency (LEP) students and provide additional support to bilingual education through competitive grants to school districts and training grants to colleges and universities. However, as discussed in chapter 10, in the 1980s bilingual education became a politically controversial issue when the Reagan administration opposed bilingual education and supported the English immersion-type programs that had been used with earlier immigrant groups. In the meantime, the issue of language, in this case the preservation of language, was a major consideration in the education of Native Americans.

Indian Education and the Drive for Self-Determination

While litigation and legislation were expanding the educational opportunities afforded Black and language minority students, Native Americans were attempting to gain greater control and assume greater responsibility for the education of their youth as well as to restore native language and culture to the curriculum. During the Kennedy and Johnson administrations of the 1960s federal Indian policy was directed at creating programs that would reduce the dependency of Indian communities on federal aid and at the same time reverse the termination policy begun in the years immediately following World War II. The goal of the termination policy was to end federal obligations to Indians and their communities and was supported by individuals from across the social and political spectrum. Some people saw the termination of federal involvement as being consistent with the civil rights movement; others believed that previous assimilations programs, including the paternalistic programs of the New Deal, had failed and that it was time to get the federal government out of Indian affairs and save the taxpayers' money (Clarkin, 2001). Despite what were in some cases positive motives, the termination policy, which in effect represented a "sink or swim" approach to assimilation, had some very negative consequences. Indians would be freed from federal supervision and control, but at the same time they would lose any sovereign rights they possessed, and Indian lands would be removed from trust status.

Most Indian communities did not support the termination policy but did support the move toward self-determination. Public and political support for self-determination grew as a result of increased Indian activism in the 1960s and, perhaps more important, activities that followed the presentation of the report of the U.S. Special Senate Sub-Committee on Indian Education, *Indian Education: A National Tragedy—A National Challenge* (1969), also known as the Kennedy Report. The report presented the results of an in-depth study of the BIA and the public school education of Native Americans; the report on the failure of the public schools is presented as a Primary Source Reading for this chapter. The opening statement of the report began what was to be an indictment of federal policy: "The dominant policy of the Federal Government toward the American Indian has been one of coercive assimilation . . . [which] has had disastrous effects on the education of Indian children." After a lengthy and very negative litany of failures the report made 60 recommendations. Among them were increased funding of Indian education and the expansion of promising programs; the inclusion of Native American language, culture, and history in the curriculum; increased involvement of Native American parents in the education of their children; and that no services to Native Americans be terminated without their consent.

President Nixon supported the recommendations of the Kennedy Report in a special message to Congress on Indian affairs in July of 1970:

> It is long past time that the Indian policies of the Federal government begin to recognize and build upon the capacities and insights of the Indian people. Both as a matter of justice and as a matter of enlightened social policy, we must begin to act on the basis of what the Indians themselves have long been telling us. The time has come to break decisively with the past and to create the conditions for a new era in which the Indian future is determined by Indian acts and Indian decisions.

Self-determination came closer to reality with the passage of the Indian Education Act of 1972 (IEA) and the Indian Self-Determination and Educational Assistance Act (ISEAA) in 1975. The IEA greatly increased parental and community participation

For Your Reflection and Analysis

How have the Indian Education Act of 1972 and the Indian Self-Determination and Educational Assistance Act of 1975 improved educational opportunities for Native Americans?

in planning and directing aid received by public schools. It also established the Office of Indian Education within the USOE. One important feature of the IEA was that it covered the urban and eastern Indians, who had historically been ignored by federal programs (Szasz, 1999). Although very limited compared to the recommendations of the Kennedy Report, the IEA was considered a major victory for Indian people (Szasz, 1999).

The ISEAA went further than the IEA, which had affected only students in the public schools. The ISEAA focused on giving Native American families and tribes greater participation in the governance and education of Native American peoples and provided for takeover of the operation of BIA schools.

As discussed in more detail in chapter 10, the victories of the 1970s promised Native Americans freedom of control over Indian education programs. However, the Indian policy set in motion by Ronald Reagan signaled that any celebration was premature.

Expanding Educational Opportunities for Mexican Americans

Mexican Americans presently and historically have been the largest Hispanic group in the United States. During the 1940s there was a large migration of Hispanics from Puerto Rico and, beginning in 1959, from Cuba. This was followed in the 1960s and 1970s by Central and South Americans fleeing economic and political instability. Nevertheless, the number of these Hispanic groups remains small compared to the number of Mexican Americans.

The Mexican American population grew significantly in the 1940s as a result of increased immigration. During World War II almost a quarter of a million Mexican workers were recruited under an agreement between the Mexican and U.S. governments to work as farm and railroad workers. The *bracero* (hired hand) program was scheduled to end when the war was over, but pressure from large growers who needed the cheap labor was successful in getting the program reinstated in 1947 and extended several more times. In 1964, in large part because of the attention paid by religious groups, labor organizations, and civil rights groups to the documented abuses of the Mexican laborers, the program was allowed to expire. Immigration records indicate that 4.8 million Mexican workers participated in the program, and an estimated 8% of them ultimately settled in the United States (Garcia, 2002). However, the end of the bracero program did not stop the flow of Mexican immigrants, both legal and illegal. In the 1970s the number of legal Mexican immigrants was more than twice what it had been during the 1950s bracero decade (640,000 vs. 300,000).

Like other immigrant groups, Mexican Americans had actively sought schooling in the United States. However, despite the fact that over the course of the 20th century they had received increased access to the public schools, the access was to the segregated schools, schools that were usually of inferior quality, with larger classes, taught by less prepared teachers, and with reduced budgets. Despite the increased access, a large portion of Mexican American students did not attend school, largely because of poverty, the mobility associated with rural employment, and discriminatory education policies (San Miguel, 1997). Some school districts openly denied admission to migrant children. Others operated schools on a shortened school day to allow the students to work the fields for part of the day (Gonzalez, 1990).

> *For Your Reflection and Analysis*
>
> *Should assimilation be a goal for everyone? Why or why not?*

The education provided Hispanic students, like that provided Native American students, was designed to promote, if not force, assimilation and deculturalization. Instruction in the segregated schools was in English, and the use of Spanish was forbidden, even on the playground. In this atmosphere many students dropped out of school, and because compulsory attendance of Mexican Americans was not enforced, the overall result was a significantly lower level of educational attainment than that of the Anglo population.

Until right after World War II the segregation of Hispanics was permitted in California and other states. Then, in 1944 Gonzalo Mendez moved his family to a farm he was to run for its Japanese owners who were in an internment camp. When the Westminister School District refused to enroll his children, he joined other parents in suing Westminister and three other school districts. In 1946 the U.S. district court rejected the school district argument that the segregation was not based on race but the need to provide special instruction to Hispanic children (a defense that had been successfully used by the Del Rio School District in Texas in 1930). In fact, the court said, the only special instruction these students needed was to learn English, and this was actually impeded by segregation (*Mendez et al. v. Westminister School District*, 1947). Accordingly, the court determined that segregation was illegal because it had no basis in state law or educational need. Although some, including the NAACP and its attorney, Thurgood Marshall, who had filed an *amicus curiae* brief in the case, were disappointed that the court did not overturn "separate but equal," the decision did have a broad impact. Encouraged by the decision, the segregation of Mexican Americans was challenged in the courts in other states, and within 2 years *de jure* segregation had been overturned in Texas and Arizona.

However, despite these and other court victories the desegregation of Hispanic children was far from being achieved, and equality of opportunity was still an unrealized dream. By the 1960s, increasing frustration with the educational inequities and biased Eurocentric curricula led to an education revolt among Mexican American young people. Encouraged by the student rights and civil rights movements, they employed many of their techniques.

In high schools they employed walkouts, sometimes called "blowouts," and boycotts to promote their demands for educational quality and equality, more relevant social science courses, bilingual and bicultural education, more raza teachers, counselors, and school board members.

At colleges and universities various techniques were employed: mass protest demonstrations, sit-ins in administration offices and other direct-confrontation tactics—usually accompanied by emotional rhetoric and sometimes attacks on university property. Some faculty members joined the students in demands for incorporating

The Chicano movement sought to improve the economic and educational condition of Mexican Americans.

Chicano history and culture into social sciences courses, admitting more raza students, creating Chicano studies programs, and increasing Chicano representation of faculties and governing boards. (Meier & Ribera, 1993, p. 220)

 For Your Reflection and Analysis

Why did the Chicano movement last for only a decade? What are some of the positive results of the movement that still exist today?

The Chicano movement, sometimes referred to as *el movimiento*, lasted for about a decade, from 1965 to 1975, and had a major impact on high school and college campuses in the Southwest. Chicano studies were introduced, the number of Chicano faculty and staff increased, and in higher education for the first time serious efforts were made to recruit and retain Chicano students. More broadly, the attention that the Chicano movement turned on education served to emphasize its importance and provided encouragement for young Chicanos to continue their education. The results were evident throughout the 1970s in the lowering of the dropout rate and the increased levels of educational attainment of the Hispanic population.

The Education of Asian Americans

The First to Come: Chinese Americans

The first Asian group to arrive in the United States in any significant numbers was the Chinese. As their numbers increased, so did the discrimination and hostility they faced; the dangers presented by the "yellow peril" screamed from newspaper headlines. Under U.S. immigration policies Chinese and other Asian immigrants could not become naturalized citizens. In many states they could not own land.

Except for a brief period (1859–1871) when San Francisco operated a segregated public school for Chinese, the only education most Chinese students received was at missionary or Chinese language schools. However, neither of these institutions satisfied the desires of Chinese parents for an American public education for their children. Six years after the closing of the Chinese public school, 1,300 Chinese Americans petitioned the California legislature for separate public schools. The petitioners noted that although they paid taxes to support education, 3,000 Chinese children were being denied a public education. Their petition was denied as was the subsequent attempt to enroll 8-year-old Mami Tape in the Spring Valley School in San Francisco in September of 1884. The state superintendent of public instruction supported the board's denial, noting that the California constitution declared Chinese to be "dangerous to the well-being of the state." However, in subsequent court action the California Supreme Court agreed with a lower court decision that to deny Mami, an American citizen, entrance to the public school would be a violation of the Fourteenth Amendment (*Tape v. Hurley*, 1885). In anticipation of the court's ruling the school district persuaded the legislature to pass a bill allowing school districts to establish segregated schools for "Mongolians," which they did (Wollenberg, 1976). Typically these schools were inferior to those attended by White students.

In some districts, Chinese and other Asian students were allowed to attend White schools. However, they were often segregated in different rooms or on different floors. In the classroom the special language needs of students were largely ignored; schools were reluctant to employ Asian American teachers and attempted to force mastery of the English language (Weinberg, 1997). In 1902 the practice of segregation was legalized by the courts of California by the *Wong Him v. Callahan* decision, which said that it was not unconstitutional to restrict attendance by Chinese students to segregated Chinese schools as long as the schools offered the same advantages as other schools.

Following World War I the rigid policy of segregation began to break down as parents became more persistent and Chinese students were regularly admitted to public high schools. However, elementary schools remained highly segregated, in large part because of housing patterns and attendance zones. Even in the years after World War II, when many middle-class Chinese moved out of segregated neighborhoods and into integrated neighborhoods, schools in the many ethnic neighborhoods (Chinatowns) remained basically segregated. Instruction in these schools was typically in English only, leading to the *Lau* case previously discussed.

Japanese Americans

At the same time that overt discrimination against Chinese children was decreasing, it was being replaced by discrimination against the Japanese. Because of tight restrictions by the Japanese government during the 19th century few Japanese migrated to America. Loosening of these restrictions in the last decade of the century led to increased immigration (see Table 9.2). As with other immigrant groups, as their numbers increased, so did the racism they experienced.

TABLE 9.2 Chinese and Japanese Immigration, 1851–1950

Year	China	Japan
1851–1860	41,397	n.a.
1861–1870	64,301	186
1871–1880	123,201	149
1881–1890	61,711	2,270
1891–1900	14,799	25,942
1901–1910	20,605	129,697
1911–1920	21,278	83,837
1921–1930	29,907	33,462
1931–1940	4,928	1,948
1941–1950	16,709	1,555

Source: U.S. Bureau of Citizenship and Immigration Services. (2004). Retrieved July 30, 2004 from USCIS Website: USCIS.gov/graphics/shared/aboutus/statistics/imm98excel/Table2_2xls.

In 1905 the San Francisco board of education passed a resolution requiring Japanese students, along with Korean and Chinese students, to leave their neighborhood schools and attend the segregated Oriental Public School. Vigorous protests by the Japanese community ensued, including a diplomatic protest that their treatment violated the favored nation treaty between the United States and Japan. President Roosevelt was able to resolve the potential international crisis and to persuade the school board to rescind the resolution by agreeing to prohibit the immigration of Japanese from Hawaii, Mexico, and Canada.

Roosevelt's gentleman's agreement neither solved the problem of Japanese immigration nor curtailed efforts to segregate Japanese students. In 1921 the California legislature amended the state education code to specifically name Japanese as a group subject to segregation. However, by the end of the decade only four districts had established separate oriental schools. In the remainder of the state about 30,000 nisei (second generation) Japanese children attended integrated schools. Although still subject to discrimination, they achieved so well and received so many honors that some White parents objected (Wollenberg, 1976).

After the Japanese bombing of Pearl Harbor, some individuals in the War Department were concerned that Japanese along the West coast might have a primary allegiance to Japan and represent a threat to the interests of the United States. They concluded that it was a military necessity to move these Japanese to the interior where they could be relocated. About two thirds of the approximately 110,000 persons subsequently relocated were American born, and 25,000 were of school age. The hastily constructed camps, although surrounded by barbed wire and guarded by armed sentries, were intended to function as normal communities with hospitals, newspapers, movie theaters, and schools. The War Relocation Agency (WRA) operated both the camps (such as the one described in the second Primary Source Reading for Chapter 8) and the schools. The schools were designed using the concepts of progressive education as understood by the WRA. The goal of the schools was to "promote an understanding of American ideas, institutions, and practices," and their primary purpose was to prepare students for reabsorption into normal community life and provide them with an education that would permit them to return to schools outside the camps without loss of credit. The WRA insisted that the schools meet the minimum accreditation standards of the state in which they were located, and all camp high schools offered a college prep curriculum (Wollenberg, 1976). The schools met for 11 months a year, in part to make up for the time lost during relocation, and in part to keep the children occupied.

Despite the good intentions of the WRA, the camp schools were always short on supplies and equipment and were never able to hire enough certified teachers. However, they did keep public school life alive in the camps and did provide a link and avenue for return to life outside the barbed wire (Wollenberg, 1976). In fact, when the Japanese students did return to the public schools after the war, although there were some problems with readjustment, overall their assimilation proceeded well and they continued to excel academically. Beginning in 1942, nisei students whose education had been interrupted were allowed to resume or begin their college education at institutions outside California. Eventually an estimated 4,000 students were allowed to leave the camps for college (James, 1985).

By the second half of the 20th century most Japanese American children attended integrated schools. But, as with the Chinese, in some communities segregation continued, perpetuated in large part by residential housing patterns.

> *For Your Reflection and Analysis*
>
> *How do you explain the consistent high academic achievement of Asian American students compared to their non-Asian counterparts?*

Gender Equity in Education

As discussed throughout this text, historically females have not been permitted to participate fully in all aspects of American society and have not been afforded the same rights and educational opportunities as males. Winning the right to vote in 1920 did not change this. And, although the Civil Rights Act of 1964 prohibited overt discrimination in employment, many doors remained closed to women, and they were denied many opportunities. It was not surprising then that in the mid-1960s, taking their cue from the civil rights movement, a number of female organizations were formed to, as stated in the 1966 mission statement of the National Organization for Women (NOW), "take action to bring women to full participation in the mainstream of American society." In the same document, education was said to be "the key to effective participation in today's economy."

The promotion of sex equity—equal treatment and equal opportunity regardless of sex—was one of the major goals of the women's rights movement. What was hoped would be a major step in that direction was taken with the passage of Title IX of the Education Amendments of 1972. Title IX provided that "no person in the United States shall, on the basis of sex, be excluded from participation in, be denied the benefits of, or be subjected to discrimination under any education program or activity receiving federal financial assistance." This included both academic programs and interscholastic athletics.

Another victory in the movement to extend civil rights to women came in the same session of Congress when Title VII of the Civil Rights of 1964, which prohibited discrimination in employment, was extended to cover academic institutions. With the legal support of Title IX and Title VII, women brought political pressure on local school districts and colleges and universities to end sex discrimination in admissions and access to courses, extracurricular activities, instructional materials, counseling and counseling materials, employment, and policies and regulations governing the treatment of students and employees.

At the time of the passage of Title IX the problem of sexism, in and out of the schools, was familiar to most females, and many males, but it had not yet been labeled. In 1973 Frazier and Sadker published one of the first books to examine and document the differential treatment of female students. In *Sexism in School and Society*, Frazier and Sadker examined a variety of research on sexist practices in the school and society and found that those practices led to the loss of academic potential, self-esteem, and occupational potential, particularly for girls and women.

The attention Frazier, Sadker, and others brought to the harm done by sexism in schools, as well as the congressional testimony surrounding Title IX, were in-

Efforts to advance women's rights were an extension of the civil rights movement.

For Your Reflection and Analysis

In what ways did males benefit from Title IX?

strumental in the passage of the Women's Educational Equity Act of 1974 (WEEA). The WEEA was enacted to promote educational equity for girls and women, including those who experience multiple discrimination based on gender, race, ethnicity, national origin, disability, or age. WEEA's major impact was on curriculum and instruction; it sought to expand programs for females in math, science, computer science, and athletics, as well as guidance and counseling activities to encourage participation in these disciplines. WEEA also provided funds to help education agencies and institutions meet the requirements of Title IX and to support programs to increase the number of female administrators.

The remainder of the 1970s saw continued legal and political pressure brought against school districts and colleges and universities to end discrimination in access; gender bias in curriculum materials, textbooks, and testing and guidance; inequality in support of athletic programs; and discrimination in employment. As a result, the number of women receiving advanced degrees and their representation across the occupations increased significantly (see Table 9.3). The doors having been opened, women entered in what has remained ever-increasing numbers.

TABLE 9.3 Percentage of Master's and Doctoral Degrees Earned by Women, by Field of Study, 1970–71 and 2001–02

Field of study	Master's degrees		Doctoral degrees	
	1970–71	2001–02	1970–71	2001–02
Total	40.1	58.7	14.3	46.3
Health professions and related sciences	55.3	77.6	16.5	63.3
Education	56.2	76.4	21.0	66.5
Psychology	40.6	76.4	24.0	68.2
English language and literature/letters	60.6	68.0	28.8	58.5
Communications	34.6	65.4	13.1	55.1
Visual and performing arts	47.4	57.6	22.2	56.0
Biological/life sciences	33.6	57.8	16.3	44.3
Social sciences and history	28.5	50.8	13.9	43.1
Business	3.9	41.1	2.8	35.4
Mathematics	27.1	42.4	7.6	29.0
Agriculture and natural resources	5.9	48.1	2.9	33.5
Physical sciences	13.3	37.6	5.6	28.0
Computer and information sciences	10.3	33.3	2.3	22.8
Engineering	1.1	21.2	0.6	17.2

Source: U.S. Department of Education, National Center for Education Statistics. (2004). *The condition of education 2004.* Washington, DC: U.S. Government Printing Office.

Expanding Access to Children With Disabilities

In the mid-1970s there were an estimated 3.7 million children with disabilities in the United States (Bernard & Mondale, 2001b). Despite these numbers most state laws allowed the expulsion or absolute exclusion from school of children who were deemed uneducable, untrainable, or otherwise unable to benefit from the regular education program. Not until two important federal court cases in the early 1970s was the right of children with disabilities to an education recognized by most states and school districts.

Both of these cases came in 1972. In *Mills v. Board of Education of the District of Columbia* it was estimated that 18,000 of the 22,000 retarded, emotionally disturbed, blind, deaf, and speech or learning disabled children in the District of Columbia were not being served. Rejecting the district's defense that it did not have the money to serve the children, the court ordered that

> no child eligible for a publicly supported education in the District of Columbia public schools shall be excluded from a regular public school assignment by a rule, policy, or practice of the Board of Education of the District of Columbia or its agents unless such child is provided (a) adequate alternative educational services suited to the child's needs, which may include special education or tuition grants, and (b) a constitutionally adequate prior hearing and periodic review of the child's status, progress, and the adequacy of any educational alternative.

The second case, *Pennsylvania Association of Retarded Citizens (PARC) v. Commonwealth of Pennsylvania* (1972), was also concerned with the fact that children with disabilities were not being provided a public education. In an out-of-court settlement the state agreed to provide a free public education to all retarded children between the ages of 6 and 21 and to establish due process procedures to resolve disputes. Following the *PARC* decision, cases were filed in over half the states seeking similar redress, and the Council for Exceptional Children prepared model legislation for adoption by states (Newman, 1998).

The decisions in *Mills* and *PARC*, combined with intense lobbying by groups representing the handicapped, special education professionals, and parents of children with disabilities, led Congress to pass the Rehabilitation Act of 1973 and the landmark Education for All Handicapped Children Act of 1975 (EHA), now known as the Individuals With Disabilities Education Act (IDEA). The Rehabilitation Act provided grants to states and public and nonpublic agencies to expand vocational training and rehabilitation services to individuals with disabilities, including the construction of rehabilitation facilities, so that they might be employed to the full extent of their capabilities. Section 504 of the act parallels Title VI of the Civil Rights Act of 1964 and states that "no otherwise qualified individual in the United States . . . shall solely by reason of his handicap, be excluded from participation in, be denied the benefits of, or be subjected to discrimination under any program or activity receiving Federal financial assistance." Under the provisions of the bill every public or private recipient of federal funds was to provide full nondiscriminatory access to individuals with disabilities. There was significant opposition to the bill because of its potential cost to institutions, agencies, and potential employers, and it was vetoed by President Nixon. The Democratic Congress overrode his veto and the bill became law; however, implementing regulations were not enacted until the Carter administration.

The second major piece of federal legislation, the EHA, often referred to as the Bill of Rights for Handicapped Children, served not only to guarantee the educational rights of children with disabilities, but also to define and expand the rights of all children. The EHA provided over $1 billion annually to be distributed through the states to local school districts to help fund educational services for children with disabilities. In addition to providing these much-needed funds for special education services, the EHA introduced a number of significant principles. Perhaps the most fundamental and important was the right of *all* children with disabilities to a "free appropriate education and related services designed to meet their unique needs." The law also required that every child receive a comprehensive, nondiscriminatory evaluation before being placed in any special education program and that an *individualized educational program* (IEP) designed to meet the individual needs of the child be prepared for every child who is to receive special educational services. Another very important provision of EHA was the extensive due process requirements designed to ensure the rights of children with disabilities to receive a free appropriate education and to protect them from improper evaluation, classification, and placement. And, although not a requirement of EHA but its implementing regulations, children with disabilities were to be educated in the *least restrictive environment.* This requirement did not require mainstreaming children with disabilities into regular classrooms (in fact, the EHA did not even mention mainstreaming), but it encouraged this practice.

Since the implementation of the EHA in 1978 the number of children in federally supported education programs has risen steadily (see Table 9.4). This has been due to the growth in the number of students classified as having a learning disability (i.e., having a disorder or delayed development in one or more of the processes of thinking, speaking, reading, writing, listening, or doing arithmetic operations), as well as the addition of autism and brain injury as categories of disability by the Individuals With Disabilities Act of 1990 (IDEA). The increase in numbers and federal support has been accompanied by increased federal requirements regarding the delivery of services and the increased advocacy by parents, professionals, and disability rights groups. A major goal (and one that has been addressed by the inclusion movement) has been to provide greater access to the general education curriculum and nonacademic activities. Although great strides have been made to promote inclusion, and despite the safeguards included in the IDEA amendments of 1997, an ongoing concern remains the disproportionate representation of racial, ethnic, and language minority students in special education programs.

 For Your Reflection and Analysis

What accounts for the disproportionate representation of minority students in classes for the learning disabled and mentally retarded?

TABLE 9.4 Children 0 to 21 Years Old Served in Federally Supported Programs for the Disabled, by Type of Disability, 1976–77 to 1999–2000

Type of disability	1976–77	1980–81	1987–88	1988–89	1989–90	1990–91
1	2	3	4	5	6	7
	Number served, in thousands					
All disabilities	3,694	4,144	4,439	4,529	4,631	4,761
Specific learning disabilities	796	1,462	1,928	1,984	2,047	2,129
Speech or language impairments	1,302	1,168	950	964	971	985
Mental retardation	961	830	580	560	547	535
Serious emotional disturbance	283	347	371	372	380	390
Hearing impairments	88	79	56	56	57	58
Orthopedic impairments	87	58	46	47	48	49
Other health impairments	141	98	45	50	52	55
Visual Impairments	38	31	22	22	22	23
Multiple disabilities	—	68	77	83	86	96
Deaf-blindness	—	3	1	1	2	1
Autism and traumatic brain injury	—	—	—	—	—	—
Developmental delay	—	—	—	—	—	—
Preschool disabled	196	231	332	357	381	390
Infants and toddlers	—	—	30	34	37	51

Source: U.S. Department of Education, National Center for Education Statistics, (2003). *Digest of Education Statistics 2002.* Washington, DC: National Center for Education Statistics.

School Finance Reform

The 1970s was a decade marked by economic uncertainty. Presidents Nixon, Ford, and Carter fought unsuccessfully to curb inflation, reduce unemployment, reduce the federal deficit, and reduce the imbalance of foreign trade. The impact of rapid inflation was sorely felt by the schools. At the same time that operating costs were spiraling, revenues were declining. The decline in revenues was a result of two forces: (1) the "revolt" of taxpayers against rising taxes, especially property taxes, which was the major source of tax revenues for the schools, and (2) a decline in enrollment, which brought about a reduction in state revenues because most states, to a large extent, base their aid to local school districts on enrollment. In 1971, for the first time since World War II, the total number of elementary and secondary students enrolled in the public schools declined.

The decline in local revenues exacerbated the inequalities between rich and poor school districts (defined as districts with a high or low assessed property evaluation per pupil). Parents in poor districts, as well as citizens groups and teacher and administrator organizations, brought renewed pressure on state legislatures to increase state funding and remedy the revenue inequalities that were reflected in inferior schools and reduced educational opportunities. When this did not work, they turned to the courts.

1991–92	1992–93	1993–94	1994–95	1995–96	1996–97	1997–98	1998–99	1999–2000
8	9	10	11	12	13	14	15	16
Number served, in thousands								
4,941	5,111	5,309	5,378	5,573	5,729	5,903	6,054	6,195
2,232	2,351	2,408	2,489	2,579	2,649	2,725	2,789	2,834
996	994	1,014	1,015	1,022	1,043	1,056	1,068	1,080
537	518	536	555	570	579	589	597	600
399	400	414	427	438	445	453	462	469
60	60	64	64	67	68	69	70	71
51	52	56	60	63	66	67	69	71
58	65	82	106	133	160	190	221	253
24	23	24	24	25	25	25	26	26
97	102	108	88	93	98	106	106	111
1	1	1	1	1	1	1	2	2
5	19	24	29	39	44	54	67	79
—	—	—	—	—	—	4	12	19
416	450	487	519	544	552	564	568	581
66	75	92	—	—	—	—	—	—

The precipitating court decision in the school finance reform movement was the landmark 1971 California Supreme Court decision in *Serrano v. Priest.* As summarized by the court, the issue was as follows:

The public school system is maintained throughout the state by a financing plan which relies heavily on local property taxes and causes substantial disparities among individual school districts in the amount of revenue available per pupil for educational purposes. Districts with smaller tax bases, therefore, are not able to spend as much money per child for education as districts with larger assessed valuations. As a result of the financing scheme, substantial disparities in the equality and extent of availability of educational opportunities exist and are perpetuated among the state's school districts. The educational opportunities made available to children in the property poor districts are substantially inferior to the educational opportunities made available to children in other districts of the state. The state school finance plan thus fails to meet the requirements of the federal and state equal protection clause. . . . Furthermore, as a direct result of the school plan system, they [parents in poor districts] are required to pay a higher tax rate than taxpayers in many other school districts in order to obtain for their children the same or lesser educational opportunities afforded children in those other districts. (p. 1244)

In its *Serrano* ruling the highest court of the most populous state said that the quality of a child's education should be determined not by the wealth of his or her community, but by the wealth of the state as a whole. To do otherwise would be to violate the equal protection clause of the state and federal constitutions.

The *Serrano* decision sent a shock wave through the education community and state legislatures. The effect was immediate and profound. *Serrano* provided the impetus for reform as many other states feared their own courts might adopt the *Serrano* standard and their own finance formulas would fall before judicial review. And, indeed, plaintiffs in other cases did use the legal standard articulated in *Serrano* in challenging their state finance systems. In fact, just weeks after the *Serrano* decision another court, this time in Minnesota, used the *Serrano* rationale in rejecting a motion to dismiss a challenge to that state's finance system (*Van Dusartz v. Hatfield, 1971*). In the same year an Arizona Superior Court declared unconstitutional the Arizona school finance system using the *Serrano* rationale (*Hollins v. Shoftstall*, 1971). (The decision was later reversed by the state supreme court.)

In 1973 another major school finance decision was reached, *San Antonio Independent School District v. Rodriguez*, this time by the U.S. Supreme Court. Demetrio P. Rodriguez filed suit in the federal district court in San Antonio, Texas, on behalf of children living in low-property-wealth districts, alleging that the state's reliance on property taxes to finance the schools created unconstitutionally permissible funding disparities between the rich and poor districts. The district court, using the *Serrano* rationale, declared the state finance system unconstitutional, but stayed its mandate to give the legislature time to act. On appeal the U.S. Supreme Court, by a five-to-four majority composed of the Nixon appointees, overturned the lower court decision. According to the Court, although education was of "grave significance" to the individual and to society, it is not a right protected by the Constitution and neither does the wealth of the district create a "suspect classification." In the absence of either of these two conditions the Court was not required to apply the more rigorous judicial review, "strict scrutiny," only to find a "rational relationship" between the state finance plan and a legitimate state purpose, which it did.

The effect of the *Rodriguez* decision, although a setback for school finance reformers because it did not yield a decision that would have had nationwide impact, did not close the door to school finance litigation or attempts to reform school finance systems. Efforts to bring about legislative reform continued, and legal action moved the fight from the federal court to the state courts. Rather than bringing action based on the federal Constitution, challenges were now based on state constitutions alleging either that education was a right under the state constitution or that the equal protection clause of the state constitution was being violated by the spending disparities among school districts, or both. Although not all legal challenges were successful, even when they were not successful, or even in states where litigation was not initiated, in many instances the attention brought to bear on the inequities spurred legislatures to enact reforms. As a result, during the 1970s over half the states reformed their school finance systems. The reforms were directed at increasing state funding, reducing per pupil expenditure disparities, providing greater taxpayer equity, recognizing the unique characteristics of districts, and expanding the educational opportunities afforded special populations.

The school finance reform movement of the 1970s combined with the increased federal participation in the funding of education of special populations to bring a major shift in the source of funds for the schools. For the first time in our nation's history, nationwide, the local school district did not provide at least half of the funds to support the schools. As Table 9.5 shows, the burgeoning number of federal education programs resulted in an increase in federal funding from 4.4% of total revenues in 1960 to 8.0% in 1970 and 9.8% in 1980; the actual dollar increase was more than 1,400%. State aid during the decade of school finance reform increased from 39.9% in 1970 to 46.8% in 1980, while average current expenditures increased from $1,677 to $2,272 (in adjusted dollars), a 35% increase, over twice the rate of growth of the general economy over the same period.

The growth of federal involvement in education was a major factor in President Jimmy Carter's ability to overcome congressional opposition and keep his campaign promise to the National Education Association to elevate the Office of Education to department status, making its secretary a member of the president's cabinet. Carter appointed Shirley Hufstadler, a federal appeals court judge, as the first Secretary of the Department of Education. The appointment of a federal judge was indicative of Carter's commitment to enforce legislation directed at protecting civil rights and promoting equality of educational opportunity (Ravitch, 1983).

 For Your Reflection and Analysis

Since 2000, many state governments and local school systems have felt pressure to provide more equitable funding for schools. This comes at a time when state governments feel more strapped for money because of the increased cost to provide health care and other social services. How will this dilemma be resolved? Who will be the winners? Who will be the losers? Explain.

The Students' Rights and Antiwar Movements

The 1960s and 1970s saw a series of urban riots and the sometimes passive, sometimes violent students' rights and anti–Vietnam War movements. College campuses were the scenes of sit-ins, marches, and even the bombing and burning of campus buildings. High school campuses were also the scene of antiwar demonstrations. One of the first major incidents came in the fall of 1964 when an estimated 1,500 students and other protestors staged a sit-in at the administration building on the University of California Berkeley campus and were removed by campus police. The movement spread to other campuses, where students demonstrated against the war, the draft, the ROTC, military and CIA recruiters, university involvement in military or defense contracts, or almost anything related to the Vietnam War or anything in support of the "war machine." In April 1965 over 25,000 people, mostly students, participated in an antiwar demonstration in Washington, D.C.

Two of the participating students were Iowa high school students Christopher Eckhardt and John Tinker. When they returned to Des Moines, they decided, along with John's sister, Mary Beth, to express their opposition to the war by wearing black armbands to school in violation of a school policy that had been adopted in anticipation

TABLE 9.5 Revenues for Public Elementary and Secondary Schools, by Source of Funds, 1919–20 to 1999–2000

	In thousands				Percentage distribution			
				Local (including intermediate)				Local (including intermediate)
School year	Total	Federal	State	intermediate)	Total	Federal	State	intermediate)
1	2	3	4	5	6	7	8	9
1919–20	$970,121	$2,475	$160,085	$807,561	100.0	0.3	16.5	83.2
1929–30	2,088,557	7,334	353,670	1,727,553	100.0	0.4	16.9	82.7
1939–40	2,260,527	39,810	684,354	1,536,363	100.0	1.8	30.3	68.0
1941–42	2,416,580	34,305	759,993	1,622,281	100.0	1.4	31.4	67.1
1943–44	2,604,322	35,886	859,183	1,709,253	100.0	1.4	33.0	65.6
1945–46	3,059,845	41,378	1,062,057	1,956,409	100.0	1.4	34.7	63.9
1947–48	4,311,534	120,270	1,676,362	2,514,902	100.0	2.8	38.9	58.3
1949–50	5,437,044	155,848	2,165,689	3,115,507	100.0	2.9	39.8	57.3
1951–52	6,423,816	227,711	2,478,596	3,717,507	100.0	3.5	38.6	57.9
1953–54	7,866,852	355,237	2,944,103	4,567,512	100.0	4.5	37.4	58.1
1955–56	9,686,677	441,442	3,828,886	5,416,350	100.0	4.6	39.5	55.9
1957–58	12,181,513	486,484	4,800,368	6,894,661	100.0	4.0	39.4	56.6
1959–60	14,746,618	651,639	5,768,047	8,326,932	100.0	4.4	39.1	56.5
1961–62	17,527,707	760,975	6,789,190	9,977,542	100.0	4.3	38.7	56.9
1963–64	20,544,182	896,956	8,078,014	11,569,213	100.0	4.4	39.3	56.3
1965–66	25,356,858	1,996,954	9,920,219	13,439,686	100.0	7.9	39.1	53.0
1967–68	31,903,064	2,806,469	12,275,536	16,821,063	100.0	8.8	38.5	52.7
1969–70	40,266,923	3,219,557	16,062,776	20,984,589	100.0	8.0	39.9	52.1
1971–72	50,003,645	4,467,969	19,133,256	26,402,420	100.0	8.9	38.3	52.8
1973–74	58,230,892	4,930,351	24,113,409	29,187,132	100.0	8.5	41.4	50.1
1975–76	71,206,073	6,318,345	31,602,885	33,284,840	100.0	8.9	44.4	46.7
1977–78	81,443,160	7,694,194	35,013,266	38,735,700	100.0	9.4	43.0	47.6
1979–80	96,881,165	9,503,537	45,348,814	42,028,813	100.0	9.8	46.8	43.4
1981–82	110,191,257	8,186,466	52,436,435	49,568,356	100.0	7.4	47.6	45.0
1983–84	126,055,419	8,576,547	60,232,981	57,245,892	100.0	6.8	47.8	45.4
1985–86	149,127,779	9,975,622	73,619,575	65,532,582	100.0	6.7	49.4	43.9
1987–88	169,581,974	10,716,687	84,004,415	74,840,873	100.0	6.3	49.5	44.1
1989–90	208,547,573	12,700,784	98,238,633	97,608,157	100.0	6.1	47.1	46.8
1991–92	234,581,384	15,493,330	108,783,449	110,304,605	100.0	6.6	46.4	47.0
1993–94	260,159,468	18,341,483	117,474,209	124,343,776	100.0	7.1	45.2	47.8
1995–96	287,702,844	19,104,019	136,670,754	131,928,071	100.0	6.6	47.5	45.9
1997–98	325,925,708	22,201,965	157,645,372	146,078,370	100.0	6.8	48.4	44.8
1999–2000	372,864,603	27,097,866	184,613,352	161,153,385	100.0	7.3	49.5	43.2

Source: U.S. Department of Education, National Center for Education Statistics. (2003). *Digest of education statistics 2002.* Washington, DC: National Center for Education Statistics.

of their actions. When they refused to remove the armbands, they were suspended. The case that followed resulted in a U.S. Supreme Court decision that has become a landmark in students' rights cases. In *Tinker v. Des Moines Independent School District* (1969) the Court ruled that "school officials do not possess absolute authority over their students. Students in schools as well as out of school are 'persons' under our Constitution. They are possessed of fundamental rights which the state must respect." The Court also ruled that symbolic dress or expression is protected under the First Amendment and that student expression cannot be abridged unless the school can show that it presents a "material and substantial" threat to the operation of the school. Following this groundbreaking case, the Supreme Court in the 1970s further expanded students' rights by establishing the due process that must be followed in student suspensions and expulsions (*Goss v. Lopez*, 1975).

The assassinations of Martin Luther King, Jr., in April 1968 and Robert F. Kennedy in June 1968 set off a round of urban riots that was echoed on college campuses. In the first 6 months of 1968 there were 221 major demonstrations on over 100 college campuses, involving 39,000 students (Manchester, 1975). In late April 1968, 1,000 students took over five buildings at Columbia University in protest of business–military recruiting on campus and the building of a new gymnasium in a public park located between the university and Harlem. Once again police were called in to remove the students. Two weeks later 500 students again occupied an administration building, put up barricades, set fires, and battered the police removing them. In the year following the violent protests at Columbia violent protests occurred

College campuses became the scene of many civil rights and antiwar demonstrations during the 1960s and 1970s.

on about 150 college campuses, including many of the nation's most select private and public universities (Ravitch, 1983).

The civil rights and students' rights movements of the 1960s brought major changes to college campuses. Students gained a much greater voice in governance, curricular requirements were liberalized, and Black college enrollment tripled.

The student protest movement, which had lost some momentum by early 1970, was revived at the end of April when President Nixon announced the invasion of Cambodia by U.S. troops. The response was demonstrations on campuses all across the nation leading to the most deadly episode of the era. When national guard troops were sent to the campus of Kent State University to quell the riots and stop the burning of campus buildings, for reasons that will never really be known, they opened fire, killing four students. The incident drew angry responses and demonstrations across the nation: 350 institutions went on strike, others closed for the remainder of the academic year. California governor Ronald Reagan closed the state college and universities for a week, and in other states police and the national guard were called in to control student demonstrations (Ravitch, 1983). Ten days after the Kent State killings two students were killed at historically Black Jackson State College when Mississippi Highway Patrol and local police fired on a student dormitory from which students were throwing rocks on them.

The students' rights and antiwar movements tended to have a negative impact on the civil rights movement through a subliminal process of guilt by association. Many people became disenchanted with the civil rights movement, "not because they disagreed with or were unsympathetic to its legitimate claim, but because the Student Rights Movement, which they strongly opposed, got its impetus, simulation, and example from the Civil Rights Movement" (Tollett, 1983, p. 57). At the height of the campus unrest President Nixon complained that the student population seemed "determined to spend its time not learning, but in blowing up buildings and burning books." His vice president, Spiro Agnew, sought to discredit the antiwar protesters by suggesting that "they take their tactics from Gandhi and their money from daddy" (Gilbert, 2001, p. xii). A campaign against demonstrations and riots and for the restoration of law and order helped put Richard Nixon in the White House in 1969 and reelect him in 1972.

Conclusion

The civil rights movement was unquestionably one of the turning points in our nation's social history. The 20 years that followed the Supreme Court decision in *Brown* were ones of struggle and euphoria for civil rights activists, minorities, women, advocates for individuals with disabilities, and all Americans interested in advancing the causes of social justice and equal educational opportunity. Despite the fact that some fought—even violently—against the changes, and the fact that many of the gains have been set back does not diminish the fact that in less than a generation the nation was able to transform the schools from exclusive to inclusive. Students who in some instances had never attended school were given the legal right not only to attend school, but also to receive a free and appropriate education. Without question, the classrooms of today are far more diverse and multicultural than classrooms were when Justice Warren declared that separate but equal has no place in American education.

That being said, segregation, sexism, and meeting the needs of language minority students have remained major issues and challenges for the schools in the decades following the 1970s and today. However, what changed, and is of monumental importance to any future gains, is the will of the federal government to promote, or even enforce, civil rights, as well as the disengagement of the courts, primarily the conservative U.S. Supreme Court, from pursuing the rights of minorities, females, and language minority students. (The courts seem to have shown more interest in protecting and expanding the rights and access of students with disabilities.)

One area in which the pursuit of equity has continued to gain ground since the 1970s is school finance, perhaps because these arguments have been advanced in state, not federal, legislatures and courts. Beginning in the 1970s state support of education increased as federal support decreased, with a concomitant reduced reliance on the local property tax and the vagaries in associated expenditures. Beginning in the 1990s the focus of school finance reform began to shift from fiscal equity to the much more complex issue of whether adequate resources and programs were available in each district for students to reach the high performance standards enacted in most states.

In the end, the War on Poverty was not won, and perhaps it was unrealistic to think it could be. The criticisms against many of the education initiatives it supported sounded much the same as those levied against education innovations in previous generations: The liberal policies of the Great Society had failed the schools. Once again the solution offered was that the schools get rid of the "frills," institute more academic rigor, and increase testing. The conservative response grew, resulting in the educational reform movement discussed in chapter 10.

For Discussion and Application

1. Of the various initiatives that were passed to fight the War on Poverty, which were most successful and which were least successful? Give reasons why.
2. Did the courts go too far or not far enough in ordering segregation remedies? Explain.
3. Compare the similarities and dissimilarities in the segregation experiences of Blacks, Mexican Americans, and Asian Americans?
4. How has the "Bill of Rights for Handicapped Children" (EHA) not only guaranteed the educational rights of children with disabilities, but also defined and expanded the rights of all children?
5. With the current budget constraints experienced by most state governments, how can the long-overdue school finance reforms be enacted?
6. Examine college yearbooks from 1960 and 2004. Compare the educational experiences of females in terms of student activities, representation in the academic disciplines, and intercollegiate sports.

Primary Source Reading

In 1952 the National Association for the Advancement of Colored People and its chief legal counsel, Thurgood Marshall, brought five cases to the U.S. Supreme Court that challenged the doctrine of "separate but equal" that the court had upheld in Plessy v. Ferguson. There were reports that the court, while not wanting to uphold segregation, was divided on the issue of whether it had the authority to overturn Plessy. The case was first argued before the court in 1952 but the court did not reach a decision, asking that the case be reargued in 1953 addressing specific issues. Just a few weeks before the scheduled reargument, Chief Justice Vinson, who was thought to be opposed to reversing Plessy, died unexpectedly. On May 17, 1954, the new chief justice, Earl Warren, delivered the historic opinion presented below.

U.S. Supreme Court
Brown v. Board of Education, 347 U.S. 483 (1954)
Brown et al. v. Board of Education of Topeka et al.
Appeal from the United States District Court for the District of Kansas. * No. 1.

Argued December 9, 1952.

Reargued December 8, 1953.

Decided May 17, 1954.

Opinion

Mr. Chief Justice Warren delivered the opinion of the Court.

These cases come to us from the States of Kansas, South Carolina, Virginia, and Delaware. They are premised on different facts and different local conditions, but a common legal question justifies their consideration together in this consolidated opinion.

In each of the cases, minors of the Negro race seek the aid of the courts in obtaining admission to the public schools of their community on a nonsegregated basis. In each instance, they had been denied admission to schools attended by white children under laws requiring or permitting segregation according to race. This segregation was alleged to deprive the plaintiffs of the equal protection of the laws under the Fourteenth Amendment. In each of the cases other than the Delaware case, a three-judge federal district court denied relief to the plaintiffs on the so-called "separate but equal" doctrine announced by this Court in *Plessy v. Ferguson*, 163 U.S. 537. Under that doctrine, equality of treatment is accorded when the races are provided substantially equal facilities, even though these facilities be separate. In the Delaware case, the Supreme Court of Delaware adhered to that doctrine, but ordered that the plaintiffs be admitted to the white schools because of their superiority to the Negro schools.

The plaintiffs contend that segregated public schools are not "equal" and cannot be made "equal," and that hence they are deprived of the equal protection of the laws. Because of the obvious importance of the question presented, the Court took jurisdiction. Argument was heard in the 1952 Term, and reargument was heard this Term on certain questions propounded by the Court.

Reargument was largely devoted to the circumstances surrounding the adoption of the 14th Amendment in 1868. It covered exhaustively consideration of the Amendment in Congress, ratification by the states, then existing practices in racial segregation, and the views of proponents and opponents of the Amendment. This discussion and our investigation convince us that, although these sources cast some light, it is not enough to resolve the problem with which we are faced. At best, they are inconclusive. The most avid proponents of the post-War Amendments undoubtedly intended them to remove all legal distinctions among "all persons born or naturalized in the United States." Their opponents, just as certainly, were antagonistic to both the letter and the spirit of the Amendments and wished them to have the most limited effect. What others in Congress and the state legislature had in mind cannot be determined with any degree of certainty.

An additional reason for the inconclusive nature of the Amendment's history, with respect to segregated schools, is the status of public education at that time. In the South, the movement toward free common schools, supported [347 U.S. 483, 490] by general taxation, had not yet taken hold. Education of white children was largely in the hands of private groups. Education of Negroes was almost nonexistent, and practically all of the race were illiterate. In fact, any education of the Negroes was forbidden by law in some states. Today, in contrast, many Negroes have achieved outstanding success in the arts and sciences as well as in the business and professional world. It is true that public school education has advanced further in the North, but the effect of the Amendment on Northern States was generally ignored in the congressional debates. Even in the North, the conditions of public education did not approximate those existing today. The curriculum was usually rudimentary; ungraded schools were common in rural areas; the school term was but three months a year in many states; and compulsory school attendance was virtually unknown. As a consequence, it is not surprising that there should be so little in the history of the Fourteenth Amendment relating to its intended effect on public education.

In the first cases in this Court construing the Fourteenth Amendment, decided shortly after its adoption, the Court interpreted it as proscribing all state-imposed discriminations against the Negro race. The doctrine of [347 U.S. 483, 491] "separate but equal" did not make its appearance in this Court until 1896 in the case of *Plessy v. Ferguson*, *supra*, involving not education but transportation. American courts have since labored with the doctrine in over half a century. In this Court, there have been six cases involving the "separate but equal" doctrine in the field of public education. In *Cumming v. County Board of Education*, 175 U.S. 528, and *Gong Lum v. Rice*, 275 U.S. 78, the validity of the doctrine itself was not challenged. In more recent cases, all on the graduate school [347 U.S. 483, 492] level, inequality was found in that specific benefits enjoyed by white students were denied to Negro students of the same educational qualifications. *Missouri ex re. Gaines v. Canada*, 305 U.S. 337; *Sipuel v. Oklahoma*, 332 U.S. 631; *Sweatt v. Painter*, 339 U.S. 629; *McLaurin v. Oklahoma State Regents*, 339 U.S. 637. In none of these cases was it necessary to reexamine the doctrine to grant relief to the Negro plaintiff. And in *Sweatt v. Painter*, *supra*, the Court expressly reserved decision on the question whether *Plessy v. Ferguson*, should be held inapplicable to public education.

In the instant cases, that question is directly presented. Here, unlike *Sweatt v. Painter*, there are findings below that the Negro and white schools involved have been equalized or are being equalized, with respect to buildings, curricula, qualifications and salaries of teachers, and other "tangible" factors. Our decision, therefore, cannot turn on merely a comparison of these tangible factors in the Negro and white schools involved in each of the cases. We must look instead to the effect of segregation itself on public education.

In approaching this problem, we cannot turn the clock back to 1868 when the Amendment was adopted, or even to 1896 when *Plessy v. Ferguson* was written. We must consider public education in the light of its full development and its present place in American life throughout [347 U.S. 483, 493] the Nation. Only in this way can it be determined if segregation in public schools deprives these plaintiffs of the equal protection of the laws.

Today, education is perhaps the most important function of state and local governments. Compulsory school attendance laws and the great expenditures for education both demonstrate our recognition of the importance of education to our democratic society. It is required in the performance of our most basic public responsibilities, even service in the armed forces. It is the very foundation of good citizenship. Today it is a principal instrument in awakening the child to cultural values, in preparing him for later professional training, and in helping him to adjust normally to his environment. In these days, it is doubtful that any child may reasonably be expected to succeed in life if he is denied the opportunity of an education. Such an opportunity, where the state has undertaken to provide it, is a right which must be made available to all on equal terms.

We come, then, to the question presented: Does segregation of children in public schools solely on the basis of race, even though the physical facilities and other "tangible" factors may be equal, deprive the children of the minority group of equal educational opportunities? We believe that it does.

In *Sweatt v. Painter, supra,* in finding that a segregated law school for Negroes could not provide them equal educational opportunities, this Court relied in large part on "those qualities which are incapable of objective measurement but which make for greatness in a law school." In *McLaurin v. Oklahoma State Regents, supra,* the Court, in requiring that a Negro admitted to a white graduate school be treated like all other students, again resorted to intangible considerations: "[his] ability to study, to engage in discussions and exchange views with other students, and, in general, to learn his profession" [347, U.S. 483, 494]. Such considerations apply with added force to children in grade and high schools. To separate them from others of similar age and qualifications solely because of their race generates a feeling of inferiority as to their status in the community that may affect their heart and minds in a way unlikely ever to be undone. The effect of this separation on their educational opportunities was well stated by a finding in the Kansas case by a court which nevertheless felt compelled to rule against the Negro plaintiffs:

Segregation of white and colored children in public schools has a detrimental effect upon the colored children. The impact is greater when it has the sanction of the law; for the policy of separating the races is usually interpreted as denoting the inferiority of the Negro group. A sense of inferiority affects the motivation of a child to learn. Segregation with the sanction of law, therefore, has a tendency to retard the educational and mental development of Negro children and to deprive them of some of the benefits they would receive in a [racially] integrated school system.

Whatever may have been the extent of psychological knowledge at the time of *Plessy v. Ferguson,* this finding is amply supported by modern authority. Any language [347 U.S. 483, 495] in *Plessy v. Ferguson* contrary to this finding is rejected.

We conclude that in the field of public education the doctrine of "separate but equal" has no place. Separate educational facilities are inherently unequal. Therefore, we hold that the plaintiffs and others similarly situated for whom the actions have been brought are by reason of the segregation complained of, deprived of the equal protection of the laws guaranteed by the Fourteenth Amendment. This disposition makes unnecessary any discussion whether such segregation also violates the Due Process Clause of the Fourteenth Amendment.

Because these are class actions, because of the wide applicability of this decision, and because of the great variety of local conditions, the formulation of decrees in these cases presents problems of considerable complexity. On reargument, the consideration of appropriate relief was necessarily subordinated to the primary question: the constitutionality of segregation in public education. We have now announced that such segregation is a denial of the equal protection of the laws. In order that we may have the full assistance of the parties in formulating decrees, the cases will be restored to the docket, and the parties are requested to present further argument . . .

It is so ordered.

Questions for Discussion

1. In what ways are segregated schools not equal, as the plaintiffs contended, even if the segregated schools are made equal in terms of facilities, curricula, qualifications and salaries of teachers, and other "tangible" factors?
2. The court in *Brown* said that the opportunity of an education "is a right which must be made available to all on equal terms." How can you reconcile this statement with a later decision of the Supreme Court in *San Antonio v. Rodriguez* that the right to an education is not a constitutionally protected right?
3. List some possible social and psychological effects of segregation on the individual.
4. What might have gone into the decision of the court to delay issuing a decree and giving the parties for the various states to give further arguments?

Primary Source Reading

Despite some improvements following the 1928 Meriam report, in 1969 the educational, social, and economic condition of the American Indian remained desperate and deplorable. The dominant policy of the Federal Government remained one of forced assimilation of the American Indian—a policy motivated, according to the authors of the following U. S. Senate subcommittee report, by a desire to exploit and expropriate Indian land and physical resources. As described in the report, the coercive assimilation policy resulted in schools that not only failed to understand the culture of the Native American, but denigrated it and blamed children for the failures of the schools. To the Indian child the school became an alien institution and a battleground where he or she attempted to maintain his integrity and identity by defeating the purposes of the school.

Indian Education: A National Tragedy

U. S. Senate Special Subcommittee on Indian Education

To thousands of Americans, the American Indian is, and always will be, dirty, lazy, and drunk. That's the way they picture him; that's the way they treat him.

A Kansas newspaper in the middle of the 19th century described Indians as "a set of miserable, dirty, blanketed, thieving, lying, sneaking, murdering, graceless, faithless, gut-eating skunks as the Lord ever permitted to infest the earth, and whose immediate and final extermination all men, except Indian agents and traders, should pray for." In its investigation into the conditions of Indian education in all parts of the country, the subcommittee found anti-Indian attitudes still prevalent today in many white communities. In every community visited by the subcommittee, there was evidence among the white population of stereotyped opinions of Indians. The subcommittee research record is full of examples verifying the presence of such attitudes.

Superior Court Judge Robert L. Winslow of Ukiah, California, told the subcommittee that in Mendocino County, California, there was a "common feeling that Indians are inferior to non-Indians." A study of Indian–white relations in Ukiah said that whites generally looked upon Pomo Indians as "lazy, shiftless, dirty, biologically and culturally inferior." A Pomo Indian testified, "Some think the Indian is not very much or probably not even human." A Southwest study found many people convinced that Apaches were hostile, mean, lazy, and dumb. An Oklahoma principal said of his Indian students "(they) are even worse than our coloreds and the best you can do is just leave them alone."

Source: U.S. Senate Committee on Labor and Public Welfare, Special Subcommittee on Indian Education. (1969). *Indian education: A national tragedy—A national challenge.* Washington, DC: U.S. Government Printing Office.

The basis for these stereotypes goes back into history—a history created by the white man to justify his exploitation of the Indian, a history the Indian is continually reminded of at school, on television, in books, and at the movies.

It is a history which calls an Indian victory a massacre and a U. S. victory an heroic feat. It is a history which makes heroes and pioneers of goldminers who seized Indian land, killed whole bands and families, and ruthlessly took what they wanted. It is a history which equates Indians and wild animals and uses the term *savages* as a synonym for Indians.

It is this kind of history—the kind taught formally in the classroom and informally on street corners—which creates feelings of inferiority among Indian students, gives them warped understanding of their cultural heritage, and propagates stereotypes.

The manner in which Indians are treated in text books—one of the most powerful means by which our society transmits ideas from generation to generation—typifies the misunderstanding the American public as a whole has regarding the Indian, and indicates how misconceptions can become a part of a person's mindset. After examining more than a hundred history texts, one historian concluded that the American Indian has been obliterated, defamed, disparaged, and disembodied. He noted that they are often viewed as subhuman wild beasts in the path of civilization, that "Indian menace" and "Indian peril" and "savage barrier" are commonly found descriptions. Other authors talk about the "idle, shiftless savage" who "was never so happy as when, in the dead of the night he roused his sleeping enemies with an unearthly yell, and massacred them by the light of their burning homes."

Textbook studies by a number of States indicate that misconceptions, myths, inaccuracies, and stereotypes about Indians are common to the curriculum of most schools. A report prepared for the subcommittee by the University of Alaska showed that: (1) 20 widely used texts contain no mention of Alaska Natives at all, and in some cases, no mention of Alaska; (2) although some textbooks provide some coverage of the Alaskan Eskimo, very few even mention Indians; and (3) many texts at the elementary and secondary level contain serious and often demeaning inaccuracies in their treatment of the Alaskan Native.

A similar study by the University of Idaho found Indians continually depicted as inarticulate, backward, unable to adjust to modern Euro-American culture, sly, vicious, barbaric, superstitious, and destined to extinction. Minnesota has for years been using an elementary school social studies text which depicts Indians as lazy savages incapable of doing little more than hunting, fishing, and harvesting wild rice. Some schools continue to use the text. California, with its progressive public school program, found in a study of 43 texts used in fourth, fifth, and eighth grades that hardly any mention at all was made of the American Indians' contribution or of his role in the colonial period, gold rush era, or mission period of California history, and, when mentioned, the reference was usually distorted or misinterpreted.

The president of the American Indian Historical Society told the subcommittee, "There is not one Indian child who has not come home in shame and tears after one of those sessions in which he is taught that his people were dirty, animal-like, something less than a human being."

For the most part, the subcommittee's field research bore out the findings of these reports. There were some examples, though, of concerned school officials providing special materials. In Grand Portage, Minnesota, for example, a husband and wife teaching team found themselves teaching Chippewa students, but without textbooks on Chippewa culture or language. So they prepared their own Chippewa texts. Textbook changes have been made in the State of California, and the State of Idaho has undertaken the development of new materials. In Tuba City, Arizona, public school officials have recognized some of the special needs of their 90 percent Indian school population and have developed bilingual programs. New York State now includes State Indian history in its sixth and seventh grade social studies programs. But these examples are the exceptions, not the rule; and the improvements rarely go far enough either in terms of quantity or quality. These are all of very recent date.

While visiting the public schools serving Indian students on the Fort Hall Reservation in Idaho, Senator Robert F. Kennedy asked if the school had any books about Indians. After a frantic search in the back closet of the school's library a school administrator came running up to the Senator with his find. It was a book entitled *Captive of the Delawares*, which had a cover picture of a white child being scalped by an Indian. When the Senator later inquired whether the culture and traditions of the Indians there were included in the school's curriculum he was informed that "there isn't any history to this tribe."

With attitudes toward Indians being shaped, often unconsciously, by educational materials filled with inaccurate stereotypes—as well as by teachers whose own education has contained those same stereotypes and historical misconceptions—it is easy to see how the "lazy, dirty, drunken" Indian becomes the symbol for all Indians. When the public looks at an Indian they cannot react rationally because they have never known the facts. They do not feel responsible for the Indian because they are convinced that the "savages" have brought their conditions upon themselves. They truly believe the Indian is inferior to them. The subcommittee found this climate of disrespect and discrimination common in off-reservation towns which educate many Indian students in their public schools. The Indian is despised, exploited, and discriminated against—but always held in check by the white power structure so that his situation will not change.

At the heart of the matter, educationally at least, is the relationship between the Indian community and the public school and the general powerlessness the Indian feels in regard to the ed-

ucation of his children. A recent report by the Carnegie Foundation described the relationship between white people, especially the white power structure and Indians as "one of the most crucial problems in the education of Indian children." The report continued: "This relationship frequently demeans the Indians, destroys their self-respect and self-confidence, develops or encourages apathy and a sense of alienation from the educational process, and deprives them of an opportunity to develop the ability and experience to control their own affairs through participation in effective local government."

One means the white power structure employs to limit Indian control, or even participation, is to prevent Indians from getting on local school boards. The subcommittee uncovered numerous instances of school districts educating Indians with no Indian members on the school board. When Ponca City, Oklahoma, Indians tried to crack the white power structure by electing an Indian to the board of an all-Indian public school, some were threatened with loss of their rented homes while others were led to believe registration procedures were extremely complicated and would place them in jeopardy of having their land taxed. The election of the Indian marked the first time in 20 years that an Indian sat on the board. Chippewas of the Leech Lake reservation in Minnesota have alleged that their school district has been redrawn to prevent Indians from being elected to the all-white school board. The Mesquakie Tribe of Tama, Iowa, sent most of their children to South Tama County public school, yet the Indians cannot vote for members of the school board.

The subcommittee does not mean to suggest that Indians are never on public school boards or that a board will necessarily be effective if it contains Indian members. There are a number of public school districts in which Indians exercise some influence in school decision-making. But the point is that there are far too many instances of school boards in districts containing Indians making policies which adversely affect

Indian students. This is sometimes due to a willful intent by the board to keep Indians in check, but more often to a lack of understanding about the Indian community and the special needs of Indian students.

History provides several examples of Indian-controlled school systems which have had great success. In the 1800's for example, the Choctaw Indians of Mississippi and Oklahoma operated about 200 schools and academies and sent numerous graduates to eastern colleges. Using bilingual teachers and Cherokee tests, the Cherokees, during the same period, controlled a school system which produced a tribe almost 100 percent literate. Children were taught to read and write in both their native language and English. Some used these skills to establish the first American Indian press, a newspaper printed in Cherokee and English. Anthropologists have determined that, as a result of this school system, the literacy level in English of western Oklahoma Cherokees was higher than the white population of either Texas or Arkansas.

But the Cherokee and Choctaw school systems were abolished when Oklahoma became a State in 1906. Now, after almost 70 years of Federal and State controlled education, the Cherokees have the following educational record: 40 percent of adult Cherokees are functionally illiterate in English; only 39 percent have completed the eighth grade; the median educational level of the tribe's adult population is only 5.5 years; dropout rates of Indian students are often as high as 75 percent. Wahrhaftig and others who have studied this dramatic decline feel that the primary cause is the almost complete alienation of the Cherokee community from the white-controlled public school systems.

The Carnegie report cited an example of the problems Indian parents face in dealing with the power structure. Indians were trying to get a course in Ponca history and culture included in the curriculum of their all-Indian public school. The superintendent's response to their request is explained in the Carnegie report:

He had reviewed the schedule and found that if the course were taught, the children would be deprived of 54 hours of subjects they needed, such as math, English, science, and so forth. Further, he said, the teachers were doing very well in incorporating Indian culture into their teaching. Besides, he didn't see the value because this was a "competitive world and their culture was going to be lost anyway and they would be better off in the long run it they knew less of it." He also said that many felt the theme of the course would be to "teach the children to hate white people."

The principal of a Chinle, Arizona, public school had similar feelings about the teaching of Navajo culture in his school. He told an Office of Economic Opportunity evaluating team that he considered it "not American" to help any "faction" perpetuate its way of life. He felt the Rough Rock Demonstration School, with its emphasis on the Navajo culture, was a "backward step" and that the country had never moved ahead by "catering" to ethnic groups.

One outcome of the Indian's powerlessness and the atmosphere of the white community in which Indians attend school is discrimination within the public schools. Indian students on the Muckleshoot Reservation, in western Washington, for example, were automatically retained an extra year in the first grade of their public school. School officials felt that, for the Indians, the first year should be a non-academic socializing experience. The Nooksack Indians of western Washington were automatically placed in a class of slow learners without achievement testing. The subcommittee found a tracking system in the Nome public schools which several officials described as highly discriminatory. The system assigned most natives to the lowest level and most whites to the highest. . . . The school superintendent in Chinle, Arizona, admitted that his district has a policy of falsifying the Indian achievement test results. He told OEO evaluators that these children were so far behind national norms that "it just wouldn't look good.

People who don't know conditions here just wouldn't understand."

Oklahomans for Indian Opportunity, a responsible Indian organization aimed at assisting Indians, reported to the subcommittee that the non-Indian teachers of northwest Oklahoma "usually are lacking in even the most elementary understanding of or respect for the Indian students. The report quotes a principal as saying. "To tell the truth, our Indians are even worse than our coloreds and the best you can do is just leave them alone." The report concludes that "in general, the teachers and administrators in the schools of northwest Oklahoma seem incapable to treating the Indian students as sensitive human beings with the same needs and desires that non-Indian people have."

Language is another area in which the Indian is discriminated against in school. The Bureau of Indian Affairs contends that one-half to two-thirds of Indian children enter school with little or no skill in the English language. Dr. B. Gaarder of the U.S. Office of Education estimated that for half the Indians in New Mexico public schools, English is a second language. Unfamiliarity with the language of the classroom becomes a tremendous handicap for the Indian student, and records indicate he immediately falls behind his Anglo classmates. Most public school teachers are not trained to teach English as a second language. The student's position is complicated by the insistence of teachers, who have no understanding of Indian culture, that he disregard the language spoken by his parents at home.

The Indian thus feels like an alien in a strange country. And the school feels it is its responsibility not just to teach skills, but to impress the "alien" Indian with the values of the dominant culture. Teachers, textbooks, and curricula, therefore, are programmed to bring about adoption of such values of American life as competitiveness, acquisition, rugged individualism, and success. But for the Indian whose culture is oriented to completely different values, school becomes the source of much conflict and tension. He is told he must be competitive, when at home he is taught the value of cooperation. At school he is impressed with the importance of individual success, but at home the value of good interpersonal relations is emphasized.

The teacher complains about him not being motivated. But anthropologist Anne M. Smith asks if he can be expected to be motivated when to do so means rejection of his parents and their teachings, as well as his religion, race, and history.

Condemned by his language and his culture, berated because his values aren't those of his teacher, treated demeaningly simply because he is Indian, the Indian student begins asking himself if he really isn't inferior. He becomes the object of a self-fulfilling prophecy which says "Indians are no good." Dr. Brewton Berry explains it thus:

> The theory is that if teachers and other members of the dominant group are convinced that the Indian is innately inferior and incapable of learning, such attitudes will be conveyed in various and subtle ways. A child will come to think of himself in the negative way and set for himself lower standards of effort, achievement, and ambition. Thus the teacher's expectation and prediction that her Indian pupils will do poorly in school and in later life become major factors in guaranteeing the accuracy of her predictions.

Study after study confirms this is exactly what the dominant society, and the dominant school society in particular, is doing. Study after study shows Indian children growing up with attitudes and feelings of alienation, hopelessness, powerlessness, rejection, depression, anxiety, estrangement, and frustration. Few studies, if any, show the public schools doing anything to change this pattern. The public school becomes a place of discomfort for the Indian student, a place to leave when he becomes 15 or 16. . . .

Substantial evidence indicates that the question of identity is uppermost in the minds of Indians and that feelings of alienation, anxiety, and inadequacy are problems with which they are trying to cope. One of the most significant of recent studies in this area is the Coleman report, the Equality of Educational Opportunity study. Among its findings were:

One-fourth of elementary and secondary schoolteachers, by their own admission, would prefer not to teach Indian children.

Indian children, more than any other group, believe themselves to be below average in intelligence.

Indian children in the 12th grade have the poorest self-concept of all minority groups tested.

The report offers evidence showing the close relationship between the achievement of disadvantaged children and the way they feel about themselves and their future. The report states, "A pupil attitude factor which appears to have a stronger relationship to achievement than do all school factors together is the extent to which an individual feels that has control over his own destiny. . . ."

What, then, happens to the student who is told he is dirty, lazy, and inferior and must undergo school experiences daily which reinforce these attitudes? The statistical data speak for themselves:

87 percent dropout rate by the 6th grade at an all-Indian public elementary school near Ponca City, Oklahoma

90 percent dropout rate in Nome, Alaska, public schools, with about one-fourth of the students (primarily Eskimo) taking two or three years to get through the first grade

21 of 28 Indian students in a Washington 8th grade were non-readers; one-third of the 123 Yakima Indians enrolled in 8th grade of a Washington public school were reading two to six grades below the median level; 70 percent Indian dropout rate; average grade was D for the Indian senior high students in public school serving Yakima Indians

62 percent Indian dropout rate in Minneapolis Public Schools; between 45 and 75 percent statewide Indian dropout rate; 70 percent Indian dropout rates in parts if California

80 percent of the 74 Indian students who entered school in three Idaho public school districts in 1956 dropped out of school before their class graduated. A 1968 study of graduates and dropouts of Lotrop High School in Fairbanks showed a 75 percent dropout rate among native students. A student transferring from a state-operated rural school had the least chance of graduating, and native students receiving the majority of their elementary education in state-operated schools had the highest dropout rate. Seventy-five percent of the native dropouts tested revealed more than enough intelligence to complete high school.

Ever since the policy of educating Indians in public schools was adopted, it was assumed that the public schools, with their integrated settings, were the best means of educating Indians. The subcommittee's public school findings—high dropout rates, low achievement levels, anti-Indian attitudes, insensitive curricula—raise serious doubts as to the validity of these assumptions.

Questions for Discussion

1. According to the Senate subcommittee report, many Native American children have felt like an "alien in a strange country." Give examples

of how the public schools have contributed to this alienation. What other groups of students might experience these same feelings in the school setting?

2. How did the educational experience of Native Americans compare with that of Asian Americans? Hispanic Americans? African Americans?

3. How do textbooks and other instructional materials in use in the schools today depict the Native American? To what do you attribute any change since the 1969 report?

CHAPTER 10

Renewed Conservatism and Reform

Education is not the means of showing people how to get what they want. Education is an exercise by means of which enough men, it is hoped, will learn to want what is worth having.

—*Ronald Reagan*
Sincerely (1976)

The liberal educational reforms that began in the 1960s had already begun to erode by the late 1970s. The renewed conservatism that accompanied the election of Ronald Reagan in 1980 brought them under direct attack. The school reform movement that followed not only brought an emphasis on standards and accountability, but also replaced a focus on equity with a focus on excellence. The view of the school as a major player in the pursuit of social justice was replaced by the view of the school as key to international competition and economic prosperity. Once again there was interest in basics and a call for reform. A series of reports on the status of public education launched a reform movement that occupied most of the 1980s and resulted in a myriad of reforms at every level of education.

The 1990s began with an unprecedented event—for the first time in our nation's history, the federal government joined state and national leaders in approving national goals for the schools. Education had assumed an unprecedented place on the political agenda and played a major role in the election of the "Education President," Bill Clinton, in 1992. Along with a host of other education legislation, the national goals proposed under President Bush were adopted under Clinton. The national goals set the stage for the development of national curriculum standards, followed by the adoption of accountability systems to ensure that the standards were being met.

Education remained on the political agenda but took a different direction with the Republican takeover of Congress in the mid-1990s. This led to renewed efforts at the federal and state levels to advance a conservative education agenda that included support for deregulation, charter schools, vouchers, and privatization, and signaled an escalation of the debates over bilingual education, multicultural education, and gender bias in the schools. The conservative education agenda was reinforced by a series of Supreme Court decisions in the mid-1990s that brought a virtual halt to court-ordered desegregation and escalated the racial and ethnic resegregation already underway.

As countless strategies were being recommended and employed to improve the public schools, various options to expand school choice were finding their way through state legislatures and the courts. In the end, the blending of the charter school movement and the privatization movement appears to have benefited both.

Conservatism Takes Center Stage

The election of Ronald Reagan in 1980 brought a resurgence of conservatism in both politics and education. Reagan's New Federalism called for reduced taxes and reduced federal spending for social programs, including education, and a decentralization of responsibility and control over domestic issues to state and local governments. It also proposed a greater involvement of the business community in both supporting schools and setting educational goals and standards. The conservative position was articulated by both the so-called New Right, which was associated with the Washington-based think tank, the Heritage Foundation, and the centrist conservatives with ties to another conservative think tank, the American Enterprise Institute.

Both the New Right and the centrist conservatives were concerned about the expanded involvement of the federal government in education. Both groups attributed the "rising tide of mediocrity" in American education to the "failed social experiments" of the 1960s and excessive federal intervention. However, although the New Right would have eliminated almost all federal involvement in education, abolished the Department of Education, and downgraded civil rights regulations, the centrist conservatives saw some federal involvement as necessary to identify the national interest in education and promote its accomplishment, to ensure the perpetuation of a common culture, and to promote educational equity, albeit on a more limited basis (Pincus, 1985).

Much of the conservative agenda regarding federal aid to education stemmed from the fact that many conservatives blamed the schools for the social unrest of the 1960s and early 1970s and for many of the social problems that were seen as undermining the moral fabric of the country. Both the New Right and centrist conservatives favored greater accountability, higher standards, tuition tax credits, increased parental choice, and an expanded role for private schools. Within the school, the New Right advocated school prayer and the elimination of all things deemed to be associated with so-called secular humanism; the centrist conservatives were more concerned that the schools teach the basic values of the American capitalist society (Pincus, 1985). Although for much of his administration, Reagan's actions, if not his words, seemed more in keeping with the centrist position, initially the Reagan administration's education agenda, as well as its rhetoric, closely followed that of the New Right.

One of the major items on Reagan's education agenda was to reduce the number, complexity, and confusion of federal education programs. As discussed in chapter 9, the 1960s and 1970s had witnessed a proliferation of federal education programs. By 1980 their number had risen to over 500 (Rosmiller, 1990). Most of these programs were directed at children not in the mainstream of the education system and were intended to supplement, not supplant, state and local funds. To ensure that both of these directives were met, a plethora of rules and regulations, often confusing and sometimes conflicting, were promulgated. As time went on and the number of programs increased, so did the disenchantment with the federal red tape, duplication, and bureaucracy that accompanied the federal aid.

In keeping with his own agenda and the 1980 Republican Party platform to "replace the crazy quilt of wasteful programs with a system of block grants that will restore decision making to local officials," one of Reagan's first major proposals was to consolidate Title I of the ESEA, the Education for All Handicapped Children Act, the Emergency School Aid Act, and the Adult Education Act into one block grant (Chapter 1), and most of the other elementary and secondary programs into a second block (Chapter 2). The legislation that Congress enacted, the National Education Consolidation and Improvement Act (ECIA) of 1981 in the end did not combine Title I with the other acts, but it did consolidate 43 elementary and secondary categorical programs into one single block grant. However, Reagan's funding proposal for the entire block was less than what had formerly been spent for the ESEA alone. In fact, in every budget request made while he was in office, President Reagan proposed reductions in federal spending for education. From fiscal years 1980 to 1989 federal funds for elementary and secondary education declined by 17% and for higher education by 27% (U.S. Department of Education, 2003). So, although the ECIA did deliver less red tape, it also delivered fewer services.

The School Reform Movement

Another major concern of the Reagan administration was to respond to concerns about quality in the schools. In the 1950s, Sputnik and technological competition with the Russians had focused attention on the education system. In the 1980s, economic competition with the Japanese and a deteriorating domestic economy brought the education system into the forefront of public debate and with it a return to the belief that education is directly linked to the economic well-being of the nation (Horn, 2002).

Although some historians question the validity of the economic justification for the call for school reform in the 1980s, the very fact that the school was seen as a tool for solving the nation's economic problems provided a purpose for the schools that overwhelmed other popular and historic purposes (Cuban & Shipp 2000). For almost 2 centuries the public schools had been expected to promote citizenship, cultivate the moral and social development of students, and unite diverse groups into one nation.

For Your Reflection and Analysis

How would you compare the move to adopt TQM and similar business practices with the efficiency movement?

In the 1980s the public schools were asked to build the human capital thought necessary for the nation to maintain its place as the world's economic leader, and other historic purposes appeared to be distractions (Cuban & Shipp, 2000). With the shift to a business purpose came an increased prominence of the business community and business principles in planning school reform. The public schools, as well as colleges and universities, struggled to find ways to apply such business beliefs as total quality management (TQM) to their operations, and business leaders became the heads of prestigious reform commissions.

In response to the concerns about the quality of the schools, as well as to their stated importance in arresting the nation's declining economic and intellectual competitiveness, President Reagan appointed a National Commission on Excellence in Education. Its report, *A Nation at Risk: The Imperative for Educational Reform* (1983), in strong and stirring language described a "rising tide of mediocrity in education"

Curriculum Content
1. High school graduation requirements should be strengthened in the Five New Basic:
    a. 4 years of English to include reading, writing, and listening skills and knowledge of our literary heritage
    b. 3 years of mathematics to include geometry, algebra, elementary statistics, and applied mathematics, plus a new curricula for those who do not plan to continue their formal education immediately
    c. 3 years of science to include: (1) the physical and biological sciences; (2) the methods of scientific inquiry and reasoning; (3) the application of scientific knowledge to everyday life; and (4) the social and environmental implications of scientific and technological development
    d. 3 years of social studies
    e. half-year of computer science to include basic computer literacy and use of computers in other subjects
2. The study of foreign language should begin in the elementary grades, plus 2 years of foreign languages in high school for college bound students.
3. The high school curriculum should provide students with programs such as the fine and performing arts and vocational education that complement the New Basics and that demand the same level of performance as the Basics.
4. The curriculum in the elementary school should provide a sound base for study in the five basics as well as the foreign languages and the arts.

Standards and Expectations
1. Grades should be indicators of academic achievement.
2. Institutions of higher education should raise their admission requirements.
3. Standardized tests of achievement should be administered at major transition points from one level of schooling to another.
4. Textbooks and other tools of learning and teaching should be upgraded and updated to assure more rigorous content.

Time
1. Students in high schools should be assigned more homework.
2. Instruction in effective study and work skills should be introduced in the early grades and continued throughout the student's schooling.
3. Districts and legislatures should consider 7-hour school days as well as an extended school year.
4. The time available for learning should be expanded through better classroom management and organization.
5. Discipline and administrative burdens on teachers should be reduced.
6. Attendance policies with clear incentives and sanctions should be used to reduce time lost through absenteeism and tardiness.

Teaching
1. Persons preparing to teach should be required to meet high educational standards, to demonstrate an aptitude for teaching, and to demonstrate competence in an academic discipline; teacher education programs should be judged by how well their graduates meet the criteria.
2. Salaries for the teaching profession should be increased and should be professionally competitive, market sensitive, and performance based.
3. School boards should adopt an 11-month contract for teachers
4. Incentives should be made to attract students to the teaching profession.

(continued)

FIGURE 10.1   Key Recommendations From *A Nation at Risk*

Source: National Commission on Excellence in Education. (1983). *A nation at risk: The imperative for educational reform.* Washington, DC: U.S. Government Printing Office, pp. 24–33.

Leadership and Fiscal Support
1. The federal government has the primary responsibility to identify the national interest in education and, in cooperation with states and localities, should help meet the needs of key groups of students.
2. The federal government should also help fund and support efforts to protect and promote that interest and meet those needs.
3. The assistance of the federal government should be provided with a minimum of administrative burden and intrusiveness
4. Citizens should provide the financial support necessary to bring about the educational reform proposed in the report.

FIGURE 10.1   (Continued)

and declared that it would have been seen as "an act of war" if any unfriendly power had imposed our education system on us. The report was particularly critical of four things: (1) the curriculum, which it said had been "homogenized, diluted, and diffused"; (2) lowered expectations in terms of grades, testing, and graduation and college entry requirements; (3) the decreased time spent on academic subjects; and (4) the teaching force and its training.

A Nation at Risk has been described by some as a "bombshell" on the American education scene, by others as a "call to action," and by still others as a "conservative call to arms" (Horn, 2002). However described, there is no question that *A Nation at Risk* was a landmark in the history of education reform in the United States. No one in the Reagan administration could have anticipated that the report recommendations (see Figure 10.1) would become the blueprint for widespread reform of education at both the state and local levels.

A Nation at Risk was followed throughout the 1980s by numerous other reports on the status of education both nationally and in the many states. The reports came from various institutions, foundations, agencies, and individuals. A number were sponsored by the business community. Collectively they are responsible for what has been referred to as the Educational Reform Movement or the Excellence Movement.

Although few educators would question the need for some school reform in the 1980s—indeed one could not cite any time in history in which the schools or any other institution could not benefit from some reform—many members of the education community questioned whether a "crisis" in education existed or whether the schools had failed, as charged in *A Nation at Risk* and other reform reports. Perhaps the most cited challenge was Berliner and Biddle's (1995) *The Manufactured Crisis: Myths, Fraud, and the Attack on America's Public Schools*, an except from which is included as a Primary Source Reading for this chapter. In *The Manufactured Crisis*, Berliner and Biddle contended that the reform reports used questionable techniques to analyze data, distorted findings, and suppressed contradictory evidence that refuted their major conclusions.

Whether true or not, the various reform reports painted a picture of an education system in crisis, and politicians, the business community, and educators turned their attention to reforming the schools. The school reform movement that followed has been characterized as having three waves (Murphy, 1990).

Reform: The First Wave

The first wave of the school reform movement, dating from 1982 to 1985, responded to the recommendations of *A Nation at Risk* and similar reports and acted on the assumption that what was wrong with the schools could be fixed by top-down state actions directed at improving achievement and accountability. These reforms reflected, in part, the corporate formula for success: "Set clear goals and high standards for employees. Restructure operations so that managers and employees who actually make the product decide how it is to be done efficiently and effectively. Then hold those managers and employees responsible for the quality of the product by rewarding those who meet or exceed their goals and punish those who fail" (Cuban, 2001, p. 178). States enacted higher graduation requirements, standardized curriculum mandates, increased the testing of both teachers and students, and raised certification requirements for teachers. School districts increased their emphasis on computer literacy, homework, and basic skills; established minimum standards for participation in athletics; and privatized selected school operations. A more detailed listing of the initiatives from the first wave of reforms is provided in Figure 10.2.

 For Your Reflection and Analysis

Which of the initiatives from the first wave of reform are still emphasized today?

Reform: The Second Wave

No sooner had the ink dried on the first wave reform measures than they came under attack for being inadequate and misdirected. According to second wave reformers (1986–1989), the first wave was wrong in trying to prop up the existing system because the system itself was the problem and needed fundamental change. As articulated by the Carnegie Forum on Education and the Economy (1986): "We do not believe the educational system needs repairing; we believe it must be rebuilt to match the drastic change in our economy if we are to prepare our children for productive lives in the 21st century" (p. 14).

The second wave of reform focused not at the state level, on state mandates and centralization of authority, but at the local level and at the structure and processes of the schools themselves. A major theme of the second wave was the redistribution of power among the critical stakeholders of the schools. The belief was that the most effective reforms were those that emanated from those closest to the students, namely, educators and parents. The recommendations from the second wave of reform, coming from such noted educators as John Goodlad, Theodore Sizer, and Ernest Boyer, called for change from the bottom up, not from the top down, and dealt with such issues as decentralization, site-based management, teacher empowerment, parental involvement, and school choice. Restructuring, the buzzword of the second wave of reform, was associated with a number of prescriptions: year-round schools, longer school days and years, recast modes of governance, alternative funding patterns, all-out commitments to technology, and various combinations of these and other proposals (Kaplan, 1990). The second wave of reform also sought to balance the first wave's concern over the impact of education on the economy and the push for excellence with a concern for equity and the disadvantaged students who might become further disadvantaged by the "new standards of excellence."

Teachers and Teaching
- Salaries—establishing or raising minimums
- Career advancement
  - Merit pay
  - Career ladders
  - Supervision of beginning teachers
- Recruitment
  - Higher standards
  - Scholarships and loans (general, minorities and women, critical subject areas)
  - Special programs in high schools
- Preparation
  - Degree structure (liberal arts degree)
  - Clinical training
  - Changes in coursework
- Testing and certification
  - Entry tests for degree programs
  - Exit tests for degree programs
  - Certification test for beginning teachers
  - Certification test for veteran teachers
  - Alternative certification
- Beginning teacher induction
- Professional development and continuing education
  - Peer visits
  - Staff development plans
  - Sabbaticals
  - Fellowships and summer employment
  - Teaching methods
  - Evaluation

Curriculum
- Increased requirements for graduation
- Core curriculum
- Greater academic focus
- More sequenced coursework
- Higher-order skills
- Citizenship component
- Computer and technology courses
- Better textbooks

(continued)

FIGURE 10.2   Initiatives From the First Wave of Educational Reform

Source: Murphy, J. (1990). The education reform movement of the 1980s: A comprehensive analysis. In J. Murphy (Ed.), *The education reform movement of the 1980s: Perspectives and cases,* copyright 1990 by McCutchan Publishing Corporation, Richmond, California. Used by permission of the publisher.

Time
- Longer school year
- Longer school day
- Better use of time
- Increased student attendance

Monitoring, Testing, and Accountability
- Evaluation of staff (principals and teachers)
- Promotion and retention standards for students
- School report cards
- Educational bankruptcy programs
- School improvement incentives and awards
- State-centered student testing programs
- State-centered testing program for professionals

New Programs
- Gifted students
- At-risk students
  - Alternative programs
  - Recapture programs
  - Substance abuse
  - Early identification of students with problems
  - Teenage parents

Extended Concepts
- Exemplary practice schools (key schools)
- Demonstration schools
- Clinical schools
- Curriculum research and development centers
- School-university partnership

FIGURE 10.2   (Continued)

The second wave reform reports also stressed increased professionalism. Proposals to accomplish this included not only teacher empowerment, but also the reform of teacher training. One of the major proposals was presented in *A Nation Prepared: Teachers for the 21st Century* (1986) by the Carnegie Forum on Education and the Economy. The forum called for the elimination of undergraduate teacher preparation, for teacher preparation to be transferred to the graduate level, and for "lead teachers" to be appointed in every school to assist in supervising and mentoring new teachers and in curriculum development. Among its other recommendations was the establishment of a system of national certification for teachers based on teaching standards established by the profession, not state departments of education. Out of this recommendation grew the National Board for Professional Teaching Standards (NBPTS). Since it began work in 1987 the NBPTS has not only developed standards for teaching but also created certification in more than 30 fields. The certification fields are structured around student development levels and subject areas (See Table

10.1). The attainment of national board certification came to be associated with teacher competency; in 2004 all states and almost 550 school districts offered financial or other incentives to teachers who received national board certification.

The same year as the Carnegie report was published, a group of deans of colleges of education, the Holmes Group, also released a plan for the reforming of teacher education. *Tomorrow's Teachers,* as it was called, also proposed that the preparation of teachers take place at the graduate level, a proposal that generated significant controversy, but limited adoption. Although a number of Holmes Group institutions did move to a 5-year teacher education program, the cost to the student, as well as to school districts when all beginning teachers entered with a master's degree, limited widescale adoption of the proposal.

For Your Reflection and Analysis

Of all the recommendations proposed by the second wave of reforms, which was the most controversial? Why?

At the same time that attempts were being made to reform teacher education, a growing shortage of teachers was plaguing the American education system. Over the objection of teachers unions, the latter part of the 1980s saw an increase in states allowing alternative routes to certification. These programs were aimed at noneducation college graduates who had an academic major in a subject matter taught in the schools. The number of states offering alternative certification programs grew from 8 states in 1986 to 46 states in 2003 (Feistritzer & Chester, 2003).

Reform: The Third Wave

Like its predecessor, the third wave of reform began in 1988 with a critique of the previous wave (Murphy, 1990). This group of reformers proposed a more comprehensive model of change than did the two previous waves. As opposed to focusing on the education system, as did the first wave, or the adults in it, as did the second wave, the third-wave reformers focused on children and looked beyond the school to a comprehensive system for delivering services to children. Third wave reformers spoke in terms of children's policies rather than school policies and envisioned a major redesign of programs for children, with both the family and the school at the center of the service wheel (Murphy, 1990). Other comparisons between the third wave and the first two waves are presented in Table 10.2.

The response of state and local education systems to the recommendations of the various reform agendas suggests that they did not concern themselves with "waves" marked by changing directions. Rather, they looked at them as a broad set of policy recommendations that they considered in time frames that reflected their own needs (Firestone, Furhman, & Kirst, 1990). In the final analysis, the recommendations that involved the least redistribution of money, status, or authority and those that were the least expensive and the least complex (e.g., increasing graduation requirements) most often were adopted, whereas those with the opposite characteristics

For Your Reflection and Analysis

What major policy changes were proposed by the third wave of reformers?

TABLE 10.1 National Board Standards and Certification by Developmental Level

Standards Subject Area	Early Childhood Through Young Adulthood: Ages 3–18+	Early Childhood: Ages 3–8	Middle Childhood: Ages 7–12	Early & Middle Childhood: Ages 3–12	Early Adolescence: Ages 11–15	Adolescence & Young Adulthood: Ages 14–18+	Early Adolescence Through Young Adulthood: Ages 11–18+
Generalist		X	X				
Art				X			X
Career and Technical Education							X
English as a New Language				X			X
English Language Arts				X	X	X	
Exceptional Needs	X						
Library Media	X						
Mathematics					X	X	
Music				X			X
Physical Education				X			X
School Counseling	X						
Science					X	X	
Social Studies-History					X	X	
World Languages Other than English	X						

Source: National Board for Professional Teaching Standards. (2004). Standards & National Board Certification/Standards. Retrieved November 13, 2004 from the NBPTS website: www.nbpts.org/standards/stds.cfm.

TABLE 10.2   Comparing the Three Waves of Educational Reform in the 1980s

	Wave 1	Wave 2	Wave 3
Metaphor	Fix the old clunker (repair)	Get a new car (restructure)	Rethink view of transportation (redesign)
Philosophy	Expand centralized controls	Empower professionals and parents	Empower students
Assumptions	Problems traceable to low standards for workers and low quality of production tools	Problems traceable to systems failure	Problems traceable to fragmented, uncoordinated approaches for taking care of children
Change model	Top down (bureaucratic model)	Bottom up (market model); lateral (professional model)	Interorganizational (interprofessional model)
Policy mechanisms	Prescription (rule making and incentives); performance measurement	Power distribution	
Focus	The system; incremental improvement	The people (professionals and parents); radical change	The child; revolutionary change
Areas	Specific pieces of quantitative requirements—standards	Governance and work structures	Delivery structure

Source: Murphy, J. (1990). The education reform movement of the 1980s: A comprehensive analysis. In J. Murphy (Ed.), *The education reform movement of the 1980s: Perspectives and cases,* copyright 1990 by McCutchan Publishing Corporation, Richmond, California. Used by permission of the publisher.

were underadopted or not adopted at all (e.g., lengthening the school year) (Firestone et al., 1990). Thus, first-wave strategies were more widely adopted than were the proposals of the second and third waves of reform.

Essentialism, Perennialism, and Progressivism Revisited

In addition to the numerous reports issued by various commissions, foundations, and organizations, education scholars from across the ideological spectrum lent their voices to the chorus of reform recommendations. Among the most influential and public were a group of essentialists scholars associated with the back to basics movement. The back to basics movement had begun in the late 1970s as a response to the perceived lack of rigor in the curriculum and the decline in standardized test scores (scores on the Scholastic Aptitude Test fell almost 60 points in the 1970s). With its emphasis on academic subjects and the transmission of a core body of knowledge, the back to basics movement was a revisitation of the essentialist positions of the 1940s and the back to basics push by Bestor, Rickover, and others.

One of the individuals most identified with the neo-essentialist movement was E. D. Hirsch, Jr. Hirsch's 1987 best-selling *Cultural Literacy: What Every American Needs to Know* became a manifesto for the back to basics movement. In *Cultural Literacy*, Hirsch identified 5,000 names, dates, facts, and concepts from the fields of art, religion, science, and culture that he maintained an individual must know to be considered educated. Cultural literacy, he claimed, had become the "common currency for social and economic exchange in our democracy" and is therefore "the only available ticket to citizenship" and "the only sure avenue of opportunity for disadvantaged children" (p. xiii). *Cultural Literacy* was such a success in the popular press that Hirsch followed it with a dictionary of cultural literacy and books about what children should know at various grade levels. Hirsch also developed a core knowledge curriculum that offered the same academic credit to students in over 1,000 core knowledge schools nationwide.

In a similar vein was Diane Ravitch and Chester Finn's *What Do Our 17-Year-Olds Know?* (1987). After analyzing the results of the history and literature sections of the National Assessment of Educational Progress (NEAP), Ravitch and Finn concluded that the students had failed in both subjects. They then advanced the essentialist position that there is a body of knowledge that is so important it should be possessed by all Americans.

Another very visible essentialist was the secretary of education during much of Reagan's second term, William Bennett. From his position Bennett designed the curriculum for the model essentialist high school, *James Madison High School* (1987) and the model elementary school, *James Madison Elementary School* (1988). According to Bennett's design, all students except those in vocational programs would have the same curriculum of high academic standards. Bennett also used his position in the Department of Education as a "bully pulpit" to advance the administration's (and his) moral crusade against abortion, and for the "Just Say No" drug policy, abstinence, and prayer in the schools.

 For Your Reflection and Analysis

What current education spokesperson best represents the essentialist position?

Separate from the neo-essentialists, but also supportive of a more traditional curriculum, were the neo-perennialists, represented by Mortimer Adler and Allan Bloom. As discussed in chapter 1, in *The Paideia Proposal: An Educational Manifesto* (1982), Adler, like Hutchins, his former colleague at the University of Chicago, opposed a differential curriculum and maintained that all students should be exposed to the same high-quality education, one that included language, literature, mathematics, natural sciences, fine arts, history, geography, and social studies. Similar to Hutchins, Adler maintained that by studying the Great Books, one can learn the enduring lessons of life. The National Paideia Center at the University of North Carolina—Greensboro was established to disseminate information and research and train educators in Paideia principles and methods.

Delivering a similar message regarding the curriculum in higher education was Allan Bloom. As also discussed in chapter 1, in *The Closing of the American Mind* (1987), Bloom stressed the importance of teaching and learning from the Great Books and the responsibility of education to transmit our cultural heritage to our children.

Another call for change and another philosophical position was represented by Theodore Sizer, the former dean of the Harvard Graduate School of Education, described by Ravitch (2000) as "the leading voice of contemporary American progressivism" (p. 418). Published shortly after *A Nation at Risk*, Sizer's *Horace's Compromise* (1984) did not offer a set of top-down reform recommendations but proposed a set of nine principles that could be individualized to guide reform in any community. Among them were that teaching and learning be personalized to the maximum extent possible and that the school staff be empowered to make the majority of educational decisions. According to Sizer, the goal of the school should be simple: to ensure that each student master a limited number of essential skills and areas of knowledge. Sizer was not concerned with the quantity of learning (in fact, he proposed that the curriculum consist of only three areas: math/sciences, history/philosophy, and the arts), but rather with the quality of learning. Sizer maintained that the central focus of the schools should be the intellect and helping students to use their minds well. Sizer established an organization called the Coalition of Essential Schools to promote his reform ideas. By the end of the century hundreds of schools nationally and internationally had become members of the coalition.

Also associated with the new progressivism was the pedagogical theory of constructivism. As explained in chapter 1, constructivism builds on the theoretical framework of Bruner and is based on the premise that learning is a process by which learners construct their own meaning and understanding by reflecting on their past experiences and accumulated knowledge. By the mid-1980s, constructivism had become the dominant idea among education theorists, who quoted Dewey and Piaget to argue that students would only be motivated to learn if they were actively involved in the learning process, constructing their own knowledge through their own experiences (Ravitch, 2000).

For Your Reflection and Analysis

What essential skills should all students master?

For Your Reflection and Analysis

Give an essentialist's example of constructivism in action.

National Goals, National Standards, and Accountability

By the end of the 1980s, despite the adoption of a myriad of reform initiatives, the reform and restructuring of education proposed by the various commissions and individuals did not appear to have produced any significant change in educational outputs. As a result, the quality of education and the perceived need to "fix it" remained major topics of public debate. Responding to the ongoing criticism of both education and his administration's failure to offer any remedies, in the fall of 1989 President Bush co-convened, with the National Governors Association, an "education summit" at Charlottesville, Virginia. Chaired by Arkansas Governor Bill Clinton, the governors agreed that the states should focus on raising student achievement, raising academic standards, and holding schools accountable for the results. There was also agreement on the creation of national education goals. Accordingly, in early 1990, the National Governors' Association and the Bush administration announced six national education goals to be accomplished by the year 2000 (see Goals 1–3 and 5–7 in Figure 10.3).

President Bush's plan to implement the goals, *America 2000: An Education Strategy*, presented to Congress in April of 1991, called for the creation of "world class standards" and a national standardized test for assessing their attainment. Bush was unable to gain congressional support for his plan, largely because of the controversy surrounding a key feature of the plan—vouchers to promote school choice—but also because he was never able to articulate how it would be funded. However, in the last 2 years of his administration he was able to provide support to the standards movement by funding grants to the professional organizations in the major subject areas to develop voluntary national standards in the arts, civics and government, foreign languages, geography, history, and science. The math standards already developed by the National Council of Teachers of Mathematics served as a model for the other groups.

The election of 1992 saw education assume a place of prominence on the political agenda that it had never held before. As observed by Terrel H. Bell, secretary of education under President Reagan:

> George Bush proclaimed himself to be the "Education President" during his successful 1988 campaign. President Bill Clinton brought the less-than-spectacular Bush record in education to the attention of the voters during the campaign of 1992 and promised to be a more effective "Education President." This has never happened in the nation's history. Education is now a major, high priority national concern, as well as a state and local responsibility. (1993, p. 595)

The Clinton administration did, in fact, attempt to keep its commitment to education. The first 2 years of the Clinton administration have been said to be the most productive in terms of major education legislation since 1965–66, and included increasing Head Start funding, reforming the student loan program, funding violence prevention programs, and supporting programs that link education and the workplace (the School to Work Opportunities Act), to name a few. Known as an education governor, Clinton came to the presidency talking excellence and accountability, the catchwords of state school reform during the 1980s (Newman, 1998).

 For Your Reflection and Analysis

Can President Clinton be considered an "education president"? Why or why not?

The Clinton plan to implement the national goals, called the Goals 2000: Educate America Act, adopted the six goals articulated by the National Governors' Association and added two new goals related to parent participation and teacher education and professional development (see Figure 10.3, Goals 4 and 8).

The adoption of Goals 2000 marked a turning point in the direction of state and federal education policy. "Emphasis shifted from educational inputs to educational outcomes and from procedural accountability to educational accountability.

1. *School Readiness.* By the year 2000, all children in America will start school ready to learn.
2. *High School Completion.* By the year 2000, the high school graduation rate will increase to at least 90 percent.
3. *Student Achievement and Citizenship.* By the year 2000, all students will leave grades 4, 8, and 12 having demonstrated competency over challenging subject matter including English, mathematics, science, foreign languages, civics and government, economics, arts, history, and geography, and every school in the United States will ensure that all students learn to use their minds well, so they may be prepared for responsible citizenship, future learning, and productive employment in our Nation's modern economy.
4. *Teacher Education and Professional Development.* By the year 2000, the Nation's teaching force will have access to programs for the continued improvement of their professional skills and the opportunity to acquire the knowledge and skills needed to instruct and prepare all American students for the next century.
5. *Mathematics and Science.* By the year 2000, United States students will be first in the world in mathematics and science achievement.
6. *Adult Literacy and Lifelong Learning.* By the year 2000, every adult American will be literate and will possess the knowledge and skills necessary to compete in a global economy and exercise the rights and responsibilities of citizenship.
7. *Safe, Disciplined, and Alcohol- and Drug-Free Schools.* By the year 2000, every school in the United States will be free of drugs, violence, and the unauthorized presence of firearms and alcohol, and will offer a disciplined environment conducive to learning.
8. *Parental Participation.* By the year 2000, every school will promote partnerships that will increase parental involvement and participation in promoting the social, emotional, and academic growth in children.

FIGURE 10.3   The National Education Goals
Source: H. R. 1804 Goals 2000 Educate America Act, Sec. 101. (1994).

Equity was reconceptualized as ensuring all students access to high-quality educational programs rather than providing supplemental and often compensatory services" (Goertz, 2001, p. 62). Included under the Goals 2000 umbrella was the reauthorization of the ESEA, the Improving America's Schools Act (IASA). A major purpose of this version of the ESEA was to encourage comprehensive reform at the state and local levels to meet the national goals. A major provision of the act required states (with the input of local school districts) to develop school improvement plans that established challenging content and performance standards, implement assessments to measure student progress in meeting these standards, and adopt

For Your Reflection and Analysis

What are some of the current issues that represent an ongoing "curriculum war"?

measures to hold schools accountable for the achievement of the standards. It also required that students with disabilities be included in state and local assessment and accountability systems. And, unlike previous federal programs, which bypassed state education policies, these initiatives were designed to be integrated with state and local reform initiatives (Goertz, 2001).

Throughout the remainder of the 1990s the calls for school reform continued, and *standards* and *accountability* became the key words in reform proposals. However, states and school districts faced a number of difficulties in their efforts to establish challenging academic standards and assessment systems. States varied widely in the scope and rigor of their standards, in what they measured, and in how they measured it. In state after state standards became the battleground for ongoing "curriculum wars" as educators and policy makers faced off over such issues as whole language versus phonics or whose history to teach (Campbell, 2000).

Objections to the standards also came from religious groups such as the Christian Coalition, who directed their criticism to what was called outcome-based education. Some of the standards included student learning outcomes that involved student values and attitudes (e.g., "give examples of your own positive and negative impact on the environment and assess their personal commitment to the environment"), which religious conservatives challenged as potentially penalizing students who gave the "wrong" answer or who gave an answer that reflected so-called family

The first national education goals, Goals 2000, were adopted during the Clinton Administration.

values (Newman, 1998). Other conservatives were concerned that the standards were being "dumbed down" and that they focused too much on minorities and women and not enough on the "Founding Fathers," or, more generally, that they reflected a liberal bias.

However, despite the challenges, and in no small part as a result of the work of the various curriculum organizations, by the end of the decade content standards were in place in 47 states along with statewide assessments in 30 states. Local school districts were expected to align their curricula with the standards, and colleges of education were expected to incorporate the standards into their curricula and instruction.

The push for standards and standards-based assessment was accompanied by the enactment in most states of so-called *high-stakes testing* to determine who would be promoted and who would graduate from high school. However, as testing was being initiated, several states experienced serious problems with test construction and, more important, with the high numbers of students who failed the tests. In most states the students who performed the poorest on the exams were low-income and minority students, especially those with limited English-speaking ability and those from low-income, mostly urban districts—the victims described in Jonathan Kozol's *Savage Inequalities* (1991).

Simultaneous with the standards and assessment movement was the accountability movement. That is, states and school districts began to issue "report cards" to parents and the general public grading schools on one or more quality or performance indicators. Although the indicators varied somewhat, student performance was always included. States varied widely in how they graded the schools, in how they measured improvement, in the assistance they provided low-performing schools, and in the penalties they enacted for continued low performance. Various schemes were devised to reward high-performing schools. Conversely, 20 states enacted legislation authorizing the state to initiate takeover action when a school was chronically underperforming and showed inadequate improvement. However, in only a limited number of cases did state officials have the political will to take such action.

School Choice

A major plank in the campaign to reform the schools in the 1990s was school choice. Support for school choice came from parents across the socioeconomic and ideological spectrum. Low-income and minority parents saw choice as a way to extend educational opportunities to students who historically had not had the resources to choose between public and private schools, or even among public schools. Other parents saw choice as providing the opportunity to protect their children from the violence in the schools or to provide them with a more academically challenging or enriching experience. Religious conservatives saw choice as a way to support schools that promoted a particular religious ideology. However, despite the fact that almost all parents and politicians supported the concept that parents should be given greater choice in the schools their children attended, how this was to be achieved was very much in debate. The most often seriously considered approaches were school vouchers, charter schools, and privatization.

Vouchers

The most intensely debated of the school choice options was vouchers, especially those that could be used at private religious schools. Voucher supporters hoped that competition would do what regulation had failed to do (Hertert, 1998). Giving financial grants to consumers and treating education as a "consumable item," subject to the forces or the market place, was presumed to force schools to operate more efficiently.

As previously noted, President Bush had unsuccessfully proposed federal vouchers as part of his America 2000 plan. In 1996 Republican presidential candidate Robert Dole proposed vouchers that could be used at private as well as public schools. Although not rejecting the concept of vouchers, the Democrats opposed their use at private schools. They argued that this would violate the separation of church and state. They also rejected any plan that would shift money from the chronically underfunded public schools to private schools and that would require taxpayers to support public schools as well as private schools. They were also concerned that vouchers would exacerbate inequities and stratification by race, color, or creed. Democrats argued that the schools should be improved, not abandoned.

With the prospect of federal vouchers in gridlock, several states considered voucher proposals. Only two states, Wisconsin and Ohio, ultimately adopted voucher proposals, with programs being initiated in Milwaukee in 1990 and Cleveland in 1995. Although the Milwaukee program initially did not include the use of the vouchers at religious schools, in 1995 it was expanded to include these schools, as had the Cleveland program from its inception. Both programs were immediately challenged in the courts. Conflicting lower court decisions regarding whether the use of the vouchers at religious schools was an unconstitutional support of religion paved the way for appeals to the U.S. Supreme Court. In 1998 the U.S. Supreme Court declined to review the Wisconsin Supreme Court's decision upholding the Milwaukee program (*Jackson v. Benson*, 1998). In 2002 the Court ruled that the Cleveland program, which was aimed at providing scholarships of up to $2,250 to attend the school of their parents' choice, was not unconstitutional as long as parents had a choice among a range of public and nonpublic schools (*Zelman v. Simmons-Harris*, 2002).

Following the *Zelman* decision, voucher supporters anticipated their widespread adoption. However this has not occurred. A major reason seems to be that the growing array of alternative school choice options (see Figure 10.4), in particular charter schools, contributed to a decreased interest in pursuing the contentious voucher alternative (Metcalf & Legan, 2002).

Charter Schools

A less controversial proposal for increasing parental choice, one that gained increasing favor in the 1990s, was charter schools. Charter schools are publicly supported schools established on the issuance of a charter (contract) from the state, local school board, or other designated entity. Charter schools are intended to give greater autonomy to the school (they are typically exempt from all state regulations except those governing health and safety and civil rights), encourage innovative programs and practices, promote efficiency through competition, and most important, provide greater choice in education programs to parents and students within the public

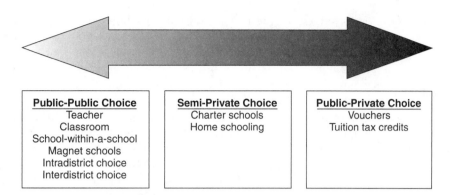

Public-Public Choice	**Semi-Private Choice**	**Public-Private Choice**
Teacher	Charter schools	Vouchers
Classroom	Home schooling	Tuition tax credits
School-within-a-school		
Magnet schools		
Intradistrict choice		
Interdistrict choice		

FIGURE 10.4   The Choice Continuum

Source: Metcalf, Kim K., Muller, Patricia A., Legan, Natalie A. (2001). *School Choice in America: The Great Debate.* Bloomington, IN: Phi Delta Kappa International, 2001, p. 4. Reprinted by permission of Phi Delta Kappa International.

school system. Although its roots can be found in the "liberal" alternative school movement of the 1960s and 1970s, charters have been widely supported by Republicans as well as Democrats.

In 1991 Minnesota became the first state to enact legislation providing for the establishment of charter schools. California followed suit the next year. Arizona, the state with the most liberal charter school legislation, came aboard in 1993. The liberalness of the Arizona law, which allows any individual or group to apply for a charter, led to many false starts and charter school closures, many times leaving students in the lurch. Teacher unions have not opposed the concept of charter schools (in fact, NEA affiliates in several states applied for charters [Newman, 1998]), but they have opposed state charter school laws that, like those in Arizona, do not require teachers in charter schools to be certified.

The Republican takeover of many state legislatures in 1994 lent support to the charter school movement, as did President Clinton in his 1997 state of the union address by pledging $100 million to help create 3,000 more charter schools by the year 2002. In fact, by 2002 over 2,500 charter schools were in operation in 37 states and the District of Columbia (U.S. Department of Education, 2003).

 For Your Reflection and Analysis

What would influence your decision to work in a charter school if you were asked to do so?

Private Contractors

Although not expanding the choice option to attending a different school, another favorite among choice advocates was to allow private contractors to bid to provide various services to the schools. The assumption was that private contractors would operate more effectively and efficiently than public schools. The practice of contracting with private companies or individuals outside the school system for services (e.g., transportation, food services, and custodial services) has been around since the establishment of the first New England schools. However, such contracts typically had not been for the delivery of instructional or administrative services. In the 1990s the push for efficiency and privatization opened the door, often over objections of teacher groups, for an expansion of the concept to include these professional domains. Some districts contracted with for-profit firms to tutor students to raise test scores or to deliver other instructional services. Other districts contracted for leadership or instructional services (e.g., Minneapolis contracted with a private firm for an employee to serve as superintendent of schools). Others went so far as to contract with for-profit firms such as Educational Alternatives Incorporated (EAI) or the Edison Schools to operate one or more schools. The success of these experiments varied. Many of the contract schools were located in disadvantaged urban areas. In a number of cases, the most public being the 2-year EAI experiment in Baltimore, either because of political controversy or underperformance, the contract was not renewed. The most successful of the private contractors was the Edison Schools, which by the end of the 1990s was operating over 100 schools in 20 states.

Although the move to contract with private, for-profit firms did not expand as widely as was originally anticipated, it was given added life by its association with the charter school movement. That is, some charter schools hired private contractors to operate the schools. In fact, in a number of states, including Arizona and Michigan, private contractors became major players in the charter school movement. In Michigan 70% of the charter schools came to be operated by education management organizations (Arsen, Plank, & Sykes, 2001). The convergence of the choice strategies has proven to benefit both.

Cultural and Gender Wars

The Republican takeover of the U.S. Congress and many state legislatures in the 1994 elections not only put Clinton's educational goals in conflict with a renewed conservative agenda but also signaled an escalation of what historian Joel Spring (2001) described as the "cultural wars." The major battles of the cultural wars were waged over bilingual education, multicultural education, and school choice. Although some indicators, such as SAT scores, had improved in the 1980s in the wake of the reform movements, large numbers of parents continued to be dissatisfied with a school system that valued diversity over diction and affirmative action over arithmetic and demanded the end of multicultural and bilingual education and affirmative action, and greater control over curriculum content and materials.

Bilingual Education Debate

Bilingual education became a major political target during the Reagan and Bush administrations. In fact, some Republicans supported a movement opposing bilingual education and promoting the adoption of English as the official language of the United States and their state and that it be the language used in conducting public affairs and voting. The movement was led by such ultraconservative groups as U.S. English, English First, and Save Our Schools. In 1981 Reagan's secretary of education withdrew the proposed federal regulations for compliance with the *Lau* decision and left it up to the states to decide which bilingual education model to support. Unlike previous administrations, Reagan supported the English immersion programs that had been used with earlier immigrant groups. The change symbolized the intractable and heated controversy surrounding bilingual education: which bilingual education program model (transition, immersion, or maintenance) works best, whether any work, or more fundamentally, whether they are needed at all.

In states such as Florida, Texas, Arizona, and California, with large numbers of language minority students who were underperforming and dropping out of school, it was clear that attention must be given to reaching these students. Many believed bilingual education was key to doing so. However, opponents of bilingual education felt that the time and money invested in bilingual education could be better spent elsewhere, that providing bilingual education actually discouraged children from using English by allowing them to function in school without it, and that bilingual education was harmful to their academic progress. They also argue that bilingual education, like multicultural education, promotes cultural separatism, not cultural unity. This argument is especially common among those who see the primary goal of the school as transmitting a core body of knowledge and the cultural values of the dominant society.

Opposition was particularly strong to bilingual maintenance programs, programs that deliver instruction in both English and the native language and seek to promote fluency in both. Critics charged that such programs produce students who speak neither language well and are not prepared to succeed in the English-dominated society. Supporters of bilingual education counterclaim that these programs are not a threat to the core academic program, but have a vital role in the reform of the education system and in the attainment of equal educational opportunity for not only language minority students, but all students.

For Your Reflection and Analysis

Where do you stand on the bilingual education debate?

The success of the opposition to the bilingual maintenance model was reflected in the 1988 amendments to the Bilingual Education Act. These amendments provided additional funding for English-only instructional programs and decreased funding for bilingual programs. The act also limited student participation in bilingual programs to 3 years.

Opposition to native language teaching continued in the 1990s and grew to include immigrant parents. Their concerns focused on the fact that children routinely remained segregated in bilingual programs for 3 years of more, and in some cases more than 6 years. Nowhere was the opposition more heated than in California. In 1994 the California voters passed Proposition 187 banning undocumented immigrants from public education as well as from receiving other social services. Supporters believed that the denial of services would decrease illegal immigration. (The proposition was later declared unconstitutional.)

Another volley in the cultural wars in California came the next year, in July 1995, when the regents of the University of California adopted a policy eliminating the consideration of race and gender from admission decisions. Then, in 1998 California voters approved another referendum, Proposition 227, the so-called English

Opposition to bilingual education grew during the 1980s and 1990s.

for the Children initiative, which mandated that limited-English-proficiency (LEP) students be taught in a special English immersion program for no more than 1 year before being mainstreamed into the regular classroom. Two years later a similar initiative, Proposition 203, was overwhelmingly approved in Arizona. Several other states have also considered English-only initiatives. Concerns and debate, far from fading, continued into the next century.

Multicultural Education Under Fire

The civil rights movement brought an increase in ethnic pride and increased pressure to recognize and respect the history and contributions of each racial and ethnic group as well as women. The curriculum began to offer such courses as cultural awareness, Black history, Native American history, and ethnic and gender studies. In the 1980s and 1990s, as the reform movement and back to basics movement sought to bring more "rigor" to the curriculum and increase graduation requirements, opposition to the place of such courses in the curriculum grew. Supporters of a basic curriculum considered these courses "frills" and argued that such a curriculum undermined cultural unity and family values and promoted radical feminism and gay rights. Perhaps equally damning, they suggested that efforts to gain equal access and equal educational opportunity were undermining the pursuit of excellence.

Beginning with the Reagan administration, excellence was counterpoised as effectively the opposite of equity, and many questioned whether the nation could have both (Bernard & Mondale, 2001c). As a result, support for programs designed to promote equity and multiculturalism was reduced. In response, proponents of multicultural education continued to argue that an excellent education is multicultural and that those who are seeking equal educational opportunities are seeking, in fact, an excellent education, not a lesser education. Many groups and individuals also expressed grave concern over the impact of the standards, testing, and accountability movements on poor and minority children and the schools they attended (e.g., the National Coalition of Advocates for Students in *Barriers to Excellence: Our Children at Risk* [1988] and Jonathan Kozol in *Savage Inequalities* [1991]). Educators and policy analysts noted the growing economic segregation, as well as the racial and ethnic re-segregation discussed later in this chapter, and documented their negative consequences. However, the continued attention given to the perceived deficits in American education ensured continued debate about the place of multicultural education in the curriculum.

 For Your Reflection and Analysis

If only one goal could be promoted, should it be excellence or equity? Explain your choice.

According to Spring (2001), the cultural wars of the late 20th century reflected "yet another battle in the centuries old effort to make English and Anglo-American Protestant culture the unifying language and culture of the United States" (p. 411). The perceived threats coming from the civil rights movement and the new wave of immigration from Mexico and Asia were different, but the war was the same.

Gender Wars

As discussed in chapter 9, beginning in the 1960s and 1970s feminist activism had brought an attention to the issue of gender equity in the schools that had resulted in significant gains in improving female representation in the curriculum, athletics, scholarships, and the professions. Throughout the 1980s and much of the 1990s the attention to gender issues in school continued to focus on the barriers and the sexism females faced in achieving equal educational opportunity. (See, for example, *Shortchanging Girls, Shortchanging America* [AAUW, 1991]; *How Schools Shortchange Girls* [AAUW, 1992]; *Hostile Hallways* [AAUW, 1993; AAUW, 2001b]; and *Gender Gaps: Where Schools Still Fail Our Children* [AAUW, 1998].)

At the same time the New Right unleashed what has come to be known as a backlash against feminism. The term has been used to describe what many believe to be attempts to undo the social and legal gains made by women and the acceptance of feminist thought in the popular culture. The backlash was a response to what was said to be the myths created by the media, popular culture, psychology, and right-wing conservatives that emphasized the mental, physical, and emotional problems and sacrifices of career women and their families, the dangers and costs of child care, the "crisis of masculinity," reverse discrimination, and so on. According to Faludi (1991), "Just as Reaganism and Thatcherism shifted political discourse far to the right and demonized liberalism, so the backlash convinced the public that women's liberation was the true contemporary scourge—the source of an endless laundry list of personal, social, and economic problems" (p. 26). Others consider the backlash as another example of the "backlash politics" that occurs when groups or sectors of society feel they are declining in their perceived importance, influence, or power (Watson, Brown, & Dawson, 1996).

The backlash against feminism has not been as visible in education as it has been in the larger society. However, it has been reflected in charges of discrimination against males and in claims that boys experience the most gender bias in the schools (see, e.g., Sommers [2000], *The War Against Boys*). The response of the American Association of University Women, *Beyond the Gender Wars* (2001a), acknowledged that both boys and girls experience sexism. Other researchers, such as David Sadker in the Primary Source Reading for this chapter, however, refuted the charge that in the gender wars boys are the victims and "girls rule." The disinterest of the first Bush administration in supporting women's equity programs and affirmative action were also reflections of, if not a backlash, the mood of the times.

Resegregation

As discussed in chapter 9, during the 1970s a number of urban districts came under court order to desegregate their schools. Many of these districts were home to poor and minority students and had tried in good faith for years to integrate the schools. They had been frustrated in their efforts by changing economic and community demographics that resulted in many urban areas becoming increasingly minority and the schools becoming resegregated.

In a series of decisions in the 1990s a more conservative Supreme Court responded to the plight of these districts. In 1991, in *Board of Education of Oklahoma City Public Schools v. Dowell* and in 1992 in *Freeman v. Pitts*, the Supreme Court ruled that court-ordered desegregation can be terminated when the school board had in good faith made efforts to comply with the court order and had, *to the extent practical*, given past history and current conditions, eliminated the vestiges of past discrimination. The decisions ended judicial oversight of desegregation plans for a number of school districts and provided these districts the opportunity to fashion new remedies that appeared more likely to be successful given the circumstances of the district.

In a landmark case in 1995, *Missouri v. Jenkins*, the Supreme Court addressed what must be done and spent in attempting to desegregate. In this case the Kansas City school system and the state of Missouri had reportedly spent $1.7 million between 1986 and 1995 on a massive desegregation plan. The Supreme Court ruled that desegregation plans should be limited in time and scope and that the goal of desegregation plans need not be to achieve racial balance but to restore control to state and local authorities as soon as possible. The Court ruled that once the district had eliminated the effects of legally imposed segregation, the schools could revert to their "natural" pattern of segregation. According to the Court, "The Constitution does not prevent individuals from choosing to live together, to work together, or to send their children to school together, as long as the state does not interfere with their choice on the basis of race" (p. 2063).

The decisions in *Dowell, Pitts,* and *Jenkins* were viewed by some as necessary corrections to judicial excesses. But many others saw them as the Court turning its back on *Brown*. Lower courts following the lead of the Supreme Court declared districts to have achieved unitary status and removed their judicial oversight. The effect of these decisions has been to encourage school districts to bring an end to busing and other desegregation strategies in favor of neighborhood schools and a steady unraveling of 25 years of progress in integration. Over 500 court-ordered and voluntary desegregation plans were eliminated.

The resegregation that has occurred has affected both Black and Hispanic students. In fact, for a number of years Hispanic American students have been more segregated than Blacks, not only by ethnicity but increasingly by language (Orfield, 2001; Orfield, Frankenberg, & Lee, 2003). Segregation by race and ethnicity is highly correlated to segregation by poverty (Orfield, 2001). In 2000, over 75% of Hispanics and 70% of Blacks attended predominately minority schools, and 37% of each attended schools that are 90 to 100% minority, an increase for Hispanics from the prebusing level of 1968 (23%)(Orfield, 2001). In effect, although the overall school enrollment has become increasingly diverse, the nation's schools are becoming increasingly segregated.

The End of a Presidency, a Decade, a Century

During President Clinton's second term, debate at the federal level continued over whether there should be a federal Department of Education, voluntary national testing, and private school choice. Toward the end of his presidency Clinton used his bully pulpit to advocate the end of so-called social promotion, a drumbeat continued by the second Bush administration (Goodlad, 2002). Faced with a larger Republican majority in Congress, and weakened by personal scandals and threats of impeachment, Clinton was able to hold off any significant reductions in federal spending for education, but he was unable to advance any of his major education proposals.

The influence of the business community on education and the emphasis on the importance of an educated workforce to international competition begun during the Reagan administration continued during the Clinton presidency. In fact, both were reinforced by a second education summit sponsored by the National Governors Association held in 1996 at IBM's Executive Conference Center in Palisades, New York. The Summit included the executives of major businesses nationwide, but basically excluded the education community. The message was clear: Professional educators had failed to bring quality to the schools, and it was someone else's turn to try—the someones who are the ultimate consumers of the output of the American education system (Lagowski, 1996).

The final year of the 20th century brought a tragedy that captured the nation's attention: the massacre at Columbine High School in Littleton, Colorado, that resulted in the death of 14 students and one teacher. As the century closed, conflict in the schools was matched by fighting in the courts. The growing conservatism of the 1990s brought renewed efforts to allow prayer in the school, to fight so-called secular humanism in the curriculum, and to elect an "education president" who shared the conservative agenda. The outcome is the topic of the next chapter.

Conclusion

The 1980s and 1990s provide perhaps the best examples a historian could ask for of history repeating itself: The schools were blamed for the ills of society and the economy and at the same time seen as a tool for the solution; a new group of essentialist scholars advocated that schools focus on the essential knowledge and skills needed to successfully function in our democratic society; and neo-perennialists called on the schools to focus on the unchanging truths or great ideas. At the same time, progressivism came to be associated with the growing educational theory of constructivism.

What was new about the reform movement that began in the 1980s was, in a way that had not been true since the common school movement, the scope of the impact. Virtually every level of the education system was the object of reform. The reforms ultimately enacted were also unprecedented in their consequences: high-stakes testing that could spell doom for teachers who could not obtain or renew certificates, students not allowed to graduate, and schools taken over by the state. And, as the schools became increasingly academic, vocational offerings were reduced. Standards and accountability were the twin pillars of the reform movement.

The proposed companion to reforming the existing education system was to give students the choice to attend any school in the district, public or private. Competition, it was argued, would force schools to be more efficient and effective in order to survive. After a number of proposals and failed attempts, voucher programs that included parochial schools were implemented by several districts and, more important, were upheld by the Supreme Court. Of greater importance—indeed it may change the face of American public education—is the charter school movement. Although overall the numbers of charter schools and students in them are small, they are one of the fastest growing educational innovations and appear to have become, possibly more rapidly than any other in American education history, an established part of the education landscape.

Some historians have interpreted the events of the 1990s—vouchers, charter schools, privatization, and the abandonment of support for education as a source of equal educational opportunity—as spelling the end of the common school (Spring, 2001). Others have taken a less pessimistic view but observe that "the age of the public school as an instrument of social policy may have reached a limit" (Rury, 2002, p. 218). Almost all share a concern about what appeared to be unrelenting criticism of the public schools as they faced the challenges inherent in educating an increasingly multicultural student body and meeting the needs of at-risk students while meeting the mandates of the federal No Child Left Behind Act discussed in the next chapter.

For Discussion and Application

1. Which, if any, American president in the period from 1960 to 2000 do you think most deserves the title "education president"? Why?
2. What are the common denominators of reform movements?
3. Of the three so-called waves of education reform, which wave had the greatest impact on education? Explain.
4. Discuss the changing role of business in education reform. Do you perceive this as a positive or negative change? Why?
5. What is your response to Joel Spring's assertion that the end of the common school is at hand?
6. Visit or read the descriptive materials from two charter schools in your area or state. Describe the extent to which they exhibit innovative programs and practices.

Primary Source Reading

According to David Berliner, professor at Arizona State University, and Bruce Biddle, professor at the University of Missouri, many of the claims made by A Nation at Risk *and other reform reports of the 1980s were based on faulty evidence and inaccurate information. As a result, the policy makers and the general American public concluded that our schools were in crisis and began to focus their energy and attention to "fixing the schools" instead of paying attention to the real problems facing education, such as how to distribute fewer resources, design appropriate curricula to meet the needs of diverse populations, and develop a system of education that provides high standards and equal opportunity for all students regardless of social class. In this excerpt from* The Manufactured Crisis *Berliner and Biddle attempt to debunk the "myth" of declining student achievement.*

The Manufactured Crisis: Myths, Fraud, and the Attack on America's Public Schools

D. C. Berliner and B. J. Biddle

This chapter is concerned with a key tenet of the Manufactured Crisis. Critics of American schools have argued that student achievement has declined sharply, that American students now lag seriously behind students in other Western countries, and that these facts are confirmed by massive evidence. America's teachers and schools are failing the nation, they say, and America is in danger of falling into the ash can of history. As we shall show, these assertions are errant nonsense. . . .

We begin with the SAT story. To be sure, *aggregate* total SAT scores obtained by the nation's high school seniors fell between about 1963 and 1975. Moreover, that decline came about because aggregate scores fell for both parts of the

Source: Berliner, D. C., & Biddle, B. J. (1995). *The manufactured crisis: Myths, fraud, and the attack on America's public schools* (pp. 14–23). Reading, MA: Addison-Wesley.

SAT—the parts that measure, respectively, verbal and mathematics achievement.

This decline has been cited as evidence that our schools were failing by many people—such as William Bennett—who were either ignorant or wanted to rubbish public education. These doomsayers argue that such a "huge" decline in SAT scores—ranging from 60 to 90 points, depending on the years used to compute the figure—was sure proof that the nation was in trouble. And to this day the press continues to report annual figures for aggregate national SAT scores (sometimes citing shifts of one or two points in those scores) as if they were a report card that can tell Americans something about the effectiveness of their schools.

This is all nonsense. Such small shifts in SAT scores are not meaningful, and by themselves aggregate SAT scores provide no information about the performance of American schools. To understand this, one must learn a bit about the SAT and its limitations.

First, how are SAT scores generated, and what does an SAT score truly mean? The SAT is taken by high school seniors and for some years has required those students to answer 138 multiple-choice questions, 78 concerned with verbal materials, 60 focused on mathematics. (It has *not* examined student knowledge of history, the sciences, the arts, the humanities, foreign languages, the social sciences, or other important subjects that high schools also teach.) Although new questions are developed for the SAT each year, those questions have been carefully checked so that each new edition of the SAT has been presumed to be equivalent to the first "standardized" form of the test, which appeared *in April of 1941.* If we believe the critics, then, the quality of the entire twelve or more years of schooling to which American students are exposed could be judged by means of a 138-item test requiring only a few hours to complete, and composed of questions designed to assess only a narrow range of student knowledge against the standards of fifty years ago!

Second, scores for the SAT are not reported as numbers of right answers but are "converted" (through obscure rules) in such a way that the scale scores earned by each student for each subtest range from 200 to 800 points. This means that the total SAT score for an individual can range from 400 to 1600 points, but this huge range of scale points actually represents a much smaller range of correct or incorrect answers. Thus, in the middle of the SAT range, a difference of one correct or incorrect answer will generate about *ten* points of difference in the SAT scale score. You may think this is absurd, but there is actually more confusion. The relation between number of correct SAT answers and scale scores also varies, depending on the number of right answers. In fact, the very talented student who correctly answers all but one of the questions on the verbal part of the SAT loses *fifty* scale points for that one error, earning a score of 750 rather than 800.

What does this mean for the interpretation of aggregate SAT scores? Such aggregates are computed by averaging the individual scale scores of many thousands of students. Since the scale scores summed in those averages come from students representing the entire talent range, it is literally impossible to compute exactly what a difference in aggregate SAT scores means in terms of average numbers of questions answered correctly on the test. But if we assume that most students answered a middling number of questions correctly, then a decline of "from 60 to 90 points" in aggregate SAT scale scores probably means that the average student answered from six to nine fewer questions correctly. Since students had to answer 138 questions in all, this means that the "terrible" decline in SAT scores was in reality a drop of perhaps 5 percent in the number of questions answered correctly. Put this way, the decline in aggregate SAT scores that began about 1963 seems a good deal less "massive." Moreover, the drop that did occur in aggregate SAT scores ceased in the mid-1970s, and there has been no evidence of a decline since then. Recent annual shifts in aggregate national scores have been minute, often amounting to only one or two scale points, which probably means that the students of America have answered, or failed to answer, one or two *tenths* of an additional SAT question.

Third, problems are also generated when one tries to figure out the meaning of *aggregate* SAT scores. The SAT was designed to predict the grade point averages of individual college freshmen and has demonstrated real, if limited, value when used for this purpose. SAT scores were never intended to be aggregated for evaluating the achievements of teachers, schools, school districts, or states, and such scores have *no* validity when used for such evaluations. The reason is that the SAT is a *voluntary* test and is typically taken only by those high school seniors interested in going to college. Moreover, the proportion of students choosing to take the SAT varies sharply across the country. For example, in 1993 the percentage of students taking the SAT varied from *less than 10 percent* in Alabama, Arkansas, Iowa, Kansas, Louisiana, Mississippi, North Dakota, Oklahoma, South Dakota, and Utah to *more than 70 percent* in Connecticut, the District of Columbia, Massachusetts, New Hampshire, New Jersey, New York, and Rhode Island.

Does this matter? Absolutely. When only a few students take the SAT, those students are likely to be people with strong high school records, who are trying to get into "the best" colleges. In contrast, when a larger proportion of students take the SAT, that proportion will include more students with weak high school records, who are merely hoping to qualify for some kind of higher education. This means, of course, that the aggregate SAT score earned by a school, school district, or state is not valid for judging the educational quality of that unit unless all, or a *representative sample*, of its students take the test. This may sound like a harsh judgment, but we are only echoing a warning that has already been circulated by the College Entrance Examination Board, which publishes the SAT.

Now, let us apply this principle to the problem of interpreting aggregate SAT scores for the nation. Widespread adoption of the SAT came about gradually, but since the mid-1960s, only about half of all eligible high school seniors in the country have taken the test each year. Aggregate national SAT scores, therefore, have never represented the nation as a whole but have always been generated by a self-selected pool of students who wanted to attend college and thought they could improve their chances by taking the test.

Moreover, the composition of students who take the SAT has varied over time. Data on the characteristics of test takers have been distributed by the College Entrance Examination Board since 1976, and these suggest how student composition has changed over the past eighteen years. The accompanying graph (Exhibit 2.3) displays the percentages of students from each of the five high school achievement ranks who chose to take the test in 1976 and 1993. As you can see, more students from the lower achievement ranks have recently opted to take the SAT. This would not matter if students from each achievement rank were equal in their abilities, but this is obviously not the case. Students who earn top high school grades also are much more likely to earn high SAT scores than students who earn mediocre high school grades. This means that even if the ability of schools to educate students remains constant across the nation, aggregate national SAT scores will fall when more students from the lower achievement ranks choose to take the test.

The proportion of students representing minority groups and differing levels of family income has also changed over time, and this has also affected aggregate SAT scores. As we noted above, the SAT was standardized to predict the college grades of students interested in entering college *in 1941*—at a time when these students were predominantly from white, Anglo-Saxon, middle- or upper-middle-class, Protestant homes where English was spoken. We should not be surprised, therefore, to learn that minority and immigrant students tend to have lower scores than the group that first took the SAT fifty years ago. (In fact, so striking is this problem that James Grouse and Dale Trusheim have recently argued that whenever decisions about college admission are based on SAT results, those decisions are *always* biased against impoverished, minority students.) Even if schools across the nation retain their abilities to educate students, aggregate national SAT scores will also

fall when more students from impoverished, minority backgrounds choose to take the test.

Finally, SAT results are also closely tied to the income earned by students' families. In fact, at present the average SAT score earned by students goes down *by fifteen points* for each decrease of $10,000 in family income. This means, of course, that whenever colleges use the SAT for making admissions decisions, they are also discriminating against students from poorer homes. And it means that aggregate SAT scores will also fall when more students from poorer families choose to take the test.

How does this help us to understand the small decline in aggregate SAT scores during the late 1960s and early 1970s? If nothing else, this decade was a period of exploding interest in higher education among groups in the population that had not aspired to college before then. Sharply larger numbers of students from the lower-achievement ranks in high schools, from minority groups, and from poorer families began to take the SAT during those years—and these decisions alone were sufficient to generate the decline in aggregate national SAT scores during these decades. Thus, the brief decline in SAT scores a generation ago provided no information whatever about the performance of American schools but was, instead, a signal that interest in higher education was spreading throughout the nation. Surely this should have been a matter for rejoicing, not alarm.

In larger terms, since the SAT is voluntary and is only taken by roughly one-half of high school seniors across the nation, aggregate national SAT scores will *always* reflect the characteristics of students who choose to take the test. And since those characteristics change over time, aggregate national scores simply *cannot* be used for making valid judgments about the performance of the nation's schools. Despite repeated claims by the critics and alarmist reports in the press, shifts in national *aggregate* SAT scores tell us nothing at all about the performance or problems in American education.

So much for *aggregate* SAT scores. But isn't it possible to discover something about the nation's educational achievements by looking at *disaggregated* SAT data? Yes, it is possible, and it can be done in various ways. For example, we can look at disaggregated SAT scores for students with stronger and weaker high school records, and we can ask, how have these different student groups fared recently in SAT scores?

Average scores for the verbal and mathematics subtests of the SAT for students from each high-school rank for the past eighteen years show, over this period verbal SAT scores remained quite constant, but scores for the mathematics subtest increased slightly for each of the five achievement ranks. (Granted, these increases were small, but they were consistent. The increase for the top rank was ten points, and for the remaining ranks the increases were thirteen, thirteen, seven, and four points respectively.) Thus, students with both strong and weak achievement records have recently been holding their own on the verbal SAT and doing slightly better in mathematics. Moreover, the top fifth of high school seniors have continued to score at a healthy level on both subtests of the SAT and still earn an aggregate score that exceeds 1000.

In addition, data have been available since 1976 concerning the race and ethnicity of students taking the SAT. Average SAT scores were nearly constant for white students, but the scores *increased* for every minority group during this period. (The slight decline for white students merely reflects the larger numbers of those students with weaker academic backgrounds who are now taking the test.

When one looks at *disaggregated* SAT data, then, one discovers the following: (1) scores for verbal achievement have been holding steady; (2) scores for mathematics achievement have shown modest recent increases; (3) white students have been holding their own; (4) students from minority homes are now earning higher average scores. The last two findings, in particular, are truly startling when compared with incessant charges leveled by the critics. How on earth can America's teachers and schools be failing the nation when SAT scores for white students have recently been

stable, the average SAT score for Native Americans has increased thirty-nine points, and average scores for blacks has gone up a whopping fifty-five points? Citizens should rejoice at this marvelous news.

A summary of the SAT story:

- The SAT is a one shot, multiple-choice test that is taken by high school seniors; the test assesses only students' knowledge of a fixed set of topics in mathematics and English against the performance standards of a group of high status, mostly male, mostly Northeastern students who wanted to enter highly selective colleges in 1941.
- SAT scale scores are not meaningful in and of themselves; large shifts in scale scores represent only small shifts in the number of SAT test questions answered correctly.
- Since the SAT is taken by only those students interested in going to college, *aggregate* SAT scores should not be used for judging the performance of schools, school districts, states, or the nation as a whole.
- *Disaggregated* SAT scores suggest that student achievement in the nation has either been steady or has been climbing over the past eighteen years.

So although critics have trumpeted the "alarming" news that aggregate national SAT scores fell during the late 1960s and the early 1970s, this decline indicates nothing about the performance of American schools. Rather, it signals that students from a broader range of backgrounds were then getting interested in college, which should have been cause for celebration, not alarm.

Questions for Discussion

1. One of the charges made by the authors is that questionable techniques had been used to analyze data, distort reports of findings, and suppress contradictory evidence concerning the

current status of schools. What safeguards can and should be used to protect the reader from any type of misinformation and disinformation?

2. Speculate on the reasons politicians, business leaders, or the parties responsible for preparing the reform reports would have manufactured the crisis.

3. Based on the Berliner and Biddle reading, do you believe that the reforms initiated in the 1980s and 1990s to increase student achievement were necessary? Give reasons why or why not.

Primary Source Reading

In this article David Sadker presents an overview of the so-called "gender war" portrayed in such books as The War Against Boys *and presents research that refutes the claim that school is a place where boys have become the victims and "girls rule." Sadker also suggests that what is needed is to make schools a more fair and equitable place for* all *students.*

As you read the article, think about your own school experiences and ask yourself whether the evidence Dr. Sadker presents reflects your own experiences.

An Educator's Primer on the Gender War

David Sadker

Several recent books, a seemingly endless series of television and radio talk shows, and a number of newspaper columns have painted a disturbing picture of schools mired in a surreptitious war on boys. In such books as *The War Against Boys* and *Ceasefire!*, readers are introduced to education

Source: Sadker, D. (2002). An educator's primer on the gender war. *Phi Delta Kappan 84* (3), 235–240, 244. David Sadker is a professor at American University, Washington, D.C., and is co-author of *Failing at Fairness.* (www.american.edu/sadker).

using war metaphors and are informed that boys are daily casualties of zealous efforts to help girls. These "schools-at-war" authors also call for more "boy-friendly" education, including increased testing, frequent classroom competitions, and the inclusion of war poetry in the curriculum—all measures intended to counter feminist influences. They also argue that sections of Title IX, the law that prohibits sex discrimination in education, be rescinded. Teachers are informed that giving extra attention to boys in classrooms and building up school libraries that are dominated by books about male characters are useful strategies to improve boys' academic performance. As one book warns, "It's a bad time to be a boy in America."

After over a quarter century of researching life in schools, I must admit that at first I thought this "gender war" was a satire, a creative way to alert people to the difficulties of creating fair schools that work for all children. Certainly boys (like girls) confront gender stereotypes and challenges, and teachers and parents must work hard every day to make schools work for all children. But these recent books and talk shows were not intended as satire; they purported to present a serious picture of schools in which girls ruled and boys were their victims.

The irony of girls waging a war on boys reminded me of a "Seinfeld" episode that featured "Bizarro World." For those of you not versed in the culture of Bizarro World, it is a Superman comics theme in which everything is opposite: up is down, in is out, and good is bad. When the popular sitcom featured an episode on Bizarro World, Kramer became polite and discovered that doors were to be knocked on, not stormed through. George went from nerdiness to cool, from dysfunctional to popular; he was rewarded with two well-adjusted parents. Elaine's self-absorption was transformed into compassion, a change that would probably lead to a hitch in the Peace Corps and stardom in her own Seinfeld spin-off, "Elaine in Africa." In this topsy-turvy transformation, the entire Seinfeld gang became well adjusted, with their ethical compasses recalibrated to do the right thing. What would schools be like, I thought, if such Bizarro World changes came to pass? What would school look like if "misguided feminists" were actually engaged in a "war against boys"? And then I thought, what if girls really did rule?

* * *

(Camera fade-in)
The statue of the great woman dominates the front lawn of suburban Alice Paul High School. (Alice Paul, of course, led the courageous fight for women to be recognized as citizens, and her efforts contributed to passage of the 19th Amendment.) By 2003, Alice Paul, Susan B. Anthony, and Hillary Rodham Clinton have become the most common names for America's schools.

The statue of Alice Paul at the entrance of the school has become a student *talis-woman*. Students rub Alice's big toe before taking the SAT or on the eve of a critical soccer match with their cross-town rivals, the Stanton Suffragettes. Although Alice Paul died in 1977, she remains a real presence on campus.

Once inside Alice Paul High School, images of famous women are everywhere. Pictures of Jeannette Rankin, Mary MacLeod Bethune, Margaret Sanger, Carry Nation, and Mia Hamm gaze down on students as they go to their classes, constant reminders of the power and accomplishments of women. There are few if any pictures of men, as if in confirmation of the old adage "It's a woman's world." Trophy cases overflow with artifacts trumpeting women's role in ending child labor, reforming schools, eliminating domestic violence, confronting alcoholism, and battling for health care reform. It is the same story in the technology and math wing of Alice Paul High, where the influence of such computer pioneers as Ada Loveless and Grace Hopper can be seen everywhere.

Few images of males can be found anywhere in the hallways—or in the textbooks. The typical history text devotes less than 5% of its content to the contributions of men, a percentage that actually shrinks in math and science texts. Other than the one or two "unusual men" who find their way into the curriculum, students learn that their world was constructed almost exclusively by and for women.

Not everyone is happy with female-dominated bulletin boards and textbooks, as school principal Anna Feminie knows all too well. (Most school principals are, of course, female, since they seem better equipped to manage demanding parents and a predominantly male faculty.) From time to time, a few vociferous parents of boys complain about the lack of male images. But Anna has been in her job for five years now, and she knows just how to handle angry parents. She makes a big show of Men's History Month. Almost magically, every March, a new crop of male figures materializes. Anna understands that Men's History Month is nothing more than a nod to political correctness. Luckily, most parents and faculty agree with Anna and feel more comfortable with the well-known female names and images from their own student days. But all that may be changing with the increased emphasis on standardized state tests. New history standards put the traditional female front and center once again, and perhaps the end of Men's History Month is in sight. And if that should come to pass, it would be just fine with principal Anna Feminie.

By 8 a.m., hallway noise is at a peak as students exchange last-minute comments before the late bell sounds. Crowds of girls rule the school's "prime real estate": main stairwells, cafeteria entrance, and the senior locker bay. In groups, the girls can be even more intimidating. Individual boys carefully weave their way around these "girl areas," looking down to avoid unwanted stares and snares. The strategy is less than effective. Sometimes the boys are forced to pretend that they do not hear those louder-than-a-whisper offensive comments. At other times, the boys rapidly sidestep the outstretched arms of some of the more aggressive girls who are trying to impress their friends. Boys at Alice Paul travel in bands for safety, like convoys at sea. They smile a lot and speak a little. Although they do not quite understand it all, they know that they are at some risk, even in their own school, and taking precautions has become second nature.

Girls dominate in classrooms as well. They shout out answers, and teachers accept their behavior as "natural," part of their more aggressive biological makeup. Not true for the boys. When boys call out, they are likely to be reminded to "raise your hand." Even when girls do not shout out, teachers call on them more often than on boys, reward them more, help them more, and criticize them more. With girls as the center of classroom attention, boys seem content to sit quietly on the sidelines: low profiles are safe profiles.

Most boys take to their quiet, second-class role with incredible grace. They enroll in the programs more suitable for their nature: the humanities and social sciences courses, as well as the typical and predictable vocational programs. Few boys are assigned to costly special education programs. While educating boys is relatively inexpensive, there are rewards associated with lower career goals, docility, and conformity. Every quarter, boys are rewarded with higher grades on report cards. Boys are also more likely to be listed on the honor roll and chosen to be the school valedictorian. Teachers appreciate boys who do their work on time, cause few disruptions, demand less in class, rarely complain, and do not need special education.

While these higher report card grades are comforting, low test scores are disturbing. When the SAT and other competitive tests roll around, boys' scores lag behind girls on both math and verbal tests. On virtually every high-stakes test that matters, including the Advanced Placement tests and later the Graduate Record Exam, girls outscore boys. Few adults wonder why boys' high report card grades are not reflected in these very important test scores.

While the athletic field offers a change of venue, it is basically the same story. At Alice Paul, boys' football, baseball, and basketball do not hold a candle to girls' field hockey and soccer. The student newspaper is filled with the exploits of the Alice Paul Amazons, as the female athletes are called. The Gentlemen Amazons draw smaller crowds and less coverage in the school paper. Funding for just one of the girls' teams can equal the entire male athletic budget. Although some parents have tried to bolster male sports, coaches, parents, and the influential state athletic association have thwarted their efforts.

Female domination of athletics is accompanied by the ringing of a cash register. A few female athletes not only have won college scholarships but also have moved into the multimillion-dollar ranks of the professionals. Amazon booster clubs have been generous to Alice Paul, funding the new athletic field, the state-of-the-art girls' training facility, and a number of athletic scholarships. The Alice Paul Amazons ignite school spirit and have won several state championships. No one was surprised five years ago when the former girls' field hockey coach, Anna Feminie, was chosen as the new principal.

If Alice Paul were alive today, she would be proud of her Amazons. Alice Paul women dominate corporate boardrooms and government offices, and many are leaders promoting social reform around the globe. And Alice herself would be no less proud of the men who graduate from her school, true partners with women at work and at home.

(Camera fade-out)

* * *

The description of the fictional Alice Paul High School is a true reflection of hundreds of studies of school life, with one obvious modification (after all, it is Bizarro World): the genders have been reversed. The idea that "girls rule" in school is not only silly, it is intentionally deceptive. So why all the recent commotion about "a war on boys"?

Certainly boys do not always fit comfortably into the school culture, but this has little to do with girls—and a lot to do with how we conduct school. In fact, both girls and boys confront different school challenges, and they respond in different ways. Girls are more likely to react to problems in a quieter and less disruptive fashion, while boys are more likely to act out—or drop out. Males of color in particular drop out of high school more often and enroll in college less frequently than either minority females or white males. Decades of studies, books, and reports have documented the school difficulties of boys generally and of boys of color in particular.

The new twist in the current debate is the scapegoating of the feminist movement. And for those who were never very comfortable with the feminist movement, these new books and their ultraconservative spokespeople have an allure. Many mainstream media fixate on the audience appeal of a "Mars versus Venus" scenario, portraying boys as hapless victims of "male-hating feminists." Even educators and parents who do not blame females for the problems boys experience still buy into the argument that girls are "ahead" in school.

But for people to believe that "girls are responsible for boys' problems," they must repress historical realities: these problems predated the women's movement. Boys' reading difficulties, for example, existed long before modern feminism was even a twinkle in Betty Friedan's eye, and the dropout rate has actually decreased since the publication of *The Feminine Mystique*. Ironically, it was female teachers who fought hard to remove corporal punishment, while promoting new instructional strategies that moved teachers beyond lecture and recitation. Women educators led the movement for more humane classrooms, and the current attack on feminism has the potential of hurting boys as well as girls.

The truth is that *both* boys and girls exhibit different strengths and have different needs, and gender stereotypes shortchange all of us. So where are we in terms of the progress made for both girls and boys in school today? And what challenges still remain? The following "Report Card" takes us beyond the phony gender war and offers a succinct update of salient research findings.

A Report Card on the Costs of Gender Bias

Grades and Tests

Females. Females receive better grades from elementary school through college, but not everyone sees this as good news. Some believe that this may be one of the "rewards" girls receive for more quiet and conforming classroom behavior.

Female test scores in several areas have improved dramatically in recent years. The performance of females on science and math achievement tests has improved, and girls now take more Advanced Placement tests than boys. Yet they lag behind males on a number of important tests, scoring lower on both the verbal and mathematics sections of the SAT, the Advanced Placement exams, and the Graduate Record Exam.

Males. Males (and students from low-income families) not only receive lower grades, but they are also more likely to be grade repeaters. Many believe that school norms and culture conflict with many male behavior patterns. The National Assessment of Educational Progress and many other exams indicate that males perform significantly below females in writing and reading achievement.

Academic Enrollment

Females. Female enrollment in science and mathematics courses has increased dramatically in recent years. Girls are more likely to take biology and chemistry as well as trigonometry and algebra II. However, boys still dominate physics, calculus, and more advanced courses, and boys are more likely to take all three core science courses—biology, chemistry, and physics.

College programs are highly segregated, with women earning between 75% and 90% of the degrees in education, nursing, home economics, library science, psychology, and social work. Women trail men in Ph.D.s (just 40% are awarded to women) and in professional degrees (42% to women). And women are in the minority at seven of eight Ivy League schools.

Computer science and technology reflect increasing gender disparities. Boys not only enroll in more such courses, but they also enroll in the more advanced courses. Girls are more likely to be found in word-processing classes and clerical support programs. Girls are also less likely to use computers outside school, and girls from all ethnic groups rate themselves considerably lower than boys on technological ability. Current software products are more likely to reinforce these gender stereotypes than to reduce them.

Males. Males have a higher high school dropout rate than females (13% to 10%), and they trail females in extracurricular participation, including school government, literary activities, and the performing arts.

Men are the minority (44%) of students enrolled in both undergraduate and graduate institutions, and they lag behind women in degree attainment at the associate (39%), bachelor's (44%), and master's (44%) levels. Although white males and females attend college in fairly equal proportions, African American and Hispanic males are particularly underrepresented at all levels of education.

Gender segregation continues to limit the academic and career majors of all students. Male college students account for only 12% of elementary education majors, 11% of special education majors, 12% of library science majors, and 14% of those majoring in social work.

Academic Interactions and Special Programs

Females. Females have fewer academic contacts with instructors in class. They are less likely to be called on by name, are asked fewer complex and abstract questions, receive less praise or constructive feedback, and are given less direction on how to do things for themselves. In short, girls are more likely to be invisible members of classrooms.

In elementary school, girls are identified for gifted programs more often than boys; however, by high school fewer girls remain in gifted programs, particularly fewer African American and Hispanic girls. Gender segregation is also evident in the low number of gifted girls found in math and science programs.

Males. Boys receive more teacher attention than females, including more negative attention. They are disciplined more harshly, more publicly, and more frequently than girls, even when they violate the same rules. Parents of male elemen-

tary school students (24%) are contacted more frequently about their child's behavior or schoolwork than parents of female students (12%), and boys constitute 71% of school suspensions.

Males account for two-thirds of all students served in special education. The disproportionate representation of males in special education is highest in the categories of emotional disturbance (78% male), learning disability (68% male), and mental retardation (58% male).

Health and Athletics

Females. About one million U.S. teenagers get pregnant each year, a higher percentage than in other Western nations. Fifty percent of adolescent girls believe that they are overweight, and 13% are diagnosed with anorexia, bulimia, or binge-eating disorder.

Girls who play sports enjoy a variety of health benefits, including lower rates of pregnancy, drug use, and depression. But despite these benefits, only 50% of girls are enrolled in high school physical education classes. Women today coach only 44% of women's college teams and only 2% of men's teams, while men serve as athletic directors for over 80% of women's programs.

Males. Males are more likely than females to succumb to serious disease and be victims of accidents or violence. The average life expectancy of men is approximately 6 years shorter than that of women.

Boys are the majority (60%) of high school athletes. Male athletes in NCAA Division I programs graduate at a lower rate than female athletes (52% versus 68%).

Career Preparation, Family, and Parenting

Females. Women dominate lower-paying careers. Over 90% of secretaries, receptionists, bookkeepers, registered nurses, and hairdressers/cosmetologists are female, and, on average, a female college graduate earns $4,000 less annually than a male college graduate. Nearly two out of three working women today do not have a pension plan.

More than 45% of families headed by women live in poverty. For African American women, that figure rises to 55%, and it goes to 60% for Hispanic women. Even when both parents are present, women are still expected to assume the majority of the household responsibilities.

Males.   Men make up 99% of corporate chief executive officers in America's 500 largest companies but account for only 16% of all elementary school teachers and 7% of nurses (although this last figure is an increase from 1% of nurses in 1972).

Women and men express different views of fatherhood. Men emphasize the need for the father to earn a good income and to provide solutions to family problems. Women, on the other hand, stress the need for fathers to assist in caring for children and in responding to the emotional needs of the family. These differing perceptions of fatherhood increase family strain and anxiety.

Even this brief overview of gender differences does little more than confirm common-sense observations: neither boys nor girls "rule in school." Sometimes, even progress can mask problems. While a great deal has been written about females attending college in greater numbers than males, this fact has at least as much to do with color as with gender. The disparity between males and females in college enrollment is shaped in large part by the serious dearth of males of color in postsecondary programs. Moreover, attendance figures provide only one indicator; enrollments in specific college majors tell a different story.

As a result of striking gender segregation in college programs, women and men follow very different career paths, with very different economic consequences. Although the majority of students are female, the college culture is still strongly influenced by male leaders. Four out of five full professors are males, more male professors (72%) are awarded tenure than female professors (52%), and, for the last 30 years, full-time male professors have consistently earned more

than their female peers. Even at the elementary and secondary levels, schools continue to be managed by male principals and superintendents. If feminists are waging a "war on boys," as some proclaim, they are being led by male generals.

It is not surprising that many educators are confused about gender issues. Both information and misinformation abound. There is little doubt that boys and school are not now—nor have they ever been—a match made in heaven. But this is a far cry from concluding that a gender war is being waged against them or that girls now "rule" in school, as one recent magazine cover proclaimed.

In the midst of the adult controversy, we can easily overlook the obvious, like asking children how they see the issue. Students consistently report that girls get easier treatment in school, are the better students, and are less likely to get into trouble. Yet school lessons are not always life lessons. When researcher Cynthia Mee asked middle school students about boys and girls, both had more positive things to say about being a boy than being a girl. When, in another study, more than a thousand Michigan elementary school students were asked to describe what life would be like if they were born a member of the opposite sex, over 40% of the girls saw advantages to being a boy, ranging from better jobs to more respect. Ninety-five percent of the boys saw no advantage to being female, and a number of boys in this 1991 study indicated they would consider suicide rather than live life as a female. While some adults may choose to argue that females are the advantaged gender, girls and boys often see the world before them quite differently.

The success of the backlash movement has taught us a great many lessons. It has reminded us of the slow pace of social change and of the power of political ideologues to set the agenda for education. How ironic that the gender debate, once thought to be synonymous with females, now hinges on how well boys are doing in school. And in the end, reframing gender equity to include boys may prove to be a very positive development. For now, it is up to America's educators to duck the barrage from the gender-war crowd and to continue their efforts to make schools fairer and more humane environments for all our students.

Discussion Questions

1. Do you agree or disagree with Sadker's conclusion that boys do not always fit comfortably into the school culture, but that this has little to do with girls and a lot to do with how we conduct school? Give reasons why.

2. What might explain the disproportionate representation of males in special education classes for emotional disturbance, learning disability, and mental retardation?

3. How do you reconcile or explain the fact that females receive better grades than males from elementary school through college, but lag behind males on the verbal and mathematics sections of the SAT, Advanced Placement exams, and the Graduate Record Examination?

CHAPTER 11

Education in a New Century

Anyone who has looked carefully at standardized tests knows they are loaded with trivia. Our children are being fed intellectual junk food, and we would do well to insist on a healthier educational diet.

—*Nel Noddings, 2004*

The new century began where the last one left off—with the public as well as the education establishment divided over issues of state and national standards, accountability, school choice, and the place of religion in the schools. In the face of rising test scores, and despite the fact that the 1990s had witnessed the unparallel economic prosperity said to have been at risk because of the quality of the schools, the cries for education reform continued into the new century.

The reform offered by the first president of the new century, George W. Bush, was embodied in his education plan, No Child Left Behind (NCLB). No Child Left Behind, the most sweeping education reform legislation since the Elementary and Secondary Education Act (ESEA) of 1965, did what a Democratic administration could never have done: created "a much larger federal presence in educational policy and funding and set the foundation for a national testing system" (Lewis, 2002, p. 423). Although debates on the merits as well as the details of the key mandates of the plan related to student testing, accountability, and teacher quality were legion, the universal concern heard in state departments of education and school districts was "unfunded mandates." States facing huge budget deficits complained that the federal government had imposed dozens of new mandates without providing them with the funds to do the job.

The impact of NCLB went beyond just what it represented in terms of an expanded federal role; it provided the framework and impetus for standards-based reform of education in state after state. The NCLB mandates for Title I schools were quickly adopted and applied to all public schools. Schools struggled to develop and deliver curricula to meet state standards, develop and administer assessments of student progress in meeting the standards, improve student achievement, staff the schools with "highly qualified" teachers, and increase accountability to various constituencies. And, they did all this against the backdrop of major changes in the demographics of the student populations, a widening of the achievement gap between minority and White students, the resegregation of schools, the challenges and opportunities presented in providing school choice, and the never-ending challenge of funding the schools equitably and adequately.

An Education President, Again

Education was again a major political issue during the 2000 elections. George W. Bush took credit for the education reform in Texas that had resulted in improved test scores, especially among minorities, during his governorship. In actuality, the major reforms had been initiated under his predecessor, a Democrat, Governor Ann Richards, although Bush did forcefully move them along. (The results were later revealed to be exaggerated.) The Democratic presidential candidate, Al Gore, never really found his voice on education during the campaign, and the Republicans were able to take the education issue from the Democrats (Lemann, 2002). The Republican platform supported private school vouchers, promoted phonics-based reading instruction, and, unlike the platforms of the previous 2 decades, did not call for the abolishment of the Department of Education. To appease the religious right, a moving force in the Republican Party, Bush did support character education and abstinence sex education. However, over the objections of the conservative wing of the party Bush pushed for mandated state standards and testing. The effect of Bush's proposals was to create "the greatest intrusion into local control of the school curriculum in the history of the federal government" (Spring, 2002, p. 11).

No Child Left Behind and the New Federal Role

The cornerstone of George W. Bush's education program was embodied in the 2001 reauthorization of the Elementary and Secondary Education Act, entitled the No Child Left Behind Act. The law, more than 1,200 pages in length, was passed with wide bipartisan support and marked a major expansion and change in the direction of federal involvement in education. It also created a vastly expanded regulatory role for states and local school districts. The goal of NCLB was to have all students achieving at grade level proficiency by 2014. NCLB's funding was directed at promoting higher achievement of low-income and minority students and holding schools accountable for the progress of all students. It was also intended to increase parental choice and increase the flexibility of school districts in directing federal dollars to areas of need.

As discussed in more detail in the sections that follow, the major provisions of NCLB were concerned with the development and implementation of "challenging" academic standards, student assessment against these standards, accountability, and teacher quality. The act required that by the end of the 2005–06 school year all students in Grades 3 through 8 be tested annually in reading and math using state-prescribed tests, that the tests be aligned with state-developed standards in these areas, and that schools make adequate yearly progress (AYP) toward reaching grade-level proficiency on the state test. The act also specified that by 2003 all teachers (and paraprofessionals) hired with Title I funds must be "highly qualified," and by 2005–06 all teachers must be highly qualified, regardless of the funding source.

The expanded role and new direction for the federal government in education created by NCLB is evident in at least four areas (Jennings, 2002). First, unlike previous federal legislation, which was limited to specific purposes or directed to children with special needs, NCLB was directed at *every* student and *every* teacher in *every* public school in the country: *All* children in Grades 3 through 8 would be tested; *all* students would be grade level proficient; and *all* teachers would be "highly qualified."

Second, NCLB changed the very underlying purpose of the federal government's involvement in education. Historically, the federal government's involvement was based on the premise that an educated citizenry would contribute to the national political and economic welfare. NCLB, however, made clear that the purpose of national support for education would no longer simply be to support additional services. Rather,

> the principal reason for the federal government's increased involvement in elementary and secondary education is to raise students' academic achievement. This sharpness of purpose is a new development, as are the detailed consequences for schools that do not measure up. (Jennings, 2002, p. 26)

The third way the role of the federal government changed and expanded with the passage of NCLB was evident in its heavy reliance on student test scores as an indicator of academic achievement and as the determinant of AYP, as well as its specification of sanctions against schools that do not make AYP in improving test scores. Finally, and monumentally important, for the first time in our nation's history the federal government became involved in determining the qualifications of instructional personnel. States still issued teaching certificates, but what it means to be a "qualified teacher" was now defined by the federal government and imposed on the states.

The initial response of the education community and the general public to NCLB was understandably mixed. Conservatives attacked the expanded federal involvement and what appeared to be a major step toward national testing and a national curriculum. Others saw NCLB simply as the Texas model on a national scale. Critics called it "unrealistic," "impossible," and an echo of the 1989 education summit's bragging declaration that U.S. students would be first in the world in math and science by 2000 (Lewis, 2002). Supporters saw the law as giving hope to a generation of children, especially those in the inner city and the academically disadvantaged (Hardy, 2002). Yet, whatever the disagreements on the merits of the law, on one thing there was no disagreement: It was "groundbreaking" legislation that "involve[d] the federal government in local education in a way it never had before" (Hardy, 2002, p. 21).

 For Your Reflection and Analysis

How realistic is the goal of having all students achieving at grade level proficiency by 2014?

Expanded State and Local Responsibilities

For more than 2 decades states had become more and more involved in issues that traditionally had been the responsibility of local school boards. In part this was perhaps a natural result of the states assuming greater financial responsibility. It was also a result of the school reform movement and the standards, testing, and accountability measures that accompanied the 1994 ESEA. NCLB expanded the state role even further. As discussed later, under NCLB, states had to develop and expand existing student assessment systems and provide technical assistance to schools identified as being "in need of improvement." Sanctions imposed on schools who continued to fail to make AYP included state takeover of the operation of the schools. In fact, this happened in Pennsylvania when the governor assumed responsibility for the operation of the Philadelphia schools.

NCLB also gave states the primary responsibility for ensuring that by 2005–06 all teachers were "highly qualified" and for making annual reports on their progress in achieving this goal. Perhaps most important, because the state, not the local school district or the federal government, has the legal responsibility to provide for education, the state is ultimately responsible for meeting the goal that all children in the state will be achieving at the proficient level by 2014. In effect, what NCLB did was to federalize actions and to further initiatives that had been taking place state by state since the school reform movement began in the 1980s. Broadly speaking, these actions and initiatives were addressed at improving student performance through the establishment of standards-based curriculum reform and assessment, improving the quality of the teaching force, and increasing accountability.

Raising the Stakes on High-Stakes Testing and Accountability

So-called "high-stakes testing" did not begin with NCLB. As discussed in previous chapters, the American public as well as the business community have increasingly sought to hold the schools accountable for student outcomes. These efforts increased during the school reform movement of the 1980s, when a number of states adopted standardized tests to determine student promotion and graduation. High-stakes testing was also given federal support by the 1994 reauthorization of the ESEA, the Improving America's Schools Act (IASA), which required states to develop statewide assessments in reading and math aligned with state standards, to use the assessment results to determine whether disadvantaged students were making adequate yearly progress in meeting the standards, to take corrective action against underperforming Title I schools, and to reward high-performing schools. However, state compliance with these requirements was uneven, and sanctions were rare; by the time NCLB was enacted, fewer than 20 states were in full compliance with IASA.

The enactment of NCLB not only toughened the IASA testing and accountability provisions, but also extended and expanded the movement through the use of a number of more prescriptive mandates. For example, the 1994 ESEA required states to set up assessment systems and to test students in Grades 3 and 8 in math and reading. NCLB required that beginning in 2005–06, students in every grade from 3 through 8 be tested annually in reading and math and one more time in Grades 10 through 12. Moreover, by the 2007–08 school year annual science assessments in grades 3 through 5, or 6 through 9, or 10 through 12 must be in place.

Although NCLB required yearly testing, it did not mandate what these tests must be, or even that they be standardized tests. But the law did say that the state tests must be aligned with state standards. NCLB also did not mandate what the proficiency levels should be on the state tests but left this decision to the state. However, far from making policy makers feel better about federal mandates, giving states the

The No Child Left Behind Act brought high-stakes testing to all states.

autonomy to decide the proficiency level of students aroused contention among many because this meant the proficiency standard could vary across the test distribution: What was judged to be proficient in one state might not be in another. As it turned out, these concerns were justified: Because of the variation in the rigor of state tests, as well as in the setting of state proficiency levels, states differed dramatically in the way they viewed school performance and categorized student proficiency. Students with the same skills may be considered proficient in one state but not in another. In the case of schools with the same student achievement and student growth, but located across the state line from each other, one may be considered underperforming and the other not (Kingsbury, Olson, Cronin, Hauser, & Houser, 2004). Because of these variations, the number of schools identified as in need of improvement varied significantly from state to state. Michigan identified over 1,500 underperforming schools and California over 1,000, whereas Wyoming and Arkansas identified none. In Florida, 87% of the schools, including 22% of the "A" schools, failed to make AYP under NCLB guidelines. Urban districts, districts serving high proportions of minority and poor students, as well as rural districts reported the highest percentage of schools in need of improvement.

 For Your Reflection and Analysis

What, if any, are the advantages of yearly testing?

A major issue for states in complying with the NCLB testing mandate was that most states did not have tests developed in reading and math at every grade level from 3 through 8, or in science. Initially a few states talked about not participating in the program and forgoing federal funds because of the expense involved in setting up and administering a testing program that would essentially more than double their existing program, but in the end all states did apply for funding.

Although states have gone forward with implementing statewide testing, concerns remain about the narrow academic focus of most state tests and whether they lead to improved learning or are even aligned with state standards. Concerns have also been raised that the tests have come to direct the curriculum rather than simply to assess student mastery of the curriculum. Other educators have voiced concern that teachers will increasingly feel the pressure to "teach to the test." Test accuracy and scoring have also come into question. In Georgia, for example, the statewide exam for fifth-graders had to be cancelled because of test errors 3 years in a row (Henriques, 2003). In Connecticut, the private firm scoring the tests made so many errors that the state had to suspend publication of school ratings (Tucker & Toch, 2004). More serious consequences befell students in Minnesota, where scoring errors resulted in 8,000 students being inaccurately failed, including 525 seniors who were denied diplomas.

Another point of contention has been NCLB's mandate that all children in all schools reach the state proficiency level by 2014. Again, by "all" the federal government meant all. Schools cannot simply show an overall improvement in test scores; they must disaggregate test scores to show AYP by race, ethnicity, poverty status, English proficiency, and disability. This requirement has been applauded by many as an attempt to ensure that attention is directed to those most in need and as a necessary step in closing the achievement gap discussed later in this chapter. However, others have expressed concern that all this testing actually will have a deleterious effect on the very students it aims to help: that in fact, research suggests that high-stakes testing tends to result in higher rates of retention and dropping out (Goldberg, 2004).

 For Your Reflection and Analysis

Is there any subgroup that should be exempt from the grade level proficiency requirement?

The accountability provisions of NCLB required that states and local school districts make public in annual report cards the results of the yearly testing, by school, for both the aggregate student population and for specific subgroups. Results were also to be presented by gender and migrant status. The report cards must identify any achievement gaps that exist between each student subgroup and the majority population. This requirement ensures that the achievement of these groups are not lost in an overall average for the school or district.

NCLB also required that state results be compared to the results from a small sample of fourth- and eighth-graders taking the National Assessment of Educational Progress (NAEP). The NAEP comparability "is supposed to ensure that states are not setting the bar too low on their standards and tests. That is, if a state shows progress on its statewide test results but does not show comparable progress on the NAEP, it would suggest that the state's standards and tests are not challenging enough" (PBS Frontline, 2003, p. 2). NCLB did not, however, provide for any penalties if this is the case, merely that the comparative results be made public. The results that have been made public show, ironically, that the largest discrepancy between NAEP scores and state scores was in Texas, home of President Bush and Secretary of Education Paige. Texas reported that 91% of its eighth-graders were proficient in math, but only 24% reached that level on the NAEP (Bracey, 2003).

Sanctions

Although NCLB did not specify what test or proficiency standards states should use, it did specify the consequences for schools that did not achieve AYP in the aggregate or for any of the major student subgroups on the test the state adopted. This provision of NCLB generated support from advocates for poor children because of its stated goal of preventing children from being trapped in underperforming or dangerous schools. And, although actual sanctions detailed in NCLB applied only to Title I schools, each state was required to have in place a state system of accountability that addresses the consequences for non-Title I schools that fail to make AYP. In practice many states adopted the same sanctions for non-Title I schools and Title I schools.

Adequate yearly progress is determined for NCLB purposes by a formula that anticipates that an additional 4 to 6% of the students will become proficient each year until 2014, when they are all expected to be proficient (Neill, 2003). An entire school can be considered not to have made AYP if even one of the subgroups in the school fails to make the targeted progress.

Racial and ethnic minority students, low-income students, students with limited English proficiency, and students with disabilities are expected to progress at a faster rate, thereby closing the achievement gap. The likelihood of this actually happening has been the subject of much skepticism given that "schools serving mostly low-income communities start with students who are less academically ready, have greater social needs . . . have fewer qualified teachers, larger class sizes, fewer library books, little technology, and dilapidated buildings" (Neill, 2003, p. 19).

According to the provisions of NCLB, any Title I school that fails to show AYP for 2 consecutive years is considered "in need of improvement." Schools in need of improvement are required to adopt a 2-year school improvement plan and are eligible for financial and technical assistance to implement the plan. NCLB stipulated that the plan focus on programs for which scientifically rigorous research has produced strong evidence of effectiveness in improving student achievement.

 For Your Reflection and Analysis

How effective are punitive incentive systems in bringing about the desired change?

Once a school has been identified as in need of improvement, the district must inform parents that their children have what is called school choice: They have the choice to transfer to another public school, including a charter school. The district must also identify the schools to which students can transfer. If all schools in the district are considered in need of improvement, the district must attempt to establish an agreement with a neighboring district to serve

For Your Reflection and Analysis

What would be the incentive for a neighboring district to accept students from an under-performing school?

the students. The sending district must provide transportation, and if sufficient funds are not available to transport all students who request a transfer, priority is given to the lowest achieving students from low-income families. Data from the first 2 years under NCLB indicated that only a very small percentage of eligible students chose to transfer (Robelen, 2004), whether because of reluctance to leave the neighborhood school, limited transfer options, or discouragement from the local school district.

If a school fails to make adequate yearly progress for a third year, students are also eligible for "supplemental education services" such as outside tutoring at district expense, after-school enrichment programs, and summer school. In contrast to the small percentage of students who have taken advantage of the transfer option, after 2 years of implementation, almost half of eligible students received supplemental educational services (Robelen, 2004). Supplemental services can be provided by the district or by supplemental service providers, over 1,000 of whom have been state approved nationwide. Although in rural areas supplemental service providers may be limited to those available online, in urban and suburban areas a wide array of contractors are available, including religious organizations. The district must pay for these services out of its Title I funds.

After 4 years of failure to make AYP the school is subject to corrective action as detailed in Figure 11.1. After 5 years, schools that do not improve could be reconstituted as charter schools, have their management taken over by private for-profit firms (e.g., Edison schools, etc.), have their teachers fired, or be taken over by the state.

Even though NCLB only went into effect in 2001–02, schools were held accountable for inadequate performance from prior years if a state testing system was already in place. As a result, in some states, with Michigan being the most dramatic example, even after only 2 years under the law, numerous districts faced the most dramatic consequences for failing to make AYP.

Although the assignment of sanctions seems to be an objective and equitable process based on a measurable standard, AYP, many educators and policy makers have considered this very equity unfair. Educators are trained to *not* treat all students the same, to recognize student differences and develop individual education plans that reflect these differences. They are critical of a system that presumes that all children can achieve at the same pace and

> does not recognize that a hungry child with a poor, single parent and a violent home may not be focused on phonics each morning . . . [and] makes no distinction between a school with well-educated parents and generous resources and an impoverished school. Both schools are held to the same standards. (Mathis, 2003, p. 685)

At the time of this writing several states are advocating that the law be changed to allow flexible education goals for each school rather than having every school in the state meet the same fixed goal.

The high-pressure atmosphere created by NCLB, with not only promotions and graduations, but also jobs, school reputations, and even real estate values at stake,

End of Year 1: Schools are identified in terms of whether each student subgroup has met or is making adequately yearly progress (AYP) toward meeting the established proficiency level on state academic standards.

End of Year 2: Schools that fail to make AYP for a second consecutive year are identified as being in need of improvement. Schools so identified are required to develop a two year improvement plan that includes professional development for teachers. Students are given the option to transfer to a higher performing public school in the district, including a charter school.

End of Year 3: Schools that fail to make AYP for a third year must not only continue their improvement efforts and provide student transfer options, they must provide supplemental services (from public or private providers) to students from low-income families who remain at the school.

End of Year 4: Schools that fail to make AYP for a fourth year must continue all of the above and are also subject to corrective action by the district. Such action must include one or more of the following: replacing staff, restructuring, implementing a new curriculum, extending the school day or year, or hiring an external advisor.

End of Year 5: Schools that fail to make AYP for five consecutive years are subject to identification for restructuring. This requires the school to plan for restructuring and/or an alternative governance arrangement, including: state take over, converting to a charter school, replacing staff, or hiring a private contactor to manage the school.

End of Year 6: Schools that still do not make AYP must implement their restructuring plan.

FIGURE 11.1 No Child Left Behind Timeline for Title I Schools in Need of Improvement

led some teachers and administrators to alter best practices and, unfortunately, a few to engage in unethical behavior, including test tampering, fudging dropout rates, pushing low-achieving students out of the school system, or classifying students under bureaucratic categories that hide their enrollment status or their failure to graduate (Goldberg, 2004). As of this writing the pressure remains high on test companies and state departments of education to create valid and reliable standards-based tests, and to administer and score them efficiently and accurately; on students to achieve at or above the proficiency level; and on teachers and schools to produce good scores to avoid loss of funding, reputations, and even jobs.

Teacher Crisis: Issues of Quantity and Quality

Just as high-stakes testing and accountability did not begin with NCLB, neither did concern about and efforts to improve teacher quality. As discussed in chapter 10, the reform movement that began the 1980s brought with it increased competency testing of teachers and increased college graduation requirements of prospective teachers. Once again, what NCLB did was to take what had been addressed on the state level and move it to the federal agenda. In what were some of its most controversial provisions NCLB required that all currently employed teachers in the core academic subjects (i.e., English, reading/language arts, mathematics, science, foreign languages, civics and government, economics, art, history and geography) be "highly qualified" by 2005–06 and that newly hired teachers be highly qualified at the time of employment.

NCLB defined "highly qualified" differently for new and experienced teachers. New elementary teachers were required to pass a "rigorous" state test in the core elementary subjects. New middle and high school teachers had to either pass a "rigorous" state test in the academic subject matter or have an academic major, graduate degree, or advance certification in the subject(s) they plan to teach. Veteran teachers had to demonstrate content knowledge by any of these means or by meeting the requirements of a "high, objective, uniform state standard of evaluation" (HOUSSE). For neither new nor veteran teachers were there requirements related to pedagogic knowledge and techniques.

For Your Reflection and Analysis

Who should pay the expense for a currently employed teacher to meet the criteria for being highly qualified?

The teacher quality requirement of NCLB reflected both the continued public concern for teacher quality and the research that suggested that teacher quality is a key variable in student achievement. It also addressed the growing concern about the alarming number of teachers teaching out-of-field or on emergency or temporary certificates. A report by the U.S. Department of Education (2003) estimated that only 50% of the English teachers in the secondary schools met the NCLB criteria for being highly qualified. Comparable figures for math, science, and social studies teachers were 47%, 55%, and 55%, respectively. More important, nationwide, secondary students in high-poverty schools were twice as likely as students in low-poverty schools to have teachers who were not licensed in the subject matter they taught (Olson, 2003).

Added to the out-of-field teachers were the tens of thousands of teachers nationwide teaching on emergency or temporary certificates. In 2001 in California alone more than 42,000 teachers, 14% of the state's teachers, were working on emergency certificates (Kerr, 2001). And, unfortunately, in California as elsewhere, data showed that low-achieving schools and schools serving low-income and minority students were most likely to have uncertified and out-of-field teachers. In California, 23% of the teachers in low-achieving schools lacked full certification compared to 6% of teachers in the highest achieving schools.

Whether the teacher quality requirements of NCLB are likely to accomplish their intended goal of ensuring that students are taught by highly qualified teachers has been the subject of intense debate, as has whether NCLB's criteria for teacher quality are sufficient. Although NCLB defined "highly qualified," it did not comment on what should be required for full state certification. The U.S. Department of Education (2003), however, noted some "promising alternatives" to current state requirements for full certification, including Teach for America and Passports to Teaching Certification. The NCLB teacher quality requirements were seen by some as actually lessening teacher quality by suggesting that individuals with subject knowledge but no professional knowledge be allowed to teach (Kaplan & Owings, 2001). Others saw them as strengthening teacher quality by requiring states to strengthen their licensure requirements, which in some cases did not even require subject matter expertise at the middle and high school levels (Rotherham & Mead, 2003).

One of the major issues surrounding the highly qualified teacher mandate was how states chose to determine the "qualifiedness" of both new and experienced teachers. The regulations implementing NCLB adopted in 2002 did not specify what constitutes "rigorous testing" or a HOUSSE, but left these determinations to the states. The result has been the perpetuation of a system of widely different requirements and practices, many of which test new teachers for only minimum competence and do not link subject matter knowledge to student academic standards or to the ability to impart knowledge to students (Rebell & Hunter, 2004). In Arkansas 5 years of successful teaching experience is considered sufficient for being classified as highly qualified, and Indiana maintains that having a license in the subject area is sufficient. New Mexico teachers, however, must first have 5 years of experience and two evaluations before moving to a second set of requirements that include being observed by two peers who teach in the subject and compiling a satisfactory portfolio of lesson plans, student achievement data, and more. As a final step two judges must agree on whether the teacher should be considered highly qualified (Keller, 2004).

Whether NCLB will lessen or strengthen teacher quality may be debated, but what is not debatable is that many districts have had a problem complying with the NCLB mandate because of a shortage of qualified teachers. Although some researchers have challenged the existence of an absolute nationwide shortage of teachers (Ingersoll, 2002), they do not argue that there will be an increased demand for teachers (as many as 2.3 million [Gursky, 2001]) in the first decade of the 21st century. The impact of the "baby boom echo"—the children of the 76 million baby boomers born between the end of World War II and 1964—was strengthened by continued immigration, pushing school enrollment beyond the record 1971 baby boom enrollment of 51.3 million. The K–12 enrollment of 53.2 million in 2000 was projected to reach 54.3 million by the year 2011, with the greatest increases in California and Texas (see Figure 11.2).

Also not in question in discussions of teacher quality was the real and pronounced shortage of teachers in certain subject areas (e.g., special education, math, and science), in certain states, and in certain types of districts, primarily rural and inner-city districts. This shortage of teachers was a major factor in the hiring of a high number of uncertified and out-of-field teachers in the classroom. For many districts, having any teacher in the classroom was a challenge; having a "highly qualified" teacher in every classroom seemed impossible, especially given the estimated 20 to 50% additional cost associated with attracting these teachers (Olson, 2003).

 For Your Reflection and Analysis

What can a district with limited resources do to attract high-quality teachers?

Enrollment (in thousands)

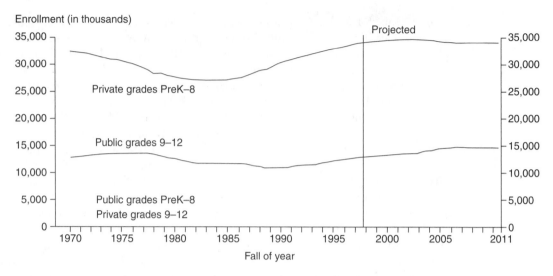

FIGURE 11.2 Public Elementary and Secondary School Enrollment, 1970–2011
Source: U.S. Department of Education, National Center for Education Statistics. (2001). *Projections of education statistics to 2011* (Figure 4). Washington, DC: U.S. Department of Education.

Funding an Adequate Education

The end of the 1980s ushered in a new era in school finance. The focus of school finance policy and legislation began to shift from the pursuit of equity in funding to the attainment of adequacy, that is, from an emphasis on ensuring equal inputs to ensuring that sufficient resources were provided to produce the level of student performance deemed to constitute an adequate education. The shift coincided with the standards-based reform movement that was growing during this same period. Beginning with the 1989 *Rose v. Council for Better Education* decision in Kentucky, a series of lawsuits were filed, and a number were successful, arguing that state funding systems did not meet state constitutional requirements to provide an adequate education. The lawsuits attempted to link school funding to the attainment of state or district proficiency standards. As a result of the impetus provided by these cases, policy makers in a number of other states initiated reform of their state finance programs in an effort to provide a sufficient level of funding to deliver an adequate education to every child in the state.

Despite the growing interest in adequacy, the financial crises and large budget deficits faced by many states resulted in a number of states actually cutting their K–12 budgets at the same time NCLB was initiated, undermining efforts to create state finance systems that would provide the support needed by those schools and students who were not making AYP. An estimate by the NEA suggested that $41.8 billion would be needed in 2004 to reach all the students eligible for services and all the schools eligible for interventions under NCLB (Hoff, 2004). These expenditures would come on top of the billions that would be required to meet the testing and accountability mandates (CNN, 2003).

For Your Reflection and Analysis

How can local school districts or the states (or even the federal government) generate the money necessary to fund NCLB?

Federal funding provides only about half the 20 to 30% increase in education expenditures estimated as necessary to meet NCLB mandates. In an attempt to support the efforts of districts to meet the mandates, the law allows districts to move up to 50% of funds to areas of greatest need. However, even with federal funds and the flexibility that NCLB allows, implementing the law remained costly for states and school districts.

The financial concerns of state governments went beyond the inadequate federal funding of NCLB mandates. State lawmakers and educators also feared that NCLB and the attention given to getting all students to the same proficiency level had "opened the door to a potential tidal wave of costly new lawsuits challenging the level and equality of state public school financing" (CNN, 2003, p. 2). Students in low-income districts could easily make the case that their poorly funded schools were set up to fail under the new requirements (Toppo, 2003). If the states are hit by this "new wave of costly lawsuits," they may in turn bring suit against the federal government to recover the funds necessary to meet NCLB mandates.

 For Your Reflection and Analysis

What would be the major issues (legal, policy, or otherwise) in a state suing the federal government for funds to support education?

Although the issues and concerns surrounding NCLB were a major focus of educators and dominated political discourse leading up to the 2004 elections, several other issues shaping the direction of public education in the United States were also receiving attention. These included changing student demographics, the growing achievement gap between minority and White students, the resegregation of the schools in many urban and suburban areas, and the continued efforts to promote school choice.

Brown + 50: What's Changed, What's Not

In the 50 years since the *Brown* decision outlawing segregation in American public schools, much has changed, but much remains the same. In 1954 we had not walked on the moon, but the majority of public school students walked to school. Fifty years later 56% of students were transported at public expense. In 1954–55, K–12 public school enrollments were 30.1 million; by 2004 they had increased by more than 50%. The expanded student population of 2004 looked very different from that of 1954–55. In 1955 Black students made up 13.5% of the student population and Hispanic students less then 5%. By 2004 Black and Hispanic representation had increased to 16.6% and 17%, respectively. In fact, Hispanics had become the fastest growing segment of the U.S. population and are expected to double in numbers by 2050.

Accompanying the growth in the student population was an almost 160% increase in the size of the instructional staff. Concomitant with the growth in the instructional staff was a significant reduction in pupil–teacher ratios at both the elementary and secondary levels (see Table 11.1).

TABLE 11.1   American Education: *Brown* + 50 Years

	1954–55	2003–04
Elementary/Secondary school enrollment		
Public	30,680,000	47,223,000
Private	4,600,000	5,944,000
Student racial/ethnic distribution (%)[1]		
American Indian	—	1.1
Asian/Pacific Islander	—	4.1
Black	13.5	16.6
White	86.5	60.2
Hispanic	—	17.0
Number of teachers		
Public	1,141,000	2,953,000
Private	145,000	390,000
Gender of teachers (%)		
Male	22	25
Female	78	75
Pupil/teacher ratios		
Public Elem.	30.2	19.1
Private Elem.	40.4	
Public Sec.	20.9	14.9
Private Sec.	15.7	
Current expenditures/pupil (in 2000 constant dollars)	1,831	7,392
Revenue sources (% of total expenditures)		
Federal	4.5	8.2
State	39.6	49.1
Local	55.9	42.7

[1]Enrollment data were not reported by other racial or ethnic groups in 1955.

Sources: National Center for Education Statistics. (2004). *Digest of Education Statistics 2002.* Washington, DC: U. S. Department of Education and National Education Association. (2004). *Estimates of School Statistics,* www.nea.org.

School funding also changed in significant ways in the 50 years since *Brown*, but it remained the same in some very important ways. Expenditures per pupil had more than doubled in constant dollars. The source of revenues changed, with the federal share and the state share increasing, while the local share decreased. Perhaps most important, funding differences between schools were no longer based on the existence of "White schools" and "Black schools." However, although this had improved as a result of 3 decades of court decisions and school finance reform, what had not changed was that significant funding differences among schools remained. These inequalities in funding, inequalities that had become most evident between rich districts and poor districts and urban districts and suburban districts, translated into inequalities of educational opportunities, inferior facilities, and the difficulty of poor districts to attract and retain "highly qualified" teachers. As in 1954, most often the schools that were on the short end of state funding in 2004 were those attended by racial and ethnic minorities and the poor.

On the positive side, 78% of African Americans completed high school in 2002, compared to only about 20% in 1954. However, as discussed in the following section, 50 years after *Brown*, race and class remained the most significant predictors of educational attainment. The resegregation of the schools only contributed to these educational differences.

The Achievement Gap

Although the half century since *Brown* saw the educational attainment and achievement of minorities improve significantly, a large achievement gap between White and ethnic minority students remained. In fact, after improving in the 1970s and 1980s, during the 1990s an increase in the gap between some subgroups occurred. For example, as seen in Table 11.2, in 1975 there was a 36-point gap between the reading scores of Black and White eighth-graders on the National Assessment of Educational Progress, and in 1973 a 46-point gap in math scores. By 1990 these differences had

TABLE 11.2 NAEP Fourth and Eighth Grade Reading and Math Scores, by Race/Ethnicity: 1973–2003

	1973	1975	1978	1980	1986	1990	2003
Fourth grade reading							
White, non-Hispanic		217		221		217	229
Black, non-Hispanic		181		189		182	198
Hispanic		183		190		189	200
Eighth grade reading							
White, non-Hispanic		262		264		262	272
Black, non-Hispanic		226		233		242	244
Hispanic		233		237		238	245
Fourth grade math							
White, non-Hispanic	225		224		227	235	243
Black, non-Hispanic	190		192		202	208	216
Hispanic	202		203		205	214	222
Eighth grade math							
White, non-Hispanic	274		272		274	276	288
Black, non-Hispanic	228		230		249	249	252
Hispanic	239		238		254	255	259

Source: http://nces.ed.gov/nationsreportcard/naepdata. Retrieved 8/15/04.

decreased to 20 and 27 points, respectively. However, in 2003 the gap in reading scores had increased to 28 points, and the gap in math scores to 36 points. As seen in Table 11.2, similar trends in the gap between NAEP scores of Whites and Hispanics also occurred.

The continuing size of the achievement gap between White and minority students and the fact that it appears to be widening is the subject of growing concern among educators and policy makers, as well as the general public. A number of strategies and programs have focused on improving minority achievement, many with promising results. And, of course, minority achievement is a central focus of NCLB. However, the concern remains that these gaps may increase unless K–12 budgets can recover from the budget cuts and stalemates of the early 2000s and unless more resources are made available and targeted to those schools and those students where they are most needed to provide an adequate education.

Resegregation

Fifty years after the Supreme Court outlawed *de jure* segregation, the nation's schools went from segregated to integrated to resegregated. The segregation of today is not mandated by law, but by economics. The dual system of today is not one of Black schools and White schools, but of rich schools with a predominantly White student body and poor schools with a predominantly minority student body.

In 2003 only 21% of White fourth-graders attended schools in which over 50% of students were eligible for free or reduced lunch (a proxy for low-income family status), compared to 71% of Blacks and 73% of Hispanics. In addition to attending schools with high concentrations of students from low-income families, in the same year 50% of Black and 56% of Hispanics fourth-graders attended schools in which 75% or more of the students in the school were minorities (National Center for Education Statistics [NCES], 2004).

While progress in the integration of African Americans that was gained in the 1960s and 1970s has been lost, the segregation of Hispanic students has surpassed that of African American students despite the rapid growth in Hispanic enrollment. This resegregation is of concern, not only because of its ethical and social repercussions, but also because the schools these students attend typically cannot offer them the same educational opportunities as the more affluent schools. They are also less able to attract and retain the highly qualified teachers needed to help these students reach established state standards. The question becomes that posed by the Harvard University Civil Rights Project (Orfield & Lee, 2004): Will the future bring "King's Dream or *Plessy*'s Nightmare?"

School Choice

Charter schools continue to be the most popular choice option. Since the first charter school opened in 1992, their numbers have grown to almost 3,000. Charter school laws have been enacted in 41 states and the District of Columbia. Charter schools are operating in 38 states, enrolling 1.5% of the total school population. The Bush administration lent its support to charter schools by suggesting that a solution for schools labeled as failing under NCLB would be to reconstitute themselves as charter schools.

Questions about the stability and standards of charter schools on one hand, and their claims of effectiveness and academic superiority on the other, has prompted a growing body of charter school research. Recent NAEP data on the performance of charter schools released in the *New York Times* (2004) seemed to indicate that charter school students have lower achievement in Grades 4 and 8 than that of students in traditional public schools. The results were immediately challenged by charter school advocacy groups who point to not only data from specific states where charter school students have been found to perform better than students in traditional schools, but also the fact that charter schools serve high proportions of minority and ill-prepared students (Center for Education Reform, 2004). Many other studies, with often conflicting results, could also be cited, but in the absence of more comprehensive and longitudinal data, the bottom line seems to be that "charter school students show no significant test score superiority (or inferiority) over comparable public school students" (Lieberman, 2004, p. 64).

Following the 2002 U.S. Supreme Court decision in *Zelman v. Simmons-Harris* many expected that voucher programs would be widely proposed. However, in the face of declining state budgets such proposals were not feasible. Only three states (Texas, Louisiana, and Colorado) considered statewide programs. Only in Colorado was the proposal adopted, and then was limited to students in Denver who score poorly in state exams. Vouchers were given some federal support in early 2004 when Congress enacted legislation to provide vouchers to nearly 2,000 students in Washington, DC. Although public support for vouchers has not increased since the mid-1990s (Rose & Gallup, 2004), support for vouchers continues to come from across the political spectrum despite the fact that, as with charter schools, the body of

Charter schools grow in numbers and continue to be the most popular choice option.

evidence does not support claims of superior achievement of voucher students on various standardized tests. Nonetheless, the belief that the introduction of the forces of the marketplace into the provision of education (i.e., school choice) will force improvement in the public schools remains strong among school choice advocates, as does the belief that increased parental choice is an unqualified good (Molnar, 2004).

Conclusion: Left (and Right) Back

The history of American education is far more than a history of people or institutions. It is primarily a history of competing views of who should be educated, what they should be taught, the purpose of schooling, and the role of the education system in a democracy. (See Ackerman's comparison of the traditionalist and progressivist views in the Primary Source Reading for this chapter.) Ravitch's (2000) history of American education in the 20th century described it as one of failed reforms by what might be described as "progressive educators" (the left) and a war between competing traditions of education. Other historians might view the same history as attempts by those with a more essentialist view of education (the right) to overhaul what to them is a failed system of public schooling.

What seems clear is that the recent past has seen the criticism of public education grow louder and the push to reform it with market-driven strategies and privatization grow stronger. What also seems clear, at least to this writer, is that the goals of NCLB, although perhaps well intended, are not likely to be achieved. Whether the data that report the large number of children labeled as failing will provide critics of the public school system the ammunition to demand its restructure, even its privatization, will be the history reported in a later edition.

For Discussion and Application

1. The eight goals included in Goals 2000 were not achieved by the year 2000. How would you rate the likelihood of the attainment of the NCLB goals? What factors influence your judgment?
2. Compare the equity and adequacy goals of school finance. To what extent are they competing or complementary?
3. Discuss the advantages and disadvantages of using high-stakes testing to determine high school graduation.
4. Identify a school in your area that was in operation in 1954. Using available documentation, and personal interviews if possible, describe the changes in the school in the years since *Brown.*
5. Choose a profession other than teaching (e.g., law, medicine, architecture) and discuss with a member of that profession the qualifications for licensure, how they have changed over the last decade, and what and by whom suggestions for improving and monitoring the profession have been made.

Primary Source Reading

The fundamental debate between progressive and traditional educators has gone on for more than a century. Ackerman suggests that the time has come for a truce and a search for common ground. According to Ackerman, both points of view can and should be recognized as complementary. To accomplish this task, he identifies a dual set of foundational principles (i.e., two tablets) with five commandments each. He also offers examples of what school would be like if both the traditional and progressive ideas were blended into a synergistic whole. As you read the following article, keep in mind your own thoughts regarding traditional and progressive ideology.

Taproots for a New Century: Tapping the Best of Traditional and Progressive Education

David B. Ackerman

In California, a coalition of "mathematically correct" parents and university professors campaigns vigorously against progressive-style "fuzzy math" and demands the return of a no-nonsense, basic-skills curriculum. In Massachusetts, the state department of education hires a consultant from New South Wales to argue for the importance of learning science content, thus doing battle with the schools of education and think tanks closer to home and their fervently espoused gospel of hands-on or "process" science. With such a belligerence evident from coast to coast and with valid insights from one side in these "wars" canceling out those of the other, might it be time to call a truce and search for common ground?

These battles in math and science and in many other areas (e.g., history versus social studies, speaking versus grammar in foreign-language

Source: Ackerman, D. B. (2003). Taproots for a new century: Tapping the best of traditional and progressive education. *Phi Delta Kappan, 84* (5), 344–349.

learning) are manifestations of a fundamental debate between progressive educators and traditionalists that has been going on for more than a century. While individual practitioners make pragmatic accommodations (a stiff dose of phonics alternating with fragrant whiffs of whole language), for the profession as a whole the progressivism-versus-traditionalism debate has reached a stalemate. Characteristically, even where one side seems to have the upper hand (for example, progressivism is dominant in most schools of education), the gospel is largely rejected elsewhere (for example, in most actual high schools).

It is easy to write off this debate as an all-too-predictable exercise in rhetorical wheel spinning, but to do so would be sad and foolish, for these two traditions represent the best we know about teaching and learning. They are the intertwined taproots of our professional outlook, the warp and woof of the fabric of beliefs that guide us when we walk into a classroom. In the best tradition of traditional education, we need to articulate the content of this debate, and in the best tradition of Deweyan progressivism, we need to work to derive useful insights. Our aim should be to break the philosophical logjam that has been obstructing us as a profession. But how can this be done?

While there can be no pat formula, there is a promising pathway, rooted in the intuition that we are dealing not with educational good and evil but with *dual virtues* that need to be boldly and imaginatively combined. The validity of this intuition would be demonstrated by the hybrid vigor of the synthesis that results. The problem is figuring out how to get to the point where points of view long at war can be recognized as essentially complementary. I see three steps as necessary for depolarizing the debate and achieving a unified outlook.

First, those who temperamentally or philosophically lean toward one side of the debate need to resist the temptation to claim the high ground by simply caricaturing the other side. Specifically, traditionalists need to stop ridiculing progressives as anti-intellectual bleeding hearts, and progressives need to stop deriding traditionalists as pedantic, insensitive crushers of freedom.

Second, we need to articulate the enduring and valid insights of both camps and engrave them on the two tablets of our new educational "10 commandments." And neither tablet is to be given mere lip service!

Third, we need to recognize and imagine educational practices in which all these "commandments" are alive and well, in which the actions inspired by traditionalism and those sparked by progressivism are orchestrated so as to produce classrooms and schools characterized philosophically by breadth of vision and functioning as learning communities that make us want to sing and shout.

To illustrate what I am suggesting, let me identify a double-barreled set of foundational principles—two tablets with five commandments each—and sketch an example or two of what school would look like if both the traditional and progressive ideas were powerfully, synergistically alive.

The Traditional Tablet

The traditionalist insists, rightly, that a developing mind deserves not intellectual junk food but the most nourishing repast we know how to serve. The traditionalist draws our attention to hierarchies of curricular importance and academic competence; the focus of instruction is on mastery of material that can ennoble a student rather than on concern for the frustration students may feel when their efforts fall short. A set of traditionalist commandments would include the following five.

1. **Thou shalt teach that which is of deepest value.** Not all topics and questions are equally worth pursuing. And, even though the idea of a canon fixed once and for all time is illusory, we must not duck the responsibility of choosing texts that will pass along to young people what Matthew Arnold famously described as "the best which has been thought and said in the world."

We obey this commandment not to show fealty to the past and certainly not to indulge in high-minded puffery but in order to be as respectful—and as educationally generous—as possible to our students *today*. We therefore invite them to partake of a cornucopia of ideas, perspectives, and vicarious experiences that have the power to lift them beyond themselves, to spark a desire to live not a commonplace existence but one that has been, as Robert Maynard Hutchins said it, "transfigured and seen through the eyes of wisdom and genius." "Thinking skills" and "learning how to learn" may have their place in the overall curriculum, but they are hollow vehicles if they are not harnessed to the "good stuff"—the novels and plays, poems and paintings, essays and sermons, and stories of mathematical and scientific discovery. These treasures, the best of the whole world's opus, must be internalized to become part of each student's sensibility and vision of life.

2. **Thou shalt teach with rigor.** The moment of temptation comes when our students—out of ignorance, laziness, or immaturity—express unclear thought, as they inevitably will. The temptation will be to let it slide, but our duty is to criticize—not heartlessly and certainly not disparagingly or compulsively, but with tactful insistence. The same high degree of plain-spoken rigor is, of course, to be applied to oneself as explicator of subtle or complex ideas and as respondent to students' questions. The motivation for rigor is not puritanical righteousness or dry-souled pedantry. The aim of rigor is joyous illumination, which is experienced by students when a powerful but initially blurry idea comes into luminous focus and subsequently helps open their minds to further enlightenment.

3. **Thou shalt uphold standards of excellence.** The same principle that requires rigor in classroom discourse manifests itself in a teacher's adherence to high standards in the evaluation of student work. While earnest effort ought to be admired, it must not be conflated with authentic achievement. Low grades may discourage a student or hurt his or her feelings, but inflated grades cheapen that same student's cultural inheritance by seeming to pass on precious intellectual goods at discount prices. The desire to encourage thus metamorphoses insidiously into acts of degradation.

4. Thou shall not kill time.   In evaluating alternative instructional methods, effectiveness—not ideology—ought to be the central criterion. And effectiveness cannot be gauged without considering the time required to achieve the results. Thus there is nothing intrinsically "bad" about a lecture or "good" about cooperative learning. The overriding question must always be: In the time available, which pedagogical pathway is likely to lead students to the biggest pot of educational gold?

Methods that require a considerable amount of time must be assessed not just in terms of their effectiveness in teaching a concept but also in light of the opportunity cost incurred when students do *not* learn whatever else they might have learned during the same time slot. The "depth versus breadth" argument simply cannot be decided on principle alone. Each teacher must decide between particular sets of tradeoffs, between small bundles of large nuggets and large bundles of small ones.

5. Remember the disciplines and keep them holy (even though they are partial).   If there is such a coherent educational aim as "knowledge integration," then the road to holistic heaven is paved with disciplinary knowledge. And discipline-based knowledge is the firm foundation of any imagined ascent into the transdisciplinary firmament. The subject disciplines provide powerful, indispensable perspectives and tools of inquiry as well as intrinsically important knowledge about the nature of human beings and the world. Pursuing knowledge integration when the knowledge base is meager is always a fatuous undertaking. An inescapable test of the validity of "thematic" approaches to curriculum, whatever their potential to motivate and spark children's imagination, is whether the disciplinary ingredients in the interdisciplinary stew maintain enough of their own flavors to become robust parts of the students' mental apparatus.

The Progressive Tablet

The progressive educator insists, rightly, that adroitness in accommodating, both psychologically and intellectually, what the student brings to the classroom is at least as important as wise selection of the most sublime material. Each student embodies a unique sensibility formed by years of interaction between genetic endowment and life experiences.

At a macro level, a student's life history affects the degree to which she sees what the teacher asks of her as being desirable, interesting, attainable, applicable to her present and future life, and worthy of strenuous effort. At a micro level, each element of the common curriculum is being assimilated within individual educational histories, resulting in classrooms characterized by multiple degrees of subject-matter mastery and a spectrum of optimal instructional levels or "zones of proximal development." Each student's mind has evolved along an idiosyncratic trajectory of learning; each student makes meaning for himself in the context of his personal history. These unique, evolving sensibilities must be cherished at least as much as the instructional content. The commandments that flow from these and related considerations might include the following five:

6. Remember that children are whole people, not deficient adults.   Children have lives of their own, on a plane of existence more fundamental than that of the institutionalized functioning of the school. Children do not depend on teachers to be able to think, pose questions, investigate, or engage with aspects of life that interest them. Each child owns her own sense of truth and desire for meaning. The task of the school is to nurture positive traits and natural proclivities, while discouraging their opposites. While students' minds may be "blank slates" on a particular topic, students are always full-fledged subjects of their unfolding life experience. Children and adults differ in accountability for their actions, but they resemble one another in desiring to understand the world and in displaying ignorance when they do not know any better.

7. Thou shalt not try to make one standard fit all.   While standards of excellence may be regarded as absolute, the performance standard for what can reasonably be expected of a particular learner at a particular time, in any given domain, may differ from that which is reasonable to expect of another learner, even one of the same age. In sports, the performances of the club pro and the average weekend golfer are benchmarked both against Tiger Woods (the best in the game) and against each player's personal best. We rightfully expect more of the club pro (and he does of himself) than we expect of the amateur. Scholastically, performance standards and expectations naturally differ for the math prodigy and the average weekday math student and, more subtly, from one math prodigy—and even one "average math student"—to the next. For, fundamentally, we teach individual young people and not categories of them.

8. Thou shalt not treat the mind of a child as though it were a receptacle.   Classroom teaching would be a breeze if a lucid explanation were sufficient to bring about a solid grasp of the material—if the teacher's knowledge could somehow be deposited into the students' minds in the way valuables can be deposited into a safe deposit box. In reality, the teacher's words alone amount to noise, not knowledge.

Mindful learning requires a mindful learner. Pearls of wisdom cannot adorn the life of the mind, nor can the next generation cash in these receivables from its inheritance, until their meaning has been extracted and understood. For students to achieve understanding, they need to do more than press the record button in class and subsequently play back the teacher's words. Students need to think about what they have heard or read. If they are successful in their efforts to learn from instruction, they will be able to paraphrase the material, draw inferences from it, and interweave it with other threads in a descriptive or explanatory tapestry. A lecture can be an effective method *if* students respond with acts of comprehension. If a student responds mindlessly, he will not understand the material. The extent to which the teacher or student is blamed is an ideological question, but, if the intention of the teacher is to deduce understanding and that of the student is to learn, then the bottom line is that both have failed.

9. Honor what children bring to the text. This commandment does not mean endorsing or being obsequious about the beliefs and attitudes that students bring to the classroom. Rather, it means taking these beliefs and attitudes respectfully into account. The moral obligation for a teacher to do so can be derived from the rather traditional philosophical premise of "respect for persons." (See Commandment 6, above.) On a practical level, it is not wise to ignore the students' background knowledge because that knowledge may systematically distort the intended meanings of the teacher's words. Students *do* interpret new information in terms of what they already believe to be true. Conflicting claims will either be rejected as invalid or stored in a special compartment of statements that are true in school—and false everywhere else. Why, except out of indolence or arrogance, should we ignore the relevant characteristics of the knowledge receivers and indulge in the myth that their minds are blank slates?

10. Thou shalt honor the student's search for holistic knowledge.   Discipline-based learning is necessary, but it is not sufficient. It is true that a student can tune in to a wide range of intellectual wavelengths that emanate from the subject disciplines. And it is important to acknowledge that each subject discipline has the potential to contribute to a student's search for truth, beauty, goodness, meaning, refined pleasure, and self-realization. But a student is a unitary being whose sensibility does not change when the bell rings and it's time to change classes. At day's end, a student wants to know not what's true in science and what truths can be gleaned from literature. But, more comprehensively, she wants to know what's true; she desires to fulfill her potential not as a mathematical thinker or an artist, but as a person. She wants a belief system that includes the lessons learned in school and those learned through everyday living. It is narrow-minded and spiritually stingy to absolve the school from its responsibility to assist students in the elusive challenge of knowledge integration, for it is the school's job to help translate the cacophonous and fragmented disciplinary babel into a versatile and ultimately harmonious and coherent set of lenses on the world.

Take Two Tablets and Bring Them to School in the Morning

Imagine a set of schools in which all 10 of these commandments or basic principles of curriculum and instruction were robustly and accountably alive. While individual teachers and schools might tack a little to the right or left, the range of tenable variations would be limited by virtue of the strength of commitment to the opposite-pulling tablet. (Of course, in the school culture, it is not the rhetorical pose that matters but the pedagogical power; it is important to recognize, for example, that some "traditional" teachers communicate tremendous personal caring and some "progressive" teachers manifest steely rigor.) The phenotypes generated by the two-tablet genotype would thus range from, say, the best "Dewey schools" to the best versions of E. D. Hirsch's "schools we deserve." Dewy-eyed progressive schools and "back-to-basics" schools that revolve around rote drill and memorization would both be rejected as unworthy caricatures.

If this set of guiding principles (or some alternative containing compelling additions, deletions, or substitutions) is valid, it can be tested, at least at the level of thought experiment. The test would be to describe a school that has eliminated one of the principles or watered it down practically beyond recognition and then to assess whether or not the educational value of the resulting program would be significantly reduced. Less globally, dialogue with this decalogue can be used to inspire good programs to become even better—to spark the creation of a science program, for example, in which hands-on investigation, superb teacher explication, and inspiring stories from the history of science are elegantly combined.

Framed more generally, the argument I am advancing here is that schools that try to impart sublime content while being largely inattentive to student individuality (and their converses) offer *substantially less value* than those that propel learners through a powerful synthesis of both sets of ideas. To use a biological metaphor, the argument is that the philosophical form of an outstanding school is akin to the double helix of DNA; *both*

the progressive and the traditional strands intertwine, reinforcing and amplifying one another. These are the kinds of schools on which we ought to set our sights.

Let us imagine, then, school programs in which

- "active learning" is understood as *mentally active* and not something necessarily requiring hopping around the classroom;
- strong disciplinary pillars exist within a set of structures that foster knowledge integration;
- the value (and limitations) of *both* "depth" and "coverage" are understood, and a balance among the tradeoffs between scope and intensity has been artfully maintained;
- students are grouped by ability when unwillingness to do so would waste their time unconscionably and grouped heterogeneously when each participant has something of genuine value *relative to the subject matter at hand* to contribute to his classmates; and
- students are evaluated on the progress they have made toward achieving *personal excellence*, the standards for which have been derived from and point toward standards of absolute excellence.

Who would not want to teach or learn in such a school? Who would not want to send a child to such a school? Who but an utter ideologue would disparage a profession that, far and wide, produced schools that beautifully exemplified these 10 commandments?

Questions for Discussion

1. Which of the 10 commandments delineated by Ackerman best describe your theory of education? Explain.
2. Using the progressive-versus-traditional debate, how has your theory of education evolved over time?
3. If you were to imagine a school that successfully blended both the progressive and traditional strands, what additional suggestions would you add to Ackerman's list?

References

Acts and Resolutions, Public and Private, of the Province of Massachusetts Bay. (1701–1750). Boston: Massachusetts Historical Society.

Adams, D. W. (1995). *Education for extinction: American Indians and the boarding school experience, 1875–1928.* Lawrence, KN: University of Kansas Press.

Adler, M. (1982). *The Paideia proposal: An educational manifesto.* New York: Macmillan.

Adler, M. (1984). *The Paideia program.* New York: Macmillan.

Adovasio, J. M., & Page, J. (2002). *The first Americans: In pursuit of archaeology's greatest mystery.* New York: Random House.

American Association of School Administrators (AASA). (1952). *The American school superintendency,* Thirtieth Yearbook. Washington, DC: Author.

American Association of University Women (AAUW). (1991). *Shortchanging girls, shortchanging America.* Washington, DC: AAUW Educational Foundation.

American Association of University Women (AAUW). (1992). *How Schools shortchange girls.* Washington, DC: AAUW Educational Foundation.

American Association of University Women (AAUW). (1993). *Hostile hallways: The AAUW survey on sexual harassment in America's Schools.* Washington, DC: AAUW Education Foundation.

American Association of University Women (AAUW). (1998). *Gender gaps: Where schools fail our children.* Washington, DC: AAUW Education Foundation.

American Association of University Women (AAUW). (2001a). *Beyond the gender wars: A conversation about girls, boys, and education.* Washington, DC: AAUW Education Foundation.

American Association of University Women (AAUW) (2001b). *Hostile hallways: Bullying, teasing and sexual harassment in school.* Washington, DC: AAUW Education Foundation.

American Indian Education Foundation. (AIEF). (2003). History and facts about Indian education. Retrieved June 9, 2003, from AIEF Web site: www.aiefprograms.org/history-facts/history.html.

American Journey: The Native American Experience. (1998). Woodbridge, CT: Primary Source Media.

Anderson, J. D. (1978). The Hampton model of normal school industrial education, 1868–1900. In V. P. Franklin & J. D. Anderson (Eds.), *New perspectives on black educational history.* Boston: G. K. Hall.

Anderson, J. D. (1988). *The education of blacks in the South, 1860–1935.* Chapel Hill: The University of North Carolina Press.

Anderson, J. D. (2001). Part three: 1950–1980, separate and unequal: Introduction. In S. Mondale & S. B. Patten (Eds.), *School, the story of American public education* (pp. 123–130). Boston: Beacon Press.

Angus, D. L., & Mirel, J. (2000). *Professionalism and the public good: A brief history of teacher certification.* Washington, DC: Thomas B. Fordham Foundation.

Apple, M. W. (2004). *Ideology and curriculum.* New York: Routledge Falmer.

Aronowitz, S. (2003). *How class works: Power and social movement.* New Haven: Yale University Press.

Arsen, D., Plank, D., & Sykes, D. (2001). *A work in progress.* Stanford, CA: Hoover Institute.

Bagley, W. C. (1938). An essentialist platform for the advancement of American education. *Educational Administration and Supervision, 24,* 241–256.

Balwin, J. (2002). Preface. In E. Foner, *Who owns history: Rethinking the past in a changing world.* (p. ix). New York: Hill and Wang.

Bell, T. H. (1993). Reflections one decade after A Nation at Risk. *Phi Delta Kappan, 74,* 592–597.

Bennett, L., Jr. (1976). *Before the Mayflower: A history of Black America.* New York: Penguin.

Bennett, W. J. (1987). *James Madison High School: A curriculum for American students.* Washington, DC: U.S. Department of Education.

Bennett, W. J. (1988). *James Madison Elementary School: A curriculum for American students.* Washington, DC: U.S. Department of Education.

Berger, M. (1947). Education in Texas during the Spanish and Mexican periods. *Southwestern Historical Quarterly, 51,* 41–53.

Berliner, D. C., & Biddle, B. J. (1995). *The manufactured crisis: Myths, fraud, and the attack on America's public schools.* Reading, MA: Addison Wesley.

Bernard, S. C., & Mondale, S. (2001a). A nation at risk? In S. Mondale & S. B. Patten (Eds.), *School, the story of American public education* (pp. 183–213). Boston: Beacon Press.

Bernard, S. C., & Mondale, S. (2001b). Why don't you go to school with us? In S. Mondale & S. B. Patten (Eds.), *School, the story of American public education* (pp. 131–170). Boston: Beacon Press.

Bernard, S. C., & Mondale, S. (2001c). You are an American. In S. Mondale & S. B. Patten (Eds.), *School, the story of American public education* (pp. 71–119). Boston: Beacon Press.

Bestor, A. E. (1953). *Educational wasteland: The retreat from learning in the public schools.* Urbana, IL: University of Illinois Press.

Bestor, A. E. (1956). *The restoration of learning.* New York: Alfred A. Knopf.

Biesta, G. J. (2001). Preparing for the incalculable: Deconstruction, justice, and the question of education. In G. J. Biesta & D. Egea-Kuehne (Eds.), *Derrida & education* (pp. 32–54). London: Routledge.

Binder, F. M. (1974). *The age of the common school, 1830–1865.* New York: John Wiley & Sons.

Blake, N., Masschelein, J. (2003). Critical theory and critical pedagogy. In N. Blake, P. Smeyers, R. Smith, & P. Standish (Eds). *The Blackwell guide to the philosophy of education.* (pp. 38–56). Malden, MA: Blackwell Publishing.

Blinderman, A. (1976). *Three early champions of education: Benjamin Franklin, Benjamin Rush, and Noah Webster.* Bloomington, IN: The Phi Delta Kappa Educational Foundation.

Bloom, A. (1987). *The closing of the American mind.* New York: Simon & Schuster.

Board of Education of Oklahoma City v. Dowell, 111 S. Ct. 630 (1991).

Bobbitt, F. (1912). The elimination of waste in education. *The Elementary School Teacher, 12,* 259–271.

Bobrick, B. (1997). *Angel in the whirlwind: The triumph of the American revolution.* New York: Simon & Schuster.

Bonner, T. N. (1963). *Our recent past: American civilization in the twentieth century.* Upper Saddle River, NJ: Prentice Hall.

Boorstin, D. J. (1958). *The Americans: The colonial experience.* New York: Random House.

Bowles, S., & Gintis, H. (1975). *Schooling in capitalist America.* New York: Basic Books.

Boylan, A. M.(1988). *Sunday school: The formation of an American institution, 1790–1880.* New Haven, CT: Yale Univesity Press.

Bracey, G. W. (2003). The 13th Bracey report on the condition of public education. *Phi Delta Kappan, 85,* 148–164.

Brendtro, L. K., Brokenleg, M., & Van Bockern, S. (1991). The circle of courage. *Beyond Behavior, 2* (1), 5–12.

Brosio, R. A. (2000). *Philosophical scaffolding for the construction of critical democratic education.* New York: Peter Lang.

Brown vs. Board of Education, 347 U.S. 463 (1954).

Bruner, J. S. (1977). *The process of education.* Cambridge: Harvard University Press.

Butler, J. D. (1966). *Idealism in education.* New York: Harper & Row.

Butts, R. F., & Cremin, L. A. (1953). *A history of education in American culture.* New York: Holt, Rinehart and Winston.

Callahan, R. E. (1962). *Education and the cult of efficiency.* Chicago: University of Chicago Press.

Campbell, J. (2000). Benjamin Rush and women's education: A revolutionary disappointment, a nation's achievement. *John and Mary's Journal, 13,* 14–19.

Cardozier, V. R. (1993). *Colleges and universities in World War II.* Westport, CT: Praeger.

Carlson, A. D. (1933, November). Deflating the schools. *Harpers, 167,* 707–713.

Carnegie Forum on Education and the Economy. (1986). *A nation prepared: Teachers for the Twenty-first century.* Washington, DC: Author.

Carnes, J. (1995). *U.S. and them: A history of intolerance in America.* New York: Oxford University Press.

Center for Education Reform. (2004). Charter connection. Retrieved September 10, 2003, from www.edreform.com/charter_schools.

Clarkin, T. (2001). *Federal Indian policy in the Kennedy and Johnson administrations, 1961–1969.* Albuquerque: University of New Mexico Press.

CNN Online. (2003, August, 10). Education law tries thin state budgets. Retrieved August 10, 2003, from www.cnfyi.printthis. clickability/com/pt.

Cohen, S. (Ed.). (1974a). *Education in the United States, A documentary history,* Volume 1. New York: Random House.

Cohen, S. S. (1974b). *A history of colonial education, 1607–1776.* New York: John Wiley & Sons.

Cole, N. M. (1956). The licensing of schoolmasters in colonial Massachusetts. *History of Education Journal, 8,* 68–74.

Coleman, M. C. (1993). *American Indian children at school, 1850–1930.* Jackson, MS: University of Mississippi Press.

Commager, H. S. (1977). *The empire of reason: How Europe envisioned and America realized the Enlightenment.* Garden City, NY: Doubleday.

Conant, J. B. (1953). *Education and liberty.* Cambridge, MA: Harvard University Press.

Conant, J. B. (1959). *The American high school today.* New York: McGraw-Hill.

Connell, W. F. (1980). *A history of education in the twentieth century.* New York: Teachers College Press, Columbia University.

Conway, J. K. (1978). Perspectives on the history of women's education in the United States. In D. R. Warren (Ed.), *History, education and public policy* (pp. 273–285). Berkley, CA: McCutchan.

Counts, G. C. (1978). *Dare the schools build a new social order?* Carbondale, IL: Southern Illinois Press. (Original work published 1932)

Counts, G. S. (1926). *The senior high school curriculum.* Chicago: University of Chicago Press.

Cremin, L. A. (1959). What happened to progressive education? *Teachers College Record, 61,* 23–29.

Cremin, L. A. (1970). *American education: The colonial experience, 1607–1783.* New York: Harper & Row.

Cremin, L. A. (1982). *American education: The national experience, 1783–1876.* New York: Harper & Row.

Cremin, L. A. (1988). *American education: The metropolitan experience, 1876–1980.* New York: Harper & Row.

Cuban, D., & Shipp, D. (2000). *Restructuring the common good: Coping with intractable American dilemmas.* Stanford, CA: Stanford University Press.

Cuban, L. (1984). *How teachers taught: Constancy and change in American classrooms, 1890–1980.* New York: Longman.

Cuban, L. (2001). Part Four: 1980–2000, The bottom line, introduction. In S. Mondale & S. B. Patten (Eds.), *School, the story of American public education* (pp. 173–182). Boston: Beacon Press.

Cubberley, E. P. (1934). *Readings in public education.* Cambridge, MA: Riverside Press.

The cult of domesticity and true womanhood. Retrieved May 17, 2003, from www.library .csi.cuny.edu/dept/history/lavender/386/ truewoman.html.

Dayton Board of Education v. Brinkman, 433 U.S. 406 (1977).

DeJong, D. H. (1993). *Promises of the past: A history of Indian education in the United States.* Golden, CO: North American Press.

Derrida, J. (1976). *Of grammatology.* (G. C. Spivak, Trans.). London: The Johns Hopkins University Press.

Dewey, J. (1899, rev. ed. 1943). *The school and society.* Chicago: The University of Chicago Press.

Dewey, J. (1916). *Democracy and education: An introduction to the philosophy of education.* New York: Macmillan.

Dewey, J. (1920). *Reconstruction in philosophy.* New York: H. Holt.

Doherty, K. M., & Skinner, R. A. (2003, January 9). State of the states. *Education Week*, pp. 75–78.

Donahoe v. Richards. 38 Me. 379 (1854).

DuBois, W. E. B. (1903). The talented tenth. In *The Negro problem.* New York: James Pott and Company.

Education Policies Commission. (1942). *A war policy for American schools.* Washington, DC: National Education Association.

Ellis, M. S., Jr. (1995). Revisionism in U.S. education: An historical inquiry, contemporary perspective, and future prediction. *Loch Haven International Review, 9,* Retrived February 10, 1999, from lhup.edu/library/ international/review/issue9.htm

Faludi, S. (1991). *Backlash: The undeclared war against women.* London: Vintage.

Feistritzer, E., & Chester, D. (2003). *Alternative teacher certification: An overview.* Retrieved June 24, 2003, from National Center for Education Information, www.ncei.com.

Firestone, W., Fuhrman, S., & Kirst, M. W. (1990). An overview of education reform since 1983. In J. Murphy (Ed.), *The education reform movement of the 1980s: Perspectives and cases* (pp. 349–364). Berkeley, CA: McCutchan.

Fithian, D. (2000). *The lyceum movement: A revolution in American education.* Retrieved June 2, 2004, from www.tncc.cc.va.us/faculty/ longt/FrienshipBook/LyceumMovemen. htm.

Foner, E. (2002). *Who owns history? Rethinking the past in a changing world.* New York: Hill and Wang.

Ford, P. L. (Ed.). (1962). *The New England primer.* New York: Columbia University Teachers College.

Foster, S. J. (2000). *Red alert: Educators confront the red scare in American public schools, 1947–1954.* New York: Peter Lang.

Frazier, N. & Sadker, M. (1973). *Sexism in school and society.* New York: Harper & Row.

Freeman v. Pitts, 112 S. Ct. 1430 (1992).

Freire, P. (1973). *Pedagogy of the oppressed.* New York: Seabury Press.

Gabella, M. S. (1994). Beyond the looking glass: Bringing sutdents into the conversation of historical inquiry. *Theory and Research in Social Education, 23*(3), 340–363.

Garcia, A. M. (2002). *The Mexican-Americans.* Westport, CT: Greenwood Press.

Garrison, J. (1994). Realism, Deweyan, pragmatism, and educational research. *Educational Researcher, 23*(1), 5–14.

Garrison, J., & Neiman, A. (2003). Pragmatism and education. In N. Blake, P. Smeyers, R. Smith, & P. Standish (Eds). *The Blackwell guide to the philosophy of education* (pp. 21–37). Malden, MA: Blackwell Publishing.

Georgia's Spanish Missions. (2003). Retrieved February 20, 2003, from http://members .aol.com/jeworth/gbomiss.htm.

Gilbert, M. J. (2001). Introduction. In M. J. Gilbert (Ed.), *The Vietnam war on campus: Other voices, more distant drums.* Westport, CT: Praeger.

Gilland, T. M. (1935). *The origins and development of the powers and duties of the city-school superintendent.* Chicago: University of Chicago Press.

Gillett, M. (1966). *A history of education: Thought and practice.* Toronto: McGraw-Hill.

Giroux, H. (2003). *The abandoned generation: Democracy beyond the culture of fear.* New York: Palgrave MacMillan.

Glubok, S. (Ed.). (1969). *Home and child life in colonial days.* New York: Macmillan.

Goertz, M. E. (2001). Redefining government roles in an era of standards-based reform. *Phi Delta Kappan, 83,* 62–66.

Goldberg, M. F. (2004). The total mess. *Phi Delta Kappan, 85,* 361–366.

Gonzalez, G. (1990). *Chicano education in the era of segregation.* Philadelphia, PA: Balch Institute Press.

Goodlad, J. (2002). Kudzu, rabbits, and school reform. *Phi Delta Kappan, 84,* 16–23.

Goss v. Lopez, 419 U. S. 565 (1975).

Graham, P. A. (1967). *Progressive education: From arcady to academe: A history of the Progressive Education Association, 1915–1955.* New York: Teachers College Press.

Graham, P. A. (1974). *Community & class in American education.* New York: John Wiley & Sons.

Graves, K. A. (2002). *Going to school during the great depression.* Mankato, MN: Capstone Press.

Gray, R., & Peterson, J. M. (1974). *Economic development of the United States.* Homewood, IL: Richard D. Irwin.

Green v. County School Board, 391 U.S. 430 (1968).

Greene, M. (1967). *Existential encounters for teachers.* New York: Random House.

Griffin v. County School Board, 377 U.S. 218 (1964).

Gurskey, D. (2001). Finding and training those 2 million teachers. *Education Digest, 66* (6), 17–23.

Gutek, G. (1988). *Philosophical and ideological perspectives on education.* Boston: Allyn and Bacon.

Gutek, G. (2004). *Philosophical and ideological voices in education.* New York: Allyn and Bacon.

Gutek, G. L. (1981). *Basic education: A historical perspective.* Bloomington, IN: Phi Delta Kappan Educational Foundation.

Gutek, G. L. (1986). *Education in the United States: An historical perspective.* Upper Saddle River, NJ: Prentice Hall.

Hakim, J. (1999a). *The first Americans.* New York: Oxford University Press.

Hakim, J. (1999b). *Making thirteen colonies.* New York: Oxford University Press.

Hale, L. (2002). *Native American handbook: A reference handbook.* Santa Barbara, CA: ABC-CLIO.

Hardy, L. (2002). A new federal role. *American School Board Journal, 189* (9), 20–24.

Hare, N., & Swift, D. W. (1976). Black education. In D. W. Swift (Ed.). *American education: A sociological view.* Boston: Houghton Mifflin.

Heffernan, H. (1968). The school curriculum in American education. In E. Fuller & J. B. Pearson (Eds.), *Education in the states: Nationwide development since 1900.* Washington, DC: National Education Association.

Henderson, J. G. (2001). *Reflective teaching: Professional artistry through inquiry* (3rd ed.). Upper Saddle River, NJ: Prentice Hall/ Merrill.

Henriques, D. B. (September 2, 2003). Rising demands for teaching push limits of its accuracy. *New York Times,* p. A-1.

Henry, N. B. (Ed.). (1945a). *American education in the postwar period, part I: Curriculum reconstruction, Forty-fourth yearbook of the National Survey for the Study of Education.* Chicago: University of Chicago Press.

Henry, N. B. (Ed.). (1945b). *American education in the postwar period, part II: Structural reorganization, Forty-fourth yearbook of the National Survey for the Study of Education.* Chicago: University of Chicago Press.

Herbst, J. (1996). *The once and future school: Three hundred and fifty years of American secondary education.* New York: Routledge.

Hertert, L. G. (1998). What the governors propose for 1998. *School Business Affairs, 64*(7), 28–52.

Hollins v. Shofstall, 515 P 2d 590 (1973).

Hirsch, E. D., Jr. (1987). *Cultural literacy: What every American needs to know.* Boston: Houghton Mifflin.

Hissong, M. C., & Hissong, C. (1930). The scientific movement and progressive education, *Education, 51,* 1–9.

Hofstadter, R. (1955). *Academic freedom in the age of the college.* New York: Columbia University Press.

Holmes Group. (1986). *Tomorrow's teachers: A report of the Holmes Group.* East Lansing, MI: Holmes Group.

Holt, J. (1981). *Teach your own.* New York: Delacorte.

Horn, R. A., Jr. (2002). *Understanding educational reform: A reference handbook.* Santa Barbara, CA: ABC-CLIO.

Hutchins, R. M. (1936). *The higher learning in America.* New Haven, CT: Yale University Press.

Illich, I. (1974). *Deschooling society.* New York: Harper & Row.

Ingersoll, R. M. (1999). The problem of under-qualified teachers in American secondary schools. *Educational Researcher, 28* (2), 26–37.

Jacobsen, D. A. (2003). *Philosophy in classroom teaching* (2nd ed.). Upper Saddle River, NJ: Prentice Hall/Merrill.

Jackson v. Benson, 578 NW 2d 602 (Wis. 1998), *cert denied* 119 S.Ct. 467 (1998).

James, T. (1985), *Excile within: The schooling of Japanese Americans, 1942–1945.* Cambridge, MA: Harvard University Press.

Jennings, J. (2002). Knocking on your door. *American School Board Journal, 189* (9), 25–27.

Kaestle, C. F. (1983). *Pillars of the republic: Common schools and American Society, 1780–1860.* New York: Hill and Wang.

Kandel, I. L. (1948). *The impact of the war upon American education.* Chapel Hill, NC: University of North Carolina Press.

Kaplan, G. (1990). Pushing and shoving in videoland U.S.A.: TV's version of education (and what to do about it). *Phi Delta Kappan, 71,* K11–K12.

Kaplan, L., & Owings, W. (2001). Teacher quality and student achievement: Recommendation for principals. *NASSP Bulletin, 85* (628), 64–73.

Katz, L. G., & Chard, S. C. (2000). *Engaging children's minds: The project approach* (2nd ed.). Stamford, CT: Ablex.

Keller, B. (2004, January 14) Rigor disputed in standards for teachers. *Education Week,* pp. 1, 14.

Kerr, C. (1963). *Uses of the university.* Cambridge, MA: Harvard University Press.

Kerr, J. (2001, July 29). 14 percent of classes have unqualified teachers, state says. *The Tribune,* San Louis Obispo County, CA, pp. A1, A11.

Keyes v. School District No. 1, 413 U.S. 189 (1973).

Kidwell, C. S., & Swift, D. W. (1976). Indian education. In D. W. Swift (Ed.), *American education: A sociological view.* Boston: Houghton Mifflin.

Kincheloe, J. (2004). *Twelve ways of looking at school.* Menlo Park, CA: Sunset Publishing.

Kincheloe, J. L., Slattery, P., & Steinberg, S. R. (2000). *Contextualizing teaching: Introduction to education and educational foundations.* New York: Longman.

King, W. (1995). *Stolen childhood: Slave youth in nineteenth century America.* Bloomington, IN: Indiana University Press.

Kingsbury, G. G., Olson, A., Cronin, J., Hauser, C., & Houser, R. (2004). *Research brief: The state of state standards.* Portland, OR: Northwest Evaluation Association.

Kirkland, E. C. (1969). *A history of American economic life* (4th ed.). New York: Appleton-Century-Crofts.

Kliebard, H. M. (1995). *The struggle for the American curriculum, 1893–1958* (2nd ed.). New York: Routledge.

Kneller, G. F. (1971). *Introduction to the philosophy of education.* New York: John Wiley & Sons.

Knight, E. W. (1952). *Fifty years of American education.* New York: The Ronald Press.

Kozol, J. (1972). *Free schools.* Boston: Houghton Mifflin.

Kozol, J. (1991). *Savage inequalities: Children in America's schools.* New York: Crown.

Kraushaar, O. F. (1976). *Private schools: From Puritans to the present.* Bloomington, IN: The Phi Delta Kappa Educational Foundation.

Lagowski, J. J. (1996). The education summit: A different signal. *Journal of Chemical Education, 73,* 383–386.

Lankshear, C., & Knobel, M. (2003). *New literacies, changing knowledge, and classroom learning.* London: Open University Press.

Lau v. Nichols, 414 U.S. 563 (1974).

Leiberman, M. (2004), Charter schools: Facts, fictions, future. *The World & I*, 19(5), 64–65.

Lemann, N. (2002, March 28). The president's big test. PBS Frontline. Retrieved September 10, 2003 from PBS Web site: www.pbs .org/wgbh/pages/frontline/shows/schools/nochild/lemann.html.

Lemlech, J., & Marks, M. B. (1976). *The American teacher: 1776–1976*. Bloomington, IN: The Phi Delta Kappa Foundation.

Lerner, M. (1962). *Education and radical humanism*. Columbus, OH: Ohio State University Press.

Lewis, A. C. (2002). New ESEA extends choice to school officials. *Phi Delta Kappan, 83*, 423–425.

Lindley, B., & Lindley, E. K. (1938). *A new deal for youth: The story of the National Youth Administration*. New York: Viking.

Littlefield, G. M. (1965). *Early schools and schoolbooks of New England*. New York: Russell & Russell.

Lyotard, J. (1985). *The postmodern condition: A report on knowledge*. Minneapolis: University of Minnesota Press.

Madsen, D. L. (1966). *The national university, enduring dream of the U.S.A.* Detroit: Wayne State University Press.

Madsen, D. L. (1974). *Early national education, 1776–1830*. New York: John Wiley & Sons.

Manchester, W. (1975). *The glory and the dream: A narrative history of America 1932–1972*. New York: Bantam Books.

Maritain, J. (1941). *Scholasticism and politics*. New York: Macmillan.

Maritain, J. (1943). *Education at the crossroads*. New Haven, CT: Yale University Press.

Marr, H. W. (1959). *The old New England academies founded before 1826*. New York: Comet Press.

Mathis, W. J. (2003). No Child Left Behind: Costs and benefits. *Phi Delta Kappan, 84*, 679–686.

McGrath, E. J. (1958). Sputnik and American education. *Teachers College Record, 59*, 379–395.

McLaren, P., & Torres, C. A. (1998). Voicing from the margins: The politics and passion of pluralism in the work of Maxine Greene. In W. Ayers & J. L. Miller (Eds.), *A light in dark times: Maxine Greene and the unfinished conversation* (190–203). New York: Teachers College Press.

McLaren, P. (2003). *Life in Schools: An introduction to critical pedagogy in the foundations of education*. Boston: Pearson/Allyn and Bacon.

McManis, J. T. (1916). *Ella Flagg Young and a half century of the Chicago public schools*. Chicago: McClurg.

Meir, M., & Ribera, F. (1993). *Mexican Americans/American Mexicans: From Conquistadors to Chicanos*. New York: Hill and Wang.

Mendez et al. v. Westminister School District of Orange County, 64 F. Supp. 544 (S.D. Cal. 1946), aff'd 161 F.2d 774 (1947).

Meriwether, C. (1978). *Our colonial curriculum*. Washington, DC: Capital.

Metcalf, K. K., & Legan, N.A. (2002). Educational vouchers: A primer. *The Clearing House, 76* (1), 25–26.

Milliken v. Bradley, 418 U.S. 717 (1974).

Mills v. Board of Education of the District of Columbia, 348 F. Supp. 866 D. D. C. (1972).

Milner, C. A., II, O'Conner, C. A., & Sandweiss, M. A. (1994). *The Oxford history of the American west*. New York: Oxford University Press.

Missouri v. Jenkins, 115 S. Ct. 2038 (1995).

Molnar, A. (September 12, 2004). Charter Schools: Do they work? No, charters are failing. *Arizona Republic*, pp. v1–v2.

Moreo, D. W. (1996). *Schools in the Great Depression*. New York: Garland.

Morris, V. C., & Pai, Y. (1976). *Philosophy in the American school*. Boston: Houghton Mifflin.

Murphy, J. (1990). The education reform movement of the 1980s: A comprehensive analysis. In J. Murphy (Ed.), *The education reform movement of the 1980s: Perspectives and cases* (pp. 3–55). Berkley, CA: McCutchan.

Nabokov, P., & Vine, D., Jr. (2000). *Native American testimony: A chronicle of Indian-White relations from prophecy to the present, 1492–2000*. New York: Penguin.

National Board of Professional Teaching Standards (NBPTS). (2003). Retrieved June 24, 2003, from www.nbpts.org.

National Center for Education Statistics (NCES). (1993). *120 Years of American education: A statistical portrait.* Washington, DC: Author.

National Center for Education Statistics (NCES). (2003). *Digest of education statistics, 2002.* Washington, DC: Author.

National Center for Education Statistics (NCES). (2004). Participation in education. Retrieved August 24, 2004 from www.nces.ed.gov/programs/coe./2004/section 1.

National Coalition of Advocates for Students (1988). *Barriers to Excellence: Our Children at Risk.* Boston, MA: Author.

National Commission on Excellence in Education. (1983). *A nation at risk: The imperative for educational reform.* Washington, DC: U.S. Government Printing Office.

National Education Association (NEA), Department of Superintendence. (1933a). *Educational leadership: Progress and possibilities, Eleventh Yearbook.* Washington, DC: Author.

National Education Association (NEA), Research Division. (1933b). *Current conditions in our nation's schools.* Washington, DC: Author.

National Policies Commission. (1941). *The Civilian Conservation Corps, the National Youth Administration, and the public schools.* Washington, DC: National Education Association.

Neill, A. S. (1960). *Summerhill: A radical approach to child rearing.* New York: Hart.

Neill, M. (2003). High stakes, high risk. *American School Board Journal, 190* (2), 18–21.

Newcomer, M. (1959). *A century of higher education for women.* New York: Harper & Brothers.

Newman, J. W. (1998). *America's teachers: An introduction of education* (3rd ed.). New York: Longman.

Noddings, N. (1992). *The challenge to care in schools: An alternative approach to education.* New York: Teachers College Press.

Noddings, N. (1995). *Philosophy of education.* Boulder, CO: Westview Press.

Noddings, N. (2004). War, critical thinking, and self-understanding, *Phi Delta Kappan, 85,* 488–495.

Oates, M. J. (1994). Catholic female academies on the frontier. *U.S. Catholic Historian, 12,* 121–136.

O'Brien, M. J. (1917). Irish schoolmasters in New England. *Catholic Historical Review, 3,* 52–71.

Ohio mileposts—Feb. 2, 1804: Coonskin library fosters learning. *OVAL Ohio Library News Digest 2/3/05.* Retrieved January 31, 2003, from www.oval.lib.us/ohlibnews/Feb03/020303.htm.

Olson, L. (2003, January 9). The great divide. *Education Week,* pp. 9–16.

Orfield, G. (2001). *Schools more separate: Consequences of a decade of resegregation.* Cambridge, MA: Harvard University, The Civil Rights Project.

Orfield, G., Frankenberg, E. D., & Lee, C. C. (2003). The resurgence of school segregation. *Educational Leadership, 60*(4), 16–20.

Orfield, G., & Lee, C. C. (2004). *Brown at 50: King's dream or Plessy's nightmare.* Cambridge, MA: The Civil Rights Project, Harvard University.

Ozmon, H. A., & Craver, S. M. (2003). *Philosophical foundations of education.* Upper Saddle River, NJ: Prentice Hall/Merrill.

Patterson, J. T. (2001). *Brown v. Board of Education: A civil rights milestone and its troubled legacy.* New York: Oxford University Press.

Payne, S. (2003). *The McGuffey readers.* Retrieved February 21, 2003, from www.nd.edu/~rbarger/www7/Mcguffey.html.

PBS Frontline. (2003). The new rules. PBS Frontline: Testing our schools: No child left behind. Retrieved September 10, 2003 from PBS Web Site: www.pbs.org/wgbh/pages/frontline/shows/schools/nochild/nclb.html.

Pennsylvania Association of Retarded Citizens (PARC) v. Commonwealth of Pennsylvania, 343 F. Supp. 279 (E.D. Pa. 1972).

Perlmann, J., Siddali, S. R., & Whitescarver, K. (1997). Literacy, schooling, and teaching among New England women, 1730–1820. *History of Education Quarterly, 37,* 117–139.

Piaget, J. (1948). *The moral judgment of the child.* New York: Free Press.

Pifer, A. (1973). *The higher education of blacks in the United States.* New York: Carnegie Corporation.

Pincus, F. L. (1985). From equity to excellence: The rebirth of educational conservatism. In B. & R. Gross (Eds.), *The great school debate: Which way for American education?* (pp. 329–344). New York: Simon & Schuster.

Plato. (1958). *The republic.* (F. Carnford, Trans.). New York: Oxford University Press.

Plessy v. Ferguson, 163 U.S. 537, 16 S. Ct. 1138 (1896).

Power, E. J. (1982). *Philosophy of education: Studies in philosophies, schooling, and educational policies.* Upper Saddle River, NJ: Prentice Hall.

President's Commission on Higher Education. (1948). *Higher education for American democracy.* New York: Harper & Brothers.

Progressive Education. (1924). *1, 2.*

Rafferty, M. (1964). *What they are doing to your children.* New York: New American Library.

Ravitch, D. (1983). *The troubled crusade—American education, 1945–1980.* New York: Basic Books.

Ravitch, D. (2000). *Left back: A century of failed school reform.* New York: Simon & Schuster.

Ravitch, D. (2001). Part Two: 1900–1950, As American as public school, introduction. In S. Mondale & S. B. Patten (Eds.), *School, the story of American public education* (pp. 63–70). Boston: Beacon Press.

Ravitch, D., & Finn, C. E. (1987). *What do our 17-year-olds know? A report on the first national assessment of history and literature.* New York: Harper & Row.

Reagan, T. (2000). *Non-Western educational traditions: Alternative approaches to educational thought and practice.* Mahwah, NJ: Lawrence Erlbaum Associates.

Rebell, M. A., & Hunter M. A. (2004). 'Highly qualified' teachers: Pretense or legal requirement? *Phi Delta Kappan, 85,* 690–696.

Rheller, T. L. (1935). *The development of the city superintendency.* Philadelphia: Theodore Lee Rheller.

Rickover, H. G. (1959). *Education and freedom.* New York: E. P. Dutton.

Rippa, S. A. (1984). *Education in a free society.* New York: Longman.

Robelen, E. W. (2004, February 4). More school districts feeling the effects of 'No Child' law. *Education Week,* p. 6.

Roberts v. City of Boston, 59 Mass. (5 Cush.) 198 (1850).

Rorty, R. (1998). *Philosophers of education: Historical perspectives.* London: Routledge.

Rose, L. C., & Gallup, A. M. (2004). The 36th annual PDK/Gallup poll of the public's attitude toward the public schools. *Phi Delta Kappa, 36,* 41–52.

Rose v. Council for Better Education, 790 S.W. 2d 186 (Ky. 1989).

Rossmiller, R. H. (1990). Federal funds: A shifting balance? In J. Underwood & D. A. Verstegen (Eds.), *The impacts of litigation and legislation on public school finance: Adequacy, equity and excellence, Tenth Annual Yearbook of the American Education Finance Association* (pp. 3–25). New York: Harper & Row.

Rotherham, A. J., & Mead, S. (2003). Teacher quality: Beyond No Child Left Behind: A response to Kaplan and Owings (2002), *NASSP Bulletin, 86,* 65–76.

Rudolph, F. (Ed.). (1965). *Essays on education in the early republic.* Cambridge, MA: Harvard University Press.

Ruenzel, D. (1997, May/June). Look who's talking. *Teacher Magazine, 8,* 26–31.

Rury, J. L. (2002). *Education and social change: Themes in the history of schooling.* Mahwah, NJ: Lawrence Erlbaum.

San Antonio Independent School District v. Rodriguez, 4 U.S. 1 (1973).

San Miguel, G., Jr. (1997). Education. In N. Kanellos (Ed.), *The Hispanic American almanac* (2nd ed., pp. 391–411). New York: Gale Research.

Sarte, J. P. (1956). *Being and nothingness* (H. Barnes, Trans.). New York: Philosophical Library.

Scheffler, I. (1960). *The language of education.* Springfield, IL: Thomas.

Serrano v. Priest, 487 P.2d 1241 (1971).

Shea, J. G. (1978). *The Catholic church in the United States.* New York: Arno Press.

Silberman, C. (1970). *Crisis in the classroom.* New York: Random House.

Sizer, T. (1984). *Horace's compromise: The dilemma of the American high school.* Boston: Houghton Mifflin.

Snyder, T. D. (1993). *120 Years of American education: A statistical profile.* Washington, DC: U.S. Department of Education, National Center for Education Statistics.

Soltis, J. F. (1978). *An introduction to the analysis of educational concepts.* Reading, MA: Addison-Wesley.

Sommers, C. H. (2000). *The war against boys: How misguided feminism is harming our young men.* New York: Touchstone.

Spangler, M. M. (1998). *Aristotle on Teaching.* Lanham, MD: Rowman & Littlefield.

Spring, J. (1970). Education and progressivism. *History of education quarterly, 10,* 53–71.

Spring, J. (1989). *The sorting machine revisited: National educational policy since 1945.* New York: David McKay.

Spring, J. (2001). *The American school 1642–2000* (5th ed.). New York: Longman.

Spring, J. (2002). *Conflict of interest: The politics of American education* (4th ed.). New York: McGraw-Hill.

Stuart et al. v. School District No. 1 of the Village of Kalamazoo, 30 Michigan 69 (1874).

Swann v. Charlotte-Mecklenburg Board of Education, 402 U.S. 1 (1971).

Szasz, M. C. (1988). *Indian education in the American colonies, 1607–1783.* Albuquerque, NM: University of New Mexico Press.

Szasz, M. C. (1999). *Education and the American Indian: The road to self-determination since 1928* (3rd ed.). Albuquerque, NM: University of New Mexico Press.

Tape v. Hurley, 66 Cal Rep. 473 (1885).

Taylor, A. (2001). *American colonies.* New York: Viking.

Thorndike, E. L. (1904). *An introduction to the theory of mental and social measurements.* New York: Teachers College, Columbia University.

Thorndike, E. L. (1918). The nature, purposes, and general methods of measurement of educational products. In *The measurement of educational products, Part II, Seventeenth Yearbook of the Society for the Study of Education.* Bloomington, IL: Public School Publishing.

Tinker v. Des Moines Independent School District, 393 U.S. 503 (1969).

Tollett, K. S. (1983). *The right to education: Reaganism, Reaganomics, or human capital?* Washington, DC: Institute for the study of Educational Policy, Howard University.

Toppo, G. (2003, January 28). Most states lag far behind "No Child Left Behind" law. *USA Today.* Retrieved September 10, 2003 from www.usatoday.com/news/education/2003-01-28-education-cover-usat_x.htm.

Tozer, S. E., Violas, P. C., & Senese, G. (2002). *School and society: Historical and contemporary perspectives* (4th ed.). Boston: McGraw-Hill.

Trustees of Dartmouth College v. Woodward, 17 U.S. (4 Wheat) 518 (1819).

Tunis, E. (1957). *Colonial living.* New York: Thomas Y. Crowell.

Tyack, D. B. (1967). *Turning points in American educational history.* Waltham, MA: Blaisdell.

Tyack, D., & Cuban, L. (1995). *Tinkering toward Utopia: A century of public school reform.* Cambridge, MA: Harvard University Press.

Tyack, D., Lowe, R., & Hansot, E. (1984). *Public schools in hard times: The great depression and recent years.* Cambridge, MA: Harvard University Press.

Ugland, R. M. (1979). "Education for Victory:" The high school Victory Corps and curricular adaptation during World War II. *History of Education Quarterly 19,* 435–451.

U.S. Bureau of the Census. (1975). *Historical statistics of the United States, colonial times to*

1970. Washington, DC: U.S. Government Printing Office, Series H 316–326.

U.S. Bureau of Education. (1918). *Cardinal Principles of Secondary Education.* Washington, DC: U.S. Government Printing Office.

U.S. Bureau of Education. (1918). *Report of the Committee on the Reorganization of Secondary Education appointed by the National Education Association.* Washington, DC: U.S. Government Printing Office.

U.S. Department of Education, National Center for Education Statistics. (2003). *Digest of education statistics 2002.* Washington, DC: U.S. Government Printing Office.

U.S. Office of Education. (2002). *Meeting the highly qualified teachers challenge: The secretary's annual report on teacher quality.* Washington, DC: Author.

U.S. Senate Special Subcommittee on Indian Education. (1969). *Indian education: A national tragedy—A national challenge.* Senate Report No.91-501. Washington, DC: U.S. Government Printing Office.

Van Dusartz v. Hatfield, 334 F. Supp. 870 (D. Minn. 1971).

Vega, M. L. C. (1984). *Legacy of Mexico to the philosophy of American Education.* Unpublished doctoral dissertation, Arizona State University, Tempe, Arizona.

Washington, B. T. (1895/1976). A moderate Negro view. In L. H. Fishel & B. Quarles (Eds.)., *The Black American, A documentary history* (pp. 342–345). Glenview, IL: Scott, Foresman.

Watras, J. (1997). *Politics, race, and schools: Race and integration, 1954–1994.* New York: Garland.

Watson-Brown, L., & Dawson, G. (1996). *The politics of gendered exclusion.* Retrieved July 3, 2004, from www.psa.ac.uk/cps/1996.

Webb, L. D., & McCarthy, M. M. (1998). Ella Flagg Young: Pioneer of democratic school administration. *Educational Administration Quarterly, 34,* 224–242.

Wecter, D. (1995). How to write history. In *A sense of history* (pp. 38–45). New York: Smithmark.

Weinberg, M. (1997). *Asian-American education: Historical backgrounds and current realities.* Mahwah, NJ: Erlbaum.

West, E. H. (1972). *The Black American and education.* Columbus, OH: Prentice Hall/Merrill.

Westheimer, J., & Kahne, J. (1993). Building school communities: An experience-based model. *Phi Delta Kappan, 75* (4), 324–328.

Williams, R. L. (2003). Land grant colleges and universities. In J. W. Guthrie (Ed.), *Encyclopedia of education* (2nd ed., pp. 1380–1384). New York: Macmillan Reference.

Wineburg, S. (1999). Thinking about history and other unnatural acts. *Phi Delta Kappan, 80,* 492–498.

Wollenberg, C. (1976). *All deliberate speed: Segregation and exclusion in California schools, 1855–1985.* Berkeley, CA: University of California Press.

Wong Him v. Callahan, 119 F. 381 (N.D. Cal. 1902).

Woodward, W. H. (1906). *Studies in education during the age of the Renaissance, 1400–1600.* Cambridge, England: Cambridge University Press.

Woody, T. (1929). *A history of women's education in the United States.* New York: Science Press.

Wraga, W. G. (2000, April). The comprehensive high school in the United States: A historical perspective. Paper presented at the annual meeting of the American Educational Research Association, April, New Orleans.

Young, H. S. (1976). *In pursuit of a profession: A historical analysis of the concept of "Professionalism" for the American public school superintendency, 1865–1973.* Doctoral dissertation, the Pennsylvania State University. College Park, PA.

Zelman v. Simmons-Harris, 122 S. Ct. 2460 (2002).

Zigler, E., & Valentine, J. (Eds.). (1979). *Project Head Start: A legacy of the War on Poverty. New people's history of the United States.* New York: The Face Press.

Zinn, H. (1980). *A people's history of the United States.* New York: Harper & Row.

Name Index

Ackerman, David B., 376, 377
Adams, D. W., 196
Adams, Jane, 218
Adler, Mortimer, 21, 22
Adovasio, J. M., 53
Agnew, Spiro, 308
Anderson, J. D., 200, 282
Angus, D. L., 150, 151, 159, 160, 192
Apple, Michael W., 34
Aquinas, Thomas, 11
Aristotle, 8, 9, 11, 26
Armstrong, Samuel Chapman, 198
Aronowitz, Stanley, 34
Arsen, D., 340
Augustine, Saint, 7, 11

Bacon, Francis, 9
Bagley, William C., 26, 229, 256
Baltimore, Lord, 83
Balwin, J., 3
Barnard, Henry, 145, 153, 158–159
Barnett, Ross, 284
Beecher, Catherine, 121, 125, 137, 145, 158–159
Bell, Terrel H., 334
Benezet, Anthony, 82
Bennett, L., Jr., 95
Bennett, William, 332
Berger, M., 51
Berkeley, William, 83
Berliner, D. C., 325, 347
Bernard, Henry, 155
Bernard, S. C., 220, 264, 300, 342
Bestor, Arthur E., 26, 263, 266, 331
Biddle, B. J., 325, 347
Biesta, G. J., 30
Binder, F. M., 122, 138, 140, 144, 155
Binet, Alfred, 228
Bishop, Nathan, 150
Blake, N., 27
Blinderman, A., 91, 111
Bloom, Allan, 22
Blow, Susan, 172, 202
Bobbitt, John Franklin, 223, 226
Bobrick, B., 84
Bonner, T. N., 214, 225
Boorstin, D. J., 78, 79, 91
Boyer, Ernest, 326
Boylan, Ann M., 115, 116
Bracey, G. W., 365
Brameld, Theodore, 29
Brendtro, L. K., 57, 58
Brokenleg, M., 57, 58
Brosio, R. A., 12
Bruner, Jerome, 31, 267, 333
Buber, Martin, 15–16
Bugenhagen, Johann, 47
Bush, George H. W., 321, 333, 334, 338
Bush, George W., 359, 360, 365
Butler, J. D., 6, 26
Butts, R. F., 72, 81, 85, 112, 173, 189

Cabot, John, 68
Callahan, R. E., 221
Calvin, John, 46–47, 70
Campbell, J., 111, 119, 336
Cardozier, V. R., 259
Carlson, A. D., 245
Carnes, J., 155, 166
Carter, James Earl, 301, 302, 305
Carter, James G., 123, 137, 144–145, 158–159
Champlain, Samuel de, 51
Chard, S. C., 23
Chester, D., 327
Clarkin, T., 291
Clinton, Dewitt, 141
Clinton, William J., 321, 333, 339, 340, 345
Cohen, S. S., 68, 79, 80, 81, 83, 84, 86, 89, 91
Cole, N. M., 94
Coleman, James, 285
Coleman, M. C., 96, 195, 196, 197
Columbus, Christopher, 47, 48
Comenius, John Amos, 9, 82
Commager, Henry Steele, 113
Comte, Auguste, 12
Conant, James, 266–267
Connell, W. F., 191
Conway, J. K., 125
Counts, G. S., 29, 182, 271
Counts, George C., 254, 256
Cramer, B., 63
Craver, S. M., 7, 11, 13, 16
Cremin, L. A., 69, 72, 76, 81, 85, 90, 108, 112, 115, 145, 152, 173, 189, 221, 231, 232, 262
Cronin, J., 363
Cuban, D., 323
Cuban, L., 180, 182, 183, 219, 222, 254, 282, 326
Cubberley, E. P., 69, 72, 89, 120, 147, 152, 154, 157, 193, 228

Daley, Richard J., 286
Darling, Noyes, 124
Darwin, Charles, 12, 228
Dawson, G., 343
DeJong, D.H., 57, 58, 195, 196
Derrida, Jacques, 29
Descartes, René, 7
Dewey, John, 3, 12, 13, 24, 27, 212, 213, 218, 224–225, 226, 229, 231, 233, 333
Dock, Christopher, 94, 97, 100
Dole, Robert, 338
DuBois, W. E. B., 170, 179, 198–200, 201, 208

Eckhardt, Christopher, 305
Eisenhower, Dwight, 269, 283
Eisner, Elliott W., 31, 37
Eliot, Charles, 177, 188

Eliot, John, 96
Ellis, Robert Byron, 284
Emerson, Ralph Waldo, 141
England, John, 155
Erasmus, Desiderius, 44, 60

Faludi, S., 343
Faubus, Orval, 283
Feistritzer, E., 327
Feltre, Vittorino da, 45
Finn, Chester, 332
Firestone, W., 329, 331
Fithian, D., 141
Foner, E., 3
Ford, Gerald, 302
Ford, P. L., 75
Foster, S. J., 268, 269
Foxe, John, 75
Franklin, Benjamin, 67, 82, 90, 110
Frazier, N., 298
Friere, Paulo, 29
Froebel, Friedrich, 116, 172, 202, 213, 223–224
Fuhrman, S., 329, 331

Gallup, A. M., 375
Garcia, A. M., 292
Garrison, J., 12
George, King of England, 125
Gilbert, Humphrey, 68
Gilbert, M. J., 308
Gilland, T.M., 149, 150
Gillett, M., 172
Giroux, Henry A., 34
Glubok, S., 72, 95
Goertz, M. E., 335, 336
Goldberg, M. F., 364, 367
Gonzalez, G., 293
Goodlad, J., 326, 345
Graham, P. A., 176, 180, 201, 226, 230, 231, 264
Grant, Ulysses S., 196
Graves, 246
Gray, R., 217
Greeley, Horace, 141
Greene, M., 17
Gursky, D., 369
Gutek, G., 8, 10, 11, 15, 18, 27, 29, 31,
Gutek, G. L., 115, 139, 140, 189, 198, 262

Hakim, J., 43, 78
Hale, L., 55, 195
Hall, G. Stanley, 182, 227
Hall, Samuel, 156
Hansot, E., 244, 245, 246, 249, 250, 252
Hardy, L., 361
Hare, N., 201
Harper, William Raney, 189
Harris, William T., 172, 202
Harvard, John, 78
Hauser, C., 363

Hauser, R., 363
Hawley, Gideon, 148
Heffernan, H., 229
Hegel, Georg Wilhelm Friedrich, 7
Heidigger, Martin, 16
Henderson, J. G., 30
Henriques, D. B., 363, 364
Henry, N. B., 258, 260
Herbart, Johann Friedrich, 190–191
Herbst, J., 76, 79, 118, 122, 123, 124, 174, 179
Hertert, L. G., 338
Hirsch, E. D., Jr., 332
Hissong, C., 231
Hissong, M. C., 231
Hoff, 369
Hofstadter, R., 124, 232
Holbrook, Joseph, 141
Holmes, Oliver Wendell, 141
Holt, John, 16
Hoover, Herbert, 244
Horn, R. A., Jr., 178, 180, 225, 323, 325
Hudson, Henry, 80
Hufstadler, Shirley, 305
Hunter, M. A., 369
Husserl, Edmund, 16
Hutchins, Robert M., 22, 263–264
Hutchinson, Anne, 142

Illich, Ivan, 29
Ingersoll, R. M., 369

Jacobsen, D. A., 10
James, T., 297
James, William, 13
James I, King of England, 68
Jefferson, Thomas, 108–110, 112, 114, 126
Jennings, J., 360, 361
Johnson, Lyndon B., 280, 281, 284, 285, 286, 287, 288, 289, 291
Jordan, K. F., 5, 287

Kaestle, C. F., 72, 111, 114, 115, 118, 142, 146
Kahne, J., 23
Kandel, I. L., 257, 259, 261
Kant, Immanuel, 7
Kaplan, L., 369
Katz, L. G., 23
Keller, B., 369
Kennedy, John F., 281, 284, 287, 291
Kennedy, Robert F., 307
Kenrick, Francis Patrick, 156
Kerr, Clark, 259
Kerr, J., 368
Kidwell, C. S., 253
Kierkegaard, Søren, 15
Kilpatrick, William H., 24, 213, 233, 255
Kincheloe, J., 27, 28, 30
Kincheloe, Joe L., 34
King, Martin Luther, Jr., 307
King, W., 95
Kingsbury, G. G., 363
Kirkland, E. C., 218
Kirkpatrick, William H., 226
Kirst, M. W., 329, 331
Kliebard, H. M., 178, 179, 181, 182, 191, 223, 227
Kneller, G. F., 6, 15
Knight, E. W., 259, 260
Knobel, M., 34
Kozol, Jonathan, 16, 337, 343
Kraushaar, O. F., 76, 80, 81, 82, 89, 119

Lagowski, J. J., 345
Lancaster, Joseph, 114
Lankshear, Colin, 34
Lee, C. C., 371
Leeuwenhoek, 88
Legan, N. A., 338
Lemann, N., 360
Lemlech, J., 157
Lerner, M., 23
Lewis, A. C., 359, 361
Lieberman, M., 375
Limbaugh, Rush, 343
Lincoln, Abraham, 2, 183
Littlefield, G. M., 70, 76, 77, 78
Locke, John, 9, 88, 90
Lowe, R., 244, 245, 246, 249, 250, 252
Luther, Martin, 45–46
Lyon, Mary, 121
Lyotard, Jean-Francois, 29

Madsen, David, 112
Manchester, W., 283, 284, 307
Mann, Horace, 136, 137, 142–144, 145, 153, 155, 158, 172
Maritain, Jacques, 22
Marks, M. B., 157
Marr, H. W., 121, 157, 158
Marshall, Thurgood, 282, 293, 310
Marx, Karl, 27
Mary II, Queen of England, 86
Masschalein, J., 27
Mather, Cotton, 95
Mathis, W. J., 366
McCarthy, Joseph, 268
McCarthy, M. M., 226
McGrath, E. J., 264, 265
McGuffey, William Holmes, 151–153
McLaren, Peter, 30, 34
McManis, J. T., 226
Mead, S., 369
Meier, M., 294
Melanchthon, Philip, 47
Mendez, Gonzalo, 293
Menendez de Aviles, Don Pedro, 48
Meredith, James, 284
Meriwether, C., 72, 78, 84, 86
Metcalf, K. K., 338
Metha, Arlene, 5, 287
Milner, C. A., II, 68, 69
Mirel, J., 150, 151, 159, 160, 192
Molnar, A., 376
Mondale, S., 220, 264, 300, 342
Moreo, D. W., 245, 246, 250, 251, 254
Morrill, Justin, 183
Morris, V. C., 10, 11, 12, 18, 19
Murphy, J., 325, 327, 329, 331
Murrow, Edward R., 287

Nabakov, P., 53, 54
Nampeyo, 57, 63
Neill, A. S., 16
Neill, M., 365
Newcomer, M., 184
Newman, J. W., 29, 300, 334, 337, 339
Newton, Isaac, 88
Nixon, Richard, 286, 301, 302, 304, 308
Noddings, Nel, 7, 13, 14, 16, 18, 358

Oates, M. J., 121
O'Brien, M. J., 92
O'Conner, C. A., 68, 69
Olson, G., 363, 368, 369
Onate, Don Juan de, 48
Orfield, G., 286, 345, 371

Orfield, J., 97
Owen, Robert, 116
Owings, W., 369
Ozman, H. A., 7, 11, 13, 16

Page, David P., 159
Page, J., 53
Pai, Y., 10, 11, 12, 21, 22
Paige, Rod, 365
Parker, Francis W., 24, 213, 224, 231
Patterson, J. M., 217
Patterson, J. T., 282
Payne, S., 152
Peabody, Elizabeth, 172
Perlman, J., 70
Pestalozzi, Johann Heinrich, 9, 143–144, 153–155, 172, 213, 223–224
Piaget, Jean, 31, 267, 333
Pierce, Charles Sanders, 13
Pifer, A., 198, 200
Pincus, F. L., 322
Plank, D., 340
Plato, 6, 7, 8, 9, 26, 35
Power, E. J., 9
Pratt, Richard Henry, 195

Quintilian, 44, 45

Rae, Noel, 98
Raikes, Robert, 115
Raleigh, Sir Walter, 68
Ravitch, Diane, 24, 214, 220, 255, 263, 264, 268, 269, 305, 308, 332, 376
Reagan, Ronald, 308, 320, 321, 322, 323, 334, 340, 341, 342
Reagan, T., 54, 55, 57
Rebell, M. A., 369
Rheller, T. L., 149
Ribera, F., 294
Richards, Ann, 360
Rickover, Hyman G., 26, 263–264, 266, 331
Riis, Jacob, 217, 233
Rippa, S. A., 109, 119, 138
Robelen, E. W., 366
Rodriguez, Demetrio P., 304
Roelasten, Adam, 80, 97
Rogers, John, 75
Roosevelt, Franklin D., 242, 244, 252, 296
Rorty, Richard, 29
Rose, L. C., 375
Rosmiller, R. H., 322
Rotherham, A. J., 369
Rousseau, Jean-Jacques, 9, 88, 213
Rudolph, F., 111
Ruenzel, D., 22
Rugg, Harold, 29, 255
Runkle, John, 179
Rush, Benjamin, 104, 105, 108, 110–112, 114, 126, 144
Russell, Bertrand, 18
Russell, Laura, 98

Sadker, David, 344, 351
Sadker, M., 298
Sandweiss, M. A., 68, 69
San Miguel, G., Jr., 293
Sartre, Jean-Paul, 16
Scheffler, Israel, 18
Schurz, Margaretha, 172
Sekerak, George, 274
Senese, G., 122, 161
Sequoyah, 195

Shea, J. G., 50
Sheldon, Edward A., 155
Shipp, D., 323
Siddali, S. R., 70
Silberman, Charles, 16
Simon, Theodore, 228
Sizer, Theodore, 25, 326, 333
Slattery, P., 27, 28, 30
Smith, William, 90
Snyder T. D., 200
Socrates, 8, 35
Soltis, Jonas, 18
Sommers, C. H., 344
Spangler, M. M., 9
Spring, J., 97, 113, 114, 156, 159, 160,
   221, 255, 265, 266, 340, 343, 360
Steinberg, S. R., 27, 28, 30
Stevens, Thaddeus, 146, 162
Steward, William H., 155–156
Stowe, Harriet Beecher, 121
Swift, D. W., 201, 253
Sykes, D., 340
Szasz, M. C., 55, 56, 58, 59, 84, 86, 292

Tallmadge, Isaac S., 283
Taylor, A., 50, 51, 53
Taylor, Frederick W., 221, 223
Terman, Lewis, 228

Thoreau, Henry David, 141
Thorndike, Edward L., 223, 228, 229, 267
Tinker, John, 305–306
Tinker, Mary Beth, 305–306
Toch, 364
Tollett, K. S., 308
Toppo, G., 371
Torres, C. A., 30
Tozer, S. E., 122, 161
Truman, Harry, 259
Tucker, 364
Tyack, David, 108, 110, 112, 139, 151,
   182, 183, 190, 192, 222, 244, 245,
   246, 249, 250, 252, 281
Tyler, Ralph, 255

Ugland, R. M., 257

Valentine, J., 288
Van Bockern, S., 57, 58
Vega, M. L. C., 48, 49, 50, 51
Verona, Guarino da, 45
Vine, D., Jr., 53, 54
Vinson, Fred, 310
Violas, P. C., 122, 161

Warren, Earl, 282, 309, 310
Washington, Booker T., 198–200, 201

Watras, J., 283, 286
Watson-Brown, L., 343
Webb, L. D., 5, 226, 287
Webster, Noah, 108, 112–113, 114
Weinberg, M., 295
West, E. H., 198
Westheimer, J., 23
Wheelock, Eleazer, 91
White, Theodore H., 66
Whitescarver, K., 70
Willard, Emma, 121, 125, 130, 158
William, Duke of Cleves, 60
William III, King of England, 86
Williams, R. L., 183, 184
Williams, Roger, 142
Wirt, William, 223
Wollenberg, C., 295, 296, 297
Woodward, Calvin, 179
Woodward, W. H., 45, 60
Woody, T., 125, 184, 188
Wraga, W. G., 178

Young, Ella Flagg, 24, 213, 224,
   225–226, 238
Young, H. S., 150

Zigler, E., 288
Zinn, Howard, 126

Subject Index

Ability grouping, 264, 266
Abolition, 110, 162, 197
Abstinence sex education, 360
Academies
   common school movement and, 137
   convent, 121
   growth of, 105, 118–119
   high schools and, 177
   in Pennsylvania, 110
   practical education and, 67
   rise of, 90–91
   state aid to, 158
   for women, 119–122
Accountability
   in the 21st century, 359
   and 1980s conservatism, 322
   in the 1990s, 333–337, 346
   and disadvantaged students, 337, 343
   essentialism and, 26
   and the No Child Left Behind Act
      (2001), 360, 362–365
Achievement gap, 359, 361, 365,
   373–374
Adequate yearly progress (AYP),
   360–361, 364, 365, 366
Administration, progressivism in,
   221–223
Adult education, 115, 221, 245
Adult Education Act, 323

Advanced placement, 266
Aesthetics. See Axiology
Affirmative action, 250, 341
African Americans
   and the achievement gap, 373–374
   as apprentices, 72
   Benjamin Rush and, 111
   civil rights and (See Civil Rights
      movement)
   during the Depression, 252
   desegregation and, 282–286
   equal educational opportunity and, 281
   as indentured servants, 68
   manual training movement and, 179
   post-Civil War to WWI, 171, 194,
      197–201
   during Reconstruction, 198
   resegregation and, 345, 373, 374
   Sunday schools and, 115, 127
   vocational education and, 180
   Works Projects Administration (WPA)
      and, 250–251
Age of Enlightenment. See
   Enlightenment
Age of Reason. See Enlightenment
Age of the University, 187
Algonquians, 54, 96
Allegory of the Cave, The, 6–7, 35
Alternative schools, 233, 339

America 2000: An Education Strategy, 334,
   338
American Association of School Adminis-
   trators, 257
American Association of University
   Women, 344
American Baptist Mission Society, 200
American Colonization Society, 197
American Council on Education, 259
American Dictionary of the English
   Language, 112
American Enterprise Institute, 322
American Experience, 43
American Federation of Labor (AFL),
   194
American Federation of Teachers (AFT),
   194, 246
American High School Today, The, 266
American Institute of Biological Sciences
   Curriculum Study Group, 266
American Institute of Instruction, 145
American Journal of Education, 125,
   140–141, 145
American Lyceum, 137, 141–142
American Missionary Association, 200
American Normal School Association,
   192
American Psychological Association
   (APA), 227

American Sunday School Union, 115, 160
American Women's Education Association, 145
Analytic philosophy, 17–19
Antioch, 184
Antitrust legislation, 218
Antiwar movement, 305, 307–308
Apprentices
  in colonial America, 69, 72, 80, 81–82
  gender and, 72
  and teacher training, 94
  transition to schools by, 89
Army Air Force College Training Program, 260
Army Specialized Training Program, 260
Articles of Confederation, 106
Asian Americans
  Chinese Americans, 290, 294–295
  equal educational opportunity and, 281
  Japanese Americans, 258, 274, 295–297
  Korean Americans, 296
Assessment. *See also* Testing and measurement
  authentic, 28
  essentialism and, 26
  and the No Child Left Behind Act, 360
  perennialism and, 22
  postmodernism and, 31
  progressivism and, 24
  social reconstructionism and, 28
  standards-based, 337
Assimilation
  common school movement and, 137
  of immigrants, 137, 139–140
  of Mexican Americans, 293
  of Native Americans, 194–195, 253, 291, 313
Atlanta Compromise, 199
Atlanta University, 200
Attendance zones, 285
Automobile, role in 20th century, 218
Axiology
  aesthetics and, 5
  analytic philosophy and, 18
  ethics and, 4
  existentialism and, 15
  idealism and, 6
  meaning of, 4–5
  pragmatism and, 12
  realism and, 9
  theistic realism and, 10–11

Baby boom, 262, 369
Back-to-basics movement, 26, 263–264, 331
Barriers to Education: Our Children at Risk, 343
Being and Nothingness, 16
Berea College, 197
Beyond the Gender Wars, 344
Bilingual education
  and the cultural wars of the 1990s, 340–342
  equal educational opportunity and, 281, 289–290
  Native Americans and, 253
Bilingual Education Act, 341
Bill of Rights, 108–109
Bill of Rights for Handicapped Children, 301

Black Codes, 197
Blacks. *See* African Americans
Blue-back speller, 113
Boarding 'round, 95, 246
Boarding schools. *See* Native Americans, boarding schools
Board of Education of Oklahoma Public Schools v. Dowell, 344
Book of Martyrs, 75
Books. *See* Textbooks
Boston English High School, 122
Boston Latin Grammar School, 76, 105
Bracero program, 292
Brown University, 91
Brown v. Board of Education of Topeka, 282, 283, 344, 371
Bryn Mawr, 184, 188
Bureau of Indian Affairs (BIA), 171, 194, 195, 196, 252–253
Business and industry
  abuses in early 20th century, 217
  influence on 1980s education reform, 323, 325
  influence on education in 1990s, 345
Busing, 285, 286, 344

Canada, French exploration and, 51–52
Cardinal Principles of Secondary Education, 178
Carnegie Forum on Education and the Economy, 326, 328
Carnegie Foundation for the Advancement of Teaching, 177
Carnegie Unit, 177
Catechisms, 46, 49, 75, 113
Categorical imperatives, 7
Categorization, realism and, 10
Certification
  and the 1980s school reform movement, 328–329
  in the 1990s, 346
  after the Civil War, 191–192
  alternative, 329
  charter schools and, 339
  in colonial America, 94
  No Child Left Behind Act and, 361, 368–369
  normal schools and, 190
  in Progressive era, 222
  state regulation of, 246
Change
  measurability of, 213
  pragmatism and, 12
  students as change agents, 27, 28
  teachers as change agents, 28
Character education
  essentialism and, 26
  and the religious right, 360
Charity kindergartens, 172
Charity schools, 72, 85–86, 115, 139
Charter schools
  in the 1990s, 337, 338–339
  and the No Child left Behind Act, 365–366
  since the 1990s, 346, 374–376
Chemical Education Material Study Group, 266
Cherokee alphabet, 195
Cheyney State College, 197
Chicago Federation of Labor (CFL), 193
Chicago Teachers Federation (CTF), 193
Child-centered education
  challenges to, 254

and the Kindergarten movement, 172
Native Americans and, 253
in progressive era, 213, 230, 232
proponents of, 224–227
and the school reform movement of the 1980s, 329
Child development, stage concept of, 267
Child labor laws, and influence on school attendance, 176
Child study movement, 213, 228–229
Chinese Americans. *See* Asian Americans
Choice
  in 21st century schools, 359, 374–376
  and the 1980s conservative agenda, 322
  and the 1980s school reform movement, 326
  in the 1990s, 334, 337–340
  existentialism and, 15, 16
  and the No Child left Behind Act, 365
  private schools and, 345
  in the Renaissance, 44
  and school desegregation, 284
Christian Coalition, 336
Christian doctrine. *See also* Religion
  idealism and, 7
  perennialism and, 22
Citizenship, 108
Civilian Conservation Corp (CCC), 249
Civil Rights Act of 1964, 284–285, 297–298
Civil Rights movement
  impact of, 308–309
  rise of, 282
  school desegregation and, 308–309
  student protests and, 308
Clark University, 227
Class issues
  Coleman Report and, 285
  dame schools and, 70
  equal educational opportunity and, 281
  female academies and, 122
  Latin Grammar Schools and, 76
  progressive education and, 230, 232
  Quaker schools and, 82
  school boards in Progressive era and, 222
  social constructivism and, 27
  social reconstructionism and, 255
  in Southern colonies, 78, 80, 84–85, 97
Classroom environment
  essentialism and, 26
  Jerome Bruner and, 267
  perennialism and the, 21
  postmodernism and, 31
  progressivism and, 24
  social reconstructionism and, 28
Closing of the American Mind, The, 22
Coaching, perennialism and, 21, 22
Coalition of Essential Schools, 333
Cognition, theory of, 267
Cold War, 243, 264
Coleman Report, 285
Collaboration
  importance of, 39–40
  postmodernism and, 31
  pragmatism and, 13–14
  progressivism and, 23, 24
Collectivism, social reconstructionism and, 255
College, Academy, and Charitable School of Pennsylvania, 91
College of Philadelphia (University of Pennsylvania), 82–83, 110

College of William and Mary, 86, 91, 109
Colloquies, 44
Colombian School, 156
Colonial American education
  17th century
    Mid-Atlantic, 79–83
    New England, 68–79
    South, 83–86
  18th century, 87–92
  legacy of, 97
  minorities and, 95–98
  teachers and, 92–95
Columbia University
  in colonial America, 81, 91
  educators from, 227, 228, 229, 254,
    256
  graduate programs at, 188
  New York College for the Training of
    Teachers at, 190
  and the Progressive Education Associ-
    ation, 231
  student protests at, 307–308
Columbine High School, 345
Committee of Ten, 177–178, 182, 219
Common School Journal, 125, 140
Common schools
  after the Civil War, 171
  curriculum and instruction in, 151–155
  description of a district school, 128–130
  failure of, 155–156
  forerunners of, 114
  funding and supervision of, 146–151
  growth of, 105, 116–118, 127
  historical context of, 138–142
  Noah Webster and, 113
  opponents of, 146, 161
  proponents of, 142–145
  teachers in, 156–160
  and town schools, 70
Communication. *See also* Language
  analytic philosophy and, 19
  growth in 20th century, 217
Communism, 264, 268–269
Community
  and Native American educational prac-
    tices, 58
  pragmatism and, 12, 13
  progressivism and, 23, 221, 225
  social reconstructionism and, 27–28
Compensatory education
  Coleman Report and, 285
  and the War on Poverty, 281
Competency
  essentialism and, 25, 26
  and Native American educational prac-
    tices, 58
Compulsory attendance, secondary
  schools, 176
Compulsory education, Massachusetts
  Education laws and, 69
Computer-assisted instruction, essentialism and, 25
Conant Report, 266
Concord Academy, 157
Conflict resolution, social reconstruc-
  tionism and, 28
Congregationalists, 200
Conservatism
  in the 1980s, 321, 322–334
  in the 1990s, 321, 334–345
  centrist, 322
  precursor to late 20th century, 309
Consolidation, 218–219, 267, 285

Constitution, Tenth Amendment, 106
Constructivism
  impact of progressivism on, 233
  and the new progressivism, 333
  postmodernism and, 31
  theory of cognition and, 267
Continental Congress, 106
Contracting, 339–340
Convent academies, 121
Cook County Normal School, 224
Cooperative education programs, 180
Cooperative learning. *See* Collaboration
Core knowledge curriculum, 332
Core values, of Native American educa-
  tional practices, 57
Corporal punishment. *See* Discipline
Cosmology, 4
Council for Exceptional Children, 300
Council on Basic Education, 263
Court schools, in the Renaissance, 45
Creek Confederacy, 54
Critical thinking
  perennialism and, 21
  postmodernism and, 30
  progressivism and, 23
  social reconstructionism and, 27
  value of, 38–39
CRSE (Commission on the Reorganization of Secondary Education),
  178–179
Cult of domesticity, 125–126
*Cultural Literacy: What Every American
  Needs to Know*, 332
Curriculum and instruction
  50/50 curriculum for Native Ameri-
    cans, 195
  in 1980s school reform movement, 326
  in academies, 119
  action-centered, 23
  analytic philosophy and, 19
  child-centered, 23 (*See also* Child-cen-
    tered education)
  classical, 124–125
  in colonial schools, 70, 72, 74–76
  in the common schools, 118–119, 137,
    151–155, 157, 159
  in the comprehensive high school,
    181–182
  core, 177, 332
  CRSE report on, 178–179
  Depression and, 246
  differential, 213, 223, 332
  in early colonial universities, 78–79,
    86, 91
  in early national period, 109, 110, 112,
    114, 115, 116, 118, 124
  English-only, 220
  equality-centered, 23
  essentialism and, 25, 256
  existentialism and, 16–17
  growth-centered, 23
  Herbartianism and, 191
  idealism and, 7–8
  influence of cognition theories on, 267
  integrated, 255
  John Locke and, 88
  in Latin Grammar Schools, 76
  life adjustment education and, 263
  Lutheran, 46
  in monitorial schools, 114
  multicultural, 342–343
  No Child Left Behind Act and, 361,
    362, 364

  peer-centered, 23
  perennialism and, 21–22
  postmodernism and, 31
  pragmatism and, 13–14
  in Progressive era, 222, 227, 230
  progressivism and, 23
  realism and, 8, 9–10
  social efficiency and, 178
  social reconstructionism and, 27
  Sputnik and, 126, 264–267
  standardization of, 177
  in teacher institutes, 160
  theistic realism and, 11
  at turn of 20th century, 219
  and Tyler Rationale, 255
  in vernacular schools, 47
  vocational, 198
  Women's Educational Equity Act of
    1974 (WEEA) and, 299
  WWII and, 257
  Yale report of 1828 and, 124–125

Dame schools, 70–71, 98–100
Dartmouth College, 96
Dayton Board of Education v. Brinkman,
  286
Decentralization
  and the 1980s school reform move-
    ment, 326
  common schools and, 117
Decoding, postmodernism and, 31
Deconstructionism, postmodernism and,
  31
Deductive logic. *See* Logic, deductive
de facto segregation, 285, 286
de jure segregation, 285, 286
Delaware, 83
Democracy
  academies and, 225
  and the comprehensive high school
    curriculum, 181–182
  John Dewey and, 225
  pragmatism and, 12, 13
  progressivism and, 24
  social reconstructionism and, 27
Democracy and Education, 225
Demonstration, theistic realism and, 11
Department of Education, 305, 332, 345
Depression of 1920s
  impact on education, 243, 244–249,
    269
  and inequality of opportunity, 254
  overview of, 244
  and social reconstructionism, 254–255
Deschooling Society, 29
Desegregation. *See* Segregation
Developmental learning, 155
Didactic teaching, perennialism and, 21
Disability rights issues
  and accountability in the 1990s, 336
  civil rights movement and, 282
  Depression and, 245
  Elementary and Secondary Education
    Act of 1965 (ESEA) and, 288
  equal educational opportunity and, 281
  expanding access and, 300–301
  legislation for, 288, 300–304
  post-Civil War academic curricula and,
    182
Discipline
  corporal punishment and, 44
  in early state universities, 124
  essentialism and, 26, 256

Discipline (*cont.*)
  and Native American educational practices, 58
  perennialism and, 21
  in the Renaissance, 44, 45
Discrimination. *See* Equality/inequality
Districts. *See* School Districts
District schools. *See* Common schools
Diversity
  impact of Civil Rights movement on, 308–309
  postmodernism and, 30
Doctrine of courtesy, 45
Dominicans, 51
Donohoe v. Richards, 156
Dutch West India Company, 80–81

Eclecticism, 25
Economic issues
  during the Age of Enlightenment, 89
  Atlanta Compromise, 199
  and the conservative school reform movement, 323
  and the Depression of 1920s, 244
  and economic growth in 20th century, 214, 217
  and finance in 21st century schools, 359
  post-Civil War growth and, 171, 174
  and poverty, 345
  resegregation and, 374
  and school finance reform, 302–304, 370–371
  and school funding since *Brown,* 372–373
  social reconstructionism and, 254–255
  in the Southern colonies, 83–84
  unfunded mandates and, 359
  the War on Poverty and, 281, 287–289
Economic Opportunity Act (EOA), 288
Edison Schools, 340, 366
Educational Alternatives Incorporated (EAI), 340
Educational Professions Development Act, 289
Educational Reform Movement, 325
Educational Testing Service, 266
Educational Wastelands, 263
Education for All Handicapped Children Act (EHA) of 1975, 300, 301, 323
Education management organizations, 340
Education of Young Children, 44
Education Policy Commission (1942), 257
Efficiency movement, 178, 213, 221–227, 245
Eight-Year Study, 232, 255
Elementary and Secondary Education Act of 1965 (ESEA), 285, 288, 323. *See also* No Child Left Behind Act
Elementary education
  1980s decline in federal funds for, 323
  Baby Boom and, 262
  in colonial America, 69–72, 74–75, 84–85, 94–95
  Depression and, 245
  impact of WWII on, 258
  and the No Child Left Behind Act, 368
  and progress since *Brown,* 371
  Reformation and, 45–47
Elementary Spelling Book, 113

Emergency School Aid Act, 323
Engineering, Science, and Management Defense Training Program, 260
English Classical School for Boys, 122
English First, 340
English High School, 122
English immersion, 290, 341, 342
English schools, 89, 90
Enlightenment
  in colonial America, 67, 87–88
  and the early national period, 108–109, 126
  Renaissance and, 44
Environment. *See* Classroom environment
Epistemology
  analytic philosophy and, 18
  existentialism and, 15
  idealism and, 6
  meaning of, 4
  pragmatism and, 12
  realism and, 8–9
  theistic realism and, 10
Equality/inequality. *See also* Civil Rights movement; Class issues; Disability rights issues; Gender equity issues; Racism
  and the 1980s school reform movement, 326
  Depression and, 254
  and equal educational opportunity, 279–319
  Mexican American schools and, 293
  and multiple discrimination, 299
  New Deal and, 254
  postmodernism and, 29, 30
  in Quaker schools, 82
  of rural school systems, 229
  separate but equal and, 126, 197, 282
  testing and, 230
  in urban schools, 233
Equal Opportunity Grants, 289
Essays, perennialism and, 22
Essentialism
  in the 1990s, 332, 345–346
  assessment and, 26
  classroom environment and, 26
  curriculum and, 25
  Eight-Year Study and, 256
  instruction and, 25
  life adjustment education and, 263
  overview of, 25
  perennialism and, 19
  proponents of, 26
  purpose of schooling and, 25
  and the school reform movement of the 1980s, 331–333
  teachers and, 26
  testing and measurement and, 229–230
Ethics. *See* Axiology
Excellence Movement, 325
Existentialism
  axiology and, 15
  educational implications of, 16–17
  epistemology and, 15
  metaphysics and, 15
  overview of, 14–15
  postmodernism and, 29
  proponents of, 15–16
Experience
  postmodernism and, 31
  progressivism and, 23
  project method and, 227
  as a way of knowing, 4

Experimentalism. *See* Pragmatism
Experts, efficiency, 222

Facilitator, teacher as, 24
Faith, realism and, 9
Family values, and objections to standards in the 1990s, 337
Federal government
  Department of Education, 332, 345
  desegregation, 282–287
  funding for vocational education, 180
  New Deal, 251–252, 270
  New Federalism, 322–323
  No Child Left Behind Act (2001), 359, 360–361
  the Northwest Ordinance, 106
  Progressive era, 213, 218, 222
  school finance reform movement of the 1970s, 305
  War on Poverty, 281, 287–289
  WWII "impact aid," 258
Finance. *See* Economic issues
Fisk University, 200
Food Production War Training Program, 258
Formative evaluation, 28
France, exploration of New World, 51–53
Franciscans, 48, 49, 50
Freeman v. Pitts, 344
Free School Act (Pennsylvania), 148
Free schools, 85–86, 113, 115, 234
Free School Society of New York City, 115
Free will. *See* Choice
Frontier movement, common schools and, 140
Frontier Thinkers, 255

Games. *See* Play
Gender equity issues
  apprentices and, 72
  Benjamin Rush and, 111
  civil rights movement and, 282
  in colonial schools, 70, 72, 82, 84, 89, 97
  in common schools, 117
  and the cultural wars of the 1990s, 343–344
  Depression and, 245
  in the early national period, 125–126, 127
  equal educational opportunity and, 281
  Erasmus and, 44
  female academies and, 119–122
  junior colleges and, 189
  in Latin Grammar Schools, 77
  Noah Webster and, 113
  and post-Civil War higher education, 171, 187
  public high schools and, 122–123
  social constructivism and, 27
  Title IX of the Educational Amendments of 1972 and, 297–298
  Title VII of the Civil Rights Act of 1964 and, 297–298
  Women's Educational Equity Act of 1974, 299
  and the women's rights movement, 297–298
Gender Gap: Where Schools Still Fail Our Children, 343
General Education Board, 198
Georgia, in colonial period, 67

Georgia Female College, 184
Gerrymandering, segregation and, 285
G.I. Bill, 262
Goals, in the 1990s, 333–337
Goals 2000: Educate America Act, 334
Goss v. Lopez, 307
Government. *See* Federal government;
   State government
Graduate education. *See* Higher
   education
Grammatical Institute of the English Lan-
   guage, 112
Great Books
   idealism and, 7, 8
   neo-perennialism and, 332
   perennialism and, 22, 264
   postmodernism and, 31
   realism and, 8
Great Migration, 68
Green v. County School Board of New Kent
   County, 285
Griffin v. County School Board, 285
Guidance counselors
   after Sputnik, 266
   in the comprehensive high school, 182
   vocational, 181

Hampton Normal and Agricultural Insti-
   tute, 198–200
Harmony, as a Native American educa-
   tional goal, 57
Hartford Female Seminary, 120, 145
Harvard University, 78, 91, 96, 124, 188,
   333
Harvard University Civil Rights Project,
   374
Hatch Act, 183
Head Start. *See* Project Head Start
Herbartianism, 191
Heritage Foundation, 322
Hermeneutics, 16
Hierarchy of knowing, 10
Higher education
   1980s decline in federal funds for, 323
   in colonial America, 67, 78–79, 81,
     84–85
   in early national period, 110, 123–124
   electives and, 188–189
   and the emergence of the modern uni-
     versity, 187–189
   enrollment in 20th century, 232
   and equal educational opportunity, 281
   expansion in the 18th century, 91
   federal grants for research and, 259
   graduate education, 188, 222, 232
   and idea of a national university, 112
   Jefferson and, 110
   and junior colleges, 171, 189, 232, 250
   and land grant colleges, 183–184
   and the National Youth Administration
     (NYA), 249–250
   placement tests for admission to, 266
   private colleges and, 125
   progressive education movement and,
     231–232
   Reformation and, 46
   Spanish, 48
   and the War on Poverty, 281
   for women after the Civil War, 184,
     187
   WWII and, 259–262
Higher Education Act of 1965, 289
High School Victory Corps, 257
High-stakes testing, 26, 337, 362–365

Hispanics
   achievement gap, 374
   Chicano movement, 293
   civil rights movement, 282, 293
   desegregation, 286
   educational opportunities for Mexican
     Americans, 292–293
   equal educational opportunity, 281
   resegregation, 345, 374
   school desegregation, 282–286
Hollins v. Shoftstall, 304
Holmes Group, 329
Horace's Compromise, 333
Hornbook, 74
Hostile Hallways, 343
Housing restrictions, segregation and,
   285
HOUSSE (high, objective, uniform state
   standard of evaluation), 368
Howard University, 200
How Schools Shortchange Girls, 343
How the Other Half Lives: Studies Among
   the Tenements of New York, 233
Humanism, in the Renaissance, 44

Idealism
   axiology and, 6
   educational implications of, 7–8
   epistemology and, 6
   essentialism and, 25
   metaphysics and, 6
   overview of, 5
   perennialism and, 19
   proponents of, 6–7
Illinois Conference Female College, 184
Immigration
   after the Civil War, 200–201
   bilingual education and, 289–290, 341
   of Chinese Americans, 294–295
   common schools and, 117, 137, 138,
     139–140, 155, 161
   increase in 20th century of, 214,
     219–220
   of Japanese Americans, 295–297
   of Mexican Americans, 292–293
   and the No Child Left Behind Act,
     369
   and urban school overcrowding in 20th
     century, 220
   vocational education and, 180, 198
Improving America's Schools Act (IASA),
   335, 362
Inclusion. *See* Equality/inequality
Indiana University, 124
Indian Education: A National Tragedy, 291
Indian Education Act of 1972 (IEA),
   291–292
Indian Emergency Conservation Work
   (IECW), 253
Indian New Deal, 252–253
Indian Removal Act of 1830, 195
Indian Reorganization Act of 1934, 253
Indian Self-Determination and Educational Assistance Act (ISEAA),
   291–292
Individualism
   and the common school movement,
     155
   existentialism and, 16–17
   and individual freedom, 218
   and Native American educational prac-
     tices, 58
   progressivism and, 220
   in the Renaissance, 44

social reconstructionism and, 255
   Thorndike and, 267
Individualized educational program
   (IEP), 301
Individualized instruction, 228
Individuals With Disabilities Education
   Act of 1990 (IDEA), 300, 301
Inductive logic. *See* Logic, inductive
Industrialization, and the common
   school movement, 137, 139
Industrial training. *See* Vocational educa-
   tion
Infant schools, 105, 116, 127
Ingram University, 184
Initiative, progressive movement and,
   218
Institutio Oratoria, 44
Instruction. *See* Curriculum and instruc-
   tion
Instrumentalism. *See* Pragmatism
Integration, progressivism and, 224
Intuition, 4, 6
Ipswich Female Seminary, 158
IQ tests. *See* Testing
Irish schoolmasters, 92
Iroquoians, 54
"I-Thou" relationship, 15–16

Jackson State College, 308
Jackson v. Benson, 338
James Madison Elementary School, 332
James Madison High School, 332
Jamestown colony, 67
Japanese Americans. *See* Immigration
Jesuits, 48, 51–52
Job Corps, 288
Johns Hopkins University, 188, 227, 285
Johnson O'Malley (JOM) Act, 253
Joliet Junior College, 189
Journals
   of education, 140–141
   postmodernism and, 31
Judaism, idealism and, 7
Judgment, value of, 38
Junior colleges. *See* Higher education
Junior high schools. *See* Secondary
   education

Kalamazoo case. *See Stuart et al. v. School*
   District No. 1 of the Village of
   Kalamazoo
Kent State University, 308
Keyes v. School District No. 1, 286
Kindergarten, 116, 171, 172–173,
   202–208, 245
Kings College (Columbia University),
   81, 91

Labor
   legislation concerning, 218
   regulation of, 213
   unions and, 218
Lab schools, 346
Land Grant College Act, 183
Land grant college movement, 183–184
Land Ordinance of 1785, 106
Language. *See also* Bilingual education
   analytic philosophy and, 17–19
   postmodernism and, 30
   preservation of Native American, 290
Language of Education, The, 18
Lanham Act of 1941, 258
Latin Grammar Schools, 45, 75, 76–77,
   84, 118, 122

Lau v. Nichols, 289–290
Laws for the Suppression of Popery, 92
Learning by doing, 213, 224, 250
Learning environment. *See* Classroom environment
Learning theories, 19–34, 267
Lectures on Schoolteaching, 157
LESA (limited English-speaking ability) youth, expanding the rights of, 289–290
Letters to the Mayors and Aldermen of All Cities of Germany in Behalf of Christian Schools, 46
Liberal arts
  progressivism and, 264
  in the Renaissance, 45
Liberalism
  in the 1960s and 1970s, 289–319, 321
  charter schools and, 339
Liberia, 197–198
Licensing. *See* Certification
Life adjustment education, 263
Lifelong learning, 11, 225. *See also* Adult education
Limited-English-Proficiency (LEP) students, 290, 342
Lincoln University, 197
Linguistic analysis. *See* Analytic philosophy
Literacy, multiple forms of, 39
Little Rock, Arkansas, 283
Local control
  and the 1980s school reform movement, 326
  and the Civil Rights Movement, 283–284
  common schools and, 137, 146
  as legacy of colonial America, 97
  New Deal and, 249, 252
  in New England colonies, 69–70, 94
  and the No Child Left Behind Act (2001), 360, 361–362
  school finance reform and, 302–305
Logic
  deductive, 4, 6, 8–9
  idealism and, 6
  inductive, 4, 23, 88
  as a way of knowing, 4
Loretto Academy, 121

Mainstreaming, 301
Manpower Development and Training Act, 288
Manual training movement, 179
Manufactured Crisis: Myths, Fraud, and the Attack on America's Public Schools, 325, 347
Mary Sharp College, 184
Massachusetts, public high schools and, 123
Massachusetts Bay Colony, 68
Massachusetts Education Laws of 1642 and 1647, 69–70, 72, 76, 123
Massachusetts Institute of Technology, 179
Massachusetts Law of 1827, 144
Mathematics, 265–266
McCarthy era, 268–269
McGuffey Readers, 152
Measurement movement, 213, 223, 228–230
Mehary Medical College, 200

Mendez et al. v. Westminster School District, 293
Meriam Report, 194, 197, 252, 253, 313
Metaphysics
  analytic philosophy and, 17
  existentialism and, 15
  idealism and, 6
  meaning of, 4
  myths as truth and, 30
  postmodernism and, 29, 30
  pragmatism and, 12
  realism and, 8
  theistic realism and, 10
Methodist Episcopal Church, 200
Mexican Americans. *See* Hispanics
Michigan State University, 188
Mid-Atlantic colonies
  Delaware, 83
  denominational variations in, 79–80
  ethnic, language, and religious differences in, 67
  New Jersey, 81
  New York (New Netherlands), 80–81, 94
  Pennsylvania, 81–83
Migrants, 288, 292–293
Military academies, 112, 118
Milliken v. Bradley, 286
Mills v. Board of Education of the District of Columbia, 300
Minnesota State University, 188
Missionaries
  French, 51–53
  Native American boarding schools and, 97
  Spanish, 48–51
Mississippi State College for Women, 184
Missouri v. Jenkins, 344
Monitorial schools
  expansion of education and, 105, 127
  Lancasterian, 114–116
Moravians, 96
Morrill Land Grant Acts, 106, 171, 183–184
Mother and Nursery Songs, 172
Mount Holyoke Female Seminary, 120
Muckrakers, 218
Multicultural education, 341, 342–343, 346
Multiplicity, postmodernism and, 30

NAACP (National Association for the Advancement of Colored People), 199, 282, 310
National Assessment of Educational Progress (NEAP), 332, 364–365
National Association of School Superintendents, 192
National Board for Professional Teaching Standards (NBPTS), 328–329
National Commission on Excellence in Education, 323
National Defense Education Act (NDEA) of 1958, 243, 265
National Education Consolidation and Improvement Act (ECIA), 323
National Foundation of the Arts and the Humanities, 289
National Herbartian Society, 191
Nationalism
  after the revolution, 105
  common school movement and, 137

and education in the early national period, 108–109
social constructivism and, 27
National Organization for Women (NOW), 297
National Paideia Center at the University of North Carolina-Greensboro, 332
National Science Foundation (NSF), 265
National Society of the Scientific Study of Education, 191
National Teacher Corps, 289
National Teachers Association (NTA), 192
National Youth Administration (NYA), 249–250
Nation at Risk: The Imperative for Educational Reform, A, 26, 126, 323–325, 333, 347
Nation Prepared: Teachers for the 21st Century, A, 328
Native Americans
  assimilation and, 194–195, 253, 291, 313
  bilingual education and, 253
  boarding schools for, 194, 195–196, 253
  in colonial America, 95–96
  Dartmouth and, 91
  day schools for, 196–197
  educational systems of, 53–59
  Elementary and Secondary Education Act of 1965 (ESEA) and, 288
  European disease and, 49
  French and, 52–53
  Indian New Deal and, 252–253
  manual training movement and, 179
  mission schools and, 48–53, 194–195
  post-Civil War, 171
  and preservation of language, 290
  and public schools, 196–197
  Quaker schools and, 82
  self-determination of, 290–292
  slave labor and, 68
  Sunday schools and, 127
  vocational education and, 197, 198
Naturalism, 88
Natural law, 9, 88
Natural rights, John Locke and, 88
Natural selection, theory of, 13
Nature, in the Renaissance, 44
Naval Academy, 118
Naval College Training Programs, 260
Nazareth Academy, 121
NEA (National Education Association), 172–173, 177–179, 192, 225, 237, 246, 257, 305
Neo-essentialism, 332
Neo-perennialism, 332–333
Neo-Thomism. *See* Theistic realism
New Deal
  Civilian Conservation Corp (CCC) and, 249
  education programs of, 249
  and Eight Year Study, 255
  and essentialism, 256
  and federal aid debate, 251–252
  impact on schools of, 243
  and the Indian New Deal, 252–253
  and inequality of opportunity, 254
  National Youth Administration (NYA) and, 249–250

Public Works Administration (PWA) and, 250
and social reconstructionism, 254–255
Works Projects Administration (WPA), 250–251
New England colonies
education in, 67, 68–69
elementary schools in, 70–72
financial support of, 77–78
higher education in, 78–79
instruction, 74–75
Latin grammar schools, 76–77
Massachusetts Education Laws of 1642 and 1647, 69–70
New England Primer, 44, 74–75, 152
New Federalism, 322
New Hampshire, 68
New Haven, 68
New Jersey, 81
New math, 265
New Netherlands. *See* New York
New Right, 322, 343, 360
New York, 80–81
New York College for the Training of Teachers. *See* Columbia University
New York State Normal School at Albany, 159
No Child Left Behind Act (2001)
and the achievement gap, 374
conservatism and, 346
essentialist position and, 26
and expanded state and local responsibilities, 361–362
and federal role, 360–361
funding and, 370–371
future success of, 376
high-stakes testing and accountability and, 362–365
impact of, 359
sanctions of, 361, 362, 365–367
and securing the national welfare, 126
teachers and, 367–369
Nonviolence, in civil rights movement, 284
Normal schools
after the Civil War, 171, 187, 189–190
common school movement and, 137
establishment of, 158–160
Horace Mann and, 143
James G. Carter and, 144
and the progressive movement, 232
Northwest Ordinance, 106–107

Oberlin, 184, 197
Objectivity, postmodernism and, 30
Object lessons, 153, 172
O'Fallon Polytechnic Institute of Washington University, 179
Office of Civil Rights, 286
Office of Indian Education, 292
Of the First Liberal Education for Children, 44
Old Deluder Satan Law, 69
Old field schools, 85–86
Ontology, 4
Oral tradition, of Native Americans, 55
Organizations, education, 140–141
Oswego Normal School, 155
Oxford Female College, 184

Paideia Proposal: An Educational Manifesto, 22, 332

Parents, and the 1980s school reform movement, 326
Parochial schools. *See also* Religion
in the 1990s, 346
in colonial New Jersey, 81
in colonial New York, 81
common schools and, 137
in the Mid-Atlantic colonies, 80
Passports to Teaching Certification, 369
Pauper schools, 72
Paying for Today and Tomorrow, 37
Peabody Fund for the Advancement of Negro Education in the South, 198
Pedagogical progressivism, 223–237
Pedagogy of the Oppressed, 29
Penal Laws of 1695, 92
Pennsylvania, 81–83, 110
Pennsylvania Association of Retarded Citizens (PARC) v. Commonwealth of Pennsylvania, 300
Pennsylvania State University, The, 188
Perennialism
in the 1990s, 332–333, 346
assessment and, 22
classroom environment and, 21
and critics of progressive education, 263
curriculum and instruction in, 21
ecclesiastical, 21
focus of, 19, 21
lay educators and, 21
proponents of, 22
purpose of schooling and, 21
role of teacher and, 22
and the school reform movement of the 1980s, 331–333
Personal narratives, 31
Phenomenology, 16
Phillips Academy, 157
Phillips Andover Academy, 91
Philosophical analysis. *See* Analytic philosophy
Philosophy. *See also* individual philosophies
branches of, 4–5
contemporary, 12–19
of education, 19–34
history and, 3
native traditions and, 55–57
traditional, 5–11
Physical Science Study Committee (PSSC), 265
Pilgrims, 68
Platooning, 223
Play
and the kindergarten movement, 172
and Native American educational practices, 58
in the Renaissance, 45
Plessy v. Ferguson, 200, 201, 282, 310–312
Plymouth Bay Colony, 68
Politics. *See also* Power
backlash against feminism and the New Right, 343–344
common school movement and, 139
corruption in, 213, 217, 232
Depression and, 246
postmodernism and, 30
Progressive movement and, 218
Population growth
in 19th century, 127
in 20th century, 214

Postmodernism, 29–34
Poverty, 345. *See also* Economic issues
Power
of church authority in reformation, 45–46
curriculum decisions and, 180
postmodernism and, 29, 31
progressive reformers and, 232
redistribution in the 1980s school reform movement, 326
social reconstructionism and, 27
unequal educational opportunities and, 281
Powhatan Confederacy, 54
Pragmatism
educational implications of, 13–14
epistemology and, 12
focus of, 12
John Dewey and, 12, 224
metaphysics and, 12
postmodernism and, 29
progressivism and, 23
proponents of, 12–13
Prayer, in 21st century schools, 359
Praying towns, 96
Preschools
and Project Head Start, 288, 334
and the War on Poverty, 281
Works Projects Administration (WPA) and, 250–251
President's Commission on Higher Education in a Democracy (1946), 259
Princeton University, 81, 91, 110
Printing press, 45, 48
Private colleges. *See* Higher education, private colleges
Private contractors. *See* Contracting
Private schools
in the 1990s, 346
and the conservative agenda, 322
New Deal and, 252
and private venture schools, 85–86, 89, 90, 119
progressive education and, 230
in the reform era, 213
and school choice, 338
school segregation and, 283
seminaries and, 137
Privatization, 326, 337–339, 346. *See also* Choice
Problem solving
John Dewey and, 224–225
postmodernism and, 31
pragmatism and, 13
progressivism and, 23
social reconstructionism and, 27
Professionalism, and the 1980s school reform movement, 328
Progressive education
in the 1990s, 333, 346
after WWI, 230–231
and changes in education, 218–221, 233
child study movement and, 227–228
critics of, 263, 269
decline of, 231, 264, 269
efficiency movement and, 221–227
essentialists and, 242
Frontier Thinkers and, 242
influence on higher education of, 231–232
measurement movement and, 228–230
proponents of, 222–223

Progressive education (*cont.*)
 and the school reform movement of
  the 1980s, 331–333
 and traditional education, 377–381
 before WWI, 221–230
Progressive Education Association
 (PEA), 231, 254, 255
Progressive era, 212–218
Progressivism, 23–25
Project Head Start, 288, 334
Project method, 23, 226–227
Property taxes. *See* Taxes, property taxes
*Proposals Relating to the Education of Youth
 in Pennsylvania*, 90
Proposition 187 (California), and bilin-
 gual education in the 1990s, 341
Proposition 203 (Arizona), and bilingual
 education in the 1990s, 341
Proposition 227 (California), and bilin-
 gual education in the 1990s, 341
Protestantism. *See* Religion
Provincial Council of Catholicity, 155
Psychological connectionism, 267
Public Law 815, 258
Public Law 874, 258
Public libraries, 115
Public School Society, 115, 155, 156
Public school systems
 dame schools as, 70–71
 high schools as, 122–123
 Jefferson and, 109–110
 Massachusetts Education laws and, 69
 Puritan education and, 69
 segregation of, 200–201
 taxation and, 77, 109
Public Works Administration (PWA),
 250
Puritans, 46, 68, 69

Quakers, 81–82, 96
Questioning. *See* Socratic method
Quotas, school integration and, 285

Racism. *See also* African Americans; Na-
  tive Americans; Slavery
 affirmative action and, 250
 Chinese Americans and, 294–295
 federal aid and, 252
 immigrants in 20th century and, 214
 Japanese Americans and, 258, 274,
  295–297
 as legacy of colonial America, 97
 Quaker schools and, 82
 social constructivism and, 27
Radcliffe College, 184
Rate bill, 146
Rationalism
 Enlightenment and, 67
 postmodernism and, 30
 realism and, 8
Reading schools, 71–72
Realism, 8–10, 9, 19, 25, 29
Recall, progressive movement and, 218
Recapitulation theory, 228
Reconstruction in Philosophy, 27
Reconstructionism. *See* Social
 reconstruction
Reconstruction period to WWI, 171–208
Red Scare, 268–269
Referendum, progressive movement and,
 218
Reform. *See* Economic issues, school fi-
  nance reform; Progressive move-

ment; School reform movement,
 1980-present
Regionalism
 impact of WWII and, 258
 as legacy of colonial America, 97
Religion. *See also* Roman Catholicism
 in 21st century schools, 359
 in the 1990s, 346
 in colonial American schools, 67,
  80–83, 86, 92
 and the common school movement,
  137, 142, 155–156, 161, 166
 idealism and, 7–8
 in the Mid-Atlantic colonies, 80, 81
 and the New Deal, 81
 in progressive era schools, 220
 Protestant Huguenots and, 51
 Protestant Reformation and, 45–48
 Sunday schools and, 116
Renaissance, 44–45
Republic, The, 6
Republican educational theorists,
 108–114, 126–127
Research, federal grants for, 259
Resegregation. *See* Segregation
Rhode Island, 68
Roberts v. City of Boston, 197
Roman Catholicism
 common schools and, 137, 155–156,
  166
 influence on U. S. education, 52
 and Irish schoolmasters, 92
 Protestants and, 45
 Thomism and, 11
Rose v. Council for Better Education, 370
Rural schools
 common school movement and,
  150–151
 Depression and, 254
 impact of WWII on, 258
 inequality and, 230, 372–373
 No Child Left Behind Act and, 363, 369
 teachers in, 118, 246
Rutgers University, 81, 91

*San Antonio Independent School District v.
 Rodriguez*, 304
Savage Inequalities, 337, 343
Save Our Schools, 340
Scholasticism, 44
School administration, 145
School and Society, The, 225
School boards
 common school movement and, 137,
  150
 corruption in 20th century, 217
 depression and, 246
 efficiency movement and, 222
 resegregation and, 344–345
 segregation and, 201
School districts
 in 1980s school reform movement, 326
 and the common school movement,
  148–149
 consolidation of, 218–219, 267
 desegregation and, 286
 in early national period, 117
 and the No Child Left Behind Act,
  360
 resegregation and, 344–345
 and school improvement plans in the
  1990s, 335–336

School finance reform. *See* Economic
 issues
School Management/Schul-lordnung, 94,
 100–103
Schoolmasters, Irish, 92
School Mathematics Study Group,
 265–266
School prayer, and the conservative
 agenda, 322
School reform movement, 1980-present
 accountability and, 333–337
 bilingual education and, 340–342
 Clinton administration and, 334–345
 conservatism, 322–323
 and essentialism, perennialism, progressivism, 331–333
 first Bush administration and, 323–324
 gender equity and, 343–344
 multicultural education and, 342–343
 and national goals and standards,
  333–337
 Reagan administration and, 323–333
 resegregation and, 344–345
 school choice and, 337–340
 second Bush administration and, 345
School superintendents
 and the common school movement,
  137, 148–150
 in Progressive era, 222, 225
 and state certification, 192
School to Work Opportunities Act, 334
Science and technology, 264
Science of education, 190, 222, 228
Scientific inquiry, 4, 67, 88, 213, 229
Scientific management, 221–222, 245
Scientific method
 and the Age of Enlightenment, 88
 postmodernism and, 29–30
 progressivism and, 23
 realism and, 9, 10
Scientific research, 4
Script, 246
Secondary education
 1980s decline in federal funds for, 323
 academies and democratization of, 119
 academies as forerunners to, 105
 after the Civil War, 171, 173–174
 in colonial America, 76–77, 81, 82, 92,
  94–95
 comprehensive high school and,
  181–182
 and compulsory attendance laws, 176
 and curriculum standardization, 177
 Depression and, 245
 growth in 20th century, 219
 and guidance counselors, 266
 impact of WWII on, 258
 junior high schools and, 171, 182–183
 manual training movement and, 179
 and the National Youth Administration
  (NYA), 249–250
 and the No Child Left Behind Act,
  368
 post-Civil War, 173–174
 and progress since *Brown*, 371
 and public school systems, 122–123
 Reformation and, 46
 Renaissance and, 45
 and the seven cardinal principles of,
  177–179
 tax support of, 174, 176
 vocational education and, 180–181
 WWII and, 257

Second Morrill Act of 1890, 183–184, 200
Secret ballot, progressive movement and, 218
Secular humanism, and the conservative agenda, 322
Segregation
  of African Americans, 282–287
  beginnings of, 197
  of Chinese Americans, 295
  and desegregation, 282–287, 344
  federal aid and, 252
  of Japanese Americans, 295–296
  of Korean Americans, 296
  by poverty, 345
  during the Reconstruction period, 200–201
  and resegregation, 286, 344–345, 359, 374
Self-actualization
  existentialism and, 17
  idealism and, 7
Self-assessment, postmodernism and, 31
Self-determination. *See* Native Americans, self-determination
Self-esteem, and Native American educational practices, 57–59
Self-expression, and the kindergarten movement, 172
Seminaries, female, 120–121, 130
Sense realism, 4, 8, 88, 172
Separate but equal
  and the cult of domesticity, 126
  and desegregation, 282
  and free and freed Blacks, 197
Separation of church and state, 49, 338
Serrano v. Priest, 303–304
Service learning, importance of, 40
Serviceman's Readjustment Act of 1944 (G.I. Bill), 262
Sexism. *See* Gender equity issues
Sexuality, social constructivism and, 27
Shays' Rebellion, 107
Shortchanging Girls, Shortchanging America, 343
Slater Fund, 198
Slavery
  abolition movement and, 110
  beginnings of, 68
  Native Americans and, 68
  in Southern colonies, 95
  and the Southern economy, 83–84
  SPG and, 86, 95
Smith College, 184
Smith-Hughes Act of 1917, 180, 189
Social Contract, 88
Social control, common school movement and, 139–140
Social efficiency movement, 222–223
Social engineering, 246
Social interaction, pragmatism and, 14
Socialism, 264
Socialization of Nampeyo, The, 63
Social promotion, 345
Social reconstructionism
  after the Depression, 254–255
  assessment and, 28
  classroom environment and, 28
  and impetus for postmodern and critical theory movements, 255
  instruction and, 27–28
  overview of, 27
  postmodernism and, 29

progressivism and, 25
proponents of, 29, 254–255
purpose of schooling and, 27
and social engineering, 246
teachers and, 28
Social reform. *See* Progressive reform era
Society for the Relief of Free Negroes Unlawfully Held in Bondage, 110
Socratic method
  essentialism and, 25
  existentialism and, 17
  idealism and, 8
  perennialism and, 21, 22
  postmodernism and, 31
  realism and, 8
Some Thoughts Concerning Education, 88
Southern colonies
  and College of William and Mary, 86
  elementary and secondary education in, 84–86
  social and economic systems in, 83–84
  social class and, 67
  teacher certification in, 94
Spain, 48–51
Special education. *See* Disability rights
SPG (Anglican Missionary Society for the Propagation of the Gospel in Foreign Parts)
  in colonial America, 80, 81, 82, 94, 95, 96
  and education of slaves, 86
Spirituality, Native Americans and, 55–56
Sputnik, 243, 264, 323
St. Joseph's Academy, 121
Stage theory of learning, 267
Standards
  in 21st century schools, 359
  in the 1990s, 346
  and curriculum wars in the 1990s, 336
  and disadvantaged students, 343
  national, 322, 333–337
  and the No Child Left Behind Act, 360
  for secondary school curriculum, 177
  and standards-based assessment, 337
State colleges, 232
State government. *See also* Local control
  and the 1980s school reform movement, 326
  common school movement and, 137, 146, 148–151
  control of education by, 46, 47, 337
  and the efficiency movement, 222
  and the No Child Left Behind Act, 359, 360, 361–362
  school finance reform and, 302–305, 309
  and school improvement plans in the 1990s, 335
  Spanish concept of church/state division and, 49
  teacher certification and, 192
  Virginia system of public schools and, 109–110
States rights, 283–284
State teachers colleges, 190
State University of Iowa, 184
Stock market crash of 1929, 243
Storytelling. *See* Oral tradition
Stuart et al. v. School District No. 1 of the Village of Kalamazoo, 174, 176
Student loan program, 334
Students. *See also* Child-centered education

analytic philosophy and, 19
existentialism and, 17
idealism and, 8
pragmatism and, 14
realism and, 9–10
theistic realism and, 11
Student's Army Training Corp, 232
Students' rights movement, 281, 305, 307–308
Suburbia, 213, 262
Suffrage
  common school movement and, 140
  progressive movement and, 218
Summa Theologica, 11
Summer school
  Depression and, 245
  Works Projects Administration (WPA) and, 250–251
Sunday and Adult School Union, 115
Sunday schools
  expansion of education and, 105
  secular purpose of, 115–116
Superintendents. *See* School superintendents
Supreme Court, 282, 284, 285
Swann v. Charlotte-Mecklenburg Board of Education, 285
Syllogism, 9

Tabula rasa, 9
Tammany Hall, 217
Tape v. Hurley, 295
Taxation
  and the common school movement, 140, 143, 146, 148
  property taxes, 109, 117, 146
  tax support for secondary schools, 174, 176
  tuition tax credits, 322
Teachers
  in 21st century schools, 359
  and the 1980s school reform movement, 326, 328–329
  academies and, 119, 120–121
  analytic philosophy and, 19
  certification of, 191–192, 346
  in charter schools, 339
  Cold War and, 265
  in colonial America, 70–71, 78, 80, 92, 94–95
  and the common school movement, 118, 137, 151, 156–160
  Depression and, 245–246
  in early national period, 111
  essentialism and, 26
  existentialism and, 17
  growth in number in 20th century, 219
  idealism and, 8
  impact of WWII on, 258
  inequalities of funding and, 372–373
  influence of cognition theories on, 267
  McCarthy era and, 268–269
  No Child Left Behind Act (2001) and, 360, 361, 362, 364, 367–369
  normal schools and training of, 159, 189–190
  organizations of, 192–194
  perennialism and, 22
  postmodernism and, 31
  pragmatism and, 14
  progressivism and, 24
  realism and, 10
  during Reconstruction, 200

Teachers (*cont.*)
  salaries of, 95, 246
  school integration and, 285
  social reconstructionism and, 28
  tenure and, 246
  theistic realism and, 11
  training of, 94, 119, 160, 190–191, 232
  unions and, 194, 226
  women as, 126, 144
  Works Projects Administration (WPA) and, 250–251
Teachers College. *See* Columbia University
Teachers colleges, 232
Teach for America, 369
Technical education. *See* Vocational education
Technology
  and the 1980s school reform movement, 326
  essentialism and, 25
Tenth Amendment, to the Constitution, 106
Tenure. *See* Teachers, tenure
Testing and measurement
  in 21st century schools, 359
  in 1980s school reform movement, 326
  Binet-Simon Scale and, 228
  critics of, 229–230
  and diagnostic tests, 26
  of disadvantaged students, 337, 343
  essentialism and, 26
  high-stakes, 26, 337, 362–365
  importance of, 40
  of IQ, 26, 228
  and the No Child Left Behind Act, 361
  performance-based, 26
  standardized, 26, 28, 182
  Stanford-Binet Intelligence Test and, 228, 229
  of teacher competency, 28
  and test construction, 228, 337
  voluntary national, 345
  and WWI, 229
Textbooks
  after Sputnik, 265–266
  in colonial schools, 74
  in common schools, 137, 151–153
  Depression and, 245
  McCarthy era and, 268–269
  in Progressive era, 222
Theistic realism, 10–11, 19
Theory. *See* Learning theories
Theory and Practice of Teaching or the Motives of Good School Keeping, 159
Theory of evolution, 228
Thomism. *See* Theistic realism
Thoughts Upon Female Education, 111
Tinker v. Des Moines Independent School District, 307
Title I of the Elementary and Secondary Education Act of 1965, 288
Title II, Educational Amendments of 1974, 290
Title IV of the Civil Rights Act of 1964, 285
Title VI of the Civil Rights Act of 1964, 284, 300–301
Title VI of the Elementary and Secondary Education Act of 1965, 288

Title VII of the Civil Rights Act of 1964, 284
Title VII of the Elementary and Secondary Education Act of 1965, 288
Title IX, Educational Amendments of 1972, 297–298
Tobacco, in colonial America, 68
Tomorrow's Teachers, 329
Total quality management (TQM), 323
Town schools. *See* Common schools
Training. *See* Teachers, training
Transportation, growth in 20th century, 217, 218
Troy Female Academy, 130, 157
Troy Female Seminary, 120
Trustees of Dartmouth College v. Woodward, 125
Truth. *See* Metaphysics
Tuskegee Institute, 198–200

Unfunded mandates, 359
Unions
  and the 1980s school reform movement, 329
  American Federation of Teachers (AFT), 194
  charter schools and, 339
  Chicago Teachers Federation (CTF), 193–194
  in Progressive era, 218, 238
  and teachers' right to unionize, 226
United States Military Academy, 118
University of Alabama, 283–284
University of California Berkeley, 305
University of Chicago, 189, 225
University of Georgia, 123
University of Iowa, 190
University of Michigan, 124
University of Mississippi, 283–284
University of North Carolina, 123–124
University of Pennsylvania, 82–83, 188
University of South Carolina, 124
University of Tennessee, 124
University of Virginia, 110
University of Wisconsin, 124
Upon the Method of Right Instruction, 44
Urban issues
  after the Civil War, 174
  and the common school movement, 137, 138, 139, 151
  Depression and, 254
  in early national period, 127
  growth of cities in the reform era and, 213, 214, 220
  inequalities of funding and, 372–373
  New Migration and, 171
  No Child Left Behind Act and, 363, 369
  rural migration and, 171
  and urban slums, 218
Ursulines, 52
U.S. English, 340
U.S. Office of Education (USOE) Wartime Commission, 257

Values. *See* Axiology
Van Dusartz v. Hatfield, 304
Vassar College, 184
Vernacular schools, 46
Vienna Circle, 17
Vietnam War, protests against, 281

Violence
  Columbine High School and, 345
  prevention programs for, 334
Virginia, in the colonial period, 68, 109–110
Vocational-Defense Training Program, 258
Vocational education
  African Americans and, 198
  after the Civil War, 171, 180–181
  in colonial America, 89
  immigrants and, 198
  Native Americans and, 197, 198
  and the New Deal, 249
  in the progressive reform era, 220
  as promoted by Martin Luther, 46
  and the War on Poverty, 281
Vocational Education Act of 1963, 288
Vocational Rehabilitation Act (VRA) of 1973, 300
Vocational Training for War Production Workers, 258
Volunteers in Service to America (VISTA), 288
Vouchers, 334, 337–338, 346, 375–376

Walton College, 200
War Against Boys, The, 344, 351
War on Poverty, 281, 287–289, 309
War Relocation Agency (WRA), 296–297
Wellesley College, 184
Western Institute for Women, 121, 145
What Do Our 17-Year-Olds Know?, 332
Whiskey Rebellion, 107
Wilberforce University, 197
William and Mary. *See* College of William and Mary
Wisconsin State University, 188
Women's Educational Equity Act of 1974, 299
Women's rights movement, 297–299
Women's suffrage. *See* Suffrage
Wong Him v. Callahan, 295
Works Projects Administration (WPA), 250–251
Work-study-play plan, 223
Work study program, 250
World War I
  international growth and, 214
  population growth and, 214
  and postwar prosperity, 243
  progressive education after, 230–231
  progressivism before, 221–230
  testing and measurement and, 229
World War II
  education and, 256–257, 262–264
  and higher education, 259–262
  impact on elementary and secondary schools, 258
  impact on schools, 243
  in Japanese American relocation camps, 258, 274
Writing schools, 71–72

Yale Report of 1828, 124–125, 177
Yale University, 78, 91, 188
Young Ladies Academy of Philadelphia, 111

Zelman v. Simmons-Harris, 338, 375
Zoning ordinances, segregation and, 285